Lecture Notes in Computer Science 16533

The series Lecture Notes in Computer Science (LNCS), including its subseries Lecture Notes in Artificial Intelligence (LNAI) and Lecture Notes in Bioinformatics (LNBI), has established itself as a medium for the publication of new developments in computer science and information technology research, teaching, and education.

LNCS enjoys close cooperation with the computer science R & D community, the series counts many renowned academics among its volume editors and paper authors, and collaborates with prestigious societies. Its mission is to serve this international community by providing an invaluable service, mainly focused on the publication of conference and workshop proceedings and postproceedings. LNCS commenced publication in 1973.

Michael Sperber · Ekaterina Komendantskaya
Editors

Functional and Logic Programming

18th International Symposium, FLOPS 2026
Tsukuba, Japan, May 26–28, 2026
Proceedings

Editors
Michael Sperber
Active Group
Tübingen, Germany

Ekaterina Komendantskaya
University of Southampton and Heriot-Watt University
Southampton, UK

ISSN 0302-9743 ISSN 1611-3349 (electronic)
Lecture Notes in Computer Science
ISBN 978-981-92-0183-9 ISBN 978-981-92-0184-6 (eBook)
https://doi.org/10.1007/978-981-92-0184-6

This Springer imprint is published by the registered company Springer Nature Singapore Pte Ltd.
The registered company address is: 152 Beach Road, #21-01/04 Gateway East, Singapore 189721, Singapore

Preface

Welcome to the *18th International Symposium on Functional and Logic Programming – FLOPS 2026*! This year's symposium continued the long tradition of bringing together researchers from the logic and functional programming communities. FLOPS's mission is to stimulate research in design, semantics, theory, applications, implementations, and teaching of declarative programming, including its theoretical advances, and its applications in language systems and tools. This year's FLOPS was hosted by the University of Tsukuba, Japan.

We were fortunate to be joined by three invited speakers:

- Kazunori Ueda, from Waseda University, Japan, with a talk on *Hierarchical Port Hypergraphs: Two Decades Toward a Unifying Structure for Declarative Languages*;
- Fritz Henglein, from the University of Copenhagen, Denmark, with an invited tutorial on *The Lean Theorem Prover*; and
- Gabriele Keller, from Utrecht University, the Netherlands, with a talk on *Accelerate – Past, Present and Future.*

FLOPs received 23 regular research paper submissions of which 12 were accepted to be published in the Springer Proceedings. We also received, and accepted for publication, two system descriptions and a declarative pearl. The accepted papers cover a range of topics in Lambda Calculus and Type Theory, Term Rewriting, Programming Language Semantics, Programming Language Compilers, Functional, Logic, and Functional-Logic Programming, SAT solving, and applications thereof. The papers were peer-reviewed by the Programme Committee of 27 members from Australia, Denmark, France, Italy, Japan, Portugal, Spain, Sweden, the UK, and the USA; from industry and academia. All papers were subject to Single-blind peer review, and each paper received at least 3 reviews. We thank all authors and reviewers for their hard work!

Two papers were marked by the PC as *Distinguished Papers*, for their quality and impact:

- Rose Bohrer. *Demonic Dynamic Logic Programming*
- Neng-fa Zhou, Chufeng Jiang, Hendrik Bierlee, and Peter Stuckey. *Dynamic Programming and Tabled Logic Programming for Encoding Single-Constant Multiplication into SAT (Declarative Pearls)*

We congratulate all authors on receiving this distinction!

Finally, we thank the local organisers, and in particular the local chair Yukiyoshi Kameyama, from the University of Tsukuba, for the excellent organisation of the event! We hope that you found the FLOPS 2026 programme interesting, stimulating, and inspiring and that the symposium provided you with the opportunity to meet with other researchers, forge new collaborations, and exchange ideas.

May 2026

Ekaterina Komendantskaya
Michael Sperber

Organization

General Chair

Yukiyoshi Kameyama	University of Tsukuba, Japan

Program Committee Chairs

Ekaterina Komendantskaya	University of Southampton and Heriot-Watt University, UK
Michael Sperber	Active Group, Germany

Steering Committee Chairs

Shin-ya Katsumata	Kyoto Sangyo University, Japan

Steering Committee

John Gallagher	Roskilde University, Denmark
Jeremy Gibbons	University of Oxford, UK
Atsushi Igarashi	Kyoto University, Japan
Michael Hanus	Christian-Albrechts-Universität zu Kiel, Germany
Yukiyoshi Kameyama	University of Tsukuba, Japan
Shin-ya Katsumata	National Institute of Informatics, Japan
Andy King	University of Kent at Canterbury, UK
Oleg Kiselyov	Tohoku University, Japan
Dale Miller	Inria Saclay, France
Keisuke Nakano	Tohoku University, Japan
Konstantinos Sagonas	Uppsala University, Sweden
Martin Sulzmann	Karlsruhe University of Applied Sciences, Germany
Makoto Tatsuta	National Institute of Informatics, Japan

Program Committee

Reynald Affeldt	AIST, Japan
Davide Ancona	University of Genoa, Italy
Lennart Augustsson	Epic Games, Sweden
Mutsunori Banbara	Nagoya University, Japan
Alessandro Bruni	ITU Copenhagen, Denmark
William Byrd	University of Alabama at Birmingham, USA
Pedro Cabalar	University of A Coruña, Spain
Youyou Cong	Institute of Science Tokyo, Japan
Matthew Daggitt	University of Western Australia, Australia
Jeremy Gibbons	Oxford University, UK
Andrew D. Gordon	Cogna and University of Edinburgh, UK
Gopal Gupta	University of Texas at Dallas, USA
Jason Hemann	Seton Hall University, USA
Mirai Ikebuchi	Kyoto University, Japan
Ranjit Jhala	University of California, San Diego, USA
Wen Kokke	Well-Typed, UK
Dale Miller	Inria Saclay - Île-de-France and the Laboratoire d'Informatique (LIX), France
Simon Peyton Jones	Epic Games, UK
Benjamin Pierce	University of Pennsylvania, USA
Michael Rawson	University of Southampton, UK
Takehide Soh	Kobe University, Japan
Theresa Swift	Universidade Nova de Lisboa, Portugal
Enrico Tassi	INRIA, France
Ekaterina Verbitskaia	JetBrains Research, The Netherlands
Christina Zeller	Active Group, Germany
Neng-Fa Zhou	Brooklyn College, USA
Akimasa Morihata	University of Tokyo, Japan

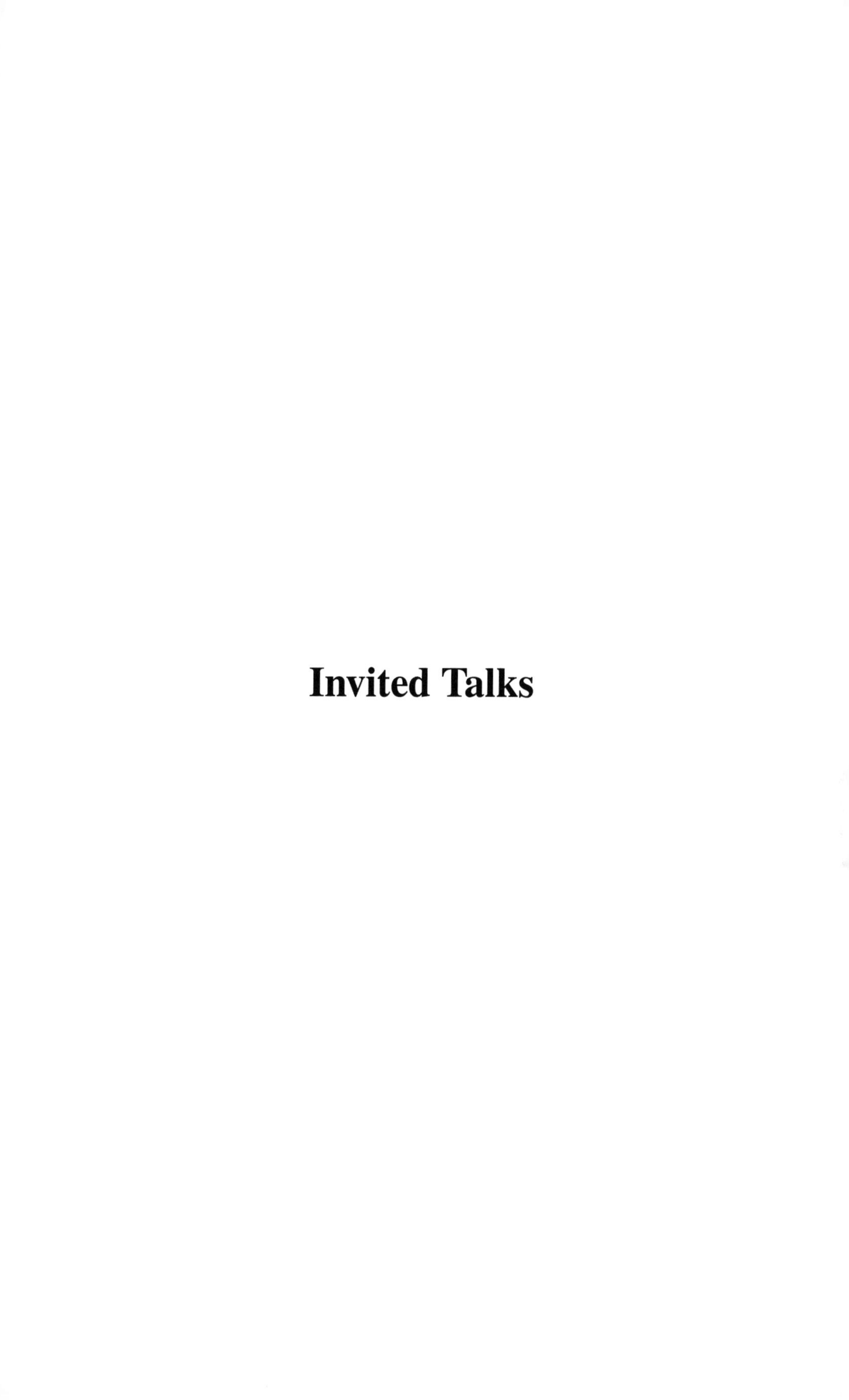

Invited Talks

Accelerate – Past, Present and Future

Gabriele Keller, Ivo Gabe de Wolff, and David van Balen

Utrecht University, Heidelberglaan 8, 3584 CS Utrecht, The Netherlands

Abstract. Accelerate, a purely functional embedded parallel array language was designed to give Haskell programmers an easy, high-level way to exploit parallel hardware. It has been around for many years, and it has seen significant changes, some on the user level, but mostly in its implementation behind the scene.

This talk briefly introduces the language, and the concept of functional parallel array languages in general. It also explores upcoming changes – now available in an experimental release – that rethink fusion, scheduling, and code generation.

Fusion optimizations typically focus on merging producer-consumer pairs to reduce intermediate structures and memory accesses. However, many approaches struggle with multiple inputs and often fail to fuse computations whose combination would be producing multiple outputs, therefor missing optimizations opportunities. Accelerate's new strategy can deal with this situation. Yet, more powerful fusion strategies complicate finding optimal solutions, as this is an NP-complete problem, so this poses additional challenges.

The new scheduling strategy, which we present, enables mixing data and task parallelism while preserving loop parallelism. In this respect, it is unlike most approaches that convert all parallelism to tasks. Preserving data-parallelism avoids task-parallel overhead and supports selfscheduling for loops, o!ering full flexibility: thread counts and distribution need not be fixed before execution.

Finally, a new backend-aware intermediate language enables architecturedependent optimizations. Together, these innovations promise to improve performance, and broaden Accelerate's applicability to modern hardware.

Hierarchical Port Hypergraphs: Two Decades Toward a Unifying Structure for Declarative Languages

Kazunori Ueda

Waseda University, Tokyo, 169-8555, Japan

Declarative languages take diverse forms with respect to data structures and control structures. They encompass a broad range of notions and paradigms, ranging from higher-order terms with binders to concurrent processes with various forms of communication.

A natural but challenging question is whether many, if not all, of these frameworks can be unified within a simple yet expressive formalism, rather than merely combined into a larger formalism. Graphs and graph rewriting provide a promising framework, since higher-order terms can be represented as tree structures augmented with edges encoding binding structures, while networks of processes can be represented as graph nodes and edges representing processes and their interconnection, respectively.

This perspective motivated us to design and implement LMNtal [7], a graph rewriting language for modeling and programming. LMNtal was conceived as an attempt to unify constraint-based concurrency (a.k.a. concurrent constraint programming) [10] and Constraint Handling Rules [1], two extensions of concurrent logic programming, within a simple setting consisting of *relations* and *zero-assignment logical variables* that connect relations (i.e., without function/constant symbols). This 'degeneration' naturally allows computation to be interpreted in terms of graphs and graph rewriting. Here, graphs are more accurately described as *port graphs* (when each variable connects exactly two ports of graph nodes) or *port hypergraphs* (when each variable may connect more than two ports), to distinguish them from ordinary graphs in graph theory.

Programming languages for graphs remain largely under-explored, presumably because graphs have poor affinity with standard PL-style inductive definitions. LMNtal addresses this issue by allowing graphs to be represented as terms modulo structural congruence, which serves as a PL counterpart of graph isomorphism.

Another key notion in LMNtal is a *membrane*, which encloses a subgraph to represent hierarchy and locality, thereby making LMNtal a language for rewriting *hierarchical port (hyper)graphs*.

Once the graph structures to be handled is established, the next step is to design appropriate language constructs for the matching and rewriting of subgraphs, including their copying and removal. LMNtal provides rich constructs for representing graph patterns based on connectivity, hierarchy, graph grammars, and quantification [2].

These constructs allow LMNtal to encode diverse formalisms including the λ-calculus with strong reduction [6, 11], distributed process calculi [5], proof nets and their reduction [3], and quantum circuit transformation [4].

On the practical side, LMNtal comes with full-fledged, compiler-based, open-source implementation [9], which supports both (i) *concurrent execution of rewrite rules* and (ii) *graph-based parallel model checking* that scales up to 10^9 states. In addition, the tool LaViT supports *visualization of graphs* and *visualization of state space of model checking*, which was proven extremely useful in *understanding* key properties of programs [8].

References

1. Früwirth, T.: Theory and practice of constraint handling rules. J. Logic Program. **37**, 95–138 (1998). https://doi.org/10.1016/S0743-1066(98)10005-5
2. Mishina, H., Ueda, K.: Introducing quantification into a hierarchical graph rewriting language. In: LOPSTR 2024. LNCS, vol. 14919, pp. 220–239. Springer Cham (2024). https://doi.org/10.1007/978-3-031-71294-4_13
3. Takyu, K., Ueda, K.: Enhancing a hierarchical graph rewriting language based on MELL cut elimination. In: PADL 2025. LNCS, vol. 15537, pp. 196–214. Springer Cham (2025). https://doi.org/10.1007/978-3-031-84924-4_13
4. Tei, K., Mishina, H., Yamamoto, N., Ueda, K.: Graph rewriting language as a platform for quantum diagrammatic calculi. In: PADL 2026. LNCS, vol. 16401, pp. 57–76. Springer Cham (2026). https://doi.org/10.1007/978-3-032-15981-6_4
5. Ueda, K.: Encoding distributed process calculi into LMNtal. Electron. Notes Theoret. Comput. Sci. **209**, 187–200 (2008). https://doi.org/10.1016/j.entcs.2008.04.012
6. Ueda, K.: Encoding the pure lambda calculus into hierarchical graph rewriting. In: RTA 2008. LNCS, vol. 5117, pp. 392–408. Springer Berlin Heidelberg (2008). https://doi.org/10.1007/978-3-540-70590-1_27
7. Ueda, K.: LMNtal as a hierarchical logic programming language. Theoret. Comput. Sci. **410**(46), 4784–4800 (2009). https://doi.org/10.1016/j.tcs.2009.07.043
8. Ueda, K., Ayano, T., Hori, T., Iwasawa, H., Ogawa, S.: Hierarchical graph rewriting as a unifying tool for analyzing and understanding nondeterministic systems. In: ICTAC 2009. pp. 349–355. Springer Berlin Heidelberg (2009). https://doi.org/10.1007/978-3-642-03466-4_24
9. Ueda, K., et al.: LMNtal: a unifying language and model checking tools, https://github.com/lmntal/
10. Ueda, K.: Logic/constraint programming and concurrency: The hard-won lessons of the Fifth Generation Computer Project. Sci. Comput. Program. **164**, 3–17 (2018). https://doi.org/10.1016/j.scico.2017.06.002
11. Yasen, A., Ueda, K.: Revisiting graph types in HyperLMNtal: A modelling language for hypergraph rewriting. IEEE Access **9**, 133449–133460 (2021). https://doi.org/10.1109/ACCESS.2021.3112903

Contents

Finite Functional Programming
or, LAMBDA: The Ultimate Predicate

Michael Arntzenius[(✉)] and Max Willsey

University of California, Berkeley, Berkeley, USA
daekharel@gmail.com, mwillsey@berkeley.edu

Abstract. We unify functional and logic programming by treating predicates as functions equipped with their support: the set of inputs whose output is nonzero. Datalog, for instance, is a language of finitely supported boolean functions. Finite support allows representing functions as input-output tables. Generalizing from boolean functions to other pointed sets neatly handles aggregation and weighted logic programming. We refer to the combination of finitely supported functions, represented as data, with higher order functions, represented as code, as *finite functional programming.* We give a simple type system to check finite support, using graded effects to check variable grounding and relevance types to model pointed sets.

Keywords: Logic programming · Functional programming · Categorical semantics · Linear types · Relevance types · Graded effects

1 Logic Programming Is (not) Functional Programming

Consider the following simple logic program to find mutual follows in a social network graph:

```
follows(john, mary).
follows(mary, john).
% ... many more follows() facts.
mutuals(X,Y) :- follows(X,Y), follows(Y,X).
```

Predicates like `follows` and `mutuals` denote functions into booleans. Following this intuition, we can translate this logic program directly into a functional one:

$$
\begin{aligned}
&\mathit{follows}, \mathit{mutuals} : \mathit{user} \to \mathit{user} \to \mathit{bool}\\
&\mathit{follows}\ x\ y = (\mathit{john} == x \text{ and } \mathit{mary} == y)\\
&\qquad\qquad\ \text{or } (\mathit{mary} == x \text{ and } \mathit{john} == y)\\
&\qquad\qquad\ \text{or} \ldots\\
&\mathit{mutuals}\ x\ y = \mathit{follows}\ x\ y \text{ and } \mathit{follows}\ y\ x
\end{aligned}
$$

However, functions in functional and imperative languages are unidirectional: they take inputs to outputs. Evaluating $\mathit{mutuals}\,x\,y$ will test whether fixed users x, y are mutuals—but unlike in logic programming, we cannot use it to enumerate mutual follows, for instance, to find the mutuals y of a fixed user x.

M. Sperber and E. Komendantskaya (Eds.): FLOPS 2026, LNCS 16533, pp. 1–18, 2026.
https://doi.org/10.1007/978-981-92-0184-6_1

For the same reason, our functional translation cannot handle existential quantifiers (also called 'projection' in databases). Consider this logic program to find actors who have appeared in the same film:

```
costars(Actor1, Actor2) :-
  stars(Film, Actor1),
  stars(Film, Actor2).
```

Since `Film` does not appear in the head of the rule, the head is derivable if there exists a `Film` satisfying the body. To embed this functionally, we could assume a function $\mathit{exists} : \forall\alpha.\,(\alpha \to \mathit{bool}) \to \mathit{bool}$:

$$\begin{aligned}&\mathit{costars} : \mathit{person} \to \mathit{person} \to \mathit{bool}\\&\mathit{costars}\ \mathit{actor1}\ \mathit{actor2} = \mathit{exists}\ (\lambda \mathit{film}.\ \mathit{stars}\ \mathit{film}\ \mathit{actor1}\ \text{and}\ \mathit{stars}\ \mathit{film}\ \mathit{actor2})\end{aligned}$$

But how can we implement *exists* for an arbitrary type α and function $f : \alpha \to \mathit{bool}$? We are stymied by unidirectionality: all we can do with f is give it inputs; since the input type is arbitrary, we cannot generate any.[1]

Logic programming implements existential quantification by rejecting input-output directionality: much as a function is a set of input-output tuples, a predicate can enumerate its tuples—or rather, those whose output is true (any non-enumerated inputs are implicitly false). We call these inputs the *support* of a predicate. If we know f's support, calculating *exists* f is simple: is the support nonempty?

This suggests we can make the direct functional translation of logic programs behave correctly if we equip functions with their support. Inspired by Datalog, we focus on finite support. Since finitely supported functions can be represented as key-value tables, we also call them *finite maps*. We make the following contributions:

1. We observe that defining a function's support requires a point in its codomain, suggesting the category Set_* of pointed sets and point preserving maps is a suitable site for the semantics of a functional logic programming language.
2. We show Set_* forms a model of relevance, a relaxation of linearity in which variables must be used at least once rather than exactly once.
3. We show finite maps form a graded monad/comonad on Set_*.
4. We construct a simply typed language λ_{FS} that can express relational algebra and some forms of aggregation, whose type system guarantees finite support.
5. We give a denotational semantics of λ_{FS} in Set_*.

Along the way we will observe other curious connections:

1. Database inner joins are point preserving maps out of the smash product $A \otimes B$ of pointed sets, while outer joins map out of the direct product $A \,\&\, B$.

[1] Of course, one can define *exists* for any finite type α by enumeration, and even for some infinite types by exploiting continuity of f [7,8]. However, our approach will be to presume, not static knowledge of the type, but dynamic knowledge of f's support.

2. Input/output modes in bottom-up logic programming correspond to procedural functions and finite maps respectively.
3. Checking a rule is well moded corresponds to an effect system for the graded monad of finite maps.

さあ始めましょう！ Let's get started!

2 Support, Pointedly

The support of a boolean function f is the set $\{x \in A : f(x) \neq \mathit{false}\}$. It will be useful to generalize beyond booleans, firstly to expose compositional structure, for instance, to define the support of a curried function $f : A \to B \to \mathit{bool}$; and secondly to generalize from boolean logic and existential quantification (or relational algebra and projection, respectively) to weighted logic programming and aggregation (or tensor algebra and contraction).

To this end we write P, Q, R for sets with a designated element ('pointed sets') and $\mathit{nil}_P \in P$ for the designated element (the 'point'). (We use A, B, C for ordinary sets.) For instance, we regard *bool* as pointed with $\mathit{nil}_{\mathit{bool}} = \mathit{false}$. We define the support of a function $f : A \to P$ into a pointed set to be $\operatorname{supp} f = \{x \in A : f(x) \neq \mathit{nil}_P\}$. If one regards nil_P as an uninteresting, default value, a function's support contains those inputs with interesting, nondefault outputs.

We write $A \Rightarrow P = \{f \in A \to P : \operatorname{supp} f \text{ is finite}\}$ for the finitely supported functions from A to P. This is a pointed set with $\mathit{nil}_{A \Rightarrow P} = \lambda x.\ \mathit{nil}_P$; the boring, default finite map is the one with empty support. What can we do with finite maps? We can of course apply them—this is lookup in a key-value table. We can also curry and uncurry them: $A \times B \Rightarrow P \cong A \Rightarrow (B \Rightarrow P)$. This converts between a single flat table $A \times B \Rightarrow P$ and a trie-like nesting of tables $A \Rightarrow B \Rightarrow P$.

But how can we manipulate the output P of a finite map $A \Rightarrow P$? Can we, for instance, compose finite maps? Unfortunately, the composition of two finite maps may not have finite support: e.g. take $\lambda x.\ x < 3 : \mathbb{N} \Rightarrow \mathit{bool}$ followed by $\mathit{not} : \mathit{bool} \Rightarrow \mathit{bool}$. The set of naturals less than three is finite; its complement is not. For the same reason, we cannot compose a finite map $g : A \Rightarrow P$ with an arbitrary function $f : P \to Q$ and expect the result to be finitely supported.

However, we *can* compose a finite map with a function f if $f(\mathit{nil}_P) = \mathit{nil}_Q$; this preserves finiteness because it can only contract our support. These are the *point preserving maps*, which we notate $P \multimap Q = \{f \in P \to Q : f(\mathit{nil}_P) = \mathit{nil}_Q\}$. These are pointed with $\mathit{nil}_{P \multimap Q} = \lambda x. \mathit{nil}_Q$. The category Set_* has pointed sets P, Q as objects and point preserving maps as morphisms; what we have just observed is that, for any set A, there is a functor $F_A : \mathrm{Set}_* \to \mathrm{Set}_*$ given by $F_A(P) = A \Rightarrow P$. If finitely supported maps are this work's *raison d'être,* point preserving maps are how we will manipulate and combine them.

2.1 Direct or/and Smash

Following logic programming, we take particular interest in two point preserving maps: boolean disjunction and conjunction. Let's start with their types. Recall

Notation	*Name*	*Elements*	*nil*
$P \mathbin{\&} Q$	direct product	$\langle p, q\rangle$ for $p \in P, q \in Q$	$\langle nil_P, nil_Q\rangle$
$P \otimes Q$	smash product	(p, q) for $p \in P, q \in Q$ modulo:	$(nil_P, q) = (p, nil_Q)$
$P \multimap Q$	point preserving maps	$f : P \to Q$ with $f(nil_P) = nil_Q$	$\lambda\_.\, nil_Q$
$A \Rightarrow P$	finite maps	$f : A \to P$ with $\operatorname{supp} f$ finite	$\lambda\_.\, nil_P$
bool	booleans	*true*, *false*	*false*
$\mathbb{N}_0$	natural numbers	0, 1, 2, 3, 4...	0
maybe A	maybe type	just a for $a \in A$, none	none

Fig. 1. Pointed sets I have known and loved

that $nil_{bool} = false$. Observe that *or* yields *nil* when both its arguments are *nil*, while *and* yields *nil* when either argument is. We can reflect this both/either distinction using distinct types. Disjunction accepts a pair which is *nil* when both components are. This is the direct product of pointed sets, $P \mathbin{\&} Q = \{\langle p, q\rangle : p \in P, q \in Q\}$ where $nil_{P\&Q} = \langle nil_P, nil_Q\rangle$. Conversely, conjunction accepts a pair which is *nil* if either component is. This is the smash product of pointed sets, $P \otimes Q = \{(p, q) : p \in P, q \in Q\}$ quotiented by $nil_{P\otimes Q} = (nil_P, y) = (x, nil_Q)$. Thus:

$$\text{or} : bool \mathbin{\&} bool \multimap bool \qquad\qquad \text{and} : bool \otimes bool \multimap bool$$

It will be useful to generalize ‘and’ to type $bool \otimes P \multimap P$, along with its mirror image ‘when’ of type $P \otimes bool \multimap P$, defined:[2]

$$\begin{aligned} true \text{ and } x = x \text{ when } true &= x \\ false \text{ and } x = x \text{ when } false &= nil_P \end{aligned}$$

Finally, we must note an important asymmetry: curried maps $f : P \multimap Q \multimap R$ must preserve *nil* in each argument separately, like ‘and’ and unlike ‘or’:

$$\begin{aligned} (f\ nil_P)\ q &= nil_{Q\multimap R}\ q = nil_R && \text{since } f : P \multimap (Q \multimap R) \text{ preserves } nil \\ (f\ p)\ nil_Q &= nil_R && \text{since } f\ p : Q \multimap R \text{ preserves } nil \end{aligned}$$

In fact, currying and uncurrying of point preserving maps forms an isomorphism $P \otimes Q \multimap R \cong P \multimap Q \multimap R$. But there is no corresponding way to curry maps $P \mathbin{\&} Q \multimap R$ (like ‘or’) that yield *nil* only when both arguments are *nil*.[3]

3 A Finitely Supported Map from Examples to Booleans

Now that we've developed enough notation (summarized in Fig. 1, along with a few more pointed sets we will introduce later), we can consider some example programs and their types. For now we rely on intuition to see that they are semantically well typed; in Sects. 4–6 we will develop typing rules. First,

[2] An edifying exercise is to verify the generalized ‘and’ is one leg of an isomorphism $bool \otimes P \cong P$; its inverse is $\lambda x.\, (true, x) : P \multimap bool \otimes P$.

[3] Phrased categorically, Set_* does not have all exponential objects.

$$
\begin{array}{rrcl}
\text{types} & A, B & ::= & P \mid A \to B \mid A \times B \mid 1 \mid \ldots \\
\text{pointed types} & P, Q & ::= & P \mathbin{\&} Q \mid P \otimes Q \mid P \multimap Q \mid A \Rightarrow Q \mid \mathit{maybe}\ A \mid \mathbb{N}_0 \\
\text{expressions} & e & ::= & t \mid x \mid \lambda x.\, e \mid e_1\, e_2 \mid (e_1, e_2) \mid \pi_i\, e \mid () \\
 & & & \text{case } e_1 \text{ of just } x \to e_2;\ \text{none} \to e_3 \mid \ldots \\
\text{pointed terms} & t, u & ::= & \mathit{nil} \mid x \mid \lambda x.\, t \mid t\, u \mid t\, x \mid t\, e \mid \langle t, u\rangle \mid \pi_i\, t \\
 & & & (t, u) \mid \text{let } (x, y) = t \text{ in } u \mid \text{just } e \mid \text{let just } x = t \text{ in } u
\end{array}
$$

Fig. 2. Syntax of λ_{FS}

$$
\begin{array}{rclcrcl}
\mathit{bool} & \longrightarrow & \mathit{maybe}\ 1 & \quad & t \text{ and } u & \longrightarrow & \text{let just } \_ = t \text{ in } u \\
\mathit{true} & \longrightarrow & \text{just } () & & \text{let } x = t \text{ in } u & \longrightarrow & \text{let } (x, y) = (t, \mathit{true}) \text{ in } (y \text{ and } u) \\
\mathit{false} & \longrightarrow & \mathit{nil} & & t \text{ when } u & \longrightarrow & \text{let } x = t \text{ in } (u \text{ and } x)
\end{array}
$$

$$
\begin{array}{rclcrcl}
\text{or} & : & \mathit{bool} \mathbin{\&} \mathit{bool} \multimap \mathit{bool} & \quad & \mathit{exists} & : & (A \Rightarrow \mathit{bool}) \multimap \mathit{bool} \\
(+) & : & \mathbb{N}_0 \mathbin{\&} \mathbb{N}_0 \multimap \mathbb{N}_0 & & \mathit{sum} & : & (A \Rightarrow \mathbb{N}_0) \multimap \mathbb{N}_0 \\
(\times) & : & \mathbb{N}_0 \otimes \mathbb{N}_0 \multimap \mathbb{N}_0 & & (=) & : & A \to (A \Rightarrow \mathit{bool})
\end{array}
$$

Fig. 3. Syntax sugar and primitive functions in λ_{FS}

let's consider some basic uses of conjunction (inner joins, in database parlance), starting with the simplest, cross product:

$$
\begin{array}{l}
\mathit{cross} : (A \Rightarrow \mathit{bool}) \multimap (B \Rightarrow \mathit{bool}) \multimap (A \Rightarrow B \Rightarrow \mathit{bool}) \\
\mathit{cross}\ f\ g\ x\ y = f\ x \text{ and } g\ y
\end{array}
$$

The type of *cross* captures something important: curried functions preserve *nil* in all arguments separately, and since $\mathit{nil}_{A \Rightarrow \mathit{bool}} = \lambda\_.\, \mathit{false}$ is the empty relation, we know from its type alone that the cross product of an empty set with any other relation is empty. Inner joins in general have this property because they use conjunction. For instance, intersection:

$$
\begin{array}{l}
\mathit{intersect} : (A \Rightarrow \mathit{bool}) \multimap (A \Rightarrow \mathit{bool}) \multimap (A \Rightarrow \mathit{bool}) \\
\mathit{intersect}\ f\ g\ x = f\ x \text{ and } g\ x
\end{array}
$$

This intersects two finite sets, but we can also more generally 'intersect' (i.e. filter) a finite set with an arbitrary function $A \to \mathit{bool}$:

$$
\begin{array}{l}
\mathit{filter} : (A \Rightarrow \mathit{bool}) \multimap (A \to \mathit{bool}) \multimap (A \Rightarrow \mathit{bool}) \\
\mathit{filter}\ f\ g\ x = f\ x \text{ and } g\ x
\end{array}
$$

We can also define the intersection of two arbitrary functions $f, g : A \to \mathit{bool}$, but this will only yield another function, not a finite map.

Let's move on to considering what we can express with the function $\mathit{exists} : (A \Rightarrow \mathit{bool}) \multimap \mathit{bool}$, now justified by the finite support of its argument:

$costars : person \Rightarrow person \Rightarrow bool$
$costars\ x\ y = exists\ (\lambda film.\ stars\ film\ x \text{ and } stars\ film\ y)$

Functions of the shape $(A \Rightarrow P) \multimap P$ represent *aggregations* into P. For instance, $sum : (A \Rightarrow \mathbb{N}_0) \multimap \mathbb{N}_0$ lets us count the number of films someone has starred in:

$filmCount : person \Rightarrow \mathbb{N}_0$
$filmCount\ actor = sum\ (\lambda film.\ 1 \text{ when } stars\ film\ actor)$

In general, for any commutative monoid of the form $(P, \oplus, nil_P)$, since $nil \oplus nil = nil$ we have $\oplus : P \,\&\, P \multimap P$. This extends to an aggregation $\bigoplus_P : (A \Rightarrow P) \multimap P$ that takes a finite map $f : A \Rightarrow P$ to the monoid sum $\bigoplus_{x \in \mathsf{supp}\, f} f(x)$. For instance, the aggregation of the monoid $(bool, or, false)$ is *exists*, while the aggregation of $(\mathbb{N}_0, +, 0)$ is *sum*.

Just as *exists* combined with $and : bool \otimes bool \multimap bool$ gave us relational composition in *costars*, summation combined with $\times : \mathbb{N}_0 \otimes \mathbb{N}_0 \multimap \mathbb{N}_0$ (which holds since $0 \times y = x \times 0 = 0 = nil_{\mathbb{N}_0}$) gives us matrix multiplication:

$matMul : (A \times B \Rightarrow \mathbb{N}_0) \multimap (B \times C \Rightarrow \mathbb{N}_0) \multimap A \times C \Rightarrow \mathbb{N}_0$
$matMul\ m\ n\ i\ k = sum\ (\lambda j.\ m\ i\ j \times n\ j\ k)$

We have already seen that $A \Rightarrow P$ is functorial in P. Given a commutative monoid aggregation over P, it is also functorial in the key space A, by aggregating the values of keys that collide under some map $f : A \to B$. For $\mathbb{N}_0$ under *sum* this is:

$map : (A \to B) \to (A \Rightarrow \mathbb{N}_0) \multimap (B \Rightarrow \mathbb{N}_0)$
$map\ f\ count\ b = sum\ (\lambda a.\ count\ a \text{ when } f\ a = b)$

Of course, finite sets $A \Rightarrow bool$ and bags $A \Rightarrow \mathbb{N}_0$ are not only functors but monads. If besides an aggregation *exists*/*sum* we have a monoid $(P, \circledast : P \otimes P \multimap P, 1)$—for *bool* this is conjunction $(bool, and, true)$, for $\mathbb{N}_0$ it is multiplication $(\mathbb{N}_0, \times, 1)$—then we can define monadic pure and join:

$pure : A \to (A \Rightarrow \mathbb{N}_0)$
$pure\ x\ a = 1 \text{ when } x = a$

$join : ((A \Rightarrow \mathbb{N}_0) \Rightarrow \mathbb{N}_0) \multimap (A \Rightarrow \mathbb{N}_0)$
$join\ nested\ a = sum\ (\lambda t.\ nested\ t \times t\ a)$

We might even dare to consider defining finitely supported predicates recursively:

$connected : person \Rightarrow person \Rightarrow bool$
$connected\ x\ y = costars\ x\ y$ or $exists\ (\lambda z.\ connected\ x\ z$ and $connected\ z\ y)$

Unfortunately we will not be able to give typing rules or semantics for this kind of recursion here. Ensuring the existence of a fixed point would seem to require some sort of monotonicity à la Datafun [3] or $\lambda_\vee$ [24], and ensuring it remains finite will be even more difficult; we leave this to future work.

Finally, let's turn our attention to the prototypical outer join: union.

$union : (A \Rightarrow bool)\ \&\ (A \Rightarrow bool) \multimap (A \Rightarrow bool)$
$union\ fg\ x = \pi_1\ fg\ x$ or $\pi_2\ fg\ x$

We saw in Sect. 2 why *union*, being a function on & pairs, cannot be curried. But why can't we destructure the pair *fg*? To explain this, we must understand the variable usage discipline that ensures functions preserve *nil*.

4 The Relevance of Being Relevant

We've seen that point preserving maps are important because they can be safely applied to the outputs of finitely supported maps while preserving finite support, and allow us to combine multiple maps either via inner joins (maps out of $\otimes$ pairs) or outer joins (maps out of & pairs). How can we statically check that maps preserve *nil*? To gain some intuition, let's look at a few simple examples and whether they preserve *nil*:

$$\begin{array}{rll} id = \lambda x.\ x & : P \multimap P & ✓ \\ three = \lambda x.\ 3 & : P \multimap \mathbb{N}_0 & ✗\ \text{NOT POINT PRESERVING} \\ dup_\otimes = \lambda x.\ (x, x) & : P \multimap P \otimes P & ✓ \\ dup_\& = \lambda x.\ \langle x, x\rangle & : P \multimap P \,\&\, P & ✓ \end{array}$$

Plainly the identity function preserves *nil*, but constant functions do not (except for $\lambda x.\ nil$). This suggests a linear type system, which ensures each variable is used exactly once; constant functions do not use their argument and so are prohibited. However, duplication does preserve *nil*, whether into $\otimes$ or & pairs: $(nil, nil) = nil$ and $\langle nil, nil\rangle = nil$. Or, consider the intersection ($\lambda x.\, f\,x$ and $g\,x$) of two maps $f, g : P \multimap bool$, which uses x twice yet still preserves *nil*. Thus the appropriate approach is a *relevant* type system, which ensures variables are used *at least once*—although as we'll see presently, what counts as 'used' can be subtle.

So far our examples fail to distinguish the behavior of $\otimes$ from &; let's fix that:

$$\begin{array}{llll}
\mathit{fst}_\otimes = \lambda p.\,\text{let}\ (x,y) = p\ \text{in}\ x & : P \otimes Q \multimap P & ✗ & \text{NOT POINT PRESERVING} \\
\mathit{fst}_\& = \lambda p.\,\pi_1\,p & : P \,\&\, Q \multimap P & ✓ & \\
\mathit{pair}_\otimes = \lambda x.\,\lambda y.\,(x,y) & : P \multimap Q \multimap P \otimes Q & ✓ & \\
\mathit{pair}_\& = \lambda x.\,\lambda y.\,\langle x,y\rangle & : P \multimap Q \multimap P \,\&\, Q & ✗ & \text{NOT POINT PRESERVING} \\
\mathit{and3}_\otimes = \lambda x.\,(x,3) & : P \multimap P \otimes \mathbb{N}_0 & ✓ & \\
\mathit{and3}_\& = \lambda x.\,\langle x,3\rangle & : P \multimap P \,\&\, \mathbb{N}_0 & ✗ & \text{NOT POINT PRESERVING}
\end{array}$$

One can verify these examples mechanically using the definitions of $\otimes$ and &, but some intuition may be helpful. To use an $\otimes$ pair (x, y) we must use both x and y, to guarantee that if either is *nil* we will propagate it. By contrast, if a & pair is *nil* then both of its components are, so we are free to use only one. This is why $\mathit{fst}_\otimes$ is invalid but $\mathit{fst}_\&$ is correct—and also why we use destructuring to eliminate $\otimes$, but projection for &. Conversely, constructing an $\otimes$ pair (t, u) uses anything used by either t or u, since if either t or u is *nil* the whole pair is, but constructing a & pair $\langle t, u\rangle$ uses only what both t and u use, since only these will force both t and u to be *nil*. This is why $\mathit{pair}_\otimes$ and $\mathit{and3}_\otimes$ are correct but $\mathit{pair}_\&$ and $\mathit{and3}_\&$ are invalid.

Since we need to mix a cartesian, structural type system for sets A, B and functions $A \to B$ with a substructural, relevant type system for pointed sets P, Q and point preserving maps $P \multimap Q$, we adapt the rules of Benton and Wadler's mixed linear/nonlinear logic LNL [5,6] to relevance rather than linearity. We use two contexts, Γ containing ordinary variables $x : A$ and Δ containing pointed set variables $x : P$; two syntactic classes of terms, ordinary e and point preserving t; and two typing judgments, $\Gamma \vdash e : A$ for functions and $\Gamma \,/\, \Delta \vdash t : P$ for point preserving maps. A few example rules:

$$\frac{\Gamma \,/\, \Delta \vdash t : P \qquad \Gamma \,/\, \Delta \vdash u : Q}{\Gamma \,/\, \Delta \vdash \langle t, u\rangle : P \,\&\, Q} \qquad \frac{\Gamma \,/\, \Delta_1 \vdash t : P \qquad \Gamma \,/\, \Delta_2 \vdash u : Q}{\Gamma \,/\, \Delta_1 \cup \Delta_2 \vdash (t, u) : P \otimes Q}$$

$$\frac{}{\Gamma \,/\, x : P \vdash x : P} \qquad \frac{\Gamma \,/\, \Delta, x : P \vdash t : Q}{\Gamma \,/\, \Delta \vdash \lambda x.\, t : P \multimap Q}$$

Observe that in the rule for & pairs $\langle t, u\rangle$ each component is checked in the same relevant context Δ, and therefore must use the same variables; but in $\otimes$ pairs (t, u), we give them different contexts Δ_1, Δ_2 which must *union* to produce the context of the whole pair. This union is a key difference from standard linear logic, which would split the contexts disjointly; it allows a variable to be used in both branches—but, unlike the & rule, does not *require* it.

5 The Other Side of the Tracks

Alas, these are not yet the typing rules we are looking for. A scant two contexts will not suffice; we have *three* kinds of function we'd like to introduce—ordinary

$A \to B$, point preserving $P \multimap Q$, and finitely supported $A \Rightarrow P$—and therefore three kinds of variable, needing three separate contexts. Besides Γ and Δ we need a context Ω of finitely supported variables $x : A, y : B, \ldots$, and our typing judgement takes the form $\Gamma \,/\, \Delta \,/\, \Omega \vdash t : P$. To understand how Ω behaves, let's revisit the examples that opened the previous section:

$$\begin{array}{rll} id = \lambda x.\, x & : P \Rightarrow P & \text{✗ NOT FINITELY SUPPORTED} \\ three = \lambda x.\, 3 & : A \Rightarrow \mathbb{N}_0 & \text{✗ NOT FINITELY SUPPORTED} \\ dup_{\otimes} = \lambda x.\, (x, x) & : P \Rightarrow P \otimes P & \text{✗ NOT FINITELY SUPPORTED} \\ dup_{\&} = \lambda x.\, \langle x, x \rangle & : P \Rightarrow P \,\&\, P & \text{✗ NOT FINITELY SUPPORTED} \end{array}$$

Oh no! What went wrong? Well, constant functions like *three* are not finite because their support is their entire possibly infinite domain ($\lambda x.\, nil$ is the only exception). Similarly, the support of id, $dup_{\otimes}$, and $dup_{\&}$ is the entire domain minus nil; we cannot generally use a finite map's input directly in its output.[4]

If $\lambda x.\, x$ is not well typed, what does our variable rule look like? How do we use variables in our finitely supported context Ω? Let's return to our source of inspiration. In bottom-up logic programming, we generate nonempty, finite relations by either (1) combining other nonempty relations or (2) using rules that refer to constants. We saw in Sect. 3 that in λ_{FS}, (1) means using point preserving maps to transform finite maps, and (2) means using equality $(=) : A \to A \Rightarrow bool$ to generate singleton finite maps. Let's consider a prototypical example of each kind:

$$\begin{array}{rll} actorOrDirector = \lambda x.\, actor\ x \text{ or } director\ x & : person \Rightarrow bool & ✓ \\ hitchcockAlone = \lambda x.\, hitchcock = x & : person \Rightarrow bool & ✓ \end{array}$$

In each case, we use the finitely supported variable x by applying a finite map to it. This, then, will serve both as our elimination rule for finite maps and our usage rule for finitely supported variables:

$$\frac{\Gamma \,/\, \Delta \,/\, \Omega, x : A \vdash t : P}{\Gamma \,/\, \Delta \,/\, \Omega \vdash \lambda x.\, t : A \Rightarrow P} \Rightarrow\mathrm{I} \qquad \frac{\Gamma \,/\, \Delta \,/\, \Omega \vdash t : A \Rightarrow P}{\Gamma \,/\, \Delta \,/\, \Omega, x : A \vdash t\, x : P} \Rightarrow\mathrm{E}$$

These rules structuralize the isomorphism $A \Rightarrow B \Rightarrow P \cong A \times B \Rightarrow P$ (which is more obvious after renaming: $\Omega \Rightarrow A \Rightarrow P \cong \Omega \times A \Rightarrow P$). Combined with the isomorphism $P \cong (1 \Rightarrow P)$, this shows that finitely supported maps form not just a functor but a *graded monad* on Set_*.

[4] We could in principle make a carve-out for maps with finite domains. As we intend to represent finite maps by tables, however, this poses a usability hazard: enumerating all 64-bit integers just because a programmer wrote $\lambda x.\, x$ is not desirable.

A (non-graded) monad is an endofunctor F with natural transformations $\mathit{pure}_\alpha : \alpha \to F\alpha$ and $\mathit{join}_\alpha : FF\alpha \to F\alpha$, satisfying certain laws which we omit for brevity. For our purposes, a *graded monad* [14,26] is a family of functors F_m where $m \in M$ is drawn from some monoid of grades $(M, \cdot, 1)$, equipped with analogues of *pure* and *join* which interact with these gradings in the following way: $\mathit{pure}_\alpha : \alpha \to F_1\alpha$ and $\mathit{join}_\alpha : F_m F_n \alpha \to F_{mn}\alpha$, again satisfying certain omitted laws.

In our case, the graded monad is $F_A P = A \Rightarrow P$, and the monoid of grades is sets under cross product.[5] This makes $\mathit{pure}_P : P \multimap (1 \Rightarrow P)$ and $\mathit{join}_P : (A \Rightarrow B \Rightarrow P) \multimap (A \times B \Rightarrow P)$ merely the forward legs of our two isomorphisms. The laws we omitted hold trivially because these maps are isomorphisms—indeed, the reverse legs of these isomorphisms also make F_A is a graded *comonad* [22]. Although almost trivial, this graded (co)monad is of practical interest because type systems for graded monads (effect systems) have been extensively studied [11].

Unfortunately, our typing rules do not all follow neatly from this connection to grading. Let's examine the rules for & and ⊗. Both are informative: the former because it is straightforward, the latter because it is not. The rules for & are:

$$\frac{\Gamma \,/\, \Delta \,/\, \Omega \vdash t : P \qquad \Gamma \,/\, \Delta \,/\, \Omega \vdash u : Q}{\Gamma \,/\, \Delta \,/\, \Omega \vdash \langle t, u\rangle : P \,\&\, Q}\,\&\,\text{I} \qquad \frac{\Gamma \,/\, \Delta \,/\, \Omega \vdash t : P_1 \,\&\, P_2}{\Gamma \,/\, \Delta \,/\, \Omega \vdash \pi_i\, t : P_i}\,\&\,\text{E}$$

Now let's consider what rules we would need to type the following examples involving ⊗ (by way of $\mathit{and} : \mathit{bool} \otimes \mathit{bool} \multimap \mathit{bool}$):

$$\begin{aligned}
&f : A \Rightarrow \mathit{bool}, g : A \Rightarrow \mathit{bool} \,/\, \cdot \,/\, x : A, y : A \vdash f\,x \text{ and } g\,y : \mathit{bool}\\
&f : A \Rightarrow \mathit{bool}, g : A \Rightarrow \mathit{bool} \,/\, \cdot \,/\, x : A \qquad\quad\; \vdash f\,x \text{ and } g\,x : \mathit{bool}\\
&f : A \Rightarrow \mathit{bool}, g : A \to \mathit{bool} \,/\, \cdot \,/\, x : A \qquad\quad\; \vdash f\,x \text{ and } g\,x : \mathit{bool}
\end{aligned}$$

Since we wish to guarantee finite support, we first ask: what is the support of each example (as a function of the supports of f, g)?

The support of fx and gy is the cross product of the supports of $f : A \Rightarrow \mathit{bool}$ and $g : A \Rightarrow \mathit{bool}$. Fortunately, the cross product of finite sets is finite. So what typing rule does this example need? We have used each variable x, y in our finite support context Ω exactly once, so it suffices to be able to split this context between the (implicit) ⊗ pair of arguments to 'and':

$$\frac{\Gamma \,/\, \Delta_1 \,/\, \Omega_1 \vdash t : P \qquad \Gamma \,/\, \Delta_2 \,/\, \Omega_2 \vdash u : Q}{\Gamma \,/\, \Delta_1 \cup \Delta_2 \,/\, \Omega_1, \Omega_2 \vdash (t, u) : P \otimes Q}$$

[5] Technically this is not a monoid, since $(A \times B) \times C$ is only isomorphic, not equal, to $A \times (B \times C)$. This technicality is not worth getting hung up on; it can be fixed in any number of ways, for instance, by taking grades to be contexts of types Ω under concatenation rather than sets themselves.

This rule does not suffice for our second example, $f\ x$ and $g\ x$, which uses the same finitely supported variable x twice. Nonetheless this has finite support, namely, the intersection of f's and g's supports. So we can relax our rules to union contexts, much like the rules for the relevant context Δ:

$$\frac{\Gamma \,/\, \Delta_1 \,/\, \Omega_1 \vdash t : P \qquad \Gamma \,/\, \Delta_2 \,/\, \Omega_2 \vdash u : Q}{\Gamma \,/\, \Delta_1 \cup \Delta_2 \,/\, \Omega_1 \cup \Omega_2 \vdash (t, u) : P \otimes Q}$$

Yet this still fails to check our final example, which filters the finite set $f : A \Rightarrow \mathit{bool}$ by an arbitrary boolean function $g : A \to \mathit{bool}$. This is unproblematic semantically: we can filter a finite set by any predicate we like and the result remains finite! The solution is a rule that breaks the rules: any variable finitely supported by t may be used unrestricted in u, so the finite support context Ω_1 for t will *jump* across the railway tracks into the unrestricted context for u:

$$\frac{\Gamma \,/\, \Delta_1 \,/\, \Omega_1 \vdash t : P \qquad \Gamma, \Omega_1 \,/\, \Delta_2 \,/\, \Omega_2 \vdash u : Q}{\Gamma \,/\, \Delta_1 \cup \Delta_2 \,/\, \Omega_1, \Omega_2 \vdash (t, u) : P \otimes Q} \otimes\text{I}$$

This rule is asymmetric: it 'grounds' variables from left to right. This choice is arbitrary—right to left is just as sound—but the symmetric variant, which allows variables finitely supported by either t or u to be used unrestricted in the other, allows circular dataflow and is unsound. For instance, there may be infinitely many x, y such that $x = y$, but for fixed x there is exactly one such y; this is why we give equality the type $A \to (A \Rightarrow \mathit{bool})$. However, if we allow each branch to ground variables used in the other, then ($x = y$ and $y = x$), though semantically identical to $x = y$, would incorrectly appear to finitely support both x and y: in the left branch, x is used to ground y, and vice-versa.

To ensure our last rule generalizes the two prior ones, we must be able to weaken a finitely supported hypothesis $x{:}A \in \Omega$ to an unrestricted one $x{:}A \in \Gamma$. Then a variable finitely supported by both t and u can simply be placed into Ω_1 in $\otimes$I. Unfortunately this doesn't yet hold: $\Rightarrow$E lets us apply finite maps $A \Rightarrow P$ to variables in Ω but not in Γ! We need an additional rule that lets us apply a finite map to an unrestricted variable x, or more generally an expression e which (as usual) may use unrestrictedly any variables finitely supported by t:[6]

$$\frac{\Gamma \,/\, \Delta \,/\, \Omega \vdash t : A \Rightarrow P \qquad \Gamma, \Omega \vdash e : A}{\Gamma \,/\, \Delta \,/\, \Omega \vdash t\, e : P} \Rightarrow\text{E}_2$$

[6] Adding Ω to e's context is also needed to allow multiple uses of a finitely supported variable among the arguments to a nested finite map, e.g. $\cdot \,/\, f : A \Rightarrow A \Rightarrow P \,/\, x : A \vdash f\, x\, x : P$.

6 Types and Semantics

We give the typing rules of λ_{FS} in Fig. 4. The attentive reader will find few surprises. As mentioned in Sect. 4, our rules borrow from adjoint calculi such as LNL [5,6] to handle the interaction between ordinary functions and point preserving functions. This corresponds semantically to an adjunction between the cartesian closed category Set (LNL's $\mathcal{C}$) and the symmetric monoidal closed category Set_* (LNL's $\mathcal{L}$). Additionally, Set_* possesses a natural family of diagonal maps $\lambda x.\, (x, x) : P \multimap P \otimes P$, making it a relevant monoidal category [16,21]. The adjunction in question consists of the free functor *maybe* : Set $\to$ Set_* and the forgetful functor $U : \mathrm{Set}_* \to \mathrm{Set}$. Our main difference from a standard adjoint calculus is our additional context Ω of finitely supported variables, which in most typing rules follows the context-hopping pattern of $\otimes$ introduction that we explored in Sect. 5.

Unsurprisingly, we interpret 'set' types as sets $[\![A]\!] \in \mathrm{Set}$, and 'pointed set' types as pointed sets $[\![P]\!] \in \mathrm{Set}_*$. We have deliberately used almost identical notation for the syntax of types and for the mathematical objects they denote. See Fig. 5 for the semantics of types and contexts. The n-ary smash product $\bigotimes_i P_i$ deserves some explanation: this denotes the pointed set $\{(x_1, \ldots, x_n) : x_1 \in P_1, \ldots, x_n \in P_n\} \uplus \{\mathit{nil}\}$ quotiented by $\forall i.\, x_i = \mathit{nil} \implies (x_1, ..., x_n) = \mathit{nil}$. The explicit addition of *nil* means that the nullary smash product, $\bigotimes\{\}$, has two elements: *nil* and the empty tuple (), which is important for interpreting the case $\Delta = \cdot$ of an empty pointed set context.

$$[\![\Gamma \vdash e : A]\!] \in [\![\Gamma]\!] \to [\![A]\!]$$
$$[\![\Gamma \,/\, \Delta \,/\, \Omega \vdash t : P]\!] \in [\![\Gamma]\!] \to [\![\Delta]\!] \multimap [\![\Omega]\!] \Rightarrow [\![P]\!]$$

We give semantics to expressions e and terms t in Fig. 6. The term semantics often depend on the splitting of the Δ and Ω contexts, so we include the conclusion of the typing judgment in the semantic brackets. For space reasons we could not include the premises, so cross-referencing with Fig. 4 is suggested. To make it clear that terms are finitely supported with respect to the context Ω, we construct all finite maps explicitly using set comprehensions as sets of input-output pairs, $x \mapsto y$.

$\boxed{\Gamma \vdash e : A}$

$$\frac{\Gamma \,/\, \cdot \,/\, \cdot \vdash t : P}{\Gamma \vdash t : P}\ \text{UI} \qquad \frac{x : A \in \Gamma}{\Gamma \vdash x : A}\ \text{EVAR} \qquad \frac{}{\Gamma \vdash () : 1}\ 1\,\text{I}$$

$$\frac{\Gamma, x : A \vdash e : B}{\Gamma \vdash \lambda x.\, e : A \to B}\ {\to}\,\text{I} \qquad \frac{\Gamma \vdash e_1 : A \to B \qquad \Gamma \vdash e_2 : A}{\Gamma \vdash e_1\, e_2 : B}\ {\to}\,\text{E}$$

$$\frac{\Gamma \vdash e_1 : A \qquad \Gamma \vdash e_2 : B}{\Gamma \vdash (e_1, e_2) : A \times B}\ \times\,\text{I} \qquad \frac{\Gamma \vdash e : A_1 \times A_2}{\Gamma \vdash \pi_i\, e : A_i}\ \times\,\text{E}_i$$

$$\frac{\Gamma \vdash e_1 : \mathit{maybe}\ A \qquad \Gamma, x : A \vdash e_2 : B \qquad \Gamma \vdash e_3 : B}{\Gamma \vdash \text{case } e_1 \text{ of just } x \to e_2;\ \text{none} \to e_3 : B}\ \text{CASE}$$

$\boxed{\Gamma \,/\, \Delta \,/\, \Omega \vdash t : P}$

$$\frac{\Gamma \vdash e : P}{\Gamma \,/\, \cdot \,/\, \cdot \vdash e : P}\ \text{UE} \qquad \frac{}{\Gamma \,/\, x : P \,/\, \cdot \vdash x : P}\ \text{VAR} \qquad \frac{}{\Gamma \,/\, \Delta \,/\, \Omega \vdash \mathit{nil} : P}\ \text{NIL}$$

$$\frac{\Gamma \,/\, \Delta, x : P \,/\, \cdot \vdash t : Q}{\Gamma \,/\, \Delta \,/\, \cdot \vdash \lambda x.\, t : P \multimap Q}\ {\multimap}\,\text{I} \qquad \frac{\Gamma \,/\, \Delta \,/\, \Omega, x : A \vdash t : P}{\Gamma \,/\, \Delta \,/\, \Omega \vdash \lambda x.\, t : A \Rightarrow P}\ {\Rightarrow}\,\text{I}$$

$$\frac{\begin{array}{c}\Gamma \,/\, \Delta_1 \,/\, \Omega_1 \vdash t : P \multimap Q \\ \Gamma, \Omega_1 \,/\, \Delta_2 \,/\, \Omega_2 \vdash u : P\end{array}}{\Gamma \,/\, \Delta_1 \cup \Delta_2 \,/\, \Omega_1, \Omega_2 \vdash t\, u : Q}\ {\multimap}\,\text{E} \qquad \frac{\Gamma \,/\, \Delta \,/\, \Omega \vdash t : A \Rightarrow P}{\Gamma \,/\, \Delta \,/\, \Omega, x : A \vdash t\, x : P}\ {\Rightarrow}\,\text{E}$$

$$\frac{\begin{array}{c}\Gamma \,/\, \Delta \,/\, \Omega \vdash t : P \\ \Gamma \,/\, \Delta \,/\, \Omega \vdash u : Q\end{array}}{\Gamma \,/\, \Delta \,/\, \Omega \vdash \langle t, u \rangle : P \,\&\, Q}\ \&\,\text{I} \qquad \frac{\begin{array}{c}\Gamma \,/\, \Delta_1 \,/\, \Omega_1 \vdash t : P \\ \Gamma, \Omega_1 \,/\, \Delta_2 \,/\, \Omega_2 \vdash u : Q\end{array}}{\Gamma \,/\, \Delta_1 \cup \Delta_2 \,/\, \Omega_1, \Omega_2 \vdash (t, u) : P \otimes Q}\ \otimes\,\text{I}$$

$$\frac{\Gamma \,/\, \Delta \,/\, \Omega \vdash t : P_1 \,\&\, P_2}{\Gamma \,/\, \Delta \,/\, \Omega \vdash \pi_i\, t : P_i}\ \&\,\text{E} \qquad \frac{\begin{array}{c}\Gamma \,/\, \Delta_1 \,/\, \Omega_1 \vdash t : P \otimes Q \\ \Gamma, \Omega_1 \,/\, \Delta_2, x : P, y : Q \,/\, \Omega_2 \vdash u : Q\end{array}}{\Gamma \,/\, \Delta_1 \cup \Delta_2 \,/\, \Omega_1, \Omega_2 \vdash \text{let } (x, y) = t \text{ in } u : Q}\ \otimes\,\text{E}$$

$$\frac{\Gamma \,/\, \Delta \,/\, \Omega \vdash t : A \Rightarrow P \qquad \Gamma, \Omega \vdash e : A}{\Gamma \,/\, \Delta \,/\, \Omega \vdash t\, e : P}\ {\Rightarrow}\,\text{E}_2$$

$$\frac{\Gamma \vdash e : A}{\Gamma \,/\, \cdot \,/\, \cdot \vdash \text{just}\, e : \mathit{maybe}\ A}\ \text{MAYBE I}$$

$$\frac{\Gamma \,/\, \Delta_1 \,/\, \Omega_1 \vdash t : \mathit{maybe}\ A \qquad \Gamma, \Omega_1, x : A \,/\, \Delta_2 \,/\, \Omega_2 \vdash u : P}{\Gamma \,/\, \Delta_1 \cup \Delta_2 \,/\, \Omega_1, \Omega_2 \vdash \text{let just } x = t \text{ in } u : P}\ \text{MAYBE E}$$

Fig. 4. λ_{FS} typing rules

$$[\![1]\!] = 1 \qquad [\![A \times B]\!] = [\![A]\!] \times [\![B]\!] \qquad [\![A \to B]\!] = [\![A]\!] \to [\![B]\!] \qquad [\![P]\!] = U[\![P]\!]$$

$$[\![P \,\&\, Q]\!] = [\![P]\!] \,\&\, [\![Q]\!] \qquad [\![P \otimes Q]\!] = [\![P]\!] \otimes [\![Q]\!] \qquad [\![P \multimap Q]\!] = [\![P]\!] \multimap [\![Q]\!]$$

$$[\![A \Rightarrow P]\!] = [\![A]\!] \Rightarrow [\![P]\!] \qquad [\![\mathit{maybe}\ A]\!] = \mathit{maybe}\ [\![A]\!] \qquad [\![\mathbb{N}_0]\!] = \mathbb{N}_0$$

$$[\![\Gamma]\!] = \prod_{x:A\in\Gamma} [\![A]\!] \qquad [\![\Delta]\!] = \bigotimes_{x:P\in\Delta} [\![P]\!] \qquad [\![\Omega]\!] = \prod_{x:A\in\Gamma} [\![A]\!]$$

Fig. 5. Semantics of types and contexts in λ_{FS}

SEMANTICS OF $\Gamma \vdash e : A$

$$\begin{aligned}
[\![t]\!]\,\gamma &= [\![t]\!]\,\gamma\,()\,() \\
[\![x]\!]\,\gamma &= \pi_x\gamma \\
[\![()]\!]\,\gamma &= () \\
[\![\lambda x.\, e]\!]\,\gamma &= \lambda x.\, [\![e]\!]\,(\gamma, x) \\
[\![e_1\ e_2]\!]\,\gamma &= [\![e_1]\!]\,\gamma\,([\![e_2]\!]\,\gamma) \\
[\![(e_1, e_2)]\!]\,\gamma &= ([\![e_1]\!]\,\gamma,\ [\![e_2]\!]\,\gamma) \\
[\![\pi_i\ e]\!]\,\gamma &= \pi_i([\![e]\!]\,\gamma)
\end{aligned}$$

$$[\![\text{case } e_1 \text{ of just } x \to e_2;\text{ none} \to e_3]\!] = \begin{cases} [\![e_2]\!]\,(\gamma, x) & \text{if } [\![e_1]\!]\,\gamma = \text{just } x \\ [\![e_3]\!]\,\gamma & \text{otherwise} \end{cases}$$

SEMANTICS OF $\Gamma \,/\, \Delta \,/\, \Omega \vdash t : P$

$$\begin{aligned}
[\![\Gamma \,/\, \cdot \,/\, \cdot \vdash e : P]\!]\,\gamma\,\delta &= \{() \mapsto [\![e]\!]\,\gamma : \delta \neq \mathit{nil}\} \\
[\![\Gamma \,/\, \Delta \,/\, \Omega \vdash \mathit{nil} : P]\!]\,\gamma\,\delta &= \{\} \\
[\![\Gamma \,/\, x : P \,/\, \cdot \vdash x : P]\!]\,\gamma\,x &= \{() \mapsto x\} \\
[\![\Gamma \,/\, \Delta \,/\, \cdot \vdash \lambda x.\, t : P \multimap Q]\!]\,\gamma\,\delta &= \{() \mapsto \lambda x.\, [\![t]\!]\,\gamma\,(\delta, x)\} \\
[\![\Gamma \,/\, \Delta \,/\, \Omega \vdash \lambda x.\, t : A \Rightarrow P]\!]\,\gamma\,\delta &= \{\omega \mapsto \{x \mapsto y : (\omega, x) \mapsto y \in [\![t]\!]\,\gamma\,\delta\} : \\
&\qquad \exists x, y.\, (\omega, x) \mapsto y \in [\![t]\!]\,\gamma\,\delta\} \\
[\![\Gamma \,/\, \Delta_1 \cup \Delta_2 \,/\, \Omega_1, \Omega_2 \vdash t\,u : Q]\!]\,\gamma\,\delta &= \{(\omega_1, \omega_2) \mapsto x\,y : \\
&\qquad \omega_1 \mapsto x \in [\![t]\!]\,\gamma\,(\pi_{\Delta_1}\delta), \\
&\qquad \omega_2 \mapsto y \in [\![u]\!]\,(\gamma, \omega_1)\,(\pi_{\Delta_2}\delta)\} \\
[\![\Gamma \,/\, \Delta \,/\, \Omega, x : A \vdash t\,x : P]\!]\,\gamma\,\delta &= \{(\omega, x) \mapsto y : \omega \mapsto f \in [\![t]\!]\,\gamma\,\delta,\ x \mapsto y \in f\} \\
[\![\Gamma \,/\, \Delta \,/\, \Omega \vdash t\,e : P]\!]\,\gamma\,\delta &= \{\omega \mapsto f([\![e]\!]\,(\gamma, \omega)) : \omega \mapsto f \in [\![t]\!]\,\gamma\,\delta\} \\
[\![\Gamma \,/\, \Delta \,/\, \Omega \vdash \langle t, u\rangle : P \,\&\, Q]\!]\,\gamma\,\delta &= \{\omega \mapsto \langle x, y\rangle : \omega \mapsto x \in [\![t]\!]\,\gamma\,\delta,\ \omega \mapsto y \in [\![u]\!]\,\gamma\,\delta\} \\
[\![\Gamma \,/\, \Delta_1 \cup \Delta_2 \,/\, \Omega_1, \Omega_2 \vdash (t, u) : P \otimes Q]\!]\,\gamma\,\delta &= \{(\omega_1, \omega_2) \mapsto (x, y) : \\
&\qquad \omega_1 \mapsto x \in [\![t]\!]\,\gamma\,(\pi_{\Delta_1}\delta), \\
&\qquad \omega_2 \mapsto y \in [\![u]\!]\,(\gamma, \omega_1)\,(\pi_{\Delta_2}\delta)\} \\
[\![\Gamma \,/\, \Delta \,/\, \Omega \vdash \pi_i\,t : P_i]\!]\,\gamma\,\delta &= \{\omega \mapsto \pi_i\,x : \omega \mapsto x \in [\![t]\!]\,\gamma\,\delta\} \\
[\![\Gamma \,/\, \Delta_1 \cup \Delta_2 \,/\, \Omega_1, \Omega_2 \vdash \text{let } (x, y) = t \text{ in } u : Q]\!]\,\gamma\,\delta &= \{(\omega_1, \omega_2) \mapsto z : \\
&\qquad \omega_1 \mapsto (x, y) \in [\![t]\!]\,\gamma\,(\pi_{\Delta_1}\delta), \\
&\qquad \omega_2 \mapsto z \in [\![u]\!]\,(\gamma, \omega_1)\,(\pi_{\Delta_2}\delta, x, y)\} \\
[\![\Gamma \,/\, \cdot \,/\, \cdot \vdash \text{just}\,e : \mathit{maybe}\ A]\!]\,\gamma\,\delta &= \{() \mapsto \text{just}\,([\![e]\!]\,\gamma) : \delta \neq \mathit{nil}\} \\
[\![\Gamma \,/\, \Delta_1 \cup \Delta_2 \,/\, \Omega_1, \Omega_2 \vdash \text{let just } x = t \text{ in } u : P]\!]\,\gamma\,\delta &= \{(\omega_1, \omega_2) \mapsto y : \\
&\qquad \omega_1 \mapsto \text{just } x \in [\![t]\!]\,\gamma\,(\pi_{\Delta_1}\delta), \\
&\qquad \omega_2 \mapsto y \in [\![u]\!]\,(\gamma, \omega_1, x)\,(\pi_{\Delta_2}\delta)\}
\end{aligned}$$

Fig. 6. Semantics of expressions and terms in λ_{FS}

7 Looking Back and Forward

There are many ways to combine logic and functional programming. Mercury [27] integrates functional programming into top-down logic programming. Functional IncA [20] embeds functional programming into Datalog via a demand transform. Flix [18] has two sublanguages, logical and functional, which can each invoke the other.

λ_{FS}, however, belongs to the subfamily of languages that integrate logical features into a functional substrate. Perhaps its best known exemplars are 'functional logic programming' languages like Curry [1] and Verse [4], where relations $A \times B \to \mathit{bool}$ become 'functions' $A \to B$ that may yield many Bs for a given A. We find this undesirable because it (a) makes multiple returns and unification into pervasive ambient effects and (b) hides the boolean-ness, losing the opportunity to generalize from *bool* to other types. λ_{FS} is closer to Datafun [3] and $\lambda_\vee$ [24], which avoid ambient effects by representing relations as finite sets, a separate type from normal functions. However, they express logical operations via loops or set comprehensions. In contrast λ_{FS} is inspired by Rel [2], where relations are defined pointwise like functions, using 'and', 'or', and 'exists'. Rel also supports arithmetic operators and aggregations, as if relations had return values. However, Rel implements this by desugaring to a Datalog-like core where the 'value' of a Rel expression is just the relation's final column. λ_{FS} reimagines this syntactic sugar semantically.

By generalizing beyond booleans, λ_{FS} moves closer to weighted logic programming languages like Dyna [9,10], ProbLog [23], or Datalog$^\circ$ [15]. Indeed, λ_{FS} is inspired by and indebted to databases research on K-relations [12], generalizing Datalog semantics from booleans to semirings, which has in turn inspired functional query languages [13,25]. Other Datalog-inspired languages like Datafun, Flix, and $\lambda_\vee$ generalize to semilattices. However, so far as we know only λ_{FS} uses pointed sets—the minimal, most general structure required to define a function's support. Semirings then emerge as a natural structure over pointed sets: we can generalize *or* and *exists* to an 'additive' commutative monoid $(P, \oplus : P \mathbin{\&} P \multimap P, \mathit{nil}_P)$ and its aggregation operator $\bigoplus : (A \Rightarrow P) \multimap P$, and similarly *and* generalizes to a 'multiplicative' monoid $(P, \circledast : P \otimes P \multimap P, \mathbf{1})$ distributing over $\oplus$.

λ_{FS} has many limitations which we would like to lift in future work:

- It lacks recursion. There are two kinds of recursion we might want: lazy functional recursion (as in recursively defined functions or codata) and bottom-up iteration until reaching a fixed point (as in Datalog's recursively defined relations). It's not obvious how these should interact semantically. $\lambda_\vee$ [24] shows how to unify them, but requires a lot of structure (semilattices, dcpos, and continuity); moreover, it seemingly cannot do stratified computation, where we compute a fixed point and then use its results in a non-monotone way.
- We did not show how to implement either our type system or our semantics. We have built a prototype, which we lack space to discuss here; it can be found at https://github.com/rntz/fslang/blob/main/fslang.rkt. As our finite

map operations are closely connected to tensor algebra, perhaps indexed streams [17] could provide an efficient implementation technique.
- Our contexts have a fixed order, $\Gamma \,/\, \Delta \,/\, \Omega \vdash P$, glossed as $\Gamma \to \Delta \multimap \Omega \Rightarrow P$. This is not fully general: because $P \multimap (A \Rightarrow Q) \not\cong A \Rightarrow (P \multimap Q)$, to write programs of the latter type naturally we would need an additional context $\Gamma/\Delta_1/\Omega/\Delta_2 \vdash P$. In general, any number of interleavings of point preserving Δ and finitely supported Ω contexts may be necessary. The best way forward may be to investigate the connection to graded effect systems: is there a grading structure that yields a (generalization of) our typing rules?
- Destructuring of & pairs would be convenient for writing outer joins, but standard linear/relevance typing rules do not permit this. We suspect it may be possible by stealing rules from the logic of bunched implications [19].
- We can apply a finite map to a finitely supported variable to ground it, $t\,x$, or to an expression to look up its value, $t\,e$. We would like to extend this to application to *patterns,* which may mix variables to ground with expressions to look up. For instance, we would like to have $\Gamma \,/\, f : A \times A \Rightarrow P \,/\, x : A \vdash f\,(x, x) : P$. Indeed, it's not obvious whether λ_{FS} can express a program equivalent to this or not.
- λ_{FS} lacks metatheory. Our semantics is a sketch; we have not proven finite support or point preservation, nor have we shown syntactic weakening or substitution. The need for $\Rightarrow \mathrm{E}_2$ should show this is surprisingly subtle.

Disclosure of Interests. The authors have no competing interests to declare that are relevant to the content of this article.

References

1. Antoy, S., Hanus, M.: Functional logic programming. Commun. ACM **53**(4), 74–85 (2010)
2. Aref, M., et al.: Rel: a programming language for relational data. In: Companion of the 2025 International Conference on Management of Data, SIGMOD/PODS 2025, pp. 283–296. Association for Computing Machinery, New York (2025). https://doi.org/10.1145/3722212.3724450
3. Arntzenius, M., Krishnaswami, N.R.: Datafun: a functional Datalog. In: Proceedings of the 21st ACM SIGPLAN International Conference on Functional Programming, pp. 214–227. ICFP 2016, ACM, New York (2016). https://doi.org/10.1145/2951913.2951948
4. Augustsson, L., et al.: The Verse calculus: a core calculus for deterministic functional logic programming. Proc. ACM Program. Lang. **7**(ICFP), 417–447 (2023). https://doi.org/10.1145/3607845
5. Benton, P.N.: A mixed linear and non-linear logic: proofs, terms and models (extended abstract). In: Pacholski, L., Tiuryn, J. (eds.) CSL 1994. LNCS, vol. 933, pp. 121–135. Springer, Cham (1994). https://doi.org/10.1007/BFB0022251
6. Benton, P.N., Wadler, P.: Linear logic, monads and the lambda calculus. In: Proceedings, 11th Annual IEEE Symposium on Logic in Computer Science, New Brunswick, New Jersey, USA, 27–30 July 1996, pp. 420–431. IEEE Computer Society (1996). https://doi.org/10.1109/LICS.1996.561458

7. Escardó, M.H.: Infinite sets that admit fast exhaustive search. In: Proceedings of the 22nd IEEE Symposium on Logic in Computer Science (LICS 2007), 10–12 July 2007, Wroclaw, Poland, pp. 443–452. IEEE Computer Society (2007). https://doi.org/10.1109/LICS.2007.25
8. Escardó, M.H.: Seemingly impossible functional programs. Blog post (2007). https://math.andrej.com/2007/09/28/seemingly-impossible-functional-programs/
9. Filardo, N.W.: Dyna 2: Towards a general weighted logic language. Ph.D. thesis, Johns Hopkins University (2017). https://www.ietfng.org/nwf/publications-and-talks/2017-thesis.html
10. Francis-Landau, M.: Declarative programming via term rewriting. Ph.D. thesis, Johns Hopkins University (2024). https://matthewfl.com/research#phd
11. Gaboardi, M., Katsumata, S.Y., Orchard, D., Breuvart, F., Uustalu, T.: Combining effects and coeffects via grading. SIGPLAN Not. **51**(9), 476–489 (2016). https://doi.org/10.1145/3022670.2951939
12. Green, T.J., Karvounarakis, G., Tannen, V.: Provenance semirings. In: Libkin, L. (ed.) Proceedings of the Twenty-Sixth ACM SIGACT-SIGMOD-SIGART Symposium on Principles of Database Systems, 11–13 June 2007, Beijing, China, pp. 31–40. ACM (2007). https://doi.org/10.1145/1265530.1265535
13. Henglein, F., Kaarsgaard, R., Mathiesen, M.K.: The programming of algebra. In: Gibbons, J., New, M.S. (eds.) Proceedings Ninth Workshop on Mathematically Structured Functional Programming, MSFP@ETAPS 2022, Munich, Germany, 2nd April 2022. EPTCS, vol. 360, pp. 71–92 (2022). https://doi.org/10.4204/EPTCS.360.4
14. Katsumata, S.Y.: Parametric effect monads and semantics of effect systems. In: Proceedings of the 41st ACM SIGPLAN-SIGACT Symposium on Principles of Programming Languages, POPL 2014, pp. 633–645. Association for Computing Machinery, New York (2014). https://doi.org/10.1145/2535838.2535846
15. Khamis, M.A., Ngo, H.Q., Pichler, R., Suciu, D., Wang, Y.R.: Convergence of Datalog over (pre-) semirings. J. ACM **71**(2), 8:1–8:55 (2024). https://doi.org/10.1145/3643027
16. Kosta, D., Petrić, Z.: Relevant categories and partial functions. Publ. l'Inst. Math. **96**, 17–23 (2007). https://doi.org/10.2298/PIM0796017D
17. Kovach, S., Kolichala, P., Gu, T., Kjolstad, F.: Indexed streams: a formal intermediate representation for fused contraction programs. Proc. ACM Program. Lang. **7**(PLDI) (2023). https://doi.org/10.1145/3591268
18. Madsen, M., Lhoták, O.: Fixpoints for the masses: programming with first-class Datalog constraints. Proc. ACM Program. Lang. **4**(OOPSLA) (2020). https://doi.org/10.1145/3428193
19. O'Hearn, P.W., Pym, D.J.: The logic of bunched implications. Bull. Symb. Log. **5**(2), 215–244 (1999). https://doi.org/10.2307/421090
20. Pacak, A., Erdweg, S.: Functional programming with Datalog. In: Ali, K., Vitek, J. (eds.) 36th European Conference on Object-Oriented Programming, ECOOP 2022, Berlin, Germany, 6–10 June 2022. LIPIcs, vol. 222, pp. 7:1–7:28. Schloss Dagstuhl - Leibniz-Zentrum für Informatik (2022). https://doi.org/10.4230/LIPICS.ECOOP.2022.7
21. Petrić, Z.: Coherence in substructural categories. Stud. Logica. **70**(2), 271–296 (2002). https://doi.org/10.1023/A:1015186718090
22. Petricek, T., Orchard, D.A., Mycroft, A.: Coeffects: a calculus of context-dependent computation. In: Jeuring, J., Chakravarty, M.M.T. (eds.) Proceedings of the 19th

ACM SIGPLAN international conference on Functional programming, Gothenburg, Sweden, 1–3 September 2014, pp. 123–135. ACM (2014). https://doi.org/10.1145/2628136.2628160
23. Raedt, L.D., Kimmig, A., Toivonen, H.: Problog: a probabilistic prolog and its application in link discovery. In: Veloso, M.M. (ed.) IJCAI 2007, Proceedings of the 20th International Joint Conference on Artificial Intelligence, Hyderabad, India, 6–12 January 2007, pp. 2462–2467 (2007). http://ijcai.org/Proceedings/07/Papers/396.pdf
24. Rioux, N., Zdancewic, S.: Functional meaning for parallel streaming. Proc. ACM Program. Lang. **9**(PLDI), 1220–1244 (2025). https://doi.org/10.1145/3729299
25. Shaikhha, A., Huot, M., Smith, J., Olteanu, D.: Functional collection programming with semi-ring dictionaries. Proc. ACM Program. Lang. **6**(OOPSLA1), 1–33 (2022). https://doi.org/10.1145/3527333
26. Smirnov, A.L.: Graded monads and rings of polynomials. J. Math. Sci. **151**, 3032–3051 (2008). https://doi.org/10.1007/s10958-008-9013-7. Translated from Zapiski Nauchnykh Seminarov POMI, vol. 349, pp. 174–210 (2007)
27. Somogyi, Z., Henderson, F., Conway, T.C.: The execution algorithm of Mercury, an efficient purely declarative logic programming language. J. Log. Program. **29**(1–3), 17–64 (1996). https://doi.org/10.1016/S0743-1066(96)00068-4

Demonic Dynamic Logic Programming

Rose Bohrer(✉)

National Institute of Advanced Industrial Science and Technology, Tokyo, Japan
rose.bohrer@aist.go.jp

Abstract. This paper introduces a logic programming language called Demonic Dynamic Logic Programming. It is based on the ground, Demonic fragment of propositional dynamic logic, a well-studied program logic. Syntax, operational semantics and proof-theoretic semantics are presented. The theoretical foundations are validated by proving theorems such as soundness and existence of uniform proofs. Applications to two-player mathematical games are discussed and a pursuit-evasion game on a graph is presented as a concrete example. By bringing program logic and logic programming together, we hope to improve reasoning about imperative programs within logic programs. Future work is discussed, including extensions to game logic which hold the potential to generate winning strategies of games.

Keywords: Logic programming · Dynamic Logic · Program Logic

1 Introduction

The vitality of logic programming (LP) as a field depends on the development of diverse LP languages with theoretical foundations in different flavors of logic. The development of specialized LP languages enables new styles of automated reasoning, simplifies modeling of new problems, and leads to richer theoretical guarantees compared to broad-purpose languages like Prolog. As examples: inductive LP enables example-driven reasoning [36], linear logic and answer-set programming excel in modeling procedural content generation problems [15,32], and finite-choice LP provides elegant performance bounds [31]. It is unsurprising, then, that LP languages based on modal logics [5,43] have received significant attention, including temporal logics [1,6,21,35] and multi-modal logics [37]. However, given the central role of program logics like Hoare logic [26] and its generalization, dynamic logic [20,24] (DL), in software correctness, it is surprising that LP languages based on them have received minimal attention. Since the 1980's, temporal LP works like Tempura [35] have acknowledged the importance of bridging this gap between LP and program logics. Compared to the successes of other specialized LP languages, the few existing works at this intersection [18,38,42] have not yet delivered comparable reasoning tools, modeling functionality, or theoretical guarantees to LP programmers.

M. Sperber and E. Komendantskaya (Eds.): FLOPS 2026, LNCS 16533, pp. 19–76, 2026.
https://doi.org/10.1007/978-981-92-0184-6_2

This paper interprets the ground, Demonic fragment of propositional dynamic logic (PDL) as an LP language, called *Demonic Dynamic Logic Programming* (DDLP). In recent years, the main impact of dynamic logics is in interactive theorem-proving, where the KeY [2] and KeYmaera X [22] provers are used to verify object-oriented software and cyber-physical systems, respectively. DDLP imports the reasoning abilities, modeling power, and guarantees of dynamic logics into the logic programming context.

By example, we demonstrate the ability to model two-player games, for which we provide invariant reasoning principles. We provide guarantees regarding soundness and the existence of uniform proofs, which are standard but essential validation for an LP language. Because PDL is a logic for program correctness, DDLP is particularly promising for the development of verified software.

This work is the first stage of a long-term effort to develop an LP language based in two-player mathematical games. The recent *Curry-Howard correspondence for games* [9–11] shows that executable code for a winning strategy of a game can be extracted from proof terms for game logic, a conservative extension of PDL. Likewise, an LP interpretation of game logic would enable programmers to model games in logic and extract provably-correct executable strategies. Because PDL is a substantial fragment of game logic, the development of DDLP is an essential step in this effort. At the same time, it is natural to defer Angelic formulas and unification variables to later work, because their proper treatment will require generating programs based on constraints discovered during search.

2 Example and Background

As our running example, we consider pursuit-evasion games on graphs (PEGs) [29]. A PEG is a game between two players, Angel and Demon, who take turns moving along the edges of a graph. In our example, Demon is the pursuer and Angel the evader. The pursuer wins if the players are ever on the same vertex, while the evader wins if they evade the pursuer indefinitely. Key applications of PEGs include network security, e.g., intrusion detection [12], and physical security and safety problems like surveillance patrol [7] and search-and-rescue [17].

Concretely, we consider a PEG on the 4-node cycle graph $A \leftrightarrow B \leftrightarrow C \leftrightarrow D$ where Angel is initially located at A and Demon is initially located at C. This PEG is depicted in Fig. 1.

Though it is a straightforward exercise to formalize the above game given the full power of game logic, DDLP is a fragment and thus requires additional care. Every DDLP program consists of a series of (e.g., predicate) declarations followed by a single *query* that the programmer asks the DDLP program to solve. The query is indicated by the `?-` symbol. As in most LP languages, identifiers starting with lowercase letters are *universally quantified symbols*, either *predicates* or *program symbols*. Many, but not all, LP languages also have *existentially-quantified symbols* which are solved for during execution and written with uppercase symbols. We leave existential symbols to future work because their solutions are entire programs in the DDLP setting.

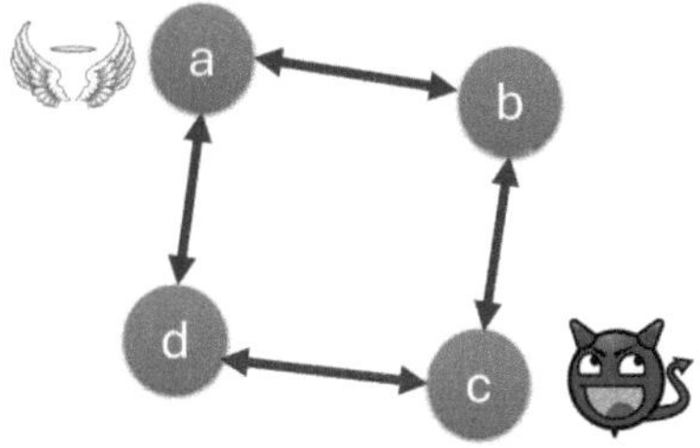

Fig. 1. Pursuit-evasion game on 4-node cycle graph where Angel avoids Demon.

For clarity, before giving declarations, we formalize the following query: The players' respective initial positions are A and C. Repeatedly, Demon takes a turn, then Angel. We ensure Angel avoids Demon at the end. This is shown through an *invariant property* that Angel avoids Demon in every repetition. Thus, our query might take the format, where each predicate of form `xy` means Angel is at x and Demon at y.

```
?- ac -> [(demon-turn;angel-turn)*@inv(ac|bd|ca|db)] (ac|bd|ca|db).
```

Completing the example requires 1) predicates for every reachable state (e.g., `ac`), 2) the player's turns `demon-turn` and `angel-turn`, and 3) a loop invariant which holds before and after every turn. Most DDLP games have these three components. The complete example is shown in Fig. 2.

The predicates are not declared before use. In this example, the reachable states are: `ab`, `ac`, `ad`,`ba`, `bc`, `bd`, `ca`, `cb`, `cd`, `da`, `db`, `dc`.

On each turn (2), players choose between two moves, metaphorically *left* or *right*. We respectively write $\ell, r, \ell a, ra$ for the left and right moves of Demon and Angel. Each move has a program symbol, defined by four clauses, each defining the resulting state for some initial state. For example, clause `[l]ab <- ac` means Demon's left move takes state (A, C) to state (A, B). The `demon-turn` moves either way nondeterministically, written `l U r`. The `angel-turn` uses tests (?) to identify the optimal reaction to Demon's move.

The invariant (3) should hold before and after every turn. The evader should maintain distance 2 or more. In the example graph, this corresponds to opposing positions, written `(ac | bd | ca | db)`.

This example (Fig. 2) uses all key DDLP features. Its query succeeds because Angel can avoid Demon. To further explain the meaning of the example, we give key cases of PDL semantics in Fig. 3; see Appendix A or the literature for details [24]. Programs use Kripke semantics: $(\omega, \nu) \in [\![\alpha]\!]$ means program α can go from state ω to state ν. Formula semantics $\omega \in [\![\phi]\!]$ describe states where formula ϕ holds. Fixed interpretation I defines program symbols c. Test $?\phi$ asserts ϕ's current truth. Operator $\cup$ picks a program, the ; operator sequences two programs, and the $*$ operator repeats a program zero or more times. Demonic modality $[\alpha]\phi$ means ϕ holds for all runs of α.

```
[l]ab <- ac. [l]bc <- bd. [l]cd <- ca. [l]da <- db.
[r]ad <- ac. [r]ba <- bd. [r]cb <- ca. [r]dc <- db.
demon-turn ::= l U r.

[la]db <- ab. [la]ac <- bc. [la]bd <- cd. [la]ca <- da.
[ra]bd <- ad. [ra]ca <- ba. [ra]db <- cb. [ra]ac <- dc.
angel-turn ::= (?ab;la U ?bc;la U ?cd;la U ?da;la) U
               (?ad;ra U ?ba;ra U ?cb;ra U ?dc;ra).

?- ac -> [(demon-turn;angel-turn)*@inv(ac|bd|ca|db)] (ac|bd|ca|db).
```

Fig. 2. DDLP implementation of PEG on 4-vertex cycle graph.

$$[\![c]\!] = I(c) \qquad [\![?\phi]\!] = \{(\omega, \omega) \mid \omega \in [\![\phi]\!]\} \qquad [\![\alpha;\beta]\!] = [\![\alpha]\!] \circ [\![\beta]\!]$$

$$[\![\alpha \cup \beta]\!] = [\![\alpha]\!] \cup [\![\beta]\!] \qquad [\![\alpha^*]\!] = \bigcup_{i \geq 0} [\![\alpha]\!] \circ \cdots \circ [\![\alpha]\!] (i \text{ times})$$

$$[\![[\alpha]\phi]\!] = \{\omega \mid \nu \in [\![\phi]\!] \text{ for all } (\omega, \nu) \in [\![\alpha]\!]\}$$

Fig. 3. Semantics of PDL

3 Syntax

A DDLP program consists of a set of *declarations* and a *query*. The query is a distinguished *rule*. A set of declarations is called a *signature* Σ.

3.1 Core Constructs

Expressions e can be either formulas ϕ, ψ or programs α, β. Programs can be symbols c, tests $?\phi$, sequences $\alpha;\beta$, choices $\alpha \cup \beta$, and loops α^*. We assume that loops are annotated with invariant formulas J, written $\alpha^*@inv(J)$, so that proof search need not identify invariants. However, we consider two annotated loops to be syntactically identical if they differ only in their invariant annotation, as it is a proof hint and not core program syntax. Formulas can be predicates p, implications $\phi \to \psi$ (equiv. $\psi \leftarrow \phi$, see `ψ :- φ` in Prolog), disjunctions $\phi \vee \psi$, (written `P | Q` in concrete syntax) conjunctions $\phi \wedge \psi$ (written `P & Q` in concrete syntax), and modalities $[\alpha]\phi$. We include explicit program quantifiers $\forall c\, \phi$ in the abstract syntax for two reasons: to make scope clear and to provide stylistic consistency between ours and others' treatments of uniform proofs [34]. The quantifier $\forall c\, \phi$ universally quantifies program symbol c in formula ϕ. When not written, they are implied to be top-level (e.g., Sect. 2).

In DL, the truth of a formula can depend on the ambient *state*, which is modified by executing programs. In DDLP, the truth value of predicates is in general state-dependent, e.g., the formula $p \to [\alpha]p$ is not true in the general case. We thus say that they are *non-rigid* symbols.

Every declaration is either an *abbreviation* or a *clause*. A non-recursive *abbreviation* $c ::= \alpha$ defines the program symbol c to be exactly equal to program α. We only abbreviate programs, but other expressions work in principle.

Two key classes of formulas are *goal formulas* G and clause formulas D; these are defined in Sect. 3.2 as their definitions are non-trivial. A context Γ is called *clause* if all its formulas are clause formulas D. For conjunctions $G = G_1 \wedge \cdots \wedge G_n$, we call each G_i a *subgoal.*

A *head* formula h is either a predicate p or has form $[c]p$ for program symbol c and predicate p. Not all *clause* formulas are allowed in predicate definitions; to simplify the operational semantics, we assume nested implications of form $A_1 \to \ldots \to A_n$ where A_n is a head formula. The disjunction of clauses with a given predicate in their head can be said to define that predicate.

3.2 Syntactic Restrictions

Uniformity of proofs [34] is an important theoretical property for LP languages, which formalizes guarantees on the structural simplicity of proofs found during proof search. As a rule, LP languages must restrict the syntax of formulas to make such guarantees possible. Identifying appropriate syntactic restrictions for DDLP is thus an important contribution to the language design. Moreover, because DDLP incorporates programs into formulas, the necessary restrictions are not immediately obvious from existing LP languages.

Take for example the LP language of first-order hereditary Harrop formulas [34, §4], which defines the clause formulas D and the goal formulas G as:

$$
\begin{aligned}
D &::= p \mid G \to p \mid \forall x\ D \mid D_1 \wedge D_2 \\
G &::= p \mid G_1 \wedge G_2 \mid G_1 \vee G_2 \mid \forall x\ G \mid \exists x\ G \mid D \to G
\end{aligned}
$$

Note that goals can include both positive and negative operators while clauses include only positive ones, and we switch between the two classes whenever we move to the left of an implication arrow. We develop the DDLP equivalent by dropping existential quantifiers and adding boxes (and true).

Programs too can be either clause (δ) or goal (γ). Loops and sequencing are prohibited in clause programs because they create nested modalities during proof search, which are not clause. The remaining cases reflect that choices behave like conjunction and tests like implication. The latter motivates an implication-like restriction on the right-hand side of a box modality in a clause.

$$
\begin{aligned}
D &::= \mathsf{true} \mid p \mid G \to p \mid \forall c\ D \mid D_1 \wedge D_2 \mid [\delta]p \\
G &::= \mathsf{true} \mid p \mid G_1 \wedge G_2 \mid G_1 \vee G_2 \mid \forall c\ G \mid D \to G \mid [\gamma]G \\
\delta &::= c \mid ?G \mid \delta_1 \cup \delta_2 \qquad \gamma ::= c \mid ?D \mid \gamma_1 \cup \gamma_2 \mid \gamma^*@inv(J) \mid \gamma_1;\gamma_2
\end{aligned}
$$

Invariant formulas J face a unique situation, as the same formula appears on both the left and right of an arrow when proving a loop invariant is preserved.

Therefore it must satisfy the requirements for both clause and goal formulas at once. Programs appearing therein, written ι, face the same situation.

$$J ::= \mathsf{true} \mid p \mid \forall c\ J \mid J \rightarrow p \mid J \wedge J \mid [\iota]p \qquad \iota ::= c \mid ?J \mid \iota \cup \iota \mid \iota^{*}@inv(J)$$

Yet Fig. 2 shows disjunctive invariants are essential for reasoning about stateful programs, so we allow extended invariant formulas $\hat{J}$ in practice: $\hat{J} = \bigvee_i J_i$. This extension complicates the uniformity theorem (Theorem 3), which is resolved by building disjunction support into the loop proof rule.

4 Proof-Theoretic Semantics

LP is programming-as-proof-search. Thus it is natural to specify the intended semantics of an LP language by presenting proof rules over which proof search is to be performed, i.e., a *proof-theoretic semantics* [33]. We present a proof-theoretic semantics for DDLP here, then move toward implementation with an operational semantics in Sect. 5. We present the rules as a constructive sequent calculus, where the judgement $\Gamma \vdash \phi$ means the single conclusion formula ϕ is constructively provable under context Γ. A context Γ is a set of assumptions, traditionally separated by commas, with $\cdot$ indicating the empty context.

The core rules used for search are presented Fig. 4. With the exception of $*R$, and Expl, most of these rules are standard in DL. In order to be self-contained, we explain the standard rules as well.

Rule Init means the antecedent and signature are provable. Rule $\top$ means the trivial formula true is provable. Rules $\wedge R$ and $\wedge L$ allow proving a conjunction from both conjuncts and recovering them. Rules $\rightarrow L$, $\cup L$, and $?L$ are likewise used to decompose the assumptions. Rules $\vee R1$ and $\vee R2$ allow proving a disjunction from either disjunct. Rule $\rightarrow R$ proves an implication by moving the assumption to the context. Though $\rightarrow R$ is standard, it is worth noting that the truth of context formulas is not generally preserved under modalities, which contrasts with, e.g., clauses in the signature Σ. Rule $?R$ proves a test by proving an implication. Rule $;R$ proves a sequential program by proving a nested modality. Rule $\cup R$ proves a choice by proving the conjunction of choices. Rule $\forall R$ proves a universal quantifier by introducing a fresh program symbol c and $\forall L$ instantiates a quantifier to a specific program α, which we restrict to a δ-program.

The rules that distinguish DDLP from a standard DL proof calculus are Expl and $*R$. Rule Expl implements explicitly-defined symbols (e.g., `demon-turn` and `angel-turn`) by substitution, replacing an identifier with its definition. Rule Expl requires preserving goal and clause restrictions. Rule Expl is unsurprising for an LP language. Rule $*R$ is thus the most distinctive rule of DDLP. The primary challenge is that loop invariants must appear on both the left and right, satisfying the syntactic restrictions for both goal and clause formulas. This rules out top-level disjunctions, which are desired in most real-world invariants. To emulate disjunctive invariants while respecting syntactic restrictions, rule $*R$ accepts a *finite set* of disjuncts J_i as parameters and proves at each step that some disjunct holds. We assume the structural rules.

$$\textsc{Init}\ \frac{\phi \in \Gamma \cup \Sigma}{\Gamma \vdash_{\Sigma} \phi} \qquad \top\ \frac{*}{\Gamma \vdash \mathsf{true}} \qquad ;R\ \frac{\Gamma \vdash [\alpha][\beta]\phi}{\Gamma \vdash [\alpha;\beta]\phi} \qquad \cup R\ \frac{\Gamma \vdash [\alpha]\phi \land [\beta]\phi}{\Gamma \vdash [\alpha \cup \beta]\phi} \qquad \land R\ \frac{\Gamma \vdash \phi \qquad \Gamma \vdash \psi}{\Gamma \vdash \phi \land \psi}$$

$$\land L\ \frac{\Gamma, \psi_1, \psi_2 \vdash \phi}{\Gamma, \psi_1 \land \psi_2 \vdash \phi} \qquad ?L\ \frac{\Gamma, \psi_1 \to \psi_2 \vdash \phi}{\Gamma, [?\psi_1]\psi_2 \vdash \phi} \qquad \cup L\ \frac{\Gamma, [\alpha]\psi \land [\beta]\psi \vdash \phi}{\Gamma, [\alpha \cup \beta]\psi \vdash \phi} \qquad \lor R1\ \frac{\Gamma \vdash \phi}{\Gamma \vdash \phi \lor \psi} \qquad \lor R2\ \frac{\Gamma \vdash \psi}{\Gamma \vdash \phi \lor \psi}$$

$$\forall L\ \frac{\Gamma, \psi(\alpha) \vdash \phi}{\Gamma, \forall c\ \psi(c) \vdash \phi}\ (\alpha \text{ is } \delta\text{-prog}) \qquad \to L\ \frac{\Gamma \vdash \psi_1 \qquad \Gamma, \psi_2 \vdash \phi}{\Gamma, \psi_1 \to \psi_2 \vdash \phi} \qquad \to R\ \frac{\Gamma, \phi \vdash \psi}{\Gamma \vdash \phi \to \psi} \qquad \forall R\ \frac{\Gamma \vdash \phi(c')}{\Gamma \vdash \forall c\ \phi(c)}$$

$$?R\ \frac{\Gamma \vdash \psi \to \phi}{\Gamma \vdash [?\psi]\phi} \qquad \textsc{Expl}\ \frac{c ::= \alpha \in \Sigma \qquad \Gamma(\alpha) \vdash \phi(\alpha)}{\Gamma(c) \vdash \phi(c)}\ (\Gamma(\alpha) \text{ clause}, \phi(\alpha) \text{ goal})$$

$$*R\ \frac{\Gamma \vdash \bigvee_i \psi_i \qquad \psi_1 \vdash [\alpha] \bigvee_j \psi_j \cdots \qquad \psi_n \vdash [\alpha] \bigvee_j \psi_j \qquad \psi_1 \vdash \phi \cdots \qquad \psi_n \vdash \phi}{\Gamma \vdash [\alpha^* @ inv(\bigvee_i \psi_i)]\phi}$$

Fig. 4. Proof-theoretic semantics, core rules.

When performing proof search over the rules of Fig. 4, we often wish to perform search in some context for flexibility, e.g., under a modality. This added flexibility requires additional rules for manipulating modalities. Moreover, the syntactic restrictions imply that for certain logical connectives, only their right-rules are employed during proof search, yet a full understanding of those connectives' meanings requires understanding the left-rules as well. We present these secondary rules in Fig. 5.

As is standard in DL, the rules M, K, and G provide generic reasoning for all program modalities. Rule M allows applying an implication under a modality if it holds in the empty context. Rule K applies a modal implication to a modal assumption to get a modal conclusion. Rule G proves a formula under a modality by proving it in the empty context. Rule M and a special case of rule G are admissible (Lemma 2), but we include both as proper rules because monotonicity is conceptually essential. Rules $\lor L$, $;L$, $*L$ are left rules that never arise during proof search due to syntax restrictions.

The omission of the cut rule is standard in LP languages because cut greatly complicates proof search. Rules M and K can also complicate proof search, so we do not employ them arbitrarily in search. Rather, they justify the soundness of applying the core rules under modalities per the operational semantics (Sect. 5). Cut elimination is often false for DLs [40], and the design of sequent calculi for DLs with cut elimination is a substantial research problem in its own right [25, 41], so we conjecture that cut elimination is false in DDLP.

This completes the introduction of the proof-theoretic semantics.

$$\text{M}\quad \frac{\phi \vdash \psi \qquad \Gamma \vdash [\alpha]\phi}{\Gamma \vdash [\alpha]\psi} \qquad \text{K}\quad \frac{\Gamma \vdash [\alpha]\phi \qquad \Gamma \vdash [\alpha](\phi \rightarrow \psi)}{\Gamma \vdash [\alpha]\psi} \qquad \text{G}\quad \frac{\phi}{[\alpha]\phi}$$

$$\vee L\quad \frac{\Gamma, \phi_1 \vdash \psi \qquad \Gamma, \phi_2 \vdash \psi}{\Gamma, \phi_1 \vee \phi_2 \vdash \psi} \qquad ;L\quad \frac{\Gamma, [\alpha][\beta]\psi \vdash \phi}{\Gamma, [\alpha;\beta]\psi \vdash \phi} \qquad *L\quad \frac{\Gamma, \psi \wedge [\alpha][\alpha^*@inv(\vee_i \psi_i)]\psi \vdash \phi}{\Gamma, [\alpha^*@inv(\vee_i \psi_i)]\psi \vdash \phi}$$

Fig. 5. Secondary rules

Implications. Proof-theoretic semantics is declarative in nature, defining the reasoning principles available in proof search, but not the operational details of search itself. We have defined reasoning principles that are strong enough to solve the example from Fig. 2.

The proof-theoretic semantics provides hints about potential challenges when developing a lower-level operational semantics (Sect. 5) and the theory of DDLP (Sect. 6). The rules G, K, and M are applicable to all modal formulas, which introduces nondeterminism in search. For modalities of program symbols, they are the only applicable rules, and are not admissible rules. This implies that a practical operational semantics needs to reason under modalities, but must take care to do so efficiently, and to expand the defining rules of a program symbol when needed to progress the proof. Because this flexibility is similar to cut, we expect uniformity may fail for the secondary rules.

5 Operational Semantics

Proof-theoretic semantics are declarative in nature, thus high-level. It is helpful to also provide an *operational semantics* which is low-level enough to describe how execution proceeds, yet abstract enough to promote analysis. The best-known operational semantics for LP is arguably (SLD-)resolution [4,19], where the proof search space is represented with a potentially-infinite tree. Small-step semantics and similar transition-system approaches, have also been used, however [3,8,13,16]. We present our semantics in small-step style, primarily to improve accessibility for readers with functional programming backgrounds.

The instantaneous state of a running program is simply a goal formula G. The goal formula G, often a conjunction of subgoals G_i, expresses what remains to be proved. All the declarations of a DDLP program are interpreted logically; we write Σ for the signature containing them all.

The small-step judgment $G \Longrightarrow_\Sigma G'$ indicates that a single step of executing signature Σ can take G to G'. In general, stepping is nondeterministic. For example, if a predicate p has multiple clauses, then the goal p has multiple step transitions, one for each clause. The nondeterminism corresponds directly to the branching present in an SLD-resolution tree [4], with each complete stepping trace corresponding to a path from root to leaf in an SLD tree.

As is standard, we write $\Longrightarrow^*$ for the transitive, reflexive closure of $\Longrightarrow$. Execution terminates successfully if execution reduces to the trivial formula true. We search for proofs, not refutations, following Miller, for example [34]. The rules of the operational semantics are listed in Fig. 6.

We explain each rule. Many of the rules are generalized to operate under an arbitrary collection of goal-specific assumptions A and an arbitrary chain of modalities $M()$. This is important to improving completeness: we often need to simplify the postcondition of a program modality through execution *first*, then apply a defining clause for the program. For simplicity, the soundness proofs assume at M contains at least one modality. Rule OpGoal applies a step to a goal in-place and $\mathsf{OpClose}$ cleans up a solved goal. Rule OpHyp resolves a goal from the assumptions A or signature Σ. Rule OpPred reduces a predicate to the assumptions of one of its defining clauses. Rule OpExpl reduces an explicitly-defined symbol to its definition. Rule $\mathsf{Op?}$, $\mathsf{Op;}$, and $\mathsf{Op}\cup$ match the rule for each program closely, except that they are generalized to operate under modalities. Rule $\mathsf{Op*}$ does not operate under modalities because it is not sound to do so. Rules $\mathsf{Op}\vee 1$ and $\mathsf{Op}\vee 2$ likewise apply disjunction reasoning soundly in context. Rule $\mathsf{Op}\wedge$ raises a conjunction over a modality to produce two subgoals. Rule $\mathsf{Op}\forall$ substitutes a top-level quantifier with a fresh program symbol. Rule $\mathsf{Op}\rightarrow$ normalizes the assumptions of implications into a conjoined assumption.

The rules ending in L decompose assumptions in the context so they may be matched to goals. Rule $\mathsf{Op}\wedge L$ reduces a conjunction assumption to assumptions of each conjunct. Rule $\mathsf{Op?}L$ reduces test assumptions to implication assumptions. Rule $\mathsf{Op}\cup L$ reduces choice assumptions to conjunction assumptions. Rule $\mathsf{Op}{\rightarrow}L$ applies an implication assumption by searching for a proof of its assumption. Rule $\mathsf{Op}\forall L$ instantiates a quantified assumption with a chosen program. In practical implementations of proof search, not all L-rules are created equal. Rules $\mathsf{Op}\wedge L$, $\mathsf{Op?}L$, and $\mathsf{Op}\cup L$ can be applied eagerly without completeness concerns nor incurring substantial proof obligations. In contrast, $\mathsf{Op}{\rightarrow}L$ incurs an obligation to prove the assumption and $\mathsf{Op}\forall L$ has the potential for incompleteness because it consumes the quantifier. For these reasons, a practical implication should consider applying $\mathsf{Op}{\rightarrow}L$ and $\mathsf{Op}\forall L$ cautiously, e.g., only when a goal unifies with the result thereof. This completes the operational semantics.

Proposition 1. *The example query in Fig. 2 succeeds according to the operational semantics. Letting Σ be the signature of all declarations and ϕ be the query, the judgement $\phi \Longrightarrow^*_\Sigma \mathsf{true}$ holds.*

Proof. See annotated execution trace in appendix.

Implications. The operational semantics reveals several challenges that deserve attention during implementation. Nondeterminism arises when selecting between clauses of predicates, selecting among nested modalities, and selecting between left vs. right rules. In rules OpGoal, $\mathsf{OpClose}$, a standard depth-first search removes nondeterministic choice between subgoals. In practice, it may be convenient to resolve modalities from the inside out, as rules applied to an inner modality leave the outer one undisturbed. Moreover, when a nested modality

$$\textsc{OpGoal}\ \frac{A \to G \Longrightarrow A' \to G'}{(A \to G) \wedge \boldsymbol{G} \Longrightarrow (A' \to G') \wedge \boldsymbol{G}} \qquad \textsc{OpClose}\ \frac{*}{\mathsf{true} \wedge \boldsymbol{G} \Longrightarrow \boldsymbol{G}} \qquad \textsc{OpHyp}\ \frac{G \in A \cup \Sigma}{A \to G \Longrightarrow_\Sigma \mathsf{true}}$$

$$\textsc{OpExpl}\ \frac{(c ::= \alpha) \in \Sigma}{A{\to}M([c]G) \Longrightarrow_\Sigma A{\to}M([\alpha]G)}\ (c \text{ is } \gamma\text{-prog}, c \notin A, G, M)$$

$$\textsc{OpPred}\ \frac{(\boldsymbol{A} \to c) \in \Sigma}{A \to M(c) \Longrightarrow_\Sigma \wedge_i(A \to M(\boldsymbol{A}_i))} \qquad \textsc{Op;}\ \frac{*}{A \to M([\alpha;\beta]G) \Longrightarrow A \to M([\alpha][\beta]G)}$$

$$\textsc{Op}\cup\ \frac{*}{A{\to}M([\alpha \cup \beta]G) \Longrightarrow A{\to}M([\alpha]G \wedge [\beta]G)} \qquad \textsc{Op?}\ \frac{*}{A \to M([?A']G) \Longrightarrow A \to M(A' \to G)}$$

$$\textsc{Op*}\ \frac{*}{A \to [\alpha^*@inv(\bigvee_i J_i)]G \Longrightarrow (A \to \bigvee_i J_i) \wedge \bigwedge_i (J_i \to [\alpha]\bigvee_j J_j) \wedge \bigwedge_i (J_i \to G)}$$

$$\textsc{Op}\vee 1\ \frac{*}{A \to M(G_1 \vee G_2) \Longrightarrow A \to M(G_1)} \qquad \textsc{Op}\vee 2\ \frac{*}{A \to M(G_1 \vee G_2) \Longrightarrow A \to M(G_2)}$$

$$\textsc{Op}\wedge\ \frac{*}{A{\to}M(G_1{\wedge}G_2) \Longrightarrow (A{\to}M(G_1)){\wedge}(A{\to}M(G_2))} \qquad \textsc{Op}\forall\ \frac{*}{A \to \forall c\, G(c) \Longrightarrow A \to G(c')}$$

$$\textsc{Op}{\to}\ \frac{*}{A \to A_1 \to G \Longrightarrow A \wedge A_1 \to G} \qquad \textsc{Op}\wedge L\ \frac{*}{A \wedge (A_1 \wedge A_2) \to G \Longrightarrow A \wedge A_1 \wedge A_2 \to G}$$

$$\textsc{Op?}L\ \frac{*}{A \wedge [?G_1]p \to G \Longrightarrow A \wedge (G_1 \to p) \to G}$$

$$\textsc{Op}\forall L\ \frac{*}{A \wedge \forall c\, A_1(c) \to G \Longrightarrow A \wedge A_1(\alpha) \to G}\ (\alpha \text{ is } \delta\text{-program})$$

$$\textsc{Op}\cup L\ \frac{*}{A{\wedge}[\alpha \cup \beta]p{\to}G \Longrightarrow A{\wedge}[\alpha]p{\wedge}[\beta]p{\to}G} \qquad \textsc{Op}{\to}L\ \frac{*}{A{\wedge}(G_1{\to}p){\to}G \Longrightarrow (A{\to}G_1){\wedge}(A{\wedge}p{\to}G)}$$

Fig. 6. Operational semantics of DDLP.

contains a program symbol, simplifying its postcondition can enable the application of a defining clause. The nondeterminism between multiple defining clauses is fundamental, as in most LP languages. Thus an implementation should employ (standard) techniques to search amongst clauses.

Both left and right rules can introduce branching, so the ordering of left and right rules can substantially impact proof search performance. This is especially true because the loop rule has $2k + 1$ branches for a k-branch invariant formula. We give heuristics for ordering, but any heuristic is likely to be slow when applied to worst-case LPs. Non-branching left rules like $\mathsf{Op}\wedge L$ should be applied early so they are not repeated on each branch. Branching left rules like $\mathsf{Op}{\rightarrow}L$ may benefit from lazy application, as many subgoals could prove without them, and eager application could create combinatorially-many branches if branching occurs on the right as well.

6 Theory

The syntax, proof-theoretic semantics, and operational semantics of DDLP are new and thus require validation. We validate them with theoretical results.

Chief among the theoretical results, soundness shows that whenever the operational semantics responds affirmatively to a query, the query formula has a model. The proof of soundness, in turn, relies on several admissible rules and a lemma characterizing invariant formulas.

Lemma 1 (Invariant formulas and programs). *We prove these claims:*

- *Every invariant formula J is clause (D).*
- *Every invariant formula J is goal (G).*
- *Every invariant program ι is clause (δ).*
- *Every invariant program ι is goal (γ).*

Proof. By simultaneous induction on the structures of J and ι.

Lemma 2 (Admissible Rules). *Monotonicity, regularity, their iterated forms, and iterated rule K are all admissible in the proof-theoretic semantics. Rule G is admissible under the added assumption that its conclusion is a goal formula with definitions c expanded.*

$$\text{Ks}\ \frac{\Gamma \vdash M(\phi) \qquad \Gamma \vdash M(\phi \rightarrow \psi)}{\Gamma \vdash M(\psi)} \qquad \text{M}\ \frac{\phi \vdash \psi \qquad \Gamma \vdash [\alpha]\phi}{\Gamma \vdash [\alpha]\psi} \qquad \text{Ms}\ \frac{\phi \vdash \psi \qquad \Gamma \vdash M(\phi)}{\Gamma \vdash M(\psi)}$$

$$\textsc{Reg}\ \frac{\Gamma \vdash [\alpha]\phi \qquad \Gamma \vdash [\alpha]\psi}{\Gamma \vdash [\alpha](\phi \wedge \psi)} \qquad \textsc{Regs}\ \frac{\Gamma \vdash M(\phi) \qquad \Gamma \vdash M(\psi)}{\Gamma \vdash M(\phi \wedge \psi)} \qquad \text{G}\ \frac{\phi}{[\alpha]\phi}$$

These lemmas enable the following soundness property, showing that whenever the operational semantics solve a query, that query is provable proof-theoretically with an appropriately strengthened context.

Theorem 1 (Soundness w.r.t. Proof-Theoretic Semantics). *Let G be a goal formula. If judgement $G \Longrightarrow_\Sigma \mathsf{true}$ holds in the operational semantics then $\cdot \vdash_\Sigma G$ holds in the proof-theoretic dynamics. More generally, let G, G' be goal formulas such that $G \Longrightarrow_\Sigma G'$. If premise $\cdot \vdash_\Sigma G'$ is derivable in proof-theoretic semantics, the conclusion $\cdot \vdash_\Sigma G'$ is derivable in proof-theoretic semantics.*

Proof. By induction on the derivation of $G \Longrightarrow_\Sigma G'$. In appendix.

The proof-theoretic semantics, in turn, are validated by proving them sound with respect to the established semantics of PDL.

Theorem 2 (Soundness w.r.t. PDL). *The proof-theoretic semantics is sound w.r.t. PDL semantics, i.e., every sequent provable in DDLP is true in PDL.*

Proof. By induction on the derivation. In appendix. Though this is a standard result for PDL, we prove soundness anew for our proof rules, because they differ slightly from prior presentations of PDL.

6.1 Operational Semantics

Lemma 3 (Goal Property). *Let Γ be a clause context, G a goal formula. Let $\mathcal{D}$ derive $\Gamma \vdash G$ without rules K and M. At every step of the derivation $\mathcal{D}$, every antecedent is a clause formula and every succedent is a goal formula.*

The rules K and M are excluded from the statement because the premises include formulas which appear nowhere in the conclusion.

Lemma 4 (Goal Preservation). *If G is a goal formula and judgement $G \Longrightarrow_\Sigma G'$ holds in the operational semantics for formula G', then G' is a goal formula.*

Proof. By induction on the derivation of $G \Longrightarrow_\Sigma G'$. In appendix.

6.2 Uniform Proofs

Well-behaved LP languages typically search for proofs that are themselves well-behaved in some sense. The notion of *uniform proof* captures an established notion of such proofs. A proof T is *uniform* if all its sequents have succedents of at most one formula and the right-rule of the top-level succedent connective is applied at each step. For technical reasons, we also allow initial sequents. That is, where T_i are proofs of the premises and the sequent is of form $A \to G$:

1. Either T is an instance of Init or:
2. If G is $G_1 \vee G_2$ then T_1 is a proof of $A \to G_1$ or $A \to G_2$
3. If G is $G_1 \wedge G_2$ then T_1 is a proof of $A \to G_1$ and T_2 is a proof of $A \to G_2$.

4. If G is $\forall c\ G'$ then T_1 is a proof of $A \rightarrow [c/c']G$ for some fresh parameter c'.
5. If G is $A' \rightarrow G'$ then T_1 is a proof of $A \wedge A' \rightarrow G'$
6. If G is $[\alpha;\beta]G$ then T_1 is a proof of $[\alpha][\beta]G$
7. If G is $[?D]G$ then T_1 is a proof of $D \rightarrow G$
8. If G is $[\alpha \cup \beta]G$ then T_1 is a proof of $[\alpha]G \wedge [\beta]G$
9. If G is $[\alpha^* @inv(\wedge_i J_i)]G$, let there be n invariant branches J_i, then there are $2n+1$ premises. Specifically T_1 proves $\bigvee_i J_i$, for each $i \in [1, n]$, have T_{1+i} proves $J_i \vdash [\alpha] \bigvee_j J_i$, and for each $i \in [1, n]$, have T_{1+n+i} proves $J_i \vdash P$.

For DDLP, the uniformity theorem holds:

Theorem 3 (Uniformity). *Let Γ be clause, G be goal, and Σ a signature. Assume without loss of generality that explicitly-defined symbols are expanded.*

If $\Gamma \vdash_\Sigma G$ has a proof using only the core fragment of the proof-theoretic semantics Fig. 4, then $\Gamma \vdash_\Sigma G$ has a uniform proof.

It is informative to compare our uniformity theorem against those of other LP languages. One purpose of uniformity is to show that execution truly *constructs a solution.* Concretely, uniformity often subsumes the disjunction property (if $\phi \vee \psi$ has a proof, either ϕ has a proof or ψ has a proof) and the existential property (if $\exists x\ \phi(x)$ has a proof, we can extract a term e such that $\phi(e)$ has a proof). Our uniformity theorem subsumes the disjunction property, i.e., it can determine *which branch* of a disjunction is proven, but DDLP has no existential property to speak of, as we omit existential quantifiers. This is an intentional scoping decision: the existential property for DDLP program quantifiers amounts to synthesizing programs during proof search, a task which can easily fill a second paper. Our focus on ground programs is likewise intentional, precedented by similar treatments for answer-set programming [23].

A second purpose of uniformity is to demonstrate that the proofs found are somehow *sufficiently simple.* For example, our uniformity proof shows that left and right rules commute, so that right rules can be raised to the top level. However, DDLP faces unique challenges here as well. The classic uniformity proofs assume proof calculi that support cut-elimination, but cut-elimination is a serious challenge for DL, and is often simply false [40]. For cut-like rules such as K, similar are expected. Thus we instead *assume* a proof tree of such rules, allowing us to pinpoint which aspects of DDLP proof-search are open-ended. In particular, when performing DDLP proof search for goals that contain program constants, it is often required to operate under a modality, a fact reflected in the modal nature of the operational rules. When a goal contains nested modalities, there is a nondeterministic choice of which modality to operate on.

6.3 Complexity and Scalability

The best-known complexity result for PDL is doubly-exponential in the complexity of formulas [20]. Even in DDLP, which annotates loop invariants, nested conditionals can branch exponentially.

We expect polynomial complexity for many practical cases; we analyze PEGs as an example. An n-vertex game has n^2 states, thus $O(n^2)$ invariant branches. There are 4 combinations of player moves, a constant factor. In each branch, the postcondition and `angel-turn`'s definition each have $O(n^2)$ cases, yielding $O(n^4)$ proof steps per state, or $O(n^6)$ overall.

This analysis highlights improvement opportunities. The branching of invariants and `angel-turn` are redundant; we believe full game logic removes the redundancy, for $O(n^4)$ complexity. The complexity is state-bound, so modeling abstractions that reduce state count are also promising.

7 Related Work

We discuss related work in DL, modal LP, theory of LP, and applications.

Dynamic Logic. DL [20,24,47] is a family of program logics; compared to Hoare logic [26], it emphasizes first-class program modalities. PDL is its complete [44], decidable [20,48] propositional fragment. Cut elimination is desirable, but DDLP does not pursue it because it fails in straightforward calculi [40], requiring bounded loops, infinitary proofs, or cyclic proofs [25,41,52].

DDLP presupposes the computational content of DL is significant. Proof-term [27] and constructive calculi for DL [40,53] support this assertion. When extended to games [45], this content amounts to games' winning strategies [9–11].

Modal Logic Programming. Because DL is a (multi-)modal logic, DDLP is indebted to previous modal LP languages [43]. Temporal LP languages like Tempura [35] and Tokio [21] are mature and numerically-indexed multimodal LP [37] has been proposed, but these do not support program logics.

Previous attempts at LP for DL have substantial limitations. DL Prolog [42] proposes Prolog's SLD-resolution with DL axioms, but does not support invariants, is not validated on examples, and only sketches soundness for two rules. Pseudo-models are computable for deterministic, test-free PDL, but this fragment is too restrictive for realistic code like that in Fig. 2. The closest work [18] proposes LP for serial PDL, but its approach and intended use differ greatly. Our work is proof-theoretic, theirs model-theoretic. We reason about programs in hopes of program verification; they reason about similarity relations in pursuit of knowledge fusion for databases. A few technical aspects are comparable, notably our syntax restrictions.

Theory of Logic Programming. DDLPs upon the rich history of LP theory. LP is often called *programming as proof search*, so proof-theoretic semantics are often primary. Yet foundations are diverse, reflecting competing definitions of LP. Least fixed point and least model semantics [4,19] are considered canonical declarative semantics, which can be adapted to Prolog specifics such as negation-as-failure [49]. Operational semantics are often secondary, e.g., clarifying implementation-level issues or extra-logical practical features [3,8,13,16].

Extending least model semantics further, stable model semantics give a meaningful definition to LP languages where proof search may not even be feasible [30,39]. Other authors argue that proof search [33] is the defining feature of an LP language, and that uniform proofs [34] capture the proofs that search should return. Uniform proofs are notable for the absence of cut and for fulling resolving disjunctions and existentials. Because DDLP admits a proof-search interpretation with uniform proofs, we provide such an interpretation, but it is not clear whether these interpretations hold for planned extensions to richer logics.

Applications. Our running example is a pursuit-evasion game on a graph (PEG). Key applications of PEGs include network security problems such as intrusion detection [12] and physical security and safety problems such as surveillance patrol [7] and search-and-rescue; in the robotics community, a wide variety of such games have been solved [17]. Theoretical work on PEGs has largely emphasized development of algorithms to solve classes of PEGs with proven performance bounds [14], but formal verification in dynamic logics has attracted attention as well [29], for PEGs of similar complexity to our example. Formal verification work increases confidence in the theory of PEGs and could contribute to verified software for applications in robotics and networks.

We compare the PEG against an implementation we wrote in Dusa [31] (see appendix, D), which is used similarly to answer-set programming. The Dusa program was 34 meaningful lines of code; DDLP was 8. Dusa running time is exponential in game length, with a significant pause for a 15-turn game. DDLP performance is independent of game length.

More broadly, PDL is a logic for regular programs, so there is potential for use in other applications of regular languages, such as finite automata [50], data stream processing [28], and software-defined networking [51].

8 Conclusion

We presented DDLP, an LP interpretation of the ground, Demonic fragment of PDL. This contributes to the theory of LP by building a bridge between LP and program logics. As a driving example, we programmed a verified-correct pursuit-evasion game in DDLP. We developed proof-theoretic and operational semantics. We proved the semantics sound and the existence of uniform proofs.

Future work will add unification based on fast game logic substitutions [46] and extend DDLP to PDL and game logic. Future work will document the ongoing prototype implementation and its applications.

A PDL Semantics

We present the semantics of PDL in greater detail here (compared to Sect. 1). The semantics of PDL for programs α is written $[\![\alpha]\!]_I$, meaning the set of transitions (ω, ν) such that program α can transition from start state ω to end state ν when all program symbols and predicates are interpreted according to interpretation I. The argument I is omitted when it is not especially relevant. The semantics of PDL for formulas ϕ is written $[\![\phi]\!]_I$, meaning the set of states ω where formula ϕ is true when all program symbols and predicates are interpreted according to interpretation I.

The states ω, ν are drawn from some set of states $\mathcal{S}$. In PDL, we typically do not imbue $\mathcal{S}$ with any extra structure. First-order DL, in contrast, often defines states as assignments of variables to (e.g., scalar) values. The interpretation I defines both predicates and program constants, which have different "types." Letting $\mathcal{P}(S)$ be the power set of a set S, we have $I(p) : \mathcal{P}(S)$ for predicates p and $I(c) : \mathcal{P}(S \times S)$ for program constants c. Note that our predicates are *flexible symbols* whose truth value differs with the state, thus they are not in general equivalent to the formulas true or false.

We give the equations for programs, where $[\![\alpha]\!]^i$ is shorthand for iterated sequential composition:

$$\begin{aligned}
[\![c]\!]_I &= I(c)\\
[\![?\phi]\!] &= \{(\omega,\omega) \mid \omega \in [\![\phi]\!]\}\\
[\![\alpha;\beta]\!] &= [\![\alpha]\!] \circ [\![\beta]\!]\\
[\![\alpha \cup \beta]\!] &= [\![\alpha]\!] \cup [\![\beta]\!]\\
[\![\alpha^*]\!] &= \bigcup_{i \geq 0} [\![\alpha]\!] \circ \cdots \circ [\![\alpha]\!] (i \text{ times}) = \bigcup_{i \geq 0} [\![\alpha]\!]^i
\end{aligned}$$

And the equations for formulas

$$\begin{aligned}
[\![p]\!]_I &= I(p)\\
[\![[\alpha]\phi]\!] &= \{\omega \mid \nu \in [\![\phi]\!] \text{ for all } (\omega,\nu) \in [\![\alpha]\!]\}\\
[\![\langle\alpha\rangle\phi]\!] &= \{\omega \mid \nu \in [\![\phi]\!] \text{ for some } (\omega,\nu) \in [\![\alpha]\!]\}\\
[\![\phi \vee \psi]\!] &= [\![\phi]\!] \cup [\![\psi]\!]\\
[\![\phi \wedge \psi]\!] &= [\![\phi]\!] \cap [\![\psi]\!]\\
[\![\mathsf{true}]\!] &= \mathcal{S}\\
[\![\phi \to \psi]\!] &= [\![\psi]\!] \cup [\![\phi]\!]^{\mathsf{C}}\\
[\![\forall c\, \phi]\!]_I &= \bigcap \{[\![\phi]\!]_J \text{ where } J = I \text{ on } \{c\}^{\mathsf{C}}\}
\end{aligned}$$

The only feature in our presentation of PDL which is not entirely standard is the explicit program quantifier $\forall c\, \phi$, which is true when ϕ is true after assigning an arbitrary program relation to the interpretation of program symbol c.

Sequents relate to formulas in the standard way. Letting $\Gamma = \phi_1, \ldots, \phi_n$ then the semantics of a sequent $\Gamma \vdash \psi$ is defined to be the semantics of the formula $\bigwedge_i \phi_i \to \psi$. However, provability of a sequent is also parameterized by a signature Σ potentially containing definitions; validity must be incorporate the signature as well. Thus, a sequent $\Gamma \vdash_\Sigma \psi$ is valid iff formula $\bigwedge_i \phi_i \to \psi$ is locally valid in all interpretations I which satisfy the signature Σ. That is, the interpretation I must make all definitions in Σ true equations.

A formula (likewise sequent) ϕ is *valid* if it $[\![\phi]\!]_I = \mathcal{S}$ for all interpretations $\mathcal{S}$, i.e., it holds in all states and interpretations A formula (likewise sequent) ϕ is *locally valid* w.r.t. interpretation I if $[\![\phi]\!]_I = \mathcal{S}$, i.e., it holds for all states under a fixed interpretation I.

Consider a rule of form

$$\frac{P_1 \cdots P_n}{C}$$

A rule is sound if all instances are sound. An instance is sound if assuming the validity of all P_i suffices to show the conclusion C is sound. A rule instance (likewise rule) is *locally sound* if for all interpretations I, assuming the local validity of all P_i in interpretation I suffices to show C is locally valid in the same interpretation I. Local soundness is strictly stronger than soundness. All rules we present are locally sound except those which instantiate some predicate or program constant.

B Proofs

Note that variable names may differ between the main paper and appendix as style conventions have evolved during preparation.

Before proving the operational semantics sound with respect to the proof-theoretic semantics, we show the proof-theoretic semantics sound with respect to PDL semantics. This theorem is not in doubt because it is a standard theorem from the DL literature. However, we provide a proof out of abundance of caution because different authors' presentation of DL may differ in the details. For example, our rules for quantifiers over programs and explicitly-defined symbols are not standard across all presentations of DL.

The coincidence lemma and substitution lemma are standard lemmas to DL soundness.

Lemma 5 (Coincidence Lemma). *Let I and J be interpretation. Prove two claims: If I and J agree on free symbols of formula ϕ, then $[\![\phi]\!]_I = [\![\phi]\!]_J$. If I and J agree on free symbols of program α, then $[\![\alpha]\!]_I = [\![\alpha]\!]_J$.*

Proof. By simultaneous induction on the structure of programs α and formulas ϕ. The IHs are quantified over all I, J that agree on free symbols of the respective program or formula.

Case program c: Show $[\![c]\!]_I = I(c) =_* J(c) = [\![c]\!]_J$. The step marked * holds because we assumed I and J agree on free symbols of c, i.e., on $\{c\}$.

Case $?\phi$: Assume IH $[\![\phi]\!]_I = [\![\phi]\!]_J$.
Show $[\![?\phi]\!]_I = \{(\omega,\omega) \mid \omega \in [\![\phi]\!]_I\} = \{(\omega,\omega) \mid \omega \in [\![\phi]\!]_J\} = [\![?\phi]\!]_J$.

Case $\alpha;\beta$: Assume IHs $[\![\alpha]\!]_I = [\![\alpha]\!]_J$ and $[\![\beta]\!]_I = [\![\beta]\!]_J$. Show $[\![\alpha;\beta]\!]_I = [\![\alpha]\!]_I \circ [\![\beta]\!]_I = [\![\alpha]\!]_J \circ [\![\beta]\!]_J = [\![\alpha;\beta]\!]_J$.

Case $\alpha \cup \beta$: Assume IHs $[\![\alpha]\!]_I = [\![\alpha]\!]_J$ and $[\![\beta]\!]_I = [\![\beta]\!]_J$. Show $[\![\alpha \cup \beta]\!]_I = [\![\alpha]\!]_I \cup [\![\beta]\!]_I = [\![\alpha]\!]_J \cup [\![\beta]\!]_J = [\![\alpha \cup \beta]\!]_J$.

Case $\alpha^*@inv(\bigvee_i \psi_i)$: Assume IHs $[\![\alpha]\!]_I = [\![\alpha]\!]_J$ and $[\![\psi_i]\!]_I = [\![\psi_i]\!]_J$ for all i. Show $[\![\alpha^*@inv(\bigvee_i \psi_i)]\!]_I = \bigcup_{i\geq 0}[\![\alpha]\!]_I^i = \bigcup_{i\geq 0}[\![\alpha]\!]_J^i = [\![\alpha^*@inv(\bigvee_i \psi_i)]\!]_J$.

Case $\phi \wedge \psi$: Assume IHs $[\![\phi]\!]_I = [\![\phi]\!]_J$ and $[\![\psi]\!]_I = [\![\psi]\!]_J$. Show $[\![\phi \wedge \psi]\!]_I = [\![\phi]\!]_I \cap [\![\psi]\!]_I = [\![\phi]\!]_J \cap [\![\psi]\!]_J = [\![\phi \wedge \psi]\!]_J$.

Case $\phi \vee \psi$: Assume IHs $[\![\phi]\!]_I = [\![\phi]\!]_J$ and $[\![\psi]\!]_I = [\![\psi]\!]_J$. Show $[\![\phi \vee \psi]\!]_I = [\![\phi]\!]_I \cup [\![\psi]\!]_I = [\![\phi]\!]_J \cup [\![\psi]\!]_J = [\![\phi \vee \psi]\!]_J$.

Case $\phi \to \psi$: Assume IHs $[\![\phi]\!]_I = [\![\phi]\!]_J$ and $[\![\psi]\!]_I = [\![\psi]\!]_J$. Show $[\![\phi \to \psi]\!]_I = [\![\psi]\!]_I \cup [\![\phi]\!]_I^{\complement} = [\![\psi]\!]_J \cup [\![\phi]\!]_J^{\complement} = [\![\phi \to \psi]\!]_J$.

Case $[\alpha]\phi$: Assume IHs $[\![\alpha]\!]_I = [\![\alpha]\!]_J$ and $[\![\phi]\!]_I = [\![\phi]\!]_J$. Show $[\![[\alpha]\phi]\!]_I = \{\omega \mid \nu \in [\![\phi]\!]_I \text{ for all } (\omega,\nu) \in [\![\alpha]\!]_I\} = \{\omega \mid \nu \in [\![\phi]\!]_J \text{ for all } (\omega,\nu) \in [\![\alpha]\!]_J\} = [\![[\alpha]\phi]\!]_J$.

Case $\forall c\, \phi$: Assume IH $[\![\phi]\!]_I = [\![\phi]\!]_J$ when I and J agree on the free symbols of ϕ, i.e., on the free variables of $\forall c\, \phi$ and potentially also $\{c\}$.

Show $[\![\forall c\, \phi]\!]_I = \bigcup\{[\![\phi]\!]_{I'} \mid I = I' \text{ on } \{c\}^{\complement}\} =_* \bigcup\{[\![\phi]\!]_{J'} \mid J = J' \text{ on } \{c\}^{\complement}\} = [\![\forall c\, \phi]\!]_J$.

The step labeled * holds by the IH on ϕ. The IH is applicable because the sets $\{I' \mid I = I' \text{ on } \{c\}^{\complement}\}$ and $\{J' \mid J \text{ on } \{c\}^{\complement}\}$ are the same set up to agreement on the free symbols of ϕ. First, they agree on the free symbols of $\forall c\, \phi$ because I and J do, and all elements agree with I and J on these symbols. Secondly, they agree on c because in both sets, c takes on every possible value.

Case formula p: Show $[\![p]\!]_I = I(p) =_* J(p) = [\![p]\!]_J$. The step marked * holds because we assumed I and J agree on free symbols of p, i.e., on $\{p\}$.

The substitution lemma relies on the notion of admissible substitution.

Definition 1 (Admissible Substitution). *A substitution of some* α_1 *for some* α_2 *is admissible if no replacement site occurs under a binder of any free symbol of* α_1 *or* α_2.

Lemma 6 (Substitution Lemma). *Let* I *be an interpretation,* ϕ *a formula, and* α, β *programs. Let variable* c *be fresh. Abbreviate* $\hat{I} = [c/[\![\alpha]\!]_I]I$. *Assume an admissible substitution. The lemma consists of the following claims. Firstly,* $[\![\phi(c)]\!]_{\hat{I}} = [\![\phi(\alpha)]\!]_I$ *and* $[\![\beta(c)]\!]_{\hat{I}} = [\![\beta(\alpha)]\!]_I$. *Secondly, let* α_1, α_2 *be programs and suppose* $[\![\alpha_1]\!]_I = [\![\alpha_2]\!]_I$. *Then* $[\![\phi(\alpha_1)]\!]_I = [\![\phi(\alpha_2)]\!]_I$ *and* $[\![\beta(\alpha_1)]\!]_I = [\![\beta(\alpha_2)]\!]_I$.

Proof. We prove the claims $[\![\phi(c)]\!]_{\hat{I}} = [\![\phi(\alpha)]\!]_I$ and $[\![\beta(c)]\!]_{\hat{I}} = [\![\beta(\alpha)]\!]_I$ by simultaneous induction on the structure of (parameterized) programs $\beta(c)$ and formulas $\phi(c)$. The remaining claims $[\![\beta(\alpha_1)]\!]_I = [\![\beta(\alpha_2)]\!]_I$ and $[\![\phi(\alpha_1)]\!]_I = [\![\phi(\alpha_2)]\!]_I$ then following from the first claims by a short direct proof.

Case argument c: Show $[\![\beta(c)]\!]_{\hat{I}} = [\![c]\!]_{\hat{I}} = \hat{I}(c) = [\![\alpha]\!]_I = [\![\beta(\alpha)]\!]_I$.

Case program $c' \neq c$: Show $[\![\beta(c)]\!]_{\hat{I}} = [\![c']\!]_{\hat{I}} = \hat{I}(c') = I(c') = [\![\beta(\alpha)]\!]_I$.

Case $?\phi$: Assume the IH $[\![\phi(c)]\!]_{\hat{I}} = [\![\phi(\alpha)]\!]_I$. Then show $[\![\beta(c)]\!] = [\![?\phi(c)]\!]_{\hat{I}} = \{(\omega,\omega) \mid \omega \in [\![\phi(c)]\!]_{\hat{I}}\} = \{(\omega,\omega) \mid \omega \in [\![\phi(\alpha)]\!]_I\} = [\![?\phi(\alpha)]\!]_I = [\![\beta(\alpha)]\!]_I$.

Case $\beta_1;\beta_2$: Assume IHs $[\![\beta_1(c)]\!]_{\hat{I}} = [\![\beta_1(\alpha)]\!]_I$ and $[\![\beta_2(c)]\!]_{\hat{I}} = [\![\beta_2(\alpha)]\!]_I$. Show $[\![\beta(c)]\!]_{\hat{I}} = [\![\beta_1(c);\beta_2(c)]\!]_{\hat{I}} = [\![\beta_1(c)]\!]_{\hat{I}} \circ [\![\beta_2(c)]\!]_{\hat{I}} = [\![\beta_1(\alpha)]\!] \circ [\![\beta_2(\alpha)]\!]_I = [\![\beta_1(\alpha);\beta_2(\alpha)]\!]_I = [\![\beta(\alpha)]\!]_I$.

Case $\beta_1 \cup \beta_2$: Assume IHs $[\![\beta_1(c)]\!]_{\hat{I}} = [\![\beta_1(\alpha)]\!]_I$ and $[\![\beta_2(c)]\!]_{\hat{I}} = [\![\beta_2(\alpha)]\!]_I$. Show $[\![\beta(c)]\!]_{\hat{c}} = [\![\beta_1(c) \cup \beta_2(c)]\!]_{\hat{I}} = [\![\beta_1(c)]\!]_{\hat{I}} \cup [\![\beta_2(c)]\!]_{\hat{I}} = [\![\beta_1(\alpha)]\!]_I \cup [\![\beta_2(\alpha)]\!]_I = [\![\beta_1(\alpha) \cup \beta_2(\alpha)]\!]_I = [\![\beta(\alpha)]\!]_I$.

Case ${\beta_1}^*@inv(\bigvee_i \psi_i)$: Assume IHs $[\![\beta_1(c)]\!]_{\hat{I}} = [\![\beta_1(\alpha)]\!]_I$ and $[\![\psi_i(c)]\!]_{\hat{I}} = [\![\psi_i(\alpha)]\!]_I$. It follows immediately that for all $i \geq 0$, we have $[\![\beta_1(c)]\!]^i_{\hat{I}} = [\![\beta_1(\alpha)]\!]^i_{I}$. Show $[\![\beta(c)]\!]_{\hat{I}} = [\![\beta_1(c)^*@inv(\bigvee_i \psi_i(c))]\!] = \bigcup_{i\geq 0}[\![\beta_1(c)]\!]^i_{\hat{I}} = \bigcup_{i\geq 0}[\![\beta_1(\alpha)]\!]^i_I = [\![\beta_1(\alpha)^*@inv(\bigvee_i \psi_i(\alpha))]\!]_I = [\![\beta(\alpha)]\!]_I$.

Case formula p: Show $[\![\phi(c)]\!]_{\hat{I}} = [\![p]\!]_{\hat{I}} = \hat{I}(p) = I(p) = [\![p]\!]_I = [\![\phi(\alpha)]\!]_I$.

Case $\phi_1 \to \phi_2$: Assume IHs $[\![\phi_1(c)]\!]_{\hat{I}} = [\![\phi_1(\alpha)]\!]_I$ and $[\![\phi_2(c)]\!]_{\hat{I}} = [\![\phi_2(\alpha)]\!]_I$. Show $[\![\phi(c)]\!]_{\hat{I}} = [\![\phi_1(c) \to \phi_2(c)]\!]_{\hat{I}} = [\![\phi_2(c)]\!]_{\hat{I}} \cup [\![\phi_1(c)]\!]^{\complement}_{\hat{I}} = [\![\phi_2(\alpha)]\!]_I \cup [\![\phi_1(\alpha)]\!]^{\complement}_I = [\![\phi_1(\alpha) \to \phi_2(\alpha)]\!]_I = [\![\phi(\alpha)]\!]_I$.

Case $\phi_1 \wedge \phi_2$: Assume IHs $[\![\phi_1(c)]\!]_{\hat{I}} = [\![\phi_1(\alpha)]\!]_I$ and $[\![\phi_2(c)]\!]_{\hat{I}} = [\![\phi_2(\alpha)]\!]_I$. Show $[\![\phi(c)]\!]_{\hat{I}} = [\![\phi_1(c) \wedge \phi_2(c)]\!]_{\hat{I}} = [\![\phi_1(c)]\!]_{\hat{I}} \cap [\![\phi_2(c)]\!]_{\hat{I}} = [\![\phi_1(\alpha)]\!]_I \cap [\![\phi_2(\alpha)]\!]_I = [\![\phi_1(\alpha) \wedge \phi_2(\alpha)]\!]_I = [\![\phi(\alpha)]\!]_I$.

Case $\phi_1 \vee \phi_2$: Assume IHs $[\![\phi_1(c)]\!]_{\hat{I}} = [\![\phi_1(\alpha)]\!]_I$ and $[\![\phi_2(c)]\!]_{\hat{I}} = [\![\phi_2(\alpha)]\!]_I$. Show $[\![\phi(c)]\!]_{\hat{I}} = [\![\phi_1(c) \vee \phi_2(c)]\!]\hat{I} = [\![\phi_1(c)]\!]_{\hat{I}} \cup [\![\phi_2(c)]\!]_{\hat{I}} = [\![\phi_1(\alpha)]\!]_I \cup [\![\phi_2(\alpha)]\!]_I = [\![\phi_1(\alpha) \vee \phi_2(\alpha)]\!]_I = [\![\phi(\alpha)]\!]_I$.

Case $\forall c'\ \phi_1$: Assume IH $[\![\phi_1(c)]\!]_{\hat{I}} = [\![\phi_1(\alpha)]\!]_I$. Assume without loss of generality that c occurs in ϕ_1. Admissibility implies that $c \neq c'$ and that c' does not appear as a free variable in α. The freshness assumption on c further implies that c does not appear as a free variable in α. Show:

$$
\begin{aligned}
&[\![\phi(c)]\!]_{\hat{I}} \\
=&[\![\forall c'\ \phi_1(c)]\!]_{\hat{I}} \\
=&\bigcap\{[\![\phi_1(c)]\!]_J \text{ where } \hat{I} = J \text{ on } \{c'\}^{\complement}\} \\
=&\bigcap\{[\![\phi_1(c)]\!]_J \text{ where } [c/[\![\alpha]\!]_I]I = J \text{ on } \{c'\}^{\complement}\} \\
=_*&\bigcap\{[\![\phi_1(c)]\!]_{[c/[\![\alpha]\!]_I]J} \text{ where } [c/[\![\alpha]\!]_I]I = J \text{ on } \{c'\}^{\complement}\} \\
=_{C1}&\bigcap\{[\![\phi_1(c)]\!]_{[c/[\![\alpha]\!]_I]J} \text{ where } I = J \text{ on } \{c'\}^{\complement}\} \\
=_{C2}&\bigcap\{[\![\phi_1(c)]\!]_{[c/[\![\alpha]\!]_J]J} \text{ where } I = J \text{ on } \{c'\}^{\complement}\} \\
=&\bigcap\{[\![\phi_1(c)]\!]_{\hat{J}} \text{ where } I = J \text{ on } \{c'\}^{\complement}\} \\
=_{IH}&\bigcap\{[\![\phi_1(\alpha)]\!]_J \text{ where } I = J \text{ on } \{c'\}^{\complement}\} \\
=&[\![\forall c'\ \phi_1(\alpha)]\!]_I \\
=&[\![\phi(\alpha)]\!]_I
\end{aligned}
$$

The step labeled $*$ is justified by idempotence of substitution in an interpretation, i.e., $J = [c/[\![\alpha]\!]_I]J$ because $J(c) = [\![\alpha]\!]_I$ already holds here from the assumption $J = \hat{I}$ on $\{c'\}^{\complement}$ for $c \neq c'$. Steps C1 and C2 are both justified by Lemma 5. In C1, c is not a free variable of α so whether I agrees with J on c has no effect on $[\![\alpha]\!]$. In C2, c' is not a free variable of α so agreement of I and J on

$\{c'\}^{\mathsf{C}}$ suffices to ensure $I = J$ on the free variables of α and thus the semantics agree. The step labeled IH holds by the inductive hypothesis.

Case $[\beta_1]\phi_1$: Assume IHs $[\![\beta_1(c)]\!]_{\hat{I}} = [\![\beta_1(\alpha)]\!]_I$ and $[\![\phi_1(c)]\!]_{\hat{I}} = [\![\phi_1(\alpha)]\!]_I$. Show $[\![\phi(c)]\!]_{\hat{I}} = [\![[\beta_1(c)]\phi_1(c)]\!]_{\hat{I}} = \{\omega \mid \nu \in [\![\phi_1(c)]\!]_{\hat{I}} \text{ for all } (\omega,\nu) \in [\![\beta_1(c)]\!]_{\hat{I}}\} = \{\omega \mid \nu \in [\![\phi_1(\alpha)]\!]_I \text{ for all } (\omega,\nu) \in [\![\beta_1(\alpha)]\!]_I\} = [\![[\beta_1(\alpha)]\phi_1(\alpha)]\!]_I = [\![\phi(\alpha)]\!]_I$.

This completes the induction. We prove the remaining claims by appeal to the first two claims.

To prove $[\![\phi(\alpha_1)]\!]_I = [\![\phi(\alpha_2)]\!]_I$, observe:

$$\begin{aligned}
&[\![\phi(\alpha_1)]\!]_I && \\
=&[\![\phi(c)]\!]_{[c/[\![\alpha_1]\!]_I]I} && \text{[By claim 1]}\\
=&[\![\phi(c)]\!]_{[c/[\![\alpha_2]\!]_I]I} && \text{[By assump.]}\\
=&[\![\phi(\alpha_2)]\!]_I && \text{[By claim 1]}
\end{aligned}$$

To prove $[\![\beta(\alpha_1)]\!]_I = [\![\beta(\alpha_2)]\!]_I$, observe:

$$\begin{aligned}
&[\![\beta(\alpha_1)]\!]_I && \\
=&[\![\beta(c)]\!]_{[c/[\![\alpha_1]\!]_I]I} && \text{[By claim 2]}\\
=&[\![\beta(c)]\!]_{[c/[\![\alpha_2]\!]_I]I} && \text{[By assump.]}\\
=&[\![\beta(\alpha_2)]\!]_I && \text{[By claim 2]}
\end{aligned}$$

We now proceed to the main PDL soundness proof.

Theorem 4 (Soundness w.r.t. PDL). *The proof-theoretic DDLP semantics is sound with respect to the semantics of PDL, i.e., every sequent provable in DDLP is true in PDL.*

Proof. It suffices to prove that every rule in the proof-theoretic semantics is sound. Soundness of DDLP with respect to PDL follows immediately by induction on the structure of derivations. Thus we proceed by cases on the rules of Fig. 4 and Fig. 5. In each case, we fix an instance of the rule, assume the premises are valid, and show the conclusion is valid. Though we need only prove soundness, most cases are *locally sound*, i.e., the conclusion holds in the same interpretation as the premises.

Case Init: $\dfrac{\phi \in \Gamma \cup \Sigma}{\Gamma \vdash_\Sigma \phi}\,\textsc{Init}$ Assume I that satisfies Σ. Fix ω such that $\omega \in [\![\Gamma]\!]$. From the premise, either $\phi \in \Gamma$ or $\phi \in \Sigma$. Proceed by cases. If $\phi \in \Gamma$, then $\omega \in [\![\Gamma]\!]$ immediately implies $\omega \in [\![\phi]\!]$, as desired. Else $\phi \in \Sigma$, then I satisfies Σ which immediately implies $\omega \in [\![\phi]\!]_I$ for all $\omega \in \mathcal{S}$, as desired.

Case $\top$: $\dfrac{*}{\Gamma \vdash \mathsf{true}}\,\top$ It suffices to show $\omega \in [\![\mathsf{true}]\!]$ which holds by definition, for all $\omega \in \mathcal{S}$.

Case $;R$: $\dfrac{\Gamma \vdash [\alpha][\beta]\phi}{\Gamma \vdash [\alpha;\beta]\phi}\;{;R}$

Assume $\omega \in [\![\Gamma]\!]$. Applying this assumption to the premise yields $\omega \in [\![[\alpha][\beta]\phi]\!]$, then reason:

$$\begin{aligned}
&\omega \in [\![[\alpha][\beta]\phi]\!]\\
\text{iff }& \mu \in [\![[\beta]\phi]\!] \text{ for all } (\omega,\mu) \in [\![\alpha]\!]\\
\text{iff }& \nu \in [\![\phi]\!] \text{ for all } (\omega,\mu) \in [\![\alpha]\!], (\mu,\nu) \in [\![\beta]\!]\\
\text{iff }& \nu \in [\![\phi]\!] \text{ for all } (\omega,\nu) \in [\![\alpha]\!] \circ [\![\beta]\!]\\
\text{iff }& \nu \in [\![\phi]\!] \text{ for all } (\omega,\nu) \in [\![\alpha;\beta]\!]\\
\text{iff }& \omega \in [\![[\alpha;\beta]\phi]\!]
\end{aligned}$$

as desired.

Case $\cup R$: $\dfrac{\Gamma \vdash [\alpha]\phi \wedge [\beta]\phi}{\Gamma \vdash [\alpha \cup \beta]\phi}\;{\cup R}$

Assume $\omega \in [\![\Gamma]\!]$. Applying this assumption to the premise yields $[\alpha]\phi \wedge [\beta]\phi$, then reason:

$$\begin{aligned}
&\omega \in [\![[\alpha]\phi \wedge [\beta]\phi]\!]\\
\text{iff }& \omega \in [\![[\alpha]\phi]\!] \cap [\![[\beta]\phi]\!]\\
\text{iff }& \nu \in [\![\phi]\!] \text{ for all } (\omega,\nu) \in [\![\alpha]\!] \text{ and } \nu \in [\![\phi]\!] \text{ for all } (\omega,\nu) \in [\![\beta]\!]\\
\text{iff }& \nu \in [\![\phi]\!] \text{ for all } (\omega,\nu) \in [\![\alpha]\!] \cup [\![\beta]\!]\\
\text{iff }& \nu \in [\![\phi]\!] \text{ for all } (\omega,\nu) \in [\![\alpha \cup \beta]\!]\\
\text{iff }& \omega \in [\![[\alpha \cup \beta]\phi]\!]
\end{aligned}$$

as desired.

Case $\wedge R$: $\dfrac{\Gamma \vdash \phi \qquad \Gamma \vdash \psi}{\Gamma \vdash \phi \wedge \psi}\;{\wedge R}$ Assume $\omega \in [\![\Gamma]\!]$. Applying this assumption to the premises yields $\omega \in [\![\phi]\!]$ and $\omega \in [\![\psi]\!]$ from which $\omega \in [\![\phi]\!] \cap [\![\psi]\!]$ and thus $\omega \in [\![\phi \wedge \psi]\!]$ as desired.

Case $\wedge L$: $\dfrac{\Gamma, \psi_1, \psi_2 \vdash \phi}{\Gamma, \psi_1 \wedge \psi_2 \vdash \phi}\;{\wedge L}$ Assume $\omega \in [\![\Gamma, \psi_1 \wedge \psi_2]\!]$, so $\omega \in [\![\Gamma]\!]$ and $\omega \in [\![\psi_1 \wedge \psi_2]\!] = [\![\psi_1]\!] \cap [\![\psi_2]\!]$ from which $\omega \in [\![\psi_1]\!]$ and $\omega \in [\![\psi_2]\!]$ immediately. Thus $\omega \in [\![\Gamma, \psi_1, \psi_2]\!]$ which can be applied to the premise, yielding $\omega \in [\![\phi]\!]$ as desired.

Case $?L$: $\dfrac{\Gamma, \psi_1 \to \psi_2 \vdash \phi}{\Gamma, [?\psi_1]\psi_2 \vdash \phi}\;{?L}$ Assume $\omega \in [\![\Gamma, [?\psi_1]\psi_2]\!]$ so $\omega \in [\![\Gamma]\!]$ and $\omega \in [\![[?\psi_1]\psi_2]\!]$. Then to apply the premise it suffices to show $\omega \in [\![\psi_1 \to \psi_2]\!]$, reasoning:

$$\begin{aligned}
&\omega \in [\![[?\psi_1]\psi_2]\!]\\
&\text{iff } \nu \in [\![\psi_2]\!] \text{ for all } (\omega, \nu) \in [\![?\psi_1]\!]\\
&\text{iff } \omega \in [\![\psi_2]\!] \text{ if } \omega \in [\![\psi_1]\!]\\
&\text{iff } \omega \in [\![\psi_2]\!] \cup [\![\psi_1]\!]^{\complement}\\
&\text{iff } \omega \in [\![\psi_1 \rightarrow \psi_2]\!]
\end{aligned}$$

from which the premise applies and immediately yields ϕ as desired.

Case $\cup L$: $\dfrac{\Gamma, [\alpha]\psi \wedge [\beta]\psi \vdash \phi}{\Gamma, [\alpha \cup \beta]\psi \vdash \phi}\ {\scriptstyle \cup L}$ Assume $\omega \in [\![\Gamma, [\alpha \cup \beta]\psi]\!]$ so $\omega \in [\![\Gamma]\!]$ and $\omega \in [\![[\alpha \cup \beta]\psi]\!]$. To apply the premise it suffices to show $\omega \in [\![[\alpha]\psi \wedge [\beta]\psi]\!]$, reasoning:

$$\begin{aligned}
&\omega \in [\![[\alpha \cup \beta]\psi]\!]\\
&\text{iff } \nu \in [\![\psi]\!] \text{ for all } (\omega, \nu) \in [\![\alpha \cup \beta]\!]\\
&\text{iff } \nu \in [\![\psi]\!] \text{ for all } (\omega, \nu) \in [\![\alpha]\!] \cup [\![\beta]\!]\\
&\text{iff } \nu \in [\![\psi]\!] \text{ for all } (\omega, \nu) \in [\![\alpha]\!] \text{ and } \nu \in [\![\psi]\!] \text{ for all } (\omega, \nu) \in [\![\beta]\!]\\
&\text{iff } \omega \in [\![[\alpha]\psi]\!] \text{ and } \omega \in [\![[\beta]\psi]\!]\\
&\text{iff } \omega \in [\![[\alpha]\psi]\!] \cap [\![[\beta]\psi]\!]\\
&\text{iff } \omega \in [\![[\alpha]\psi \wedge [\beta]\psi]\!]
\end{aligned}$$

from which the premise applies and immediately yields ϕ as desired.

Case $\vee R1$: $\dfrac{\Gamma \vdash \phi}{\Gamma \vdash \phi \vee \psi}\ {\scriptstyle \vee R1}$ Assume $\omega \in [\![\Gamma]\!]$. Applying this assumption to the premise yields $\omega \in [\![\phi]\!] \subseteq [\![\phi]\!] \cup [\![\psi]\!] = [\![\phi \vee \psi]\!]$ as desired.

Case $\vee R2$: $\dfrac{\Gamma \vdash \psi}{\Gamma \vdash \phi \vee \psi}\ {\scriptstyle \vee R2}$

Assume $\omega \in [\![\Gamma]\!]$. Applying this assumption to the premise yields $\omega \in [\![\psi]\!] \subseteq [\![\phi]\!] \cup [\![\psi]\!] = [\![\phi \vee \psi]\!]$ as desired.

Case $\forall L$: $\dfrac{\Gamma, \phi(\alpha) \vdash \psi}{\Gamma, \forall c\, \phi(c) \vdash \psi}\ {\scriptstyle \forall L}$ Fix I and assume $\omega \in [\![\Gamma, \forall c\, \phi(c)]\!]_I$, so $\omega \in [\![\Gamma]\!]_I$ and $\omega \in [\![\forall c\, \phi(c)]\!]_I$. Define $J = [c/[\![\alpha]\!]_I]I$, then $I = J$ on $\{c\}^{\complement}$ by construction. By definition, $[\![\forall c\, \phi]\!]_I = \bigcap\{[\![\phi]\!]_J \text{ where } J = I \text{ on } \{c\}^{\complement}\}$ and by construction of J, have $[\![\forall c\, \phi]\!]_I \subseteq [\![\phi(c)]\!]_J$. By Lemma 6, $[\![\phi(c)]\!]_J = [\![\phi(\alpha)]\!]_I$, thus $\omega \in [\![\phi(\alpha)]\!]_I$. Combined with $\omega \in [\![\Gamma]\!]_I$, the premise applies, yielding $\omega \in [\![\psi]\!]_I$ as desired.

Case $\rightarrow L$: $\dfrac{\Gamma \vdash \phi_1 \qquad \Gamma, \phi_2 \vdash \psi}{\Gamma, \phi_1 \rightarrow \phi_2 \vdash \psi}\ {\scriptstyle \rightarrow L}$

Assume $\omega \in [\![\Gamma, \phi_1 \rightarrow \phi_2]\!]$ so $\omega \in [\![\Gamma]\!]$ and $\omega \in [\![\phi_1 \rightarrow \phi_2]\!]$. Because $\omega \in [\![\Gamma]\!]$, the first premise applies, yielding $\omega \in [\![\phi_1]\!]$, i.e., $\omega \notin [\![\phi_1]\!]^{\complement}$. By definition $\omega \in$

$[\![\phi_1 \rightarrow \phi_2]\!] = [\![\phi_2]\!] \cup [\![\phi_1]\!]^{\mathsf{C}}$. From $\omega \notin [\![\phi_1]\!]^{\mathsf{C}}$ it immediately follows that $\omega \in [\![\phi_2]\!]$. Combined with $\omega \in [\![\Gamma]\!]$, the second premise now applies, yielding $\omega \in [\![\psi]\!]$ as desired.

Case $\rightarrow R$: $\dfrac{\Gamma, \phi \vdash \psi}{\Gamma \vdash \phi \rightarrow \psi}\ {\rightarrow}R$

Assume $\omega \in [\![\Gamma]\!]$. By law of excluded middle, either $\omega \in [\![\phi]\!]$ or $\omega \in [\![\phi]\!]^{\mathsf{C}}$.

If $\omega \in [\![\phi]\!]$ then $\omega \in [\![\Gamma, \phi]\!]$ so the premise applies, yielding $\omega \in [\![\psi]\!]$ as desired. Else, $\omega \in [\![\phi]\!]^{\mathsf{C}} \subseteq [\![\psi]\!] \cup [\![\phi]\!]^{\mathsf{C}} = [\![\phi \rightarrow \psi]\!]$ as desired.

Case $\forall R$: $\dfrac{\Gamma \vdash \phi(c')}{\Gamma \vdash \forall c\ \phi(c)}\ \forall R$ where c' is fresh.

Fix I and assume $\omega \in [\![\Gamma]\!]_I$. Let $J = [c'/R]I$ for arbitrary transition relation R. Because c' is fresh, c' is not mentioned in Γ and $\omega \in [\![\Gamma]\!]_J$ holds for all such J. Applying the premise yields $\omega \in [\![\phi(c')]\!]_J$ for all such J. That is, for all R, we have $\omega \in [\![\phi(c')]\!]_{[c'/R]I}$ so $\omega \in \bigcap_R [\![\phi(c')]\!]_{[c'/R]I} = \bigcap \{[\![\phi(c')]\!]_J$ where $J = I$ on $\{c'\}^{\mathsf{C}}\} = [\![\forall y\ \phi(c')]\!]_I$. By renaming, $\omega \in [\![\forall x\ p(x)]\!]_I$ as desired.

Case $?R$: $\dfrac{\Gamma \vdash \psi \rightarrow \phi}{\Gamma \vdash [?\psi]\phi}\ ?R$

Assume $\omega \in [\![\Gamma]\!]$. Applying this assumption to the premise yields $\omega \in [\![\psi \rightarrow \phi]\!] = [\![\phi]\!] \cup [\![\psi]\!]^{\mathsf{C}}$. Expanding the definition of the conclusion, it suffices to show $\nu \in [\![\phi]\!]$ for all $(\omega, \nu) \in [\![?\psi]\!]$. By definition of $[\![?\psi]\!]$ we have $(\omega, \nu) \in [\![?\psi]\!]$ iff $\omega = \nu$ and $\omega \in [\![\psi]\!]$. Thus $\omega \notin [\![\psi]\!]^{\mathsf{C}}$ and from $\omega \in [\![\phi]\!] \cup [\![\psi]\!]^{\mathsf{C}}$ we have $\omega \in [\![\phi]\!]$ or equivalently $\nu \in [\![\phi]\!]$ as desired.

Case $*R$: $\dfrac{\Gamma \vdash \vee_i \psi_i \qquad \psi_1 \vdash [\alpha] \vee_j \psi_j \cdots \psi_n \vdash [\alpha] \vee_j \psi_j \qquad \psi_1 \vdash \phi \cdots \psi_n \vdash \phi}{\Gamma \vdash [\alpha^* @inv(\vee_i \psi_i)]\phi}\ {*}R$

Let n be the number of branches in the invariant. Assume $\omega \in [\![\Gamma]\!]$. To prove the conclusion, we prove $\nu \in [\![\phi]\!]$ for all $(\omega, \nu) \in [\![\alpha^* @inv(\bigvee_i \psi_i)]\!] = \bigcup_{i \geq 0} [\![\alpha]\!] \circ \cdots \circ [\![\alpha]\!] (i$ times), which we equivalently notate $\bigcup_{i \geq 0} [\![\alpha]\!]^i$. We prove the intermediate claim that $\nu \in [\![\bigvee_i \psi_i]\!]$. We proceed by induction on the (least) i for which $(\omega, \nu) \in [\![\alpha]\!]^i$.

Base case $i = 0$: If $(\omega, \nu) \in [\![\alpha]\!]^0$ then $\nu = \omega$ and it suffices to show $\omega \in [\![\bigvee_i \psi_i]\!]$, which follows immediately from applying $\omega \in [\![\Gamma]\!]$ to the first premise.

Inductive case $i = k + 1$: If $(\omega, \nu) \in [\![\alpha]\!]^{k+1}$ then there exists μ such that $(\omega, \mu) \in [\![\alpha]\!]^k$ and $(\mu, \nu) \in [\![\alpha]\!]$. Moreover, the inductive hypothesis asserts that $\mu \in [\![\bigvee_i \psi_i]\!]$, thus $\mu \in [\![\psi_j]\!]$ for some j. Proceed by cases on j. Apply $\mu \in [\![\psi_j]\!]$ to premise $1 + j$ to obtain $\mu \in [\![[\alpha] \bigvee_i \psi_i]\!]$, which expands to $\nu' \in [\![\bigvee_i \psi_i]\!]$ for all $(\mu, \nu') \in [\![\alpha]\!]$. Setting $\nu' = \nu$ we obtain $\nu \in [\![\bigvee_i \psi_i]\!]$, which completes the inductive case and the induction.

From the claim $\nu \in [\![\bigvee_i \psi_i]\!]$ observe $\nu \in [\![\psi_i]\!]$ for some i. Applying this fact to premise $1 + n + i$ yields $\nu \in [\![\phi]\!]$ as desired.

Case Expl: $\dfrac{c ::= \alpha \in \Sigma \qquad \Gamma(\alpha) \vdash \phi(\alpha)}{\Gamma(c) \vdash \phi(c)}$ Expl ($\Gamma(\alpha)$ clause, $\phi(\alpha)$ goal)

Fix I that satisfies $c ::= \alpha$ and assume $\omega \in \Gamma(c)$. Because I satisfies $c ::= \alpha$ we have $[\![c]\!]_I = [\![\alpha]\!]_I$. By Lemma 6, then, $\omega \in \Gamma(\alpha)$, which applies to the second premise, yielding $\omega \in \phi(\alpha)$. By Lemma 6 again, $\omega \in \phi(c)$ as desired.

Case K: $\dfrac{\Gamma \vdash [\alpha]\phi \qquad \Gamma \vdash [\alpha](\phi \to \psi)}{\Gamma \vdash [\alpha]\psi}$ K

Assume $\omega \in [\![\Gamma]\!]$. Applying this assumption to the premises yields $\omega \in [\![[\alpha]\phi]\!]$ and $\omega \in [\![[\alpha](\phi \to \psi)]\!]$. The first expands to $\nu \in [\![\phi]\!]$ for all $(\omega, \nu) \in [\![\alpha]\!]$. Fix any such ν. The second expands to $\nu' \in [\![\phi \to \psi]\!]$ for all $(\omega, \nu') \in [\![\alpha]\!]$. Set $\nu' = \nu$, then $\nu \in [\![\phi \to \psi]\!]$ iff $\nu \in [\![\psi]\!] \cup [\![\phi]\!]^{\complement}$ and because $\nu \notin [\![\phi]\!]^{\complement}$ we conclude $\nu \in [\![\psi]\!]$. Because this argument held for all $(\omega, \nu) \in [\![\alpha]\!]$ we conclude $\omega \in [\![[\alpha]\psi]\!]$ as desired.

Case G: $\dfrac{\phi}{[\alpha]\phi}$ G Fix state ω. Suffices to show $\nu \in [\![\phi]\!]$ for all $(\omega, \nu) \in [\![\alpha]\!]$. Fix any such ν, then $\nu \in [\![\phi]\!]$ is immediate from the premise.

Case $\vee L$: $\dfrac{\Gamma, \phi_1 \vdash \psi \qquad \Gamma, \phi_2 \vdash \psi}{\Gamma, \phi_1 \vee \phi_2 \vdash \psi}$ $\vee L$ Assume $\omega \in [\![\Gamma, \phi_1 \vee \phi_2]\!]$ then $\omega \in [\![\Gamma]\!]$ and $\omega \in [\![\phi_1 \vee \phi_2]\!]$, from which either $\omega \in [\![\phi_1]\!]$ or $\omega \in [\![\phi_2]\!]$. Consider each case. If $\omega \in [\![\phi_1]\!]$ then $\omega \in [\![\Gamma, \phi_1]\!]$ and the first premise applies, yielding $\omega \in [\![\psi]\!]$ as desired. Else $\omega \in [\![\phi_2]\!]$ so $\omega \in [\![\Gamma, \phi_2]\!]$ and the second premise applies, yielding $\omega \in [\![\psi]\!]$ as desired.

Case $;L$: $\dfrac{\Gamma, [\alpha][\beta]\psi \vdash \phi}{\Gamma, [\alpha;\beta]\psi \vdash \phi}$ $;L$ Assume $\omega \in [\![\Gamma, [\alpha;\beta]\psi]\!]$, then $\omega \in [\![\Gamma]\!]$ and $\omega \in [\![[\alpha;\beta]\psi]\!]$. Expanding definitions yields:

$$\begin{aligned}
&\nu \in [\![\psi]\!] \text{ for all } (\omega, \nu) \in [\![\alpha;\beta]\!]\\
\text{iff } &\nu \in [\![\psi]\!] \text{ for all } (\omega, \nu) \in [\![\alpha]\!] \circ [\![\beta]\!]\\
\text{iff } &\nu \in [\![\psi]\!] \text{ for all } (\omega, \mu) \in [\![\alpha]\!], (\mu, \nu) \in [\![\beta]\!]\\
\text{iff } &\mu \in [\![[\beta]\psi]\!] \text{ for all } (\omega, \mu) \in [\![\alpha]\!]\\
\text{iff } &\omega \in [\![[\alpha][\beta]\psi]\!]
\end{aligned}$$

Thus $\omega \in [\![\Gamma, [\alpha][\beta]\psi]\!]$ and the premise applies, yielding $\omega \in [\![\phi]\!]$ as desired.

Case $*L$: $\dfrac{\Gamma, \psi \wedge [\alpha][\alpha^*@inv(\vee_i \psi_i)]\psi \vdash \phi}{\Gamma, [\alpha^*@inv(\vee_i \psi_i)]\psi \vdash \phi}$ $*L$

Assume $\omega \in [\![\Gamma, [\alpha^*@inv(\vee_i \psi_i)]\psi]\!]$, then we obtain $\omega \in [\![\Gamma]\!]$ as well as $\omega \in [\![[\alpha^*@inv(\vee_i \psi_i)]\psi]\!]$. Expanding definitions, get $\nu \in [\![\psi]\!]$ for all $(\omega, \nu) \in [\![\alpha^*@inv(\vee_i \psi_i)]\!] = \bigcup_{i \geq 0} [\![\alpha]\!] \circ \cdots \circ [\![\alpha]\!] (i \text{ times})$, which we equivalently notate $\bigcup_{i \geq 0} [\![\alpha]\!]^i$. Considering $i = 0$, we have $(\omega, \omega) \in \bigcup_{i \geq 0} [\![\alpha]\!]^i$ so $\omega \in [\![\psi]\!]$. Now consider all $i > 0$, i.e., of form $1 + k$. Then $(\omega, \nu) \in [\![\alpha]\!]^{1+k} = [\![\alpha]\!] \circ [\![\alpha]\!]^k$ and there exists μ such that $(\omega, \mu) \in [\![\alpha]\!]$ and $(\mu, \nu) \in [\![\alpha]\!]^k$ and $\nu \in [\![\psi]\!]$. Because k is arbitrary, we have $\nu \in [\![\phi]\!]$ for all $(\mu, \nu) \in \bigcup_{i \geq 0} [\![\alpha]\!]^i = [\![\alpha^*@inv(\vee_i \psi_i)]\!]$ and thus $\mu \in [\![[\alpha^*@inv(\vee_i \psi_i)]\psi]\!]$. Because the argument holds for any such μ, we have $\omega \in [\![[\alpha][\alpha^*@inv(\vee_i \psi_i)]\psi]\!]$. Combined with the assumptions and the $i = 0$ case we have $\omega \in [\![\Gamma, \psi \wedge [\alpha][\alpha^*@inv(\vee_i \psi_i)]\psi]\!]$ so the premise applies, yielding $\omega \in [\![\phi]\!]$ as desired.

This completes the induction.

We use the following lemmas in the soundness proof:

Lemma 7 (Admissible Rules). *Monotonicity, regularity, their iterated forms, and iterated rule K are all admissible in the proof-theoretic semantics. Rule G is admissible under the added assumption that its conclusion is a goal formula with definitions c expanded.*

$$\text{Ks}\ \frac{\Gamma \vdash M(\phi) \qquad \Gamma \vdash M(\phi \to \psi)}{\Gamma \vdash M(\psi)} \qquad \text{M}\ \frac{\phi \vdash \psi \qquad \Gamma \vdash [\alpha]\phi}{\Gamma \vdash [\alpha]\psi} \qquad \text{Ms}\ \frac{\phi \vdash \psi \qquad \Gamma \vdash M(\phi)}{\Gamma \vdash M(\psi)}$$

$$\text{Reg}\ \frac{\Gamma \vdash [\alpha]\phi \qquad \Gamma \vdash [\alpha]\psi}{\Gamma \vdash [\alpha](\phi \wedge \psi)} \qquad \text{Regs}\ \frac{\Gamma \vdash M(\phi) \qquad \Gamma \vdash M(\psi)}{\Gamma \vdash M(\phi \wedge \psi)} \qquad \text{G}\ \frac{\phi}{[\alpha]\phi}$$

Proof. First consider the iterated rule Ks.

The admissibility proof proceeds by induction on the number k of nested modalities in M, starting with a base case of $k = 1$.

Base case $k = 1$, where $M(\phi) \equiv [\alpha]\phi$ for some α. Then rule Ks reduces directly to K.

$$\text{K}\ \frac{\Gamma \vdash [\alpha]\phi \qquad \Gamma \vdash [\alpha](\phi \to \psi)}{\Gamma \vdash [\alpha]\psi}$$

Inductive case $k = j + 1$, where $M(\phi) \equiv [\alpha]M'(\phi)$ for some α and some M' of length j. Inductive hypothesis: The following rule is admissible:

$$\text{IH}\ \frac{\Gamma \vdash M'(\phi) \qquad \Gamma \vdash M'(\phi \to \psi)}{\Gamma \vdash M'(\psi)}$$

We want to show the following rule is admissible:

$$\frac{\Gamma \vdash [\alpha]M'(\phi) \qquad \Gamma \vdash [\alpha]M'(\phi \to \psi)}{\Gamma \vdash [\alpha]M'(\psi)}$$

Let $\Gamma' \equiv M'(\psi \to \psi), M'(\phi)$.

First derive a branch $\mathcal{B}_1$:

$$\dfrac{\mathcal{D}_2\;\dfrac{*}{\Gamma \vdash [\alpha]M'(\phi \to \psi)} \qquad \to\!R\;\dfrac{\mathrm{IH}\;\dfrac{\textsc{Init}\;\dfrac{*}{\Gamma' \vdash M'(\phi)} \qquad \textsc{Init}\;\dfrac{*}{\Gamma' \vdash M'(\phi \to \psi)}}{M'(\phi \to \psi), M'(\phi) \vdash M'(\psi)}}{\vdash M'(\phi \to \psi) \to (M'(\phi) \to M'(\psi))}}{\Gamma \vdash [\alpha](M'(\phi) \to M'(\psi))}\;\mathrm{M}$$

Then we give a derivation:

$$\mathrm{K}\;\dfrac{\mathcal{D}_1\;\dfrac{*}{\Gamma \vdash [\alpha]M'(\phi)} \qquad \mathcal{B}_1}{\Gamma \vdash [\alpha]M'(\psi)}$$

This completes the proof for Ks.

Claim: M is admissible. $\overset{\mathrm{M}}{\dfrac{\phi \vdash \psi \qquad \Gamma \vdash [\alpha]\phi}{\Gamma \vdash [\alpha]\psi}}$

The proof relies on G and K. Let $\mathcal{D}_1$ be a derivation of $\phi \vdash \psi$ and $\mathcal{D}_2$ a derivation of $\Gamma \vdash [\alpha]\phi$.

$$\mathrm{K}\;\dfrac{\mathcal{D}_2\;\dfrac{*}{\Gamma \vdash [\alpha]\phi} \qquad \mathrm{W}\;\dfrac{\mathrm{G}\;\dfrac{\to\!R\;\dfrac{\mathcal{D}_1\;\dfrac{*}{\phi \vdash \psi}}{\vdash \phi \to \psi}}{\vdash [\alpha](\phi \to \psi)}}{\Gamma \vdash [\alpha](\phi \to \psi)}}{\Gamma \vdash [\alpha]\psi}$$

Now consider the iterated rule Ms. Let $\mathcal{D}_1$ be a derivation of $\phi \vdash \psi$ and $\mathcal{D}_2$ be a derivation of $\Gamma \vdash M(\phi)$. The admissibility proof proceeds by induction on the number k of nested modalities in M, starting with a base case of $k = 1$.

Base case $k = 1$, where $M(\phi) \equiv [\alpha]\phi$ for some α. This case holds immediately by a single application of M:

$$\mathrm{M}\;\dfrac{\phi \vdash \psi \qquad \Gamma \vdash [\alpha]\phi}{\Gamma \vdash [\alpha]\psi}$$

Inductive case $k = j + 1$, where $M(\phi) \equiv [\alpha]M'(\phi)$ for some α and some M' of length j. Inductive hypothesis: The following rule is admissible:

$$\mathrm{IH}\;\dfrac{\phi \vdash \psi \qquad \Gamma \vdash M'(\phi)}{\Gamma \vdash M'(\psi)}$$

We wish to show the following rule admissible:

$$\frac{\phi \vdash \psi \qquad \Gamma \vdash [\alpha]M'(\phi)}{\Gamma \vdash [\alpha]M'(\psi)}$$

We give a derivation:

$$\text{M}\ \frac{\text{IH}\ \dfrac{\text{Init}\ \dfrac{*}{M'(\phi) \vdash M'(\phi)} \qquad \mathcal{D}_1\ \dfrac{*}{\phi \vdash \psi}}{M'(\phi) \vdash M'(\psi)} \qquad \mathcal{D}_2\ \dfrac{*}{\Gamma \vdash [\alpha]M'(\phi)}}{\Gamma \vdash [\alpha]M'(\psi)}$$

This completes the proof for Ms.

Now consider rules Reg and Regs. In the following derivation of Reg, let $\mathcal{D}_1$ be a derivation of $\Gamma \vdash [\alpha]P$ and $\mathcal{D}_2$ be a derivation of $\Gamma \vdash [\alpha]Q$.

$$\text{K}\ \frac{\mathcal{D}_1\ \dfrac{*}{\Gamma \vdash [\alpha]P} \qquad \text{M}\ \dfrac{\mathcal{D}_2\ \dfrac{*}{\Gamma \vdash [\alpha]Q} \qquad \to R\ \dfrac{\wedge R\ \dfrac{\text{Init}\ \dfrac{*}{P, Q \vdash P} \qquad \text{Init}\ \dfrac{*}{P, Q \vdash Q}}{P, Q \vdash P \wedge Q}}{Q \vdash P \to P \wedge Q}}{\Gamma \vdash [\alpha](P \to P \wedge Q)}}{\Gamma \vdash [\alpha](P \wedge Q)}$$

Now consider the general case:

$$\text{Regs}\ \frac{\Gamma \vdash M(P) \qquad \Gamma \vdash M(Q)}{\Gamma \vdash M(P \wedge Q)}$$

Abbreviate $\mathcal{B}_1$ by

$$\text{Ks}\ \frac{\mathcal{D}_1\ \dfrac{*}{\Gamma \vdash M(P)} \qquad \text{Ms}\ \dfrac{\mathcal{D}_2\ \dfrac{*}{\Gamma \vdash M(Q)} \qquad \to R\ \dfrac{\wedge R\ \dfrac{\text{Init}\ \dfrac{*}{P, Q \vdash P} \qquad \text{Init}\ \dfrac{*}{P, Q \vdash Q}}{P, Q \vdash P \wedge Q}}{Q \vdash P \to P \wedge Q}}{\Gamma \vdash M(P \to P \wedge Q)}}{\Gamma \vdash M(P \wedge Q)}$$

This completes the proof for regularity.

Now consider the rule G. By the goal formula assumption, we can ignore the case $\alpha \equiv c$ without loss of generality.

Claim: G is admissible. $\overset{\text{G}}{\dfrac{P}{[\alpha]P}}$

By induction on the structure of α.
Case $?Q$
Then prove

$$\dfrac{\dfrac{\dfrac{\vdash P}{Q \vdash P}\,\mathrm{W}}{\vdash Q \rightarrow P}\,{\rightarrow}R}{\vdash [?Q]P}\,?R$$

Case $\alpha;\beta$
Assume inductive hypotheses on α and β.
Then prove

$$\dfrac{\dfrac{\dfrac{P}{\vdash [\beta]P}\,\mathrm{IH2}}{\vdash [\alpha][\beta]P}\,\mathrm{IH1}}{\vdash [\alpha;\beta]P}\,;R$$

Case $\alpha \cup \beta$
Assume inductive hypotheses on α and β.
Then prove

$$\dfrac{\dfrac{\dfrac{P}{\vdash [\alpha]P}\,\mathrm{IH1} \quad \dfrac{P}{\vdash [\beta]P}\,\mathrm{IH2}}{\vdash [\alpha]P \wedge [\beta]P}\,{\wedge}R}{\vdash [\alpha \cup \beta]P}\,{\cup}R$$

Case $\alpha^*@inv(\bigvee_i J_i)$
Assume inductive hypothesis on α. Then prove (note we allow the invariant to change)

$$\dfrac{\vdash P \quad \dfrac{\dfrac{\dfrac{P}{\vdash [\alpha]P}\,\mathrm{IH}}{P \vdash [\alpha]P}\,\mathrm{W}}{\vdash P \rightarrow [\alpha]P}\,{\rightarrow}R \quad \dfrac{\dfrac{*}{P \vdash P}\,\textsc{Init}}{\vdash P \rightarrow P}\,{\rightarrow}R}{\vdash [\alpha^*@inv(P)]P}\,{*}R$$

Theorem 5 (Soundness w.r.t. Proof-Theoretic Semantics). *Let G be a goal formula. If judgement $\wedge_i \Gamma_i \rightarrow G \Longrightarrow_\Sigma \mathsf{true}$ holds in the operational semantics then $\Gamma \vdash_\Sigma G$ holds in the proof-theoretic dynamics. More generally, let G_i, G_i' be goal formulas and D_i, D_i' clause formulas. Let* $\mathbf{D}$ *denote* *the interpretation of clause formula D as a context. Now assume such that* $\wedge_i(D_i \to G_i) \Longrightarrow_\Sigma \wedge_i(D_i' \to G_i')$, *then if all premises* $\boldsymbol{D_i'} \vdash_\Sigma G_i'$ *are derivable in the proof-theoretic semantics, then all conclusions* $\boldsymbol{D_i} \vdash_\Sigma G_i$ *are derivable in the proof-theoretic semantics.*

Proof. By induction on the derivation of $\wedge_i(G_i \to D_i) \Longrightarrow_\Sigma \wedge_i(G_i' \to D_i')$.

Case OpGoal: The inductive hypothesis says that if $A' \vdash G'$ is derivable, so is $A \vdash G$. Assume derivations $\mathcal{D}_1$ of $A' \vdash G'$ and $\mathcal{D}_2$ of $\vdash \hat{G}$. Assume without loss of generality that $\hat{G}$ is an implication, i.e., is not a conjunction thereof. Derive $A \vdash G$ and $\vdash \hat{G}$.

The IH on $\mathcal{D}_1$ yields $A \vdash G$. Then $\mathcal{D}_2$ is already a derivation of $\vdash \hat{G}$.

Case OpClose: Assume a derivation $\mathcal{D}$ of $\vdash \hat{G}$. Derive $\vdash$ true and $\vdash \hat{G}$ from $\mathcal{D}$. Then $\vdash$ true is immediate by rule $\top$ and $\vdash \hat{G}$ is immediate from $\mathcal{D}$.

Case OpHyp: Assume a derivation $\mathcal{D}$ of $\vdash$ true. Assume the side condition $G \in A \cup \Sigma$. Derive $\boldsymbol{A} \vdash G$.

$$\textsc{Init}\ \frac{*}{\boldsymbol{A} \vdash_\Sigma G}$$

where the side condition is reused in Init.

Case OpPred: Assume derivations $\mathcal{D}_i$ of each $\boldsymbol{A} \vdash M(A_i)$. Assume the side condition $(\wedge_i A_i \to p) \in \Sigma$. Derive $\boldsymbol{A} \vdash M(p)$. Goals with unbound index variables indicate collections of goals, e.g., $A \vdash M(A_i)$ represents one goal for each value of i. The use of K, for example, implies that M is a non-empty modality chain, which we implicitly assume as documented in Sect. 5. Dropping this assumption in future work is desirable for reasons of elegance, but will require either the addition of a cut rule or modification of the rule(s) for initial sequents so that cut-like reasoning is no longer required.

$$\textsc{K}\ \frac{\textsc{Reg}\ \dfrac{\mathcal{D}_i\ \dfrac{*}{\boldsymbol{A} \vdash M(A_i)}}{\boldsymbol{A} \vdash M(\wedge_i A_i)} \qquad \textsc{W}\ \dfrac{\textsc{G}\ \dfrac{\textsc{Init}\ \dfrac{*}{\vdash \wedge_i A_i \to p}}{\vdash M(\wedge_i A_i \to p)}}{\boldsymbol{A} \vdash M(\wedge_i A_i \to p)}}{\boldsymbol{A} \vdash M(p)}$$

Case OpExpl: Assume a derivation $\mathcal{D}$ of $\boldsymbol{A} \vdash M([\alpha]G)$. Assume the side condition $(c ::= \alpha) \in \Sigma$ where $c \notin A, G, M$. Derive $\boldsymbol{A} \vdash M([c]G)$.

Define $P(c') \equiv M([c']G)$ and $\Gamma(c') \equiv \boldsymbol{A}$ where c' is a fresh variable. Applying rule Expl on Γ and P yields

$$\textsc{Expl}\ \frac{\Gamma(\alpha) \vdash P(\alpha)}{\Gamma(c) \vdash P(c)}$$

Observe that $(\Gamma(\alpha) \vdash P(\alpha)) \equiv (\boldsymbol{A} \vdash M([\alpha]G))$ by construction and because c' was fresh. Thus $\mathcal{D}$ fulfills the premise of Expl, yielding $\Gamma(c) \vdash P(c)$. Now observe $(\Gamma(c) \vdash P(c)) \equiv (\boldsymbol{A} \vdash M([c]G))$ by construction, completing the case.

Case Op?: Assume a derivation $\mathcal{D}$ of $\boldsymbol{A} \vdash M(P \to G)$. Derive $\boldsymbol{A} \vdash M([?P]G)$.

$$\dfrac{\mathcal{D}\,\dfrac{*}{\boldsymbol{A} \vdash M(P \to G)} \qquad ?R\,\dfrac{\textsc{Init}\,\dfrac{*}{P \to G \vdash P \to G}}{P \to G \vdash [?P]G}}{\boldsymbol{A} \vdash M([?P]G)}\,\mathrm{M}$$

Case OpSeq: Assume proof $\mathcal{D}$ of $\boldsymbol{A} \vdash M([\alpha][\beta]G)$. Derive $\boldsymbol{A} \vdash M([\alpha;\beta]G)$.

$$\dfrac{\mathcal{D}\,\dfrac{*}{\boldsymbol{A} \vdash M([\alpha][\beta]G)} \qquad ;R\,\dfrac{\textsc{Init}\,\dfrac{*}{[\alpha][\beta]G \vdash [\alpha][\beta]G}}{[\alpha][\beta]G \vdash [\alpha;\beta]G}}{\boldsymbol{A} \vdash M([\alpha;\beta]G)}\,\mathrm{M}$$

Case Op∪: Assume a derivation $\mathcal{D}$ of $\boldsymbol{A} \vdash M([\alpha]G \wedge [\beta]G)$. Derive $\boldsymbol{A} \vdash M([\alpha \cup \beta]G)$.

$$\dfrac{\mathcal{D}\,\dfrac{*}{\boldsymbol{A} \vdash M([\alpha]G) \wedge M([\beta]G)} \qquad \cup R\,\dfrac{\textsc{Init}\,\dfrac{*}{[\alpha]G \wedge [\beta]G \vdash [\alpha]G \wedge [\beta]G}}{[\alpha]G \wedge [\beta]G \vdash [\alpha \cup \beta]G}}{\boldsymbol{A} \vdash M([\alpha \cup \beta]G)}\,\mathrm{M}$$

Case Op∗: Assume derivations of the premises, specifically, $\mathcal{B}$ deriving $\boldsymbol{A} \vdash \bigvee_i J_i$, $\mathcal{C}_i$ deriving each $J_i \vdash [\alpha] \bigvee_j J_j$, $\mathcal{D}_i$ deriving each $J_i \vdash G$.

Derive $\boldsymbol{A} \vdash [\alpha^*@inv(\bigvee_i J_i)]G$. In the following derivation, goals with unbound index variables denote collections of goals in a small abuse of notation. For example, where $J_i \vdash G$ appears as the premise of a rule, we mean a collection of premises, one for each such i.

$$*R\,\dfrac{\mathcal{B} \qquad \mathcal{C}_i \qquad \mathcal{D}_i}{\boldsymbol{A} \vdash [\alpha^*@inv(\bigvee_i J_i)]G}$$

Case $\mathsf{Op}\vee 1$: Assume a derivation $\mathcal{D}$ of $\boldsymbol{A} \vdash M(B)$. Derive $\boldsymbol{A} \vdash M(B \vee C)$.

$$\textsc{M}\ \dfrac{\mathcal{D}\ \dfrac{*}{\boldsymbol{A} \vdash M(B)} \quad \vee R1\ \dfrac{\textsc{Init}\ \dfrac{*}{B \vdash B}}{B \vdash B \vee C}}{\boldsymbol{A} \vdash M(B \vee C)}$$

Case $\mathsf{Op}\vee 2$: Assume a derivation $\mathcal{D}$ of $\boldsymbol{A} \vdash M(C)$. Derive $\boldsymbol{A} \vdash M(B \vee C)$.

$$\textsc{M}\ \dfrac{\mathcal{D}\ \dfrac{*}{\boldsymbol{A} \vdash M(C)} \quad \vee R2\ \dfrac{\textsc{Init}\ \dfrac{*}{C \vdash C}}{C \vdash B \vee C}}{\boldsymbol{A} \vdash M(B \vee C)}$$

Case $\mathsf{Op}\wedge$: Assume derivations $\mathcal{D}_1$ of $\boldsymbol{A} \vdash M(B)$ and $\mathcal{D}_2$ of $\boldsymbol{A} \vdash M(C)$. Derive $\boldsymbol{A} \vdash M(B \wedge C)$.

$$\textsc{Reg}\ \dfrac{\mathcal{D}_1\ \dfrac{*}{\boldsymbol{A} \vdash M(B)} \quad \mathcal{D}_2\ \dfrac{*}{\boldsymbol{A} \vdash M(C)}}{\boldsymbol{A} \vdash M(B \wedge C)}$$

Where Reg refers to Lemma 2, rule Regs.

Case $\mathsf{Op} \rightarrow$: Assume a derivation $\mathcal{D}$ of $\boldsymbol{A}, B \vdash C$. Derive $\boldsymbol{A} \vdash B \rightarrow C$.

$$\rightarrow R\ \dfrac{\mathcal{D}\ \dfrac{*}{\boldsymbol{A}, B \vdash C}}{\boldsymbol{A} \vdash B \rightarrow C}$$

Case $\mathsf{Op}\forall$: Assume a derivation $\mathcal{D}$ of $\boldsymbol{A} \vdash P(c)$ where c is a fresh program symbol. Derive $\boldsymbol{A} \vdash \forall c'\ P(c')$.

$$\forall R\ \dfrac{\boldsymbol{A} \vdash P(c)}{\boldsymbol{A} \vdash \forall P(c')}$$

where c is a fresh program symbol.

Case $\mathsf{Op}\wedge L$: Assume a derivation $\mathcal{D}$ of $\boldsymbol{A}, A_1, A_2 \vdash B$. Derive $\boldsymbol{A}, (A_1 \wedge A_2) \vdash B$.

$$\wedge L\ \dfrac{\mathcal{D}\ \dfrac{*}{\boldsymbol{A}, A_1, A_2 \vdash B}}{\boldsymbol{A}, A_1 \wedge A_2 \vdash B}$$

Case $\mathsf{Op}?L$: Assume a derivation $\mathcal{D}$ of $\boldsymbol{A}, (P \to p) \vdash B$. Derive $A, [?P]p \vdash B$.

$$?L\ \dfrac{\mathcal{D}\ \dfrac{*}{\boldsymbol{A}, P \to p \vdash B}}{\boldsymbol{A}, [?P]p \vdash B}$$

Case $\mathsf{Op}\cup L$: Assume a derivation $\mathcal{D}$ of $\boldsymbol{A}, [\alpha]p \wedge [\beta]p \vdash B$. Derive $\boldsymbol{A}, [\alpha \cup \beta]p \vdash B$.

$$\cup L\ \dfrac{\mathcal{D}\ \dfrac{*}{\boldsymbol{A}, [\alpha]p \wedge [\beta]p \vdash B}}{\boldsymbol{A}, [\alpha \cup \beta]p \vdash B}$$

Case $\mathsf{Op}{\to}L$: Assume derivations $\mathcal{D}_1$ of $\boldsymbol{A} \vdash B$ and $\mathcal{D}_2$ of $\boldsymbol{A}, p \vdash C$. Derive $\boldsymbol{A}, B \to p \vdash C$.

$$\to L\ \dfrac{\mathcal{D}_1\ \dfrac{*}{\boldsymbol{A} \vdash B} \quad \mathcal{D}_2\ \dfrac{*}{\boldsymbol{A}, p \vdash C}}{\boldsymbol{A}, (B \to p) \vdash C}$$

Case $\mathsf{Op}\forall L$: Assume a derivation $\mathcal{D}$ of $\boldsymbol{A}, P(\alpha) \vdash B$ for some program α. Derive $\boldsymbol{A}, \forall c\ P(c) \vdash B$.

$$\forall L\ \dfrac{\mathcal{D}\ \dfrac{*}{\boldsymbol{A}, P(\alpha) \vdash B}}{\boldsymbol{A}, \forall c\ P(c) \vdash B}$$

Lemma 8 (Invariant formulas and programs). *The lemma consists of four claims:*

- *Every invariant formula J is clause (D).*
- *Every invariant formula J is goal (G).*
- *Every invariant program ι is clause (δ).*
- *Every invariant program ι is goal (γ).*

Proof. By simultaneous induction on the structures of J and ι.

Case (formula) p: By definition, p is clause. By definition, p is goal.

Case true: By definition, true is clause. By definition, true is goal.

Case $J \to p$: Inductive hypotheses: (a) J is clause, (b) J is goal. By definition, $J \to p$ is clause if J is goal (b) and p is atomic, which is immediately true. By definition, $J \to p$ is goal if J is clause (a) and p is goal, which is immediately true.

Case $J_1 \wedge J_2$: Inductive hypotheses: (a) J_1 is clause, (b) J_1 is goal, (c) J_2 is clause, (d) J_2 is goal. By definition, $J_1 \wedge J_2$ is clause if both J_1 and J_2 are (a) (c). By definition, $J_1 \wedge J_2$ is goal if both J_1 and J_2 are (b) (d).

Case $\forall c\ J$: Inductive hypotheses: (a) J is clause, (b) J is goal. By definition, $\forall c\ J$ is clause if J is goal (a). By definition, $\forall c\ J$ is goal if J is goal (b).

Case $[\iota]p$: Inductive hypotheses: (a) ι is clause, (b) ι is goal. By definition, $[\iota]p$ is clause if ι is clause (a) and p is atomic, which is immediately true. By definition, $[\iota]p$ is goal if ι is goal (b) and p is goal, which is immediately true.

Case $?J$: Inductive hypotheses: (a) J is clause, (b) J is goal. By definition, $?J$ is clause if J is goal (b). By definition, $?J$ is goal if J is clause (a).

Case c (program): By definition, c is goal. By definition, c is clause.

Case $\iota_1 \cup \iota_2$: Inductive hypotheses: (a) ι_1 is clause, (b) ι_1 is goal, (c) ι_2 is clause, (d) ι_2 is goal. By definition, $\iota_1 \cup \iota_2$ is clause if both ι_1 and ι_2 are (a) (c). By definition, $\iota_1 \cup \iota_2$ is goal if both ι_1 and ι_2 are (b) (d).

Case $\iota^*@inv(J)$: Inductive hypotheses: (a) ι is clause, (b) ι is goal. Case assumption: (c) J is invariant. By definition, $\iota^*@inv(J)$ is clause if ι is clause (a) and J is invariant (c). By definition, $\iota^*@inv(J)$ is goal if ι is goal (b) and J is invariant (c).

By induction, the proof is complete.

Lemma 9 (Goal Property). *Let Γ be a clause context, let G be a goal formula. Consider any derivation $\mathcal{D}$ of $\Gamma \vdash G$ which is free of rules K and M. At every step of the derivation $\mathcal{D}$, every antecedent is a clause formula and every succedent is a goal formula.*

Proof. By induction on the derivation $\mathcal{D}$.

Cases Init $\top$: These cases hold vacuously because there are no premises of the form $\Gamma \vdash P$.

Case W X C: The premises have identical succedents to the conclusion and the antecedents are subsets or permutations, thus are clause formulas as required.

Case $\vee L$: The antecedent rule to which $\vee L$ is applied must have form $A \vee B$ which immediately contradicts the assumption that D was a context of clause formulas. The case holds vacuously.

Case G: $$\text{G}\ \frac{\vdash \phi}{\vdash [\alpha]\phi}$$

Since $[\alpha]\phi$ is a goal formula, so is ϕ as desired.

Case $\wedge R$: $$\wedge R\ \frac{\Gamma \vdash \phi \qquad \Gamma \vdash \psi}{\Gamma \vdash \phi \wedge \psi}$$

Since $\phi \wedge \psi$ is a goal formula, both ϕ and ψ are, as desired.

Case $\wedge L$: $$\wedge L\ \frac{\Gamma, \psi_1, \psi_2 \vdash \phi}{\Gamma, \psi_1 \wedge \psi_2 \vdash \phi}$$

Since $\psi_1 \wedge \psi_2$ is a clause formula, both ψ_1 and ψ_2 are, as desired.

Case $\vee R1$: $\dfrac{\Gamma \vdash \phi}{\Gamma \vdash \phi \vee \psi}\ \vee R1$

Since $\phi \vee \psi$ is a goal formula, so is ϕ, as desired.

Case $\vee R2$: $\dfrac{\Gamma \vdash \psi}{\Gamma \vdash \phi \vee \psi}\ \vee R2$

Since $\phi \vee \psi$ is a goal formula, so is ψ, as desired.

Case $\rightarrow L$: $\dfrac{\Gamma \vdash \psi_1 \qquad \Gamma, \psi_2 \vdash \phi}{\Gamma, \psi_1 \rightarrow \psi_2 \vdash \phi}\ \rightarrow L$

Since $\psi_1 \rightarrow \psi_2$ is a clause formula, ψ_1 is a goal formula, as desired. Moreover, ψ_2 is of form x, which implies ψ_2 is a clause formula, as desired.

Case $\rightarrow R$: $\dfrac{\Gamma, \phi \vdash \psi}{\Gamma \vdash (\phi \rightarrow \psi)}\ \rightarrow R$

Since $\phi \rightarrow \psi$ is a goal formula, ψ is a goal formula and ϕ is a clause formula, as desired.

Case $\forall L$: $\dfrac{\Gamma, \psi(\alpha) \vdash \phi}{\Gamma, \forall c\, \psi(c) \vdash \phi}\ \forall L$

Since $\forall c\, \psi(c)$ is a clause formula, so is $\psi(c)$. A side condition on $\forall L$ requires that α is a δ-program, so that $\psi(\alpha)$ is a clause formula as desired.

Case $\forall R$: $\dfrac{\Gamma \vdash \phi(c')}{\Gamma \vdash \forall c\, \phi(c)}\ \forall R$

Since $\forall c\, \phi(c)$ is a goal formula, so is $\phi(c)$. A straightforward induction shows that renaming preserves goal formulas, so $\phi(c')$ is a goal formula as desired.

Case $?R$: $\dfrac{\Gamma \vdash (\psi \rightarrow \phi)}{\Gamma \vdash [?\psi]\phi}\ ?R$

Since $[?\psi]\phi$ is a goal formula, $?\psi$ is a γ-program, which implies ψ is a clause formula, and ϕ is a goal formula as desired.

Case $;R$: $\dfrac{\Gamma \vdash [\alpha][\beta]\phi}{\Gamma \vdash [\alpha;\beta]\phi}\ ;R$ Since $[\alpha;\beta]\phi$ is a goal formula, $\alpha;\beta$ is a γ-program and ϕ is a goal formula. Then α and β are γ-programs, so $[\beta]\phi$ is a goal formula and then $[\alpha][\beta]\phi$ is a goal formula as desired.

Case $\cup R$: $\dfrac{\Gamma \vdash [\alpha]\phi \wedge [\beta]\phi}{\Gamma \vdash [\alpha \cup \beta]\phi}\ \cup R$ Since $[\alpha \cup \beta]\phi$ is a goal formula, $\alpha \cup \beta$ is a γ-program and ϕ is a goal formula. Then α and β are γ-programs, thus $[\alpha]\phi$ and $[\beta]\phi$ are goal formulas, finally $[\alpha]\phi \wedge [\beta]\phi$ is a goal formula as desired.

Case $*R$: $$\frac{\Gamma \vdash \vee_i \psi_i \qquad \psi_1 \vdash [\alpha] \vee_j \psi_j \cdots \psi_n \vdash [\alpha] \vee_j \psi_j \qquad \psi_1 \vdash P \cdots \psi_n \vdash P}{\Gamma \vdash [\alpha^* @inv(\vee_i \psi_i)]\phi} *R$$

Since $[\alpha^* @inv(\bigvee_i \psi_i)]\phi$ is a goal formula, α is a γ-program, every ψ_i is an invariant formula, and ϕ is a goal formula. Every invariant formula is both a clause formula and goal formula by Lemma 1. Then $\bigvee_i \psi_i$ is a goal formula as desired in the first premise. In the middle premises: every ψ_i is a clause formula as desired. Because $\bigvee_j \psi_j$ is a goal formula then $[\alpha] \bigvee_j \psi_j$ is a goal formula as desired. In the final premises: Every ψ_i is a clause formula and ϕ is a goal formula as desired.

Case Expl: $$\frac{c ::= \alpha \in \Sigma \qquad \Gamma(\alpha) \vdash \phi(\alpha)}{\Gamma(c) \vdash \phi(c)} \text{Expl} \quad (\Gamma(\alpha) \text{ clause}, \phi(\alpha) \text{ goal})$$ In the absence of any restriction, substitution can violate the clause and goal properties. For this reason, Expl explicitly requires a side condition that $\Gamma(\alpha)$ is clause and $\phi(\alpha)$ is goal, from which the desired property is immediate.

Lemma 10 (Goal Preservation). *If G is goal and judgement $G \Longrightarrow_\Sigma G'$ holds in the operational semantics for formula G', then G' is a goal formula.*

Proof. By induction on the derivation of $G \Longrightarrow_\Sigma G'$.

Case OpGoal: $$\frac{A \to G \Longrightarrow A' \to G'}{(A \to G) \wedge \hat{G} \Longrightarrow (A' \to G') \wedge \hat{G}} \text{OpGoal}$$

Assume the IH: If $A \to G$ is a goal formula, so is $A' \to G'$. We assume that $(A \to G) \wedge \hat{G}$ is a goal formula, thus $A \to G$ is goal and $\hat{G}$ is goal. We can then apply the IH, yielding that $A' \to G'$ is goal and moreover $(A' \to G') \wedge \hat{G}$ is goal as desired.

Case OpClose: $$\frac{*}{\mathsf{true} \wedge \hat{G} \Longrightarrow \hat{G}} \text{OpClose}$$

Assume $\mathsf{true} \wedge \hat{G}$ is goal, then conjunct $\hat{G}$ is goal as desired.

Case OpHyp: $$\frac{G \in A \cup \Sigma}{A \to G \Longrightarrow \mathsf{true}} \text{OpHyp}$$

Assume $A \to G$ is goal. We do not use the assumption. Observe true is goal by definition.

Case OpPred: $$\frac{(\boldsymbol{A} \to p) \in \Sigma}{A \to M(p) \Longrightarrow_\Sigma \wedge_i (A \to M(A_i))} \text{OpPred}$$

Assume $A \to M(p)$ is goal, then A is clause and M is a γ-modality chain. By the assumption $\boldsymbol{A} \to p$ we have that A_i is a head formula for each i. Every head formula A_i is goal, then $M(A_i)$ is goal, $A \to M(A_i)$ is goal, and $\wedge_i (A \to M(A_i))$ is goal, as desired.

Case OpExpl: $$\frac{(c ::= \alpha) \in \Sigma}{A \to M([c]G) \Longrightarrow_\Sigma A \to M([\alpha]G)} \text{OpExpl} \quad \text{where } c \notin A, G, M.$$

Assume $A \rightarrow M([c]G)$ is goal, then A is clause, G is goal, and M is a γ-modality chain. By syntactic restriction, α is a γ-program, so $[\alpha]G$ is goal, then $M([\alpha]G)$ and $A \rightarrow M([\alpha]G)$ are too, as desired.

Case Op?: $\dfrac{*}{A \rightarrow M([?P]G) \Longrightarrow A \rightarrow M(P \rightarrow G)}$ Op?

Assume $A \rightarrow M([?P]G)$ is goal, then A is clause, G is goal, and M is a γ-modality chain. Because $?P$ is γ then P is clause. Therefore $P \rightarrow G$ is goal, $M(P \rightarrow G)$ is goal, and $A \rightarrow M(P \rightarrow G)$ is goal as desired.

Case Op;: $\dfrac{*}{A \rightarrow M([\alpha;\beta]G) \Longrightarrow A \rightarrow M([\alpha][\beta]G)}$ Op;

Assume $A \rightarrow M([\alpha;\beta]G)$ is goal. Then G is goal, A is clause, $\alpha;\beta$ is a γ-program, and M is a γ-modality chain. Therefore α and β are γ-programs. Therefore $[\alpha][\beta]G$ is goal and so are $M([\alpha][\beta]G)$ and $A \rightarrow M([\alpha][\beta]G)$ as desired.

Case Op∪: $\dfrac{*}{A \rightarrow M([\alpha \cup \beta]G) \Longrightarrow A \rightarrow M([\alpha]G \wedge [\beta]G)}$ Op∪

Assume $A \rightarrow M([\alpha \cup \beta]G)$ is goal, then A is clause, G is goal, M is a γ-modality chain, and $\alpha \cup \beta$ is a γ-program. Therefore α and β are γ-programs. Therefore $[\alpha]G$ and $[\beta]G$ are goal, as are $[\alpha]G \wedge [\beta]G$, $M([\alpha]G \wedge [\beta]G)$, and $A \rightarrow M([\alpha]G \wedge [\beta]G)$ as desired.

Case Op∗:

Op∗

$$\frac{*}{A \rightarrow [\alpha^*@inv(\bigvee_i J_i)]G \Longrightarrow (A \rightarrow \bigvee_i J_i) \wedge \bigwedge_i (J_i \rightarrow [\alpha] \bigvee_j J_j) \wedge \bigwedge_i (J_i \rightarrow G)}$$

Assume $A \rightarrow [\alpha^*@inv(\bigvee_i J_i)]G$ is goal. Then A is clause, G is goal, and $\alpha^*@inv(\bigvee_i J_i)$ is a γ-program, from which α is a γ-program and J_i is a J-formula for every i.

To prove the case it suffices to show (1) $A \rightarrow \bigvee_i J_i$ is goal, (2) $\bigwedge_i (J_i \rightarrow [\alpha] \bigvee_j J_j)$ is goal, and (3) $\bigwedge_i (J_i \rightarrow G)$ is goal. By Lemma 1 every J_i is both clause and goal, from which $\bigvee_i J_i$ is goal and $A \rightarrow \bigvee_i J_i$ is goal, proving (1). Because $\bigvee_j J_j$ is goal and α is a γ-program, then $[\alpha] \bigvee_j J_j$ is goal. Because every J_i is clause, it follows that every $J_i \rightarrow [\alpha] \bigvee_j J_j$ is goal and therefore $\bigwedge_i (J_i \rightarrow [\alpha] \bigvee_j J_j)$ is goal, proving (2). Likewise, because G is goal and every J_i is clause, then every $J_i \rightarrow G$ is goal and thus $\bigwedge_i (J_i \rightarrow G)$ is goal, proving (3).

Case Op∨1: $\dfrac{*}{A \rightarrow M(G_1 \vee G_2) \Longrightarrow A \rightarrow M(G_1)}$ Op∨1

Assume $A \rightarrow M(G_1 \vee G_2)$ is goal, then A is clause, M is a γ-modality chain, and $G_1 \vee G_2$ is goal, from which G_1 and G_2 are each goal. Then $M(G_1)$ is goal and because A is clause, we have $A \rightarrow M(G_1)$ is goal as desired.

Case Op∨2: $\dfrac{*}{A \rightarrow M(G_1 \vee G_2) \Longrightarrow A \rightarrow M(G_2)}$ Op∨2

Assume $A \rightarrow M(G_1 \vee G_2)$ is goal, then A is clause, M is a γ-modality chain, and $G_1 \vee G_2$ is goal, from which G_1 and G_2 are each goal. Then $M(G_2)$ is goal and because A is clause, we have $A \rightarrow M(G_2)$ is goal as desired.

Case Op$\wedge$: $$\frac{*}{A \rightarrow M(G_1 \wedge G_2) \Longrightarrow (A \rightarrow M(G_1)) \wedge (A \rightarrow M(G_2))}\ \textsc{Op}\wedge$$

Assume $A \rightarrow M(G_1 \wedge G_2)$ is goal, then A is clause, M is a γ-modality chain, and $G_1 \wedge G_2$ is goal, from which G_1 and G_2 are each goal. Then $M(G_1)$ and $M(G_2)$ are both goal, then $A \rightarrow M(G_1)$ and $A \rightarrow M(G_2)$ are both goal, and finally $(A \rightarrow M(G_1)) \wedge (A \rightarrow M(G_2))$ is goal as desired.

Case Op$\forall$: $$\frac{*}{A \rightarrow \forall c\, G(c) \Longrightarrow A \rightarrow G(c')}\ \textsc{Op}\forall$$

Assume $A \rightarrow \forall c\, G(c)$ is goal, then A is clause and $\forall c\, G(c)$ is goal and $G(c)$ is goal. Renaming preserves goal formulas, so $G(c')$ is goal and so is $A \rightarrow G(c')$ as desired.

Case Op $\rightarrow$: $$\frac{*}{A \rightarrow A_1 \rightarrow G \Longrightarrow A \wedge A_1 \rightarrow G}\ \textsc{Op}\rightarrow$$

Assume $A \rightarrow A_1 \rightarrow G$ is goal, then G is goal and A and A_1 are clause. Then $A \wedge A_1$ is clause so $A \wedge A_1 \rightarrow G$ is goal as desired.

Case Op$\wedge L$: $$\frac{*}{A \wedge (A_1 \wedge A_2) \rightarrow G \Longrightarrow A \wedge A_1 \wedge A_2 \rightarrow G}\ \textsc{Op}\wedge L$$

Assume $A \wedge (A_1 \wedge A_2) \rightarrow G$ is goal, then G is goal and A, A_1, A_2 are clause. Then $A \wedge A_1 \wedge A_2$ is clause and $A \wedge A_1 \wedge A_2 \rightarrow G$ is goal as desired.

Case Op$?L$: $$\frac{*}{A \wedge [?G_1]p \rightarrow G \Longrightarrow A \wedge (G_1 \rightarrow p) \rightarrow G}\ \textsc{Op}?L$$

Assume $A \wedge [?G_1]p \rightarrow G$ is goal, then G is goal, A is clause, and $[?G_1]p$ is clause, from which p is clause and G_1 is goal. Then $G_1 \rightarrow p$ is clause, $A \wedge (G_1 \rightarrow p)$ is clause, and $A \wedge (G_1 \rightarrow p) \rightarrow G$ is goal as desired.

Case Op$\forall L$: $$\frac{*}{A \wedge \forall c\, A_1(c) \rightarrow G \Longrightarrow A \wedge A_1(\alpha) \rightarrow G}\ \textsc{Op}\forall L$$

Assume $A \wedge \forall c\, A_1(c) \rightarrow G$ is goal so G is goal, A is clause, and $\forall c\, A_1(c)$ is clause, from which $A_1(c)$ is clause. From the side condition that α is a δ-program, then substitution preserves causality so $A_1(\alpha)$ is clause. Thus $A \wedge A_1(\alpha)$ is clause and $A \wedge A_1(\alpha) \rightarrow G$ is goal as desired.

Case Op$\cup L$: $$\frac{*}{A \wedge [\alpha \cup \beta]p \rightarrow G \Longrightarrow A \wedge [\alpha]p \wedge [\beta]p \rightarrow G}\ \textsc{Op}\cup L$$

Assume $A \wedge [\alpha \cup \beta]p \rightarrow G$ is goal, so G is goal, A is clause, and $[\alpha \cup \beta]p$ is clause. Then p is clause and α and β are δ-programs. Thus $[\alpha]p$ and $[\beta]p$ are clause, so $A \wedge [\alpha]p \wedge [\beta]p$ is clause, so $A \wedge [\alpha]p \wedge [\beta]p \rightarrow G$ is goal.

$$\text{Case Op}{\to}L\text{:}\quad \textsc{Op}{\to}L\,\frac{*}{A\wedge(G_1\to p)\to G \Longrightarrow (A\to G_1)\wedge(A\wedge p\to G)}$$

Assume $A \wedge (G_1 \to p) \to G$ is goal. Then G is goal, A is clause, and $G_1 \to p$ is clause, from which G_1 is goal and p is clause. Then $A \wedge p$ is clause, $A \wedge p \to G$ is goal, $A \to G_1$ is goal, and finally $(A \to G_1) \wedge (A \wedge p \to G)$ is goal as desired.

Theorem 6 (Uniformity). *Let Γ be clause, G be goal, and Σ a signature. Assume without loss of generality that explicitly-defined symbols have already been expanded.*

If $\Gamma \vdash_\Sigma G$ has a proof using only the core fragment of the proof-theoretic semantics Fig. 4, then $\Gamma \vdash_\Sigma G$ has a uniform proof.

Proof. Proceed by induction, e.g., on the height h of the derivation. A uniform proof can end in any one of the following right rules: Init, $\vee R1$, $\vee R2$, $\wedge R$, $\to R$, $?R$, $;R$, $\cup R$, or $*R$, $\forall R$. Without loss of generality, suppose either (1) a one-step proof or (2) some uniform premises are extended with one more rule, resulting in a non-uniform proof. In case (1), the only option is an instance of Init, which is uniform by definition.[1] Otherwise, consider case (2). Because the right-rules are syntax-directed, the only final rules that can result in a non-uniform proof are the left rules $\wedge L$, $?L$, $\cup L$, $\to L$, and $\forall L$. It suffices to show that all such pairs of right and left rules commute. After commutation, the final rule is the appropriate right-rule, and the inductive hypothesis ensures uniformity holds inductively for every step of the resulting derivation.

Thus we proceed by cases.

Case for $\vee R1$ and $\wedge L$: Commute from

$$\wedge L\,\dfrac{\vee R1\,\dfrac{\Gamma, A, B \vdash C}{\Gamma, A, B \vdash C \vee D}}{\Gamma, A \wedge B \vdash C \vee D} \quad\text{to}\quad \vee R1\,\dfrac{\wedge L\,\dfrac{\Gamma, A, B \vdash C}{\Gamma, A \wedge B \vdash C}}{\Gamma, A \wedge B \vdash C \vee D}$$

Case for $\vee R1$ and $?L$: Commute from

$$?L\,\dfrac{\vee R1\,\dfrac{\Gamma, A \to B \vdash C}{\Gamma, A \to B \vdash C \vee D}}{\Gamma, [?A]B \vdash C \vee D} \quad\text{to}\quad \vee R1\,\dfrac{?L\,\dfrac{\Gamma, A \to B \vdash C}{\Gamma, [?A]B \vdash C}}{\Gamma, [?A]B \vdash C \vee D}$$

Case for $\vee R1$ and $\cup L$: Commute from

$$\cup L\,\dfrac{\vee R1\,\dfrac{\Gamma, [\alpha]A \wedge [\beta]A \vdash C}{\Gamma, [\alpha]A \wedge [\beta]A \vdash C \vee D}}{\Gamma, [\alpha \cup \beta]A \vdash C \vee D} \quad\text{to}\quad \vee R1\,\dfrac{\cup L\,\dfrac{\Gamma, [\alpha]A \wedge [\beta]A \vdash C}{\Gamma, [\alpha \cup \beta]A \vdash C}}{\Gamma, [\alpha \cup \beta]A \vdash C \vee D}$$

Case for $\vee R1$ and $\to L$: Commute from

$$\to L\,\dfrac{\Gamma \vdash A \quad \vee R1\,\dfrac{\Gamma, p \vdash B}{\Gamma, p \vdash B \vee C}}{\Gamma, A \to p \vdash B \vee C} \quad\text{to}\quad \vee R1\,\dfrac{\to L\,\dfrac{\Gamma \vdash A \qquad \Gamma, p \vdash B}{\Gamma, A \to p \vdash B}}{\Gamma, A \to p \vdash B \vee C}$$

[1] This definition differs slightly from Miller's. Suppose a proof of some $\boldsymbol{A} \to p \in \Sigma$. We prove this directly from the signature. Miller instead loads the signature into the antecedent, after which the left implication rule can be applied to $\boldsymbol{A} \to p$, creating a proof where initial sequents are pushed to leaves instead of the root.

Case for $\vee R1$ and $\forall L$ Commute from

$$\forall L\ \frac{\vee R1\ \frac{\Gamma, P(\alpha) \vdash B}{\Gamma, P(\alpha) \vdash B \vee C}}{\Gamma, \forall c\ P(c) \vdash B \vee C} \quad \text{to} \quad \vee R1\ \frac{\forall L\ \frac{\Gamma, P(\alpha) \vdash B}{\Gamma, \forall c\ P(c) \vdash B}}{\Gamma, \forall c\ P(c) \vdash B \vee C}$$

Case for $\vee R2$ and $\wedge L$: Commute from

$$\wedge L\ \frac{\vee R2\ \frac{\Gamma, A, B \vdash D}{\Gamma, A, B \vdash C \vee D}}{\Gamma, A \wedge B \vdash C \vee D} \quad \text{to} \quad \vee R2\ \frac{\wedge L\ \frac{\Gamma, A, B \vdash D}{\Gamma, A \wedge B \vdash D}}{\Gamma, A \wedge B \vdash C \vee D}$$

Case for $\vee R2$ and $?L$: Commute from

$$?L\ \frac{\vee R2\ \frac{\Gamma, A \to B \vdash D}{\Gamma, A \to B \vdash C \vee D}}{\Gamma, [?A]B \vdash C \vee D} \quad \text{to} \quad \vee R2\ \frac{?L\ \frac{\Gamma, A \to B \vdash D}{\Gamma, [?A]B \vdash D}}{\Gamma, [?A]B \vdash C \vee D}$$

Case for $\vee R2$ and $\cup L$: Commute from

$$\cup L\ \frac{\vee R2\ \frac{\Gamma, [\alpha]A \wedge [\beta]A \vdash D}{\Gamma, [\alpha]A \wedge [\beta]A \vdash C \vee D}}{\Gamma, [\alpha \cup \beta]A \vdash C \vee D} \quad \text{to} \quad \vee R2\ \frac{\cup L\ \frac{\Gamma, [\alpha]A \wedge [\beta]A \vdash D}{\Gamma, [\alpha \cup \beta]A \vdash D}}{\Gamma, [\alpha \cup \beta]A \vdash C \vee D}$$

Case for $\vee R2$ and $\to L$: Commute from

$$\to L\ \frac{\Gamma \vdash A \quad \vee R2\ \frac{\Gamma, p \vdash D}{\Gamma, p \vdash C \vee D}}{\Gamma, A \to p \vdash C \vee D} \quad \text{to} \quad \vee R2\ \frac{\to L\ \frac{\Gamma \vdash A \quad \Gamma, p \vdash D}{\Gamma, A \to p \vdash D}}{\Gamma, A \to p \vdash C \vee D}$$

Case for $\vee R2$ and $\forall L$ Commute from

$$\forall L\ \frac{\vee R2\ \frac{\Gamma, P(\alpha) \vdash C}{\Gamma, P(\alpha) \vdash B \vee C}}{\Gamma, \forall c\ P(c) \vdash B \vee C} \quad \text{to} \quad \vee R2\ \frac{\forall L\ \frac{\Gamma, P(\alpha) \vdash C}{\Gamma, \forall c\ P(c) \vdash C}}{\Gamma, \forall c\ P(c) \vdash B \vee C}$$

Case for $\wedge R$ and $\wedge L$: Commute from

$$\wedge L\ \frac{\wedge R\ \frac{\Gamma, A, B \vdash C \quad \Gamma, A, B \vdash D}{\Gamma, A, B \vdash C \wedge D}}{\Gamma, A \wedge B \vdash C \wedge D} \quad \text{to} \quad \wedge R\ \frac{\wedge L\ \frac{\Gamma, A, B \vdash C}{\Gamma, A \wedge B \vdash C} \quad \wedge L\ \frac{\Gamma, A, B \vdash D}{\Gamma, A \wedge B \vdash D}}{\Gamma, A \wedge B \vdash C \wedge D}$$

Case for $\wedge R$ and $?L$: Commute from

$$?L\ \frac{\wedge R\ \frac{\Gamma, A \to B \vdash C \quad \Gamma, A \to B \vdash D}{\Gamma, A \to B \vdash C \wedge D}}{\Gamma, [?A]B \vdash C \wedge D}$$

to

$$\wedge R\ \frac{?L\ \frac{\Gamma, A \to B \vdash C}{\Gamma, [?A]B \vdash C} \quad ?L\ \frac{\Gamma, A \to B \vdash D}{\Gamma, [?A]B \vdash D}}{\Gamma, [?A]B \vdash C \wedge D}$$

Case for $\wedge R$ **and** $\cup L$: Commute from

$$\cup L \dfrac{\wedge R \dfrac{\Gamma, [\alpha]A \wedge [\beta]A \vdash C \qquad \Gamma, [\alpha]A \wedge [\beta]A \vdash D}{\Gamma, [\alpha]A \wedge [\beta]A \vdash C \wedge D}}{\Gamma, [\alpha \cup \beta]A \vdash C \wedge D}$$

to

$$\wedge R \dfrac{\cup L \dfrac{\Gamma, [\alpha]A \wedge [\beta]A \vdash C}{\Gamma, [\alpha \cup \beta]A \vdash C} \qquad \cup L \dfrac{\Gamma, [\alpha]A \wedge [\beta]A \vdash D}{\Gamma, [\alpha \cup \beta]A \vdash D}}{\Gamma, [\alpha \cup \beta]A \vdash C \wedge D}$$

Case for $\wedge R$ **and** $\rightarrow L$: Commute from

$$\rightarrow L \dfrac{\Gamma \vdash A \qquad \wedge R \dfrac{\Gamma, p \vdash C \qquad \Gamma, p \vdash D}{\Gamma, p \vdash C \wedge D}}{\Gamma, A \rightarrow p \vdash C \wedge D}$$

to

$$\wedge R \dfrac{\rightarrow L \dfrac{\Gamma \vdash A \qquad \Gamma, p \vdash C}{\Gamma, A \rightarrow p \vdash C} \qquad \rightarrow L \dfrac{\Gamma \vdash A \qquad \Gamma, p \vdash D}{\Gamma, A \rightarrow p \vdash D}}{\Gamma, A \rightarrow p \vdash C \wedge D}$$

Case for $\wedge R$ **and** $\forall L$ Commute from

$$\forall L \dfrac{\wedge R \dfrac{\Gamma, P(\alpha) \vdash C \qquad \Gamma, P(\alpha) \vdash D}{\Gamma, P(\alpha) \vdash C \wedge D}}{\Gamma, \forall c\, P(c) \vdash C \wedge D}$$

to

$$\wedge R \dfrac{\forall L \dfrac{\Gamma, P(\alpha) \vdash C}{\Gamma, \forall c\, P(c) \vdash C} \qquad \forall L \dfrac{\Gamma, P(\alpha) \vdash D}{\Gamma, \forall c\, P(c) \vdash D}}{\Gamma, \forall c\, P(c) \vdash C \wedge D}$$

Case for $\rightarrow R$ **and** $\wedge L$: Commute from

$$\wedge L \dfrac{\rightarrow R \dfrac{\Gamma, A, B, C \vdash D}{\Gamma, A, B \vdash C \rightarrow D}}{\Gamma, A \wedge B \vdash C \rightarrow D}$$

to

$$\rightarrow R \dfrac{\wedge L \dfrac{\Gamma, A, B, C \vdash D}{\Gamma, A \wedge B, C \vdash D}}{\Gamma, A \wedge B \vdash C \rightarrow D}$$

Case for $\rightarrow R$ **and** $?L$: Commute from

$$?L \dfrac{\rightarrow R \dfrac{\Gamma, A \rightarrow B, C \vdash D}{\Gamma, A \rightarrow B \vdash C \rightarrow D}}{\Gamma, [?A]B \vdash C \rightarrow D}$$

to

$$\rightarrow R \dfrac{?L \dfrac{\Gamma, A \rightarrow B, C \vdash D}{\Gamma, [?A]B, C \vdash D}}{\Gamma, [?A]B \vdash C \rightarrow D}$$

Case for $\to R$ and $\cup L$: Commute from

$$\cup L\ \dfrac{\to R\ \dfrac{\Gamma, [\alpha]A \land [\beta]A, C \vdash D}{\Gamma, [\alpha]A \land [\beta]A \vdash C \to D}}{\Gamma, [\alpha \cup \beta]A \vdash C \to D} \quad \text{to} \quad \to R\ \dfrac{\cup L\ \dfrac{\Gamma, [\alpha]A \land [\beta]A, C \vdash D}{\Gamma, [\alpha \cup \beta]A, C \vdash D}}{\Gamma, [\alpha \cup \beta]A \vdash C \to D}$$

Case for $\to R$ and $\to L$: Commute from

$$\to L\ \dfrac{\Gamma \vdash A \quad \to R\ \dfrac{\Gamma, B, C \vdash D}{\Gamma, B \vdash C \to D}}{\Gamma, A \to B \vdash C \to D} \quad \text{to} \quad \to R\ \dfrac{\to L\ \dfrac{\text{W}\ \dfrac{\Gamma \vdash p}{\Gamma, C \vdash p} \qquad \Gamma, B, C \vdash D}{\Gamma, A \to B, C \vdash D}}{\Gamma, A \to B \vdash C \to D}$$

An astute reader may be concerned that W increases the height of the derivation, because it is easier to argue our induction is well-founded if height does not increase. However, W is an admissible rule whose standard implementation is height-preserving, thus this derivation is indeed height-preserving.

Case for $\to R$ and $\forall L$ Commute from

$$\forall L\ \dfrac{\to R\ \dfrac{\Gamma, P(\alpha)C, \vdash D}{\Gamma, P(\alpha) \vdash C \to D}}{\Gamma, \forall c\, P(c) \vdash C \to D} \quad \text{to} \quad \to R\ \dfrac{\forall L\ \dfrac{\Gamma, P(\alpha), C \vdash D}{\Gamma, \forall c\, P(c), C \vdash D}}{\Gamma, \forall c\, P(c) \vdash C \land D}$$

Case for $?R$ and $\land L$: Commute from

$$\land L\ \dfrac{?R\ \dfrac{\Gamma, A, B \vdash C \to D}{\Gamma, A, B \vdash [?C]D}}{\Gamma, A \land B \vdash [?C]D} \quad \text{to} \quad ?R\ \dfrac{\land L\ \dfrac{\Gamma, A, B \vdash C \to D}{\Gamma, A \land B \vdash C \to D}}{\Gamma, A \land B \vdash [?C]D}$$

Case for $?R$ and $?L$: Commute from

$$?L\ \dfrac{?R\ \dfrac{\Gamma, A \to B \vdash C \to D}{\Gamma, A \to B \vdash [?C]D}}{\Gamma, [?A]B \vdash [?C]D} \quad \text{to} \quad ?R\ \dfrac{?L\ \dfrac{\Gamma, A \to B \vdash C \to D}{\Gamma, [?A]B \vdash C \to D}}{\Gamma, [?A]B \vdash [?C]D}$$

Case for $?R$ and $\cup L$: Commute from

$$\cup L\ \dfrac{?R\ \dfrac{\Gamma, [\alpha]A \land [\beta]A \vdash C \to D}{\Gamma, [\alpha]A \land [\beta]A \vdash [?C]D}}{\Gamma, [\alpha \cup \beta]A \vdash [?C]D} \quad \text{to} \quad ?R\ \dfrac{\cup L\ \dfrac{\Gamma, [\alpha]A \land [\beta]A \vdash C \to D}{\Gamma, [\alpha \cup \beta]A \vdash C \to D}}{\Gamma, [\alpha \cup \beta]A \vdash [?C]D}$$

Case for $?R$ and $\to L$: Commute from

$$\to L\ \dfrac{\Gamma \vdash A \quad ?R\ \dfrac{\Gamma, B \vdash C \to D}{\Gamma, B \vdash [?C]D}}{\Gamma, A \to B \vdash [?C]D} \quad \text{to} \quad ?R\ \dfrac{\to L\ \dfrac{\Gamma \vdash A \qquad \Gamma, B \vdash C \to D}{\Gamma, A \to B \vdash C \to D}}{\Gamma, A \to B \vdash [?C]D}$$

Case for $?R$ and $\forall L$ Commute from

$$\forall L\ \dfrac{?R\ \dfrac{\Gamma, P(\alpha) \vdash C \to D}{\Gamma, P(\alpha) \vdash [?C]D}}{\Gamma, \forall c\, P(c) \vdash [?C]D} \quad \text{to} \quad ?R\ \dfrac{\forall L\ \dfrac{\Gamma, P(\alpha) \vdash C \to D}{\Gamma, \forall c\, P(c) \vdash C \to D}}{\Gamma, \forall c\, P(c) \vdash [?C]D}$$

Case for $;R$ and $\land L$: Commute from

$$\land L\ \dfrac{;R\ \dfrac{\Gamma, A, B \vdash [\alpha][\beta]C}{\Gamma, A, B \vdash [\alpha;\beta]C}}{\Gamma, A \land B \vdash [\alpha;\beta]C} \quad \text{to} \quad ;R\ \dfrac{\land L\ \dfrac{\Gamma, A, B \vdash [\alpha][\beta]C}{\Gamma, A \land B \vdash [\alpha][\beta]C}}{\Gamma, A \land B \vdash [\alpha;\beta]C}$$

Case for $;R$ and $?L$: Commute from

$$\dfrac{\dfrac{\Gamma, A \to B \vdash [\alpha][\beta]C}{\Gamma, A \to B \vdash [\alpha;\beta]C}\;{;R}}{\Gamma, [?A]B \vdash [\alpha;\beta]C}\;{?L} \quad \text{to} \quad \dfrac{\dfrac{\Gamma, A \to B \vdash [\alpha][\beta]C}{\Gamma, [?A]B \vdash [\alpha][\beta]C}\;{?L}}{\Gamma, [?A]B \vdash [\alpha;\beta]C}\;{;R}$$

Case for $;R$ and $\cup L$: Commute from

$$\dfrac{\dfrac{\Gamma, [\alpha]A \wedge [\beta]A \vdash [\alpha'][\beta']C}{\Gamma, [\alpha]A \wedge [\beta]A \vdash [\alpha';\beta']C}\;{;R}}{\Gamma, [\alpha \cup \beta]A \vdash [\alpha';\beta']C}\;{\cup L} \quad \text{to} \quad \dfrac{\dfrac{\Gamma, [\alpha]A \wedge [\beta]A \vdash [\alpha'][\beta']C}{\Gamma, [\alpha \cup \beta]A \vdash [\alpha'][\beta']C}\;{\cup L}}{\Gamma, [\alpha \cup \beta]A \vdash [\alpha';\beta']C}\;{;R}$$

Case for $;R$ and $\to L$: Commute from

$$\dfrac{\Gamma \vdash A \quad \dfrac{\Gamma, p \vdash [\alpha][\beta]C}{\Gamma, p \vdash [\alpha;\beta]C}\;{;R}}{\Gamma, A \to p \vdash [\alpha;\beta]C}\;{\to L} \quad \text{to} \quad \dfrac{\dfrac{\Gamma \vdash A \qquad \Gamma, p \vdash [\alpha][\beta]C}{\Gamma, A \to p \vdash [\alpha][\beta]C}\;{\to L}}{\Gamma, A \to p \vdash [\alpha;\beta]C}\;{;R}$$

Case for $;R$ and $\forall L$ Commute from

$$\dfrac{\dfrac{\Gamma, P(\alpha) \vdash [\alpha][\beta]C}{\Gamma, P(\alpha) \vdash [\alpha;\beta]C}\;{;R}}{\Gamma, \forall c\, P(c) \vdash [\alpha;\beta]C}\;{\forall L} \quad \text{to} \quad \dfrac{\dfrac{\Gamma, P(\alpha) \vdash [\alpha][\beta]C}{\Gamma, \forall c\, P(c) \vdash [\alpha][\beta]C}\;{\forall L}}{\Gamma, \forall c\, P(c) \vdash [\alpha;\beta]C}\;{;R}$$

Case for $\cup R$ and $\wedge L$: Commute from

$$\dfrac{\dfrac{\Gamma, A, B \vdash [\alpha]C \wedge [\beta]C}{\Gamma, A, B \vdash [\alpha \cup \beta]C}\;{\cup R}}{\Gamma, A \wedge B \vdash [\alpha \cup \beta]C}\;{\wedge L} \quad \text{to} \quad \dfrac{\dfrac{\Gamma, A, B \vdash [\alpha]C \wedge [\beta]C}{\Gamma, A \wedge B \vdash [\alpha]C \wedge [\beta]C}\;{\wedge L}}{\Gamma, A \wedge B \vdash [\alpha \cup \beta]C}\;{\cup R}$$

Case for $\cup R$ and $?L$: Commute from

$$\dfrac{\dfrac{\Gamma, A \to B \vdash [\alpha]C \wedge [\beta]C}{\Gamma, A \to B \vdash [\alpha \cup \beta]C}\;{\cup R}}{\Gamma, [?A]B \vdash [\alpha \cup \beta]C}\;{?L} \quad \text{to} \quad \dfrac{\dfrac{\Gamma, A \to B \vdash [\alpha]C \wedge [\beta]C}{\Gamma, [?A]B \vdash [\alpha]C \wedge [\beta]C}\;{?L}}{\Gamma, [?A]B \vdash [\alpha \cup \beta]C}\;{\cup R}$$

Case for $\cup R$ and $\cup L$: Commute from

$$\dfrac{\dfrac{\Gamma, [\alpha]A \wedge [\beta]A \vdash [\alpha']C \wedge [\beta']C}{\Gamma, [\alpha]A \wedge [\beta]A \vdash [\alpha' \cup \beta']C}\;{\cup R}}{\Gamma, [\alpha \cup \beta]A \vdash [\alpha' \cup \beta']C}\;{\cup L} \quad \text{to} \quad \dfrac{\dfrac{\Gamma, [\alpha]A \wedge [\beta]A \vdash [\alpha']C \wedge [\beta']C}{\Gamma, [\alpha \cup \beta]A \vdash [\alpha']C \wedge [\beta']C}\;{\cup L}}{\Gamma, [\alpha \cup \beta]A \vdash [\alpha' \cup \beta']C}\;{\cup R}$$

Case for $\cup R$ and $\to L$: Commute from

$$\dfrac{\Gamma \vdash A \quad \dfrac{\Gamma, p \vdash [\alpha]C \wedge [\beta]C}{\Gamma, p \vdash [\alpha \cup \beta]C}\;{\cup R}}{\Gamma, A \to p \vdash [\alpha \cup \beta]C}\;{\to L} \quad \text{to} \quad \dfrac{\dfrac{\Gamma \vdash A \qquad \Gamma, p \vdash [\alpha]C \wedge [\beta]C}{\Gamma, A \to p \vdash [\alpha]C \wedge [\beta]C}\;{\to L}}{\Gamma, A \to p \vdash [\alpha \cup \beta]C}\;{\cup R}$$

Case for $\cup R$ and $\forall L$ Commute from

$$\dfrac{\dfrac{\Gamma, P(\alpha) \vdash [\alpha]C \wedge [\beta]C}{\Gamma, P(\alpha) \vdash [\alpha \cup \beta]C}\;{\cup R}}{\Gamma, \forall c\, P(c) \vdash [\alpha \cup \beta]C}\;{\forall L} \quad \text{to} \quad \dfrac{\dfrac{\Gamma, P(\alpha) \vdash [\alpha]C \wedge [\beta]C}{\Gamma, \forall c\, P(c) \vdash [\alpha]C \wedge [\beta]C}\;{\forall L}}{\Gamma, \forall c\, P(c) \vdash [\alpha \cup \beta]C}\;{\cup R}$$

Case for $*R$ and $\wedge L$: Commute from

$$
\frac{\Gamma, A, B \vdash \bigvee_i J_i \qquad J_i \vdash [\alpha] \bigvee_j J_j \qquad J_i \vdash P}{\dfrac{\Gamma, A, B \vdash [\alpha^* @inv(\bigvee_i J_i)]C}{\Gamma, A \wedge B \vdash [\alpha^* @inv(\bigvee_i J_i)]C} \wedge L} *R
$$

to

$$
\frac{\dfrac{\Gamma, A, B \vdash \bigvee_i J_i}{\Gamma, A \wedge B \vdash \bigvee_i J_i} \wedge L \qquad J_i \vdash [\alpha] \bigvee_j J_j \qquad J_i \vdash P}{\Gamma, A \wedge B \vdash [\alpha^* @inv(\bigvee_i J_i)]C} *R
$$

Case for $*R$ and $?L$: Commute from

$$
\frac{\Gamma, A \rightarrow B \vdash \bigvee_i J_i \qquad J_i \vdash [\alpha] \bigvee_j J_j \qquad J_i \vdash P}{\dfrac{\Gamma, A \rightarrow B \vdash [\alpha^* @inv(\bigvee_i J_i)]C}{\Gamma, [?A]B \vdash [\alpha^* @inv(\bigvee_i J_i)]C} ?L} *R
$$

to

$$
\frac{\dfrac{\Gamma, A \rightarrow B \vdash \bigvee_i J_i}{\Gamma, [?A]B \vdash \bigvee_i J_i} ?L \qquad J_i \vdash [\alpha] \bigvee_j J_j \qquad J_i \vdash P}{\Gamma, [?A]B \vdash [\alpha^* @inv(\bigvee_i J_i)]C} *R
$$

Case for $*R$ and $\cup L$: Commute from

$$
\frac{\Gamma, [\alpha]A \wedge [\beta]A \vdash \bigvee_i J_i \qquad J_i \vdash [\alpha] \bigvee_j J_j \qquad J_i \vdash P}{\dfrac{\Gamma, [\alpha]A \wedge [\beta]A \vdash [\alpha^* @inv(\bigvee_i J_i)]C}{\Gamma, [\alpha \cup \beta]A \vdash [\alpha^* @inv(\bigvee_i J_i)]C} \cup L} *R
$$

to

$$\cup L\ \dfrac{\dfrac{\Gamma, [\alpha]A \wedge [\beta]A \vdash \bigvee_i J_i}{\Gamma, [\alpha \cup \beta]A \vdash \bigvee_i J_i} \qquad J_i \vdash [\alpha] \bigvee_j J_j \qquad J_i \vdash P}{\Gamma, [\alpha \cup \beta]A \vdash [\alpha^* @inv(\bigvee_i J_i)]C}\ {*R}$$

Case for $*R$ and $\rightarrow L$: Commute from

$$\rightarrow L\ \dfrac{\Gamma \vdash A \qquad {*R}\ \dfrac{\Gamma, p \vdash \bigvee_i J_i \qquad J_i \vdash [\alpha] \bigvee_j J_j \qquad J_i \vdash P}{\Gamma, p \vdash [\alpha^* @inv(\bigvee_i J_i)]C}}{\Gamma, A \rightarrow p \vdash [\alpha^* @inv(\bigvee_i J_i)]C}$$

to

$${*R}\ \dfrac{\rightarrow L\ \dfrac{\Gamma \vdash A \qquad \Gamma, p \vdash \bigvee_i J_i}{\Gamma, A \rightarrow p \vdash \bigvee_i J_i} \qquad J_i \vdash [\alpha] \bigvee_j J_j \qquad J_i \vdash P}{\Gamma, A \rightarrow p \vdash [\alpha^* @inv(\bigvee_i J_i)]C}$$

Case for $*R$ and $\forall L$ Commute from

$$\forall L\ \dfrac{{*R}\ \dfrac{\Gamma, P(\alpha) \vdash \bigvee_i J_i \qquad J_i \vdash [\alpha] \bigvee_j J_j \qquad J_i \vdash P}{\Gamma, P(\alpha) \vdash [\alpha^* @inv(\bigvee_i J_i)]C}}{\Gamma, \forall c\ P(c) \vdash [\alpha^* @inv(\bigvee_i J_i)]C}$$

to

$${*R}\ \dfrac{\forall L\ \dfrac{\Gamma, P(\alpha) \vdash}{\Gamma, \forall c\ P(c) \vdash \bigvee_i J_i} \qquad J_i \vdash [\alpha] \bigvee_j J_j \qquad J_i \vdash P}{\Gamma, \forall c\ P(c) \vdash [\alpha^* @inv(\bigvee_i J_i)]C}$$

Case for $\forall R$ and $\wedge L$ Commute from

$$\wedge L \frac{\forall R \frac{\Gamma, A, B \vdash P(c')}{\Gamma, A, B \vdash \forall c\, P(c)}}{\Gamma, A \wedge B \vdash \forall c\, P(c)} \quad \text{to} \quad \forall R \frac{\wedge L \frac{\Gamma, A, B \vdash P(c')}{\Gamma, A \wedge B \vdash P(c')}}{\Gamma, A \wedge B \vdash \forall c\, P(c)}$$

Case for $\forall R$ and $?L$ Commute from

$$?L \frac{\forall R \frac{\Gamma, A \to B \vdash P(c')}{\Gamma, A \to B \vdash \forall c\, P(c)}}{\Gamma, [?A]B \vdash \forall c\, P(c)} \quad \text{to} \quad \forall R \frac{?L \frac{\Gamma, A \to B \vdash P(c')}{\Gamma, [?A]B \vdash P(c')}}{\Gamma, [?A]B \vdash \forall c\, P(c)}$$

Case for $\forall R$ and $\cup L$ Commute from

$$\cup L \frac{\forall R \frac{\Gamma, [\alpha]A \wedge [\beta]A \vdash P(c')}{\Gamma, [\alpha]A \wedge [\beta]A \vdash \forall c\, P(c)}}{\Gamma, [\alpha \cup \beta]A \vdash \forall c\, P(c)} \quad \text{to} \quad \forall R \frac{\cup L \frac{\Gamma, [\alpha]A \wedge [\beta]A \vdash P(c')}{\Gamma, [\alpha \cup \beta]A \vdash P(c')}}{\Gamma, [\alpha \cup \beta]A \vdash \forall c\, P(c)}$$

Case for $\forall R$ and $\to L$ Commute from

$$\to L \frac{\Gamma \vdash A \qquad \forall R \frac{\Gamma, p \vdash P(c')}{\Gamma, p \vdash \forall c\, P(c)}}{\Gamma, A \to p \vdash \forall c\, P(c)} \quad \text{to} \quad \forall R \frac{\to L \frac{\Gamma \vdash A \qquad \Gamma, p \vdash P(c')}{\Gamma, A \to p \vdash P(c')}}{\Gamma, A \to p \vdash \forall c\, P(c)}$$

Case for $\forall R$ and $\forall L$ Commute from

$$\forall L \frac{\forall R \frac{\Gamma, Q(\alpha) \vdash P(c')}{\Gamma, Q(\alpha) \vdash \forall c\, P(c)}}{\Gamma, \forall c''\, Q(c'') \vdash \forall c\, P(c)} \quad \text{to} \quad \forall R \frac{\forall L \frac{\Gamma, Q(\alpha) \vdash P(c')}{\Gamma, \forall c''\, Q(c'') \vdash P(c')}}{\Gamma, \forall c''\, Q(c'') \vdash \forall c\, P(c)}$$

C Example Execution Trace

To validate the operational semantics, we perform a step-by-step execution trace of the example program and its query. We use ^ or < to indicate the next step and numbers for numbered subgoals. We indicate finished branches with *. Reasons are given in [square brackets].

```
?- ac -> [(demon-turn; angel-turn)*@inv(ac|bd|ca|db)](ac|bd|ca|db).
^(1) (ac | bd |  ca | db) <[Init] *
 (2) (ac | bd | ca | db) <[Init] *
 (3) ac -> [(demon-turn; angel-turn)](ac | bd | ca | db)
 (4) bd -> [(demon-turn; angel-turn)](ac | bd | ca | db)
 (5) ca -> [(demon-turn; angel-turn)](ac | bd | ca | db)
 (6) db -> [(demon-turn; angel-turn)](ac | bd | ca | db)

 (3) ac -> [(demon-turn; angel-turn)](ac | bd | ca | db)
^[Rigid] ac -> [((L U R); angel-turn)](ac | bd | ca | db)
^[Seq] ac -> [L U R][angel-turn](ac | bd | ca | db)
^[Choice] (7) ac -> [L][angel-turn](ac | bd | ca | db)
          (8) ac -> [R][angel-turn](ac | bd | ca | db)

(7) ac -> [L][angel-turn](ac | bd | ca | db)
```

```
^[Rigid] ac -> [L][?ab; LA U ?bc; LA U ?cd ; LA U ?da; LA
    U ?ad; RA U ?ba; RA U ?cb; RA U ?dc; RA](ac|bd|ca|db)
^[Choice,Mon]
  (7a) ac -> [L][?ab; LA](ac | bd | ca | db)
^[Seq,Mon] ac -> [L][?ab][LA](ac | bd | ca | db)
^[Or,Mon] ac -> [L][?ab][LA]db
^[Test,Mon] ac -> [L](ab -> [LA]db)
^[WL,Init,Mon] *
  (7b) ac -> [L][?bc; LA](ac | bd | ca | db)
^[Seq,Mon] ac -> [L][?bc][LA](ac | bd | ca | db)
^[Or,Mon] ac -> [L][?bc][LA]ac
^[Test,Mon] ac -> [L](bc -> [LA]ac)
^[WL,Init,Mon] *
  (7c) ac -> [L][?cd; LA](ac | bd | ca | db)
^[Seq,Mon] ac ->[L][?cd][LA](ac | bd | ca | db)
^[Or,Mon] ac -> [L][?cd][LA]bd
^[Test,Mon] ac -> [L](cd -> [LA]bd)
^[WL,Init,Mon] *
  (7d) ac -> [L][?da; LA](ac | bd | ca | db)
^[Seq,Mon] ac -> [L][?da][LA](ac | bd | ca | db)
^[Or,Mon] ac -> [L][?da][LA]ca
^[Test,Mon] ac -> [L](da -> [LA]ca)
^[WL,Init,Mon] *
  (7e) ac -> [L][?ad; RA](ac | bd | ca | db)
^[Seq,Mon] ac -> [L][?ad][RA](ac | bd | ca | db)
^[Or,Mon] ac -> [L][?ad][RA]bd
^[Test,Mon] ac -> [L](ad -> [RA]bd)
^[WL,Init,Mon] *
  (7f) ac -> [L][?ba; RA](ac | bd | ca | db)
^[Seq,Mon] ac -> [L][?ba][RA](ac | bd | ca | db)
^[Or,Mon] ac -> [L][?ba][RA]ca
^[Test,Mon] ac -> [L](ba -> [RA]ca)
^[WL,Init,Mon] *
  (7g) ac -> [L][?cb; RA](ac | bd | ca | db)
^[Seq,Mon] ac -> [L][?cb][RA](ac | bd | ca | db)
^[Or,Mon] ac -> [L][?cb][RA]db
^[Test,Mon] ac -> [L](cb -> [RA]db)
^[WL,Init,Mon] *
  (7h) ac -> [L][?dc; RA](ac | bd | ca | db)
^[Seq,Mon] ac -> [L][?dc][RA](ac | bd | ca | db)
^[Or,Mon] ac -> [L][?dc][RA]ac
^[Test,Mon] ac -> [L](dc -> [RA]ac)
^[WL,Init,Mon] *

(8) ac -> [R][angel-turn](ac | bd | ca | db)
```

```
^[Rigid] ac -> [R][?ab; LA U ?bc; LA U ?cd; LA U ?da; LA
   U ?ad; RA U ?ba; RA U ?cb; RA U ?dc; RA](ac|bd|ca|db)
^[Choice,Mon]
 (8a) ac -> [R][?ad; RA](ac | bd | ca | db)
^[Seq,Mon] ac -> [R][?ad][RA](ac | bd | ca | cb)
^[Or,Mon] ac -> [R][?ad][RA]bd
^[Test,Mon] ac -> [R](ad -> [RA]bd)
^[WL,Init,Mon] *
 (8b) ac -> [R][?ba; RA](ac | bd | ca | db)
^[Seq,Mon] ac -> [R][?ba][RA](ac | bd | ca | db)
^[Or,Mon] ac -> [R][?ba][RA]ca
^[Test,Mon] ac -> [R](ba -> [RA]ca)
^[WL,Init,Mon] *
 (8c) ac -> [R][?cb; RA](ac | bd | ca | db)
^[Seq,Mon] ac -> [R][?cb][RA](ac | bd | ca | db)
^[Or,Mon] ac -> [R][?cb][RA]db
^[Test,Mon] ac -> [R](cb -> [RA]db)
^[WL,Init,Mon] *
 (8d) ac -> [R][?dc; RA](ac | bd | ca | db)
^[Seq,Mon] ac -> [R][?dc][RA](ac | bd | ca | db)
^[Or,Mon] ac -> [R][?dc][RA]ac
^[Test,Mon] ac -> [R](dc -> [RA]ac)
^[WL,Init,Mon] *
 (8e) ac -> [R][?ab; LA](ac | bd | ca | db)
^[Seq,Mon] ac -> [R][?ab][LA](ac | bd | ca | db)
^[Or,Mon] ac -> [R][?ab][LA]db
^[Test,Mon] ac -> [R](ab -> [LA]db)
^[WL,Init,Mon] *
 (8f) ac -> [R][?bc; LA](ac | bd | ca | db)
^[Seq,Mon] ac -> [R][?bc][LA](ac | bd | ca | db)
^[Or,Mon]  ac -> [R][?bc][LA]ac
^[Test,Mon] ac -> [R](bc -> [LA]ac)
^[WL,Init,Mon] *
 (8g) ac -> [R][?cd; LA](ac | bd | ca | db)
^[Seq,Mon] ac -> [R][?cd][LA](ac | bd | ca | db)
^[Or,Mon] ac -> [R][?cd][LA]bd
^[Test,Mon] ac -> [R](cd -> [LA]bd)
^[WL,Init,Mon] *
 (8h) ac -> [R][?da; LA](ac | bd | ca | db)
^[Seq,Mon] ac -> [R][?da][LA](ac | bd | ca | db)
^[Or,Mon] ac -> [R][?da][LA]ca
^[Test,Mon] ac -> [R](da -> [LA]ca)
^[WL,Init,Mon] *


 (4) bd -> [(demon-turn; angel-turn)](ac | bd | ca | db)
```

```
~[Rigid] bd -> [(L U R); angel-turn](ac | bd | ca | db)
~[Seq] bd -> [L U R][angel-turn](ac | bd | ca | db)
~[Choice]
 (9) bd -> [L][angel-turn](ac | bd | ca | db)
 (10) bd -> [R][angel-turn](ac | bd | ca | db)

(9) bd -> [L][angel-turn](ac | bd | ca | db)
~[Rigid] bd -> [L][?ab; LA U ?bc; LA U ?cd ; LA U ?da; LA
    U ?ad; RA U ?ba; RA U ?cb; RA U ?dc; RA](ac|bd|ca|db)
~[Choice,Mon]
  (9a) bd -> [L][?bc; LA](ac | bd | ca | db)
~[Seq,Mon] bd -> [L][?bc][LA](ac | bd | ca | db)
~[Or,Mon] bd -> [L][?bc][LA]ac
~[Test,Mon] bd -> [L](bc -> [LA]ac)
~[WL,Pred,Mon] *
  (9b) bd -> [L][?ab; LA](ac | bd | ca | db)
~[Seq,Mon] bd -> [L][?ab][LA](ac | bd | ca | db)
~[Or,Mon] bd -> [L][?ab][LA]db
~[Test,Mon] bd -> [L](ab -> [LA]db)
~[WL,Pred,Mon] *
  (9c) bd -> [L][?cd; LA](ac | bd | ca | db)
~[Seq,Mon] bd -> [L][?cd][LA](ac | bd | ca | db)
~[Or,Mon] bd -> [L][?cd][LA]bd
~[Test,Mon] bd -> [L](cd -> [LA]bd)
~[WL,Pred,Mon] *
  (9d) bd -> [L][?da; LA](ac | bd | ca | db)
~[Seq,Mon] bd -> [L][?da][LA](ac | bd | ca | db)
~[Or,Mon] bd -> [L][?da][LA]ca
~[Test,Mon] bd -> [L](da ->[LA]ca)
~[WL,Pred,Mon] *
  (9e) bd -> [L][?ad; RA](ac | bd | ca | db)
~[Seq,Mon] bd -> [L][?ad][RA](ac | bd | ca | db)
~[Or,Mon] bd -> [L][?ad][RA]bd
~[Test,Mon] bd -> [L](ad -> [RA]bd)
~[WL,Pred,Mon] *
  (9f) bd -> [L][?ba; RA](ac | bd | ca | db)
~[Seq,Mon] bd -> [L][?ba][RA](ac | bd | ca | db)
~[Or,Mon] bd -> [L][?ba][RA]ca
~[Test,Mon] bd -> [L](ba -> [RA]ca)
~[WL,Pred,Mon] *
  (9g) bd -> [L][?cb; RA](ac | bd | ca | db)
~[Seq,Mon] bd -> [L][?cb][RA](ac | bd | ca | db)
~[Or,Mon] bd -> [L][?cb][RA]db
~[Test,Mon] bd -> [L](cb -> [RA]db)
~[WL,Pred,Mon] *
```

```
  (9h) bd -> [L][?dc; RA](ac | bd | ca | db)
^[Seq,Mon] bd -> [L][?dc][RA](ac | bd | ca | db)
^[Or,Mon] bd -> [L][?dc][RA]ac
^[Test,Mon] bd -> [L](dc -> [RA]ac)
^[WL,Pred,Mon] *

(10) bd -> [R][angel-turn](ac | bd | ca | db)
^[Rigid] bd -> [R][?ab; LA U ?bc; LA U ?cd ; LA U ?da; LA
   U ?ad; RA U ?ba; RA U ?cb; RA U ?dc; RA](ac|bd|ca|db)
^[Choice,Mon]
 (10a)  bd -> [R][?ba; RA](ac | bd | ca | db)
  ^[Seq,Mon] bd -> [R][?ba][RA](ac | bd | ca | db)
  ^[Or,Mon] bd -> [R][?bc][RA]ca
  ^[Test,Mon] bd -> [R](bc -> [RA]ca)
  ^[WL,Pred,Mon] *
 (10b) bd -> [R][?ad; RA](ac | bd | ca | db)
  ^[Seq,Mon] bd -> [R][?ad][RA](ac | bd | ca | db)
  ^[Or,Mon] bd -> [R][?ad][RA]bd
  ^[Test,Mon] bd -> [R](ad -> [RA]bd)
  ^[WL,Pred,Mon] *
 (10c) bd -> [R][?cb; RA](ac | bd | ca | db)
  ^[Seq,Mon] bd -> [R][?cb][RA](ac | bd | ca | db)
  ^[Or,Mon]  bd -> [R][?cb][RA]db
  ^[Test,Mon] bd -> [R](cb -> [RA]db)
  ^[WL,Pred,Mon] *
 (10d) bd -> [R][?dc; RA](ac | bd | ca | db)
  ^[Seq,Mon] bd -> [R][?dc][RA](ac | bd | ca | db)
  ^[Or,Mon] bd -> [R][?dc][RA]ac
  ^[Test,Mon] bd -> [R](dc -> [RA]ac)
  ^[WL,Pred,Mon] *
 (10e) bd -> [R][?ab; LA](ac | bd | ca | db)
  ^[Seq,Mon] bd -> [R][?ab][LA](ac | bd | ca | db)
  ^[Or,Mon] bd -> [R][?ab][LA]db
  ^[Test,Mon] bd -> [R](ab -> [LA]db)
  ^[WL,Pred,Mon] *
 (10f) bd -> [R][?bc; LA](ac | bd | ca | db)
  ^[Seq,Mon] bd -> [R][?bc][LA](ac | bd | ca | db)
  ^[Or,Mon] bd -> [R][?bc][LA]ac
  ^[Test,Mon] bd -> [R](bc -> [LA]ac)
  ^[WL,Pred,Mon] *
 (10g) bd -> [R][?cd; LA](ac | bd | ca | db)
  ^[Seq,Mon] bd -> [R][?cd][LA](ac | bd | ca | db)
  ^[Or,Mon] bd -> [R][?cd][LA]bd
  ^[Test,Mon] bd -> [R](cd -> [LA]bd)
  ^[WL,Pred,Mon] *
```

```
 (10h) bd -> [R][?da; LA](ac | bd | ca | db)
  ^[Seq,Mon] bd -> [R][?da][LA](ac | bd | ca | db)
  ^[Or,Mon] bd -> [R][?da][LA]ca
  ^[Test,Mon] bd -> [R](da -> [LA]ca)
  ^[WL,Pred,Mon] *
 (5) ca -> [(demon-turn; angel-turn)](ac | bd | ca | db)
^[Rigid] ca -> [(L U R); angel-turn](ac | bd | ca | db)
^[Seq] ca -> [L U R][angel-turn](ac | bd | ca | db)
^[Choice]
 (11) ca -> [L][angel-turn](ac | bd | ca | db)
 (12) ca -> [R][angel-turn](ac | bd | ca | db)

(11) ca -> [L][angel-turn](ac | bd | ca | db)
^[Rigid] ca -> [L][?ab; LA U ?bc; LA U ?cd ; LA U ?da; LA
   U ?ad; RA U ?ba; RA U ?cb; RA U ?dc; RA](ac|bd|ca|db)
^[Choice,Mon]
 (11a) ca -> [L][?cd; LA](ac | bd | ca | db)
^[Seq,Mon] ca -> [L][?cd][LA](ac | bd | ca | db)
^[Or,Mon] ca -> [L][?cd][LA]bd
^[Test,Mon] ca -> [L](cd -> [LA]bd)
^[WL,Pred,Mon] *
 (11b) ca -> [L][?ab;LA](ac | bd | ca | db)
^[Seq,Mon] ca -> [L][?ab][LA](ac | bd | ca | db)
^[Or,Mon] ca -> [L][?ab][LA]db
^[Test,Mon] ca -> [L](ab -> [LA]db)
^[WL,Pred,Mon] *
 (11c) ca -> [L][?bc;LA](ac | bd | ca | db)
^[Seq,Mon] ca -> [L][?bc][LA](ac | bd | ca | db)
^[Or,Mon] ca -> [L][?bc][LA]ac
^[Test,Mon] ca -> [L](bc -> [LA]ac)
^[WL,Pred,Mon] *
 (11d) ca -> [L][?da;LA](ac | bd | ca | db)
^[Seq,Mon] ca -> [L][?da][LA](ac | bd | ca | db)
^[Or,Mon] ca -> [L][?da][LA]ca
^[Test,Mon] ca -> [L](da -> [LA]ca)
^[WL,Pred,Mon] *
 (11e) ca -> [L][?ad;RA](ac | bd | ca | db)
^[Seq,Mon] ca -> [L][?ad][RA](ac | bd | ca | db)
^[Or,Mon] ca -> [L][?ad][RA]bd
^[Test,Mon] ca -> [L](ad -> [RA]bd)
^[WL,Pred,Mon] *
 (11f) ca -> [L][?ba;RA](ac | bd | ca | db)
^[Seq,Mon] ca -> [L][?ba][RA](ac | bd | ca | db)
^[Or,Mon] ca -> [L][?ba][RA]ca
^[Test,Mon] ca -> [L](ba -> [RA]ca)
```

```
^[WL,Pred,Mon] *
 (11g) ca -> [L][?cb;RA](ac | bd | ca | db)
^[Seq,Mon] ca -> [L][?cb][RA](ac | bd | ca | db)
^[Or,Mon] ca -> [L][?cb][RA]db
^[Test,Mon] ca -> [L](cb -> [RA]db)
^[WL,Pred,Mon] *
 (11h) ca -> [L][?dc;RA](ac | bd | ca | db)
^[Seq,Mon] ca -> [L][?dc][RA](ac | bd | ca | db)
^[Or,Mon] ca -> [L][?dc][RA]ac
^[Test,Mon] ca -> [L](dc -> [RA]ac)
^[WL,Pred,Mon] *

(12) ca -> [R][angel-turn](ac | bd | ca | db)
^[Rigid] ca -> [R][?ab; LA U ?bc; LA U ?cd ; LA U ?da; LA
   U ?ad; RA U ?ba; RA U ?cb; RA U ?dc; RA](ac|bd|ca|db)
^[Choice,Mon]
(12a) ca -> [R][?cb; RA](ac | bd | ca | db)
^[Seq,Mon] ca -> [R][?cb][RA](ac | bd | ca | db)
^[Or,Mon] ca -> [R][?cb][RA]db
^[Test,Mon] ca -> [R](cb -> [RA]db)
^[WL,Pred,Mon] *
(12b) ca -> [R][?ad; RA](ac | bd | ca | db)
^[Seq,Mon] ca -> [R][?ad][RA](ac | bd | ca | db)
^[Or,Mon] ca -> [R][?ad][RA]bd
^[Test,Mon] ca -> [R](ad -> [RA]bd)
^[WL,Pred,Mon] *
(12c) ca -> [R][?ba; RA](ac | bd | ca | db)
^[Seq,Mon] ca -> [R][?ba][RA](ac | bd | ca | db)
^[Or,Mon]  ca -> [R][?ba][RA]ca
^[Test,Mon] ca -> [R](ba -> [RA]ca)
^[WL,Pred,Mon] *
(12d) ca -> [R][?dc; RA](ac | bd | ca | db)
^[Seq,Mon] ca -> [R][?dc][RA](ac | bd | ca | db)
^[Or,Mon]  ca -> [R][?dc][RA]ac
^[Test,Mon] ca -> [R](dc -> [RA]ac)
^[WL,Pred,Mon] *
(12e) ca -> [R][?ab; LA](ac | bd | ca | db)
^[Seq,Mon] ca -> [R][?ab][LA](ac | bd | ca | db)
^[Or,Mon]  ca -> [R][?ab][LA]db
^[Test,Mon] ca -> [R](ab -> [LA]db)
^[WL,Pred,Mon] *
(12f) ca -> [R][?bc; LA](ac | bd | ca | db)
^[Seq,Mon] ca -> [R][?bc][LA](ac | bd | ca | db)
^[Or,Mon]  ca -> [R][?bc][LA]ac
^[Test,Mon] ca -> [R](bc -> [LA]ac)
```

```
^[WL,Pred,Mon] *
(12g) ca -> [R][?cd; LA](ac | bd | ca | db)
^[Seq,Mon] ca -> [R][?cd][LA](ac | bd | ca | db)
^[Or,Mon]  ca -> [R][?cd][LA]bd
^[Test,Mon] ca -> [R](cd -> [LA]bd)
^[WL,Pred,Mon] *
(12h) ca -> [R][?da; LA](ac | bd | ca | db)
^[Seq,Mon] ca -> [R][?da][LA](ac | bd | ca | db)
^[Or,Mon]  ca -> [R][?da][LA]ca
^[Test,Mon] ca -> [R](da -> [LA]ca)
^[WL,Pred,Mon] *

 (6) db -> [(demon-turn; angel-turn)](ac | bd | ca | db)
^[Rigid] db -> [(L U R); angel-turn](ac | bd | ca | db)
^[Seq] db -> [L U R][angel-turn](ac | bd | ca | db)
^[Choice]

 (13) db -> [L][angel-turn](ac | bd | ca | db)
^[Rigid] db -> [L][?ab; LA U ?bc; LA U ?cd ; LA U ?da; LA
   U ?ad; RA U ?ba; RA U ?cb; RA U ?dc; RA](ac|bd|ca|db)
^[Choice,Mon]
 (13a) db -> [L][?da; LA](ac | bd | ca | db)
^[Seq,Mon] db -> [L][?da][LA](ac | bd | ca | db)
^[Or,Mon] db -> [L][?da][LA]ca
^[Test,Mon] db -> [L](da -> [LA]ca)
^[WL,Pred,Mon] *
 (13b) db -> [L][?ab; LA](ac | bd | ca | db)
^[Seq,Mon] db -> [L][?ab][LA](ac | bd | ca | db)
^[Or,Mon] db -> [L][?ab][LA]db
^[Test,Mon] db -> [L](?ab -> [LA]db)
^[WL,Pred,Mon] *
 (13c) db -> [L][?bc; LA](ac | bd | ca | db)
^[Seq,Mon] db -> [L][?bc][LA](ac | bd | ca | db)
^[Or,Mon] db -> [L][?bc][LA]ac
^[Test,Mon] db -> [L](bc -> [LA]ac)
^[WL,Pred,Mon] *
 (13d) db -> [L][?cd; LA](ac | bd | ca | db)
^[Seq,Mon] db -> [L][?cd][LA](ac | bd | ca | db)
^[Or,Mon] db -> [L][?cd][LA]bd
^[Test,Mon] db -> [L](cd -> [LA]bd)
^[WL,Pred,Mon] *
 (13e) db -> [L][?ad; RA](ac | bd | ca | db)
^[Seq,Mon] db -> [L][?ad][RA](ac | bd | ca | db)
^[Or,Mon] db -> [L][?ad][RA]bd
^[Test,Mon] db -> [L](ad -> [RA]bd)
```

```
^[WL,Pred,Mon] *
 (13f) db -> [L][?ba; RA](ac | bd | ca | db)
^[Seq,Mon] db -> [L][?ba][RA](ac | bd | ca | db)
^[Or,Mon] db -> [L][?ba][RA]ca
^[Test,Mon] db -> [L](ba -> [RA]ca)
^[WL,Pred,Mon] *
 (13g) db -> [L][?cb; RA](ac | bd | ca | db)
^[Seq,Mon] db -> [L][?cb][RA](ac | bd | ca | db)
^[Or,Mon] db -> [L][?cb][RA]db
^[Test,Mon] db -> [L](cb -> [RA]db)
^[WL,Pred,Mon] *
 (13h) db -> [L][?dc; RA](ac | bd | ca | db)
^[Seq,Mon] db -> [L][?dc][RA](ac | bd | ca | db)
^[Or,Mon] db -> [L][?dc][RA]ac
^[Test,Mon] db -> [L](dc -> [RA]ac)
^[WL,Pred,Mon] *
^[Seq,Mon] db -> [L][?da][LA](ac | bd | ca | db)
^[Or,Mon] db -> [L][?da][LA]ca
^[Test,Mon] db -> [L](da -> [LA]ca)
^[WL,Pred,Mon] *

 (14) db -> [R][angel-turn](ac | bd | ca | db)
^[Rigid] db -> [R][?ab; LA U ?bc; LA U ?cd ; LA U ?da; LA
   U ?ad; RA U ?ba; RA U ?cb; RA U ?dc; RA](ac|bd|ca|db)
^[Choice,Mon]
 (14a) db -> [R][?dc; RA](ac | bd | ca | db)
^[Seq,Mon] db -> [R][?dc][RA](ac | bd | ca | db)
^[Or,Mon] db -> [R][?dc][RA]ac
^[Test,Mon] db -> [R](dc -> [RA]ac)
^[WL,Pred,Mon] *
 (14b) db -> [R][?ad; RA](ac | bd | ca | db)
^[Seq,Mon] db -> [R][?ad][RA](ac | bd | ca | db)
^[Or,Mon] db -> [R][?ad][RA]bd
^[Test,Mon] db -> [R](ad -> [RA]bd)
^[WL,Pred,Mon] *
 (14c) db -> [R][?ba; RA](ac | bd | ca | db)
^[Seq,Mon] db -> [R][?ba][RA](ac | bd | ca | db)
^[Or,Mon] db -> [R][?ba][RA]ca
^[Test,Mon] db -> [R](ba -> [RA]ca)
^[WL,Pred,Mon] *
 (14d) db -> [R][?cb; RA](ac | bd | ca | db)
^[Seq,Mon] db -> [R][?cb][RA](ac | bd | ca | db)
^[Or,Mon] db -> [R][?cb][RA]db
^[Test,Mon] db -> [R](cb -> [RA]db)
^[WL,Pred,Mon] *
```

```
 (14e) db -> [R][?ab; LA](ac | bd | ca | db)
^[Seq,Mon] db -> [R][?ab][LA](ac | bd | ca | db)
^[Or,Mon] db -> [R][?ab][LA]db
^[Test,Mon] db -> [R](ab -> [LA]db)
^[WL,Pred,Mon] *
 (14f)db -> [R][?bc; LA](ac | bd | ca | db)
^[Seq,Mon] db -> [R][?bc][LA](ac | bd | ca | db)
^[Or,Mon] db -> [R][?bc][LA]ac
^[Test,Mon] db -> [R](bc -> [LA]ac)
^[WL,Pred,Mon] *
 (14g) db -> [R][?cd; LA](ac | bd | ca | db)
^[Seq,Mon] db -> [R][?cd][LA](ac | bd | ca | db)
^[Or,Mon] db -> [R][?cd][LA]bd
^[Test,Mon] db -> [R](cd -> [LA]bd)
^[WL,Pred,Mon] *
 (14h) db -> [R][?da; LA](ac | bd | ca | db)
^[Seq,Mon] db -> [R][?da][LA](ac | bd | ca | db)
^[Or,Mon] db -> [R][?da][LA]ca
^[Test,Mon] db -> [R](da -> [LA]ca)
^[WL,Pred,Mon] *
```

D Pursuit-Evasion Game in Dusa

```
# Pursuit evasion game

#builtin INT_MINUS minus
#builtin NAT_SUCC suc

max_time is 15.

time max_time.
time (minus N 1) :-
  time N, N > 0.

edge 0 1.
edge 0 3.
edge 1 2.
edge 1 0.
edge 2 3.
edge 2 1.
edge 3 0.
edge 3 2.

 at 0 0 is 0.
```

```
 at 0 1 is 2.
 at (suc K) P is? M :-
   time K,
   at K P is N,
   edge N M.

away 0 2.
away 1 3.
away 2 0.
away 3 1.

stay_away 0 :-
  at 0 0 is U,
  at 0 1 is V,
  away U V.

stay_away (suc K) :-
  stay_away K,
  at K 0 is U,
  at K 1 is V,
  away U V.

#demand stay_away (suc (suc max_time)).
```

References

1. Aguado, F., et al.: Linear-time temporal answer set programming. Theory Pract. Log. Program. **23**(1), 2–56 (2023). https://doi.org/10.1017/S1471068421000557
2. Ahrendt, W., Beckert, B., Bubel, R., Hähnle, R., Schmitt, P.H., Ulbrich, M.: Deductive Software Verification - The KeY Book. Springer, Cham (2016)
3. Andrews, J.H.: A logical semantics for depth-first Prolog with ground negation. Theor. Comput. Sci. **184**(1–2), 105–143 (1997). https://doi.org/10.1016/S0304-3975(96)00138-7
4. Apt, K.R., Van Emden, M.H.: Contributions to the theory of logic programming. J. ACM **29**(3), 841–862 (1982)
5. Balbiani, P., del Cerro, L.F., Herzig, A.: Declarative semantics for modal logic programs. In: Proceedings of the International Conference on Fifth Generation Computer Systems, FGCS 1988, Tokyo, Japan, 28 November–2 December 1988, pp. 507–514. OHMSHA Ltd. Tokyo and Springer (1988)
6. Baudinet, M.: Temporal logic programming is complete and expressive. In: Conference Record of the Sixteenth Annual ACM Symposium on Principles of Programming Languages, Austin, Texas, USA, 11–13 January 1989, pp. 267–280. ACM Press (1989). https://doi.org/10.1145/75277.75301
7. Bhattacharya, S., Başar, T., Falcone, M.: Surveillance for security as a pursuit-evasion game. In: Poovendran, R., Saad, W. (eds.) GameSec 2014. LNCS, vol. 8840, pp. 370–379. Springer, Cham (2014). https://doi.org/10.1007/978-3-319-12601-2_23

8. Billaud, M.: Simple operational and denotational semantics for Prolog with cut. Theor. Comput. Sci. **71**(2), 193–208 (1990). https://doi.org/10.1016/0304-3975(90)90197-P
9. Bohrer, B., Platzer, A.: Constructive game logic. In: Müller, P. (ed.) ESOP 2020. LNCS, vol. 12075, pp. 84–111. Springer, Cham (2020). https://doi.org/10.1007/978-3-030-44914-8_4
10. Bohrer, B., Platzer, A.: Constructive hybrid games. In: Peltier, N., Sofronie-Stokkermans, V. (eds.) IJCAR 2020, Part I. LNCS (LNAI), vol. 12166, pp. 454–473. Springer, Cham (2020). https://doi.org/10.1007/978-3-030-51074-9_26
11. Bohrer, R., Platzer, A.: Refining constructive hybrid games. In: Ariola, Z.M. (ed.) 5th International Conference on Formal Structures for Computation and Deduction, FSCD 2020, 29 June–6 July 2020, Paris, France (Virtual Conference). LIPIcs, vol. 167, pp. 14:1–14:19. Schloss Dagstuhl - Leibniz-Zentrum für Informatik (2020). https://doi.org/10.4230/LIPICS.FSCD.2020.14
12. Bonato, A., Pralat, P., Wang, C.: Pursuit-evasion in models of complex networks. Internet Math. **4**(4), 419–436 (2007). https://doi.org/10.1080/15427951.2007.10129149
13. Börger, E., Rosenzweig, D.: A mathematical definition of full Prolog. Sci. Comput. Program. **24**(3), 249–286 (1995). https://doi.org/10.1016/0167-6423(95)00006-E
14. Borie, R.B., Tovey, C.A., Koenig, S.: Algorithms and complexity results for pursuit-evasion problems. In: Boutilier, C. (ed.) IJCAI 2009, Proceedings of the 21st International Joint Conference on Artificial Intelligence, Pasadena, California, USA, 11–17 July 2009, pp. 59–66 (2009). http://ijcai.org/Proceedings/09/Papers/021.pdf
15. Brewka, G., Eiter, T., Truszczyński, M.: Answer set programming at a glance. Commun. ACM **54**(12), 92–103 (2011)
16. de Bruin, A., de Vink, E.P.: Continuation semantics for PROLOG with cut. In: Díaz, J., Orejas, F. (eds.) CAAP 1989. LNCS, vol. 351, pp. 178–192. Springer, Heidelberg (1989). https://doi.org/10.1007/3-540-50939-9_132
17. Chung, T.H., Hollinger, G.A., Isler, V.: Search and pursuit-evasion in mobile robotics - a survey. Auton. Robots **31**(4), 299–316 (2011). https://doi.org/10.1007/S10514-011-9241-4
18. Dunin-Ke, B., Nguyen, L.A., Szałas, A., et al.: Tractable approximate knowledge fusion using the horn fragment of serial propositional dynamic logic. Int. J. Approximate Reasoning **51**(3), 346–362 (2010)
19. van Emden, M.H., Kowalski, R.A.: The semantics of predicate logic as a programming language. J. ACM **23**(4), 733–742 (1976). https://doi.org/10.1145/321978.321991
20. Fischer, M.J., Ladner, R.E.: Propositional dynamic logic of regular programs. J. Comput. Syst. Sci. **18**(2), 194–211 (1979)
21. Fujita, M., Kono, S., Tanaka, H., Moto-oka, T.: Tokio: logic programming language based on temporal logic and its compilation to Prolog. In: Shapiro, E. (ed.) ICLP 1986. LNCS, vol. 225, pp. 695–709. Springer, Heidelberg (1986). https://doi.org/10.1007/3-540-16492-8_119
22. Fulton, N., Mitsch, S., Quesel, J.-D., Völp, M., Platzer, A.: KeYmaera X: an axiomatic tactical theorem prover for hybrid systems. In: Felty, A.P., Middeldorp, A. (eds.) CADE 2015. LNCS (LNAI), vol. 9195, pp. 527–538. Springer, Cham (2015). https://doi.org/10.1007/978-3-319-21401-6_36
23. Gelfond, M., Lifschitz, V.: The stable model semantics for logic programming. In: Kowalski, R.A., Bowen, K.A. (eds.) Logic Programming, Proceedings of the

Fifth International Conference and Symposium, Seattle, Washington, USA, 15–19 August 1988 (2 Volumes), pp. 1070–1080. MIT Press (1988)

24. Harel, D., Kozen, D., Tiuryn, J.: Dynamic logic. ACM SIGACT News **32**(1), 66–69 (2001)
25. Hill, B., Poggiolesi, F.: A contraction-free and cut-free sequent calculus for propositional dynamic logic. Stud. Logica. **94**(1), 47–72 (2010). https://doi.org/10.1007/S11225-010-9224-Z
26. Hoare, C.A.R.: An axiomatic basis for computer programming. Commun. ACM **12**(10), 576–580 (1969)
27. Kamide, N.: Strong normalization of program-indexed lambda calculus (2010)
28. Kong, L., Mamouras, K.: StreamQL: a query language for processing streaming time series. Proc. ACM Program. Lang. **4**(OOPSLA), 183:1–183:32 (2020). https://doi.org/10.1145/3428251
29. Li, W.: Formal verification of the winning strategies of pursuit-evasion games. Technical report (2022). Master's thesis
30. Marek, V.W., Truszczyński, M.: Stable models and an alternative logic programming paradigm. In: Apt, K.R., Marek, V.W., Truszczynski, M., Warren, D.S. (eds.) The Logic Programming Paradigm. Artificial Intelligence, pp. 375–398. Springer, Hidelberg (1999). https://doi.org/10.1007/978-3-642-60085-2_17
31. Martens, C., Simmons, R.J., Arntzenius, M.: Finite-choice logic programming. Proc. ACM Program. Lang. **9**(POPL), 362–390 (2025). https://doi.org/10.1145/3704849
32. Miller, D.: Overview of linear logic programming. Linear Logic Comput. Sci. **316**, 119–150 (2004)
33. Miller, D.: A survey of the proof-theoretic foundations of logic programming. Theory Pract. Log. Program. **22**(6), 859–904 (2022). https://doi.org/10.1017/S1471068421000533
34. Miller, D., Nadathur, G., Pfenning, F., Scedrov, A.: Uniform proofs as a foundation for logic programming. Ann. Pure Appl. Log. **51**(1–2), 125–157 (1991). https://doi.org/10.1016/0168-0072(91)90068-W
35. Moszkowski, B.C.: Executing Temporal Logic Programs. Cambridge University Press (1986)
36. Muggleton, S., De Raedt, L.: Inductive logic programming: theory and methods. J. Log. Program. **19**, 629–679 (1994)
37. Nguyen, L.A.: Multimodal logic programming. Theor. Comput. Sci. **360**(1–3), 247–288 (2006). https://doi.org/10.1016/J.TCS.2006.03.026
38. Nguyen, L.A.: On the deterministic Horn fragment of test-free PDL. Adv. Modal Logic **6**, 373–392 (2006)
39. Niemelä, I.: Logic programs with stable model semantics as a constraint programming paradigm. Ann. Math. Artif. Intell. **25**(3), 241–273 (1999)
40. Nishimura, H.: Semantical analysis of constructive PDL. Publ. Res. Inst. Math. Sci. **18**(2), 847–858 (1982)
41. Oda, Y.: A study of cut-elimination for a non-labelled cyclic proof system for propositional dynamic logics. arXiv preprint arXiv:2512.15075 (2025)
42. Olmedo-Aguirre, J.O., Morales-Luna, G.: A dynamic logic-based modal Prolog. In: 2012 11th Mexican International Conference on Artificial Intelligence, pp. 3–8. IEEE (2012)
43. Orgun, M.A., Ma, W.: An overview of temporal and modal logic programming. In: Gabbay, D.M., Ohlbach, H.J. (eds.) ICTL 1994. LNCS, vol. 827, pp. 445–479. Springer, Heidelberg (1994). https://doi.org/10.1007/BFb0014004

44. Parikh, R.: The completeness of propositional dynamic logic. In: Winkowski, J. (ed.) MFCS 1978. LNCS, vol. 64, pp. 403–415. Springer, Heidelberg (1978). https://doi.org/10.1007/3-540-08921-7_88
45. Parikh, R.: The logic of games and its applications. In: North-Holland Mathematics Studies, vol. 102, pp. 111–139. Elsevier (1985)
46. Platzer, A.: Uniform substitution at one fell swoop. In: Fontaine, P. (ed.) CADE 2019. LNCS (LNAI), vol. 11716, pp. 425–441. Springer, Cham (2019). https://doi.org/10.1007/978-3-030-29436-6_25
47. Pratt, V.R.: Semantical considerations on Floyd-Hoare logic. In: 17th Annual Symposium on Foundations of Computer Science (SFCS), pp. 109–121. IEEE (1976)
48. Pratt, V.R.: A practical decision method for propositional dynamic logic (preliminary report). In: Proceedings of the Tenth Annual ACM Symposium on Theory of Computing, pp. 326–337 (1978)
49. Rondogiannis, P., Wadge, W.W.: Minimum model semantics for logic programs with negation-as-failure. ACM Trans. Comput. Log. **6**(2), 441–467 (2005). https://doi.org/10.1145/1055686.1055694
50. Sipser, M.: Introduction to the theory of computation. ACM SIGACT News **27**(1), 27–29 (1996)
51. Soulé, R., et al.: Merlin: a language for managing network resources. IEEE/ACM Trans. Netw. **26**(5), 2188–2201 (2018). https://doi.org/10.1109/TNET.2018.2867239
52. Wansing, H.: Displaying the modal logic of consistency. J. Symb. Log. **64**(4), 1573–1590 (1999). https://doi.org/10.2307/2586798
53. Wijesekera, D., Nerode, A.: Tableaux for constructive concurrent dynamic logic. Ann. Pure Appl. Logic **135**(1–3), 1–72 (2005)

Breccia: A Functional DSL Compiled to Egglog for Test Input Generation

Peter Boyland[1](✉), Sarah Canto Hyatt[1], Kyle Dewey[2], and Ben Hardekopf[1]

[1] University of California Santa Barbara, Santa Barbara, CA 93106, USA
boyland@ucsb.edu

[2] California State University Northridge, Northridge, CA 91330, USA

Abstract. Some prominent efforts within fuzz testing to automatically generate test inputs with complex invariants (e.g., well-typed programs for fuzzing compilers) have exploited logical satisfaction, such as using Prolog to describe constraints and generate satisfying instances. However, using Prolog has met with resistance from the community due to the difficulty of writing Prolog descriptions with acceptable performance. We propose an alternative logic programming-based approach: Datalog. While Datalog improves on the "effective programmability" of Prolog, it has its own issues: it is less expressive than Prolog, its bottom-up evaluation strategy requires keeping all generated terms in memory, and while it is easier to program effective generators in Datalog than Prolog, it still requires a specific style and has hidden pitfalls (such as bounding). We introduce Breccia, a functional DSL for generating objects with complex invariants that compiles to Egglog, a Datalog language extended with equality saturation. We show that Breccia is expressive enough to describe interesting objects such as well-typed programs with non-trivial type systems, and that equality saturation can greatly improve the performance of the resulting Egglog generator. We compare Breccia against Prolog implementations of similar generators in order to understand the tradeoffs involved.

Keywords: Generation · Prolog · Datalog · Equality Saturation · Fuzzing

1 Introduction

The problem that we address in this paper is test input generation for fuzzing systems under test. While some systems can be profitably fuzzed using random bitstrings as inputs [27], others require inputs satisfying complex constraints. For example, if fuzzing a compiler, it is unlikely that a randomly-generated bitstring is a syntactically valid and well-typed program, and such programs are needed to test deeper compiler components. One way to generate inputs satisfying constraints is to treat generation as a logic satisfiability problem, encoding input constraints as SAT or SMT formulas [26,36] or Prolog programs [11,13–15].

M. Sperber and E. Komendantskaya (Eds.): FLOPS 2026, LNCS 16533, pp. 77–99, 2026.
https://doi.org/10.1007/978-981-92-0184-6_3

Our attention is on the last strategy: writing Prolog programs to check if constraints on an input hold, and then running the program "backwards" to generate inputs satisfying those constraints. This is a theoretically elegant solution; for example, we can write a typechecker in Prolog and use it both to typecheck existing programs or create new ones. However, the reality is unfortunately not so elegant. Prolog's execution model is very sensitive to how programs are written, including constraint order and how constraints are described. Directly transcribing systems of constraints (like type systems) into Prolog is unlikely to create a usable generator; the program is more likely to run infinitely without generating any satisfying terms. In practice, writing Prolog-based generators requires in-depth reasoning about the input domain being generated, and Prolog programs must be carefully designed and optimized in ways that make generators look and behave very differently from acceptors. This issue has given Prolog a reputation for being difficult to use for test input generation [3,6,19].

In this paper we investigate a different approach to using logic programming for test input generation: using Datalog rather than Prolog. Datalog's bottom-up evaluation strategy (as opposed to Prolog's top-down strategy) means that it is much less sensitive to how a program is written. Datalog also features a fixpoint semantics wherein all satisfying terms and subterms are kept in memory, avoiding recomputation if any subterm is needed again. Even simple fuzzing problems reuse subterms, and memoization dramatically improves fuzzer performance [12,22]. With Datalog, this memoization is transparent and fully automatic. Of course, Datalog is also less expressive than Prolog, leading to our first research question: **RQ1: is Datalog expressive enough to describe interesting, non-trivial constraints for test input generation?**

Datalog's fixpoint semantics is a double-edged sword, because it requires all terms to be kept in memory. This contrasts with Prolog, whose depth-first search strategy means that as satisfying terms are computed, they can be output and then "forgotten", without consuming further memory. Our answer to this problem is to use *e-graphs* [29], as used in *equality saturation* [38], to store computed terms. E-graphs are a data structure for compactly storing congruence classes, and we exploit their capabilities to address Datalog's higher memory usage. In fact, e-graphs can do more than just reduce memory consumption: by defining congruence classes specific to the domain being generated, we should be able to significantly improve the generation rate. For example, if generating well-typed programs, we could define types as congruence classes so that all `int`-typed expressions are considered equivalent. If some expression e_1 uses an `int`-typed subexpression e_2, then our generator only needs to generate e_1 using the `int` congruence class rather than all expressions in that congruence class. This approach leads to our second research question: **RQ2: Can e-graphs and equality saturation significantly improve the performance of a Datalog-based generator?**

While Datalog is easier to use than Prolog for describing generators, Datalog still requires a rather particular style to transcribe constraints into programs. Datalog has pitfalls that can be easy to fall into, such as properly bounding generation to ensure termination. To address this issue we follow other work that has created domain-specific functional languages that compile to Datalog [30]. In our case, we have designed *Breccia*: a functional DSL for writing constraint-based generators. Breccia compiles to Egglog [42], a Datalog implementation that incorporates e-graphs and equality saturation. The compilation to Egglog automatically ensures bounding and inserts proper uses of equality saturation, based on the Breccia description.

Both the Prolog and Breccia generators that we investigate are *bounded exhaustive* generators, that is, they confine themselves to a finite subset of the infinite space of possible terms and fully explore that finite space. Bounded exhaustive generation relies on the *small scope hypothesis* [21], which states that a high percentage of bugs can be revealed by exploring all test inputs within some small scope (e.g., bounded by size of input). To compare the Prolog and Breccia generators, we investigate their respective generation rates and also run a mini-fuzzing campaign on three of our example languages to demonstrate their ability to detect bugs.

In the remainder of this paper we:

- Describe how to use Datalog for test input generation (Sect. 2);
- Describe how to optimize Datalog generation using e-graphs (Sect. 3);
- Describe the Breccia generator DSL and compiler (Sect. 4);
- Evaluate Breccia by comparing it against Prolog-based generators for a series of statically-typed languages including simply-typed lambda calculus, System F, and Featherweight Java (Sect. 5);
- Discuss various related works (Sect. 7).

The Breccia implementation and all generators used in the evaluation are available at https://github.com/pllab/breccia.

2 Generation Using Datalog

Datalog[1] generation is a good fit for constraints that are *compositional*, i.e., a term's constraint-satisfaction depends only on its subterms and how it composes them. For example, type systems are defined using inductive rules over the AST, such that a term's well-typedness depends on the types of its subterms and how they are composed into a new term. Other possible good fits include sorted lists, binary search trees, red-black trees, heaps, and B-trees [13,22,35]. On the other hand, non-compositional problems, such as generating specific integers or bitstrings matching some user-specified criteria, would be a poor fit, as would any problem with an unpredictable global context. We will illustrate Datalog generation using the running example of the simply-typed lambda calculus (STLC) [7]; see Fig. 1a for its abstract syntax and Fig. 1b for its typing rules. We

[1] We assume a modern version of Datalog extending the original definition [5] with features like algebraic datatypes (e.g., Egglog [42]). This added expressiveness comes at the cost of possible non-termination; the programmer must ensure termination.

incrementally build a Datalog generator for well-typed STLC terms in the rest of this section.[2] We demonstrate that this process is straightforward, though it requires some extra bookkeeping. While STLC is simple, our evaluation (Sect. 5) shows that more complex type systems can be handled similarly.

$$\begin{aligned} \tau \in \mathit{Type} &::= \iota \mid \tau \to \tau \\ e \in \mathit{Exp} &::= x \in \mathit{Var} \\ &\mid \lambda x{:}\tau \,.\, e \\ &\mid e_1\ e_2 \end{aligned}$$

(a) Syntax (where ι is some base type).

$$\frac{\Gamma(x) = \tau}{\Gamma \vdash x : \tau}\ \text{VAR} \qquad \frac{\Gamma[x \mapsto \tau_1] \vdash e : \tau_2}{\Gamma \vdash \lambda x{:}\tau_1 \,.\, e : \tau_1 \to \tau_2}\ \text{ABS} \qquad \frac{\Gamma \vdash e_1 : \tau_1 \to \tau_2 \qquad \Gamma \vdash e_2 : \tau_1}{\Gamma \vdash e_1\ e_2 : \tau_2}\ \text{APP}$$

(b) Typing (where $\Gamma : \mathit{Var} \to \mathit{Type}$).

Fig. 1. Simply-Typed λ-Calculus

2.1 Generation Strategy

We begin by defining datatypes for the terms being generated; for STLC this is `Type` (Fig. 2) and `Exp` (Fig. 3). We deviate from the formal definition by associating each variable with its type explicitly, making generation easier as (1) we do not need to track the context Γ; and (2) since we generate terms bottom-up, variables are effectively used before being declared, so they must have known types. Variable names are represented with integers instead of strings.

```
datatype Type =
| Base
| Arr(Type, Type)
```

Fig. 2. STLC Types

```
datatype Exp =
| Var(Int, Type)
| Abs(Var, Exp)
| App(Exp, Exp)
```

Fig. 3. STLC Expressions

The general strategy for a Datalog generator is to start with the base cases of an inductive definition and then build larger, more complex terms while ensuring that each new term satisfies the required contraints. Each base case is an initial fact, and each inductive case is a rule taking existing terms and building bigger terms. We start with types and defining the predicate `type` : `Type`, i.e., `type` will be a Datalog relation stating that its argument is a well-defined STLC type per Fig. 2. According to Fig. 2, `Base` is a well-formed type, giving us our initial fact `type(Base)`. Also from Fig. 2, if `type(t1)` and `type(t2)`, then `type(Arr(t1,t2))`, giving us a rule composing types into larger types.

[2] The description is abstracted for space; see Appendix A for the full code listing.

For types we only need well-formedness, but for terms we need both well-formedness and well-typedness. The typing judgement defined in Fig. 1b is expressed with a predicate `well-typed` : `Exp` × `Type`; note that since we explicitly associate each variable with its type we do not need the Γ argument, so the Datalog relation `well-typed` only takes an STLC expression and its type. The base case is VAR, so the rule is that if `i` is an integer and `type(t)` then `well-typed(Var(i,t), t)`; that is, the type of some variable `i` associated with type `t` is `t`. Thus each generated type has some number of variables associated with it.

Finally, we translate the ABS and APP rules to build larger well-typed terms. For ABS, the rule is that if `well-typed(Var(i,t1),t1)` and `well-typed(e, t2)`, then `well-typed(Abs(Var(i,t1),e), Arr(t1,t2))`. For APP, the rule is that if `well-typed(e1,Arr(t1,t2))` and `well-typed(e2,t2)`, then `well-typed( App(e1,e2),t2)`. With these rules, we can generate an unbounded number of well-typed STLC terms.

The translation from the typing rules to Datalog was straightforward, but inexact: typing is usually top-down (i.e., starting from the AST root), while generation is bottom-up (starting from the AST leaves). Accommodating the difference requires some mechanical changes during the translation.

2.2 Tracking Extra Information

The generator described in the prior subsection generates both open terms (i.e., containing free variables) and closed terms (i.e., with no free variables). It also allows for abstractions with unused parameters. For the sake of example, if we wish to only generate closed terms using all parameters, then we must track the free variables in a term. Doing so is again straightforward: we change `well-typed`'s signature to `well-typed` : `Exp`×`Type`×`Freelist`, where `Freelist` is a list of `Var`. This signature states that the given expression has the given type and contains the given free variables.

We modify the base VAR rule to be `well-typed(Var(i,t),t,[Var(i,t)])`. We modify the `abs` rule to require the parameter `Var(i,t)` to be contained in the body's free variables, and the freelist of the resulting term is the original freelist without the parameter. The APP rule leaves the freelist as-is. Our overall output is `output` : `Exp` × `Type`, where if `well-typed(e,t,[])`, then `output(e,t)`; this thus only outputs closed terms. While tracking this additional information is straightforward, it is not as simple as it may seem; we need helpers for updating tracked information (e.g., adding/removing variables to/from freelists, and checking if a variable is contained within) that entail a lot of boilerplate. To see this boilerplate, we can compare the STLC Datalog generator in Appendix A (that does not track any of this information) with the STLC Datalog generator created by compiling the accompanying artifact's Breccia STLC generator into Datalog, and note all the additional functions required to implement freelists and operations on freelists.

2.3 Bounding Generation

The generator in the prior subsection generates an unbounded number of well-typed closed terms. To ensure termination, we must make the term space finite via bounds. For STLC, unboundedness appears in variables (due to integers) and in types and terms (due to arbitrary sizes). To bound variables, VAR is modified to require that `i` must be a member of a fixed finite set. To bound types and terms, we modify all rules to enforce the term/type size to be $< k$ for some fixed k. Varying these bounds independently from each other explores different parts of the generation space. These modifications are again straightforward, but entail yet more boilerplate.

3 E-Graphs and Equality Saturation

The Datalog generator from Sect. 2 creates large sets of facts representing generated terms, and they must all be present in memory simultaneously for bottom-up generation to work correctly. Since the search space contains billions of terms even after bounding, this is concerning. To address this concern, we turn to e-graphs and equality saturation. We begin with a brief overview of these two concepts and then discuss how we can make use of them in a Datalog generator.

3.1 Background

An *e-graph* is a compact structure for representing congruence classes [29]; it has been applied to automated theorem proving [34] and to the *equality saturation* [38] technique. Equality saturation starts with a set of rewrite rules from terms to equivalent terms, and a set of initial terms stored in an e-graph. From there, the current terms in the e-graph are matched against the left-hand sides of the rewrite rules, and any rules that apply are used to rewrite matched terms to new terms. The new terms are then added to the e-graph by *unifying* them with the original terms they were derived from.[3] This process repeats until a fixpoint is reached.

This idea has obvious parallels with Datalog semantics, and Egglog [42] was created to combine Datalog and equality saturation. Egglog implements the fact database using e-graphs. Egglog rules can specify in their conclusion that two terms should be considered equivalent, and the e-graph will represent this fact efficiently. Egglog conditions and rules apply to congruence classes of terms instead of individual terms, greatly speeding up the processing of equivalent terms.

[3] Egglog's unification is a directive saying the given terms are equivalent no matter what they are, and cannot fail. This differs from Prolog's unification, which enforces equality constraints, and fails on syntactically distinct terms.

3.2 Application to Generation

By defining equivalences between generated terms, we can exploit Egglog to optimize generation. Doing so is trivial: we add a single rule per equivalence relation stating that any two matching terms are equivalent. The question is what terms to make equivalent, which must be determined on a per-generator basis. For STLC and other statically-typed languages, the obvious choice is to define two terms of the same type to be equivalent. For STLC, this means adding a rule saying that if `well-typed(e1,t)` and `well-typed(e2,t)`, then `e1` $\equiv$ `e2`. Generators for other kinds of terms can define their own equivalences; for example, when generating red-black trees we could consider all trees with the same height and root color to be equivalent.

4 Breccia Design and Compilation

Datalog generators require lots of boilerplate to track required information and bound generated terms. To address this, we designed Breccia: a functional DSL that compiles to Egglog. Here we describe Breccia and how it is compiled.

4.1 The Breccia Language

We illustrate Breccia by using it to implement our running STLC example; a complete formal syntax of Breccia is in Appendix B. We begin by defining bounds as integer ranges:

```
bound TSize = 1..5
bound VarInt = 1..2
bound ESize = 1..10
```

`TSize`, `VarInt`, and `ESize` are types describing integer values within the given ranges. We next define the STLC datatypes, using mostly standard syntax. Keyword `bounded_by` specifies a bound on datatype instances, and `tracking` is used to associate some additional information with each datatype instance.

```
datatype Type bounded_by (sz: TSize) tracking () = {
  Base | Arr(Type, Type)  }

datatype Freelist = { Nil | Cons(VarInt, Type, Freelist) }

datatype Exp bounded_by (sz:ESize) tracking (fv:Freelist,ty:Type) = {
  Var(VarInt, Type) | Lam(Type, VarInt, Exp) | App(Term, Term) }
```

A `Type` is bounded by `TSize`, and does not track anything (the `tracking` keyword is still needed). Given a `Type` instance `ty`, its size can be accessed using `ty.sz`. A `Freelist` is an auxiliary (not exhaustively generated) unbounded structure which tracks no additional information because it is auxiliary. An `Exp` is bounded by `ESize` and tracks (i.e., associates) both the list of free variables in the given expression and the expression's type; given a Exp named e its tracked information can be acessed using e.sz, e.fv, and e.ty.

For the bounded datatypes being generated (Type and Exp), we must define how to compute bounds:

```
def Type.bound -> TSize = { self match {
  Base() => 1 | Arr(t1, t2) => 1 + t1.sz + t2.sz }}

def Exp.bound -> ESize = { self match {
  Var(_,_) => 1 | Lam(_,_,e) => 1 + e.sz |
  App(e1, e2) => 1 + e1.sz + e2.sz }}
```

Such bound definitions need only be defined once and the compiler will insert bounds checks wherever needed, i.e., whenever the generator attempts to build a Type or Exp, the compiler will insert a call to the appropriate bound function and check that the resulting term does not exceed the bound. We must also define helper functions to manipulate the auxiliary freelist; these are standard functional definitions for dealing with lists; see fv_contains, fv_remove, and fv_append in the accompanying Breccia code examples.

Now we can define the actual generators for Type and Exp. The '#' prepending Type and Exp allow tracked information to be accessed:

```
generator base_ty() -> #Type = { Base tracking () }

generator arr_ty(t1: #Type, t2: #Type) -> #Type = {
  Arr(t1, t2) tracking ()  }

generator var(id: VarInt, ty: #Type) -> #Exp = {
  Var(id, ty) tracking (fv: Cons(id, ty, Nil()), ty: ty) }

generator lam(ty: #Type, id: VarInt, e: #Exp) -> #Exp = {
  if (fv_contains(e.fv, id, ty)) {
    let new_fv = fv_remove(e.fv, id, ty)
    Lam(ty, id, e) tracking (fv: new_fv, ty: Arr(ty, e.ty))
  }}

generator app(e1: #Exp, e2: #Exp) -> #Exp = {
  filter e1.ty is Arr(t1, t2)
  if (t1 == e2.ty) {
    App(e1, e2) tracking (fv: fv_append(e1.fv, e2.fv), ty: t2)
  }}
```

A generator takes existing terms and bounds, and potentially checks that some criteria holds on them using if (e.g., lam and app) and filter (e.g., app). Helper functions are used to check and manipulate tracked information. Generators can either silently fail (resulting in no new terms), or generate a new term with some specific tracked information. Bounding is implicit, with checks inserted by the compiler based on the bounding definitions (e.g., Type.bound and Exp.bound). We must also indicate which terms should be unified, and when:

```
unify (e1 e2 : #Exp) when { e1.ty == e2.ty && e1.size == e2.size}
```

There is no main entry point to the program; generators are applied when facts matching their parameters are generated. Bounds parameters such as VarInt are generated automatically.

4.2 Compiling to Egglog

Breccia datatypes are translated almost one-to-one into Egglog datatypes, minus the bounded_by and tracking annotations. The tracking information is compiled into a predicate specific to that datatype, associating each instance of that datatype with its tracked information; accessing tracked information via dot notation (e.g., e.ty) compiles into an access of the associated argument position of that predicate. Bounds declarations (e.g., bound VarInt 1..2) are translated into a series of facts stating that each value in the range is valid (e.g., (VarInt 1) and (VarInt 2)). Functions (def s) and function calls are compiled using the strategy from Pacak et al. [30], wherein return values are lifted to be parameters in Prolog style; we refer the reader to that paper for details. The unify directive is compiled into a rule whose conditions are derived from its body and whose conclusion unifies the relevant terms.

Each generator is translated into a control-flow tree (CFT) such that each non-failure execution path in the generator becomes a path from the CFT root to one of its leaves; the Breccia syntax disallows paths to converge, guaranteeing a tree. Each parameter of a bound type (e.g., id : VarInt in lam) is translated into a condition at the CFT root (e.g., (VarInt id)), ensuring that the translated Egglog rules will be instantiated with each possible value of the bound.

Internal CFT nodes consist of binding operators (let, filter, match) or function calls. An if expression is expanded to let x = guard; match x {...} before being translated into the CFT, where x is a fresh variable and guard is a boolean-valued expression. A binding node for some variable x to some $\langle pattern \rangle$ translates into an Egglog condition "$x = \langle pattern \rangle$". When generating conditions, we consider a single path in the CFT, thus $\langle pattern \rangle$ is only one branch of a match expression; filter is essentially a match with only one branch. Each function call node results in an Egglog rule per Pacak et al. [30], along with a condition on the return value; the rule also collects the conditions of all binding and call nodes along the path from the CFT root to the current call node.

CFT leaves are datatype constructor calls, i.e., newly-generated terms. Each leaf results in an Egglog rule whose conditions are collected from all binding and call nodes from the CFT root to the leaf, and whose conclusion is a variant of the newly-generated term. Leaves generating a datatype <T> actually conclude with a constructor call to a datatype <T>Valid, which has the same arguments as the <T> being generated. We use <T>Valid in order to insert bounds checks using the user-provided `T.bound` function. The relevant `T.bound` function is called with the `<T>Valid` value to see if the result is valid for that bound. If it is, then we create a <T>-value from the arguments of the `<T>Valid` value, i.e., we create the desired term specified by the generator.

4.3 Optimizing Compilation

A naive implementation of the compiler creates many unnecessary rules and suboptimal conditions. We apply several optimizations during compilation in order to improve the resulting Egglog program:

Eliminate Trivial Conditions. Trivially-satisfied conditions are deleted. For trivially-unsatisfied conditions we prune the containing subtree, avoiding the generation of rules that would never fire.

Copy Propagation. If a variable x is bound to e and used exactly once, then e can be inlined wherever x was used, reducing the number of variables required.

Prune Bounds Checks. If a generation function always increases a given bound (which is often the case) then we can aggressively filter out candidate generations that would definitely violate the bounds. We insert a condition that checks if the input terms have bounds such that the generated component must violate its bounds, and if so fail immediately rather than generating the new object and then rejecting it after the fact.

Collapse Independent Calls. Two function calls are *independent* if the arguments of one call do not depend on the return value of the other. Sequential independent calls in a CFT are combined into a single rule during compilation instead of making a separate rule for each of them. This optimization reduces the number of rules as well as the size of the rules associated with the later calls.

5 Evaluation

5.1 Answering the Research Questions

The two research questions posed in Sect. 1 were:

- **RQ1: is Datalog expressive enough to describe interesting, non-trivial constraints for test input generation?**
- **RQ2: Can e-graphs and equality saturation significantly improve the performance of a Datalog-based generator?**

To answer RQ1, we implement generators for five different statically-typed languages in Breccia: STLC [7], the simply-typed lambda calculus; System F [17,33] (SysF) which adds parametric polymorphism to STLC; Featherweight Java [20] (FJ-cast), an object-oriented language with subtype polymorphism;

an alternate version of Featherweight Java that removes casting[4] (FJ-nocast); and an alternative version of Featherweight Java that replaces subtype polymorphism with generics (FJ-gen). These languages explore a range of realistic type system features and demonstrate that Breccia can encode them all. The language implementations are available with the Breccia code.

To answer RQ2, we evaluate the generation rate of our Breccia implementations both with equality saturation ("union") and without ("no union", i.e., just Datalog), using types as equivalence classes in all cases.[5] We also implement generators for all five languages in Prolog in order to get a sense of the relative performance between Prolog and Datalog generation.

Comparing the Breccia and Prolog generators directly is difficult. Breccia generates terms bottom-up in contrast to Prolog's top-down, necessitating different generation algorithms for Breccia and Prolog. We must somehow bound the state space of these algorithms to ensure a finite space of generated programs, and because these algorithms are necessarily different, different components end up needing bounds. For example, the Breccia-based generators separately bound the sizes of types and expressions, as both of these must be built up separately in a bottom-up fashion. However, the Prolog-based generators tightly couple the generation of types and expressions, necessitating only a single bound. Therefore the comparison is not "apples to apples", and is only presented to give a rough idea of their relative performance.

All generators needed multiple bounds, leading to a many-dimensional state space which is difficult to comprehensively evaluate. Within a generation strategy (Breccia or Prolog), we selected bounds such that only one specific bound was varied at a time relative to another data point; this gives a glimpse into the effect of each specific bound on the state space. We also attempted to select bounds that would explore different parts of the state space, leading to different sets of generated programs which looked relatively different.

Breccia results are shown in Table 1 (STLC and SysF), Table 2 (FJ-cast and FJ-nocast), and Table 3 (FJ-gen); we use tables instead of graphs as the results vary wildly in magnitude. The generation rates for STLC and SysF (Table 1) reach as high as billions of terms per second. On the slower end, FJ-cast and FJ-nocast (Table 2) are generally dozens per second, with FJ-gen in between. In all cases, Datalog successfully generates many terms with complex invariants, and does so at least sufficiently fast for fuzzing, leading us to conclude that RQ1 is true. Furthermore, in all cases, equality saturation improves the generation rate, with STLC and SysF (Table 1) seeing even orders of magnitude improvements; this leads us to conclude that RQ2 is also true. Altogether, generation rates and equality saturation's effectiveness vary significantly. There is another surprising

[4] Casting makes every type trivially inhabitable, significantly changing the space of valid progams, and making well-typed program generation far simpler.

[5] Results were obtained on an AWS EC2 m5.2xlarge instance (8 vCPUs, Intel Xeon Platinum 8175M @ 2.50GHz, 32 GB RAM) running Ubuntu 24.04 (kernel 6.14.0-1015-aws). Experiments were run 10 times, the highest and lowest results were discarded, and the remaining were averaged.

Table 1. Breccia generation rates (#terms/s) for STLC and SysF; the other columns specify the bounds used. Bound (6-2-9) for STLC union is highlighted as it is unusually slow compared to the other STLC union results.

type size	# vars	expr size	STLC union	STLC no union	SysF # type vars	SysF union	SysF no union
3	2	10	12.7m	132.1k	2	94.7b	414.8k
4	2	14	1.9b	536.3k	2	2996.6b	335.2k
5	2	10	2.5m	209.0k	1	2.7b	258.2k
6	2	9	415.4k	129.9k	2	89.1m	124.2k
6	2	10	2.5m	210.6k	5	192.9k	13.2k
6	2	12	55.4m	309.3k	2	391.2m	276.4k
6	2	15	4.5b	236.0k	2	564.5m	302.2k
6	5	10	168.8m	168.6k	2	85.4m	39.7k
9	2	10	3.4m	518.3k	2	3.3k	2.9k

observation: within STLC union, bound (6-2-9) is notably slower than others; the relevant row is highlighted in Table 1. The next row shows that the greater STLC bound (6-2-10) is faster, as is SysF, despite these being more complex. To explain why, we also look at generation rate over time (Fig. 4).

Figure 4 takes a representative sample of languages and bounds, and plots their generation rate over time. Time is on the x-axis, the number of generated terms is on the y-axis, and both are log scale. The log scale is because, in an unbounded space, generators produce exponentially more terms as the bound linearly increases; this follows directly from terms being recursively defined. At log scale, we thus expect to see straight lines for unbounded spaces. The lines for STLC (6-2-15) and SysF (2-3-2-10) roughly follow this pattern, while the others all plateau at some point, some faster than others. In particular, STLC (6-2-9) and FJ-cast plateau quickly, and FJ-gen also plateaus but later than others.

Multiple bounds are used for each language, describing a multi-dimensional space. We hypothesize that the bounds are interacting with generation in interesting and unpredictable ways. In particular, we may reach a point where most existing terms, if used as components to generate a new term, will cause the new term to violate the bounds and be discarded; thus only a small number of valid new terms may be generated at each step, greatly slowing the generation rate. This would at least partially explain the poor performance of the FJ generators vs. STLC, as by having many more bounding parameters, the FJ generators would have many more opportunities to hit this issue. If and when this happens, and whether the slow-down is gradual or quick, is a function of the bounds and the space being explored. Characterizing this behavior is an interesting question to explore in future work.

We also briefly look at the generation rates for Prolog, shown in Table 4 (STLC and SysF), Table 5 (FJ-cast and FJ-nocast), and Table 6 (FJ-gen). Prolog, due to its top-down generation strategy, outputs terms and then discards

Table 2. Breccia generation rates (#terms/s) for FJ-nocast and FJ-cast; the other columns specify the bounds used.

language	# classes	# fields	class ids	var ids	expr size	num meth	# args	# vars	class depth	union rate	no union rate
FJ-nocast	2	2	2	2	5	6	2	2	2	14.5	9.2
	2	2	2	2	6	1	2	2	2	54.7	17.0
	2	2	2	2	9	1	2	2	2	53.6	29.0
	2	2	2	2	12	1	2	2	2	53.3	28.7
	2	6	2	2	5	2	2	2	2	113.4	21.3
	3	2	2	2	6	2	2	2	1	172.6	11.3
	3	2	2	2	6	2	2	2	3	113.2	21.8
	3	2	4	4	7	2	3	4	2	17.4	9.1
	4	3	3	3	6	3	4	3	3	16.7	14.8
	6	2	3	2	5	2	2	2	3	74.0	16.8
FJ-cast	2	2	2	2	5	6	2	2	2	36.1	31.8
	2	2	2	2	6	1	2	2	2	81.2	73.5
	2	2	2	2	9	1	2	2	2	82.3	71.2
	2	2	2	2	12	1	2	2	2	76.8	73.4
	2	6	2	2	5	2	2	2	2	53.5	48.7
	3	2	2	2	6	2	2	2	1	81.3	71.9
	3	2	2	2	6	2	2	2	3	52.0	49.9
	3	2	4	4	7	2	3	4	2	76.1	78.6
	4	3	3	3	6	3	4	3	3	85.3	44.1
	6	2	3	2	5	2	2	2	3	106.7	53.9

Table 3. Breccia generation rates (#terms/s) for FJ-gen; the other columns specify the bounds used.

# classes	# fields	class ids	var ids	expr size	num meth	# args	# vars	class depth	# class vars	union rate	no union rate
2	2	2	2	5	6	2	2	2	2	76.5	35.0
2	2	2	2	6	1	2	2	2	2	2.5k	379.1
2	2	2	2	9	1	2	2	2	2	2.5k	384.9
2	2	2	2	12	1	2	2	2	2	2.5k	379.7
2	6	2	2	5	2	2	2	2	2	23.5	55.8
3	2	2	2	6	2	2	2	1	2	70.8	177.9
3	2	2	2	6	2	2	2	3	2	19.7	5.8
3	2	4	4	7	2	3	4	2	2	87.7	30.2
4	3	3	3	6	3	4	3	3	2	103.0	35.8
6	2	3	2	5	2	2	2	3	2	51.8	19.8

them, whereas Datalog stores all generated terms in memory. As a point of interest, we investigated how much of the Prolog generation time was due to specifically to I/O, and include those numbers in the tables. That is, we measure both raw generation rate, as well as generation plus the cost to write programs to disk We see that Prolog generation is consistently orders of magnitude faster for FJ-nocast, FJ-cast, and FJ-gen (Tables 5 and 6 compared to Table 2), but orders of magnitude slower for STLC and SysF (Table 4 compared to Table 1)—however, we again must be wary of drawing conclusions due to the inherently different generation approach Prolog uses. The I/O cost of writing out terms is very large, but unavoidable in fuzzing using Prolog. The variance in generation rate across

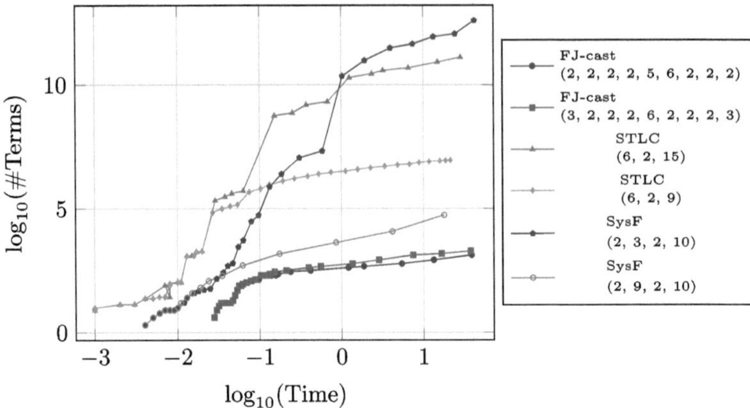

Fig. 4. Log Time (seconds) vs Log #Terms

the Prolog generators is much lower than it is for Breccia; we hypothesize this is because bounding issues are a well-known issue with Prolog generation, and we specifically bounded the Prolog code so as to mitigate this issue.

Table 4. Prolog generation rates (#terms/s) for STLC and SysF; the other columns specify the bounds used. Bounds (4-3) and (5-3) were not measured for SysF.

init bound	# vars	STLC no IO	STLC with IO	SysF no IO	SysF with IO
4	3	357.9k	175.1k	/	/
5	3	351.6k	162.5k	/	/
5	5	354.3k	163.3k	99.6k	60.9k
6	3	346.9k	152.0k	94.4k	54.0k
7	7	340.5k	141.7k	85.9k	53.1k
9	3	328.0k	126.0k	71.6k	42.8k
9	9	323.4k	125.7k	76.4k	47.4k
11	11	312.1k	112.9k	69.8k	43.6k
13	3	305.3k	103.5k	53.8k	33.8k

Table 5. Prolog generation rates (#terms/s) for FJ-nocast and FJ-cast; the other columns specify the bounds used.

language	# classes	# fields	num meth	# vars	term bound	no IO rate	with IO rate
FJ-nocast	2	4	2	4	3	365.7k	16.0k
	2	4	2	4	5	290.3k	14.6k
	2	4	2	4	8	314.9k	13.1k
	2	4	2	4	12	307.1k	11.6k
	2	4	2	12	5	378.6k	7.6k
	2	4	6	4	5	324.0k	7.5k
	2	12	2	4	5	305.9k	8.4k
	4	6	4	6	5	261.2k	4.1k
	6	4	2	4	5	128.0k	6.0k
FJ-cast	2	4	2	4	3	352.3k	15.1k
	2	4	2	4	5	307.1k	14.8k
	2	4	2	4	8	287.3k	12.5k
	2	4	2	4	12	284.0k	11.5k
	2	4	2	12	5	370.9k	8.7k
	2	4	6	4	5	295.5k	7.3k
	2	12	2	4	5	313.1k	8.5k
	4	6	4	6	5	197.9k	4.3k
	6	4	2	4	5	97.1k	5.5k

Table 6. Prolog generation rates (#terms/s) for FJ-gen; the other columns specify the bounds used.

# classes	# fields	num meth	NumParams	# type vars	ExpBound	TypeBound	no IO rate	with IO rate
2	2	5	1	1	3	6	71.0k	9.7k
3	2	2	1	1	3	6	83.8k	12.0k
3	2	5	1	1	3	6	59.5k	7.7k
3	2	5	1	1	3	8	62.0k	7.9k
3	4	5	1	1	3	6	60.9k	7.3k

5.2 A Mini-Fuzzing Campaign

To investigate the bug-finding capability of our generators we ran a mini-fuzzing campaign for two of our example languages: we chose STLC as a representative of functional languages and FJ-nocast as a representative of OOP languages. For STLC we implemented an interpreter, and for FJ-nocast we implemented a compiler (both with a type checker in the front-end). For each implementation we manually created a number of mutants, each with a different injected fault. We then selected a set of bounds and used the generated terms from both the Prolog and Breccia generators to fuzz the implementations, tracking how many of the injected faults were found. The results are shown in Table 7. We see that both the Prolog and Breccia generators find roughly the same number of bugs (the differences are because, again, the bounding strategies are different between Prolog and Breccia and so they aren't exploring exactly the same space of programs).

Table 7. Fuzzing Results.

Language Fuzzed	Generator w/bounds	#Faults found/Total faults
STLC	Breccia (7,3,2)	6 / 7
	Prolog (3,3)	7 / 7
FJ-nocast	Breccia (2,2,1,0,2,0,0,0,2)	14 / 14
	Prolog (2,1,1,1,1)	13 / 14

6 Limitations and Threats to Validity

All of the benchmarks presented in Sect. 5 deal with programs which are inherently compositional in nature (e.g., expressions contain subexpressions). We have not evaluated Breccia on non-compositional problems. Breccia's compositional nature is best suited to problems wherein it is straightforward to determine if a larger term is valid given some previously-generated valid subterms. Problems requiring state outside of a local group of terms are more challenging to encode, though not impossible, and likely have implications for performance.

Our evaluation does not consider dynamically-typed languages, though Breccia is applicable to such languages— ASTs are inherently compositional, and so syntactically valid programs in any language is doable in Breccia. Prior work using Prolog has generated JavaScript using a rudimentary type system to avoid uninteresting behavior [14], and Breccia can be used in the same way.

The bounds chosen in our evaluation were chosen to explore different parts of the state space of possible programs. However, we did not comprehensively search the space of possible bounds, making these choices somewhat arbitrary.

7 Related Work

7.1 Fuzzing Using Logic Programming Variants

Both Grygiel et al. [18] and Tarau [37] use Prolog to generate well-typed terms in the simply-typed lambda calculus [7]. However, this was for the purpose of studying properties of the terms and distributions over them, as opposed to using them for testing purposes. Dewey et al. [14] introduce the idea of using Prolog to generate programs for fuzzing. They later apply this idea to fuzzing Rust [15], student assignments [11], and a custom Scala-inspired language [10], as well as generating complex data structures with non-trivial invariants [13]. However, multiple works argue that Prolog-based fuzzing is too difficult to use, too limited, or too sensitive to optimizations to be widely applicable [3,6,19].

Luck [23] is a DSL for property-based testing [8], which has a semantics combining top-down Prolog-style backtracking with constraint solving. This semantics is exposed to the user through a functional interface, and users can work with concrete and symbolic data. Breccia, in contrast, performs bottom-up generation with equality saturation. Breccia's bottom-up nature imparts a very different approach to writing generators, and presents an arguably simpler interface, since user-exposed data is always concrete.

7.2 Functional Languages and Datalog

Pacak et al. [31] define a DSL for describing type systems which compiles to a Datalog-based incremental typechecker. Pacak et al. [30] later describe shortcomings in Datalog as a user-level programming language and use those shortcomings to motivate Functional IncA, a functional programming language with algebraic data types and sets that compiles to Datalog. Neither approach can be used for generating inputs based on constraints (including type systems). Other works, such as Flix [24,25], Datafun [2], Formulog [4], and Flan [1] either extend Datalog with functional language constructs or embed Datalog inside a functional language, usually designed for a specific purpose such as program analysis. Again, none of these languages support generating inputs based on constraints.

7.3 Equality Saturation and Egglog

Willsey et al. introduce Egg [40], a modern e-graph library for equality saturation. Zhang et al. introduce Egglog [42], which unifies Datalog and equality saturation into a single fixpoint reasoning system. Equality saturation has been applied across many domains [9,16,28,32,39,41]. None of these works apply equality saturation to the problem of input generation.

A Datalog Generator for Simply-Typed λ-Calculus

```
;; Simply-typed lambda calculus in egglog

;; Define types in STLC (Figure 2)
(datatype type
  (Base)                ;; Base type
  (Arr type type))      ;; Function type: t1 -> t2

;; Define expressions in STLC (Figure 3)
(datatype exp
  (Var i64 type)        ;; Variables: Var(Int, Type)
  (Abs exp exp)         ;; Lambda abstraction: Abs(Var, Exp)
  (App exp exp))        ;; Application: App(Exp, Exp)
```

```
;; Predicates for well-formedness and well-typedness
(relation type (type i64))           ;; type : Type, with size
(relation welltyped (exp type i64))  ;; well-typed : Exp x Type, with size

;; Bounds
(relation maxsize (i64))
(relation maxidx (i64))
(relation valididx (i64))

(maxsize 4)
(maxidx 1)

;; Generate valid variable indices
(valididx 1)
(rule
  ((valididx i) (maxidx m) (> m i))
  ((valididx (+ i 1))))

;; Base case: Base is a well-formed type
(type (Base) 1)

;; Inductive case: if type(t1) and type(t2), then type(Arr(t1,t2))
(rule
  ((maxsize m)
   (type t1 s1)
   (type t2 s2)
   (> m (+ s1 s2)))
  ((type (Arr t1 t2) (+ 1 (+ s1 s2)))))

;; Base case for var: if i is an integer and type(t),
;; then welltyped(Var(i,t), t)
(rule
  ((type t s) (valididx i))
  ((welltyped (Var i t) t 1)))

;; Rule for abs: if welltyped(Var(i,t1),t1) and welltyped(e,t2),
;; then welltyped(Abs(Var(i,t1),e), Arr(t1,t2))
(rule
  ((welltyped (Var i t1) t1 s1)
   (welltyped e t2 s2)
   (maxsize m)
   (> m (+ s1 s2)))
  ((welltyped (Abs (Var i t1) e) (Arr t1 t2) (+ 1 (+ s1 s2)))))

;; Rule for app: if welltyped(e1,Arr(t1,t2)) and welltyped(e2,t1),
;; then welltyped(App(e1,e2),t2)
(rule
  ((welltyped e1 (Arr t1 t2) s1)
   (welltyped e2 t1 s2)
   (maxsize m)
   (> m (+ s1 s2)))
  ((welltyped (App e1 e2) t2 (+ 1 (+ s1 s2)))))
```

```
;; Equality saturation: two terms of the same type are equivalent
(rule
  ((welltyped e1 t s1) (welltyped e2 t s2))
  ((union e1 e2)))

(run 10000)
(print-function welltyped 100000)
(print-size welltyped)
```

B Breccia Syntax

```
Program        ::= Declaration*

Declaration    ::= BoundDecl | DatatypeDecl | GenTypeDecl | NormalFuncDecl
                 | BoundFuncDecl | GenFuncDecl

BoundDecl      ::= bound Id = Integer .. =? Integer

DatatypeDecl   ::= datatype Id = { Variant+ }

GenTypeDecl    ::= datatype Id  bounded_by ( Param* ) \
                   tracking ( Param* ) = { Variant+ }

Variant        ::= | Id [( TypeList )]
TypeList       ::= Type [, Type]*

NormalFuncDecl ::= def Id ( FuncParams ) -> Type = { Block }

BoundFuncDecl  ::= def Id.bound -> Id = { Block }

GenFuncDecl    ::= generator Id ( FuncParams ) -> # Id = { Block }

FuncParams     ::= [Param [, Param]*]
Param          ::= Id : TypeRef
TypeRef        ::= Type | # Type

Type           ::= Int | Bool | Id

Block          ::= Statement* Expr

Statement      ::= LetStmt | FilterStmt

LetStmt        ::= let Id = Expr Newline

FilterStmt     ::= filter Expr is Pattern Newline

Expr           ::= IfExpr | MatchExpr | GenReturnExpr | BinaryExpr | Term
```

```
IfExpr          ::= if ( Condition ) { Block } [else { Block }]

MatchExpr       ::= Expr match { MatchCase* }

MatchCase       ::= | Pattern => Expr

GenReturnExpr   ::= Id [( Args )] tracking ( Id : Expr [, Id : Expr]* )

BinaryExpr      ::= Term Operator Term

Term            ::= Id | Integer | true | false | fail | FuncCall
                  | ConstructorCall | FieldAccess | ( Expr )

FuncCall        ::= Id ( Args )
ConstructorCall::= Id ( Args )
FieldAccess     ::= Id . Id
Args            ::= [Expr [, Expr ]*]

Pattern         ::= Id ( [PatternList] ) | Id | _

PatternList     ::= Pattern [, Pattern]*

Condition       ::= Expr CompOperator Expr
Operator        ::= + | - | || | &&
CompOperator    ::= == | != | < | > | <= | >=
```

References

1. Abeysinghe, S., Xhebraj, A., Rompf, T.: Flan: an expressive and efficient datalog compiler for program analysis. Proc. ACM Program. Lang. **8**(POPL), 2577–2609 (2024)
2. Arntzenius, M., Krishnaswami, N.R.: Datafun: a functional Datalog. In: Proceedings of the 21st ACM SIGPLAN International Conference on Functional Programming, pp. 214–227 (2016)
3. Awar, N.A., Jain, K., Rossbach, C.J., Gligoric, M.: Programming and execution models for parallel bounded exhaustive testing. Proc. ACM Program. Lang. **5**(OOPSLA) (2021). https://doi.org/10.1145/3485543, https://doi-org.libproxy.csun.edu/10.1145/3485543
4. Bembenek, A., Greenberg, M., Chong, S.: Formulog: datalog for SMT-based static analysis. Proc. ACM Program. Lang. **4**(OOPSLA), 1–31 (2020)
5. Ceri, S., Gottlob, G., Tanca, L., et al.: What you always wanted to know about Datalog (and never dared to ask). IEEE Trans. Knowl. Data Eng. **1**(1), 146–166 (1989)
6. Chaliasos, S., Sotiropoulos, T., Spinellis, D., Gervais, A., Livshits, B., Mitropoulos, D.: Finding typing compiler bugs. In: Proceedings of the 43rd ACM SIGPLAN International Conference on Programming Language Design and Implementation, pp. 183–198. PLDI 2022, Association for Computing Machinery, New York, NY, USA (2022). https://doi.org/10.1145/3519939.3523427

7. Church, A.: A formulation of the simple theory of types. J. Symb. Log.c **5**(2), 56–68 (1940). http://www.jstor.org/stable/2266170
8. Claessen, K., Hughes, J.: QuickCheck: a lightweight tool for random testing of haskell programs. In: Proceedings of the Fifth ACM SIGPLAN International Conference on Functional Programming, pp. 268–279. ICFP '00, ACM, New York, NY, USA (2000). https://doi.org/10.1145/351240.351266, http://doi.acm.org/10.1145/351240.351266
9. Coward, S., Constantinides, G.A., Drane, T.: Automating constraint-aware datapath optimization using E-Graphs. In: 2023 60th ACM/IEEE Design Automation Conference (DAC), pp. 1–6. IEEE (2023)
10. Dewey, K.: Automated Black Box Generation of Structured Inputs for Use in Software Testing, Chapter 7. Ph.D. thesis, University of California, Santa Barbara, USA (2017). http://www.escholarship.org/uc/item/9362s6mg
11. Dewey, K., Conrad, P., Craig, M., Morozova, E.: Evaluating test suite effectiveness and assessing student code via constraint logic programming. In: Proceedings of the 2017 ACM Conference on Innovation and Technology in Computer Science Education, pp. 317–322. ITiCSE '17, ACM, New York, NY, USA (2017). https://doi.org/10.1145/3059009.3059051, http://doi.acm.org/10.1145/3059009.3059051
12. Dewey, K., Hairapetian, S., Gavrilov, M.: MiMIs: simple, efficient, and fast bounded-exhaustive test case generators. In: 2020 IEEE 13th International Conference on Software Testing, Validation and Verification (ICST), pp. 51–62 (2020). https://doi.org/10.1109/ICST46399.2020.00016
13. Dewey, K., Nichols, L., Hardekopf, B.: Automated data structure generation: refuting common wisdom. In: Proceedings of the 37th International Conference on Software Engineering - Volume 1, pp. 32–43. ICSE '15, IEEE Press, Piscataway, NJ, USA (2015). http://dl.acm.org/citation.cfm?id=2818754.2818761
14. Dewey, K., Roesch, J., Hardekopf, B.: Language fuzzing using constraint logic programming. In: Proceedings of the 29th ACM/IEEE International Conference on Automated Software Engineering, pp. 725–730. ASE '14, ACM, New York, NY, USA (2014). https://doi.org/10.1145/2642937.2642963, http://doi.acm.org/10.1145/2642937.2642963
15. Dewey, K., Roesch, J., Hardekopf, B.: Fuzzing the rust typechecker using CLP. In: Proceedings of the 2015 30th IEEE/ACM International Conference on Automated Software Engineering (ASE), pp. 482–493. ASE '15, IEEE Computer Society, Washington, DC, USA (2015). https://doi.org/10.1109/ASE.2015.65, http://dx.doi.org/10.1109/ASE.2015.65
16. Fallin, C.: Cranelift RFC: Middle-end optimization framework based on e-graphs (2022). https://github.com/bytecodealliance/rfcs/blob/main/accepted/cranelift-egraph.md, bytecode Alliance RFC
17. Girard, J.Y.: Une extension de L'interpretation de gödel a L'analyse, et son application a L'elimination des coupures dans L'analyse et la theorie des types. In: Fenstad, J. (ed.) Proceedings of the Second Scandinavian Logic Symposium, Studies in Logic and the Foundations of Mathematics, vol. 63, pp. 63–92. Elsevier (1971). https://doi.org/10.1016/S0049-237X(08)70843-7, https://www.sciencedirect.com/science/article/pii/S0049237X08708437
18. Grygiel, K., Lescanne, P.: Counting and generating lambda terms. CoRR **abs/1210.2610** (2012). http://arxiv.org/abs/1210.2610
19. Hyatt, S.C., Dewey, K.: Mutation-based fuzzing of the swift compiler with incomplete type information. In: 2025 IEEE Conference on Software Testing, Verification and Validation (ICST), pp. 58–68 (2025).https://doi.org/10.1109/ICST62969.2025.10989032

20. Igarashi, A., Pierce, B., Wadler, P.: Featherweight Java: a minimal core calculus for Java and GJ. In: Proceedings of the 14th ACM SIGPLAN Conference on Object-Oriented Programming, Systems, Languages, and Applications, pp. 132–146. OOPSLA '99, Association for Computing Machinery, New York, NY, USA (1999). https://doi.org/10.1145/320384.320395
21. Jackson, D., Damon, C.A.: Elements of style: analyzing a software design feature with a counterexample detector. SIGSOFT Softw. Eng. Notes **21**(3), 239–249 (1996). https://doi.org/10.1145/226295.226322
22. Kuraj, I., Kuncak, V., Jackson, D.: Programming with enumerable sets of structures. In: Proceedings of the 2015 ACM SIGPLAN International Conference on Object-Oriented Programming, Systems, Languages, and Applications, pp. 37–56. OOPSLA 2015, ACM, New York, NY, USA (2015).https://doi.org/10.1145/2814270.2814323, http://doi.acm.org/10.1145/2814270.2814323
23. Lampropoulos, L., Gallois-Wong, D., Hriţcu, C., Hughes, J., Pierce, B.C., Xia, L.Y.: Beginner's luck: a language for property-based generators. In: Proceedings of the 44th ACM SIGPLAN Symposium on Principles of Programming Languages, pp. 114–129. POPL '17, Association for Computing Machinery, New York, NY, USA (2017). https://doi.org/10.1145/3009837.3009868
24. Madsen, M., Lhoták, O.: Fixpoints for the masses: programming with first-class Datalog constraints. Proc. ACM Program. Lang. **4**(OOPSLA), 1–28 (2020)
25. Madsen, M., Yee, M.H., Lhoták, O.: From Datalog to flix: a declarative language for fixed points on lattices. ACM SIGPLAN Notices **51**(6), 194–208 (2016)
26. Marinov, D., Khurshid, S.: TestEra: a novel framework for automated testing of java programs. In: Proceedings of the 16th IEEE International Conference on Automated Software Engineering, p. 22. ASE '01, IEEE Computer Society, Washington, DC, USA (2001). http://dl.acm.org/citation.cfm?id=872023.872551
27. Miller, B.P., Fredriksen, L., So, B.: An empirical study of the reliability of UNIX utilities. Commun. ACM **33**(12), 32–44 (1990). https://doi.org/10.1145/96267.96279, http://doi.acm.org/10.1145/96267.96279
28. Nandi, C., et al.: Synthesizing structured CAD models with equality saturation and inverse transformations. In: Proceedings of the 41st ACM SIGPLAN Conference on Programming Language Design and Implementation, pp. 31–44 (2020)
29. Nelson, G., Oppen, D.C.: Fast decision procedures based on congruence closure. J. ACM (JACM) **27**(2), 356–364 (1980)
30. Pacak, A., Erdweg, S.: Functional programming with datalog. In: Ali, K., Vitek, J. (eds.) 36th European Conference on Object-Oriented Programming (ECOOP 2022). Leibniz International Proceedings in Informatics (LIPIcs), vol. 222, pp. 7:1–7:28. Schloss Dagstuhl – Leibniz-Zentrum für Informatik, Dagstuhl, Germany (2022). https://doi.org/10.4230/LIPIcs.ECOOP.2022.7, https://drops.dagstuhl.de/entities/document/10.4230/LIPIcs.ECOOP.2022.7
31. Pacak, A., Erdweg, S., Szabó, T.: A systematic approach to deriving incremental type checkers. Proc. ACM Program. Lang. **4**(OOPSLA), 1–28 (2020)
32. Panchekha, P., Sanchez-Stern, A., Wilcox, J.R., Tatlock, Z.: Automatically improving accuracy for floating point expressions, pp. 1–11. PLDI '15, Association for Computing Machinery, New York, NY, USA (2015). https://doi.org/10.1145/2737924.2737959
33. Reynolds, J.C. Towards a theory of type structure. In: Robinet, B. (ed.) Programming Symposium. LNCS, vol. 19, pp. 408–425. Springer, Berlin, Heidelberg (1974). https://doi.org/10.1007/3-540-06859-7_148

34. Rümmer, P.: E-matching with free variables. In: Bjørner, N., Voronkov, A. (eds.) Logic for Programming, Artificial Intelligence, and Reasoning. LPAR 2012. LNCS, vol. 7180, pp. 359–374. Springer, Berlin, Heidelberg (2012). https://doi.org/10.1007/978-3-642-28717-6_28
35. Senni, V., Fioravanti, F.: Generation of test data structures using constraint logic programming. In: Proceedings of the 6th international conference on Tests and Proofs, pp. 115–131. TAP'12, Springer-Verlag, Berlin, Heidelberg (2012). https://doi.org/10.1007/978-3-642-30473-6_10, http://dx.doi.org/10.1007/978-3-642-30473-6_10
36. Takashima, Y., Martins, R., Jia, L., Păsăreanu, C.S.: SyRust: automatic testing of Rust libraries with semantic-aware program synthesis. In: Proceedings of the 42nd ACM SIGPLAN International Conference on Programming Language Design and Implementation, pp. 899–913. PLDI 2021, Association for Computing Machinery, New York, NY, USA (2021). https://doi.org/10.1145/3453483.3454084
37. Tarau, P.: On type-directed generation of lambda terms. In: Technical Communications of the 31st International Conference on Logic Programming, ICLP 2015, August 31 - September 4, 2015, Cork, Ireland (2015)
38. Tate, R., Stepp, M., Tatlock, Z., Lerner, S.: Equality saturation: a new approach to optimization. In: Proceedings of the 36th Annual ACM SIGPLAN-SIGACT Symposium on Principles of Programming Languages, pp. 264–276 (2009)
39. VanHattum, A., Nigam, R., Lee, V.T., Bornholt, J., Sampson, A.: Vectorization for digital signal processors via equality saturation. In: Proceedings of the 26th ACM International Conference on Architectural Support for Programming Languages and Operating Systems, pp. 874–886 (2021)
40. Willsey, M., Nandi, C., Wang, Y.R., Flatt, O., Tatlock, Z., Panchekha, P.: Egg: fast and extensible equality saturation. Proc. ACM Program. Lang. **5**(POPL), 1–29 (2021)
41. Yang, Y., Phothilimthana, P., Wang, Y., Willsey, M., Roy, S., Pienaar, J.: Equality saturation for tensor graph superoptimization. In: Smola, A., Dimakis, A., Stoica, I. (eds.) Proceedings of Machine Learning and Systems, vol. 3, pp. 255–268 (2021). https://proceedings.mlsys.org/paper_files/paper/2021/file/cc427d934a7f6c0663e5923f49eba531-Paper.pdf
42. Zhang, Y., et al.: Better together: unifying datalog and equality saturation. Proc. ACM Program. Lang. **7**(PLDI), 468–492 (2023)

Finding Programming Faults Even When Large Parts of the Code Have Disappeared

Quinten Cabo[1,2(✉)] and Sven-Bodo Scholz[1]

[1] Radboud University, Nijmegen, The Netherlands
{Quinten.Cabo,SvenBodo.Scholz}@ru.nl
[2] Leiden University, Leiden, The Netherlands
q.m.j.cabo@liacs.leidenuniv.nl

Abstract. This paper proposes a debugging technique for functional programming languages that enables debugging of highly optimised code even if the code that actually is executed is very different from its original specification. We suggest a combination of virtual shadow stacks, uniqueness types, as well as pre- and post conditions for functions. Using this combination, we can trace bugs through function calls that may no longer exist at runtime at all. We describe how this approach is realised in the functional array language SaC and we demonstrate how we can enrich virtual stack traces with partial argument information such as array dimensionality or shape.

Keywords: Debbugging · Functional Array Programming · Optimising Compilers

1 Introduction

Debugging programs in the context of compiler optimisations is a challenge. Optimisations can shuffle parts of the code around, modify, or eliminate them entirely; functions may be specialised or inlined, recursion may be transformed into loops, the list goes on. As a result, the code that is ultimately executed may no longer be easily related to the original program. Functional languages are particularly prone to such extensive changes as their semantics is based on referential transparency, enabling context-free substitutions at a large scale. This renders step-wise debugging on the source code difficult if not impossible. While in many languages this added debugging challenge can be avoided by disabling the optimisations, in highly optimising languages this can quickly become cumbersome if not infeasible due to excessive runtime demands. In particular functional array languages such as SaC [28], Futhark [16] or Accelerate [8] rely on the compiler's capability to perform rather far-reaching program transformations which turn the declarative style into resource-efficient imperative code. For these languages, it is not uncommon that the difference in runtime between unoptimised and optimised code are several orders of magnitude. As a consequence, debugging unoptimised code is only possible for parts of the code or for miniaturised problem sizes.

M. Sperber and E. Komendantskaya (Eds.): FLOPS 2026, LNCS 16533, pp. 100–117, 2026.
https://doi.org/10.1007/978-981-92-0184-6_4

As an illustrating example for the challenges of debugging in the context of extensive program optimisation, consider the following SaC program:

```
1  inline
2  double[m:shp] mean (double[n,m:shp] a) | n > 0 {
3      return rsum (1, a) / tod (n);
4  }
5
6  inline
7  int[n] foo (double[.,n:shp] a, double[.,n:shp] b) {
8      return shape (mean (a) + mean (b));
9  }
10
11 int main () {
12     int n;
13
14     ntok, n = TermFile::scanf ("%d");
15     /* left extent unknown until runtime */
16     a = genarray ([n,1000], 1d);
17     b = genarray ([2000,1000], 1d);
18     res = foo (a, b);
19     StdIO::print (res);
20
21     return 0;
22 }
```

The key element of this example is the function `mean` (lines 1–4). It computes the element-wise mean across the left-most axis of (m+1)-dimensional arrays. To avoid division by `0` errors, the function definition comes with a pre-condition [1] `n > 0` where `n` relates to the extent of the argument array `a` within the left-most axis.

We use this function in the context of a contrived function `foo` (lines 6–9), which applies it to two arrays `a` and `b`, element-wise sums up the results, but only returns the shape of the result of these function applications. Given that we allow the extent of the left-most axis of the array `a` to be provided at runtime only (line 14 in `main`), there is no way to prove or disprove the required pre-condition of the first call to `mean` inside of `foo` statically.

The SaC compiler transforms this program into code which essentially only consists of:

```
int main () {
    int n;
    ntok, n = TermFile::scanf ("%d");
    conditionalAbort (n < 0);
    StdIO::print ([1000]);
    return 0;
}
```

When providing `0` as input, we obtain:

```
*** SAC runtime error
*** In ./Example2.sac, line 2, column 1
*** Type pattern pre-condition ( n >0) of mean failed
```

Trying to identify which problem or line of code in the original program has triggered the runtime error is challenging. Using a C debugger on the generated C code is only of limited help, as the optimised code no longer directly resembles the original specification: as can be seen from the example above, all function calls have disappeared, none of the arrays exist in the generated code and even the problematic division on line 3 is no longer part of the program, only the precondition check and the corresponding error message remain.

Traditionally, the only way to get more information about the context of the failing application of `mean` is to disable the optimisations that eliminated the explicit function calls and then try to use a C debugger on the generated code. While this surely is feasible for our toy example, for more realistic examples, the introduced overhead quickly is so big that debugging unoptimised code is no longer an option.

In this paper, we propose an approach towards debugging such optimised code based on the idea of maintaining a virtual call graph that corresponds to an execution of the naive, unoptimised program. The virtual stack (inspired by shadow stacks from cybersecurity [7]) reflects the programmer's mental model of the original call sequence, as it would result from running the non-optimised code. Rather than attempting to reconstruct eliminated structure, this approach preserves call structure explicitly in the code that is optimised by the compiler. Once an error has occurred, the current virtual stack can be printed as a stack trace in error messages or even dynamically inspected.

While the concept of such virtual stacks sounds appealing from the perspective of fault localisation, it immediately poses the question whether, or to which degree, it undermines the optimisation potential of the compiler; after all, it reintroduces the overhead of accounting for the full call stack. The main performance gains in functional array languages stem from the avoidance of the creation of intermediate arrays. In this context, this implies that our shadow stacks surely must not require all arguments to be materialised. If that was the case, most likely, the resulting performance would be close to that of the unoptimised code. The beauty of using virtual stacks is that we can allow the programmer to choose how much argument information, if any, should be generated.

The key challenge of this approach then lies in the necessity to keep the virtual stack construction and maintenance in the program while still allowing the compiler to optimise away function calls and entire arguments. We achieve this by relying on the functional semantics in general and by using uniqueness types to ensure that the order of function calls matches their syntactic order in the source code. Using this approach, we can generate high quality semantically correct stack traces even when corresponding runtime calls no longer exist in the code that is executed.

In essence, our compiled code surrounds each function call with calls to runtime functions that handle the virtual stack. In case the functions themselves are no longer needed, these calls pertaining to the virtual stack still remain unless all checks between virtual function calls and virtual returns can be statically resolved by the compiler. Our example is optimised into a sequence of calls to these stack functions surrounding the pre-condition check. Even with these functions injected, neither the array `a` nor the array `b` materialise at runtime. Nevertheless, upon inputting the value `0`, we now obtain the following error message:

```
*** Stack trace:
[1] main called foo<[0,1000],[2000,1000]>(a,b) at ./flops.sac:18:11 correctly
        (the predicates held)
    foo tried to call mean<[0,1000]>(a) at ./flops.sac:8:19 but the predicates of
        mean did not hold.

*** SAC runtime error
*** In ./simple.sac, line 1, column 1
*** Type pattern pre-condition (n >0) of mean failed
```

Here, we can see precisely which of the calls to `mean` went wrong (the one in line 8 position 19) and why as the shape of the arguments are shown between angular brackets.

The individual contributions of this paper are:

- A sketch of the program transformation that injects the handling of the virtual stack. The key insight here is that this approach can piggy-back on SaC's global objects which are based on the uniqueness types in SaC.
- A description of the runtime support needed for handling the stack structure.
- A description of the virtual stack structure that is trying to keep the memory requirements to a minimum by taking extra care of recursive function calls.
- A rendering mechanism for constructing stack-trace error messages.
- A discussion about the implications of the virtual stack mechanism on the optimisation potential including some indicative performance evaluations.

A full-fledged implementation in the SaC compiler available on www.sac-home.org.

2 Uniqueness Types in SaC

This section briefly reviews SaC's uniqueness types and their associated language constructs, as they form the foundation that allows us to integrate virtual stack bookkeeping into the data flow of SaC programs without inhibiting optimisations.

SaC supports uniqueness types [29] in order to enable a static guarantee of a linear chain of data dependencies between stateful objects. Uniqueness types have to be explicitly introduced in SaC through special modules referred-to as *classes*. As an example, consider the class `rterror` from SAC's prelude. It provides a uniqueness type of the same name that is implemented as a boolean value. The only way a value of a unique type can come into existence in SaC is through a constructor function defined in that very class. In case of the class `rterror`, this is a function named `new`:

```
rterror new (bool state) {
    return (rterror)state;
}
```

The uniqueness-property of the type `rterror` ensures that any variable of that type can only be referenced once. As a consequence, any function that gets such an argument either consumes it or has to update it; a function such as

```
rterror invert (rterror old) {
    return new (!(bool)old);
}
```

implements an update. It can be used like any other function, as long as the uniqueness property is not violated. For example,

```
    err = new (false);
    err = invert (err);
    err = invert (err);
```

is legal because every call semantically creates a new unique `err`, while

```
1       err = new (false);
2       err2 = invert (err);
3       err3 = invert (err); // Same err used for a second time!
```

is not legal as the variable `err` defined in line 1 is referred to twice. Since writing such sequences is tedious and error-prone, SaC supports two syntactical shortcuts: reference parameters and global objects.

2.1 Reference Parameters

Reference Parameters allow programmers to omit the return values of functions that modify unique objects. This can be achieved by prefixing such a unique argument with the &-symbol. Using this syntactical shortcut, we can define

```
void invert (rterror &old) {
    old = new (!(bool)old);
}
```

With this definition, the legal sequence from above can be written as

```
    err = new (false);
    invert (err);
    invert (err);
```

The compiler will transform this to the initial version shown above by inserting the omitted left-hand-sides. Note here, that the use of a reference parameter makes it impossible to introduce the uniqueness violation shown earlier.

2.2 Global Objects

Taking the idea of syntactical shortcuts even further, SaC supports a notion of *Global Objects*. A global object is a unique object that is created prior to the program start and that is passed by the compiler to all functions that modify it. Using this construction, we can now introduce a global object and avoid using the explicit parameters in our function `invert` entirely:

```
objdef rterror TheControlFlow = new (false);

void invert () {
    TheControlFlow = new (!(bool)TheControlFlow);
}
```

Again, the compiler will insert the missing code in order to convert calls of the form `invert ()` into `TheControlFlow = invert (TheControlFlow)`. The main difference to the re-write for reference parameters is that the compiler analyses the entire call graph and makes sure all global objects are propagated as deep into the call graph as needed.

As with reference parameters, the transformation of global objects ensures that the compiler inserts all data dependencies required to transform the very much imperatively looking function applications into purely functional ones. All data dependencies are explicit, enabling the full repertoire of program optimisations on the transformed code. More technical detail on how these transformations are defined and implemented can be found in [13,17].

3 Running Example

To present all features of the virtual stack we extend the example from the introduction into the following slightly more complicated program:

```
use StdIO : {scanf, print};
use Array: all;

inline double[m:shp] mean (double[n,m:shp] a) | n > 0 {
    return rsum (1, a) / tod (n);
}

inline double bar (double[.,n:shp] a) {
      return bar (mean (a));
}

inline double bar (double d) {
    return d;
}

int main () {
    int n;
    ntok, n = scanf ("%d");
    a = genarray ([10, 20, 30, 40, 50, n], 1d);
    res = bar (a);
    print (res);
    return 0;
}
```

Like the introductory example, this program also makes use of the `mean` function. However, now we use a function `bar` to apply `mean` in a recursive manner, reducing the dimensionality of the result until we are left with a scalar value. If one provides an input of 0, with our proposed virtual stacks, we generate the following error message:

```
*** Stack trace:
[1] bar<[10,20,30,40,50,0]>(a) at ./flops.sac:20:11
[2] bar<[20,30,40,50,0]>(mean(a)) at ./flops.sac:9:14
[3] bar<[30,40,50,0]>(mean(a)) at ./flops.sac:9:14
[4] bar<[40,50,0]>(mean(a)) at ./flops.sac:9:14
[5] bar<[50,0]>(mean(a)) at ./flops.sac:9:14
[6] bar<[0]>(mean(a)) at ./flops.sac:9:14
    bar tried to call mean<[0]>(a) at /flops.sac:9:19
        but the predicates of mean did not hold.

*** SAC runtime error
```

```
*** In ./Example3.sac, line 4, column 1
*** Type pattern pre-condition (n >0) of mean failed
```

Here, we see the entire stack trace, including shape information of the arguments provided in angular brackets right behind the name of the function that is being called. This improves vastly over the error message without the stack trace.

The program transformations that we propose in this paper can generate these stack traces while still allowing the compiler to aggressively optimise the program. In particular, every naïve execution of `bar(a)`, conceptually performs $\prod \texttt{shape}(a)$ many additions before the recursive call on `a` with the outer axis dropped. For an array of shape `[10, 20, 30, 40, 50, n]`, this corresponds to $(12\text{M} + 1, 2\text{M} + 60\text{K} + 2\text{K} + \dots) * n$, i.e., millions of additions even for $n = 1$. The SaC compiler is able to produce an optimised version that is unrecognisable from the original program but still computes the correct result with only $150+n$ additions, as the values of the array `a` are statically known. However, the virtual stack trace would still have you believe that it is actually the naïve version that is running. We will refer to this example throughout the paper while describing the sequence of transformations applied to generate these stack traces without compromising the optimiser's ability to eliminate the underlying computation.

4 Virtual Stack Traces

To maintain the virtual stack at runtime we introduce a push and a pop function. Both of these are defined in the prelude class `rterror`[1] mentioned earlier:

```
external void stackPop ();
    #pragma effect TheControlFlow

external void stackPush (char[.] funname, char[.] filename, int line,
                         int column, char[.] callExpr, int arity, ...);
    #pragma effect TheControlFlow
```

Both these functions are implemented in C, using SaC's FFI. The `#pragma effect TheControlFlow` notifies the compiler that these functions need to be treated in the same way as a SaC-implemented function that modifies the global object `TheControlFlow`. As explained in Sect. 2, this leads to the compiler-driven insertion of `TheControlFlow` into the data-flow of the program, effectively sequentialising all calls to `stackPush` and `stackPop`. Our goal is to prepend each function application specified by the programmer with a call to `stackPush` and to append a call to `stackPop` to keep track of the call graph as it was before the compiler starts to optimise.

Beyond recording the call graph, each push call can include additional argument information such as argument dimensionality and shape which are provided as additional arguments to `stackPush`. If the compiler can infer the dimensionality and shape of an argument, then this information is directly passed to `stackPush` as literal values. Otherwise, the compiler generates additional

[1] The name `rterror` (runtime error) stems from the fact that all checks of pre and post conditions do operate on the same state.

references to the corresponding arguments and invokes the intrinsic functions `_shape_A` and `_dim_A` on them to compute their shape and dimensionality at runtime.

While this in principle could force the materialisation of the arguments the compiler's optimisations are geared towards optimising the actual argument computation away if the values are not needed otherwise. A formal basis for such optimisations is the binding scope analysis described in [14].

4.1 A-Normalisation

SaC functions are sequences of assignments. Naïvely inserting our pushes and pops into these assignment chains is not sufficient because arguments to functions may themselves be function calls. See for instance line 9 of our running example with `bar(mean(a))` on line 19 of the running example. Simply wrapping the outer call to `bar` would omit the inner call to `mean` from the stack trace. To correctly surround programmer-written function applications with pushes and pops we need to have assignment chains into a flattened form without nested function calls. To that end we A-normalise [26] the code. This transformation lifts all sub-expressions into separate assignments. Fortunately, the SaC compiler already does A-normalisation because this transformation is needed to introduce the global objects. The following code shows an A-normalised version of the function `bar` of the running example:

```
inline double bar (double[.,n:shp] a) {
    A1 = mean (a);
    A2 = bar (A1);
    return A2;
}

inline double bar (double d) {
    return d;
}
```

Now that we have the code in A-normal form we can easily insert the push and pop operations including their inferred arguments:

```
inline double bar (double[.,n:shp] a) {
    stackPush ("mean", "flops.sac", 11, 18, "mean (a)", 1, _dim_A (a), _shape_A (a));
    A1 = mean (a);
    stackPop ();
    stackPush ("bar", "flops.sac", 11, 14, "bar (mean (a))", 1, _dim_A (A1), _shape_A (A1));
    A2 = bar (A1);
    stackPop ();
    return A2;
}

inline double bar (double d) {
    return d;
}
```

The functions `mean` and `main` are being processed accordingly.

4.2 Runtime Checks

Runtime checks are injected before object expansion as well. For our example, this leads to an injection of a call to a function `conditionalAbort` implemented in the class `rterror`:

```
external void SAC_exit (int status);
    #pragma effect TheControlFlow


inline void conditionalAbort (bool p) {
    if (_not_S_ (p)) {
        SAC_exit (1);
    }
}
```

For our function `bar`, this results in:

```
inline double bar (double[.,n:shp] a) {
    conditionalAbort (n > 0);
    stackPush ("mean", "flops.sac", 11, 18, "mean (a)", 1, _dim_A (a), _shape_A (a));
    A1 = mean (a);
    stackPop ();
    stackPush ("bar", "flops.sac", 11, 14, "bar (mean (a))", 1, _dim_A (A1),
               _shape_A (A1));
    A2 = bar (A1);
    stackPop ();
    return A2;
}

inline double bar (double d) {
    return d;
}
```

4.3 Inserting Global Objects

As described in Sect. 2, global objects such as `TheControlFlow` are being injected into the data-flow of the given program. Each `stackPush(...)` is transformed into `TheControlFlow = stackPush(TheControlFlow, ...)`. Likewise, the calls to `stackPop` and to `conditionalAbort` are being adjusted. This transformation makes the stack operations as well as all runtime checks data-dependent on each other, preventing the compiler from eliminating them [12] and enforcing a strict sequence on all pushes, pops as well as all runtime checks that potentially affect `TheControlFlow`.

Because the stack functions do not require the function arguments, imposing a strict sequence on the virtual stack operations does not imply a strictly sequential execution of the program itself. The ordering is introduced solely via the explicit passing of the global object, all computation that is not required for the stack operations remains independent and may still be as aggressively optimised as before. As a consequence, the inherent concurrency of SaC programs is preserved [17].

We optionally allow shape and rank information to be added to the push operations. While this potentially creates some data dependencies and potentially could inhibit some optimisation, the restriction to shapes and ranks typically minimises this interaction as can be observed in the running example.

The following code illustrates how the running example is transformed when we insert the global objects. Again, we only look at the two instances of the function `bar`. To improve readability, we abbreviate `TheControllFlow` as `TCF`.

```
1   inline rterror, double bar (rterror TCF, double[.,n:shp] a) {
2       TCF = conditionalAbort (TCF, n > 0);
3       TCF = stackPush (TCF, "mean", "flops.sac", 11, 18, "mean (a)", 1,
4                        _dim_A (a), _shape_A (a));
5       TCF, A1 = mean (TCF, a);
6       TCF = stackPop (TCF);
7       TCF = stackPush (TCF, "bar", "flops.sac", 11, 14, "bar (mean (a))", 1,
8                        _dim_A (A1), _shape_A (A1));
9       TCF, A2 = bar (TCF, A1);
10      TCF = stackPop (TCF);
11      return TCF, A2;
12  }
13
14  inline rterror, double bar (rterror TCF, double d) {
15      return TCF, d;
16  }
```

We can see how the effect pragma of the functions `stackPush` and `stackPop` as well as the function `conditionalAbort` are leading to additional arguments and return values of all functions involved. Since the function `mean` is calling further functions, `TCF` is being propagated to that function as well. The most surprising change may be that the second instance of `bar` in lines 14–16 also receives `TCF` as an additional argument. Although the function itself does neither call `stackPush` nor `stackPop`, its signature still got extended. This happens due to the fact that there exists at least one overloaded instance of `bar` that indeed requires this extension.

Once all the functions are being inlined and possibly statically dispatched, the compiler will optimise such superfluous arguments away. Likewise, we optimise subsequent push and pop optimisations away if there is no conditional abort between them.

4.4 Runtime Support

Beyond inserting the pushes and pops into the A-normalised code, no additional compiler support is required because we can rely on the global objects. The complexity of managing, maintaining, and rendering the shadow stack can reside entirely in library code. In our implementation the stack functions are part of the `rterror` module shipped with the SaC compiler. We implement these functions in C using the SaC FFI [18,22] to avoid SaC's homogeneity restriction, which requires arrays to be uniform in both element type and shape. In C the virtual stack can be represented as an array of structs containing variable-length data without being constrained by this rule. On the C side we use the following data structures to store the virtual stack in memory.

```
typedef struct {
    int* array;
    int length;
    int capacity;
} IntStack;
```

```
typedef struct {
    StackFrame* array;
    StackFrame* top;
    int capacity;
} FrameStack;
```

```
struct StackFrame {
   char *funname;
   char *filename;
   int   line;
   int   col;
   char *source_expr;
   int   arity;
   int   recursiveCalls;
}
```

```
struct VirtualStack {
  struct FrameStack frames;
  struct IntStack dims;
  struct IntStack shapes;
  struct {
    bool compact;
    bool show_shapes;
    /* Ommited for brevity */
  } flags;
}
```

Together these data structures are designed to support pushing and popping functions frames with a variable number of arguments, and to unwind the complete virtual stack bottom-up in order to render it into string.

The virtual stack is represented by a single global `VirtualStack` structure which includes some boolean configuration flags that control how the stack trace is rendered, as well as three separate stacks that together encode the full virtual stack. The first of these three stacks is the `FrameStack` stored in the `frames` field of `VirtualStack`. Each `StackFrame` in the `FrameStack` represents one function call pushed using `stackPush` and stores all metadata associated with that call. The remaining two stacks, `IntStack dims` and `IntStack shapes`, store the dimensionality and shape of function arguments as a flat, dynamically sized sequence of integers to avoid per-argument heap allocation. By separating the call stack from the argument stacks, `StackFrame` is fixed-size. This allows for efficient allocations and iteration of call frames while still supporting function calls with varying numbers of arguments with arbitrary rank and shape.

When a new function call is pushed, a new `StackFrame` is appended to the `FrameStack`, growing the underlying array if necessary. The `arity` argument specifies the number of arguments of the pushed call which forms the coherence between the three stacks. Based on the pushed `arity`, we know there will be $2 \cdot arity$ variadic arguments passed to the push function. For each argument, its dimensionality is pushed onto the `dims` stack. The dimensionality then determines how many integers to read and push to the `shapes` stack. Because SaC may reclaim the memory backing string arguments passed to the runtime, the push operation copies all passed in strings.

Popping a frame reverses the effects of a push operation. First, we free all the strings associated with the topmost `StackFrame`. Next, we pop the argument information associated with the frame from the `dims` and `shapes` stacks. For `dims` we simply pop `arity` elements. To figure out how many values to pop from `shapes`, we have to compute *dimsum*, the sum of the dimensionalities of all arguments that belong to a frame. Because `shapes` stores one integer per dimension, *dimsum* is exactly the total number of shape entries associated with the frame.

$$dimsum = \sum_{i=0}^{\texttt{arity}-1} D_i$$

where `arity` is the number of arguments of the topmost frame, D is the segment of `dims` belonging to the topmost `StackFrame`, and D_i is the dimensionality of the i-th argument in this segment, with $0 \leq i < arity$. Finally, after popping *dimsum* elements from the `shapes` stack, the frame stack pointer `top` is decremented by 1 to remove the topmost `StackFrame`.

Recursion Compression. An important property of our virtual stack implementation is that recursive function calls can be tracked with negligible overhead. When a function call is pushed, the runtime checks whether the call is recursive by comparing the new frame with the topmost `StackFrame`. This comparison is performed without allocating heap memory and includes each argument's dimensionality and shape. If the new call is identical to the topmost frame, we only increment `recursiveCalls` on the topmost frame instead of pushing a new frame. This prevents the stack from growing during recursive calls. During a pop we simply check the recursion counter on the top frame. If it is positive, we just decrement the counter and keep the frame. Only if the counter is zero do we free the frame as described above.

The recursive call compression can be observed in the `bar` function of the running example. Because the dimensionality of the argument of `bar` is different for each call there is no recursion compression in the stack trace in Sect. 3. However if we disable dimensionality and shape tracking we get

```
*** Stack trace:
[1] bar(a) at ./Flops.sac:20:11
[2] bar(mean(a)) at ./Flops.sac:9:14 recursively 4 times
    bar tried to call mean(a) at ./Flops.sac:9:19
        but the predicates of mean did not hold.
```

5 Performance Evaluation

To get an idea of the overhead that our virtual stack approach introduces, we perform a few runtime experiments. In particular, we are interested in two questions: (i) what is the overhead of stack traces when compiling with or without checks enabled? and (ii) how do stack traces and optimisation compare to unoptimised code? While the former gives an idea of the runtime price for getting better error messages, the latter will demonstrate how this approach compares to approaches that rely on a close resemblance of the executed code to original specification.

We chose four benchmarks from an earlier performance study presented in [6]: Attention, Naïve N-Body, MultiGrid, and Quickhull. We consider them representative for a wide range of compute intensive applications. For each benchmark we measure all combinations of three binary factors: optimisation (enabled/disabled), virtual stack instrumentation (enabled/disabled), and runtime checks (enabled/disabled), resulting in eight configurations per benchmark.

All benchmarks were compiled using SaC version 2.1.0-PuurGeluk-225-g0c291 and GCC version 11.4.0. We run the code on an Intel(R) Core(TM) i7-10870H CPU @ 2.20GHz (8 physical cores, 16 logical cores), 62.5 GB RAM, running Pop!_OS 22.04 LTS (Linux kernel 6.17.9-76061709-generic). For each configuration, we performed one warm-up execution followed by ten timed runs and report the mean runtime in seconds in Table 1.

Note that to make a fair comparison we only actually disable the most disruptive optimisations that would prevent traditional stack unwinding from working well. This can be compared to running a C compiler with the -Og flag. The most important optimisations that we disable are loop folding [27], with-loop scalarization [15] and function inlining [3]. To disable these optimisations we compile the SaC programs with the -maxwlur 1 -nomemrt -noWLF -noWLS -noINL -maxspec 0 flags.

Table 1. Benchmark runtimes in seconds with small problem sizes.

Configuration	Flash Attention (d = 10, N = 1k)	N-Body (N=1k, I=10)	Multigrid (S)	Quickhull (1M rect)
noopt	7.447 ± 0.808	2.566 ± 0.136	15.906 ± 1.318	>1h ±
noopt stack	7.639 ± 0.020	17.396 ± 0.159	15.322 ± 0.119	>1h ±
noopt check	14.566 ± 0.283	5.238 ± 0.639	36.914 ± 0.311	>1h ±
noopt check stack	21.154 ± 0.189	66.441 ± 1.890	64.491 ± 2.774	>1h ±
opt	0.005 ± 0.000	0.015 ± 0.000	0.009 ± 0.000	0.018 ± 0.000
opt stack	0.006 ± 0.000	0.015 ± 0.000	0.009 ± 0.000	0.019 ± 0.001
opt check	1.253 ± 0.003	0.425 ± 0.004	1.257 ± 0.004	0.141 ± 0.001
opt check stack	1.258 ± 0.004	0.434 ± 0.001	1.268 ± 0.005	0.921 ± 0.016

Table 2. Benchmark runtime in seconds with large problem sizes.

Configuration	Flash Attention (d=100 N=10k)	N-Body (N=10k I=100)	Multigrid (W)	Quickhull (1M circle)
opt	1.740 ± 0.008	11.468 ± 0.067	4.035 ± 0.048	0.019 ± 0.000
opt stack	1.742 ± 0.009	11.428 ± 0.018	4.090 ± 0.124	0.020 ± 0.000
opt check	945.606 ± 27.572	364.555 ± 5.134	639.006 ± 31.416	0.135 ± 0.002
opt check stack	879.622 ± 22.791	362.878 ± 7.147	604.506 ± 21.037	1.085 ± 0.003

Looking at Table 1 we can observe that all optimised versions, even those that include a virtual stack, are typically at least an order of magnitude faster than any non-optimised version. In the case of Quickhull, our fully instrumented optimised version including checks and stack traces finishes below one second while any of the non optimised version requires more than an hour. This gives a clear indication that the avenue towards non optimised debugging is not an option.

Enabling the virtual stack introduces only modest overhead across the optimised configurations, the additional cost typically ranges between 1% and 20% without runtime checks, and remains below approximately 2% when runtime checks are enabled.

To better understand the large relative overhead of the virtual stack in the non-optimised setting, particularly for N-Body, we investigated the generated intermediate code. We observed that, without the ability to inline functions, the compiler can no longer eliminate certain unnecessary pushes and pops which leads to a significant increase in runtime. This shows that the efficiency of the virtual stack depends on the presence of other optimisation passes to remove unnecessary stack operations and that we could be smarter about where to instrument pushes and pops. As soon as we allow inlining the overhead of the virtual stack in N-Body disappears.

The 20% increase figure stems from extremely short runtimes (on the order of milliseconds), where small absolute differences translate into larger percentage changes. Since nearly all the optimised runtimes are well below second we repeated the optimised configuration for larger problem sizes. We can not repeat this exercise for the non-optimised versions because that would simply take too long. The results of these experiments can be found in Table 2.

For the large problem sizes of most of our benchmarks, the overhead of the virtual stack is negligible when runtime checks are disabled. In the Flash Attention and Multigrid benchmarks, the mean runtime of the stack-enabled version is even slightly lower than the baseline. Inspection of the generated code shows that the stack-enabled versions indeed contain solely additional code for push and pop operations. We conclude that these differences stem from the noise in our measurements or some artefact of the C compiler that is used for the generation of the machine code.

The impact of the virtual stack on Quickhull with runtime checks enabled is substantially larger than the other benchmarks. Further experimentation reveals that this overhead does originate from the shape arguments of our virtual stack as compiling with `-st-exclude-dim-shapes` and `-st-exclude-source-calls` reduces the mean runtime to approximately 0.7 s.

6 Related Work

Various different approaches for debugging in the context of aggressive compiler optimisations have been described in the literature.

Most of them are designed for strict imperative languages and build on the idea to enrich the generated code with debug symbols which can be used to relate the stack back to the original program specification. To cope with code optimisations, debug symbol systems such as DWARF [10] offer complex encodings of changes that the compiler has performed on the source code enabling improved debugging such as the work in [21]. Despite these techniques, after more advanced optimisations, the symbols are often incomplete and imprecise if available at all [5] and rarely prioritised [20]. Instead of trying to even further enrich the debug symbols we depart from classical debug symbols entirely, creating tailor-made accounting.

As an alternative to enriching debug symbols, there exists work on dynamic de-optimisation [19]. The central idea of that work is to only switch the portion of the program being inspected into an unoptimised computation. This gives programmers source-level debugging while leaving the remainder of the program optimised. It builds on the idea of interrupt points where switches between optimised and non-optimised code can be made. While this works well on mildly optimised code, the kind of transformations possible in functional array languages would most-likely render the blocks between possible interrupt points too large to enable unoptimised execution at all.

A lot of work has evolved around assertions that the programmer can embed in source code, like preconditions and postconditions [25], or contracts [11,23,24]. While this work is very similar to the type pattern in SaC [1], they do not help with the problem of optimisations that radically modify the execution as facilitated by referential transparency. Our proposed solution fills that gap.

In the context of declarative languages there has also been a lot of work on debugging as well. Most of the work in that context tackles the challenges introduced by non-strict evaluation orders. Work such as [2,4,9] looks at different approaches towards creating traces which are conceptually similar to our virtual stacks but they rely on different mechanisms to maintain argument data of function calls. The main difference here is that our focus lies on dealing with optimised programs, our arguments may not materialise at all. Being focussed on arrays, we can provide valuable information by just including array shapes without the need to materialise the arrays themselves.

7 Conclusion

We propose virtual stacks as complement for pre- and post-conditions when debugging highly optimised functional array programs. As it turns out, the support of uniqueness types and global objects in SaC allows us to keep the implementation effort rather low: An injection of calls into a small set of runtime library functions suffices. The necessary data dependencies are generated by the object mechanism of SaC without requiring any sophisticated additional program manipulations.

Although the support for global objects might be rather unique to SaC, the underlying idea is not, and we expect that this work could be carried over with little additional effort into any declarative language that supports states and state updates in a sound fashion. What would be needed is an injection of the required dependencies akin to the treatment of global objects in SaC.

In contrast to the other approaches we are aware of, the key innovation is that our stack traces do not require us to undo any optimisations. Programs still run fully optimised and can even execute on parallel architectures. It should be noted, however, that all possible sources of runtime errors need to be injected into the dependency chain of the global object that we pass around.

The only runtime overhead introduced by our approach is the housekeeping of the virtual stack. The price we pay in terms of programmer convenience is that we choose not to provide argument values for programmer inspection as this would most likely inhibit, depending on the granularity of the program, quite some optimisation potential. Instead, we enable the programmer to opt into recording argument shapes, which typically only has very little effect on the overall performance but provides key debugging insights.

Practical experiences show that this approach is very effective for typical SaC codes and that the overhead introduced, even when including shape information, is negligible. Our performance experiments indicate that the key to good performance is a static resolution of runtime checks and not the overhead of our stack traces. Therefore, we consider the improvement of optimisations aimed at eliminating runtime checks statically to be the most promising avenue for future work.

Acknowledgements. The research reported in this paper has been partly funded by BMK, BMDW, and the State of Upper Austria in the frame of the SCCH competence center INTEGRATE (FFG grant no. 892418) part of the FFG COMET Competence Centers for Excellent Technologies Programme.

References

1. Aaldering, J., Scholz, S.B., Gastel, B.V.: Type patterns: pattern matching on shape-carrying array types. In: Proceedings of the 35th Symposium on Implementation and Application of Functional Languages, IFL 2023. Association for Computing Machinery, New York (2024). https://doi.org/10.1145/3652561.3652572
2. Adams, S., Hanson, C., the MIT Scheme Team: MIT/GNU scheme user's manual chapter 5: debugging. Free Software Foundation/Massachusetts Institute of Technology, Boston (2020). https://www.gnu.org/software/mit-scheme/documentation/stable/mit-scheme-user.pdf
3. Aho, A.V., Ullman, J.D., Sethi, R.: Compilers: Principles, Techniques, and Tools. Addison-Wesley Pub. Co., Reading (1988)
4. Allwood, T., Peyton Jones, S., Eisenbach, S.: Finding the needle: stack tracing for GHC. In: ACM Symposium on Haskell. ACM (2009). https://www.microsoft.com/en-us/research/publication/finding-the-needle-stack-tracing-for-ghc/
5. Assaiante, C., D'Elia, D.C., Di Luna, G.A., Querzoni, L.: Where did my variable go? Poking holes in incomplete debug information. In: Proceedings of the 28th ACM International Conference on Architectural Support for Programming Languages and Operating Systems, ASPLOS 2023, vol. 2, pp. 935–947. Association for Computing Machinery, New York (2023). https://doi.org/10.1145/3575693.3575720
6. van Balen, D., et al.: Comparing parallel functional array languages: programming and performance (2025). https://arxiv.org/abs/2505.08906
7. Burow, N., Zhang, X., Payer, M.: SoK: shining light on shadow stacks. In: 2019 IEEE Symposium on Security and Privacy (SP), pp. 985–999 (2019). https://doi.org/10.1109/SP.2019.00076

8. Chakravarty, M.M., Keller, G., Lee, S., McDonell, T.L., Grover, V.: Accelerating Haskell array codes with multicore GPUs. In: Proceedings of the Sixth Workshop on Declarative Aspects of Multicore Programming, DAMP 2011, pp. 3–14. Association for Computing Machinery, New York (2011). https://doi.org/10.1145/1926354.1926358
9. Chitil, O., Runciman, C., Wallace, M.: Freja, hat and hood - a comparative evaluation of three systems for tracing and debugging lazy functional programs. In: Mohnen, M., Koopman, P. (eds.) IFL 2000. LNCS, vol. 2011, pp. 176–193. Springer, Heidelberg (2001). https://doi.org/10.1007/3-540-45361-X_11
10. DWARF Debugging Information Format Committee: DWARF Debugging Information Format version 5 (2017). Vversion 5.0
11. Foster, S., Cavalcanti, A., Canham, S., Woodcock, J., Zeyda, F.: Unifying theories of reactive design contracts. Theor. Comput. Sci. **802**, 105–140 (2020). https://doi.org/10.1016/j.tcs.2019.09.017, https://www.sciencedirect.com/science/article/pii/S0304397519305614
12. Grelck, C.: Single assignment C (SAC) high productivity meets high performance. In: Zsók, V., Horváth, Z., Plasmeijer, R. (eds.) CEFP 2011. LNCS, vol. 7241, pp. 207–278. Springer, Heidelberg (2012). https://doi.org/10.1007/978-3-642-32096-5_5
13. Grelck, C., Scholz, S.B.: Classes and objects as basis for I/O in SaC. In: Johnsson, T. (ed.) 7th International Workshop on Implementation of Functional Languages (IFL 1995), Båstad, Sweden, pp. 30–44. Chalmers University of Technology, Gothenburg (1995). sac-classes-objects-bastad-95.pdf
14. Grelck, C., Scholz, S.-B., Shafarenko, A.: A binding scope analysis for generic programs on arrays. In: Butterfield, A., Grelck, C., Huch, F. (eds.) IFL 2005. LNCS, vol. 4015, pp. 212–230. Springer, Heidelberg (2006). https://doi.org/10.1007/11964681_13
15. Grelck, C., Scholz, S.-B., Trojahner, K.: With-loop scalarization – merging nested array operations. In: Trinder, P., Michaelson, G.J., Peña, R. (eds.) IFL 2003. LNCS, vol. 3145, pp. 118–134. Springer, Heidelberg (2004). https://doi.org/10.1007/978-3-540-27861-0_8
16. Henriksen, T., Serup, N.G.W., Elsman, M., Henglein, F., Oancea, C.E.: Futhark: purely functional GPU-programming with nested parallelism and in-place array updates. In: Proceedings of the 38th ACM SIGPLAN Conference on Programming Language Design and Implementation, PLDI 2017, pp. 556–571. Association for Computing Machinery, New York (2017). https://doi.org/10.1145/3062341.3062354
17. Herhut, S., Scholz, S.B., Grelck, C.: Controllling chaos—on safe side-effects in data-parallel operations. In: Chakravarty, M., Peterson, L. (eds.) 4th Workshop on Declarative Aspects of Multicore Programming (DAMP'09), Savannah, USA, pp. 59–67. ACM Press (2009). https://doi.org/10.1145/1481839.1481847
18. Herhut, S.B.S.S., Penczek, F., Grelck, C., Shinkarov, A., Viessmann, H.N.: Single assignment C tutorial (2025). https://www.sac-home.org/_media/docs:tutorial.pdf
19. Hölzle, U., Chambers, C., Ungar, D.: Debugging optimized code with dynamic deoptimization. In: Proceedings of the ACM SIGPLAN 1992 Conference on Programming Language Design and Implementation, PLDI 1992, pp. 32–43. Association for Computing Machinery, New York (1992). https://doi.org/10.1145/143095.143114

20. Kell, S., Stinnett, J.R.: Source-level debugging of compiler-optimised code: ill-posed, but not impossible. In: Proceedings of the 2024 ACM SIGPLAN International Symposium on New Ideas, New Paradigms, and Reflections on Programming and Software, Onward! 2024, pp. 38–53. Association for Computing Machinery, New York (2024). https://doi.org/10.1145/3689492.3690047
21. Li, Y., Ding, S., Zhang, Q., Italiano, D.: Debug information validation for optimized code. In: Proceedings of the 41st ACM SIGPLAN Conference on Programming Language Design and Implementation, PLDI 2020, pp. 1052–1065. Association for Computing Machinery, New York (2020). https://doi.org/10.1145/3385412.3386020
22. Marcussen-Wulff, N., Scholz, S.B.: On interfacing sac modules with c programs. In: Mohnen, M., Koopman, P. (eds.) 12th International Workshop on Implementation of Functional Languages (IFL 2000), Aachen, Germany. Aachener Informatik-Berichte, vol. AIB-00-7, pp. 381–386. Technical University of Aachen (2000), c-interface-aachen-00.pdf
23. McKim, J.: Programming by contract. Computer **29**(3), 109–111 (1996). https://doi.org/10.1109/2.485902
24. Meyer, B.: Design by Contract. Prentice Hall, Upper Saddle River (2002)
25. Rosenblum, D.: A practical approach to programming with assertions. IEEE Trans. Software Eng. **21**(1), 19–31 (1995). https://doi.org/10.1109/32.341844
26. Sabry, A., Felleisen, M.: Reasoning about programs in continuation-passing style. SIGPLAN Lisp Pointers **V**(1), 288–298 (1992). https://doi.org/10.1145/141478.141563
27. Scholz, S.-B.: With-loop-folding in Sac-condensing consecutive array operations. In: Clack, C., Hammond, K., Davie, T. (eds.) IFL 1997. LNCS, vol. 1467, pp. 72–91. Springer, Heidelberg (1998). https://doi.org/10.1007/BFb0055425
28. Scholz, S.B.: Single assignment C: efficient support for high-level array operations in a functional setting. J. Funct. Program. **13**(6), 1005–1059 (2003). https://doi.org/10.1017/S0956796802004458
29. de Vries, E., Plasmeijer, R., Abrahamson, D.M.: Uniqueness typing simplified. In: Chitil, O., Horváth, Z., Zsók, V. (eds.) IFL 2007. LNCS, vol. 5083, pp. 201–218. Springer, Heidelberg (2008). https://doi.org/10.1007/978-3-540-85373-2_12

Unifying Hindsight and Foresight
Lazy Cost Analysis as Functional Logic Programming

Nicholas Coltharp[1], Steven Libby[2], Laura Israel[3], and Yao Li[1(✉)]

[1] Portland State University, Portland, Oregon, USA
liyao@pdx.edu
[2] University of Portland, Portland, Oregon, USA
[3] University of Konstanz, Konstanz, Germany

Abstract. Clairvoyance semantics and demand semantics are both pure and time-cost equivalent to lazy evaluation, offering alternatives to the stateful natural semantics of lazy evaluation for analyzing computation cost. Unfortunately, clairvoyance semantics is simple but hard to execute, and demand semantics is executable but complicated. In this paper, we propose a novel approach for unifying these two semantics using functional logic programming. We propose (1) a logical clairvoyance translation, which translates lazy functional programs to functional logic programs where the computation cost is reified, and (2) a logical demand translation, which is a simple extension to the logical clairvoyance translation. We prove that these two translations correctly implement clairvoyance and demand semantics respectively using Agda. We also conduct case studies on examples including insertion sort and Okasaki's banker's queue using Curry/KiCS2 to show how these translations can be used in practice.

Keywords: Functional Logic Programming · Lazy Evaluation · Cost Analysis

1 Introduction

Lazy evaluation is demand-driven, performing only those operations required to compute a final result [15]. This gives programmers the luxury of writing highly compositional code that performs comparably to, or even better than, code written in an eagerly-evaluated language [13]. Sadly, as a "side-effect," it presents challenges for performance analysis.

For example, consider the Haskell functions `take` and `(++)`, which respectively take the length-n prefix of a list and concatenate two lists. Suppose that we want to evaluate the following code:

```
take 2 ([1,2,3] ++ [4,5])
```

In a lazy language like Haskell, such an expression is evaluated only insofar as its result *demands*. Suppose that we try to print just the first element of the result: we run `take` and `(++)` once to obtain `1`. Now suppose that we save the result

M. Sperber and E. Komendantskaya (Eds.): FLOPS 2026, LNCS 16533, pp. 118–138, 2026.
https://doi.org/10.1007/978-981-92-0184-6_5

```
take :: Int -> [a] -> [a]
takeC :: Int -> [a]^A -> P([a]^A, ℕ)
takeD :: Int -> [a] -> [a]^A -> ([a]^A, ℕ)

(++) :: [a] -> [a] -> [a]
appendC :: [a]^A -> [a]^A -> P([a]^A, ℕ)
appendD :: [a] -> [a] -> [a]^A -> (([a]^A, [a]^A), ℕ)
```

Fig. 1. The Haskell type signatures of `take`, `(++)`, and their respective clairvoyance and demand translations. $\mathcal{P}$ is the power set operator. The superscript ^{A} denotes the *approximation* of a type.

in a variable and, in the future, try to print the whole thing: at that point in time, we evaluate `take` and `(++)` "one level deeper" to obtain the second element, `2`, and `take` again to obtain the end of the list, `[]`. These computations are evaluated *on demand* and *out of order*, and they are *interleaved.* Thus, even in a pure language like Haskell, the performance characteristics of the computation are inherently *stateful*: the amount of work required to evaluate a given expression depends on what has been evaluated previously. Together, these characteristics mean that one cannot generally analyze a piece of lazy code in isolation; instead, one must consider the whole program. This makes performance analysis difficult.

How can we bring locality, purity, order, and compositionality to lazy computation time costs when these properties are fundamentally missing? Some recent work proposes that, instead of working with the stateful natural semantics of lazy evaluation [15], we can use a simpler *alternative semantics* that is equivalent to lazy evaluation in terms of computation cost. Here, we focus on two such semantics: clairvoyance semantics [8,17] and demand semantics [2,30].

Clairvoyance Semantics. Clairvoyance semantics, or clairvoyant call-by-value, builds on the observation that, for analyzing computation costs, it matters only *whether* a computation cost is incurred, not *when.* Clairvoyance semantics evaluates terms eagerly, but when there is a lazy operation, it makes a *nondeterministic* choice to either evaluate the computation or skip it.

To evaluate `take 2 ([1,2,3] ++ [4,5])` in clairvoyance semantics, we first evaluate `[1,2,3] ++ [4,5]`. Each recursive function application is then nondeterministically evaluated or skipped. The possible results of `[1,2,3] ++ [4,5]` are `1:`$\bot$, `1:2:`$\bot$, $\cdots$, `[1,2,3,4,5]`, where $\bot$ represents a value whose evaluation is skipped. Next, we run `take 2` over all the nondeterministic results of `[1,2,3] ++ [4,5]`. If a branch gets "stuck," *e.g.*, forcing the second element from `take 2 (1:`$\bot$`)` , we discard it. In the end, one computation branch will have succeeded in the same amount of time as a standard lazy evaluation.

Clairvoyance semantics can be used as a recipe for a mechanical translation from a pure program to a program with reified computation costs [17]. We show pseudo type signatures of translated `take` and `(++)` in Fig. 1 as `takeC` and `appendC`, respectively. These translated functions use *approximations* of lists, denoted as `[a]`^{A} . They represent lists that are potentially "less evaluated", like `1:`$\bot$. We defer a formal definition of approximations to Sect. 3.2. A natural number ($\mathbb{N}$) in the result represents the associated computation cost. Because the evaluation is nondeterministic, each translated function returns a power set of result-cost pairs. We can use these translated functions to formally reason about the computation cost of lazy programs, as illustrated by Li *et al.* [17]

One major drawback of this approach is that power sets in return types make execution expensive. This makes it hard to use clairvoyance semantics in testing.

Demand Semantics. Demand semantics builds on the observation that, given a function's input and a demand on its output, we can evaluate the minimal input demand required for such an output demand *deterministically.*

In our example of `take 2 ([1,2,3] ++ [4,5])`, we first consider a demand on the output, *e.g.*, `1:`$\bot$, where $\bot$ represents parts of the list that are not evaluated. We then run the `take` function "backward" to find that the minimal input demand required for `take 2` is also `1:`$\bot$. We then run the `(++)` function "backward" as well to find that the minimal input demands required for the two input lists are `1:`$\bot$ and $\bot$, respectively. Throughout this process, the associated computation cost is also evaluated and carried.

Demand semantics is also useful as a translation strategy [30]. We show pseudo type signatures of the translated functions `takeD` and `appendD` in Fig. 1. As in the clairvoyance translation, we use a natural number in the result to represent computation cost. The demand translation also uses approximations like `1:`$\bot$, but it uses them to represent demands. For example, the input of `takeD` includes the input of `take` (`Int` and `[a]`), a demand on `take`'s output (`[a]`^{A}). The return type of `takeD` is the minimal demand on its input (`[a]`^{A}) and the cost ($\mathbb{N}$). Note that the `Int` datatype is not lazy, so there is no demand on it.

Because these demand functions are deterministic, computation costs are easy to test. Unfortunately, the demand translation is more complicated than the clairvoyance translation, because the "backward" direction of a function can be complex. This complexity makes it challenging to develop tools to formally reason about code under demand semantics.

Our Contributions. It is unsatisfying that, although we have two semantics that model lazy computation costs, they are very different and we have to choose between them depending on what we need. In this paper, we propose a novel approach of *unifying* these two semantics using *functional logic programming.* In this new approach, we translate a lazy functional program to a functional logic program that models clairvoyance semantics via a *logical clairvoyance translation.* This functional logic program can then be extended to obtain a new program that encodes demand semantics via a *logical demand translation* using a simpler wrapper. This simple wrapper shows that there is a simple connection between clairvoyance semantics and demand semantics. In other words, these two independently proposed semantics are two sides of the same coin. We show this connection both in theory and in practice.

```
data T a = Undefined | Thunk a

takeC :: Int -> T (List a) -> Tick (List a)
takeC n xsT = do
  tick
  fcase n `compare` 0 of
    EQ -> return Nil
    GT -> do
      xs <- force xsT
      fcase xs of
        Nil -> return Nil
        x :~ xsT' -> (x:~) <$> thunk (takeC (n - 1) xsT')

takeD :: Approx a => Int -> T (List a) -> List a -> Tick (T (List a))
takeD n xsT ysD
    | takeC n xsTD =:= Tick (ysD, c)
    = Tick (xsTD, c)
  where xsTD = approx xsT
        c free
```

Fig. 2. The logical clairvoyance translation (`takeC`) and logical demand translation (`takeD`) of the `take` function, implemented in Curry.

We show an example of translating the Haskell `take` function to Curry [10] in Fig. 2. Function `takeC` is the result of a logical clairvoyance translation, while `takeD` is the result of a logical demand translation.

The `takeC` function takes an `Int` and a `T (List a)`. The `T` datatype represents a value that could be $\bot$ (represented by `Undefined`). `List a` is the approximation of `[a]`: `Nil` is the empty list, and the `:~` operator is the cons operator on `List a`. The function returns a new `List a` inside a `Tick` monad, which encodes the computation cost associated with the returned `List a`. The function works similarly to `take` for the most part. The key to implementing clairvoyance semantics is the recursive call `thunk (takeC n' xsT')`, which unfolds to:

```
pure Undefined ? fmap Thunk (takeC n' xsT')
```

That is, we use Curry's nondeterministic choice operator `?` to either skip the evaluation and return `Undefined` (*i.e.*, $\bot$), or to evaluate the recursive call and wrap the result inside a `Thunk` constructor.

The `takeD` function is implemented in terms of `takeC`. The core of `takeD` is its guard condition: `takeC n xsTD =:= Tick (ysD, c)`, where `n` and `ysD` are `takeD`'s arguments, and `xsTD` and `c` are logic variables (also known as free variables). In this way, `takeD` computes the input `xsTD` and parts of the output `c` of `takeC`, given the rest of its output `ysD`. Put differently, `takeD` is an *inversion* of `takeC`. In addition, we require `xsTD` to be an approximation of `xsT`, another argument of `takeD`, so that it either is `xsT`, or is "less evaluated" than `xsT`.

Thanks to functional logic programming compilers, we now have a simple way of executing clairvoyance semantics. Our work also proposes a simpler way to encode demand semantics.

More concretely, we make the following contributions:

- We propose and formalize two methods that translate functional programs to functional logic programs that reify lazy computation costs: a logical clairvoyance translation that encodes clairvoyance semantics, and a logical demand translation that wraps the logical clairvoyance translation and encodes demand semantics (Sect. 2).
- We formally prove that the logical clairvoyance translation and the logical demand translation are correct with respect to clairvoyance and demand semantics, respectively. All theorems and proofs are mechanized in the proof assistant Agda [22] (Sect. 3).
- We conduct case studies by manually translating lazy Haskell programs, including insertion sort and Okasaki's banker's queue [23], to Curry [10] based on our translation strategies. We evaluate the performance of translated code using the KiCS2 Curry compiler [4], showing that logical demand translation trades off performance for simplicity, but the performance is usable for lazy cost analysis while allowing for simpler code (Sect. 4).

In addition, we discuss related work in Sect. 5, discuss limitations and conclude in Sect. 6. All the Agda formalizations and Curry code of this paper can be found in our publicly available artifact:

https://doi.org/10.5281/zenodo.18808172

2 Logical Clairvoyance Translation and Logical Demand Translation

In this section, we define two languages: a simple functional language **B** (Sect. 2.1) and a simple functional logic language **L** (Sect. 2.2). Next, we develop two translations from **B** to **L**: a *logical clairvoyance translation* which produces terms modeling clairvoyance semantics [8,17], and a *logical demand translation*, which is a wrapper around the logical clairvoyance translation, which produces terms modeling demand semantics [2,30] (Sect. 2.3).

2.1 The Base Language B

We show the syntax of the base language **B** in Fig. 3. Language **B** is a simply typed calculus with booleans, lists, and lazy thunks (*i.e.*, suspended computations). Its terms include variables, `let`-bindings, conditionals, and recursion based on `foldr`. In addition, it contains `lazy` and `force` operators, which wrap a computation in a lazy thunk and force a computation from a thunk, respectively. Finally, the `tick` operator incurs one unit of computation cost. These explicit operators decouple our analysis from any particular evaluation model.

$$
\begin{array}{lcl}
A & ::= & \texttt{Bool} \mid \texttt{List}\ A \mid \texttt{Thunk}\ A \\
t & ::= & x \mid \texttt{let}\ x\ \texttt{=}\ t\ \texttt{in}\ t \mid \texttt{true} \mid \texttt{false} \mid \texttt{if}\ t\ \texttt{then}\ t\ \texttt{else}\ t \\
 & \mid & \texttt{[]} \mid t\ \texttt{::}\ t \mid \texttt{foldr(}\lambda xx.t\texttt{,}\ t\texttt{,}\ t\texttt{)} \mid \texttt{lazy}\ t \mid \texttt{force}\ t \mid \texttt{tick}\ t
\end{array}
$$

Typing

$$
\frac{\Gamma \vdash^{\mathbf{B}} t_1 : A \qquad \Gamma \vdash^{\mathbf{B}} t_2 : \texttt{Thunk (List } A\texttt{)}}{\Gamma \vdash^{\mathbf{B}} t_1\ \texttt{::}\ t_2 : \texttt{List}\ A}\text{CONS}
$$

$$
\frac{\Gamma, x_1 : A, x_2 : \texttt{Thunk}\ B \vdash^{\mathbf{B}} t_1 : B \qquad \Gamma \vdash^{\mathbf{B}} t_2 : B \qquad \Gamma \vdash^{\mathbf{B}} t_3 : \texttt{List}\ A}{\Gamma \vdash^{\mathbf{B}} \texttt{foldr(}\lambda x_1 x_2 . t_1\texttt{,}\ t_2\texttt{,}\ t_3\texttt{)} : B}\text{FOLDR}
$$

$$
\frac{\Gamma \vdash^{\mathbf{B}} t : A}{\Gamma \vdash^{\mathbf{B}} \texttt{lazy}\ t : \texttt{Thunk}\ A}\text{LAZY} \qquad
\frac{\Gamma \vdash^{\mathbf{B}} t : \texttt{Thunk}\ A}{\Gamma \vdash^{\mathbf{B}} \texttt{force}\ t : A}\text{FORCE} \qquad
\frac{\Gamma \vdash^{\mathbf{B}} t : A}{\Gamma \vdash^{\mathbf{B}} \texttt{tick}\ t : A}\text{TICK}
$$

Fig. 3. The syntax of language **B** and typing rules related to lazy thunks and costs.

Note that language **B** does not have higher-order functions or general recursion because demand semantics does not support these features [2,30].

Most of the typing rules for language **B** are standard, so we omit them. We show the typing rules for thunks and computation costs in Fig. 3. Notably, lists are lazy: the cons of lists t_1 `::` t_2 takes a term t_1 of type A and a term t_2 of type `Thunk (List` A`)`, so the tail of a list must always be wrapped in a `Thunk`. Similarly, the "function" argument to `foldr` always requires that its second parameter be wrapped in a `Thunk`.

We can give language **B** a denotational semantics $[\![t]\!](\gamma)$ for any term t in an environment γ by simply ignoring all operations related to lazy evaluation and computation costs:

$$
[\![\texttt{lazy}\ t]\!](\gamma) = [\![\texttt{force}\ t]\!](\gamma) = [\![\texttt{tick}\ t]\!](\gamma) = [\![t]\!](\gamma)
$$

2.2 The Logic Language L

We show the syntax of language **L** in Fig. 4. Compared to **B**, language **L** has more types: unit `Unit`, natural numbers `Nat`, and products A `*` B. We need natural numbers and products to represent computation costs associated with values, and we need products and the unit type to represent environments. Note that the types of language **L** are a superset of the types of **B**. As a consequence, any valid typing context for **B** is also a valid typing context for language **L**.

Language **L** has introduction and elimination forms for all of the new types. In particular, the `lazy` and `force` operators from **B** have been replaced by constructors `thunk` and `undefined`, and eliminator `case`. The `thunk` operator reduces its argument and wraps it in a **thunk** value; `undefined` reduces to the

$$
\begin{array}{lcl}
A & ::= & \texttt{Unit} \mid \texttt{Bool} \mid \texttt{Nat} \mid A \texttt{ * } A \mid \texttt{List } A \mid \texttt{Thunk } A \\
t & ::= & x \mid \texttt{let } x \texttt{ = } t \texttt{ in } t \mid \texttt{()} \mid \texttt{true} \mid \texttt{false} \mid \texttt{if } t \texttt{ then } t \texttt{ else } t \\
 & \mid & t \texttt{ == } t \mid t \texttt{ <= } t \mid \texttt{(}t\texttt{, } t\texttt{)} \mid \texttt{fst } t \mid \texttt{snd } t \mid \texttt{thunk } t \mid \texttt{undefined} \\
 & \mid & \texttt{case } t \texttt{ of thunk } x \texttt{ => } t\texttt{; undefined => } t \mid n \mid t \texttt{ + } t \mid \texttt{[]} \mid t \texttt{ :: } t \\
 & \mid & \texttt{foldr(}\lambda x x.t\texttt{, } t\texttt{, } t\texttt{)} \mid t \texttt{ ? } t \mid \texttt{free } A \mid \texttt{fail}
\end{array}
$$

Typing

$$\frac{\Gamma \vdash^{\mathbf{L}} t : A}{\Gamma \vdash^{\mathbf{L}} \texttt{thunk } t : \texttt{Thunk } A} \qquad \frac{}{\Gamma \vdash^{\mathbf{L}} \texttt{undefined} : \texttt{Thunk } A}$$

$$\frac{\Gamma \vdash^{\mathbf{L}} t_1 : \texttt{Thunk } A \qquad \Gamma, x : A \vdash^{\mathbf{L}} t_2 : B \qquad \Gamma \vdash^{\mathbf{L}} t_3 : B}{\Gamma \vdash^{\mathbf{L}} \texttt{case } t_1 \texttt{ of thunk } x \texttt{ => } t_2\texttt{; undefined => } t_3 : B}$$

$$\frac{}{\Gamma \vdash^{\mathbf{L}} \texttt{free } A : A} \qquad \frac{\Gamma \vdash^{\mathbf{L}} t_1 : A \qquad \Gamma \vdash^{\mathbf{L}} t_2 : A}{\Gamma \vdash^{\mathbf{L}} t_1 \texttt{ ? } t_2 : A} \qquad \frac{}{\Gamma \vdash^{\mathbf{L}} \texttt{fail} : A}$$

Fig. 4. The syntax and typing rules of the logic language **L**.

special value $\bot$; `case` discriminates between these two cases. In the logical clairvoyance translation, the `thunk` and `undefined` constructors indicate whether a computation is evaluated or not; in the logical demand translation, they indicate whether a computation is demanded or not.

Language **L** also has constructs for logic programming. Free terms (`free`) may evaluate to any value of a specified type; they can be thought of as "anonymous logic variables". The choice operator (`?`) evaluates nondeterministically to either of its operands. Failure (`fail`) never evaluates to anything.

Finally, **L** has two new relational operators, `==` and `<=`. The `==` operator indicates equality, as usual. The `<=` does *not* indicate the standard order on natural numbers; rather, it indicates the *definedness* relation. Given two values a, a', we write a`<=`a', pronounced "a is less defined than a'," if a has the same shape as a', but with some **thunk** parts possibly replaced by $\bot$.

We define a simple logic language instead of using a specific functional logic language like Curry [10,28] or the Verse calculus [1] to keep our approach generally applicable.

We show the semantic rules of **L** that are related to the choice operator (`?`) and free terms in Fig. 4. Note that this semantics is eager, and due to `fail`, it is partial.

Derived Terms in **L**. We use **L** to implement functional logic programs that "carry" a computation result and its associated computation cost. To encapsulate operations related to computation costs, we define some derived term constructs in **L** in Fig. 5. We use `return` t to lift t to a computation that costs 0. We use x `<-` t_1`;` t_2 to chain computations t_1 and t_2 while accumulating their costs. We use `foldM(`$\lambda x_1 x_2.t_1$`,` t_2`,` t_3`)` to chain a list of computations, accumulating all of their costs. The `foldM` operation employs an auxiliary construct `transpose`,

$$
\begin{aligned}
\texttt{M}\ A &= A\ \texttt{*}\ \texttt{Nat}\\
\texttt{return}\ t &= \texttt{(}t\texttt{, 0)}\\
x\ \texttt{<-}\ t_1\texttt{;}\ t_2 &= \texttt{let}\ z_1\ \texttt{=}\ t_1\ \texttt{in}\\
&\quad\ \texttt{let}\ x\ \texttt{= fst}\ t_1\ \texttt{in}\\
&\quad\ \texttt{let}\ z_2\ \texttt{=}\ t_2\ \texttt{in}\\
&\quad\ \texttt{(fst}\ z_2\texttt{, snd}\ z_1\ \texttt{+ snd}\ z_2\texttt{)}\\
\texttt{foldM(}\lambda x_1 x_2.t_1\texttt{,}\ t_2\texttt{,}\ t_3\texttt{)} &= \texttt{foldr(}\lambda x_1 z_2.x_2\ \texttt{<- transpose}\ z_2\texttt{;}\ t_1\texttt{,}\ t_2\texttt{,}\ t_3\texttt{)}\\
\texttt{transpose}\ t &= \texttt{case}\ t\ \texttt{of}\\
&\quad\ \texttt{thunk}\ z_1\ \texttt{-> (}z_2\ \texttt{<-}\ z_1\texttt{; return (thunk}\ z_2\texttt{));}\\
&\quad\ \texttt{undefined -> return undefined}\\
\texttt{assert}\ t_1\ \texttt{in}\ t_2 &= \texttt{if}\ t_1\ \texttt{then}\ t_2\ \texttt{else fail}
\end{aligned}
$$

$$
\frac{\Gamma \vdash^{\mathbf{L}} t : A}{\Gamma \vdash^{\mathbf{L}} \texttt{return}\ t : \texttt{M}\ A}
\qquad
\frac{\Gamma \vdash^{\mathbf{L}} t_1 : \texttt{M}\ A \qquad \Gamma, x : A \vdash^{\mathbf{L}} t_2 : \texttt{M}\ B}{\Gamma \vdash^{\mathbf{L}} x\ \texttt{<-}\ t_1\texttt{;}\ t_2 : \texttt{M}\ B}
$$

$$
\frac{\Gamma, x_1 : A, x_2 : \texttt{Thunk}\ B \vdash^{\mathbf{L}} t_1 : \texttt{M}\ B \qquad \Gamma \vdash^{\mathbf{L}} t_2 : \texttt{M}\ B \qquad \Gamma \vdash^{\mathbf{L}} t_3 : \texttt{List}\ A}{\Gamma \vdash^{\mathbf{L}} \texttt{foldM(}\lambda x_1 x_2.t_1\texttt{,}\ t_2\texttt{,}\ t_3\texttt{)} : \texttt{M}\ B}
$$

$$
\frac{\Gamma \vdash^{\mathbf{L}} t : \texttt{Thunk (M}\ A\texttt{)}}{\Gamma \vdash^{\mathbf{L}} \texttt{transpose}\ t : \texttt{M (Thunk}\ A\texttt{)}}
\qquad
\frac{\Gamma \vdash^{\mathbf{L}} t_1 : \texttt{Bool} \qquad \Gamma \vdash^{\mathbf{L}} t_2 : A}{\Gamma \vdash^{\mathbf{L}} \texttt{assert}\ t_1\ \texttt{in}\ t_2 : A}
$$

Fig. 5. Derived constructs in **L** and their typing rules. Readers who are familiar with monads might recognize that `M` is a writer monad [20,29].

which converts terms of type `Thunk (M` A`)` to terms of type `M (Thunk` A`)`. In addition, we define `assert`, which ensures that a given condition holds, causing the computation to fail otherwise.

We show all the typing rules related to these derived terms in Fig. 5.

2.3 Logical Clairvoyance Translation and Logical Demand Translation

We define the logical clairvoyance translation $\mathbb{C}\lfloor\cdot\rfloor$ in Fig. 6. The logical clairvoyance translation translates terms in **B** to terms in **L** that simulate clairvoyance semantics. Values and variables are translated using `return`. Variable bindings (`let`) and conditionals (`if`) are translated via sequencing (`·` `<-` `·;` `·`). Folds (`foldr`) are translated to the derived term construct `foldM`. Readers familiar with monads might recognize that this is essentially a monadic translation [20,24,29] with adaptations for the `Thunk` type [17].

The most important cases of the translation are those for `lazy` and `force`. When the original term is `lazy` t, we use the nondeterministic choice operator `?` to either skip the inner term (`return undefined`) or evaluate the inner term and wrap the result inside a `thunk`. When the original term is `force` t, we first evaluate t and then pattern match on the result z_1: if z_1 evaluates to `thunk` z_2, then we return z_2; otherwise, we `fail`. Note that `fail` only terminates the current computation branch, so any branches where z_1 evaluates to

Logical Clairvoyance Translation:

$$\mathbb{C}\lfloor x \rfloor = \texttt{return}\ x \qquad \mathbb{C}\lfloor \texttt{[]} \rfloor = \texttt{return []}$$

$$\mathbb{C}\lfloor \texttt{let}\ x\ \texttt{=}\ t_1\ \texttt{in}\ t_2 \rfloor = x\ \texttt{<-}\ \mathbb{C}\lfloor t_1 \rfloor\texttt{;}\ \mathbb{C}\lfloor t_2 \rfloor$$

$$\mathbb{C}\lfloor t_1\ \texttt{::}\ t_2 \rfloor = z_1\ \texttt{<-}\ \mathbb{C}\lfloor t_1 \rfloor\texttt{;}\ z_2\ \texttt{<-}\ \mathbb{C}\lfloor t_2 \rfloor\texttt{; return (}z_1\ \texttt{::}\ z_2\texttt{)}$$

$$\mathbb{C}\lfloor \texttt{foldr(}\lambda x_1 x_2.t_1\texttt{,}\ t_2\texttt{,}\ t_3\texttt{)} \rfloor = z\ \texttt{<-}\ \mathbb{C}\lfloor t_3 \rfloor\texttt{; foldM(}\lambda x_1 x_2.\mathbb{C}\lfloor t_1 \rfloor\texttt{,}\ \mathbb{C}\lfloor t_2 \rfloor\texttt{,}\ z\texttt{)}$$

$$\mathbb{C}\lfloor \texttt{lazy}\ t \rfloor = \texttt{return undefined ?}\ z\ \texttt{<-}\ t\texttt{; return (thunk}\ z\texttt{)}$$

$$\mathbb{C}\lfloor \texttt{force}\ t \rfloor = z_1\ \texttt{<-}\ t\texttt{; case}\ z_1\ \texttt{of}$$
$$\texttt{thunk}\ z_2\ \texttt{=> return}\ z_2\texttt{; undefined => fail}$$

$$\mathbb{C}\lfloor \texttt{tick}\ t \rfloor = \texttt{let}\ z\ \texttt{=}\ \mathbb{C}\lfloor t \rfloor\ \texttt{in (fst}\ z\texttt{, snd}\ z + 1\texttt{)}$$

Logical Demand Translation:

$$\mathbb{D}_{x_1:A_1,\ldots,x_n:A_n}\lfloor t \rfloor = \texttt{let}\ x_1'\ \texttt{= free}\ A_1\ \texttt{in assert}\ x_1'\ \texttt{<=}\ x_1\ \texttt{in}$$
$$\vdots$$
$$\texttt{let}\ x_n'\ \texttt{= free}\ A_n\ \texttt{in assert}\ x_n'\ \texttt{<=}\ x_n\ \texttt{in}$$
$$\texttt{let}\ z\ \texttt{=}\ \mathbb{C}\lfloor t' \rfloor\ \texttt{in}$$
$$\texttt{assert fst}\ z\ \texttt{==}\ y\ \texttt{in ((}x_1'\texttt{, ...,}\ x_n'\texttt{), snd}\ z\texttt{)}$$
$$\text{where } t' = t[x_1'/x_1, \ldots, x_n'/x_n].$$

Fig. 6. The logical clairvoyance translation $\mathbb{C}\lfloor\cdot\rfloor$ and logical demand translation $\mathbb{D}_\Gamma\lfloor\cdot\rfloor$.

a `thunk` will continue. To `tick` a computation, we simply run it and increment its accumulated cost by 1. This translation correctly models sharing—a feature that typically poses a challenge to cost analysis—because the result term in **B** eagerly evaluates each value only once in every nondeterministic branch.

We also define the logical demand translation $\mathbb{D}_\Gamma\lfloor t \rfloor$ from **B** to **L** in Fig. 6.

In general, the logical demand translation operates on open terms with an arbitrary number of free variables, but we can build an intuition for how it works by considering terms with just one free variable. Let $t(x)$ be a term in **L** with one free variable x. Intuitively, the demand semantics interpretation of t is a term $t'(x, y)$ that takes the original parameter x and a new *demand* parameter y representing the demand on $t(x)$. The term $t'(x, y)$ computes the minimal demand on x needed to produce y. From this specification, we can see that $t'(x, y)$ acts as an *inverse* of $t(x)$ in the parameter y. In general, any term $t(x)$ has a canonical inverse term $t^{-1}(y)$ given by

$$t^{-1}(y) = \texttt{let}\ x\ \texttt{= free}\ A\ \texttt{in assert}\ t(x)\ \texttt{==}\ y\ \texttt{in}\ x.$$

The logical demand translation *extends* such an inversion: $t'(x, y)$ does not just produce any value inverse to y, it produces one that is less defined than x. We add this constraint:

$$t'(x, y) = \texttt{let}\ x'\ \texttt{= free}\ A\ \texttt{in assert}\ x'\ \texttt{<=}\ x\ \texttt{in}$$
$$\texttt{assert}\ t(x')\ \texttt{==}\ y\ \texttt{in}\ x'.$$

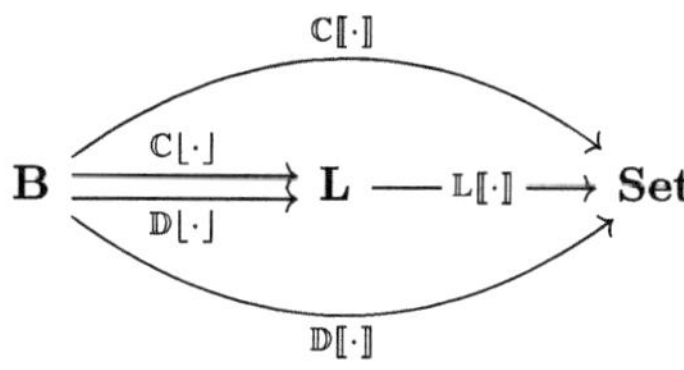

Fig. 7. An overview of our work. $\mathbb{C}[\![\cdot]\!]$ and $\mathbb{D}[\![\cdot]\!]$ respectively represent clairvoyance and demand semantics; $\mathbb{L}[\![\cdot]\!]$ is the semantics of **L**; $\mathbb{C}\lfloor\cdot\rfloor$ and $\mathbb{D}\lfloor\cdot\rfloor$ are term translations. All arrows from **B** to **Set** commute (up to a suitable notion of equivalence).

The missing piece is that the logical demand translation must turn terms in **B** into terms in **L**. We can achieve this by composing t' with some previously-defined translation. As we show in Sect. 3, the logical clairvoyance translation is exactly the translation that we need. After adjusting for the fact that the logical clairvoyance translation produces terms of type `M`, we arrive at the single-variable case of the logical demand translation:

$$\begin{aligned}\mathbb{D}\lfloor t\rfloor(x,y) = {} & \texttt{let } x' \texttt{ = free } A \texttt{ in assert } x' \texttt{ <= } x \texttt{ in} \\ & \texttt{let } z \texttt{ = } \mathbb{C}\lfloor t\rfloor(x') \texttt{ in assert fst } z \texttt{ == } y \texttt{ in} \\ & (x'\texttt{, snd } z\texttt{).}\end{aligned}$$

Extending this translation to multiple variables gives us the translation in Fig. 6.

Notably, the demand semantics of Bjerner and Holmström [2] and Xia *et al.* [30] define how to invert every term explicitly, whereas we simply rely on logic variable resolution techniques such as narrowing.

We prove that logical clairvoyance translation and logical demand translation preserve the well-typedness of the original term in **B**:

Theorem 1. *If* $\Gamma \vdash^{\mathbf{B}} t : A$, *then* $\Gamma \vdash^{\mathbf{L}} \mathbb{C}\lfloor t\rfloor : \texttt{M}\ A$.

Theorem 2. *If* $\Gamma \vdash^{\mathbf{B}} t : A$, *then* $\Gamma, x : A \vdash^{\mathbf{L}} \mathbb{D}_{\Gamma}\lfloor t\rfloor : \texttt{M}\ |\Gamma|$.

The operation $|\cdot|$ turns typing contexts into product types. Both theorems are formalized and proven in Agda.

3 Correctness

In this section, we prove that logical clairvoyance translation and logical demand translation correctly implement clairvoyance semantics and demand semantics, respectively. All of our proofs are mechanized in the Agda proof assistant [22]. Our proofs rely on the equivalence between clairvoyance and demand semantics proven by Xia *et al.* [30, Section 3.3], which we axiomatize in our formalization.

We show an overview of how we formally prove correctness theorems in Fig. 7. We first define clairvoyance semantics $\mathbb{C}[\![\cdot]\!]$ on **B**. We then show that starting from a term t in **B**, we can translate it to a term in **L** using the logical clairvoyance translation $\mathbb{C}\lfloor t\rfloor$ that has the same meaning as $\mathbb{C}[\![t]\!]$. We also prove a similar theorem relating demand semantics to the logical demand translation.

3.1 The Logical Clairvoyance Translation

Clairvoyance semantics is a big-step operational semantics with the judgment schema $\gamma\ ; t \Downarrow^{\mathbb{C}}_{c} v$. Intuitively, c is the number of `ticks` encountered while evaluating t to v. Our semantics is similar to the original clairvoyance semantics of Hackett and Hutton [8]. Like their semantics, ours is based on improvement theory [21]. The most significant difference is that our calculus has explicit `lazy` and `force` operators. Therefore, whereas Hackett and Hutton introduce nondeterminism at `let` bindings, we must introduce it at `lazy` terms. Readers can find detailed definitions of our clairvoyance semantics in Appendix B and in our artifact.

Theorem 3 (Correctness of the logical clairvoyance translation). $\gamma\ ; t \Downarrow^{\mathbb{C}}_{c} v$ *if and only if* $\gamma\ ; \lfloor t \rfloor \Downarrow^{\mathbb{L}} (v, c)$.

3.2 The Logical Demand Translation

Demand semantics is a deterministic semantics that interprets a term t as a function $\mathbb{D}[\![t]\!]$ that takes two arguments: an *exact* evaluation context γ (containing only values with no $\bot$ parts) and an *approximation* value that represents the demand on the result of $[\![t]\!](\gamma)$. It produces a list γ^A of minimal demands on γ and a computation cost. Intuitively, demand semantics computes "how much" of the input γ is required to compute a desired "amount" of the output $[\![t]\!](\gamma)$ and how much it costs to perform the computation.

We omit detailed definitions of demand semantics on **B**, as it is essentially the same as that of Xia *et al.* [30]. Interested readers can refer to them in Appendix C and in our artifact.

Lemma 1 (Semantics of the logical demand translation). $\gamma, y^A \mapsto a^A\ ; \mathbb{D}_\Gamma \lfloor t \rfloor \Downarrow^{\mathbb{L}} (|\gamma^A|, c)$ *if and only if (1)* $\gamma^A \leq \gamma$, *and (2)* $\gamma^A\ ; t \Downarrow^{\mathbb{C}}_{c} a^A$.

Proof. By construction, applying Theorem 3.

We can now establish the correctness of the logical demand translation via two theorems: adequacy and soundness.

Theorem 4 (Adequacy of the logical demand translation). *Define* $(\gamma^A, c) = \mathbb{D}[\![t]\!](\gamma, a^A)$ *and let* $\gamma^{A'} \geq \gamma^A$. *Then there exists some* $a^{A'} \geq a^A$ *such that* $\gamma, y^A \mapsto a^{A'}\ ; \mathbb{D}_\Gamma \lfloor t \rfloor \Downarrow^{\mathbb{L}} (\gamma^{A'}, c)$.

Theorem 5 (Soundness of the logical demand translation). *If* $\gamma, y^A \mapsto a^A\ ; \mathbb{D}_\Gamma \lfloor t \rfloor \Downarrow^{\mathbb{L}} (|\gamma^A|, c)$, *then* $\mathbb{D}[\![t]\!](\gamma, a^A) \leq (\gamma^A, c)$.

The proofs of these theorems depend on Lemma 1 and the theorems of cost existence and cost minimality in Xia *et al.* [30].

```
newtype Tick a =
  Tick { runTick :: (a, Int) }

data T a = Undefined | Thunk a

thunk :: Applicative f =>
  f a -> f (T a)
thunk m =
  pure Undefined ? Thunk <$> m

force :: Applicative f =>
  T a -> f a
force (Thunk x) = pure x
```

```
data List a =
  Nil | (:~) a (T (List a))

class Data a => Approx a where
  (<~) :: a -> a -> Bool

approx :: a -> a
approx x | y <~ x = y where y free

instance Approx a => Approx (T a) where
  Undefined <~ _         = True
  Thunk _   <~ Undefined = False
  Thunk x   <~ Thunk y   = x <~ y
```

Fig. 8. Key definitions for implementing the logical clairvoyance semantics and the logical demand semantics in Curry. See Fig. 2 for the definitions of `thunk` and `T`.

4 Case Studies

To show that the logical clairvoyance translation and logical demand translation work in practice, we conduct some case studies by manually applying these translation strategies on classical Haskell functions and implementing all translated functions in Curry [10]. These examples include appending lists, insertion sort, and Okasaki's banker's queue [23]. We use the KiCS2 Curry compiler [4] to test these implementations. We discuss the details of our implementation in this section.

In addition, we evaluate the performance of translated logical demand functions. Our results show that, although there are slowdowns compared with the specialized demand translation of Xia *et al.* [30], they achieve acceptable performance despite being much simpler. All the code of our case studies can be found in our publicly-available artifact.

Foundations. We begin by building a framework for representing the logical clairvoyance semantics and the logical demand semantics in Curry.

We show key definitions of this framework in Fig. 8. We represent approximation types using the `Approx` typeclass. The typeclass contains an `<~` operator, which indicates its left-hand operand approximates its right-hand operand. The other method, `approx`, nondeterministically returns a value that approximates its argument. We include a default implementation of `approx` using free variables, but a specialized implementation can be much faster. The `Approx` typeclass depends on the `Data` typeclass, which is required for free variables. The `List` type models lazy lists: `Nil` is the empty list, and the `:~` operator produces a new list by adding an element to the front of a (thunked) list.

The `Tick` datatype is a product type which uses an `Int` to represent the computation cost associated with its value. It is essentially a writer monad [20, 29]. `List a` is the approximation type of lists `[a]`. These types have all of the expected typeclass instances; *e.g.*, `Tick` is a `Monad`. These definitions are standard, and we omit them for brevity.

Examples Implemented. We manually apply the logical clairvoyance translation and logical demand translation on classical Haskell functions and implement all translated functions in Curry. Examples include appending lists, insertion sort, and Okasaki's banker's queue [23]. Interested readers can view an insertion sort case study in Appendix E, and more in our publicly available artifact.

Running Computations. All the translated functions can be executed using the KiCS2 Curry compiler, including all the logical clairvoyance functions. In our implementation, we arrange our definitions so that the less-defined result is always on the left branch of a search tree; thus, by using Curry's *search tree* package [3], we can always find the least result via a depth-first search.

Guards vs. Generators. In Curry, there are two ways of implementing logical demand functions: guards and generators. Although they are semantically equivalent, there is a huge performance difference. Naïvely, we can implement `takeD` as follows:

```
takeD' :: Approx a => Int -> T (List a) -> List a -> Tick (T (List a))
takeD' xsT ysD |  xsTD <~ xsT
               && takeC n xsTD =:= Tick (ysD, c)
               =  Tick (xsTD, c)
  where xsTD, c free
```

In contrast to the definition in Fig. 2, we use the `<~` operator in a guard condition in `takeD'` to assert that `xsTD` is an approximation of `xsT`. In this case, Curry must "guess" a valid input demand, performing poorly. On the other hand, our implementation in Fig. 2 uses a generator `approx` defined for the `List` datatype, which is more efficient.

Performance. Although the logical demand translation is simpler than the original demand translation, the question remains whether it is reasonably efficient, as it depends on the logical clairvoyance translation and free variables. To evaluate this, we ran `insertionSortD` on lists of the form `[n, n-1 .. 1]` with sizes ranging from 1 to 100, demanding the full list each time. We also ran `pushPopD`, the logical demand translation of a function that pushes n elements onto a banker's queue [23] and then pops them all. We show the result of our performance evaluation in Fig. 9. All experiments were performed on an AMD Ryzen 3900X running Linux 6.12.58 using the built-in timing functionality of KiCS2 (version 3.5.0), taking the average of 10 executions.

Asymptotically, `insertionSortD` appears to run in $O(n^3)$ time: a cubic interpolation estimates it well. This asymptotic bound is shared by the original demand translation. However, the constants are much worse: `insertionSortD` takes 6.44 s on a 100-element list, while the original demand translation version in Curry is fast enough that its runtime cannot be reliably measured. Meanwhile, the `pushPopD` function takes 12.30 seconds to execute on 10 elements.

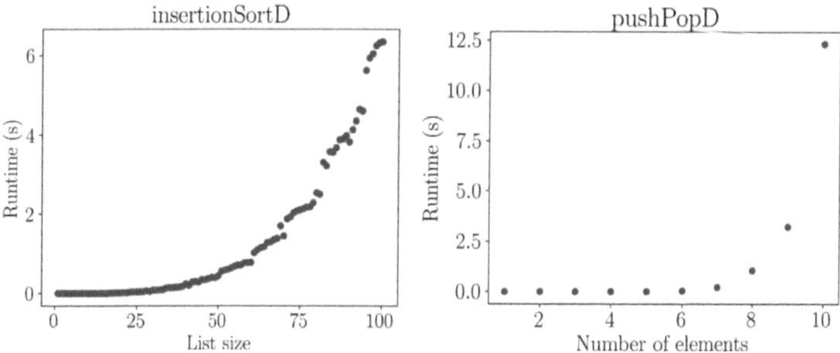

Fig. 9. The runtime of `insertionSortD` and `pushPopD`.

This result is not surprising, as the original demand semantics is specialized to computing minimal input demands, but the logical demand translation is built on a general-purpose logic language. In other words, logical demand functions trade off performance for simplicity. However, the performance is still useful for cost analysis. We discuss this in more detail in Sect. 6.

5 Related Work

Lazy Cost Analysis. Existing research on lazy cost analysis can be divided into roughly three different approaches. The first approach, represented by work on Iris$^{\$}$ [19,25], deals with mutable heaps directly, but requires using special programming logics like the separation logic [26]. The second approach, represented by LiquidHaskell [9,14], uses a graded monad proposed by Danielsson [6] to track computation cost. However, this approach needs to deal with sharing manually. The third approach utilizes alternative semantics, such as clairvoyance semantics [8,17] and demand semantics [2,30], that are equivalent to lazy evaluation in terms of computation cost. In contrast to the natural semantics of lazy evaluation [15], these semantics reify computation cost in pure and eager semantics, so we can use them to reason about lazy computation cost without being concerned with mutable heaps, sharing, or our-of-order executions.

Clairvoyance semantics was proposed by Hackett and Hutton [8], who proved its equivalence with Launchbury's semantics. Li *et al.* extended clairvoyance semantics to a typed setting and mechanized it in Rocq, along with a framework for mechanically reasoning computation costs [17]. Demand semantics was proposed by Bjerner and Holmström [2]. Xia *et al.* later extended it to a typed setting and proved its equivalence to clairvoyance semantics, in forms of cost existence and cost minimality theorems [30]. We rely on these results in our correctness theorems in Sect. 3. They further use demand semantics to mechanically verify amortized costs and persistence of two of Okasaki's data structures: the banker's queue and the implicit queue [23] in Rocq. Recently, a third semantics, memorist semantics, was proposed by Li *et al.* [16]. Memorist semantics works by tracking all the computation dependencies. As it works differently than clairvoyance semantics and demand semantics, it is unclear if there's a connection we can draw like in this paper.

There has also been work on applying property-based testing to lazy computation cost analysis, such as Foner *et al.* [7] and Lorenzen [18]. We leave it as future work to extend our work to property-based testing frameworks in Curry like EasyCheck [5] and CurryCheck [11].

Functional Logic Programming. We implemented our examples in Curry, but most of the techniques in this paper are not specific to Curry. Other functional logic languages, such as Verse [1] or Mercury [27], could also have proven sufficient. Because **L** uses eager evaluation, we could have even translated to a pure logic language such as Prolog [12]. However, the search tree traversal employed in this work is Curry-specific [3].

6 Conclusion and Future Work

We have shown that clairvoyance and demand semantics are two sides of the same coin using logic programming as an intermediary. This connection is both theoretically interesting and practically useful: it demonstrates that functional logic programming concepts have value in seemingly unrelated areas. We also obtained an executable clairvoyance semantics and a simpler demand semantics built on functional logic programming semantics.

As discussed in Sect. 4, our technique is slow with even modestly-sized inputs. Although unfortunate, this may be acceptable for most applications. A major motivation behind this line of research was the desire to find a lightweight representation of demand functions that could be used to test their asymptotic bounds (constants included) *before* trying to formally verify them. For this purpose, it usually suffices to test quite small inputs, where our technique performs quite well in absolute (wall-clock) terms. However, some applications seem to perform much worse than others for reasons that we do not yet understand. Further investigation is left as future work.

Acknowledgement. We thank all FLOPS 2026 reviewers for their constructive and insightful comments. We thank Alex Hodges and Xing Li for their feedback to a draft of this paper. This research idea was initially sparked by a discussion after a remote talk given by Shiwei Weng at Portland State University.

A The Evaluation Semantics of B

$$
\begin{aligned}
[\![x]\!](\gamma) &= \gamma(x)\\
[\![\texttt{let } x \texttt{ = } t_1 \texttt{ in } t_2]\!](\gamma) &= [\![t_2]\!](\gamma, x \mapsto [\![t_1]\!](\gamma))\\
[\![\texttt{true}]\!](\gamma) &= \mathbf{true}\\
[\![\texttt{false}]\!](\gamma) &= \mathbf{false}\\
[\![\texttt{if } t_1 \texttt{ then } t_2 \texttt{ else } t_3]\!](\gamma) &= \begin{cases} [\![t_2]\!](\gamma) & \text{if } [\![t_1]\!](\gamma) = \mathbf{true}\\ [\![t_3]\!](\gamma) & \text{otherwise}\end{cases}\\
[\![\texttt{[]}]\!](\gamma) &= \varepsilon\\
[\![t_1 \texttt{ :: } t_2]\!](\gamma) &= \mathbf{cons}([\![t_1]\!](\gamma), [\![t_2]\!](\gamma))\\
[\![\texttt{foldr(}\lambda x_1 x_2 . t_1\texttt{, } t_2\texttt{, } t_3\texttt{)}]\!](\gamma) &= [\![\lambda x_1 x_2 . t_1]\!]_{\text{foldr}}(t_2, \gamma, [\![t_3]\!](\gamma))\\
[\![\texttt{lazy } t]\!](\gamma) &= [\![t]\!](\gamma)\\
[\![\texttt{force } t]\!](\gamma) &= [\![t]\!](\gamma)\\
[\![\texttt{tick } t]\!](\gamma) &= [\![t]\!](\gamma)
\end{aligned}
$$

$$
\begin{aligned}
[\![\lambda x_1 x_2 . t_1]\!]_{\text{foldr}}(t_2, \gamma, \mathbf{nil}) &= [\![t_2]\!](\gamma)\\
[\![\lambda x_1 x_2 . t_1]\!]_{\text{foldr}}(t_2, \gamma, \mathbf{cons}(v_1, v_2)) &= [\![t_1]\!](\gamma, x_1 \mapsto v_1, x_2 \mapsto [\![\lambda x_1 x_2 . t_1]\!]_{\text{foldr}}(t_2, \gamma, v_2))
\end{aligned}
$$

B The Clairvoyance Semantics of B

$$
\frac{\gamma(x) = v}{\gamma \,;\, x \Downarrow^{\mathbb{C}}_{0} v}\ \textsc{C-Var}
\qquad
\frac{\gamma \,;\, t_1 \Downarrow^{\mathbb{C}}_{c_1} v_1 \qquad \gamma, x \mapsto v_1 \,;\, t_2 \Downarrow^{\mathbb{C}}_{c_2} v_2}{\gamma \,;\, \texttt{let } x \texttt{ = } t_1 \texttt{ in } t_2 \Downarrow^{\mathbb{C}}_{c_1+c_2} v_2}\ \textsc{C-Let}
$$

$$
\frac{}{\gamma \,;\, \texttt{true} \Downarrow^{\mathbb{C}}_{0} \mathbf{true}}\ \textsc{C-True}
\qquad
\frac{}{\gamma \,;\, \texttt{false} \Downarrow^{\mathbb{C}}_{0} \mathbf{false}}\ \textsc{C-False}
$$

$$
\frac{\gamma \,;\, t_1 \Downarrow^{\mathbb{C}}_{c_1} \mathbf{true} \qquad \gamma \,;\, t_2 \Downarrow^{\mathbb{C}}_{c_2} v}{\gamma \,;\, \texttt{if } t_1 \texttt{ then } t_2 \texttt{ else } t_3 \Downarrow^{\mathbb{C}}_{c_1+c_2} v}\ \textsc{C-If-True}
\qquad
\frac{\gamma \,;\, t_1 \Downarrow^{\mathbb{C}}_{c_1} \mathbf{false} \qquad \gamma \,;\, t_3 \Downarrow^{\mathbb{C}}_{c_3} v}{\gamma \,;\, \texttt{if } t_1 \texttt{ then } t_2 \texttt{ else } t_3 \Downarrow^{\mathbb{C}}_{c_1+c_3} v}\ \textsc{C-If-False}
$$

$$
\frac{}{\gamma \,;\, \texttt{[]} \Downarrow^{\mathbb{C}}_{0} \mathbf{nil}}\ \textsc{C-Nil}
\qquad
\frac{\gamma \,;\, t_1 \Downarrow^{\mathbb{C}}_{c_1} v_1 \qquad \gamma \,;\, t_2 \Downarrow^{\mathbb{C}}_{c_1} v_2}{\gamma \,;\, t_1 \texttt{ :: } t_2 \Downarrow^{\mathbb{C}}_{c_1+c_2} \mathbf{cons}(v_1, v_2)}\ \textsc{C-Cons}
$$

$$
\frac{\gamma \,;\, t_3 \Downarrow^{\mathbb{C}}_{c_1} v_1 \qquad \gamma \,;\, \lambda x_1 x_2 . t_1, t_2, v_1 \Downarrow^{\mathbb{C}\text{-foldr}}_{c_2} v_2}{\gamma \,;\, \texttt{foldr(}\lambda x_1 x_2 . t_1\texttt{, } t_2\texttt{, } t_3\texttt{)} \Downarrow^{\mathbb{C}}_{c_1+c_2} v_2}\ \textsc{C-Foldr}
$$

$$
\frac{\gamma \,;\, t \Downarrow^{\mathbb{C}}_{c} v}{\gamma \,;\, \texttt{lazy } t \Downarrow^{\mathbb{C}}_{c} \mathbf{thunk}\ v}\ \textsc{C-Lazy-Result}
\qquad
\frac{}{\gamma \,;\, \texttt{lazy } t \Downarrow^{\mathbb{C}}_{0} \bot}\ \textsc{C-Lazy-Undefined}
$$

$$
\frac{\gamma \,;\, t \Downarrow^{\mathbb{C}}_{c} \mathbf{thunk}\ v}{\gamma \,;\, \texttt{force } t \Downarrow^{\mathbb{C}}_{c} v}\ \textsc{C-Force}
\qquad
\frac{\gamma \,;\, t \Downarrow^{\mathbb{C}}_{c} v}{\gamma \,;\, \texttt{tick } t \Downarrow^{\mathbb{C}}_{c+1} v}\ \textsc{C-Tick}
$$

C The Demand Semantics of B

$$
\begin{aligned}
\mathbb{D}[\![x]\!](\gamma, a) &= (\{x \mapsto a\}, 0) \\
\mathbb{D}[\![\texttt{let } x = t_1 \texttt{ in } t_2]\!](\gamma, a) &= (d_1, c_1) \sqcup (d_2, c_2) && \text{where } ((d_2, x \mapsto b), c_2) = \\
&&& \mathbb{D}[\![t_2]\!](\gamma, x \mapsto [\![t]\!](\gamma)) \\
&&& \text{and } (d_1, c_1) = \mathbb{D}[\![t_1]\!](\gamma, b) \\
\mathbb{D}[\![\texttt{tick } t]\!](\gamma, a) &= (d, c + 1) && \text{where } (d, c) = \mathbb{D}[\![t]\!](\gamma, a) \\
\mathbb{D}[\![\texttt{lazy } t]\!](\gamma, \bot) &= (\bot, 0) \\
\mathbb{D}[\![\texttt{lazy } t]\!](\gamma, \textbf{thunk } a) &= \mathbb{D}[\![t]\!](\gamma, a) \\
\mathbb{D}[\![\texttt{force } t]\!](\gamma, a) &= \mathbb{D}[\![t]\!](\gamma, \textbf{thunk } a) \\
\mathbb{D}[\![\texttt{true}]\!](\gamma, a) &= (\bot_\gamma, 0) \\
\mathbb{D}[\![\texttt{false}]\!](\gamma, a) &= (\bot_\gamma, 0) \\
\mathbb{D}[\![\texttt{[]}]\!](\gamma, a) &= (\bot_\gamma, 0) \\
\mathbb{D}[\![t_1 :: t_2]\!](\gamma, a) &= \mathbb{D}[\![t_1]\!](\gamma, a) \sqcup \mathbb{D}[\![t_2]\!](\gamma, a) \\
\mathbb{D}[\![\texttt{foldr}(\lambda x_1 x_2.t_1, t_2, t_3)]\!](\gamma, b) &= (d', c) \sqcup \mathbb{D}[\![t]\!](\gamma, b') && \text{where } (g, b', c) = \\
&&& \mathbb{D}[\![\lambda x_1 x_2.t_1]\!]_{\mathrm{foldr}}(t_2, \gamma, [\![t_3]\!](\gamma), b) \\
\mathbb{D}[\![\lambda x_1 x_2.t_1]\!]_{\mathrm{foldr}}(t_2, \gamma, \textbf{nil}, b) &= (d, \textbf{nil}, c) && \text{where } (d, c) = \mathbb{D}[\![t_2]\!](\gamma, b) \\
\mathbb{D}[\![\lambda x_1 x_2.t_1]\!]_{\mathrm{foldr}}(t_2, \gamma, \textbf{cons}(v_1, v_2), b) &= (g_1 \sqcup g_2, \textbf{cons}(a', d), c_1 + c_2) \\
&\text{where } ((g_1, x_1 \mapsto a', x_2 \mapsto b'), c_1) = \mathbb{D}[\![t_1]\!](\gamma, x_1 \mapsto v_1, x_2 \mapsto [\![\lambda x_1 x_2.t_1]\!]_{\mathrm{foldr}}(t_2, \gamma, v_2), b) \\
&\text{and } (g_2, d, c) = \mathbb{D}[\![\lambda x_1 x_2.t_1]\!]_{\mathrm{foldr}'}(t_2, \gamma, v_2, b') \\
\mathbb{D}[\![\lambda x_1 x_2.t_1]\!]_{\mathrm{foldr}'}(t_2, \gamma, v, \bot) &= \bot \\
\mathbb{D}[\![\lambda x_1 x_2.t_1]\!]_{\mathrm{foldr}'}(t_2, \gamma, v, \textbf{thunk } b) &= (g, \textbf{thunk } d, c) && \text{where } (g, d, c) = \\
&&& \mathbb{D}[\![\lambda x_1 x_2.t_1]\!]_{\mathrm{foldr}}(t_2, \gamma, v, b)
\end{aligned}
$$

In the above, $\sqcup$ means "least upper bound." In the first instance, it applies to the approximations of a fixed exact value e. It is then extended to approximation environments: if $g_1, g_2 \prec \gamma$, then $g_1 \sqcup g_2$ is the elementwse least upper bound of g_1 and g_2. Finally, it is extended to pairs (g, c), where $g \prec \gamma$ and $c \in \mathbb{N}$, as

$$(g_1, c_1) \sqcup (g_2, c_2) = (g_1 \cup g_2, c_1 + c_2).$$

If e is an exact value, then $\bot_e$ means the least approximation of e. If γ is an exact environment, then $\bot_\gamma$ means the least environment approximating γ.

$$\bot_{\mathbf{tt}} = \mathbf{tt} \qquad \bot_{\mathbf{false}} = \mathbf{false} \qquad \bot_{\mathbf{true}} = \mathbf{true} \qquad \bot_n = n$$

$$\bot_{(e_1, e_2)} = (\bot_{e_1}, \bot_{e_2}) \qquad \bot_{\mathbf{nil}} = \mathbf{nil} \qquad \bot_{\mathbf{cons}(e_1, e_2)} = \mathbf{cons}(\bot_{e_1}, \bot_{e_2})$$

D The Semantics of L

$$\frac{\gamma\ ;\ t \Downarrow^{\mathbb{L}} v}{\gamma\ ;\ \texttt{thunk}\ t \Downarrow^{\mathbb{L}} \textbf{thunk}\ v}\ \text{L-RESULT} \qquad \frac{}{\gamma\ ;\ \texttt{undefined} \Downarrow^{\mathbb{L}} \bot}\ \text{L-UNDEFINED}$$

$$\frac{\gamma\ ;\ t_1 \Downarrow^{\mathbb{L}} \textbf{thunk}\ v_1 \qquad \gamma, x \mapsto v_1\ ;\ t_2 \Downarrow^{\mathbb{L}} v_2}{\gamma\ ;\ \texttt{case}\ t_1\ \texttt{of thunk}\ x\ \texttt{=>}\ t_2\texttt{; undefined =>}\ t_3 \Downarrow^{\mathbb{L}} v_2}\ \text{L-CASE-RESULT}$$

$$\frac{\gamma\ ;\ t_1 \Downarrow^{\mathbb{L}} \bot \qquad \gamma\ ;\ t_3 \Downarrow^{\mathbb{L}} v}{\gamma\ ;\ \texttt{case}\ t_1\ \texttt{of thunk}\ x\ \texttt{=>}\ t_2\texttt{; undefined =>}\ t_3 \Downarrow^{\mathbb{L}} v}\ \text{L-CASE-UNDEFINED}$$

$$\frac{\gamma\ ;\ t_1 \Downarrow^{\mathbb{L}} v \qquad \gamma\ ;\ t_2 \Downarrow^{\mathbb{L}} v}{\gamma\ ;\ t_1\ \texttt{==}\ t_2 \Downarrow^{\mathbb{L}} \textbf{true}}\ \text{L-EQ-TRUE} \qquad \frac{\gamma\ ;\ t_1 \Downarrow^{\mathbb{L}} v_1 \qquad \gamma\ ;\ t_2 \Downarrow^{\mathbb{L}} v_2 \qquad v_1 \neq v_2}{\gamma\ ;\ t_1\ \texttt{==}\ t_2 \Downarrow^{\mathbb{L}} \textbf{false}}\ \text{L-EQ-FALSE}$$

$$\frac{\gamma\ ;\ t_1 \Downarrow^{\mathbb{L}} v_1 \qquad \gamma\ ;\ t_2 \Downarrow^{\mathbb{L}} v_2 \qquad v_1 \leq v_2}{\gamma\ ;\ t_1\ \texttt{<=}\ t_2 \Downarrow^{\mathbb{L}} \textbf{true}}\ \text{L-APPROX-TRUE}$$

$$\frac{\gamma\ ;\ t_1 \Downarrow^{\mathbb{L}} v_1 \qquad \gamma\ ;\ t_2 \Downarrow^{\mathbb{L}} v_2 \qquad v_1 \not\leq v_2}{\gamma\ ;\ t_1\ \texttt{<=}\ t_2 \Downarrow^{\mathbb{L}} \textbf{false}}\ \text{L-APPROX-FALSE}$$

$$\frac{v : A}{\gamma\ ;\ \texttt{free}\ A \Downarrow^{\mathbb{L}} v}\ \text{L-FREE} \qquad \frac{\gamma\ ;\ t_1 \Downarrow^{\mathbb{L}} v}{\gamma\ ;\ t_1\ \texttt{?}\ t_2 \Downarrow^{\mathbb{L}} v}\ \text{L-CHOICE-L} \qquad \frac{\gamma\ ;\ t_2 \Downarrow^{\mathbb{L}} v}{\gamma\ ;\ t_1\ \texttt{?}\ t_2 \Downarrow^{\mathbb{L}} v}\ \text{L-CHOICE-R}$$

$$\frac{\gamma\ ;\ t_3 \Downarrow^{\mathbb{L}} v_1 \qquad \gamma\ ;\ \lambda x_1 x_2.t_1, t_2, v_1 \Downarrow^{\mathbb{L}\text{-foldr}} v_2}{\gamma\ ;\ \texttt{foldr}(\lambda x_1 x_2.t_1,\ t_2,\ t_3) \Downarrow^{\mathbb{L}} v_2}\ \text{L-FOLDR}$$

$$\frac{\gamma\ ;\ t_2 \Downarrow^{\mathbb{L}} v}{\gamma\ ;\ \lambda x_1 x_2.t_1, t_2, \textbf{nil} \Downarrow^{\mathbb{L}\text{-foldr}} v}\ \text{L-FOLDR-NIL} \qquad \frac{\gamma, x_1 \mapsto v_1, x_2 \mapsto \bot\ ;\ t_1 \Downarrow^{\mathbb{L}} v}{\gamma\ ;\ \lambda x_1 x_2.t_1, t_2, \textbf{cons}(v_1, \bot) \Downarrow^{\mathbb{L}\text{-foldr}} v}\ \text{L-FOLDR-UNDEFINED}$$

$$\frac{\gamma\ ;\ \lambda x_1 x_2.t_1, t_2, \textbf{thunk}\ v_2 \Downarrow^{\mathbb{L}\text{-foldr}} v_3 \qquad \gamma, x_1 \mapsto v_1, x_2 \mapsto \textbf{thunk}\ v_3\ ;\ t_1 \Downarrow^{\mathbb{L}} v}{\gamma\ ;\ \lambda x_1 x_2.t_1, t_2, \textbf{cons}(v_1, v_2) \Downarrow^{\mathbb{L}\text{-foldr}} v}\ \text{L-FOLDR-RESULT}$$

E Full Case Study on Insertion Sort

A classic fact about lazy evaluation is that one can efficiently find the n smallest elements in a list by first sorting it and then taking a length-n prefix (provided that one uses a sufficiently lazy sorting algorithm). To test this, we first define insertion sort in clairvoyance semantics (`insertionSortC`).

```
insertC :: Ord a => a -> List a -> Tick (List a)
insertC x ys = do
  tick
  fcase ys of
    Nil -> do
      ys' <- nilC
      return (x :~ ys')
    y :~ ysT' ->
      if x <= y then do
        ysT <- thunk (return ys)
        return (x :~ ysT)
      else do
        ysT'' <- with ysT' (insertC x)
```

```
      return (y :~ ysT'')

insertionSortC :: Ord a => List a -> Tick (List a)
insertionSortC xs = do
  tick
  fcase xs of
    Nil -> return Nil
    x :~ xsT' -> do
      ysT' <- with xsT' insertionSortC
      ys' <- force ysT'
      insertC x ys'
```

Next, we define `nminC` as a composition of `takeC` and `insertionSortC`, along with its demand-semantics counterpart `nminD`.

```
nminC :: Ord a => Int -> T (List a) -> Tick (List a)
nminC n xsT = takeC n =<< with xsT insertionSortC

nminD :: (Ord a, Approx a) => Int -> T (List a) -> List a -> Tick (T (List a))
nminD n xsT ysTD | nminC n xsTD =:= Tick (ysTD, c)
                 = Tick (xsTD, c)
  where xsTD = approx xsT
        c free
```

Now, how much does it cost to sort a 3-element list?

```
> insertionSortDG (fromList [3, 2, 1]) (fromList [1, 2, 3]) :: Tick (List Int)
(Tick ((:~ 3 (Thunk (:~ 2 (Thunk (:~ 1 (Thunk Nil)))))),10))
```

If we demand the entire result, we incur a cost of 10 ticks. What if we just want the first element?

```
> someValueWith dfsStrategy $ nminDG 1 (Thunk (fromList [3, 2, 1])) (fromList [1])
    :: Tick (T (List Int))
(Tick ((Thunk (:~ 3 (Thunk (:~ 2 (Thunk (:~ 1 (Thunk Nil))))))),9))
```

The resulting computation only costs 9 ticks.

References

1. Augustsson, L., et al.: The Verse calculus: a core calculus for deterministic functional logic programming. Proc. ACM Program. Lang. **7**(ICFP), 417–447 (2023). https://doi.org/10.1145/3607845
2. Bjerner, B., Holmström, S.: A composition approach to time analysis of first order lazy functional programs. In: Stoy, J.E. (ed.) Proceedings of the Fourth International Conference on Functional Programming Languages and Computer Architecture, FPCA 1989, London, UK, 11–13 September 1989, pp. 157–165. ACM (1989). https://doi.org/10.1145/99370.99382
3. Braßel, B., Hanus, M., Huch, F.: Encapsulating non-determinism in functional logic computations. J. Funct. Log. Program. (2004). http://danae.uni-muenster.de/lehre/kuchen/JFLP/articles/2004/S04-01/A2004-06/JFLP-A2004-06.pdf
4. Braßel, B., Hanus, M., Peemöller, B., Reck, F.: KiCS2: a new compiler from curry to haskell. In: Kuchen, H. (ed.) WFLP 2011. LNCS, vol. 6816, pp. 1–18. Springer, Heidelberg (2011). https://doi.org/10.1007/978-3-642-22531-4_1
5. Christiansen, J., Fischer, S.: EasyCheck—test data for free. In: Garrigue, J., Hermenegildo, M.V. (eds.) FLOPS 2008. LNCS, vol. 4989, pp. 322–336. Springer, Heidelberg (2008). https://doi.org/10.1007/978-3-540-78969-7_23

6. Danielsson, N.A.: Lightweight semiformal time complexity analysis for purely functional data structures. In: Necula, G.C., Wadler, P. (eds.) Proceedings of the 35th ACM SIGPLAN-SIGACT Symposium on Principles of Programming Languages, POPL 2008, San Francisco, California, USA, 7–12 January 2008, pp. 133–144. ACM (2008). https://doi.org/10.1145/1328438.1328457
7. Foner, K., Zhang, H., Lampropoulos, L.: Keep your laziness in check. Proc. ACM Program. Lang. **2**(ICFP), 102:1–102:30 (2018). https://doi.org/10.1145/3236797
8. Hackett, J., Hutton, G.: Call-by-need is clairvoyant call-by-value. Proc. ACM Program. Lang. **3**(ICFP), 114:1–114:23 (2019). https://doi.org/10.1145/3341718
9. Handley, M.A.T., Vazou, N., Hutton, G.: Liquidate your assets: reasoning about resource usage in liquid haskell. Proc. ACM Program. Lang. **4**(POPL), 24:1–24:27 (2020). https://doi.org/10.1145/3371092
10. Hanus, M.: Functional logic programming: from theory to curry. In: Voronkov, A., Weidenbach, C. (eds.) Programming Logics. LNCS, vol. 7797, pp. 123–168. Springer, Heidelberg (2013). https://doi.org/10.1007/978-3-642-37651-1_6
11. Hanus, M.: CurryCheck: checking properties of curry programs. In: Hermenegildo, M.V., Lopez-Garcia, P. (eds.) LOPSTR 2016. LNCS, vol. 10184, pp. 222–239. Springer, Cham (2017). https://doi.org/10.1007/978-3-319-63139-4_13
12. Hanus, M.: From logic to functional logic programs. Theory Pract. Log. Program. **22**(4), 538–554 (2022). https://doi.org/10.1017/S1471068422000187
13. Hughes, J.: Why functional programming matters. Comput. J. **32**(2), 98–107 (1989). https://doi.org/10.1093/comjnl/32.2.98
14. Kastner, J.: Liquid-structures (2022). https://github.com/john-h-kastner/liquid-structures, open-source code on GitHub
15. Launchbury, J.: A natural semantics for lazy evaluation. In: Deusen, M.S.V., Lang, B. (eds.) Conference Record of the Twentieth Annual ACM SIGPLAN-SIGACT Symposium on Principles of Programming Languages, Charleston, South Carolina, USA, January 1993, pp. 144–154. ACM Press (1993). https://doi.org/10.1145/158511.158618
16. Li, X., Li, Y., Schachte, P., Rizkallah, C.: The memorist tale: every thunk every cost all at once. In: Programming Languages and Systems - 35th European Symposium on Programming, ESOP 2026, Held as Part of the International Joint Conferences on Theory and Practice of Software, ETAPS 2026, Turin, Italy, 11–16 April 2026, Proceedings. Lecture Notes in Computer Science. Springer, Heidelberg (2026). https://doi.org/10.1007/978-3-032-22720-1_17
17. Li, Y., Xia, L., Weirich, S.: Reasoning about the garden of forking paths. Proc. ACM Program. Lang. **5**(ICFP), 1–28 (2021). https://doi.org/10.1145/3473585
18. Lorenzen, A.: Lightweight testing of persistent amortized time complexity in the credit monad. In: Morris, J.G., Xie, N. (eds.) Proceedings of the 18th ACM SIGPLAN International Haskell Symposium, Haskell 2025, Singapore, 12–18 October 2025, pp. 80–93. ACM (2025). https://doi.org/10.1145/3759164.3759351
19. Mével, G., Jourdan, J.-H., Pottier, F.: Time credits and time receipts in iris. In: Caires, L. (ed.) ESOP 2019. LNCS, vol. 11423, pp. 3–29. Springer, Cham (2019). https://doi.org/10.1007/978-3-030-17184-1_1
20. Moggi, E.: Notions of computation and monads. Inf. Comput. **93**(1), 55–92 (1991). https://doi.org/10.1016/0890-5401(91)90052-4
21. Moran, A., Sands, D.: Improvement in a lazy context: an operational theory for call-by-need. In: Appel, A.W., Aiken, A. (eds.) POPL '99, Proceedings of the 26th ACM SIGPLAN-SIGACT Symposium on Principles of Programming Languages, San Antonio, TX, USA, 20–22 January 1999, pp. 43–56. ACM (1999). https://doi.org/10.1145/292540.292547

22. Norell, U.: Dependently typed programming in Agda. In: Kennedy, A., Ahmed, A. (eds.) Proceedings of TLDI'09: 2009 ACM SIGPLAN International Workshop on Types in Languages Design and Implementation, Savannah, GA, USA, 24 January 2009, pp. 1–2. ACM (2009). https://doi.org/10.1145/1481861.1481862. http://dl.acm.org/citation.cfm?id=1481861
23. Okasaki, C.: Purely Functional Data Structures. Cambridge University Press, Cambridge (1999)
24. Petricek, T.: Evaluation strategies for monadic computations. In: Chapman, J., Levy, P.B. (eds.) Proceedings Fourth Workshop on Mathematically Structured Functional Programming, MSFP@ETAPS 2012, Tallinn, Estonia, 25 March 2012. EPTCS, vol. 76, pp. 68–89 (2012). https://doi.org/10.4204/EPTCS.76.7
25. Pottier, F., Guéneau, A., Jourdan, J.H., Mével, G.: Thunks and debits in separation logic with time credits. Proc. ACM Program. Lang. **8**(POPL) (2024). https://hal.science/hal-04238691/file/main.pdf
26. Reynolds, J.C.: Separation logic: a logic for shared mutable data structures. In: 17th IEEE Symposium on Logic in Computer Science (LICS 2002), Copenhagen, Denmark, 22–25 July 2002, Proceedings, pp. 55–74. IEEE Computer Society (2002). https://doi.org/10.1109/LICS.2002.1029817
27. Somogyi, Z., Henderson, F.: The design and implementation of Mercury. In: Joint International Conference and Symposium on Logic Programming (1996)
28. Tolmach, A.P., Antoy, S.: A monadic semantics for core Curry. In: Brim, L., Grumberg, O. (eds.) 12th International Workshop on Functional and Constraint Logic Programming, WFLP 2003, in connection with RDP'03, Federated Conference on Rewriting, Deduction and Programming, Boulder, Colorado, USA, 14 July 2003. Electronic Notes in Theoretical Computer Science, vol. 86, pp. 16–34. Elsevier (2003). https://doi.org/10.1016/S1571-0661(04)80691-1
29. Wadler, P.: Comprehending monads. Math. Struct. Comput. Sci. **2**(4), 461–493 (1992). https://doi.org/10.1017/S0960129500001560
30. Xia, L., et al.: Story of your lazy function's life: a bidirectional demand semantics for mechanized cost analysis of lazy programs. Proc. ACM Program. Lang. **8**(ICFP), 30–63 (2024). https://doi.org/10.1145/3674626

A Fine-Grained Small-Step Semantics for Interleaving Search

Brysen Pfingsten(✉) and Jason Hemann

Seton Hall University, South Orange, NJ, USA
{pfingsbr,jason.hemann}@shu.edu

Abstract. We present a deterministic small-step operational semantics for miniKanren that explicitly represents the evolving search tree during execution. This semantics models interleaving and goal scheduling with fine granularity, exposing each evaluation step—goal activation, suspension, resumption, and success. This approach supports reasoning about miniKanren's interleaving search behavior, helping users understand surprising answer orders and operational effects. A reference implementation undergirds an interactive visualizer that renders the search tree as it develops and lets users step through execution; we treat this tool as a consumer and demonstration of the semantics. Our semantics and tool are illustrated by example and validated through property-based testing.

Keywords: miniKanren · Redex · operational semantics · search visualization

1 Introduction

Interleaving depth-first search addresses the incompleteness of pure depth-first exploration in logic and relational languages. By periodically suspending and resuming branches, interleaving strategies [22] are intended to prevent a single infinite path from indefinitely blocking progress elsewhere, while retaining much of the efficiency of pure depth-first search. However, interleaving fundamentally changes the operational behavior of search. For instance, consider the query in Fig. 1. Under a traditional depth-first execution model, such as Prolog's, this query produces answers in the syntactic order suggested by the program text. In miniKanren implementations like those described by Friedman et al. [15] and Hemann and Friedman [18], this query produces `'(fish turtle dog cat)`.

With interleaving search, execution becomes a finely interwoven process in which goals are repeatedly suspended, resumed, and reordered according to scheduler decisions. Small differences in goal structure, ordering, or the placement of delay points can dramatically affect answer order and runtime cost. As a consequence, programmers can find the order of answers unintuitive and search difficult to reason through. Implementers, likewise, may struggle to predict the consequences of seemingly minor changes to scheduling policy. Without a precise operational account, the reasons behind such outcomes can be difficult to

M. Sperber and E. Komendantskaya (Eds.): FLOPS 2026, LNCS 16533, pp. 139–155, 2026.
https://doi.org/10.1007/978-981-92-0184-6_6

```
(defrel (same x y) (== x y))

(run* (q)
  (conde
    [(conde
       [(same q 'turtle)]
       [(same q 'cat)]
       [(== q 'dog)])]
    [(same q 'fish)]))
```

```
same(X,Y) :- X = Y.

?- ( ( same(Q,turtle)
     ; same(Q,cat)
     ; Q = dog
     )
   ; same(Q,fish)
   ).
```

Fig. 1. Definitions and uses of `same`, in a miniKanren-style and Prolog concrete syntax.

explain. Existing declarative debugging techniques [6,31] offer limited help here, as they abstract away precisely the scheduling behavior that gives rise to these effects.

The challenge is therefore to understand the *operational dynamics* of interleaving: when goals are expanded, when they are suspended, how they are resumed, and how these choices shape the evolving search space. In this paper, we present a **fine-grained, deterministic small-step operational semantics** for interleaving depth-first search, developed using miniKanren as a running example. The key design choice is representational: the *remaining search space* is reified as an explicit search-tree term. Interleaving, suspension, and resumption are realized as explicit rewrites of this search-tree structure, rather than as implicit meta-level scheduling decisions. Our semantics operates at an intra-goal level, exposing the internal decision points that determine how interleaving proceeds, unlike prior semantic accounts of miniKanren [26,28].

We mechanize the semantics in PLT Redex [12,23] and use the mechanization both as an executable reference and as a platform for property-based validation (e.g., determinism and preservation of well-formedness). We also use it to drive an interactive search-tree stepper that makes the semantics' search-structure rewrites observable during execution. A prototype implementation is available online (minikanrenredex-prod.shu.edu) and the source is on GitHub[1].

The remainder of the paper proceeds as follows. Section 2 reviews miniKanren's syntax, gives a high-level intuitive comparison of miniKanren's operational semantics to that of Prolog, and reprises interleaving search strategies. Section 3 defines our formal small-step semantics explicitly, explaining the search-tree representation and detailed reduction rules. Section 4 describes the integration of an interactive visualizer with the Redex semantics, and Sect. 5 walks through the running example and shows how answer order emerges. Finally, Sect. 6 situates our contributions within existing work on operational models of logic program execution and search, and Sect. 7 discusses future directions and potential extensions of this approach. Throughout we use Friedman et al. [15]'s concrete miniKanren syntax.

[1] https://github.com/brysenPfingsten/mk-redex-viz.

2 Background

In this section, we re-introduce miniKanren and its semantics informally, by way of a contrast with Prolog and traditional logic programming, before presenting the formal reduction rules.

2.1 MiniKanren's Simplified Execution Model

Compared with traditional Prolog-style logic languages, core miniKanren is smaller and makes more operational choices explicit. At a high level, relation calls are suspended at delay points and resumed across disjunctive branches; this scheduling intuition is what we formalize in Sect. 3. The language assumes a fixed set of relational definitions with no dynamic `assert` or `retract`. Calls to undefined relations or relation-arity mismatches are treated as errors, and can in some cases be caught statically by the host language. Unlike Prolog, miniKanren has no implicit head unification for relations. The programmer writes each predicate directly in a form of program completion [7,25]. Relations are invoked via explicit parameter substitution (akin to β-reduction in functional languages), and all unification is done explicitly via goals.

The miniKanren term language is first-order, meaning relations themselves are not in the domain of terms and there are no higher-order relations. The programmer explicitly introduces new logic variables. Lexical variables (local to a relation) and logical variables (introduced implicitly by `fresh`) have clearly disjoint scopes. Associating a lexical variable with its corresponding logic variable can also be modeled by β-substitution.

The core language is small enough that the example in Fig. 1 exercises most of the miniKanren language forms. Negation is generally disallowed, and in most dialects limited to a handful of negated primitive constraints on terms [16,24]. The miniKanren programming community emphasizes pure, cut-free declarative programming, which aligns with many modern Prolog best practices [32]. Even the miniKanren arithmetic suite [21] is implemented as library routines over bit-vectors that behave reasonably in all modes. Host-language macro extension facilities are used to provide less cumbersome surface forms that de-sugar to the core. User-level host-language macros scratch much the same itch as meta-programming in Prolog.

3 Language and Semantics

In this section, we present our model of miniKanren execution, which we define by a reduction semantics. We assume familiarity with standard reduction semantics terminology and notation, as described in, e.g., the PLT Redex textbook [12]. Readers primarily interested in the visualization aspects or high-level intuition may skip ahead without significant difficulty.

Unlike typical miniKanren implementations that use implicit streams of answers, our semantics encodes the evolving search tree and its relation environment in a single expression. The main technical contribution described in this section is treating a nondeterministic search process as a deterministic state transition system over a tree. We get a deterministic single-step transition that still models nondeterministic search, by threading the whole search tree through states. We first describe the grammar of programs, relations, and search trees, then explain the reduction rules and how they realize the standard miniKanren search strategy.

3.1 Language

Figure 2 shows the grammar of our core language. Our grammar consists of a core microKanren-like language extended with explicit constructs to represent the state of the search: notably, a search-tree (S) data structure is a component of the program. A program is a pair **prg** Σ S where Σ is the *relation environment* and S is a *search tree*. As usual, each relation definition in Σ is given as $r(L) \leftrightarrow G$ with r a relation name, L a list of syntactic variables (parameters), and G a goal that constitutes the relation's body.

Programs	$\ni p := \texttt{prg}\ \Sigma\ S$
Environments	$\ni \Sigma := r(L) \leftrightarrow G\ \ldots$
Parameter Lists	$\ni L := x\ \ldots$
Search Trees	$\ni S := \texttt{empty} \mid G\,\sigma \mid S \rightarrow S \mid S \leftarrow S \mid S + S \mid S \times G \mid \texttt{go}\ S \mid \texttt{delay}\ S$
Goals	$\ni G := \top \mid t \equiv t \mid r(t\ldots) \mid G \vee G \mid G \wedge G \mid \exists(L)\,G$
Constants	$\ni c$
Variables	$\ni x, y$
Relation Names	$\ni r$
Logic Variables	$\ni l_i$
Terms	$\ni t := c \mid x \mid l_i \mid t : t$
States	$\ni \sigma := (\theta, i)$
Substitutions	$\ni \theta := (l_i \mapsto t)\ \ldots$

Fig. 2. Core grammar of our language.

We assume the existence of several pairwise-disjoint infinite sets: syntactic variables, relation names, logic variables (written l_n, which denotes the nth logic variable introduced in a given state), and constants. The full term language consists of the closure of a binary cons constructor : over the union of the syntactic variables, logic variables, and constants. Our miniKanren language provides a primitive goal $\top$ that always succeeds, and five primitive constructors for term equations, relation calls, binary conjunction, binary disjunction, and variable introduction.

A pair of a goal G and a *state* σ is itself a search tree. A state σ is a pair (θ, i) where θ is a *substitution* mapping logic variables to terms and i is a numeric counter used to generate fresh logic variables, ensuring that each newly introduced variable is unique. To initialize the computation, the programmer's `(run (L) G ....)` query is transformed into an existentially quantified fresh goal ∃ (L) G ..., and injected into a pair with the *initial state*. The initial state consists of an empty substitution and a fresh variable count of 0.

Every leaf node of a search tree is either of the form $G\,\sigma$ or EMPTY (failure). Complex search trees are built from simpler search trees using search tree combinators. Binary constructors $S \rightarrow S$ and $S \leftarrow S$ represent pointed disjunctions, where the arrow depicts the search ordering of its children. The operator $+$ is the answer-stream constructor; terms of the form $S+S$ record produced answers while retaining the remaining search tree. S × G represents a conjunction of a search tree with a goal. Computation proceeds first down the left child; the goal on the right-hand side does not have a state because its state is determined by the search down the left-hand side. Special constructors `delay S` and `go S` mark the "delay points" for interleaving where the engine can suspend/resume goals.

We specify a set of evaluation contexts in Fig. 3 that identify the next reducible subexpression within a program. The program context E_P focuses on the search tree inside a program; all reductions occur within the search tree. An answer stream context E_A brings the focus to the search tree just below the sequence of finished answers. A search context E_S brings the focus to the node within the search tree that is to be reduced. Intuitively, this context descends into the search tree following the directive of disjunctions and the tree component of conjunctions. Finally, we define E, the composition of the previous three contexts to locate within a program the next search tree node to reduce.

PROGRAM CONTEXT	$\ni E_P := \mathbf{prg}\ \Sigma\ \square$
ANSWER CONTEXT	$\ni E_A := \square \mid (\top\,\sigma) + E_A$
SEARCH CONTEXT	$\ni E_S := \square \mid E_S \leftarrow S \mid S \rightarrow E_S \mid E_S \times G$
COMPOSITE CONTEXT	$\ni E := E_P[E_A[E_S[\square]]]$

Fig. 3. Evaluation contexts.

3.2 Semantics

Figure 4 presents the small-step reduction rules for our μKanren-inspired language. We model the miniKanren search behavior described in Hemann and Friedman [18]. In our semantics, the program state contains an explicit representation of the entire search tree as it is being explored. The benefit is that the reduction rules can manipulate this tree structure to simulate goal interleaving (for example, by propagating `delay` markers upward and reorienting pointed disjunctions so suspended computations are resumed in a fair order). Our semantics explicitly represents individual steps within the execution of each miniKanren goal, such as initiating the evaluation of a goal, suspending it, resuming it, and ultimately completing it (success or failure). We refer to these individual evaluation points as intra-goal evaluation steps. Most of the reduction rules in our semantics use the E context. The exceptions are those that match on the relation environment (Proceed) and those that must occur just below the answer stream (InvokeDelay, PromoteLeft/Right). We write answer nodes as $(\top\,\sigma)$.

DistrDisj
$$E[(G_1 \vee G_2)\,\sigma] \longrightarrow E[(G_1\,\sigma) \leftarrow (G_2\,\sigma)]$$

DistrConj
$$E[(G_1 \wedge G_2)\,\sigma] \longrightarrow E[(G_1\,\sigma) \times G_2]$$

LeftAnsConj
$$E[((\top\,\sigma) \leftarrow S) \times G] \longrightarrow E[((\top\,\sigma) \times G) \leftarrow (S \times G)]$$

RightAnsConj
$$E[(S \rightarrow (\top\,\sigma)) \times G] \longrightarrow E[(S \times G) \rightarrow ((\top\,\sigma) \times G)]$$

AssocRightLeft
$$E[S_1 \rightarrow ((\top\,\sigma) \leftarrow S_2)] \longrightarrow E[(\top\,\sigma) \leftarrow (S_1 \rightarrow S_2)]$$

AssocRightRight
$$E[S_2 \rightarrow (S_1 \rightarrow (\top\,\sigma))] \longrightarrow E[(S_2 \rightarrow S_1) \rightarrow (\top\,\sigma)]$$

AssocLeftLeft
$$E[((\top\,\sigma) \leftarrow S_1) \leftarrow S_2] \longrightarrow E[(\top\,\sigma) \leftarrow (S_1 \leftarrow S_2)]$$

AssocLeftRight
$$E[(S_1 \rightarrow (\top\,\sigma)) \leftarrow S_2] \longrightarrow E[(S_1 \leftarrow S_2) \rightarrow (\top\,\sigma)]$$

SuccConj
$$E[(\top\,\sigma) \times G] \longrightarrow E[G\,\sigma]$$

PruneConj
$$E[\texttt{empty} \times G] \longrightarrow E[\texttt{empty}]$$

PruneLeft
$$E[\texttt{empty} \leftarrow S] \longrightarrow E[S]$$

PruneRight
$$E[S \rightarrow \texttt{empty}] \longrightarrow E[S]$$

SubstFresh
$$\frac{i' = i + |x\ldots| \qquad G' = G[x\ldots/l_i\ldots]}{E[(\exists\,(x\ldots)\,G)\,(\theta, i)] \longrightarrow E[G'\,(\theta, i')]}$$

Delay
$$E[r(t_1\ldots)\,\sigma] \longrightarrow E[\texttt{delay}\ (\texttt{go}\ r(t_1\ldots)\,\sigma)]$$

Proceed
$$\frac{G' = G[x\ldots/t\ldots]}{(\texttt{prg}\ (\ldots r(x\ldots) \leftrightarrow G\ldots)\ E_A[E_S[\texttt{go}\ r(t\ldots)\,\sigma]]) \longrightarrow (\texttt{prg}\ (\ldots r(x\ldots) \leftrightarrow G\ldots)\ E_A[E_S[G'\,\sigma]])}$$

UnifySucc
$$\frac{\theta' = \mathrm{unify}(t_1, t_2, \theta)}{E[((t_1 \equiv t_2)\,(\theta, i))] \longrightarrow E[(\top\,(\theta', i))]}$$

UnifyFail
$$\frac{\mathrm{unify}(t_1, t_2, \theta)\ \text{is undefined}}{E[((t_1 \equiv t_2)\,(\theta, i))] \longrightarrow E[\texttt{empty}]}$$

DelayConj
$$E[((\texttt{delay}\ S)\ \times\ G)] \longrightarrow E[(\texttt{delay}\ (S\ \times\ G))]$$

DelayLeft
$$E[((\texttt{delay}\ S_1) \leftarrow S_2)] \longrightarrow E[(\texttt{delay}\ (S_1 \rightarrow\ S_2))]$$

DelayRight
$$E[(S_1 \rightarrow\ (\texttt{delay}\ S_2))] \longrightarrow E[(\texttt{delay}\ (S_1 \leftarrow\ S_2))]$$

InvokeDelay
$$E_P[E_A[(\texttt{delay}\ S)]] \longrightarrow E_P[E_A[S]]$$

PromoteLeft
$$E_P[E_A[((\top\,\sigma) \leftarrow S)]] \longrightarrow E_P[E_A[((\top\,\sigma) + S)]]$$

PromoteRight
$$E_P[E_A[(S \rightarrow (\top\,\sigma))]] \longrightarrow E_P[E_A[((\top\,\sigma) + S)]]$$

Fig. 4. microKanren language semantics.

The Assoc* rules are structural reassociations of pointed disjunctions around answer nodes; for example, AssocRightLeft rewrites $S_1 \rightarrow ((\top\,\sigma) \leftarrow S_2)$ into $(\top\,\sigma) \leftarrow (S_1 \rightarrow S_2)$. These rules preserve branch order while reshaping the tree so PromoteLeft/Right can apply.

We limit the amount of interleaving by introducing delay points only at relation invocations (Delay). This results in a more biased, less interleaved search than Rozplokhas et al.'s [29] model. Figure 5 shows a trace demonstrating how delay and forcing of delays behaves on a small example.

$$\begin{array}{ll}
\texttt{prg}\,(\texttt{same}(x,y) \leftrightarrow x \equiv y)\ (\exists(p)\ \texttt{same}(p,\texttt{'cat}))\ (\emptyset,0) & \\
\texttt{prg}\,(\texttt{same}(x,y) \leftrightarrow x \equiv y)\ \texttt{same}(0,\texttt{'cat})\ (\emptyset,1) & [\textsc{SubstFresh}] \\
\texttt{prg}\,(\texttt{same}(x,y) \leftrightarrow x \equiv y)\ \texttt{delay}(\texttt{go}(\texttt{same}(0,\texttt{'cat})\ (\emptyset,1))) & [\textsc{Delay}] \\
\texttt{prg}\,(\texttt{same}(x,y) \leftrightarrow x \equiv y)\ \texttt{go}(\texttt{same}(0,\texttt{'cat})\ (\emptyset,1)) & [\textsc{InvokeDelay}] \\
\texttt{prg}\,(\texttt{same}(x,y) \leftrightarrow x \equiv y)\ 0 \equiv \texttt{'cat}\ (\emptyset,1) & [\textsc{Proceed}] \\
\texttt{prg}\,(\texttt{same}(x,y) \leftrightarrow x \equiv y)\ \top\ ((0 \mapsto \texttt{'cat}),1) & [\textsc{UnifySucc}]
\end{array}$$

Fig. 5. Worked example trace: evaluating $(\exists(p)\ \texttt{same}(p,\texttt{'cat}))$ under our semantics.

We now sketch a disjunctive trace illustrating fair interleaving via step-wise promotion and resumption. Subtrees are wrapped with `delay`; the delay operator is then bubbled upward, interleaving disjunctions (DelayLeft/Right) and bypassing conjunctions (DelayConj). At the answer-stream tail, InvokeDelay releases the suspension and evaluation continues. No Go rule exists: `go` is introduced by Delay and consumed by Proceed. Figure 6 shows a trace for a disjunctive query with two `same` calls. The query variable has already been substituted in and the relation environment is omitted. The answer-stream constructor $+$ is result-level and does not schedule evaluation.

$$\begin{array}{ll}
(\texttt{same}(0,\texttt{'cat}) \vee \texttt{same}(0,\texttt{'dog}))\ (\emptyset,1) & \\
(\texttt{same}(0,\texttt{'cat})\ (\emptyset,1)) \leftarrow (\texttt{same}(0,\texttt{'dog})\ (\emptyset,1)) & [\textsc{DistrDisj}] \\
\texttt{delay}(\texttt{go}(\texttt{same}(0,\texttt{'cat})\ (\emptyset,1))) \leftarrow \texttt{same}(0,\texttt{'dog})\ (\emptyset,1) & [\textsc{Delay}] \\
\texttt{delay}(\texttt{go}(\texttt{same}(0,\texttt{'cat})\ (\emptyset,1)) \rightarrow \texttt{same}(0,\texttt{'dog})\ (\emptyset,1)) & [\textsc{DelayLeft}] \\
\texttt{go}(\texttt{same}(0,\texttt{'cat})\ (\emptyset,1)) \rightarrow \texttt{same}(0,\texttt{'dog})\ (\emptyset,1) & [\textsc{InvokeDelay}] \\
\texttt{go}(\texttt{same}(0,\texttt{'cat})\ (\emptyset,1)) \rightarrow \texttt{delay}(\texttt{go}(\texttt{same}(0,\texttt{'dog})\ (\emptyset,1))) & [\textsc{Delay}] \\
\texttt{delay}(\texttt{go}(\texttt{same}(0,\texttt{'cat})\ (\emptyset,1)) \leftarrow \texttt{go}(\texttt{same}(0,\texttt{'dog})\ (\emptyset,1))) & [\textsc{DelayRight}] \\
\texttt{go}(\texttt{same}(0,\texttt{'cat})\ (\emptyset,1)) \leftarrow \texttt{go}(\texttt{same}(0,\texttt{'dog})\ (\emptyset,1)) & [\textsc{InvokeDelay}] \\
0 \equiv \texttt{'cat}\ (\emptyset,1) \leftarrow \texttt{go}(\texttt{same}(0,\texttt{'dog})\ (\emptyset,1)) & [\textsc{Proceed}] \\
\top\ ((0 \mapsto \texttt{'cat}),1) \leftarrow \texttt{go}(\texttt{same}(0,\texttt{'dog})\ (\emptyset,1)) & [\textsc{UnifySucc}] \\
\top\ ((0 \mapsto \texttt{'cat}),1) + \texttt{go}(\texttt{same}(0,\texttt{'dog})\ (\emptyset,1)) & [\textsc{PromoteLeft}] \\
\top\ ((0 \mapsto \texttt{'cat}),1) + 0 \equiv \texttt{'dog}\ (\emptyset,1) & [\textsc{Proceed}] \\
\top\ ((0 \mapsto \texttt{'cat}),1) + \top\ ((0 \mapsto \texttt{'dog}),1) & [\textsc{UnifySucc}]
\end{array}$$

Fig. 6. Trace for `(conde ((same q 'cat)) ((same q 'dog)))`.

3.3 Novel Design Choices

Our semantics reifies the remaining search space as an explicit search-tree term. All scheduling behavior—interleaving, suspension, and resumption—is expressed as object-level rewrites of this tree rather than as meta-level control. As a result, the reduction relation is deterministic (unique next step from any well-formed configuration), even though it models nondeterministic search by explicitly retaining alternative branches in the tree.

Explicit Answer Stream. Successful goals are not immediately removed from the search, unlike in Rozplokhas et al. [29]. Instead, a success is represented as $(\top\, \sigma)$ and remains in the structure until it is lifted to the top-level answer stream (PromoteLeft/Right). We model the answer stream as a sequence of these answer nodes accumulated with the + operator. This allows the user to inspect each answer as it is produced and to see it in context. It also preserves a record of answers which can be useful for understanding the progress of the search. While success is explicitly modeled, failure is not. Upon unification failing (UnifyFail), that subtree is promptly pruned from the tree (PruneConj, PruneLeft/Right). This behavior mimics miniKanren's quiet refutation.

Pointed Disjunction (Railway Model). We represent disjunctions in a symmetric, bidirectional way to preserve the relative orderings of disjuncts upon interleaving (DelayLeft/Right). We refer to this as the *railway model* because the two branches of a disjunction are like a switch in railway tracks where evaluation can proceed down either side. In the grammar, these are represented as $\leftarrow$ and $\rightarrow$. Traditionally, a singular left-biased disjunction is used and interleaving involves swapping the two disjuncts. Visually and textually, this makes it more difficult to retain information about the search tree and requires the user to recalibrate to its new shape. While changing a $\leftarrow$ to a $\rightarrow$ or vice versa is a subtle syntactic shift, it promotes better structural correspondence between successive reductions—particularly when evaluation contexts are made explicit. As seen in Fig. 4, this combinatorially affects the number of certain reduction steps (AssocLeftLeft, etc., PromoteLeft/Right, Left/RightAnsConj, DelayLeft/Right, PruneLeft/Right); however, a smaller, correctness-preserving semantics could be derived by collapsing the bidirectional disjunctions into a single unoriented disjunction operator.

Delayed Relation Expansion. In addition to the `delay` operator, we also use a special `go` operator that wraps relation invocations. This thunk-like form prevents the immediate expansion of a relation's body (Delay) until it is scheduled for evaluation (Proceed). By delaying unnecessary expansion, we avoid exploding the search tree too early, making the focus on the current evaluation less cluttered while maintaining a more intuitive conceptualization of the actual goal being suspended (i.e., a relation call with certain arguments rather than whatever its goal body may be). This choice minimizes relation-body expansion until a call is resumed (see Sect. 5 for an example).

Table 1 highlights where our design choices situate us within a broader design space. Each row corresponds to a concrete rule family in Fig. 4: delay placement is controlled by where Delay/InvokeDelay are introduced, interleaving representation is controlled by pointed-disjunction rules (DelayLeft/Right, Assoc*, PromoteLeft/Right), and relation-expansion timing is controlled by whether calls are wrapped in `go` before Proceed. Reading the table this way makes the comparison operational rather than purely terminological: changing one row means changing a localized rule cluster and predictably shifts fairness, branch-order bookkeeping, or search-tree growth.

Table 1. Orthogonal design choices in interleaving logic programming semantics.

Axis	Alternatives	This semantics
Delay placement	Every goal Just relation entry After answer	Just relation entry
Interleaving representation	Tree swapping Railway model	Railway model
Relation expansion timing	Eager expansion Delayed expansion	Delayed expansion

Semantic Properties We subjected our reduction semantics to mechanized validation using PLT Redex. We defined a well-formedness judgment for program configurations (e.g., delayed goals always carry a valid state, substitutions and indices are coherent, and fresh-variable introduction respects distinctness and scope). Using this judgment, we tested a collection of semantic invariants by randomized generation of well-formed configurations and systematic exploration of their immediate reductions. This style of executable validation is well-suited to reduction semantics with many interacting rules, where unintended overlaps or corner cases can be difficult to identify by inspection alone.

- **Determinism (unique decomposition).** From any well-formed configuration, either the configuration is final (no further search remains), or there is exactly one next reduction step. Equivalently, there is a unique decomposition of the program into an evaluation context and a redex. Evaluation contexts select a unique reduction position, and the rule heads are syntactically disjoint at that position (by outer constructor and context form), so two different rules cannot apply simultaneously to the same well-formed configuration. This property ensures that our semantics defines a deterministic small-step transition system, even though it models a nondeterministic search process. We validated determinism by randomly generating well-formed configurations and checking that Redex never produced two distinct successor configurations from the same starting point.
- **Syntactic preservation (well-formedness preservation).** Well-formedness is preserved by every reduction step: if a configuration is well-formed, then any immediate successor configuration is also well-formed. This invariant guarantees that the explicit search-tree structure, delay markers, substitutions, and states introduced by the semantics are maintained consistently throughout execution. We validated preservation by stepping randomly generated well-formed configurations and rechecking the well-formedness judgment on the resulting configurations.
- **Scheduler invariants (delay propagation and resumption).** Our semantics reifies suspension and resumption using explicit `delay` and `go` constructs together with corresponding tree-rewrite rules (e.g., DelayConj, DelayLeft/Right, InvokeDelay). A key invariant is that delayed sub-

trees are propagated monotonically through the search tree and cannot become stranded beneath conjunctions or disjunctions. Whenever a delayed subtree reaches the head position beneath the answer stream, it becomes eligible for resumption. We validated these scheduler invariants by randomized testing, confirming that the delay machinery interacts correctly with evaluation contexts and does not introduce stuck non-final configurations.

Together, these mechanized checks suggest that the reduction rules in Fig. 4 faithfully capture the intended structure of interleaving search and scheduler behavior. They also serve as an executable reference against which future extensions to the language or search strategy can be validated.

Alternative Interleaving Strategies. Our semantics implements interleaved exploration of different branches of the search tree. Here, "interleaving" means scheduling among alternatives (disjunctive branches), not reordering conjunctive subgoals within a single branch. Conjunction remains left-to-right. Under the standard condition that some delay occurs along every cycle in the call graph, no single disjunct or recursive path monopolizes computation, and no potential solution is starved indefinitely. Under this condition, interleaving is intended to preserve completeness even in the presence of infinite branches.

Various miniKanren implementations differ in where they place delay points. These choices directly impact the search order, and thus impact query efficiency.

Common choices include:

- Every relation call. This was the choice in the original microKanren paper [17].
- Every `conde` and `fresh`, and after producing an answer. This was the choice in the first edition of Friedman et al. [14], and the `faster-miniKanren` implementation.
- Atop each relation definition. This was the choice of Friedman et al. [15], and the version we model in Sect. 3.
- Between every goal evaluation. Rozplokhas et al. [29] choose this to achieve maximally fair interleaving.

Many more options are possible. It is not clear that there is a single best choice, and finding reasonable metrics for comparing them remains an open problem.

A key benefit of reduction semantics is their modularity [13]. In our case, this means we can easily swap out reduction relations to explore different search strategies. Accordingly, we introduce an alternative semantics that incorporates Prolog's depth-first search while remaining within the same framework. This semantics constitutes a modified subset of the system presented in Fig. 4, obtained by eliminating all rules involving $\rightarrow$ or `delay` and removing the `go` within Proceed.

4 Semantics-Driven Visualization

In this section, we describe how these semantics support an interactive visualizer. We built an interactive visualizer on top of the Redex semantics that renders the evolving search tree and supports forward/backward stepping. We provide a web-based interface with a custom tree visualization that uses the executable semantics in our Redex model.

4.1 Architecture

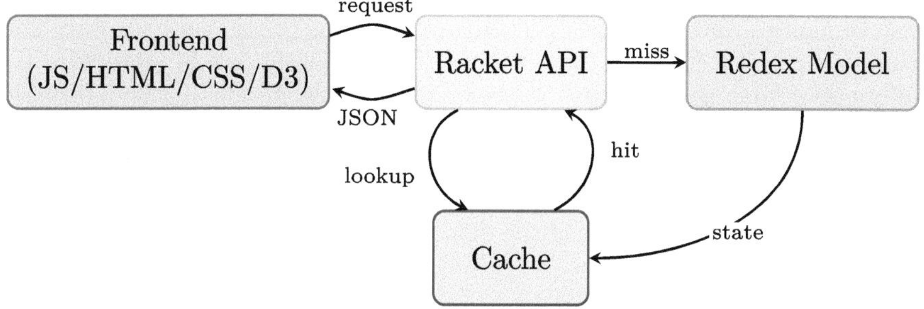

Fig. 7. The architecture of our visualizer.

Figure 7 shows the high-level architecture of the visualizer. A user sends a request from the frontend to the backend API. The user begins by selecting a reduction semantics (currently either μKanren-style interleaving or depth-first search). The user then submits a program written in the concrete syntax of Friedman et al. [15]. Additionally, the user can explore different semantics over the same program. Upon receiving a new program, a check leveraging `hosted-minikanren` and the `syntax-spec` frontend [1] supplemented by a custom well-formed judgment is performed to detect static errors. This will capture errors such as illegal expressions, parentheses mismatches, relation arity mistakes, and binding errors. Once a valid program is entered, it is transpiled to the language of our model, loaded, and execution proceeds incrementally: each step forward applies a single reduction rule from the model, serializes the updated search tree as JSON, and transmits it to the front end for rendering via the D3 library [5]. We cache previous states, allowing users to step backwards and forwards through the history. If the forward cache is empty and the user requests to step forward, the current program is stepped and cached, and the new program is sent to the front end. This methodology is similar to other examples in the literature such as Bernstein and Stark [2] and Kamburjan et al. [20].

5 Visualizing Reductions

As discussed in Sect. 1, understanding why programs produce answers in specific orders is crucial for reasoning about logic programs effectively. In this section, we demonstrate how to leverage our custom visualizer to inspect and understand search behaviors clearly. By stepping through evaluation with interleaving semantics, users can directly observe how different operational semantics influence the order of answers.

5.1 Using the Visualizer

Using this visual representation of our semantics, we explore why the program in Sect. 1 produces answers in the order it does. Figure 8 shows execution of the same program, but with interleaving semantics. The first divergence between these semantics and the depth-first one occurs after four steps: we have substituted our query variable (now `#(0)`), distributed the initial state over two conjunctions, but now the first relation call is delayed. This delay interleaves disjunctions as it is propagated up until it reaches the top of the tree. Evaluation proceeds down the other side and again delays a relation call. One can already see the railway model and lazy relation expansions at this point. Although interleaving has occurred, the ordering of the disjuncts remains consistent. Additionally,

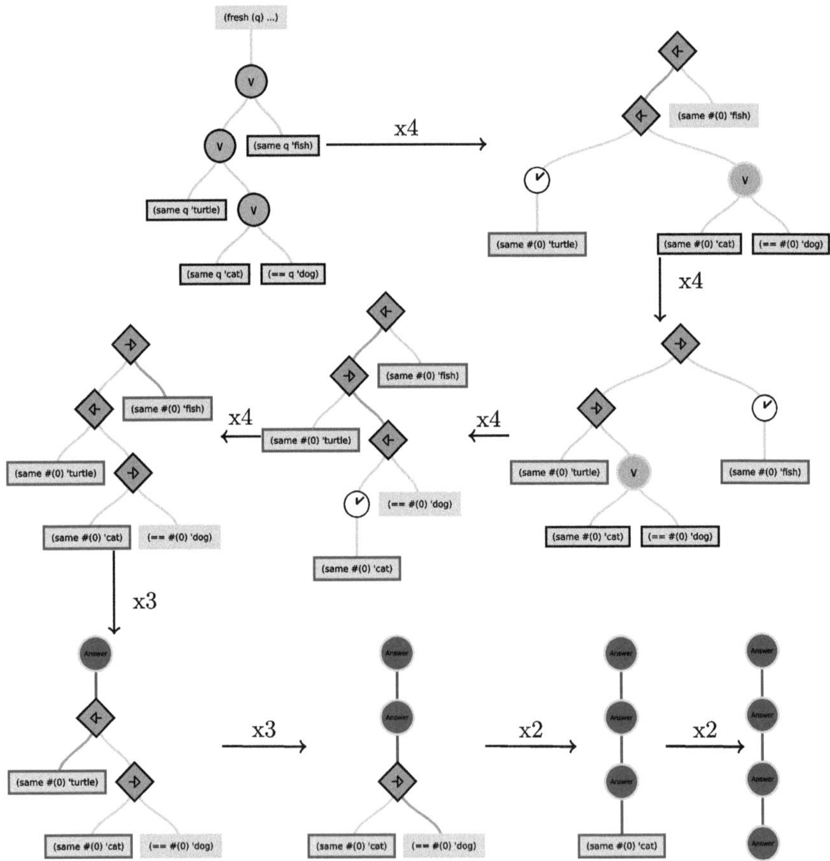

Fig. 8. Evaluation showing interleaving behavior.

the goals highlighted in green and marked as ready to proceed by the scheduler have not been expanded. Again, the delay is propagated up and evaluation now proceeds through two disjunctions to yet another relation call. The process repeats and evaluation is now focused on `(same #(0) 'fish)` which will succeed and produce the first answer, `'fish`. Evaluation continues down the left side of the tree where `(same #(0) 'turtle)` is encountered and produces the second answer, `'turtle`. Next, the right side of the final disjunction, `(== #(0) 'dog)`, immediately succeeds without delay since it is not a relation call and yields the third answer, `'dog`. The last goal, `(same #(0) 'cat)`, succeeds and produces the final answer, `'cat`.

6 Related Work

6.1 Operational Semantic Models for MiniKanren

Several prior efforts have proposed formal or mechanized models of miniKanren execution. Rosenblatt et al. [26] describe a first-order version of miniKanren and used it to implement a stepper that supports user-directed exploration. Their goal is a tooling-friendly representation of miniKanren's goals and search state. Their approach supports interactive stepping and human-guided search, but does not formalize the search order or represent the interleaving scheduler explicitly. The stepping operates at the goal level, and is interpreted by an underlying engine rather than being grounded in a formal reduction semantics.

Rozplokhas and Boulytchev [27] present a certified operational semantics for miniKanren, formalized and proved correct in Coq (now Rocq). They model a simpler interleaving structure in order to obtain clean proofs of fairness and completeness. By contrast, we aim to model the operational behavior of mainstream miniKanren implementations more directly, including the concrete points at which goals are delayed, resumed, and reordered. Rather than abstracting away these details, we make them explicit in the semantics so they can be inspected and compared.

Host Language Embeddings of Fair Backtracking. Nondeterministic choice, backtracking, and fair interleaving also have a long history in functional semantics, particularly via host-language embeddings. Functional accounts based on monads and continuations provide implementations and semantic explanations of backtracking and fair interleaving [19,22,30] inside a lazy functional host. These approaches explain and implement interleaving by exploiting features of the host language—such as laziness, continuations, or delimited control—rather than by modeling the search strategy directly in the object language.

Our work is complementary: we give an explicit *reduction semantics* for miniKanren itself, in a first-order, strict setting, where suspension and resumption are reified in the semantic state rather than delegated to the host language. A natural alternative would be meta-interpretation over an existing engine;

instead, we state these scheduler effects directly as a PLT Redex reduction relation. This lets us reuse Redex's execution and property-based validation workbench without building custom tooling around a meta-interpreter, while still making the interleaving structure observable for inspection and comparison.

Inter-derivable Semantic Artifacts for Interleaving Backtracking. A separate but closely related line of work studies the correspondence between reduction semantics, abstract machines, and continuation-based interpreters. Felleisen [11] and subsequent work by Danvy and collaborators establish a systematic pipeline relating structural operational semantics, evaluation-context reductions, small-step abstract machines, and continuation-passing interpreters via refocusing, defunctionalization, and transition compression [8–10].

In the logic programming setting, Biernacki and Danvy [4] show how a Prolog-like logic engine can be derived by defunctionalizing a continuation-based interpreter with explicit success and failure continuations. Wand and Vaillancourt [33] further relate continuation-based, depth-first, and other models of backtracking, clarifying how different control regimes correspond.

Our contribution fits into this lineage by addressing a gap in the relationship for interleaving backtracking. While the inter-derivability of semantic artifacts is well understood for lambda-calculus-based functional languages, these correspondences for interleaved search have received less attention. By giving a fine-grained reduction semantics that reifies the residual search space and scheduler behavior, we provide a concrete starting point from which one can derive abstract machines and continuation-based interpreters for interleaving depth-first search, and relate them back to streams-based and continuation-based implementations. Our semantics provides a convenient starting point for applying refocusing/defunctionalization in the interleaving-search setting.

Strategy-Generic Accounts of Nondeterminism. Our reduction rules make the scheduler explicit and thus easy to vary, but one can also ask for a *strategy-generic* semantics in which nondeterministic choice is represented uniformly and the policy is factored out. Biernacka et al. [3] introduce zipper-based semantics for nondeterminism in λ-calculus and process calculi; adapting such a formulation to miniKanren may provide a uniform representation of "the rest of the search" while varying strategy through a separate policy component.

7 Conclusions and Future Work

In this work we present a fine-grained, deterministic small-step operational semantics for interleaving logic programming, developed using miniKanren as a case study. By reifying the remaining search space as an explicit syntactic search tree, the semantics exposes interleaving, suspension, and resumption decisions that are typically implicit in language implementations. This representation makes it possible to reason concretely about surprising answer orders and performance pathologies, and to validate semantic invariants such as determinism and preservation using mechanized testing in PLT Redex.

While the interactive visualizer described in this paper was an important motivating application, we view it primarily as one consumer of the semantics rather than its central contribution. More broadly, we treat the semantics itself as an analytic and pedagogical artifact: a notional machine whose design choices shape how programmers understand and reason about interleaving execution.

One direction for future work frames the semantics itself as an object of design and comparison. Our framework supports multiple, semantically distinct presentations of interleaving search—for example, different treatments of disjunction (railroad-style versus subtree flipping), alternative placements of delay points, or eager versus deferred expansion of relation calls. Because these choices are realized directly in the reduction semantics and exposed through visualization, they provide a controlled setting for studying how different operational models affect users' understanding of program behavior. Such studies would treat semantic design decisions, rather than surface UI features, as the primary focus. Concretely, we plan controlled studies comparing relation-level and small-step views, as well as railway-orientation versus subtree-flipping presentations.

A second direction concerns the derivation of other semantic artifacts from the reduction semantics presented here. Given its explicit evaluation contexts and deterministic small-step structure, the semantics appears well suited as a starting point for following the refocusing / transition-compression pipeline [10]. More broadly, we want a systematic route from evaluation-context reductions to abstract machines, continuation-passing interpreters, and corresponding natural semantics for interleaved DFS. Pursuing these derivations would help clarify the relationships among different operational accounts of miniKanren and situate interleaved depth-first execution of logic programming within a broader semantic landscape. We would also like to increase confidence in the semantics through machine-checked metatheory in a proof-oriented framework (e.g., Rocq or the K Framework), in the spirit of Rozplokhas and Boulytchev [27], complementing our current randomized Redex validation with proof-level guarantees.

Finally, interleaving in logic programming also parallels models of controlled concurrency, which likewise involve suspension, resumption, and deterministic scheduling over nondeterministic choices. Exploring these connections may help relate logic-programming execution models to general theories of nondeterminism and concurrency.

Acknowledgements. Thanks to Michael Ballantyne, Dmitry Boulytchev, and our reviewers. This research has been supported by NSF grant CCF-2348408.

References

1. Ballantyne, M., King, A., Felleisen, M.: Macros for domain-specific languages. Proc. ACM Program. Lang. **4**(OOPSLA) (2020). https://doi.org/10.1145/3428297
2. Bernstein, K.L., Stark, E.W.: Operational semantics of a focusing debugger. Electron. Notes Theor. Comput. Sci. **1**, 13–31 (1995). https://doi.org/10.1016/S1571-0661(04)80002-1, mFPS XI, Mathematical Foundations of Programming Semantics, Eleventh Annual Conference

3. Biernacka, M., Biernacki, D., Lenglet, S., Schmitt, A.: Non-deterministic abstract machines. In: 33rd International Conference on Concurrency Theory, CONCUR 2022, Warsaw, Poland, 12–16 September 2022, pp. 7:1–7:24 (2022). https://doi.org/10.4230/LIPICS.CONCUR.2022.7
4. Biernacki, D., Danvy, O.: From interpreter to logic engine by defunctionalization. In: Bruynooghe, M. (ed.) LOPSTR 2003. LNCS, vol. 3018, pp. 143–159. Springer, Heidelberg (2004). https://doi.org/10.1007/978-3-540-25938-1_13
5. Bostock, M., Ogievetsky, V., Heer, J.: D^3 data-driven documents. IEEE Trans. Visual Comput. Graphics **17**(12), 2301–2309 (2011). https://doi.org/10.1109/TVCG.2011.185
6. Caballero, R., Riesco, A., Silva, J.: A survey of algorithmic debugging. ACM Comput. Surv. **50**(4) (2017). https://doi.org/10.1145/3106740
7. Clark, K.L.: Negation as failure. In: Logic and Data Bases, Symposium on Logic and Data Bases, Centre d'études et de recherches de Toulouse, France, 1977, pp. 293–322 (1977). https://doi.org/10.1007/978-1-4684-3384-5_11
8. Danvy, O.: From reduction-based to reduction-free normalization. Electron. Notes Theor. Comput. Sci. **124**(2), 79–100 (2005). https://doi.org/10.1016/j.entcs.2005.01.007
9. Danvy, O.: Defunctionalized interpreters for programming languages. SIGPLAN Not. **43**(9), 131–142 (2008). https://doi.org/10.1145/1411203.1411206
10. Danvy, O., Nielsen, L.R.: Refocusing in reduction semantics. BRICS Report Series **11**(26) (2004). https://doi.org/10.7146/brics.v11i26.21851
11. Felleisen, M.: Calculi of λ_v-CS conversion: a syntactic theory of control and state in imperative higher-order programming languages. Ph.D. thesis, Indiana Univ., Bloomington, IN (1987)
12. Felleisen, M., Findler, R.B., Flatt, M.: Semantics Engineering with PLT Redex, 1st edn. MIT Press (2009). ISBN 0262062755
13. Felleisen, M., Hieb, R.: The revised report on the syntactic theories of sequential control and state. Theoret. Comput. Sci. **103**(2), 235–271 (1992). https://doi.org/10.1016/0304-3975(92)90014-7
14. Friedman, D.P., Byrd, W.E., Kiselyov, O.: The Reasoned Schemer. MIT Press, Cambridge (2005). https://doi.org/10.7551/mitpress/5801.001.0001
15. Friedman, D.P., Byrd, W.E., Kiselyov, O., Hemann, J.: The Reasoned Schemer, 2nd edn. MIT Press (2018). ISBN 0262535513
16. Hemann, J.: Constraint microKanren in the CLP Scheme. Ph.D. thesis, Indiana University, Bloomington (2020). https://scholarworks.iu.edu/dspace/handle/2022/25183
17. Hemann, J., Friedman, D.P.: μKanren: a minimal functional core for relational programming. In: Proceedings of Scheme 2013 (2013). https://schemeworkshop.org/2013/papers/HemannMuKanren2013.pdf
18. Hemann, J., Friedman, D.P.: Nearly macro-free microkanren. In: Chang, S. (ed.) Trends in Functional Programming, pp. 72–91, Springer, Heidelberg (2023). https://doi.org/10.1007/978-3-031-38938-2_5
19. Hinze, R.: Deriving backtracking monad transformers. In: Proceedings of the Fifth ACM SIGPLAN International Conference on Functional Programming (ICFP) 2000, Montreal, Canada, 18–21 September 2000, pp. 186–197 (2000). https://doi.org/10.1145/351240.351258
20. Kamburjan, E., Klungre, V.N., Schlatte, R., Johnsen, E.B., Giese, M.: Programming and debugging with semantically lifted states. In: Verborgh, R., et al. (eds.) ESWC 2021. LNCS, vol. 12731, pp. 126–142. Springer, Cham (2021). https://doi.org/10.1007/978-3-030-77385-4_8

21. Kiselyov, O., Byrd, W.E., Friedman, D.P., Shan, C.: Pure, declarative, and constructive arithmetic relations (declarative pearl). In: Garrigue, J., Hermenegildo, M.V. (eds.) FLOPS 2008. LNCS, vol. 4989, pp. 64–80. Springer, Heidelberg (2008). https://doi.org/10.1007/978-3-540-78969-7_7
22. Kiselyov, O., Shan, C., Friedman, D.P., Sabry, A.: Backtracking, interleaving, and terminating monad transformers: (functional pearl). In: Proceedings of ICFP 2005, pp. 192–203, Association for Computing Machinery (2005). https://doi.org/10.1145/1086365.1086390
23. Klein, C., et al.: Run your research: on the effectiveness of lightweight mechanization. In: Proceedings of the 39th ACM SIGPLAN-SIGACT Symposium on Principles of Programming Languages, POPL 2012, Philadelphia, Pennsylvania, USA, 22–28 January 2012, pp. 285–296 (2012). https://doi.org/10.1145/2103656.2103691
24. Lassez, J.L., McAloon, K.: Independence of negative constraints. In: Díaz, J., Orejas, F. (eds.) CAAP 1989. LNCS, vol. 351, pp. 19–27. Springer, Heidelberg (1989). https://doi.org/10.1007/3-540-50939-9_122
25. Lloyd, J., Topor, R.: Making prolog more expressive. J. Logic Program. **1**(3), 225–240 (1984). https://doi.org/10.1016/0743-1066(84)90011-6
26. Rosenblatt, G., Zhang, L., Byrd, W.E., Might, M.: First-order minikanren representation: great for tooling and search. In: Proceedings of the miniKanren and Relational Programming Workshop, ICFP Workshop 2019, Association for Computing Machinery (2019), miniKanren Workshop, held with ICFP 2019
27. Rozplokhas, D., Boulytchev, D.: Certified semantics for disequality. In: Proceedings of the 2020 miniKanren and Relational Programming Workshop (2020). http://hdl.handle.net/2047/D20413639
28. Rozplokhas, D., Vyatkin, A., Boulytchev, D.: Certified semantics for miniKanren. In: Proceedings of the 2019 miniKanren and Relational Programming Workshop, pp. 80–98 (2019). http://nrs.harvard.edu/urn-3:HUL.InstRepos:41307116
29. Rozplokhas, D., Vyatkin, A., Boulytchev, D.: Certified semantics for relational programming. In: Oliveira, B.C.S. (ed.) APLAS 2020. LNCS, vol. 12470, pp. 167–185. Springer, Cham (2020). https://doi.org/10.1007/978-3-030-64437-6_9
30. Seres, S.: The algebra of logic programming. Ph.D. thesis, University of Oxford, UK (2001). http://ethos.bl.uk/OrderDetails.do?uin=uk.bl.ethos.365466
31. Shapiro, E.: Algorithmic Program Debugging. MIT Press, United States (1983). ISBN 0262192187
32. Triska, M.: The power of prolog. Online Book (2025). https://www.metalevel.at/prolog. Accessed 15 July 2025
33. Wand, M., Vaillancourt, D.: Relating models of backtracking. In: Proceedings of the Ninth ACM SIGPLAN International Conference on Functional Programming, ICFP 2004, Snow Bird, UT, USA, 19–21 September 2004, pp. 54–65 (2004). https://doi.org/10.1145/1016850.1016861

More Fun with Monoids
Declarative Pearl

Oleg Kiselyov(✉)

Tohoku University, Sendai, Japan
oleg@okmij.org
https://okmij.org/ftp/

Abstract. Playing with monoids and discovering for oneself how frequently they turn up in various guises and how much is expressed by them is a delight. Not only it brightens the day of important but frankly boring data analytics. Not only it challenges to discover efficient (with the constant time and space operation) monoids, which demands ingenuity. In the words of Guy Steele, inventing efficient associative combining operators is *a very big deal*. An efficient monoid opens up parallel implementations – not just parallel but embarrassingly parallel: The input sequence arbitrarily partitioned among workers, all running in parallel with no races, dependencies or even memory bank conflicts. This is the ideal for multi-core, GPU or distributed processing.

In this paper we show why monoids are a big deal, and also a big fun – even more than expected. Horner rule and Boyer-Moore majority voting – commonly regarded as prototypically inherently sequential – turn out monoids, and hence embarrassingly parallelizable. As we generalize monoids to observable monoids, we discover a new, vertical way to combine them, enabling efficient iterated grouping and aggregation directly on raw deserialized (big) data, on multicore or multi-processor.

1 Introduction

A monoid is mere an addition, taken broadly. That summing up a sequence is a monoid application should not be any more surprising than the realization we speak prose. What is, perhaps, surprising, is that many, many more query and accumulation tasks – looking through data and collecting the findings – turn out to be represented as a *reduction* with an associative combining operation that also has a neutral element: in other words, as a monoid reduction, or map-reduce.[1] Monoids are also a cornerstone of mathematics: after all, Category Theory is a study of fancy drawn monoids.

As Steele stressed in his ICFP 2009 keynote [11], a monoid reduction is not a mere theoretical curiosity. Like the Σ notation in Math, it specifies what should be reduced up, but not how. Unlike an accumulating for-loop (or, fold), reduce does not commit us to a particular evaluation strategy. It can be performed sequentially, but also, more importantly, in parallel – in fact, embarrassingly

[1] Throughout the paper reduction always means monoid reduction.

M. Sperber and E. Komendantskaya (Eds.): FLOPS 2026, LNCS 16533, pp. 156–172, 2026.
https://doi.org/10.1007/978-981-92-0184-6_7

parallel, in a Google MapReduce-like way. Therefore, efficient monoids – constant space and time operation – are a big deal, Steele exhorted.

In this paper, after reminding monoids and monoid reductions, we find *unexpected* fun:

- Efficient monoid and matrix presentation of the familiar Horner rule, Sect. 3 – finding a connection to semidirect product;
- Boyer-Moore majority voting, originally and typically presented as inherently sequential, as a monoid reduction: Sect. 4. The challenge is not in finding the reduction but in ascertaining that, despite the apparent non-associativity, it is the proper monoid reduction after all. For the first time we give the complete proof.
- A new, vertical, way of composing monoids, giving an efficient, embarrassingly parallel way to repeatedly group and aggregate big data: Sect. 5.

In all the cases we find both interesting theoretical connections – and efficient, practical algorithms.

The paper uses the Math notation, and hence applicable to any programming language: for example, the accompanying code implements all algorithms in OCaml.[2]

2 Monoids

For notation and reference, this warm-up section reminds various monoids and monoidal reductions.

Monoid per se hardly needs any introduction: it is a set M (called 'carrier set') with a binary associative operation $\odot$ that has a neutral element $\emptyset$, a member of M – overall, notated as a triple $(M, \odot, \emptyset)$, sometimes with an attached name for reference. The associativity and neutrality are formally written as the identities (equational laws):

$$x \odot (y \odot z) = (x \odot y) \odot \mathrm{z} \qquad \emptyset \odot x = x \odot \emptyset = x$$

where x, y and z are arbitrary elements of M. The identities betray that there is one more thing to a monoid – so ubiquitous and familiar that it is rarely mentioned explicitly: the equivalence relation denoted by '=' above, the equality. In Sect. 4 we see why it may be worth talking about explicitly.[3] In a programming language, e.g., OCaml, monoid is notated as a signature

```
module type monoid = sig type t    val zero : t    val op : t → t → t end
```

(In other languages, it corresponds to a trait or class.)

Examples of monoids are abound:

[2] http://okmij.org/ftp/Algorithms/map-monoid-reduce.html.

[3] The failure to explicitly account for the equality leads to apparent contradictions and complications to avoid them, as seen in [5].

- Sum (int, $+, 0$) and Prod (int, $*, 1$), where int is a set of integers – or a range of them that contains 0 and 1, with appropriately defined addition and multiplication: e.g., 64-bit integers;
- Min ($M, \min, e_{max}$) and Max ($M, \max, e_{min}$), where M is a totally ordered set with the minimal e_{min} and maximal e_{max} elements: e.g., 64-bit integers;
- Some (bool, $\vee$, false) and All (bool, $\wedge$, true), where bool is {false, true}.
- EF_α ($\alpha \to \alpha, \cdot, \mathrm{id}$) and EF'_α ($\alpha \to \alpha, \rhd, \mathrm{id}$) for an arbitrary type α, where '$\cdot$' and '$\rhd$' are the ordinary (right-to-left) and the left-to-right function composition, resp., and id is the identity function.

Listing of the monoids in pairs should have hinted at their connections. There are many more. A particularly important, 'faithful' connection is called monoid homomorphism. Technically, a monoid homomorphism from $(M, \odot, \emptyset)$ to $(M', \odot', \emptyset')$ is a mapping $h : M \to M'$ that "commutes with operations":

$$h(x \odot y) = (h\,x) \odot' (h\ \ y) \qquad h\,\emptyset = \emptyset'$$

As an example, negation is a homomorphism between Some and All, justified by the De Morgan law (see also Ex. 1 in the Appendix of the full paper).

If $a_0, \ldots, a_{n-1}$ is an integer sequence such as an array, its summation is the familiar $\sum_{i=0}^{n-1} a_i$. It reduces a sequence of integers to a single integer, by repeatedly applying the Sum monoid operation, using 0 for the empty array. Such a summarizing of a sequence of monoid elements to a single element is called (monoid) reduction. One may say the reduction 'wedges in' the monoid operation between each element of the sequence – which is how it is often explained in APL, where the reduce operation first appeared [8]. The Σ notation tells what is to be done (sum up – or, generally, reduce up – a sequence of monoid elements using the monoid operation) – but not how. Therefore, Steele [11] has urged using reduce as far as possible, because it decouples the algorithm from the execution strategy. The strategy (sequential, parallel, distributed) and data partitioning can be chosen later, depending on circumstances.

Indeed, on one hand, $\sum_{i=0}^{n-1} a_i$ may be implemented as a sequential reduction

$$\sum_{i=0}^{n-1} a_i = (((0 + a_0) + a_1) + \ldots + a_{n-1}) \tag{1}$$

which corresponds to the familiar accumulating for-loop, or left fold. For example, in OCaml:

```
let reduce (type a) (module M: monoid with type t = a) (a: a array) =
  let s = ref M.zero in for i=0 to length a −1 do s := M.op !s a.(i) done; !s
```

The monoid to reduce with is specified as a first-class module. This loop is exactly the implementation of Array.fold_left M.op M.zero a

One may also implement the reduction (for $n > 2$) as

$$\sum_{i=0}^{n-1} a_i = \left(\sum_{i=0}^{n'-1} a_i\right) + \left(\sum_{i=n'}^{n-1} a_i\right)$$

where $0 < n' < n$. That is, one may split the sequence into two – or, more, and not necessarily equal – parts, reduce the parts and then combine the results with the monoid operation. The part reductions are independent, and may be carried out in parallel. A part can be reduced sequentially, or by splitting it again. Although the recursive splitting is theoretically appealing, in practice[4] one cuts the sequence by the number of available workers (cores) – assigning each (non-overlapping) slice to a core. Each core does its work in parallel, without communicating or snooping on the neighbors. There is no even read conflicts, no wasting of the memory bandwidth on repeatedly feeding the same data to different processors. Monoid reduction can hence be carried out not just in parallel – *embarrassingly in parallel.*

The sequence elements do not have to be themselves monoid elements: only mappable to them. As an example, take an array a of elements of some type α and find out how many of its elements satisfy a given predicate $p : \alpha \to \mathsf{bool}$. The answer is $\Sigma f(a_i)$ where f is defined as $f(x) = (p\,x\ ?\ 1 : 0)$ (using the C-like notation for conditional expression). In programming terms, it corresponds to mapping f on an array – producing an array of integers – which can then be Sum-reduced. A database-minded reader might immediately see the query

SELECT COUNT (*) FROM widgets WHERE cnt=1 (2)

given the table widgets containing, among other columns, cnt for the inventory count. Indeed database queries are an example of monoid reduction, as was well pointed in [5].

That reduction is often preceded by mapping – called together map-reduce – is not an accident. Let's look at the monoid $(M, \odot, \emptyset)$ as an abstract data type. When M is abstract, the only elements we can get hold of are those constructible with the monoid operations: $\emptyset$, $\emptyset \odot \emptyset$, etc.; that is, the mere $\emptyset$. We need so-called generators, to bring in other M elements. In abstract algebra [3], generators are introduced as a (possibly infinite) set of M elements. A better way, easier to implement and maintaining the M abstraction, is to regard generators as an injective mapping *gen* from an index set I to M. We hence come to a so-called *collection monoids* [5]: $(M, \odot, \emptyset, I, gen)$. Whereas M may be abstract, I is concrete. The monoids $(M, \odot, \emptyset)$ considered so far such as Sum, Min, are all representable as collection monoids: $(M, \odot, \emptyset, M, \mathrm{id})$ – called primitive monoids in [5]. An example of a non-primitive monoid is a list[5] α^* of elements of some type α: $(\alpha^*, +\!\!+, [], \alpha, -^1)$ where $-^1 : \alpha \to \alpha^*$ produces a singleton list. (If α is a type (set), α^* is the set of all finite sequences made of elements of α. We also use α and α^* as common nouns, which also denote sets, in English: "an α element",

[4] "Performance testing showed little gains from recursive partitioning: the big win was from splitting the working set in buckets that fit in L2/L3-per core." User pkhuong on https://lobste.rs/c/f5cxf9.

[5] By 'list' in this paper we mean a general sequence, such as native lists, sequences (module Stdlib.Seq), dynamic arrays of OCaml, as well as strings, etc. for specific sequence types.

"a list α^*", "for some α^*", etc.) Every list is either the empty list $[]$, a singleton list x^1, or obtained from them via the list concatenation $+\!\!+$ (sometimes we denote sequence concatenation by juxtaposition, as common for multiplication). Technically, one says that $(\alpha^*, +\!\!+, [], \alpha, -^1)$ is a generated monoid.

With the collection monoid $(M, \odot, \emptyset, \alpha, gen)$, an α^* sequence may be reduced to a single value by applying gen to each element and $(M, \odot, \emptyset)$-reducing the resulting monoid sequence. Map-reduce is hence a reduction with a collection monoid. The earlier example (2) of counting widgets whose inventory count is one is hence the reduction with the collection monoid $(\mathsf{int}, +, 0, \mathsf{widget}, f)$ with f as defined earlier. As another example, finding the inventory count of all widgets except wrenches is the reduction of the widget table with the collection monoid $(\mathsf{int}, +, 0, \mathsf{widget}, g)$ where $g(w) = (\pi_{name}\, w = \text{"wrench"}\ ?\ 0 : \pi_{cnt}\, w)$ where π_{cnt} extracts the value of the cnt column from the record widget.

One may have noticed something strange from the two examples. The table of widgets (e.g., represented as widget^*) is itself a collection monoid. Let's write the above map-reduce as h: a function that takes a table and returns an integer. That is, h maps the carrier set of the collection monoid widget^* to the carrier set of $(\mathsf{int}, +, 0, \mathsf{widget}, g)$. Furthermore, as easy to see

$$h\,[] = 0 \qquad h\,(l_1 +\!\!+ l_2) = (h\,l_1) + (h\,l_2) \qquad h\,w^1 = g\,w$$

That is, *map-reduce is a (collection) monoid homomorphism.* This is the so-called First Homomorphism theorem.[6] The insight that a monoid corresponds to a stretch of an input sequence would come very helpful.

If we truly take monoid as an abstract data type, i.e., M abstract, then the reduction result, an element of M, can be used only with the monoid operations. We cannot, say, print it out. We have to extend the monoid once again, adding an observation $obs : M \to O$ observing a monoid element as a value of some concrete observation type O. The observation is a sort of an 'inverse' of a generator. The *observable monoid* is hence $(M, \odot, \emptyset, I, gen, O, obs)$. Interestingly, neither abstract algebra nor [5] seem to mention it. Any collection monoid $(M, \odot, \emptyset, I, gen)$ can be trivially observed: $(M, \odot, \emptyset, I, gen, M, \mathrm{id})$. A non-trivial observable monoid is described next.

Map-reduce in the general form – mapping a sequence $a_0, \ldots, a_{n-1}$ by the function gen, reducing it and then observing the result by obs – is then a homomorphism from the α^* collection monoid to the $(M, \odot, \emptyset, \alpha, gen, O, obs)$ observable monoid. In [11], it is called the *conjugate transform.* To present this general map-reduce it is hence sufficient to specify the observable monoid – which is how we would treat map-reduce from now on. See the accompanying code for translations of this notation to sequential and parallel code.

6 which is often stated in reverse: every list homomorphism is representable as map-reduce.

2.1 Fold as Map-Reduce

If map-reduce is so useful, can any sequence processing be done as map-reduce? A sequence processing can be understood as a state machine (not necessarily finite: the number of states may not be bound a priori), formally written as (α, σ, d, s_0) but often abbreviated in this paper to just (d, s_0). It starts in the initial state $s_0 : \sigma$; the transition function $d : \alpha \times \sigma \to \sigma$ maps the current input α and the current state σ to a new state. The run of the state machine over the input sequence (say, represented as a list $l : \alpha^*$) is what is called the left fold: in OCaml terms, List.fold_left (Fun.flip d) s0 l. (We often call (α, σ, d, s_0) or (d, s_0) as (left) fold, leaving the input sequence implicit.) The question is: can the fold be represented as map-reduce for some monoid? The answer is yes, and somewhat no.

First of all, if σ and α are the same and d is associative, the left fold is the homomorphism: see (1) for an example.

Generally, the left fold is an instance of map-reduce, unconditionally, as the following example of the run of the state machine (d, s_0) over the sequence $a_1, \ldots, a_4$ demonstrates:

$$\begin{aligned}&d(a_4, d(a_3, (a_2, d(a_1, s_0)))) = (((s_0 \mathrel{|\!\!>} d\,a_1) \mathrel{|\!\!>} d\,a_2) \mathrel{|\!\!>} d\,a_3) \mathrel{|\!\!>} d\,a_4\\&= s_0 \mathrel{|\!\!>} (d\,a_1 \rhd d\,a_2 \rhd d\,a_3 \rhd d\,a_4)\end{aligned}$$

where '$\mathrel{|\!\!>}$' is the left-to-right application (the argument is on the left), and, to remind, '$\rhd$' is the left-to-right function composition. We also implicitly curried d. All in all, left-folding of the state machine (α, σ, d, s_0) over α^* is map-reduce to the observable monoid $(\sigma{\to}\sigma, \rhd, \mathrm{id}, \alpha, d, \sigma, \lambda h.\, h\, s_0)$: or, the conjugate transform with EF'_σ.

A homomorphism from a monoid to EF_α (or EF'_α) is particularly important and has a particular name: *monoid action.* Folding is hence called the iterated action.

Unfortunately, this theoretically appealing answer is of little practical use. As the example demonstrates, the EF'_σ-reduction result is $(d\,a_1 \rhd d\,a_2 \rhd d\,a_3 \rhd d\,a_3)$: generally,[7] a big closure made from composing individual $d\,a_i$ closures. The observation applies this closure to s_0. The composed closure $d\,a_1 \rhd d\,a_2 \rhd d\,a_3 \rhd d\,a_3$ has the same structure as the original sequence $a_1, \ldots, a_4$ – and hence the same size (actually, a few times larger: not only do we have to store the list elements themselves, we have to store the function pointers d, plus the overhead). In effect we have built an intermediate data structure of unbounded size. Although composing the closures can be parallelized, the useful work of transforming the state is done only at observation, when the big closure composition is finally applied to the initial state s_0 – at which point the transition function is applied step-by-step, sequentially, just like in the original fold. This general representation of fold in terms of map-reduce only wastes time and space.

The problem hence is not merely to represent sequence processing as map-reduce, but do so *efficiently*, without undue and unbounded overhead. In other

[7] The word generally here carries a lot of weight.

words, we need to find not just any observable monoid but an efficient observable monoid, whose operations (*gen* and $\odot$) are constant time and space.[8] As Steele [11] noted, this is often non-trivial and requires ingenuity: see below.

In algebra, fold being an iterated monoid action is trivial and obvious, but seemingly not so in programming, where it is sometimes called 'the trick' [7].

3 Horner Rule

Horner rule, or schema, is a widely-used sequential algorithm to efficiently evaluate a polynomial. A similar accumulating pattern also frequently occurs in parsing. Although the algorithm is, on the face of it, inherently sequential, it turns out an efficient map-reduce. Our reduction is more general and flexible than the other ways to parallelize the Horner rule. The section also demonstrates that finding an efficient monoid is not obvious, and the insight that a monoid value corresponds to a sub-sequence helps.

To remind, Horner rule is an efficient technique to evaluate a polynomial such as

$$aw^4 + bw^3 + cw^2 + dw + e \tag{3}$$

at a particular value of w as

$$((((0 + a)w + b)w + c)w + d)w + e \tag{4}$$

Like (3), the Horner rule (4) has the same number of overt multiplications; however, the naive evaluation of (3) also requires computing powers of w. The Horner rule also needs just a single accumulator.[9]

One comes across Horner rule every time one parses (or, 'reads') a number: converts a sequence of digits $a_0, \ldots, a_n$ – a (decimal) representation of a number – to the corresponding number: i.e., evaluates $\sum a_i w^{n-i}$ at $w = 10$.

One may have recognized – e.g., by contrasting (1) with (4) – in Horner rule a state machine processing (left fold) over a sequence of polynomial coefficients, with the initial state 0 and the transition function $d(a, s) = sw + a$ – which is not associative, however.

To intuit the Horner monoid, consider a sequence of digits $1, 2, 3, 4, 5$. Each singleton subsequence is a base-10 number: 1_{10}, 2_{10}, etc. The subsequence $1, 2, 3$ is 123_{1000} and the subsequence $4, 5$ is the base-100 number 45_{100}. The whole sequence is then

$$12345_{100,000} = 123_{1000} \times 100 + 45_{100}$$

The number corresponding to a (sub)sequence of decimal digits $a_0, \ldots, a_n$ may itself be thought of as a 'digit', in base 10^n. The monoid operation is then converting the 'two-digit' mixed-base number (digit p_1 in base b_1 and digit p_2 in

---

[8] In the present paper, we consider arithmetic operations constant time and space.

[9] and so is particularly suitable for calculating by hand – which is probably not as important these days.

base b_2) to the single-digit base-$b_1 b_2$ number (representing the concatenation of the corresponding digit sequences).

The Horner monoid is hence the set of pairs (p, b), which represent the value of a polynomial with coefficients $a_0, \ldots, a_n$ at some fixed w. Specifically, $p = \sum a_i w^{n-i}$ and $b = w^n$. Formally, the monoid is:

$$(\mathsf{int} \times \mathsf{int}, \odot_H, (0,1)) \text{ where } (p_1, b_1) \odot_H (p_2, b_2) = (p_1 b_2 + p_2, b_1 b_2)$$

The neutral element is obvious, the associativity of $\odot_H$ is less so. One may prove it by a simple if slightly tedious calculation. A different presentation makes the associativity trivial. Observe:

$$\begin{pmatrix} b_1 & 0 \\ p_1 & 1 \end{pmatrix} \begin{pmatrix} b_2 & 0 \\ p_2 & 1 \end{pmatrix} = \begin{pmatrix} b_1 b_2 & 0 \\ p_1 b_2 + p_2 & 1 \end{pmatrix}$$

Therefore, the Horner monoid is a monoid whose carrier is 2×2 matrices with 0 1 in the second column; its operation is the obviously associative matrix multiplication.

Overall, the evaluation of the polynomial with integer coefficients $a_0, \ldots, a_n$ at w is the homomorphism (map-reduce) with the observable monoid

$$(\mathsf{int} \times \mathsf{int}, \odot_H, (0,1), \mathsf{int}, \lambda x.(x, w), \mathsf{int}, \pi_1)$$

(where π_1 takes out the first component of a pair). The monoid is efficient. Thus, the Horner rule is expressed as map-reduce and can hence be efficiently evaluated embarrassingly in parallel.

The construction generalizes to any polynomial ring. The matrix presentation hints at a further generalization: the Horner monoid is an instance of a so-called (outer) semidirect product. Let M $(M, \odot_M, \emptyset_M)$ and N $(N, \odot_N, \emptyset_N)$ be monoids and ϕ a homomorphism from M to $\mathsf{EF}_\mathsf{N}^\mathsf{N}$, where $\mathsf{EF}_\mathsf{N}^\mathsf{N}$ (usually written as Aut(N)) is a monoid whose carrier are not just any $N \to N$ functions but isomorphisms from N to itself. (That is, ϕ is an action by M on N that is automorphism on N). Their semidirect product by ϕ is the monoid $\mathsf{N} \rtimes_\phi \mathsf{M}$ $(N \times M, \odot_{NM}, (\emptyset_N, \emptyset_M))$ where[10]

$$(n_1, m_1) \odot_{NM} (n_2, m_2) = (\phi(m_2)(n_1) \odot_N n_2,\ m_1 \odot_M m_2)$$

Therefore, the fold $(N, N, d, \emptyset_N)$ with $d(n, s) = \phi(m)(s) \odot_N n$ for some $m \in M$ is a semidirect product homomorphism. For the Horner monoid, N is Sum and M is Prod, with the action ϕ being multiplication.

Related Work. In discussions of the Horner monoid, the parallel prefix problem and the famous parallel scan of Blelloch [1] inevitably come up. Horner rule does not require reporting of intermediate results, however. Our monoid reduction differs from Blelloch's even-odd interleaving. It also differs from monoid-cached

---

[10] Often semidirect product is defined as an isomorphic/flipped version.

trees of [11]: Horner map-reduce needs no special data structures and can work with plain arrays, spread across available cores, as demonstrated in the accompanying code.

Since Horner rule is pervasive in polynomial evaluation, there have been many techniques to parallelize it. The most common is the even/odd splitting of polynomial coefficients (described in [4, Fig. 2c] and credited to K.Ralston). Although it may well fit for SIMD processing, the even/odd splitting is bad for multicore since it creates read contention (bank conflicts) and wastes cache and memory bandwidth. Our monoid reduce lets us assign different memory banks to different cores, for their exclusive, conflict-free access.

On the other hand, Estrin's scheme [4, Fig. 2b] – binomial grouping – may be seen as a very particular instance of our monoid construction. Our monoid reduction allows however for arbitrary grouping, hierarchically if desired, and of not necessarily of the same size.

4 Boyer-Moore Majority

Boyer-Moore majority voting is the algorithm for finding the majority element in a sequence – that is, the element that occurs more than half of the time [2]. The algorithm requires one pass over the sequence and the constant amount of working space. It is important to keep in mind that the return value is the majority element *if it exists*. The algorithm *in general* cannot tell if the sequence has majority: if not, the algorithm returns an arbitrary element, not necessarily the most frequent. One may, therefore, need the second pass over the sequence to count the occurrences of the returned element and verify it is indeed the majority. The second pass may be avoided or be unnecessary in some cases.

The Boyer-Moore algorithm is called a prototypical streaming algorithm and is inherently sequential – at least, was presented as such [2]. It may be surprising, therefore, that it may also be presented as a reduction and hence performed just as efficiently in parallel – in fact, embarrassingly in parallel. The monoid reduction is simple. What is complex is convincing ourselves that it indeed works and does the right thing, in all cases.

The Boyer-Moore algorithm, originally and typically, is presented as a sequential state machine processing $(\alpha, \mathsf{int} \times \alpha, d, (0, \alpha_*))$ where α_* is an arbitrary inhabitant of α and the transition function is

$$d(a, (c, m)) = \begin{cases} (1,a) & \text{if } c = 0 \\ (c{+}1,m) & \text{if } a = m \\ (c{-}1,m) & \text{otherwise} \end{cases} \tag{5}$$

The state is the non-negative counter c and the candidate majority m (which is irrelevant if $c = 0$). At the end of the algorithm, when the entire sequence is scanned, m is the majority element, if the sequence has one. If the counter c at the end is more than the half of the sequence length, the sequence definitely has majority. Otherwise, we have to make another pass through the sequence to verify that m is indeed the majority. The verification pass may be unnecessary if we have prior knowledge that the majority exists – or if we are satisfied with any element if it does not.

The generalization to the monoid reduction comes to mind immediately: Boyer-Moore majority is the homomorphism to the efficient observable monoid:

$$(\mathsf{int} \times \alpha, \odot_{BM}, (0, \alpha_*), \alpha, \lambda x.\,(1, x), \pi_2) \qquad \text{where} \tag{6}$$

$$(c_1, m_1) \odot_{BM} (c_2, m_2) = \begin{cases} (c_2, m_2) & \text{if } c_1 = 0 \\ (c_1, m_1) & \text{if } c_2 = 0 \\ (c_1 + c_2, m_1) & \text{if } m_1 = m_2 \\ (c_1 - c_2, m_1) & \text{if } m_1 \neq m_2 \text{ and } c_1 \geq c_2 \\ (c_2 - c_1, m_2) & \text{if } m_1 \neq m_2 \text{ and } c_1 < c_2 \end{cases}$$

(where π_2 projects the second component of a pair). The original sequential algorithm is the particular instance.

That $(0, \alpha_*)$ is the neutral element of $\odot_{BM}$ is clear. But is the operation really associative? Let's check:

$$((2, a) \odot_{BM} (3, b)) \odot_{BM} (2, c) = (1, c) \qquad (2, a) \odot_{BM} ((3, b) \odot_{BM} (2, c)) = (1, a)$$

Unfortunately, (6) is not a monoid.

Yet the victory was so near: (6) does seem to work. One may *feel* that (6) is 'morally right'. There is a big difference, however, between the feeling and the rigorous proof: only the latter gives the conviction that the algorithm does work, *in all the cases.*

Let us start from scratch, with the most naive and inefficient, but uncontroversially correct way of finding majority of a sequence: count the occurrences of each element and pick the one with the largest count. If the sequence has the majority, the picked element is certainly it. What we have outlined may be taken as the specification of the majority algorithm – formalized as the homomorphism to the observable monoid:

$$(\{\{\alpha\}\}, =, \cup, \{\{\}\}, \alpha, \lambda x.\{\{x\}\}, \alpha, \text{argmax}) \tag{7}$$

where the carrier is the multiset (bag), the operation is the multiset union and argmax returns the bag element with the maximal occurrence count (or an arbitrary inhabitant of α if the bag is empty). Multiset is a monoid, for certain. We have explicitly written the equality operation – omnipresent but hardly ever mentioned explicitly. We shall see why it should be taken seriously. In our case, the equality '=' is the standard multiset equality: two multisets are equal if they contain the same elements with the same occurrence count (multiplicity).

Inspired by the correctness proof of the original Boyer-Moore algorithm [2], we introduce a particular realization P of a multiset: a partitioning into a multiset of mismatched pairs, that is, pairs (x, y) with $x \neq y$. There may be a remainder: one or several copies of an element that cannot be paired up. The realization P is hence a triple (c, m, p) where $p = \{\{(x, y) \mid x \neq y\}\}$, c is the number of copies of the left unpaired element, and m is that left out element.

When $c = 0$, m is disregarded and arbitrary. Let

$$|(c, m, p)| \triangleq \{\{x \mid (x, y) \in p\}\} \cup \{\{y \mid (x, y) \in p\}\} \cup \bigcup_{i=0}^{c} \{\{m\}\}$$

be the multiset that (c, m, p) represents (or: being a partition of). The partitioning is not unique: for example, the multiset $\{\{a, b, c, c, c\}\}$ may be partitioned either as $(1, c, \{\{(a, c), (b, c)\}\})$ or $(3, c, \{\{(a, b)\}\})$, or $(3, c, \{\{(b, a)\}\})$, etc.

P is meant to be a realization of multiset. In particular, the empty multiset is realized as $(0, \alpha_*, \{\{\}\})$ (to be called $P_\varnothing$) and the singleton $\{\{x\}\}$ as $(1, x, \{\{\}\})$. For equality, we define

$$P_1 \approx P_2 \text{ just in case } |P_1| = |P_2|$$

Clearly, '$\approx$' is an equivalence relation. The multiset union likewise may be computed directly on P, as $\odot_P$:

$$(c_1, m_1, p_1) \odot_P (c_2, m_2, p_2) = \begin{cases} (c_2, m_2, p_1 \cup p_2) & \text{if } c_1 = 0 \\ (c_1, m_1, p_1 \cup p_2) & \text{if } c_2 = 0 \\ (c_1 + c_2, m_1, p_1 \cup p_2) & \text{if } m_1 = m_2 \\ (c_1 - c_2, m_1, p_1 \cup p_2 \cup \bigcup_{i=0}^{c_2} \{\{(m_1, m_2)\}\}) & \text{if } m_1 \neq m_2 \text{ and } c_1 \geq c_2 \\ (c_2 - c_1, m_2, p_1 \cup p_2 \cup \bigcup_{i=0}^{c_1} \{\{(m_1, m_2)\}\}) & \text{if } m_1 \neq m_2 \text{ and } c_1 < c_2 \end{cases} \quad (8)$$

It is easy to verify that

$$|P_1 \odot_P P_2| = |P_1| \cup |P_2|$$

since $P_1 \odot_P P_2$ preserves all elements in $|P_1|$ and $|P_2|$, including their multiplicities. All in all, P does indeed feel like a multiset. To be precise,

Proposition 1. *$(P, \approx, \odot_P, P_\varnothing)$ is a monoid. Furthermore, $|-|$ is the homomorphism from* P *$(P, \approx, \odot_P, P_\varnothing, \alpha, \lambda x.(1, x, \{\{\}\}))$ to $(\{\{\alpha\}\}, =, \cup, \{\{\}\}, \alpha, \lambda x.\{\{x\}\})$.*

The proof follows from the observations made about $\odot_P$: it is associative *provided* P are equated using their $|-|$, that is, using '$\approx$' as equality. Therefore, we explicitly wrote the employed equality relation in the definition of the monoid.

Earlier we have specified the task of finding the majority of the sequence α^* as the homomorphism from the collection monoid α^* to $(\{\{\alpha\}\}, =, \cup, \{\{\}\}, \alpha, \lambda x.\{\{x\}\})$ (followed by the observation of the resulting bag). Proposition 1 shows that this homomorphism may be decomposed into the homomorphism to P followed by $|-|$. (Homomorphisms compose.)

Therefore, instead of reducing α^* by $(\{\{\alpha\}\}, =, \cup, \{\{\}\}, \alpha, \lambda x.\{\{x\}\})$, we may reduce by P, and then take $|-|$ of the result. The desired is not the whole resulting multiset, however, but its element with the largest occurrence count: that is, the observation of the multiset by argmax.

Let us consider observations of P. The representation P has an appealing property:

Lemma 1 (Representation). *If the multiset $|(c, m, p)|$ has majority, then $c > 0$ and m is the majority element.*

For the proof, let p be a finite multiset of pairs (x, y) with $x \neq y$ and let $|p|$ be the multiset collecting the first and the second components of the pairs:

$$|p| = \{\{x \mid (x, y) \in p\}\} \cup \{\{y \mid (x, y) \in p\}\}$$

If p has n pairs, $|p|$ has $2n$ element occurrences, not all of them necessarily distinct. However, no element of $|p|$ occurs more than n times: that is, $|p|$ does not have majority. Otherwise, by the pigeonhole principle, p must contain a pair (x, x) for some x. Turning to the representation (c, m, p), if $|(c, m, p)|$ has the majority, it may only be m, and $c > 0$.

As the corollary to the representation lemma,

$$\text{argmax}(|P|) = \pi_2 P \text{ provided } |P| \text{ has majority} \tag{9}$$

where $\pi_2(c, m, p) = m$. Therefore, majority of the sequence may be obtained as the homomorphism to the observable monoid

$$(P, \approx, \odot_P, P_\varnothing, \alpha, (1, x, \{\{\}\}), \alpha, \pi_2) \tag{10}$$

This reduction implements the specification (7). The overall proof is depicted on Fig. 1 in the Appendix of the full paper.

The final step is to note that the observation π_2 of (10) extracts out only one component of (c, m, p), namely, m. (One may also be interested in c). However, p, although needed for defining $|-|$ and $\approx$, it is not used in the calculation of c and m, as one can see from (8). Therefore, *as far as calculations of the observable result go*, the component p is irrelevant – ghost – and may be disregarded. If we drop p, we end up with (6) – the result we first intuited.

In the upshot, the majority can be found as reduction by (6), considering it as a monoid. It is just as efficient as the original Boyer-Moore algorithm: one pass over the sequence using constant and small working space. However, the input may be split arbitrarily among available workers, who would do the search in parallel, without any interference or dependencies. Majority voting can be done embarrassingly in parallel.

Our proofs are inspired by Boyer and Moore's original proofs. They however used induction, which is appropriate for the sequential algorithm. We, in contrast, relied on the algebraic and equational reasoning and the pigeonhole principle – but no induction.[11]

Related Work. Meertens [9] was first to derive (6), but noted that "something funny is going on here. ... the operator is not associative. This can be seen by considering the different ways to compute h on a bag of three distinct candidates. According to the current definitions this would mean that h is not a proper bag homomorphism." His paper then *informally* argued (invoking indeterminism)

[11] It may seem that induction is the only proof method used in computer science: many widely used textbooks present nothing but induction. Mathematics has many other proof methods.

that it is not required for consistency. We have demonstrated, formally, that there is a proper homomorphism after all – provided we are explicit about the equality. That equality, '$\approx$', however, cannot be defined using (6) alone: there is not enough information. Therefore, we had to extend it to (10) and then argue the extension is computationally irrelevant. That was the key and our contribution.

An attempt to apply the third homomorphism theorem to intuit (6) is thwarted for the same reason: processing a sequence using (5) left-to-right and right-to-left generally gives different results, so the theorem does not apply.

5 Nested Grouping-Aggregation

Another instructive example of the monoid reduction is nested grouping and aggregation – a typical problem in data analysis. That grouping and aggregation per se are expressible as a homomorphism, or map-reduce, was insightfully articulated by Fegaras and Maier in their pioneering paper on monoid comprehensions [5]. In our case, however, the result of a grouping-aggregation is grouped-aggregated again – and again.

The running example is an Advent of Code 2022 problem, summarized as: The input is a sequence of numbers separated by '|' into chunks where each chunk contains multiple comma-separated numbers. The task is to compute the sum of each chunk and find the maximum across all chunks. A sample input is as follows:

```
100,200,300|400|500,600|700,800,900|1000
```

Some proposed solutions used their language `split` operation to split the input string by '|' into chunks, then split each chunk by commas into digit sequences, convert each sequence to a number, sum them and find the maximum. Each splitting round corresponds to a full traversal of the sequence, which has to be loaded in memory. We have previously described the optimal sequential – streaming – solution, which is single-pass and constant space, and handles input of arbitrary size (which may exceed the available memory).[12] Curiously, it also featured monoids. However, their composition was not explicated. Here we show that 'piling up' particular monoids still gives a monoid – and hence the embarrassingly parallel processing. Specifically, the input can be split arbitrarily, for example

```
100,20    0,300|40    0|500,600    |700,800    ,900|1000
```

haphazardly cutting through the numbers and delimiters. We may hence assign a slice of input (in whole number of pages, except the last slice) to a worker, not worrying about how or if the data are aligned with page boundaries. The workers (CPU cores) may then all run in parallel, in constant memory, with no dependencies or races – with the assured linear speed-up. Such a processing is also fitting for GPU. The map-reduce can also be done sequentially, in a streaming fashion – which is how each worker does it.

[12] https://okmij.org/ftp/Algorithms/nested-aggregation.html.

One may have noticed that the problem involves the already familiar monoids: Horner (to read the number), Sum and Max. They are composed, however, in an unusual, nested manner, not found in Algebra textbooks: delimiters somehow have to be accounted for. Besides the theoretical interest, the problem has many practical applications. For example, a similar nested monoid composition can be used, say, to find ten most frequent words in a UTF-8–encoded text file – without loading the file in memory, without prior decoding, and utilizing all available cores or the GPU.

To build intuition, let's consider a simpler problem: a sequence of items of type α, separated by commas. The task is to group up the items between the delimiters: formally, convert the sequence $(\alpha+\delta)^*$ to $(\alpha^{*\uparrow})^*$ where a sequence $\alpha^{*\uparrow}$ is a maximal delimiter-free subsequence of the original $(\alpha+\delta)^*$. Here, δ is the type (set) of delimiters, currently consisting of just comma.

We observe:

$$(\alpha+\delta)^* = (\alpha^*\delta^*)^* = \alpha^* + \alpha^*\delta(\alpha^*\delta)^*\alpha^* = \alpha^* + \alpha^*\delta(\alpha^{*\uparrow}\delta)^*\alpha^*$$

using the almost standard algebra. Addition, however, means a sequence choice (co-product, or the either data type); inl and inr appearing later are the co-product constructors. The multiplication is sequence concatenation, and non-commutative. In words: A sequence $(\alpha+\delta)^*$ either has no delimiters, has one (when $(\alpha^*\delta)^*$ is empty) or more than one. In the latter case, the α^* sub-sequences between the delimiters are maximal. This representation is closed under concatenation ('multiplication'):

$$\begin{aligned}
&(\alpha+\delta)^* = (\alpha+\delta)^*(\alpha+\delta)^* \\
&= (\alpha^* + \alpha^*\delta(\alpha^{*\uparrow}\delta)^*\alpha^*)(\alpha^* + \alpha^*\delta(\alpha^{*\uparrow}\delta)^*\alpha^*) \\
&= \alpha^* + \alpha^*\delta(\alpha^{*\uparrow}\delta)^*\alpha^* + \alpha^*\delta(\alpha^{*\uparrow}\delta)^*\alpha^*\alpha^*\delta(\alpha^{*\uparrow}\delta)^*\alpha^* = \alpha^* + \alpha^*\delta(\alpha^{*\uparrow}\delta)^*\alpha^*
\end{aligned} \tag{11}$$

Since $(\alpha+\delta)^*$ is a collection monoid, so is $\alpha^* + \alpha^*\delta(\alpha^{*\uparrow}\delta)^*\alpha^*$ – which is either a α^* sequence, or the tuple (l,d,c,r) where l and r are α^* sequences, c is a $(\alpha^{*\uparrow}\delta)^*$ sequence, and d is a delimiter. As before, the monoid stands for a $(\alpha+\delta)^*$ subsequence. When it stands for the complete sequence, this representation lets us extract the maximal delimiter-free subsequences:

$$obs_{ms}(x) = \begin{cases} u^1 & \text{if } x = \mathsf{inl}\, u \\ l^1 c r^1 & \text{if } x = \mathsf{inr}\,(l,d,c,r) \end{cases}$$

(recall, x^1 is the singleton sequence containing x) All in all, the problem is solved as the homomorphism to the observable monoid

$$(\alpha^* + \alpha^*\delta(\alpha^{*\uparrow}\delta)^*\alpha^*, \odot_{ms}, \mathsf{inl}[], \alpha+\delta, gen_{ms}, (\alpha^{*\uparrow})^*, obs_{ms})$$

where

$$gen_{ms} = \begin{cases} \mathsf{inl}\, u & \text{if } x = \mathsf{inl}\, u \\ \mathsf{inr}([],d,[],[]) & \text{if } x = \mathsf{inr}\, d \end{cases}$$

$$x \odot_{ms} y = \begin{cases} \mathsf{inl}\, uv & \text{if } x = \mathsf{inl}\, u, y = \mathsf{inl}\, v \\ \mathsf{inr}(ul,d,c,r) & \text{if } x = \mathsf{inl}\, u, y = \mathsf{inr}\,(l,d,c,r) \\ \mathsf{inr}(l,d,c,rv) & \text{if } x = \mathsf{inr}\,(l,d,c,r), y = \mathsf{inl}\, v \\ \mathsf{inr}(l_1,d_1,c_1(r_1 l_2 d_2)^1 c_2,r_2) & \text{if } x = \mathsf{inr}\,(l_1,d_1,c_1,r_1), y = \mathsf{inr}\,(l_2,d_2,c_2,r_2) \end{cases}$$

The implementation of $\odot_{ms}$ is read directly from (11). It is a complicated version of sequence concatenation, taking into account that α^* subsequences flanked by delimiters must be maximal.

The warm-up example can be easily generalized, to a sequence $(\alpha+\delta)^*$ of α items interspersed with the delimiters δ. Suppose there is a homomorphism from α^* to the observable monoid $(M, \odot_M, \emptyset_M, \alpha, gen_M, O, obs_M)$. Then $(\alpha+\delta)^*$ can be converted to $(O+\delta')^*$ (where $\delta' \subset \delta$) as a homomorphism with the observable monoid

$$(M + M \times \delta' \times (O + \delta')^* \times M, \odot, \mathsf{inl}\, \emptyset_M, \alpha, gen, (O + \delta')^*, obs)$$

whose operations generalize the warm-up example, inserting M operations as appropriate. For the lack of space, we only show

$$gen(x) = \begin{cases} \mathsf{inl}\, gen_M\, u & \text{if } x = \mathsf{inl}\, u \\ \mathsf{inl}\, \emptyset_M & \text{if } x = \mathsf{inl}\, d \text{ and } d \notin \delta' \\ \mathsf{inr}(\emptyset_M, d, [], \emptyset_M) & \text{if } x = \mathsf{inr}\, d,\, d \in \delta' \end{cases}$$

The mapping $(\alpha+\delta)^*$ to $(O+\delta')^*$ can be iterated. At the end, when all allowable delimiters are accounted for, δ' is empty and we obtain O^*, which can be aggregated with the appropriate collection monoid as usual. See the accompanying code for how this composition looks in Ocaml. The code then composes Horner, Sum and Max monoids to solve the Advent of Code 2022 problem – efficiently and in the single pass. There is also a small benchmark, of the sequential and parallel reductions with thus composed monoid.

Related Work. Our problem is reminiscent of the one in [11], which also used chunks and segments. However, we had to grapple with the triple-nesting of the chunked processing – three times more complex – and hence derived the general vertical monoid composition.

6 Related Work

Monoid is an algebraic structure, to which the general theory and constructions (generators, generated algebra, free algebra, etc.) apply. Our particular way of introducing generators, as a mapping from an index set, seems more programmatically convenient. It also suggest a mapping from a carrier set to some other set, of observations – which is not part of the standard presentation of algebras. We showed how useful it is. Since a group is a monoid, quite a few group-theoretic constructions (e.g., direct and semidirect products) apply to monoids as well.

This paper has been inspired by Guy Steele's invited talk at ICFP 2009 [11]. He urged using reduce (rather than fold) as much as possible, because it is flexible and decouples the algorithm from the execution strategy. As an old-school talk, it dwelt on data structures such as conc and finger trees, suitable for recursive subdivision and reduction. However, monoid reductions (homomorphisms) are profitable even with ordinary flat arrays and files, as we have demonstrated in the (appendix of the) paper. In fact, in today's multi-core and GPGPU processing, flat, non-hierarchical data partitioning is just as good, if not better.

The other inspiration was the paper by Fegaras and Maier [5], which proposed monoid comprehensions and showed how they express database queries, not just over plain relational but also object-relational databases. The paper also introduced collection monoids – but not observable monoids. The paper, unfortunately, neglected to note that a monoid (implicitly) also contains the equality as one of its operations. The omission leads to a complication in their formalism and a restriction on homomorphism (which is ad hoc and limits the generality – after all, monoids may satisfy the variety of other laws, other than idempotency and commutativity).

A useful technique to if not derive then intuit a monoid reduction is the third homomorphism theorem [6,10]: if the sequential processing of a sequence left-to-right and right-to-left gives the same results, it is necessarily a homomorphism and can be written as a monoid reduction. Although the theorem is not constructive, it does give a specification for the monoid operation, which helps in finding it.

Parallel processing algorithms are a vast area; one may specifically note Guy Blelloch's work and his famous prefix sum [1]. None of it particularly applies to the present paper, however.

7 Conclusions

There is just enough space for a simple conclusion. Guy Steele's [11] final thoughts are particularly apt (emphasis his):

- Associative combining operators are a VERY BIG DEAL
- Inventing (and proving) new combining operators is a very, very big deal

As a future work, it is tantalizing to look for deeper mathematical connections for the vertical monoid composition in Sect. 5 – and apply it to more practical problems, such as querying and aggregating values associated with specific keys in a JSON file, without parsing and loading it in memory and using all available cores.

Acknowledgement. I am very grateful to the participants of the WG2.1 meeting #83 for many comments – in particular, to James McKinna, Jeremy Gibbons, Patrik Jansson, Johan Jeuring, Lambert Meertens and Zhenjiang Hu. Comments by anonymous reviewers are appreciated.

This work was partially supported by JSPS KAKENHI Grants Numbers 21K11821 and 22H03563.

References

1. Blelloch, G.E.: Parallel thinking. In: Reed, D.A., Sarkar, V. (eds.) Proceedings of the 14th ACM SIGPLAN Symposium on Principles and Practice of Parallel Programming, PPOPP 2009, Raleigh, NC, USA, 14–18 February 2009, pp. 1–2. ACM (2009). https://doi.org/10.1145/1504176.1504177
2. Boyer, R.S., Moore, J.S.: Mjrty—a fast majority vote algorithm. In: Boyer, R.S. (ed.) Automated Reasoning: Essays in Honor of Woody Bledsoe, pp. 105–117. Springer, Dordrecht (1991). https://doi.org/10.1007/978-94-011-3488-0_5
3. Burris, S., Sankappanavar, H.P.: A Course in Universal Algebra. Graduate Texts in Mathematics, vol. 78. Springer, New York (1981). https://doi.org/10.1007/978-1-4613-8130-3, http://www.math.uwaterloo.ca/~snburris/htdocs/UALG/univ-algebra2012.pdf
4. Estrin, G.: Organization of computer systems: the fixed plus variable structure computer. In: Papers Presented at the 3–5 May 1960, Western Joint IRE-AIEE-ACM Computer Conference, IRE-AIEE-ACM 1960 (Western), pp. 33–40. Association for Computing Machinery, New York (1960). https://doi.org/10.1145/1460361.1460365
5. Fegaras, L., Maier, D.: Towards an effective calculus for object query languages. In: Carey, M.J., Schneider, D.A. (eds.) Proceedings of the 1995 ACM SIGMOD International Conference on Management of Data, pp. 47–58. ACM Press (1995). https://doi.org/10.1145/223784.223789
6. Gibbons, J.: The third homomorphism theorem. J. Funct. Program. **6**(4), 657–665 (1996). https://doi.org/10.1017/S0956796800001908
7. Gibbons, J.: Origami programming for fun and profit. In: ECOOP tutorial (2019). http://www.cs.ox.ac.uk/people/jeremy.gibbons/publications/ecoop2019.pdf
8. Iverson, K.E.: A Programming Language. Wiley, New York (1962)
9. Meertens, L.: Reducing hopeful majority. Squiggolist **1**(1), 5 (1989). https://www.kestrel.edu/people/meertens/publications/papers/Reducing_hopeful_majority.pdf
10. Morita, K., Morihata, A., Matsuzaki, K., Hu, Z., Takeichi, M.: Automatic inversion generates divide-and-conquer parallel programs. In: Ferrante, J., McKinley, K.S. (eds.) Proceedings of the ACM SIGPLAN Conf. Programming Language Design and Implementation, pp. 146–155. ACM (2007). https://doi.org/10.1145/1250734.1250752
11. Steele, G.: Organizing functional code for parallel execution or, foldl and foldr considered slightly harmful (2009). ICFP 2009, Keynote

Optimizing Mesh Booleans by Being Lazy (System Description)

Chun Kit Lam(✉)

HKUST, Kowloon, Hong Kong
cklamaq@ust.hk

Abstract. Mesh Boolean operations (union, difference, intersection) enable the combination of simpler shapes into complex forms, and are essential in modeling software such as OpenSCAD, a popular functional programming language in the Maker community. Although these operations are intuitive to users, existing implementations often suffer from performance or robustness issues. Manifold is a new open source library designed for robust and efficient mesh Boolean operations. It is up to hundreds of times faster than traditional methods using exact arithmetic, and more robust than conventional float-based techniques. In this paper, we describe a crucial design decision that enabled this level of performance while maintaining a simple user-facing API: implementing a functional and lazy API design, coupled with expression tree rewriting before evaluation. Manifold has recently been integrated into projects such as OpenSCAD (nightly builds), Blender, and has bindings for various languages.

Keywords: Applications · Computational Geometry

1 Introduction

Manifold is a high-performance C++ library designed for robust mesh Booleans and more generally, complex Constructive Solid Geometry (CSG) operations. It is started by Emmett Lalish and is currently lead by him and the author. It is actively developed, with over 70 contributors, 1.8k stars on GitHub, and 4 releases on average every year. Manifold is used by many popular projects. For example, OpenSCAD added Manifold as a new backend in March 2023. Projects such as Godot Engine and Blender also added Manifold back in November 2024 and April 2025 respectively. The python binding in PyPI has a monthly download count of over 1M according to PyPI stats, as of December 2025.

Constructive Solid Geometry (CSG) uses Boolean operations to combine solids into complex forms. Basically, CSG can be described by the grammar shown in Fig. 3, where the Boolean operations are left-associative and 3D affine transformations are represented as 4-by-4 matrices. Figure 1 shows the result of the CSG expression $s \circ c \circ (r_1\ c) \circ (r_2\ c)$ with different operators $\circ$, where s is a sphere, c is a cylinder, r_1 and r_2 are rotation operators. Figure 2 shows the

M. Sperber and E. Komendantskaya (Eds.): FLOPS 2026, LNCS 16533, pp. 173–184, 2026.
https://doi.org/10.1007/978-981-92-0184-6_8

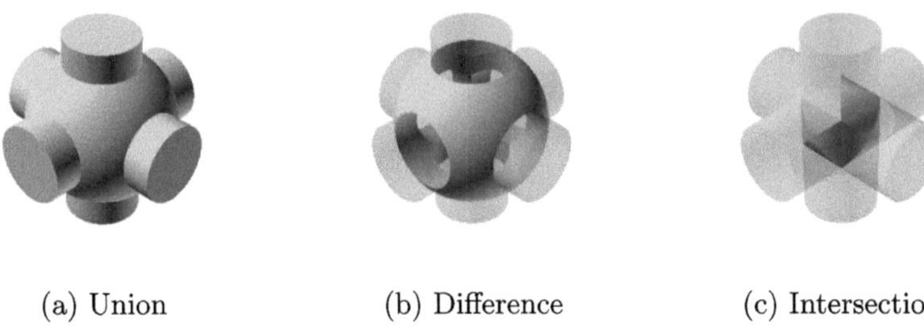

(a) Union (b) Difference (c) Intersection

Fig. 1. CSG Examples with OpenSCAD's logo. The yellow solid is the result. (Color figure online)

```
1 c0 = cylinder(62.5, 50)
2 c1 = c0.rotate(90, 0, 0)
3 c2 = c0.rotate(0, 90, 0)
4 logo = sphere(50) - c0 - c1 - c2
5 export_mesh(logo.to_mesh(), "logo.3mf")
6 print(logo.surface_area())
```

Fig. 2. Manifold's Python API Example

Python code for Fig. 1b, with additional code to export the mesh to a file and print the surface area of the mesh. Variable `logo` stores the result, line 5 exports the mesh to file `logo.3mf`, and line 6 prints the surface area of the result.

In this article, we will focus on the API design and AST rewriting optimizations in Manifold. By making the API lazy, the library can perform optimizations with AST rewriting. This approach is simple yet effective, but is largely ignored by most imperative programmers. In other libraries and older version of Manifold, everything is *eagerly* evaluated. This means that the CSG expression in Fig. 2 must be evaluated as `((sphere(50) - c0) - c1) - c2`, with no room for high-level optimizations. Instead of evaluating CSG expressions eagerly, Manifold's API is lazy. This means that Line 1–4 only build the AST, line 5 evaluates the CSG operations and outputs the mesh, while line 6 prints the surface area of the mesh that was evaluated in the previous line. This allows high-level optimizations to take place. For example, the library may choose to evaluate the expression as `((sphere(50) - c2) - c1) - c0` or `sphere(50) - ((c0 + c1) + c2)`, depending on cost heuristics. While it may not matter for this small

$$
\begin{array}{rrcl}
\text{Solid} & m & ::= & p \mid m \circ m \mid t\, m \\
\text{Boolean Operation} & \circ & ::= & \cup \mid - \mid \cap \\
\text{3D Affine Transformation} & t & \in & \mathbb{R}^{4\times 4} \\
\text{Primitive/Atom} & p & ::= & \ldots
\end{array}
$$

Fig. 3. CSG Grammar

example, as we will see in Sect. 3, high-level optimizations can provide order-of-magnitude performance improvement for complex CSG examples.

While this article is mostly about the optimizations in Manifold, we believe the idea of providing a functional and lazy API on top of an imperative API, with advanced optimizations based on AST rewriting, is also applicable to other libraries. We also hope that this article can encourage research on DSL design and optimizations for solid modeling, which there is not yet a good DSL for complex modeling.

	Boolean Operations	
$\cup, -, \cap$	$M \to M \to M$	Mesh Booleans
	Transformations	
translate, scale, rotate	$M \to \mathbb{R}^3 \to M$	Common Affine Transforms
transform	$M \to \mathbb{R}^{3\times 4} \to M$	Affine Transform
warp	$M \to (\mathbb{R}^3 \to \mathbb{R}^3) \to M$	Vertex Transform
	Constructors	
from_mesh	Mesh $\to M$	Construct a Manifold mesh object from a raw mesh
sphere	$\mathbb{R} \to M$	Sphere constructor
cube	$\mathbb{R}^3 \to M$	Rectangular cuboid constructor
	Miscellaneous	
to_mesh	$M \to$ Mesh	Get mesh output
decompose	$M \to$ List M	Decompose the mesh into disjoint components.
surface_area	$M \to \mathbb{R}$	Surface area of the mesh
volume	$M \to \mathbb{R}$	Volume of the mesh
genus	$M \to \mathbb{N}$	Genus of the mesh

Fig. 4. Manifold Public APIs

2 Implementation of Manifold

In this section, we will briefly discuss the implementation of Manifold, focusing on the API design, the AST rewriting algorithm and optimizations for variadic Boolean operations.

Manifold's source code is available on GitHub and is licensed under Apache 2.0. Manifold is implemented in C++, with parallel algorithms implemented using the TBB library [14] that supports nested parallelism and load balancing. Parallelization is optional, and can be turned off for targets with no parallelization support. Apart from regular native targets, it can also compile to WASM with Emscripten [18]. There is an online playground where users can model using JavaScript/TypeScript locally via the WASM bindings.

2.1 API Design

Figure 4 shows a selected subset of public APIs of Manifold, where M is an abstract data type for a Manifold object. The transformation APIs are similar to the affine transformation in the CSG grammar, the constructors are the primitives, and the miscellaneous APIs are for IO or querying information about the mesh. Boolean operations and transformations are lazy[1], meaning that they only build the CSG AST, and real computation only happens when the user calls the miscellaneous methods.

While a functional and lazy API seems intuitive, this is rather unique for computational geometry libraries in imperative programming languages. In fact, the original API of Manifold was eager, similar to CGAL [8], JSCAD [2] and other libraries. The change was proposed in 2022 in issue #114 to enable optimizations based on graph rewriting, and was originally considered a niche optimization by other developers. The changes were implemented in pull request #131 and merged after showing significant speedup for benchmarks from OpenSCAD. This change enabled optimizations based on AST rewriting, and the API becomes simpler because users no longer have to worry about mutations and the cost of copying. As we will see in Sect. 3, such a design decision enabled order-of-magnitude performance gains for complex CSG operations.

Note on Correctness and Determinism. Because Manifold is using an inexact algorithm, the correctness criteria for Manifold is that the output has to be topologically valid, and the vertex positions of the mesh is within a certain error tolerance from the ideal output. This means that for the same input, there can be multiple valid outputs. In Manifold, we guarantee that with a fixed library version and fixed input, the output should be bitwise identical. We can treat Boolean operations as commutative and associative for the purpose of optimizing CSG operations, even when the actual algorithm does not satisfy this requirement. We only need to ensure that 1) the rewriting algorithm is deterministic, 2) the evaluation result for variadic Boolean is also deterministic.

[1] Currently, only affine transformations are lazy, because other transformations are not amenable to algebraic transformations described in Sect. 2. However, it is trivial to change the API if needed.

$$\begin{array}{rrcl} \text{Node} & n & ::= & t\,p \mid \bigcirc\overline{n} - \overline{n} \\ \text{Variadic Boolean Operation} & \bigcirc & ::= & \cup \mid \cap \\ \text{Primitive/Atom} & p & ::= & \ldots \\ \text{Affine Transformation} & t & \in & \mathbb{R}^{4\times 4} \\ \\ \text{Shorthand} & \bigcirc\overline{n} & = & \bigcirc\overline{n} - \varnothing \end{array}$$

Fig. 5. Normalized AST Syntax with Variadic Boolean Operations

$$\boxed{[\![\, m \,]\!]_t = n}$$

$$\textsc{Atom}\quad \frac{}{[\![\, p \,]\!]_t = \cup\,(t\,p)} \qquad \textsc{Transform}\quad \frac{}{[\![\, t_0\ m \,]\!]_t = [\![\, m \,]\!]_{t\times t_0}}$$

$$\textsc{Subtraction-1}\quad \frac{[\![\, m_0 \,]\!]_t = \bigcirc\overline{n_0} - \overline{n_0}' \qquad [\![\, m_1 \,]\!]_t = \cup\,\overline{n_1}}{[\![\, m_0 - m_1 \,]\!]_t = \bigcirc\overline{n_0} - (\overline{n_0}', \overline{n_1})}$$

$$\textsc{Subtraction-2}\quad \frac{[\![\, m_0 \,]\!]_t = \bigcirc\overline{n_0} - \overline{n_0}'}{[\![\, m_0 - m_1 \,]\!]_t = \bigcirc\overline{n_0} - (\overline{n_0}', [\![\, m_1 \,]\!]_t)}$$

$$\textsc{Variadic-1}\quad \frac{[\![\, m_0 \,]\!]_t = \bigcirc\overline{n_0} \qquad [\![\, m_1 \,]\!]_t = \bigcirc\overline{n_1}}{[\![\, m_0 \bigcirc m_1 \,]\!]_t = \bigcirc(\overline{n_0}, \overline{n_1})}$$

$$\textsc{Variadic-2}\quad \frac{i \in \{0, 1\} \qquad [\![\, m_i \,]\!]_t = \bigcirc\overline{n_i}}{[\![\, m_0 \bigcirc m_1 \,]\!]_t = \bigcirc(\overline{n_i}, [\![\, m_{1-i} \,]\!])}$$

$$\textsc{Variadic-3}\quad \frac{}{[\![\, m_0 \bigcirc m_1 \,]\!]_t = \bigcirc([\![\, m_0 \,]\!]_t, [\![\, m_1 \,]\!]_t)}$$

Fig. 6. AST Rewriting Algorithm

2.2 AST Rewriting

We now present the details of the AST rewriting algorithm. It rewrites a CSG expression into an equivalent expression with *variadic* Boolean operations. These variadic Boolean operations can be optimized using heuristics that will be explained below, and the goal of the rewriting algorithm is to maximize the arity of the operations. This allows us to optimize the variadic Boolean operations using the techniques in the next section. The input to the algorithm is a CSG expression, using the grammar in Fig. 3, and the output is a normalized AST with variadic Boolean operations. The grammar of the normalized AST is shown in Fig. 5. $\overline{n}$ denotes a list of nodes, $\bigcirc\overline{n_0} - \overline{n_1}$ is interpreted as the result of performing variadic Boolean operation $\bigcirc$ on $\overline{n_0}$ and then subtracting $\overline{n_1}$. For example, $\cup\,(p_0, p_1, p_2) - (p_3, p_4)$ is interpreted as $(p_0 \cup p_1 \cup p_2) - p_3 - p_4$. We use the shorthand $\bigcirc\overline{n}$ for $\bigcirc\overline{n} - \varnothing$. Transformations can only be applied to atoms.

Figure 6 shows the rules for the rewriting algorithm. It rewrites a CSG expression m with an affine transformation t into $[\![\, m \,]\!]_t$. At the top level, we rewrite m into $[\![\, m \,]\!]_I$ where I is the identity matrix, i.e., no transformation at the top level. The algorithm applies the rewriting rules to the AST bottom-up, with rules applied from top-left to botton-right. Transformations are combined and propagated to the atoms with rules Transform and Atom. Rule Subtraction-1 flattens subtraction expressions such as $(a - b) - (c \cup d)$ into $a - (b \cup c \cup d)$, where the right operand in the original expression is a union. If we have $c \cap d$ instead of $c \cup d$, we can only perform partial flattening and get $a - (b \cup (c \cap d))$ with rule SUBTRACTION-2. For union and intersection, they are handled with rules VARIADIC-1, VARIADIC-2 and VARIADIC-3, where the first rule corresponds to the case with the most flattening, and the last rule corresponds to the case where no flattening can be done. For example, $(a \cup b) \cup (c \cup d)$ is flattened into $a \cup b \cup c \cup d$ using rule VARIADIC-1. $(a \cap b) \cup (c \cup d)$ can be partially flattened by rule VARIADIC-2 into $(a \cap b) \cup c \cup d$. Rule VARIADIC-3 corresponds to the case where the operation is different from the operation in both operands, such as $(a \cup b) \cap (c \cup d)$, which cannot be flattened.

In the implementation, the recursive algorithm is rewritten to a loop to avoid stack overflow. Instead of an expression tree, the implementation works with a directed acyclic graph with shared nodes. To avoid duplicated work, shared nodes are not flattened, i.e., they are treated as if they are atoms. For example, if we have $x = a \cup (b \cup (c \cup d))$ with no sharing, the rewriting algorithm will flatten x into $a \cup b \cup c \cup d$. However, if $y = b \cup (c \cup d)$ is shared, the algorithm will only flatten y as $b \cup c \cup d$ and evaluate that, and then evaluate $x = a \cup y$. This is somewhat reminiscent of Perceus [15], where in-place updates are performed only when the reference is not shared. In our case, flattening is performed only when the node is not shared, though this restriction is only related to performance instead of affecting soundness.

```
# heap ordered by mesh size
worklist = Heap(inputs)
lock = Lock()
def worker(i):
  while True:
    with lock:
      if len(worklist) < 2:
        break
      a = worklist.pop()
      b = worklist.pop()

    result = op(a, b)

    with lock:
      worklist.push(result)

# run k workers
execute(worker, k)
```

(a) Simple Non-deterministic Variant

```
worklist = Heap(inputs)
tmp = [None] * 2 * k
def worker(i):
  a = tmp[2 * i]
  b = tmp[2 * i + 1]
  if b == None:
    return
  tmp[2 * i] = op(a, b)

while len(worklist) > 1:
  for i in range(2 * k):
    # assume pop returns None
    # if worklist is empty
    tmp[i] = worklist.pop()
  execute(worker, k)
  for i in range(k):
    result = tmp[2 * i]
    if result != None:
      worklist.push(result)
```

(b) Deterministic Variant

Fig. 7. Parallel Variadic Boolean Algorithm in Pseudocode

2.3 Variadic Boolean Optimizations

Reordering and Parallelization. A simple heuristic for optimizing variadic Booleans is to compute Booleans on smaller meshes first. The idea is that the Boolean routine takes time proportional to the size of the resulting mesh, and the output mesh should also be small when the inputs are small. Note that this is merely a heuristic, because the actual complexity of the Boolean algorithm is complicated and depends on structure of the input meshes. While the internal of Boolean operations involve parallel algorithms, a single Boolean operation may not be able to fully utilize all cores, especially when the input meshes are small. Hence, in addition to reordering, we can perform multiple Boolean operations in parallel to further improve performance by increasing core utilization.

A simple version of this algorithm is shown in Fig. 7, where `worklist` is a heap that initially contains all the input meshes to the variadic Boolean operation, ordered by mesh size. The `pop` operation pops a mesh from the `worklist` with the smallest size and returns `None` when the `worklist` is empty. The `push` operation pushes a mesh into the `worklist`. The `with lock:` construct acquires a lock, performs some operations, and releases the lock upon exit. The statement `execute(worker, k)` spawns k worker threads, each executing the function `worker`, with parameter `i` equals to the thread id from 0 to $k-1$, and returns when all worker threads finished executing the function. The issue with this algorithm is that it is non-deterministic: Boolean results may be added to the `worklist` and consumed by another thread in an arbitrary order. Because Boolean operations are not truely commutative and associative, the result of this algorithm depends on the scheduling behavior, which is non-deterministic and violates our determinism guarantees.

A deterministic variant of this algorithm is shown in Fig. 7b. Instead of having a loop in each worker thread, each worker thread only performs one Boolean operation, with the two operands stored in the $(2i)$-th and $(2i+1)$-th element of the `tmp` array. The `tmp` array may have insufficiently many elements, in which case the $(2i+1)$-th element is `None` and no Boolean operation is performed. In the main loop, we fill the `tmp` array with the smallest $2k$ meshes from the `worklist`. We then run k worker threads in parallel to compute the results, adding the results back to the `worklist` and repeat until there is only one result left. This algorithm variant is deterministic for any fixed k because the order is fully determined. This can be slightly less efficient than the simpler variant, but we decided determinism is more important than slight performance gains. Empirical tests showed that $k = 4$ is sufficient to get high core utilization for a modern CPU with 32 threads when combined with parallel algorithms inside the Boolean routine. This value is used regardless of the number of threads in the CPU, so the result is deterministic on machines with different hardware configurations.

Composing Disjoint Unions. Another simple optimization is to optimize *disjoint* unions. If a variadic union contains only disjoint operands, it can be replaced with a compose operation which is significantly faster than actual union operations.

In Manifold, we optimize variadic unions by grouping operands into groups, each contains pairwise disjoint meshes. We compose each group as disjoint union, and use the general variadic Boolean algorithm previously mentioned to union the result from each group.

Algorithm	Robustness	Parallel	Remarks
Manifold	Inexact	Yes	
Corefinement	Inexact	No	
Arrangement	Exact	Yes	Segfaults under higher optimization settings.

Fig. 8. Comparison of Algorithms

Algorithm	Threads	Average Time (ms)	Maximum Time (ms)	Failures
Manifold	1	33.1	989.8	0
Manifold	16	11.6	97.5	0
Arrangement	1	1628.3	Timeout	8 Timeouts
Arrangement	16	245.3	Timeout	1 Timeout
Corefinement	1	27.6	1024.7	1 Bug

Fig. 9. Statistics for One-Shot Booleans

3 Benchmark Results

We now present benchmark results showing the performance of Manifold, and the importance of the AST rewriting and variadic Boolean optimizations.

Setup. The benchmarks below are run on a PC running Linux 6.17.5, with an AMD 9950X CPU (16 cores, 4.3GHz) and 128GB of RAM. For better performance consistency, frequency boost and simultaneous multithreading (SMT) are disabled. Unless otherwise specified, each binary is compiled using GCC 14.2.1 with `-O3 -march=native` and profile-guided optimizations (PGO) enabled. For single-threaded results, Manifold is compiled with `MANIFOLD_PAR=OFF` because some of the parallel algorithms can introduce overhead when parallelization is not available.

Performance of One-Shot Boolean Operations. We evaluate the performance of one-shot Boolean operations of Manifold using the benchmark set from EMBER [17] containing 1000 test cases, where each test case computes the difference between two manifold meshes from the Thingi10K dataset [19], each with 1,000 to 100,000 faces without self-intersections. Each test case is run with a 60 s timeout (60,000 ms). We compare Manifold against that of CGAL 5.6.2 corefinement [8] with the Epick kernel, and exact mesh arrangement in [7], which we shall refer to as *corefinement* and *arrangement* respectively. We cannot include EMBER in our benchmark because EMBER is not open source.

Figure 8 shows the summary of the algorithms compared in this benchmark. Manifold is inexact but robust, in the sense that it may produce meshes with small self-intersections, but those are valid input for itself, and the topology is guaranteed to be correct. *Corefinement* with the exact predicate inexact construction kernel (Epick) is an inexact method, meaning that it may fail due to rounding errors. *Arrangement* is a state-of-the-art exact method for mesh Boolean. *Corefinement* only supports single-threaded execution, while Manifold and *arrangement* supports multithreading. *Arrangement* is built with `-O2` and without PGO because it segfaults under higher optimization settings.

Figure 9 shows the statistics for this benchmark. The exact method, i.e., *Arrangement*, is much slower than the other methods. In particular, there are 8 timeouts when run with a single thread, and 1 timeout when run with 16 threads. CGAL's corefinement is on average 16% faster than Manifold on a single thread, because Manifold performs more bookkeeping for robustness. However, Manifold supports parallelization, and becomes around 40% faster on average, and 90% faster for larger meshes where parallelization is more effective.

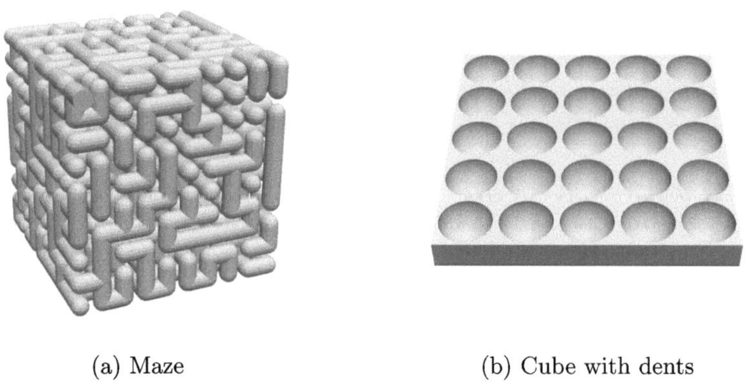

(a) Maze (b) Cube with dents

Fig. 10. Models from OpenSCAD users in PR #4533

Effect of AST Rewriting and Variadic Boolean Optimizations. We evaluate the effectiveness of AST rewriting, and variadic Boolean optimizations via an ablation study. We run Manifold on complex models from OpenSCAD users, and

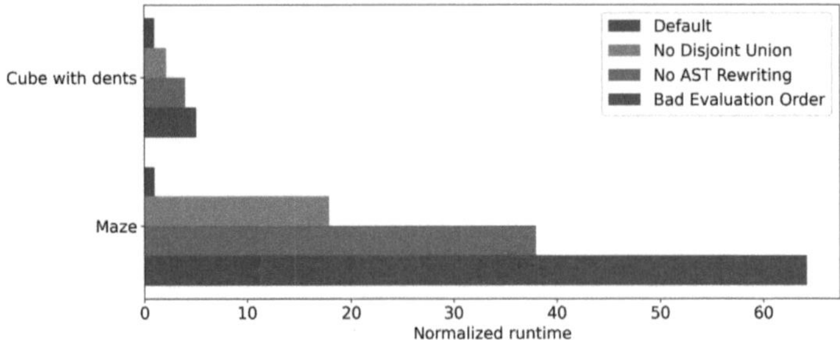

Fig. 11. Normalized Runtime

compare the results with optimizations disabled. Figure 10 shows the models, where Fig. 10a is a complex model with 2001 components, while Fig. 10b is a relatively simple model with only 26 components. Figure 11 shows the runtime with the respective optimizations disabled, normalized such that the runtime with all optimizations enabled is 1. The "No AST Rewriting" variant implies no disjoint union, because the Boolean operations are no longer variadic. The "Bad Evaluation Order" variant is with disjoint union disabled but AST rewriting enabled, and evaluating the variadic Boolean in a left-to-right order, ignoring the original order in the AST (which is right leaning in these benchmarks, i.e., $a+(b+(c+\ldots)))$. The first three results showed that our AST rewriting and variadic Boolean optimizations are useful in improving performance, especially when the input model is complex. The bad evaluation order result showed that the evaluation order has a significant effect on the performance of CSG evaluation.

4 Related Work

We now briefly discuss other libraries or domains with a DSL-like API design and introduce some popular solid modeling libraries.

DSL-Like API. One of the most popular example is database systems, which typically uses SQL or custom DSL for queries/updates. They perform query optimizations [10] with the DSL for better query performance. From an API perspective, users typically use builder pattern to build and cache the SQL statement, which is different from the style used in Manifold, i.e., results are just lazily evaluated. In the field of AI, libraries such as TensorFlow [6] can perform lazy evaluation and optimize based on the AST. TensorFlow 2 shifted to eager evaluation by default because this makes it easier to interact with other Python APIs, but users can still use the `tf.function` decorator to compile a function to a callable TensorFlow graph for optimizations. Implicit modeling libraries or languages such as libfive [12] and Fidget [11] provide a DSL-like API to build the Signed-Distance Function (SDF), and interpret them in different domains such as scalar and interval. They can perform optimization that are either static or dynamic.

Popular Solid Modeling Libraries. We will focus on popular end-user facing solid modeling libraries, i.e., not only implements the algorithm but are used by end-users. OpenSCAD [4] is one of the most popular example, which provides a scripting language for CSG operations. 3D printing websites such as Thingiverse and Maker World provide services for running OpenSCAD scripts online. The main problem with this language is that it is not well optimized, and geometries are not values, making it impossible to perform introspection on the result of geometry operations. There are many related projects such as JSCAD [2] and ImplicitCAD [1], where the latter is implemented in Haskell and models solids using SDFs instead of meshes. ImplicitCAD claims to be faster than OpenSCAD because it uses SDFs, but it becomes slower when the mesh quality increases due to the nature of SDF to mesh conversion. Also, the performance claim was based on older version of OpenSCAD, and OpenSCAD became much faster after using Manifold as its default backend in nightly versions. For NURBS-based modeling (Non-Uniform Rational Basis Spline) that can represent curved surfaces exactly, there are build123d [16] and CadQuery [5] which are Python bindings to the Open Cascade library [3]. There are a lot of custom languages and libraries for implicit modeling. For example there are libfive [12], curv [9], ImplicitCAD [1], sdf [13], and Fidget [11]. Curv compiles to GPU shader for preview using the sphere tracing algorithm, and compiles to C++ for faster SDF evaluation for mesh conversion. Fidget implements its own JIT, with SIMD evaluation.

5 Conclusion and Future Work

We presented the API design, algorithms for AST rewriting and variadic Boolean optimization in Manifold. We presented benchmarks that showed the importance of the optimizations. The widespread adoption by popular projects such as OpenSCAD and Blender also showed that Manifold is reliable and performant in the real world.

Future work will focus on enhancing heuristics for variadic Booleans and implementing value-based redundancy elimination. For example, it may be possible to have more accurate estimates for the cost of operations via querying the precomputed bounded volume hierarchy (BVH) of the meshes. We also want to extend the optimizations for other solid modeling approaches such as SDF, which is supported by Manifold albeit with not much optimizations. The primary problem is that one has to define a DSL to optimize SDFs, but this increases friction because users will have to learn and use such a DSL. This is particularly annoying when the host language does not support operator overloading, such as TypeScript/JavaScript, the language used for the manifoldcad playground. One solution might be to use reflection in the host language, for example it is possible to serialize a function in languages such as JavaScript, which can then be parsed into the DSL for optimizations.

References

1. ImplicitCAD. https://implicitcad.org/
2. JSCAD. https://github.com/jscad/OpenJSCAD.org
3. Open cascade technology. https://occt3d.com/
4. OpenSCAD. https://openscad.org/
5. CadQuery (2025). https://doi.org/10.5281/zenodo.14590990
6. Abadi, M., et al.: Tensorflow: a system for large-scale machine learning. In: 12th USENIX Symposium on Operating Systems Design and Implementation (OSDI 2016), pp. 265–283 (2016)
7. Cherchi, G., Pellacini, F., Attene, M., Livesu, M.: Interactive and robust mesh booleans. ACM Trans. Graph. **41**(6) (2022). https://doi.org/10.1145/3550454.3555460
8. Coeurjolly, D., et al.: Polygon mesh processing. In: CGAL User and Reference Manual. CGAL Editorial Board, 6.0.1 edn. (2024). https://doc.cgal.org/6.0.1/Manual/packages.html#PkgPolygonMeshProcessing
9. Doug, M.: curv. https://codeberg.org/doug-moen/curv
10. Jarke, M., Koch, J.: Query optimization in database systems. ACM Comput. Surv. (CsUR) **16**(2), 111–152 (1984)
11. Keeter, M.: Fidget. https://github.com/mkeeter/fidget
12. Keeter, M.: libfive. https://github.com/libfive/libfive
13. Fogleman, M.: SDF. https://github.com/fogleman/sdf
14. Pheatt, C.: Intel® threading building blocks. J. Comput. Sci. Coll. **23**(4), 298 (2008)
15. Reinking, A., Xie, N., de Moura, L., Leijen, D.: Perceus: garbage free reference counting with reuse. In: Proceedings of the 42nd ACM SIGPLAN International Conference on Programming Language Design and Implementation, pp. 96–111 (2021)
16. Maitland, R.: build123d: A Python-based parametric CAD library (2025). https://doi.org/10.5281/zenodo.14872323
17. Trettner, P., Nehring-Wirxel, J., Kobbelt, L.: Ember: exact mesh booleans via efficient & robust local arrangements. ACM Trans. Graph. **41**(4) (2022). https://doi.org/10.1145/3528223.3530181
18. Zakai, A.: Emscripten: an llvm-to-javascript compiler. In: Proceedings of the ACM International Conference Companion on Object Oriented Programming Systems Languages and Applications Companion, OOPSLA 2011, pp. 301–312. Association for Computing Machinery, New York, NY, USA (2011). https://doi.org/10.1145/2048147.2048224
19. Zhou, Q., Jacobson, A.: Thingi10k: a dataset of 10,000 3D-printing models. arXiv preprint arXiv:1605.04797 (2016)

Computing Supported Models via Transformation to Stable Models: A System Description

Fang Li[1(✉)] and Gopal Gupta[2]

[1] Oklahoma Christian University, Edmond, OK, USA
fang.li@oc.edu

[2] University of Texas at Dallas, Richardson, TX, USA
gupta@utdallas.edu

Abstract. Supported models offer a semantics for logic programs that relaxes the minimality constraint of stable models while maintaining logical consistency through a support condition. Despite their theoretical significance since 1988, supported models lack practical computational tools integrated with modern Answer Set Programming (ASP) infrastructure. We present a transformation-based method that enables computation of supported models using standard stable model solvers. Our approach transforms any ground logic program into an equivalent program whose stable models correspond exactly to the supported models of the original program. We implement this transformation as a preprocessor for Clingo and demonstrate applications in software verification, medical diagnosis, and planning where supported models enable valuable exploratory reasoning beyond stable models.

Keywords: Answer Set Programming · Supported Models · Program Transformation · Knowledge Representation · Exploratory Reasoning

1 Introduction

Answer Set Programming (ASP) is a declarative paradigm for solving complex combinatorial search and reasoning problems [3]. Its foundation in stable model semantics [9] identifies solutions as minimal models satisfying program rules. While effective for many applications, the strict minimality requirement can limit the discovery of non-minimal but logically consistent solutions that may be valuable in exploratory reasoning scenarios.

1.1 Motivation and Problem Statement

Stable model semantics enforces minimality: atoms are false unless they are proven to be true. This conservative approach is appropriate when seeking optimal or most parsimonious solutions. However, modern applications often require exploring richer solution spaces where non-minimal interpretations provide value:

M. Sperber and E. Komendantskaya (Eds.): FLOPS 2026, LNCS 16533, pp. 185–201, 2026.
https://doi.org/10.1007/978-981-92-0184-6_9

- **Software verification**: Testing systems under all consistent component configurations, including redundant states, ensures comprehensive coverage beyond minimal scenarios.
- **Medical diagnosis**: Physicians consider multiple co-occurring conditions in differential diagnosis, not just the minimal set explaining symptoms, as patients often present with comorbidities.
- **Planning and resource allocation**: Non-minimal plans with redundant steps or over-provisioned resources may offer greater robustness and reliability in production environments.

Supported models, introduced by Apt, Blair, and Walker [1], address this limitation by relaxing minimality while preserving a crucial property: every true atom must be *supported* by some rule whose body is satisfied. This ensures that conclusions are justified by the program's rules while permitting non-minimal models. Marek and Subrahmanian [14] proved that every stable model is a supported model, but not conversely.

1.2 Existing Approaches and Limitations

Computing supported models is theoretically well-understood through Clark's Completion [4]: the supported models of a program Π coincide exactly with the classical models of its completion Comp(Π). This enables computation via propositional satisfiability (SAT) solvers by transforming Π to Comp(Π) and finding its models.

However, this approach requires: (1) generating Clark's Completion as a separate preprocessing step, (2) interfacing with a SAT solver requiring additional tool-chain infrastructure, and (3) translating between logic program rules and propositional CNF formulas.

For practitioners already invested in the ASP ecosystem with highly optimized solvers like Clingo [8], this necessitates maintaining separate tool-chains. Modern ASP solvers provide no direct support for computing supported models despite their theoretical importance.

1.3 Our Contribution

We present a transformation-based approach that enables computation of supported models within the ASP paradigm itself. Our method transforms any ground logic program into an equivalent ASP program whose stable models correspond exactly to the original program's supported models. This allows direct use of standard ASP solvers without requiring external SAT solvers or completion-based transformations.

Our key contributions are:

1. **Novel ASP-to-ASP transformation**: A polynomial-time transformation that decouples conjunctive rule bodies using auxiliary atoms, enabling stable model solvers to capture all supported models (Sect. 3).

2. **Correctness proof**: Formal proof establishing a bijection between supported models of the original program and stable models of the transformed program (Theorem 3).
3. **Practical implementation**: A preprocessor for Clingo that automates the transformation, enabling seamless integration with existing ASP workflows (Sect. 4).
4. **Application demonstrations**: Concrete examples in software testing, medical diagnosis, and planning showing how supported models enable exploratory reasoning capabilities beyond stable models (Sect. 6).
5. **Comparative analysis**: Discussion of the relationship to Clark's Completion and the complementary nature of our ASP-based approach versus SAT-based methods (Sect. 5.1).

2 Background

2.1 Answer Set Programming Fundamentals

An ASP program Π consists of rules of the form:

$$h \leftarrow b_1, \ldots, b_m, \text{not } c_1, \ldots, \text{not } c_n$$

where h, b_i, c_j are atoms and not represents negation as failure (default negation). The set of all atoms appearing in Π is denoted $\text{atoms}(\Pi)$.

For a rule r, we denote: $\text{head}(r) = h$ (the rule head), $\text{body}^+(r) = \{b_1, \ldots, b_m\}$ (positive body literals), $\text{body}^-(r) = \{c_1, \ldots, c_n\}$ (negated body literals), and $\text{body}(r)$ for the entire body condition.

An *interpretation* is a set of atoms $M \subseteq \text{atoms}(\Pi)$. An atom a is *true* in M if $a \in M$, and *false* otherwise. A rule r is *satisfied* in M if whenever $\text{body}^+(r) \subseteq M$ and $\text{body}^-(r) \cap M = \emptyset$ (i.e., the body is satisfied), then $\text{head}(r) \in M$. An interpretation M is a *model* of Π if every rule in Π is satisfied in M.

2.2 Stable Model Semantics

The stable model semantics [9] defines solutions to answer set programs. For a ground program Π and interpretation M, the *Gelfond-Lifschitz reduct* Π^M is constructed by: (1) removing all rules containing a negative literal not c with $c \in M$, and (2) removing all remaining negative literals from rule bodies. The reduct Π^M is a positive (negation-free) program. An interpretation M is a *stable model* of Π if and only if M is the least (minimal) model of Π^M. The minimality requirement ensures that atoms are false unless they are proven true, implementing a form of closed-world reasoning.

2.3 Supported Models

We now formally define supported models following Apt, Blair, and Walker [1]; Apt and Bol [2] provide a comprehensive survey of this semantics and its place among alternatives for logic programs with negation.

Definition 1 (Supported Model). *Given a ground logic program Π, an interpretation $M \subseteq \text{atoms}(\Pi)$ is a* supported model *of Π if:*

1. *M is a model of Π (i.e., M satisfies all rules in Π), and*
2. *For each atom $a \in M$, there exists a rule $r \in \Pi$ such that:*
   - $\text{head}(r) = a$
   - $\text{body}^+(r) \subseteq M$ *(all positive body literals are true)*
   - $\text{body}^-(r) \cap M = \emptyset$ *(all negative body literals are satisfied)*

We say such a rule r supports *atom a in M.*

The support condition requires that every true atom has an active justification: some rule deriving it must have its body satisfied. This prevents atoms from being arbitrarily true without derivation, ensuring logical consistency.

For non-ground programs, this definition applies to the grounded program obtained by instantiating rules over the Herbrand universe.

Theorem 1 (Relationship to Stable Models [14]). *Every stable model of a logic program is a supported model. The converse does not hold in general.*

Example 1. Consider the program Π:

$$p \leftarrow q, \text{not } r$$
$$q \leftarrow p$$

The empty set $\emptyset$ is both a stable model and a supported model (vacuously satisfying both conditions).

The set $M = \{p, q\}$ is a supported model but not a stable model. It is supported because p is supported by the first rule ($q \in M$, $r \notin M$) and q is supported by the second rule ($p \in M$), and both rules are satisfied. However, the reduct Π^M contains $p \leftarrow q$ and $q \leftarrow p$, whose least model is $\emptyset \neq M$, so M is not a stable model.

This illustrates how supported models capture cyclic dependencies that are consistent but non-minimal.

2.4 Clark's Completion

Clark's Completion [4] provides an alternative characterization of supported models. For a program Π, the completion $\text{Comp}(\Pi)$ is a propositional theory obtained by: for each atom a, collecting all rules with head a (say $a \leftarrow \text{body}_1(a)$, $\ldots$, $a \leftarrow \text{body}_k(a)$), and forming the completed definition $a \leftrightarrow (\text{body}_1(a) \vee \cdots \vee \text{body}_k(a))$. If no rules derive a, the completion includes $a \leftrightarrow \bot$ (i.e., $\neg a$).

A fundamental result relates supported models to classical logic:

Theorem 2 ([1,4]). *An interpretation M is a supported model of Π if and only if M is a classical model of Comp(Π).*

This connection enables computing supported models via SAT solvers: generate $\text{Comp}(\Pi)$ and find its satisfying assignments. Our work provides an alternative approach within the ASP paradigm.

3 Transformation Method

We now present our main contribution: a transformation enabling computation of supported models via stable model solvers.

3.1 The Transformation

The key insight is to decouple conjunctive rule bodies using auxiliary atoms that represent "the body is disabled" (i.e., the body evaluates to false). For each rule r, we introduce an auxiliary atom $\_dm\_r$ that is true exactly when the body of r is not satisfied.

Definition 2 (Transformation). *Let Π be a ground logic program. The* transformed program *$T(\Pi)$ is constructed as follows. For each rule r in Π of the form:*

$$h \leftarrow l_1, \ldots, l_m, \text{not } l_{m+1}, \ldots, \text{not } l_n$$

we generate the following rules in $T(\Pi)$:

$$h \leftarrow \text{not } \_dm\_r \tag{1}$$
$$\_dm\_r \leftarrow \text{not } l_i \quad \text{for each } i \in \{1, \ldots, m\} \tag{2}$$
$$\_dm\_r \leftarrow l_j \quad \text{for each } j \in \{m+1, \ldots, n\} \tag{3}$$

Remark 1. The rules (2) and (3) implement De Morgan's law for negating a conjunction: $\neg(l_1 \wedge \cdots \wedge l_m \wedge \neg l_{m+1} \wedge \cdots \wedge \neg l_n) \equiv \neg l_1 \vee \cdots \vee \neg l_m \vee l_{m+1} \vee \cdots \vee l_n$. Rule (1) states that h can be derived when $\_dm\_r$ is false, i.e., when the original body is satisfied.

Example 2. Consider the rule:

$$p \leftarrow q, r, \text{not } s$$

The transformation produces:

$$p \leftarrow \text{not } \_dm\_r$$
$$\_dm\_r \leftarrow \text{not } q$$
$$\_dm\_r \leftarrow \text{not } r$$
$$\_dm\_r \leftarrow s$$

The auxiliary atom $\_dm\_r$ is true when the body fails: when q is false, or r is false, or s is true. Otherwise, $\_dm\_r$ is false and p can be derived via the first rule.

3.2 Correctness

We now prove that our transformation correctly captures supported models.

Theorem 3 (Transformation Correctness). *Let Π be a ground logic program. An interpretation $M \subseteq \text{atoms}(\Pi)$ is a supported model of Π if and only if*

$$M' = M \cup \{\_dm\_r \mid r \in \Pi \textit{ and } M \not\models \text{body}(r)\}$$

is a stable model of $T(\Pi)$.

Proof. We prove both directions.

($\Rightarrow$) Supported model to stable model:
Let M be a supported model of Π. Define:

$$M' = M \cup \{\_dm\_r \mid r \in \Pi \text{ and } M \not\models \text{body}(r)\}$$

We show M' is a stable model of $T(\Pi)$ by proving it equals the least model of the reduct $(T(\Pi))^{M'}$.

Step 1: M' is a model of $T(\Pi)$.
Consider any rule in $T(\Pi)$:

Case 1: Rule $h \leftarrow \text{not } \_dm\_r$ from some $r : h \leftarrow \text{body}(r)$ in Π.
If $\_dm\_r \in M'$, the rule is satisfied (body false). If $\_dm\_r \notin M'$, then by construction of M', we have $M \models \text{body}(r)$. Since M is a model of Π and the body of r is satisfied in M, we must have $h \in M \subseteq M'$, so the rule is satisfied.

Case 2: Rule $\_dm\_r \leftarrow \text{not } l_i$ for $l_i \in \text{body}^+(r)$.
If $l_i \in M'$, the rule is satisfied (body false). If $l_i \notin M'$, then $l_i \notin M$ (since $M \subseteq M'$ for original atoms), so $M \not\models \text{body}(r)$ (positive literal l_i fails). By construction, $\_dm\_r \in M'$, so the rule is satisfied.

Case 3: Rule $\_dm\_r \leftarrow l_j$ for $l_j \in \text{body}^-(r)$.
If $l_j \notin M'$, the rule is satisfied (body false). If $l_j \in M'$, then $l_j \in M$, so $M \not\models \text{body}(r)$ (negated literal fails). By construction, $\_dm\_r \in M'$, so the rule is satisfied.
Thus M' is a model of $T(\Pi)$.

Step 2: M' is the least model of $(T(\Pi))^{M'}$.
The reduct $(T(\Pi))^{M'}$ is obtained by removing rules with not $\_dm\_r$ where $\_dm\_r \in M'$, removing rules with not l_i where $l_i \in M'$, and removing all remaining negative literals.

The reduct contains: for each r with $M \models \text{body}(r)$, since $\_dm\_r \notin M'$, rule $h \leftarrow \text{not } \_dm\_r$ becomes fact $h \leftarrow$ in the reduct. For each r with $M \not\models \text{body}(r)$, since $\_dm\_r \in M'$, rule $h \leftarrow \text{not } \_dm\_r$ is removed from the reduct. For rules defining $\_dm\_r$: if there exists $l_i \in \text{body}^+(r)$ with $l_i \notin M'$, then rule $\_dm\_r \leftarrow \text{not } l_i$ becomes fact $\_dm\_r \leftarrow$. Similarly, if there exists $l_j \in \text{body}^-(r)$ with $l_j \in M'$, then rule $\_dm\_r \leftarrow l_j$ remains in the reduct with body satisfied.

Let N be the least model of $(T(\Pi))^{M'}$.

Claim: $N = M'$.

For any original atom $a \in \text{atoms}(\Pi)$: if $a \in M$, then there exists rule r with $\text{head}(r) = a$ and $M \models \text{body}(r)$ (since M is a supported model, a has support), and this rule contributes fact $a \leftarrow$ to the reduct, so $a \in N$. If $a \notin M$ but $a \in N$, then there exists rule r with $\text{head}(r) = a$ contributing fact $a \leftarrow$ to the reduct, meaning $M \models \text{body}(r)$; since M is a model of Π, this implies $a \in M$, a contradiction. Thus $N \cap \text{atoms}(\Pi) = M$.

For any auxiliary atom $\_dm\_r$: if $M \not\models \text{body}(r)$, then $\_dm\_r \in M'$ by construction, and some rule defining $\_dm\_r$ has its body satisfied in M, contributing fact $\_dm\_r \leftarrow$ to the reduct, so $\_dm\_r \in N$. If $M \models \text{body}(r)$, then $\_dm\_r \notin M'$ by construction, and no rule defining $\_dm\_r$ contributes a fact to the reduct, so $\_dm\_r \notin N$.

Therefore $N = M'$, establishing that M' is the least model of $(T(\Pi))^{M'}$, hence a stable model of $T(\Pi)$.

($\Leftarrow$) Stable model to supported model:

Let M' be a stable model of $T(\Pi)$. Define $M = M' \cap \text{atoms}(\Pi)$.

Step 1: M is a model of Π.

Consider any rule $r : h \leftarrow \text{body}(r)$ in Π. The transformed program contains $h \leftarrow \text{not } \_dm\_r$.

Since M' is a model of $T(\Pi)$, either $\_dm\_r \in M'$ or $h \in M'$.

Case 1: If $\_dm\_r \in M'$, then the rules generating $\_dm\_r$ imply that either some $l_i \in \text{body}^+(r)$ has $l_i \notin M'$ (hence $l_i \notin M$), or some $l_j \in \text{body}^-(r)$ has $l_j \in M'$ (hence $l_j \in M$). In either case, $M \not\models \text{body}(r)$, so rule r is satisfied in M.

Case 2: If $\_dm\_r \notin M'$, then $h \in M'$ (since the rule $h \leftarrow \text{not } \_dm\_r$ must be satisfied), hence $h \in M$. Moreover, $\_dm\_r \notin M'$ means no rule generating $\_dm\_r$ has its body satisfied in M', which means $M \models \text{body}(r)$. Since $h \in M$ and $M \models \text{body}(r)$, rule r is satisfied in M.

Therefore M is a model of Π.

Step 2: Every atom in M has support.

Let $a \in M \subseteq M'$. Since M' is a stable model, it is a supported model of $T(\Pi)$ (by Theorem 1). Thus a has a supporting rule in $T(\Pi)$.

The only rules in $T(\Pi)$ with head a (where $a \in \text{atoms}(\Pi)$) are of the form $a \leftarrow \text{not } \_dm\_r$ for some rule r with $\text{head}(r) = a$ in Π.

For such a rule to support a in M', we need the body satisfied, i.e., $\_dm\_r \notin M'$. This means $M \models \text{body}(r)$ (as established above).

Therefore a has a supporting rule r in Π with $\text{head}(r) = a$ and $M \models \text{body}(r)$, establishing that M is a supported model of Π.

3.3 Complexity Analysis

Proposition 1. *For a ground program Π with n rules and m total literals across all rule bodies, the transformed program $T(\Pi)$ has $O(n + m)$ rules and $O(n + |\text{atoms}(\Pi)|)$ atoms. The transformation is computable in polynomial time.*

Proof. For each rule r in Π with k_r literals in its body, we generate one rule of form head(r) $\leftarrow$ not $\_dm\_r$ and k_r rules defining $\_dm\_r$ (one per body literal).

Total rules: $n + \sum_{r \in \Pi} k_r = n + m = O(n + m)$.

Total atoms: original $|\text{atoms}(\Pi)|$ atoms plus n new auxiliary atoms $\_dm\_r$ (one per rule) $= O(n + |\text{atoms}(\Pi)|)$.

The transformation processes each rule once and generates a linear number of output rules, requiring $O(n + m)$ time.

4 Implementation and Algorithm

We have implemented our transformation as a Python preprocessor for Clingo, the state-of-the-art ASP solver. The implementation is publicly available at https://github.com/fanglioc/ConsistencyModelSemantics and archived at DOI: 10.5281/zenodo.18600333.

Implementation Scope. The current implementation operates on *grounded* ASP programs. The rationale for this design choice and path forward are discussed in Sect. 5.2.

4.1 Algorithm

Algorithm 1. Computing Supported Models

Require: Ground logic program Π
Ensure: Set of supported models $\mathcal{M}$
$\mathcal{M} \leftarrow \emptyset$
$\Pi' \leftarrow$ TRANSFORM(Π) ▷ Apply transformation from Definition 2
$\mathcal{M}' \leftarrow$ CLINGO(Π', 0) ▷ Compute all stable models using Clingo
for each stable model $M' \in \mathcal{M}'$ **do**
  $M \leftarrow M' \cap \text{atoms}(\Pi)$ ▷ Project to original vocabulary
  if $M \notin \mathcal{M}$ **then**
    $\mathcal{M} \leftarrow \mathcal{M} \cup \{M\}$ ▷ Collect unique supported model
  end if
end for
return $\mathcal{M}$

The algorithm transforms Π per Definition 2, computes all stable models of the transformed program using Clingo, and projects out auxiliary atoms to obtain supported models. By Theorem 3, this correctly computes all supported models of Π.

4.2 Implementation Details

Our Python implementation consists of approximately 300 lines of code and includes: a parser that reads grounded ASP programs in Clingo's text format, a transformer that applies Definition 2 to generate $T(\Pi)$, a Clingo interface that invokes Clingo as a subprocess and parses output, a projector that filters auxiliary atoms from stable models, and an output formatter that displays supported models in human-readable format.

The tool accepts command-line options for controlling the number of models to compute (specific count or all), specifying output format (text, JSON, or Clingo format), and enabling verbose mode for debugging.

4.3 Usage Example

Consider the input program `example.lp`:

```
p :- q, not r.
q :- p.
```

Step 1: Ground the program (if needed):

```
gringo example.lp > example_ground.lp
```

Step 2: Compute supported models:

```
python supported_models.py example_ground.lp
```

Output:

```
Supported Model 1: {}
Supported Model 2: {p, q}
```

The tool automatically generates the transformed program (with auxiliary atoms $\_dm\_r1$ and $\_dm\_r2$), computes its stable models using Clingo, and projects the results to obtain the supported models of the original program.

4.4 Performance Considerations

The transformation introduces $O(n)$ auxiliary atoms and $O(n+m)$ rules (Proposition 1). Modern ASP solvers like Clingo are highly optimized for programs with thousands of rules and atoms. In our experiments, programs with up to 100 rules transform and solve in under 1 s, and Clingo's optimizations (e.g., component analysis, clause learning) apply effectively to transformed programs. For very large programs, the bottleneck is typically grounding rather than our transformation or stable model computation.

5 Discussion and Related Concepts

5.1 Relationship to Clark's Completion

The supported models of a logic program Π coincide exactly with the classical models of its Clark's Completion Comp(Π) (Theorem 2). This establishes a well-known connection between supported model semantics and classical propositional logic.

Given this connection, one might ask: *Why develop a new ASP-based transformation when Clark's Completion already provides a method for computing supported models via SAT solvers?*

Comparing the Approaches. The Clark's Completion approach generates Comp(Π), converts to conjunctive normal form, invokes a SAT solver to find all satisfying assignments, and interprets each as a supported model. Our ASP transformation instead transforms Π to $T(\Pi)$, invokes Clingo to find all stable models, and projects auxiliary atoms to obtain supported models.

Complementary Nature and Advantages. These approaches are complementary. Clark's Completion with SAT benefits from mature, highly optimized SAT solvers with decades of development. Our ASP transformation offers seamless integration for researchers already using Clingo, preserves ASP program structure enabling use of ASP-specific features (constraints, optimization, aggregates) in future extensions, provides a unified framework where both stable and supported models are computed within the same paradigm, and offers pedagogical clarity through auxiliary atoms *_dm_r* that explicitly represent "rule r is disabled".

Prior Computational Approaches. Before our work, computing supported models relied on fixpoint-based interpreters implementing the support condition directly, transformation to Clark's Completion followed by SAT solving, or specialized theorem provers for logic programs. Our transformation complements these approaches by enabling computation within standard ASP infrastructure, making supported models accessible to the ASP community without requiring specialized tools.

Theoretical Relationship. Both approaches compute the same models (supported models of Π) via different paths, as illustrated in Fig. 1. Our contribution provides the ASP-based path, expanding the toolkit available to ASP practitioners.

5.2 The Grounding Restriction

Our current implementation operates on grounded logic programs. This is an implementation-based restriction, not a fundamental theoretical limitation.

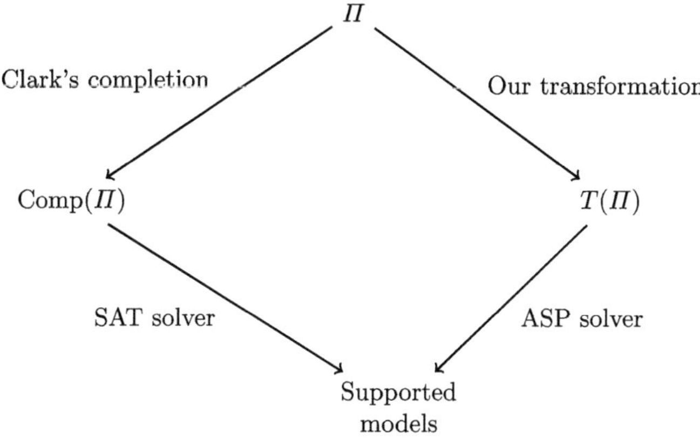

Fig. 1. Two paths for computing supported models of a logic program Π.

Why the Restriction Exists. ASP solvers like Clingo internally perform two steps: grounding (the gringo component instantiates rules over the Herbrand universe) and solving (the clasp component computes stable models of the ground program). Our transformation operates on the ground program after grounding, fitting naturally into the pipeline as shown in Fig. 2.

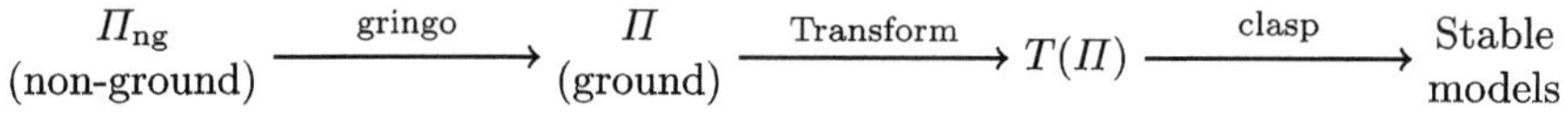

$$\underset{\text{(non-ground)}}{\Pi_{\text{ng}}} \xrightarrow{\text{gringo}} \underset{\text{(ground)}}{\Pi} \xrightarrow{\text{Transform}} T(\Pi) \xrightarrow{\text{clasp}} \begin{array}{c}\text{Stable}\\ \text{models}\end{array}$$

Fig. 2. The supported model computation pipeline.

Why this is not a Fundamental Limitation. The transformation can, in principle, be integrated into the grounding phase. We implemented it as a post-grounding preprocessor for simplicity, transparency, and modularity. Future work will integrate the transformation into the ASP system's front-end to handle non-ground programs transparently.

6 Applications

We now demonstrate domains where supported models enable valuable exploratory reasoning beyond stable models. The following examples use standard ASP syntax as accepted by Clingo, where `:-` corresponds to $\leftarrow$ and `not` denotes default negation.

6.1 Software Verification: Comprehensive Test Generation

In software testing, generating all possible system states consistent with component behaviors ensures comprehensive test coverage, including redundant configurations that may occur in practice.

Example 3 (Redundant Systems Testing). Consider a system with primary and backup components:

```
% Components can be activated externally (self-supporting)
pri :- pri.
bak :- bak.

% System state rules
run :- pri.
run :- bak.
red :- pri, bak.
```

The self-referential rules `pri :- pri` and `bak :- bak` model components that can be activated by external triggers or preexisting conditions (e.g., hardware initialization, operator commands). Such rules create supported but non-minimal models.

Stable Models: Only $\emptyset$ (no components active, the minimal model).

Additional Supported Models:

- {`pri`, `run`} (only primary active),
- {`bak`, `run`} (only backup active),
- {`pri`, `bak`, `run`, `red`} (both active in redundant configuration).

Testing only the stable model (empty system) misses critical scenarios: Does the system behave correctly when only primary is active? Does backup correctly take over when primary fails? What happens when both components are simultaneously active? Supported models enumerate all these configurations for comprehensive test suites.

6.2 Medical Diagnosis: Differential Diagnosis Generation

Physicians routinely consider multiple co-occurring conditions when diagnosing patients. Supported models naturally capture this exploratory reasoning.

Example 4 (Comorbidity Exploration). Consider a diagnostic knowledge base:

```
% Conditions can be hypothesized (for exploratory
    diagnosis)
infection :- infection.
inflammation :- inflammation.
allergy :- allergy.

```

```
% Symptom manifestation rules
fever :- infection.
fever :- inflammation.
cough :- infection.
cough :- allergy.
fatigue :- infection.
fatigue :- inflammation.
```

Stable Models: Only ∅ (no conditions assumed).

Supported Models Include: {`infection`, `fever`, `cough`, `fatigue`} (infection alone), {`inflammation`, `fever`, `fatigue`} (inflammation alone), {`allergy`, `cough`} (allergy alone), as well as all pairwise and triple combinations of conditions with their associated symptoms.

Real patients often present with multiple conditions. Enumerating all supported models provides a differential diagnosis for further investigation through lab tests, imaging, or patient history.

6.3 Planning: Alternative Resource Allocations

In resource allocation and planning, exploring all valid allocations helps identify robust solutions with redundancy.

Example 5 (Server Allocation with Redundancy). Consider allocating servers to tasks:

```
% Servers can be allocated (choice of allocation)
s1 :- s1.
s2 :- s2.
s3 :- s3.

% Task completion rules
tA :- s1. tA :- s2.
tB :- s2. tB :- s3.
all :- tA, tB.
```

Stable Models: Only ∅ (no allocation).

Supported Models Include:

- {`s2`, `tA`, `tB`, `all`} (minimal: server 2 handles both tasks),
- {`s1`, `s2`, `tA`, `tB`, `all`} (redundant for task A),
- {`s2`, `s3`, `tA`, `tB`, `all`} (redundant for task B),
- {`s1`, `s2`, `s3`, `tA`, `tB`, `all`} (maximum redundancy).

In production systems, the minimal allocation creates a single point of failure. Enumerating all supported models enables selection of an allocation balancing reliability against cost based on operational requirements.

In general, supported models are valuable when exploration over optimization is the goal, when non-minimal scenarios are realistic, when hypothesis generation or comprehensive coverage is required, or when self-referential reasoning is present. Stable models remain appropriate when minimality corresponds to optimality or when closed-world reasoning is desired.

7 Related Work

7.1 Alternative ASP Semantics

Several alternative semantics for logic programs have been proposed. Well-founded semantics [18] computes a unique three-valued model (atoms can be true, false, or undefined), providing polynomial-time reasoning; however, it loses the flexibility of multiple answer sets and cannot enumerate alternative solutions. Partial stable models [16] extend stable models to three-valued logic, allowing undefined atoms, which is conceptually similar to supported models in relaxing requirements but uses a different formalism. L-stable models [6] and other preferred model semantics define preference orderings among models; supported models can be seen as relaxing preferences for minimality. Coinductive ASP [10,17] extends standard ASP to capture greatest fixed-point semantics, enabling reasoning about infinite structures and cyclic definitions; it naturally captures non-minimal models for positive cycles but requires specialized solvers with co-logic programming capabilities.

Our work is complementary to these semantics, focusing specifically on supported models and their practical computation using standard ASP infrastructure.

7.2 ASP Extensions and Expressiveness

Modern ASP supports various extensions enhancing expressiveness. Choice rules like `{p} :- body` allow non-deterministic inclusion of atoms but require explicit annotation for each choice point, whereas our transformation systematically generates all supported models without manual specification. Disjunctive ASP allows rules with disjunctive heads, increasing expressiveness but still maintaining stable model semantics; our transformation applies to normal (non-disjunctive) programs. Aggregate atoms and optimization statements could potentially be combined with supported models in future extensions.

Our transformation provides a systematic method to explore non-minimal models through supported semantics without requiring manual annotations or program restructuring.

7.3 Program Transformations in ASP

Program transformation is a well-established technique in ASP. Strong equivalence [13] preserves answer sets under all contexts, enabling modular transformations; our transformation preserves supported models but changes stable model semantics. Shifting [11] and other normal form transformations standardize program structure; our transformation similarly restructures programs but for semantic rather than syntactic purposes. Completion-based transformations like the one by Fages [7] relate logic programs to classical logic; our work shares the goal of capturing supported models but stays within the ASP paradigm.

Our transformation is novel in providing an ASP-to-ASP translation that changes the class of models captured (from stable to supported) while enabling computation with standard solvers.

7.4 Knowledge Representation Applications

ASP has been applied to diverse domains. Configuration and synthesis [15] benefit from exploring alternative valid configurations, where supported models could enumerate options. Planning [12] typically seeks optimal plans, but supported models could generate backup plans or alternatives. Diagnosis [5] naturally involves considering multiple explanatory hypotheses, aligning with our medical diagnosis example.

Our application examples demonstrate how supported models enable exploratory reasoning in these domains, complementing traditional stable model approaches.

8 Conclusion and Future Work

We presented a transformation-based method for computing supported models using standard ASP solvers. Our approach bridges the gap between theoretical semantics (supported models, defined in 1988) and practical tools (modern ASP solvers optimized for stable models since the 1990s).

Our key contributions include a polynomial-time ASP transformation (Definition 2) with a formal correctness proof (Theorem 3), a practical open-source implementation as a Python preprocessor for Clingo (Sect. 4), a comparative analysis with Clark's Completion, and application demonstrations in software verification, medical diagnosis, and resource allocation.

8.1 Future Directions

Several promising directions for future work include the following.

Integration with ASP Front-End. Integrating the transformation directly into the grounder would enable transparent handling of non-ground programs with variables, eliminating the current implementation-based restriction (Sect. 5.2).

Empirical Performance Evaluation. A systematic benchmark comparison between our ASP-based transformation and the established Clark's Completion with SAT solver approach would quantify performance trade-offs across diverse problem domains.

Extension to Disjunctive Programs. Our current transformation applies to normal logic programs. Extending to disjunctive programs (rules with disjunctive heads) would broaden applicability.

Preference-Based Filtering and Incremental Computation. While our method enumerates all supported models, applications often benefit from ranking or filtering models based on domain-specific preferences. Additionally, algorithms for incrementally generating supported models one at a time would improve responsiveness and memory efficiency.

Hybrid Stable/Supported Semantics. Some applications might benefit from stable model semantics for certain predicates while using supported semantics for others. Investigating program annotations or transformations enabling such hybrid reasoning would combine the strengths of both approaches.

Connection to Coinductive ASP. Both supported models and coinductive ASP capture non-minimal solutions for cyclic definitions. Exploring the theoretical relationship and potential practical integration between these approaches could yield new insights and tools.

Supported models offer a valuable alternative to stable models for applications requiring exploratory reasoning. By providing accessible computational tools and demonstrating concrete applications, we hope to encourage broader adoption and further research into relaxed semantics for logic programming.

References

1. Apt, K.R., Blair, H.A., Walker, A.: Towards a theory of declarative knowledge. In: Minker, J. (ed.) Foundations of Deductive Databases and Logic Programming, pp. 89–148. Morgan Kaufmann (1988)
2. Apt, K.R., Bol, R.N.: Logic programming and negation: a survey. J. Logic Program. **19–20**, 9–71 (1994)
3. Baral, C.: Knowledge Representation, Reasoning and Declarative Problem Solving. Cambridge University Press (2003)
4. Clark, K.L.: Negation as failure. In: Gallaire, H., Minker, J. (eds.) Logic and Data Bases, pp. 293–322. Plenum Press, New York (1978)
5. Eiter, T., Fink, M., Greco, G., Lembo, D.: Answer set programming for data integration. In: Logic Programming and Nonmonotonic Reasoning, 7th International Conference, LPNMR 2003, pp. 393–405. Springer (2003)
6. Eiter, T., Leone, N., Sacca, D.: On the partial semantics for disjunctive deductive databases. Ann. Math. Artif. Intell. **19**(1–2), 59–96 (1997)
7. Fages, F.: Consistency of Clark's completion and existence of stable models. Methods Logic Comput. Sci. **1**(1), 51–60 (1994)
8. Gebser, M., Kaminski, R., Kaufmann, B., Schaub, T.: Clingo = asp + control: preliminary report. arXiv preprint arXiv:1405.3694 (2014)
9. Gelfond, M., Lifschitz, V.: The stable model semantics for logic programming. In: 5th Conference on Logic Programming, vol. 88, pp. 1070–1080 (1988)
10. Gupta, G., et al.: Coinductive answer set programming or consistency-based computing. In: Co-LP 2012-A Workshop on Coinductive Logic Programming (2012)

11. Janhunen, T.: Representing normal programs with clauses. In: Logics in Artificial Intelligence, 9th European Conference, JELIA 2004, pp. 358–370. Springer (2004)
12. Lifschitz, V.: Answer set programming and plan generation. Artif. Intell. **138**(1–2), 39–54 (2002)
13. Lifschitz, V., Pearce, D., Valverde, A.: Strongly equivalent logic programs. ACM Trans. Comput. Log. **2**(4), 526–541 (2001)
14. Marek, V.W., Subrahmanian, V.S.: The relationship between stable, supported, default and autoepistemic semantics for general logic programs. Theoret. Comput. Sci. **103**(2), 365–386 (1992)
15. Nogueira, M., Balduccini, M., Gelfond, M., Watson, R., Barry, M.: An A-Prolog decision support system for the space shuttle. In: Practical Aspects of Declarative Languages, 3rd International Symposium, PADL 2001, pp. 169–183. Springer (2001)
16. Przymusinski, T.C.: Stable semantics for disjunctive programs. N. Gener. Comput. **9**(3), 401–424 (1991)
17. Simon, L., Mallya, A., Bansal, A., Gupta, G.: Co-logic programming: extending logic programming with coinduction. In: Automata, Languages and Programming, 34th International Colloquium, ICALP 2007, pp. 472–483. Springer (2007)
18. Van Gelder, A., Ross, K.A., Schlipf, J.S.: The well-founded semantics for general logic programs. J. ACM **38**(3), 619–649 (1991)

Probabilistic Linear Logic Programming with an Application to Bayesian Network Computations

Matteo Acclavio[1] and Roberto Maieli[2](✉)

[1] University of Southern Denmark, Odense, Denmark
[2] Roma TRE University, Rome, Italy
maieli@uniroma3.it

Abstract. Bayesian networks are a canonical formalism for representing probabilistic dependencies, yet their integration within logic programming frameworks remains a nontrivial challenge, mainly due to the complex structure of these networks.

In this paper, we propose *probLO* (*probabilistic Linear Objects*) an extension of Andreoli and Pareschi's LO language which embeds Bayesian network representation and computation within the framework of multiplicative additive linear logic programming. The key novelty is the use of multi-head Prolog-like methods to reconstruct network structures, which are not necessarily trees, and the operation of *slicing*, standard in the literature of linear logic, enabling internal numerical probability computations without relying on external semantic interpretation.

Keywords: Bayesian Networks · Focusing Proofs · Linear Logic · Logic Programming · Probabilities · Sequent Calculus

1 Introduction

Probabilistic logic programming (PLP) has emerged as a key paradigm for integrating structured logical knowledge with uncertain information [9]. However, representing and reasoning about probabilistic dependencies in a Bayesian network [19,30] within logic programming frameworks remains a nontrivial challenge due to the complex structure of these networks, where variables can have multiple parents nodes and child nodes. In fact, most existing approaches in probabilistic logic programming [9,11,15,20,32,34], relies on classical or Horn-clause logic as their logical framework, where each method typically has the head made of a single atom, thus suggesting a tree-like structure of dependencies. Furthermore, the absences of cyclic dependencies in Bayesian networks suggests that, even if a variable can be influenced by multiple parent variables, its use in a computation should be linear, i.e., each variable should be computed once in a given query.

R. Maieli—Supported by the INdAM-GNSAGA Research Group.

M. Sperber and E. Komendantskaya (Eds.): FLOPS 2026, LNCS 16533, pp. 202–219, 2026.
https://doi.org/10.1007/978-981-92-0184-6_10

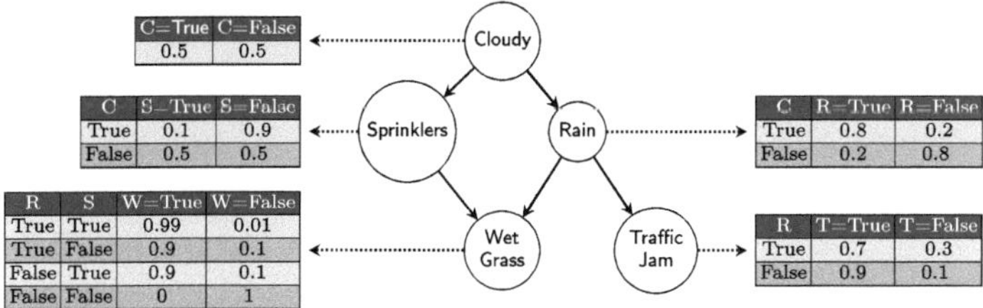

Fig. 1. A Bayesian Network representing the set of random variables (Cloudy (C), Sprinklers (S), Rain (R), WetGrass (W), and TrafficJam (T)).

In this paper, we introduce the *probabilistic Linear Objects language* (or *probLO*, for short) to embed Bayesian network representation and computation within the framework of logic programming. The probLO language is an extension of Andreoli and Pareschi's *Linear Objects language* (or LO) [6,7], a logic programming language grounded in *linear logic* [16]. The operational semantics of LO is derived from Andreoli's theory of *focused proofs* [5], and it refines the well-known correspondence between computation and proof search articulated in Miller's *Uniform Proofs* [29].

The choice of linear logic as the underlying logical framework is motivated by its inherent resource sensitivity, which aligns well with the intuition that we should resolve the conditional probability of each node of Bayesian network only once per computation. Therefore, the specific selection of LO becomes necessary because of the possibility of defining *multi-head clauses* (or *methods*) otherwise, it would become quite difficult to represent the complex dependencies of Bayesian networks without resorting to redundancy or auxiliary constructs. In LO, each method can be interpreted as a *bipole formula* [5] of linear logic, and its application in an execution corresponds to the application of a (derivable) *synthetic rule* in a proof search, or equivalently, to joining the *positive* (or synchronous) and *negative* (or asynchronous) phases together in the proof search that focuses on the bipole:

$$\overbrace{\underbrace{[h_{X_1},\ldots,h_{X_n}]}_{\texttt{multi-head}} :- \underbrace{[b_{Y_1},\ldots,b_{Y_m}]}_{\texttt{body}}}^{\texttt{LO method}} \rightsquigarrow \overbrace{\underbrace{(h^{\perp}_{X_1}\otimes\cdots\otimes h^{\perp}_{X_n})}_{\text{multi-head}}\otimes\underbrace{(b_{Y_1}\parr\cdots\parr b_{Y_m})}_{\text{body}}}^{\texttt{bipole}} \quad (1)$$

To understand why the possibility of multi-head clauses is crucial to represent Bayesian networks, let us briefly recall some basic notions about them. A Bayesian network is a graphical model that represents a set of random variables and their conditional dependencies via a directed acyclic graph, where each node represents a random variable, and the directed edges represent the conditional dependencies between these variables. See Fig. 1 for an example of a simple Bayesian network. Each row of the *conditional probability table* associated to a node specifies the *conditional probability* $\mathsf{Pr}(\mathsf{X} \mid \mathsf{Y}_1,\ldots,\mathsf{Y}_m)$ that the variable X takes a specific value, given some *evidences*, i.e., given that the parent variables $\mathsf{Y}_1, \ldots, \mathsf{Y}_m$ take specific values. In the general case, conditional probabilities for random variables $\mathsf{X}_1, \ldots, \mathsf{X}_n$, given evidences random variables $\mathsf{Y}_1, \ldots, \mathsf{Y}_m$, are defined by the following law, known as Bayes' Theorem,

$$\mathsf{Pr}(\mathsf{X}_1, \ldots, \mathsf{X}_n \mid \mathsf{Y}_1, \ldots, \mathsf{Y}_m) = \frac{\mathsf{Pr}(\mathsf{X}_1, \ldots, \mathsf{X}_n, \mathsf{Y}_1, \ldots, \mathsf{Y}_m)}{\mathsf{Pr}(\mathsf{Y}_1, \ldots, \mathsf{Y}_m)} \tag{2}$$

where $\mathsf{Pr}(\mathsf{X}_1, \ldots, \mathsf{X}_n, \mathsf{Y}_1, \ldots, \mathsf{Y}_m)$ is the *joint probability* of $\mathsf{X}_1, ..., \mathsf{X}_n, \mathsf{Y}_1, ..., \mathsf{Y}_m$, and $\mathsf{Pr}(\mathsf{Y}_1, \ldots, \mathsf{Y}_m)$ is the *marginal probability* that $\mathsf{Y}_1, \ldots, \mathsf{Y}_m$ happen, regardless of the values of $\mathsf{X}_1, \ldots, \mathsf{X}_n$.

Our driving intuition on the need of multi-head methods to represent conditional probabilities is that, as in conditional probabilities, we can interpret the outcomes $\mathsf{X}_1, \ldots, \mathsf{X}_n$ as being *produced* simultaneously given the evidences $\mathsf{Y}_1, \ldots, \mathsf{Y}_m$; thus, we can represent their computation in a logic programming framework by means of *multi-head methods* having $\mathsf{X}_1, \ldots, \mathsf{X}_n$ as head and Y_1, $\ldots$, Y_m as body. In probLO, we can interpret conditional probabilities as multi-head methods annotated with a probability value $p \in [0, 1]$, using a syntax inspired by the one adopted in ProbLog [10,15] as shown in Eq. (3).

$$\underbrace{\mathsf{Pr}(\mathsf{X}_1, \ldots, \mathsf{X}_n \mid \mathsf{Y}_1, \ldots, \mathsf{Y}_m) = p}_{\text{conditional probability}} \quad \rightsquigarrow \quad \underbrace{p}_{\text{probability}} \quad :: \underbrace{[X_1, \ldots, X_n]}_{\text{multi-head}} :- \underbrace{[Y_1, \ldots, Y_m]}_{\text{body}} \tag{3}$$

The effect of the probabilistic annotation is to modify the operational semantics of the method application in such a way that, when the method is applied during a proof search (*expansion* phase), the probability of the conclusion $q \cdot p$ is obtained by multiplying the probability of the premises q by the probability p of the method, as shown in Eq. (4).

$$\mathsf{exp}\frac{q :: \ \mathsf{P}; \ \Gamma, b_1, \ldots, b_m}{q \cdot p :: \ \mathsf{P}, \mathtt{T}; \ \Gamma, h_1, \ldots, h_n} \qquad \text{where } p :: [\mathtt{h}_1, \ldots, \mathtt{h}_\mathtt{n}] :- [\mathtt{b}_1, \ldots, \mathtt{b}_\mathtt{m}] \in \mathtt{T} \tag{4}$$

As a first application of probLO, we show how to represent Bayesian networks, and how to compute joint and marginal probabilities directly within the logic programming framework without relying on an external semantic interpretation. We show how derivations in probLO naturally mimic the process of computing over a Bayesian network where probabilities, annotating the current state, are updated according to rules of the operational semantics, each corresponding to the application of a conditional probability defined in the network (see Fig. 2).

Contributions of the Paper. In this paper, we show (Theorem 2) how it is possible to characterize the property of a directed graph being acyclic within the framework of (purely multiplicative) LO. Then we introduce probLO, an extension of LO with probabilistic reasoning capabilities, and we show how to represent

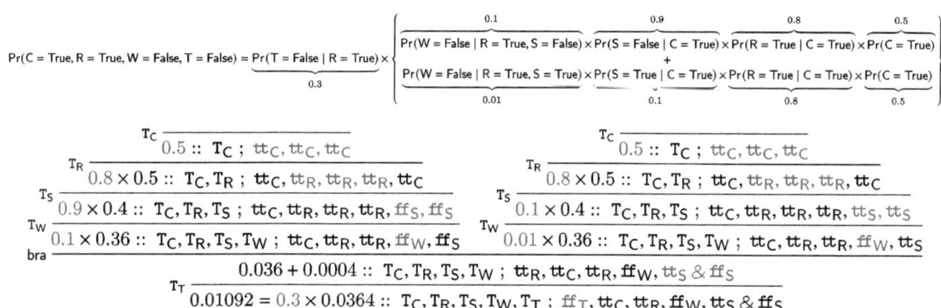

Fig. 2. The arithmetic expression of a possible way to compute the marginal probability $\mathsf{Pr}(\mathsf{C} = \mathsf{True}, \mathsf{R} = \mathsf{True}, \mathsf{W} = \mathsf{False}, \mathsf{T} = \mathsf{False})$, and the corresponding probLO derivation. In the derivation, each application of a method $\mathtt{T}_{\mathsf{X}}$ corresponds to the multiplication of the probability of the premises by the probability in the row of the conditional probability table of X corresponding to the values of the evidences in the premises; the branching step corresponds to the sum in the arithmetic expression above.

Bayesian networks in probLO using multi-head probabilistic methods. Finally, we show (Theorem 3) how to compute joint and marginal probabilities directly within the logic programming framework of probLO, without relying on an external semantic interpretation.

Paper Structure. In Sect. 2, we recall the logical foundations underlying our work, starting from the evolution of linear logic programming toward resource-sensitive computation, as well as basic definitions in probability theory and Bayesian networks. In Sect. 3, we recall the results on LO, and we show how to encode a graph traversal algorithm to detect the absence of cycles in a directed graph in LO, thus characterizing directed acyclic graphs. In Sect. 4, we introduce probLO, and we show how to represent computations in Bayesian networks within this framework. We conclude with Sect. 5 where we discuss some related works and future research directions. Due to space limitations, the proofs of the main results are not contained in the paper, but can be found in the extended version of this paper [3].

2 Background

In this section, we provide the necessary background linear logic and focussing proof search, and we recall some basic definitions in probability theory and Bayesian networks.

2.1 Multiplicative Additive Linear Logic

Linear Logic (LL) [16] is a refinement of Classical Logic that has raised a lot of interest in computer research, especially because of its resource sensitive-nature.

$$\text{AX}\,\frac{}{\vdash A, A^\perp} \quad \otimes\,\frac{\vdash \Gamma, A \quad \vdash B, \Delta}{\vdash \Gamma, A \otimes B, \Delta} \quad \parr\,\frac{\vdash \Gamma, A, B}{\vdash \Gamma, A \parr B} \quad \&\,\frac{\vdash \Gamma, A \quad \vdash \Gamma, B}{\vdash \Gamma, A \& B} \quad \oplus_1\,\frac{\vdash \Gamma, A}{\vdash \Gamma, A \oplus B} \quad \oplus_2\,\frac{\vdash \Gamma, B}{\vdash \Gamma, A \oplus B} \quad \text{mix}\,\frac{\vdash \Gamma \quad \vdash \Delta}{\vdash \Gamma, \Delta}$$

Fig. 3. Sequent calculus rules for $\mathsf{MALL}^{\mathsf{mix}}$.

In this paper, we are interested in the fragment of LL called *Multiplicative and Additive Linear Logic with mix* ($\mathsf{MALL}^{\mathsf{mix}}$) [25] in which we have two kinds of connectives: **multiplicative** connectives ($\otimes$ and $\parr$) and **additive** connectives ($\&$ and $\oplus$). The former connectives model purely linear usage of resources, while the latter allow to express some tamed form of structural rules, allowing to duplicate or discard resources in a controlled way. The **mix** rule allows combining two derivations that do not share any resource. It can be considered in the context of logic programming as it allows to model independent and computations with separated resources [1,4,12,14,21,22].

We consider **formulas** defined from a countable set of **atoms** $\mathbb{A}$ as follows:[1]

$$A, B ::= a \mid a^\perp \mid A \otimes B \mid A \parr B \mid A \& B \mid A \oplus B \qquad \text{with } a, a^\perp \in \mathbb{A} \tag{5}$$

and we may denote by $\bigoplus_{i=1}^n A_i$ the formula $A_1 \oplus (A_2 \oplus (\cdots \oplus A_n) \cdots)$.

A **sequent** Γ is a multiset of formulas. A **sequent system** is a set of inference rules as the ones in Fig. 3. We recall the sequent systems $\mathsf{MLL}^{\mathsf{mix}} = \{\mathsf{AX}, \parr, \otimes, \mathsf{mix}\}$ and $\mathsf{MALL}^{\mathsf{mix}} = \mathsf{MLL}^{\mathsf{mix}} \cup \{\&, \oplus_1, \oplus_2\}$. A **derivation** in a sequent system Sys of a sequent Γ is a finite tree of sequent with root Γ built according to the inference rules from in Sys. We say that a sequent Γ is **provable** in a sequent system Sys (written $\vdash_{\mathsf{Sys}} \Gamma$) if there exists a derivation of Γ using only the rules of Sys.

In the following we adopt the logical framework provided by *focusing*, while avoiding its technical intricacies.[2] For this reason, we simply define special formulas, called *bipoles*, that will be used to represent logic programming methods in the next subsections, and we introduce the notion of *synthetic inference rule* that will be used to define the operational semantics of logic programming in terms of proof search in the next subsections.

Definition 1. *A (multiplicative)* ***bipole*** *is a formula of the form $P \otimes N$ with P a* ***positive monopole*** *(i.e., a formula built using only negated atoms and $\otimes$) and N a* ***negative monopole*** *(i.e., a formula built using only atoms and $\parr$).*[3] *A* ***degenerate bipole*** *is a positive monopole.*

---

[1] Note that we do not consider the (linear) negation $\cdot^\perp$ being a connective, but rather an *involutive* relation between atoms, which extends to formula via the following De Morgan laws: $(A^\perp)^\perp = A$ and $(A \otimes B)^\perp = (A^\perp \parr B^\perp)$, and $(A \parr B)^\perp = (A^\perp \otimes B^\perp)$.

[2] For a detailed introduction to focusing and focusing LP, we refer the interested reader to [2,5–7,17,24,28].

[3] The choice of using negated atoms ($h_i^\perp$) in positive monopoles (resp., atoms (b_i) in negative monopoles) is a convention we adopt to allow easier readability of goals which, dually, are made simply of atoms.

We associate to each bipole ***synthetic inference rules*** *as follows:*

$$\mathcal{F} = (h_1^\perp \otimes \cdots \otimes h_n^\perp) \otimes (b_1 \parr \cdots \parr b_m) \quad \rightsquigarrow \quad \mathcal{F}\,\frac{\vdash \Gamma, b_1, \ldots, b_m}{\vdash \Gamma, (h_1^\perp \otimes \cdots \otimes h_n^\perp) \otimes (b_1 \parr \cdots \parr b_m), h_1, \ldots, h_n}$$
$$\mathcal{F} = (h_1^\perp \otimes \cdots \otimes h_n^\perp) \rightsquigarrow \mathcal{F}^{\mathsf{mix}}\,\frac{\vdash \Gamma}{\vdash \Gamma, (h_1^\perp \otimes \cdots \otimes h_n^\perp), h_1, \ldots, h_n} \quad \text{and} \quad \mathcal{F}^{\mathsf{mix}}\,\frac{}{\vdash (h_1^\perp \otimes \cdots \otimes h_n^\perp), h_1, \ldots, h_n} \tag{6}$$

The ***synthetic calculus*** $\mathsf{S}_\mathcal{B}$ *for a multiset of bipoles* $\mathcal{B} = \{\mathcal{F}_1, \ldots, \mathcal{F}_n\}$ *is the set all synthetic inference rules of Eq.* (6) *associated to these bipoles.*

The fact that each bipole can be seen as an elementary instruction of proof search is underlined by the following Propositions 1 and 2, showing that provability can be reduced to provability using only synthetic inference rules associated to bipoles, corresponding to phases of a focused proof search. It can be shown that the synthetic inference rule associated to a bipole is derivable in $\mathsf{MLL}^{\mathsf{mix}}$ and $\mathsf{MALL}^{\mathsf{mix}}$. Notice that the need of mix is crucial to derive the synthetic rule for degenerate bipoles in when the rule is not a leaf of the derivation.

Proposition 1. *Each synthetic rule associated to a bipole is derivable in* $\mathsf{MLL}^{\mathsf{mix}}$.

Proof. It suffices to consider the open derivations below on the left hand side for the non-degenerate case and the one on the right hand side for the first rule for the degenerate case.

$$\otimes\,\frac{\parr\,\dfrac{\vdash \Gamma, b_1, \ldots, b_m}{\vdash \Gamma, (b_1 \parr \cdots \parr b_m)} \quad \otimes\,\dfrac{\mathsf{AX}\,\dfrac{}{\vdash h_1^\perp, h_1} \;\cdots\; \mathsf{AX}\,\dfrac{}{\vdash h_n^\perp, h_n}}{\vdash h_1^\perp \otimes \cdots \otimes h_n^\perp, h_1, \ldots, h_n}}{\vdash \Gamma, (h_1^\perp \otimes \cdots \otimes h_n^\perp) \otimes (b_1 \parr \cdots \parr b_m), h_1, \ldots, h_n} \qquad \mathsf{mix}\,\frac{\vdash \Gamma \quad \otimes\,\dfrac{\mathsf{AX}\,\dfrac{}{\vdash h_1^\perp, h_1} \;\cdots\; \mathsf{AX}\,\dfrac{}{\vdash h_n^\perp, h_n}}{\vdash h_1^\perp \otimes \cdots \otimes h_n^\perp, h_1, \ldots, h_n}}{\vdash \Gamma, h_1^\perp \otimes \cdots \otimes h_n^\perp, h_1, \ldots, h_n} \tag{7}$$

The other rule for the degenerate case is the same as the sub-derivation on the right-premise of the mix-rule in the derivation above on the right.

Proposition 2. *Let* $\mathcal{C} = \bigoplus_{i=1}^k \mathcal{F}_i$ *with* $\mathcal{F}_1, \ldots, \mathcal{F}_k$ *bipoles of the form* $\mathcal{F}_i = (h_1^\perp \otimes \cdots \otimes h_n^\perp) \otimes (b_1^i \parr \cdots \parr b_{m_i}^i)$ *for all* $i \in \{1, \ldots, k\}$. *Then the following synthetic inference rule is derivable in* $\mathsf{MALL}^{\mathsf{mix}}$:

$$\mathcal{C}\,\frac{\vdash \Gamma, b_1^i, \ldots, b_{m_i}^i}{\vdash \Gamma, \bigoplus_{i=1}^k \mathcal{F}_i, h_1, \ldots, h_n}\; i \in \{1, \ldots, k\} \quad \text{and} \quad \mathcal{C}\,\frac{}{\vdash \bigoplus_{i=1}^k \mathcal{F}_i, h_1, \ldots, h_n}\; \begin{array}{c}\text{exists } i \in \{1, \ldots, k\} \\ \text{s.t. } m_i = 0\end{array} \tag{8}$$

Proof. Similar to the derivations in (7), but each starting with some applications of the rule $\oplus$ to select the appropriate bipole $\mathcal{F}_i$ among $\mathcal{F}_1, \ldots, \mathcal{F}_k$.

2.2 Probability and Bayesian (Boolean) Networks

In this section, we recall some preliminary notions on probability for discrete variables and Bayesian networks to fix the notation used in the rest of the paper. For the sake of simplicity, in the following, we restrict to considering only the case of **random (Boolean) variables**, taking values True or False, but the entire approach can easily be adapted and extended to encompass arbitrary discrete variables. For each random variable X, we denote by $\mathbf{X}$ the set containing the two **events**, $\mathsf{X} = \mathsf{True}$ and $\mathsf{X} = \mathsf{False}$, in which X takes the value True or False respectively, and by x any event in $\mathbf{X}$.

Definition 2. *Let* $\mathsf{X}_1,\ldots,\mathsf{X}_n,\mathsf{Y}_1,\ldots,\mathsf{Y}_m,\mathsf{Z}_1,\ldots,\mathsf{Z}_k$ *be random variables.*

- *A* ***probability distribution*** *for* X *is a function* $\mathsf{Pr}(\mathbf{X})$ *assigning a probability in* $[0,1]\subset\mathbb{R}$ *to each* $x\in\mathbf{X}$ *in such a way* $\mathsf{Pr}(\mathsf{X}=\mathit{True})+\mathsf{Pr}(\mathsf{X}=\mathit{False})=1$.
- *A* ***joint probability distribution*** *of the variables* $\mathsf{X}_1,\ldots,\mathsf{X}_n$ *is a probability distribution for the set of events* $\mathbf{X}_1\times\cdots\times\mathbf{X}_n$. *Variables* $\mathsf{X}_1,\ldots,\mathsf{X}_{k-1}$ *and* $\mathsf{X}_k,\ldots,\mathsf{X}_n$ *are* ***independent*** *if* $\mathsf{Pr}(x_1,\ldots,x_n)=\mathsf{Pr}(x_1,\ldots,x_{k-1})\mathsf{Pr}(x_k,\ldots,x_n)$ *for all* $(x_1,\ldots,x_n)\in\mathbf{X}_1\times\cdots\times\mathbf{X}_n$.
- *The* ***conditional distribution*** $\mathsf{Pr}(\mathsf{X}_1,\ldots,\mathsf{X}_n\mid\mathsf{Y}_1,\ldots,\mathsf{Y}_m)$ *of the variables* $\mathsf{X}_1,\ldots,\mathsf{X}_n$ *given the* ***evidences*** $\mathsf{Y}_1,\ldots,\mathsf{Y}_m$ *is defined as the probability distribution such that, fixed* $y_1\in\mathbf{Y}_1,\ldots,y_m\in\mathbf{Y}_m$ *with* $\mathsf{Pr}(y_1,\ldots,y_m)>0$, *we have* $\mathsf{Pr}(x_1,\ldots,x_n\mid y_1,\ldots,y_m)=\frac{\mathsf{Pr}(x_1,\ldots,x_n,y_1,\ldots,y_m)}{\mathsf{Pr}(y_1,\ldots,y_m)}$ *for all* $x_1\in\mathbf{X}_1,\ldots,x_n\in\mathbf{X}_n$.[4]
- *The* ***marginal probability*** *of variables* $\mathsf{X}_1,\ldots,\mathsf{X}_n$ *with respect to* $\mathsf{Y}_1,\ldots,\mathsf{Y}_m$ *is the sum of the probability distributions over* $\mathsf{X}_1,\ldots,\mathsf{X}_n$ *over all possible values of* $\mathsf{Y}_1,\ldots,\mathsf{Y}_m$, *that is,* $\sum_{y_1\in\mathbf{Y}_1,\ldots,y_m\in\mathbf{Y}_m}P(\mathsf{X}_1,\ldots,\mathsf{X}_n,y_1,\ldots,y_m)$. *The* ***marginal probability of the events*** $x_1\in\mathsf{X}_1,\ldots,x_n\in\mathsf{X}_n$ *with respect to* $\mathsf{Y}_1,\ldots,\mathsf{Y}_m$ *is the sum* $\sum_{y_1\in\mathbf{Y}_1,\ldots,y_m\in\mathbf{Y}_m}P(x_1,\ldots,x_n,y_1,\ldots,y_m)$.

A *Bayesian network* is a probabilistic graphical model representing a set of random variables and their conditional dependencies via a directed acyclic graph. The interest of Bayesian networks lies in the fact that they allow to represent joint probability distributions in a compact way, by exploiting conditional independencies between variables explicitly encoded in the network structure. They allow to efficiently compute marginal and conditional probability distributions of interest by exploiting these independencies.

Definition 3. *A* ***graph*** *is a pair* $\mathcal{G}=\langle V,\rightharpoonup\rangle$ *made of a set of vertices* V *and a set* $\rightharpoonup\subset V\times V$ *of edges. A* ***simple path*** $\mathcal{G}$ *is a sequence of* distinct *vertices* $v_1,\ldots,v_n$ *such that* $(v_i,v_{i+1})\in\rightharpoonup$ *for all* $i\in\{1,\ldots,n-1\}$. *A graph is* ***acyclic*** *if it contains no simple path* $v_1,\ldots,v_n$ *such that* $(v_n,v_1)\in\rightharpoonup$. *A* ***root*** *(resp.* ***leaf****) is a vertex* v *such that there is no* (v',v) *(resp.* (v,v')*) in* $\rightharpoonup$ *for any* $v'\in V$.

A ***Bayesian Network*** *is a triple* $\mathcal{B}=\langle V_{\mathcal{B}},\rightharpoonup_{\mathcal{B}},\mathcal{P}_{\mathcal{B}}\rangle$ *such that* $V_{\mathcal{B}}$ *is a set of random variables,* $\rightharpoonup_{\mathcal{B}}\subset V_{\mathcal{B}}\times V_{\mathcal{B}}$ *is a set of edges such that* $\langle V_{\mathcal{B}},\rightharpoonup_{\mathcal{B}}\rangle$ *form a directed acyclic graph, and* $\mathcal{P}_{\mathcal{B}}$ *is a map associating to each variable* $\mathsf{X}\in V_{\mathcal{B}}$ *a* ***conditional probability table*** *whose rows consist of a possible assignment of values to the variables in the set of* ***parents*** *of* X *(denoted* π_{X}*), together with the corresponding conditional probabilities for the events* $\mathsf{X}=\mathit{True}$ *and* $\mathsf{X}=\mathit{False}$ *as follows, where* $\pi_{\mathsf{X}}=\{\mathsf{Y}_1,\ldots,\mathsf{Y}_n\}$:

Row table:

$\mathsf{Y}_1=v_1$	$\cdots$	$\mathsf{Y}_n=v_n$	$\mathsf{Pr}(\mathsf{X}=\mathit{True}\mid\mathsf{Y}_1=v_1,\ldots,\mathsf{Y}_n=v_n)$	$\mathsf{Pr}(\mathsf{X}=\mathit{False}\mid\mathsf{Y}_1=v_1,\ldots,\mathsf{Y}_n=v_n)$

[4] We can always reduce (complex) conditional probabilities to a sequence of so-called *simple* conditional probabilities (i.e., conditional probabilities of a single variable given a set of other variables) by iteratively applying the *chain rule* of conditional probabilities, $\mathsf{Pr}(\mathsf{X},\vec{\mathsf{Y}}\mid\vec{\mathsf{Z}})=\mathsf{Pr}(\mathsf{X}\mid\vec{\mathsf{Y}},\vec{\mathsf{Z}})\cdot\mathsf{Pr}(\vec{\mathsf{Y}}\mid\vec{\mathsf{Z}})$.

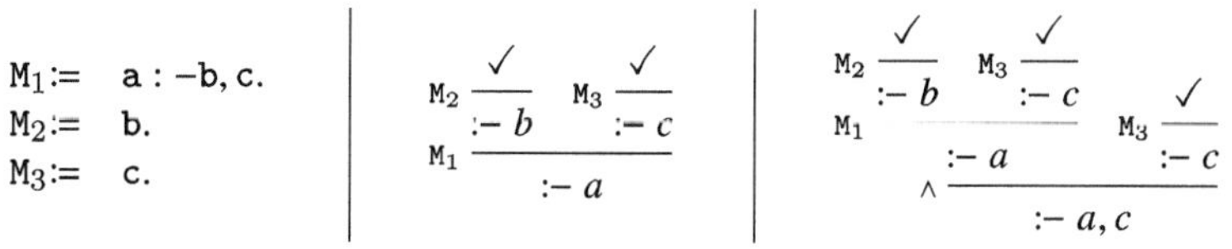

```
M1:=  a : −b, c.
M2:=  b.
M3:=  c.
```

$$\mathtt{M_1}\ \dfrac{\mathtt{M_2}\ \dfrac{\checkmark}{:\!-\ b} \quad \mathtt{M_3}\ \dfrac{\checkmark}{:\!-\ c}}{:\!-\ a}$$

$$\wedge\ \dfrac{\mathtt{M_1}\ \dfrac{\mathtt{M_2}\ \dfrac{\checkmark}{:\!-\ b} \quad \mathtt{M_3}\ \dfrac{\checkmark}{:\!-\ c}}{:\!-\ a} \quad \mathtt{M_3}\ \dfrac{\checkmark}{:\!-\ c}}{:\!-\ a, c}$$

Fig. 4. A Prolog program made of three methods $\mathtt{M_1}$, $\mathtt{M_2}$ and $\mathtt{M_3}$, and the representation of the computation of the two queries : −a. and : −a, c..

We represent Bayesian networks as in Fig. 1, where nodes represent variables and directed edges represent dependencies between them, while conditional probability tables are connected to the corresponding nodes with dashed lines, and, to avoid ambiguities, they include an extra row to indicate the order of the variables in the parent set we are considering.

In a Bayesian network $\mathcal{B} = \langle V, \rightharpoonup, \mathcal{P} \rangle$, the joint probability distribution of all variables in $\vec{\mathsf{X}}$ can be computed as the product of the conditional probability distributions of each variable given its parents in the graph $\langle \vec{\mathsf{X}}, \rightharpoonup \rangle$. This takes the name of *Factorization Theorem* (Theorem 1).

Theorem 1. *If* $\mathcal{B} = \langle V, \rightharpoonup, \mathcal{P} \rangle$ *is a Bayesian Network, then* $\prod_{\mathsf{X} \in V} \mathsf{Pr}(\mathsf{X} \mid \pi_{\mathsf{X}})$.

3 From Logic Programming to Linear Objects

Logic programming originated with Prolog [8], a language grounded in Horn clause logic and based on a goal-directed proof procedure (SLD-resolution). Prolog's computational interpretation relies on *unrestricted* reuse of program clauses, implicitly assuming that logical resources can be consumed arbitrarily many times. While this assumption is suitable for many symbolic tasks, it limits Prolog's expressiveness when modeling computations where resource usage matters as, e.g., state changes, process calculi, or probabilistic reasoning. For example, in Fig. 4 we show a simple Prolog program and two queries solved using it: while the first uses each method only once, the second query requires to use one of the methods twice to derive the goal.

The introduction of linear logic provided a refined logical foundation where resources are treated explicitly: in linear logic, propositions are consumed when used (unless marked as reusable). This perspective leads naturally to programming languages where the flow of computation corresponds to the controlled consumption and production of resources. Linear logic programming thus differs fundamentally from classical logic programming: instead of deriving consequences from static facts, it orchestrates a dynamic evolution of states represented as multisets of linear formulas.

Exploiting these ideas, Andreoli and Pareschi introduced **Linear Objects** (LO) [6,7], a logic programming language grounded in the multiplicative-additive fragment of linear logic (MALL). In LO, methods are Prolog-like multi-head clauses where both preconditions and post-conditions are represented as multisets of linear formulas (see Equation (1)). Its operational semantics is defined

$$\mathsf{exp}\ \frac{\mathsf{P}\ ;\ b_1,\ldots,b_m,\Gamma}{\mathsf{P},[\mathtt{h_1},\ldots,\mathtt{h_n}] \coloneq [\mathtt{b_1},\ldots,\mathtt{b_m}]\ ;\ h_1,\ldots,h_n,\Gamma} \qquad \mathcal{F}\ \frac{\vdash \Delta_{\mathsf{P}}, b_1,\ldots,b_m,\Gamma}{\vdash \Delta_{\mathsf{P}}, h_1^{\perp}\otimes\cdots\otimes h_n^{\perp}\otimes b_1 \parr\cdots\parr b_m, h_1,\ldots,h_n,\Gamma}$$

$$\mathsf{exp}^{\mathsf{mix}}\ \frac{\mathsf{P}\ ;\ \Gamma}{\mathsf{P},[\mathtt{h_1},\ldots,\mathtt{h_n}] \coloneq [.]\ ;\ h_1,\ldots,h_n,\Gamma} \qquad \mathcal{F}^{\mathsf{mix}}\ \frac{\vdash \Delta_{\mathsf{P}},\Gamma}{\vdash \Delta_{\mathsf{P}}, h_1^{\perp}\otimes\cdots\otimes h_n^{\perp}, h_1,\ldots,h_n,\Gamma}$$

$$\mathsf{term}\ \frac{}{[\mathtt{h_1},\ldots,\mathtt{h_n}] \coloneq [.]\ ;\ h_1,\ldots,h_n} \qquad \mathcal{F}\ \frac{}{\vdash h_1^{\perp}\otimes\cdots\otimes h_n^{\perp}, h_1,\ldots,h_n}$$

Fig. 5. Rules of the operational semantics of the multiplicative fragment of LO, and the corresponding synthetic inference rules.

$$\mathcal{F}_1 := a^{\perp}\otimes(b\parr c) \qquad \mathcal{F}_2 := b^{\perp} \qquad \mathcal{F}_3 := c^{\perp}$$

$$\mathcal{F}_1\ \dfrac{\mathcal{F}_2^{\mathsf{mix}}\ \dfrac{\mathcal{F}_3\ \dfrac{}{\vdash c^{\perp}, c}}{\vdash b^{\perp}, c^{\perp}, b, c}}{a^{\perp}\otimes(b\parr c), b^{\perp}, c^{\perp}, a} \qquad \mathcal{F}_3\ \dfrac{\mathcal{F}_1\ \dfrac{\mathcal{F}_2^{\mathsf{mix}}\ \dfrac{\vdash c}{\vdash b^{\perp}, b, c}}{\vdash a^{\perp}\otimes(b\parr c), b^{\perp}, a}}{\vdash a^{\perp}\otimes(b\parr c), b^{\perp}, c^{\perp}, a, c}$$

Fig. 6. The bipoles associated to the methods in Fig. 4, and two derivations in the synthetic sequent calculus reminding the one for the two queries in the same figure. Here the rightmost one get stuck because the method $\mathcal{F}_3 = c^{\perp}$ can only be used once.

in terms of proof search in linear logic: a state of the system is represented as a sequent containing the current multiset of goals and the current methods available to the program program itself, and a program execution corresponds to a proof search in linear logic, where the execution of each method corresponds to the application of a synthetic inference rule associated to a bipole formula representing the method. See Fig. 5 for the rules of the operational semantics of the multiplicative fragment of LO and the corresponding synthetic inference rules in $\mathsf{MLL}^{\mathsf{mix}}$. For example, the two Prolog queries in Fig. 4 are in a purely multiplicative fragment of LO as shown in Fig. 6. Here is possible to see how the first query can be solved by using each method once, while the second query get stuck because method $\mathtt{M_3}$ cannot be used twice.

In this section, we recall a small fragment of LO enriched with the mix rule, corresponding to the multiplicative fragment of linear logic $\mathsf{MLL}^{\mathsf{mix}}$ (Fig. 5), and we show (Sect. 3.1) how execution of a purely multiplicative LO program can characterize the absence of cycles in directed graphs.

3.1 From Exploring Trees to Exploring Directed Acyclic Graphs Using LO

We construct the encoding of a directed graph $\mathcal{G} = \langle V, \rightharpoonup \rangle$ by associating to each node v of a graph an atom a_v. Then, if the node v has parents $u_1,\ldots,u_n$ and m child nodes, we define a bipole containing literals representing 'half edges' connecting the node to its parents and child nodes. More precisely, we associate to the node v the bipole $\mathcal{F}_v$ made of the *tensor* ($\otimes$) of $m+1$ copies of $a_v^{\perp}$ together with the *par* ($\parr$) of all atoms $a_{u_1},\ldots,a_{u_n}$, as shown in Eq. (9) below.

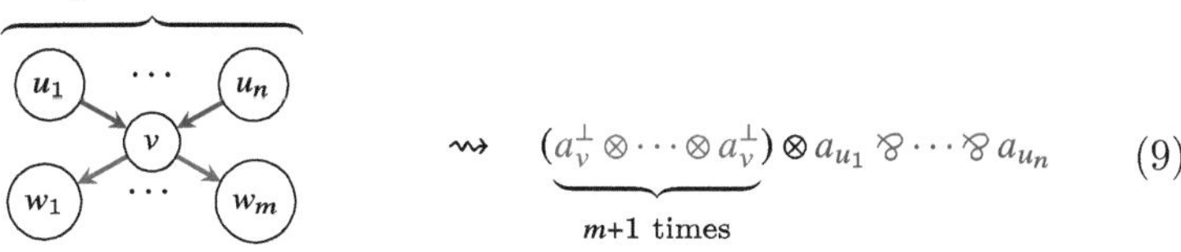

$$\rightsquigarrow \quad \underbrace{(a_v^\perp \otimes \cdots \otimes a_v^\perp)}_{m+1 \text{ times}} \otimes a_{u_1} \parr \cdots \parr a_{u_n} \tag{9}$$

Definition 4. *Let $\mathcal{G} = \langle V, \rightharpoonup \rangle$ be a graph, and $\mathbb{A}$ a set of atoms containing a subset of atoms $\{a_v \mid v \in V\}$ in one-to-one correspondence with V. The* ***encoding*** *of $\mathcal{G}$ is the multiset of bipoles $\Gamma_{\mathcal{G}}$ containing a bipole $\mathcal{F}_v$ for each $v \in V$ defined as Eq. (9). Note that the bipole of each root node is degenerate.*

Theorem 2. *Let $\mathcal{G} = \langle \{v_1, \ldots, v_n\}, \rightharpoonup \rangle$ be a graph. Then, $\mathcal{G}$ is acyclic iff $\vdash_{\mathsf{MLL}^{\mathsf{mix}}} \Gamma_{\mathcal{G}}, a_{v_1}, \ldots, a_{v_n}$.*

Proof (Sketch of Proof). There is a one-to-one correspondence between the sequence of nodes explored in a leaf-to-root traversal of the graph $\mathcal{G}$ and the sequence of bipoles used in a proof of $\vdash_{\mathsf{MLL}^{\mathsf{mix}}} \Gamma_{\mathcal{G}}, a_{v_1}, \ldots, a_{v_n}$.

Corollary 1. *Determining whether a set $\Gamma_{\mathcal{G}}$ of n bipoles that encodes a graph describes a directed acyclic graph can be decided in* LO *(with* mix*) in linear time.*

Proof. It follows from the proof of Theorem 2 after remarking that the expansion rules are reversible (see [26]) and that each method can be used at most once.

Remark 1. The derivation we construct to prove Theorem 2 reproduces a graph traversal from leaves to the roots. The multi-headed nature of the methods allows us to process the presence of multiple triggering conditions (in this case, if all children have been processed) without the need of aggregating this information in a single condition. This prevents the risk of creating races on (linear) resources that could potentially lead to deadlocks.

At the same time, we observe that if at any point the exploration of the graph could be separated into two independent explorations, then we could introduce a branching point in the search (and in the derivation using the mix-rule). However, such a branching point cannot be safely created preemptively because it could lead to deadlocks if resources are separated in the wrong way. For this reason, the mix rule is pushed into the rule $\mathsf{exp}^{\mathsf{mix}}$ of the operational semantics of LO, which allows handling multi-rooted graphs without the need of preemptively guessing how to separate the exploration of the graph into independent branches.

4 From LO to probLO

We introduce probLO, a probabilistic extension of LO suitable to model and reason about Bayesian networks. We start by defining the syntax of methods, conditionals, tables and programs. To simplify the presentation for the purpose of modeling Boolean Bayesian networks[5], we introduce a typing discipline on the atoms we use in our programs, and we limit the definition of probLO-conditionals to the case required to model simple conditional probability distributions of Boolean variables: we only allow two atoms per basic type, and we define conditionals to be made of two methods, each for one of the two Boolean values.

Definition 5. *Let* $\mathsf{X}_1, \ldots, \mathsf{X}_n$ *be random Boolean variables. For each variable* X_i*, we define two distinct atoms* $\mathtt{tt}_{\mathsf{X}_i}$ *and* $\mathtt{ff}_{\mathsf{X}_i}$ *of* ***type*** X_i*.*

A ***simple (Boolean) probLO-method*** *of* ***type*** $\mathsf{X}_1 \times \cdots \times \mathsf{X}_n :- \mathsf{Y}_1, \ldots, \mathsf{Y}_m$ *is a LO-method with* ***multi-head*** $[\mathtt{h}_1, \ldots, \mathtt{h}_\mathtt{n}]$ *of* ***length*** n *and* ***body*** $[\mathtt{b}_1, \ldots, \mathtt{b}_\mathtt{m}]$ *of* ***length*** m *annotated with a probability value* $p \in [0, 1]$ *written as follows:*

$$\mathtt{M} = p :: \overbrace{[\mathtt{h}_1, \ldots, \mathtt{h}_\mathtt{n}]}^{\textit{multi-head}} :- \overbrace{[\mathtt{b}_1, \ldots, \mathtt{b}_\mathtt{m}]}^{\textit{body}} \qquad \textit{or} \qquad \mathtt{M} = p :: \overbrace{[\mathtt{h}_1, \ldots, \mathtt{h}_\mathtt{n}]}^{\textit{multi-head}} :- [\overbrace{\quad\cdot\quad}^{\textit{empty body}}] \tag{10}$$

A ***probLO-method*** *of type* $\mathsf{X}^n \times \mathsf{Y}_1 \times \cdots \times \mathsf{Y}_m$ *is a multiset of simple probLO-methods of type* $\mathsf{X}^n \times \mathsf{Y}_1 \times \cdots \times \mathsf{Y}_m$*. A probLO-method is*

- *a (Boolean)* ***probLO-conditional*** *for the variable* X *if it is made of two simple methods with the same body and sum of their probability being 1:*

$$\mathsf{C}_{\mathsf{X}}^{\mathtt{b}_1, \ldots, \mathtt{b}_\mathtt{m}} = \begin{bmatrix} p_1 :: [\mathtt{tt}_\mathsf{X}, \ldots, \mathtt{tt}_\mathsf{X}] :- [\mathtt{b}_1, \ldots, \mathtt{b}_\mathtt{m}], \\ p_2 :: [\mathtt{ff}_\mathsf{X}, \ldots, \mathtt{ff}_\mathsf{X}] :- [\mathtt{b}_1, \ldots, \mathtt{b}_\mathtt{m}] \end{bmatrix} \quad \textit{with } p_1 + p_2 = 1 \textit{ (and heads of the same length)} \tag{11}$$

- *a* ***probLO-table*** *if it can be split into probLO-conditionals, one for each possible body* $[\mathtt{b}_1, \ldots, \mathtt{b}_\mathtt{m}]$ *(where each* $\mathtt{b}_\mathtt{i}$ *is of type* Y_i *for* $i \in \{1, \ldots, m\}$*).*

A ***(probLO-)program*** P *is a multiset of probLO tables.*

Remark 2. Even if we adopt the same way to annotate probabilities as in ProbLog [10,15], we weight methods with probabilities, not only facts. Note also that our probLO-conditionals do not support a constructor in which we can inject the choice directly in the head of a method. In fact, each method could be seen as a formula of the form $\bigoplus_{i=1}^{k}((h_i^\perp \otimes \cdots \otimes h_i^\perp) \otimes (b_1^i \parr \cdots \parr b_m^i))$ and each conditional could be seen as a formula $\left(\bigoplus_{i=1}^{2}(h_i^\perp \otimes \cdots \otimes h_i^\perp)\right) \otimes (b_1 \parr \cdots \parr b_m)$, which is similar to the way methods in LPADs [34] are defined. We opt to keep the syntax simple, and to avoid including an additional constructor in probLO, in order to get simple methods as purely multiplicative formulas.

The intuition behind a probLO-table is that it represents a conditional probability table of a variable X given some evidences $\mathsf{Y}_1, \ldots, \mathsf{Y}_m$. Each probLO-conditional in the probLO-table represents the two possible outcomes of the variable X (True or False) given a specific assignment of values to the evidences $\mathsf{Y}_1, \ldots, \mathsf{Y}_m$ represented by the body of the methods in the conditional. We later show when modeling Bayesian networks that, during the program execution, the current goal in the state allows it to uniquely choose a single simple method

[5] The syntax we present can be easily generalized to arbitrary discrete variables.

$$\text{term}\ \frac{}{p :: \mathsf{T}\ ;\ h_1, \ldots, h_n}\ \dagger \qquad \text{bra}\ \frac{p :: \mathsf{P}\ ;\ \Gamma, A \quad q :: \mathsf{P}\ ;\ \Gamma, B}{p + q :: \mathsf{P}\ ;\ \Gamma, A \,\&\, B}$$

$$\text{exp}^{\text{mix}}\ \frac{q :: \mathsf{P}\ ;\ \Gamma}{q \cdot p :: \mathsf{P}, \mathtt{T}\ ;\ \Gamma, h_1, \ldots, h_n}\ \dagger \qquad \text{exp}\ \frac{q :: \mathsf{P}\ ;\ \Gamma, b_1, \ldots, b_m}{q \cdot p :: \mathsf{P}, \mathtt{T}\ ;\ \Gamma, h_1, \ldots, h_n}\ \ddagger$$

$$\dagger := p :: [\mathtt{h}_1, \ldots, \mathtt{h}_n] \text{ :- } [.] \in \mathtt{T} \qquad \ddagger := p :: [\mathtt{h}_1, \ldots, \mathtt{h}_n] \text{ :- } [\mathtt{b}_1, \ldots, \mathtt{b}_m] \in \mathtt{T}$$

Fig. 7. Rules of the operational semantics of probLO. Both rules term and exp may instead be annotated by the method M applied by the rule.

every time a probLO-table is called (Lemma 1). At the same time, the use of probLO-tables instead of multiple simple probLO-modules allows for having a general-purpose goal-independent program that can adapt to the given goal, without the need to hard-code the specific goal in the program itself.

In probLO, we want to keep the same operational semantics of LO, where the usage of each method prevents its reuse, but we also want to extend it to account for the probabilistic nature of the methods. Therefore, in addition to keeping track of the current state of the program —i.e., its current goal and the currently available methods— we also want to keep track of the probability of reaching the current state from the program's initial state.

To this aim, we represent a state of a probLO program as a **weighted sequent** of the form $p :: \mathsf{P}\ ;\ \Gamma$ with p a probability value, P a probLO program and Γ a multiset of atoms representing the current goal. In Fig. 7 we show the rules of the operational semantics of probLO. Derivations in this system are built bottom-up and represent the possible executions of a probLO program. The probability value annotating the sequent root of a derivation has to be interpreted as the probability of successfully reaching the initial goal. We may also annotate these rules with the method M applied by the rule instead of term and exp. The rule bra is used to process goals containing additive conjunctions (&) that represent uncertain events; it splits the current execution into two sub-executions, one for each branch of the conjunction, summing up their probabilities.

Remark 3. If we forget about probability, we can easily see that each rule in the operational semantics of probLO corresponds to a synthetic rule in $\mathsf{MALL}^{\mathsf{mix}}$. In particular, the rules term and exp correspond to the synthetic rules in Eq. (8), while the rule bra corresponds to an instance of the rule & for the additive conjunction. Notice also that the 'probabilistic' part of the inference is not in the choice of which simple method to select in the case of tables, but in the application of the simple method itself. In fact, the selection of the simple method is completely deterministic and driven by the current state of the program. Said differently, the probabilistic nature of probLO is not in the choice of which method to apply, as if the connective $\oplus$ had a probabilistic nature (as in [18]), but in the success of the application itself.

4.1 Encoding Bayesian Networks in probLO

We now show how to encode Bayesian networks into probLO programs as one of the possible applications, using probLO-tables to model probabilistic choices. At the same time, we use additive connectives in the goal to represent the uncertainty on the values of Boolean variables: if the value of a Boolean variable X is unknown, we represent this as a 'superposition' of its possible values.

Notation 1. *From now on, we assume that the set of atoms* $\mathbb{A}$ *always includes a pair of atoms,* $\mathtt{tt}_{\mathsf{X}}$ *and* $\mathtt{ff}_{\mathsf{X}}$*, for each Boolean variable* X *we may consider, representing the events* X = *True and* X = *False in* $\mathbf{X}$*, respectively. To simplify the notation, we denote by* $\mathtt{w}_{\mathsf{X}}$ *an element in* $\{\mathtt{tt}_{\mathsf{X}}, \mathtt{ff}_{\mathsf{X}}\}$*, assuming that the corresponding* $x \in \mathbf{X}$ *is specified by the context.*

Definition 6 (Encoding Bayesian Networks in ***probLO*****).** *Let* $\mathcal{B} = \langle V, \rightharpoonup, \mathcal{P}\rangle$ *be a Bayesian network. We define the following for each variable* $\mathsf{X} \in V$ *with parents* $\{\mathsf{Y}_1, \ldots, \mathsf{Y}_h\}$ *and* m *children:*

1. *the simple probLO-method of type* $\mathbf{X} :- \mathbf{Y}_1 \times \cdots \times \mathbf{Y}_h$ *that is associated to the row of the conditional probability table of* X *for the event* $\langle x, y_1, \ldots, y_h\rangle \in \mathbf{X} \times \mathbf{Y}_1 \times \cdots \times \mathbf{Y}_h$*:*
$$\mathtt{M}_{\mathsf{X}}^{\langle x,y_1,\ldots,y_h\rangle} = [\mathtt{w}_{\mathsf{X}}, \ldots, \mathtt{w}_{\mathsf{X}}] :- [\mathtt{w}_{\mathsf{Y}_1}, \ldots, \mathtt{w}_{\mathsf{Y}_h}][\mathsf{Pr}(x \mid y_1, \ldots, y_h)] \tag{12}$$
where the multi-head contains $m+1$ *copies of* $\mathtt{w}_{\mathsf{X}}$*, and where* $\mathtt{w}_{\mathsf{Z}}$ *is either the atom* $\mathtt{tt}_{\mathsf{Z}}$ *(if* Z = *True) or* $\mathtt{ff}_{\mathsf{Z}}$ *(if* Z = *False) for each* $\mathsf{Z} \in \{\mathsf{X}, \mathsf{Y}_1, \ldots, \mathsf{Y}_h\}$*;*
2. *the probLO-table that is associated to the conditional probability table of the variable* X*:*
$$\mathtt{T}_{\mathsf{X}} = \begin{bmatrix} \mathtt{M}_{\mathsf{X}}^{\langle x^1,y_1^1,\ldots,y_h^1\rangle}, \\ \vdots \\ \mathtt{M}_{\mathsf{X}}^{\langle x^{2^h},y_1^{2^h},\ldots,y_h^{2^h}\rangle} \end{bmatrix} \quad \text{where } \{\langle x^i, y_1^i, \ldots, y_h^i\rangle \mid i \in \{1, \ldots, 2^{h+1}\}\} = \mathbf{X} \times \mathbf{Y}_1 \times \cdots \times \mathbf{Y}_h \tag{13}$$

The program $\mathsf{P}_{\mathcal{B}}$ *associated to* $\mathcal{B}$ *is the multiset of tables containing the table* $\mathtt{T}_{\mathsf{X}}$ *for each variable* $\mathsf{X} \in V$*.*

Example 1 The program associated to the Bayesian network in Fig. 1 is the multiset of tables $[\mathtt{T}_{\mathsf{C}}, \mathtt{T}_{\mathsf{W}}, \mathtt{T}_{\mathsf{T}}, \mathtt{T}_{\mathsf{S}}, \mathtt{T}_{\mathsf{R}}]$ where each table is defined in Fig. 8.

In the encoding of a Bayesian network $\mathcal{B}$ into a probLO-program $\mathsf{P}_{\mathcal{B}}$, as in Definition 6, each probLO-table $\mathtt{T}_{\mathsf{X}}$ is the encoding of the entire conditional probability table of the variable X in $\mathcal{B}$. However, although the interpretation of the method in $\mathsf{MALL}^{\mathsf{mix}}$ involves a synthetic rule that includes a non-deterministic choice enforced by the connective $\oplus$ (see, Eq. (8)), this choice can be made fully deterministic in each possible execution of the program $\mathsf{P}_{\mathcal{B}}$ by introducing suitable constraints into the program's initial goal. We can observe indeed that, if a derivation that uses a program $\mathsf{P}_{\mathcal{B}}$ with a goal containing an atom $\mathtt{w}_{\mathsf{X}} \in \{\mathtt{tt}_{\mathsf{X}}, \mathtt{ff}_{\mathsf{X}}\}$, for some variable X in V, has a state containing both atoms $\mathtt{tt}_{\mathsf{X}}$ and $\mathtt{ff}_{\mathsf{X}}$ then, this derivation cannot be successful anymore. We refer to this property as the *Boolean consistency* in the following.

Conditional probability	probLO Method	Conditional	Table
$\mathsf{Pr}(\mathsf{C} = \mathsf{True}) = 0.5$	$\mathtt{M}_{\mathsf{C}}^{\langle \mathsf{C=True} \rangle} = 0.5 :: [\mathtt{tt}_\mathsf{C}, \mathtt{tt}_\mathsf{C}, \mathtt{tt}_\mathsf{C}] :- [.]$	C_C	$\mathtt{T}_\mathsf{C}$
$\mathsf{Pr}(\mathsf{C} = \mathsf{False}) = 0.5$	$\mathtt{M}_{\mathsf{C}}^{\langle \mathsf{C=False} \rangle} = 0.5 :: [\mathtt{ff}_\mathsf{C}, \mathtt{ff}_\mathsf{C}, \mathtt{ff}_\mathsf{C}] :- [.]$		
$\mathsf{Pr}(\mathsf{R} = \mathsf{True} \mid \mathsf{C} = \mathsf{False}) = 0.2$	$\mathtt{M}_{\mathsf{R}}^{\langle \mathsf{R=True,C=False} \rangle} = 0.2 :: [\mathtt{tt}_\mathsf{R}, \mathtt{tt}_\mathsf{R}, \mathtt{tt}_\mathsf{R}] :- [\mathtt{ff}_\mathsf{C}]$	$\mathsf{C}_\mathsf{R}^{\mathtt{ff}_\mathsf{C}}$	$\mathtt{T}_\mathsf{R}$
$\mathsf{Pr}(\mathsf{R} = \mathsf{False} \mid \mathsf{C} = \mathsf{False}) = 0.8$	$\mathtt{M}_{\mathsf{R}}^{\langle \mathsf{R=False,C=False} \rangle} = 0.8 :: [\mathtt{ff}_\mathsf{R}, \mathtt{ff}_\mathsf{R}, \mathtt{ff}_\mathsf{R}] :- [\mathtt{ff}_\mathsf{C}]$		
$\mathsf{Pr}(\mathsf{R} = \mathsf{True} \mid \mathsf{C} = \mathsf{True}) = 0.8$	$\mathtt{M}_{\mathsf{R}}^{\langle \mathsf{R=True,C=True} \rangle} = 0.8 :: [\mathtt{tt}_\mathsf{R}, \mathtt{tt}_\mathsf{R}, \mathtt{tt}_\mathsf{R}] :- [\mathtt{tt}_\mathsf{C}]$	$\mathsf{C}_\mathsf{R}^{\mathtt{tt}_\mathsf{C}}$	
$\mathsf{Pr}(\mathsf{R} = \mathsf{False} \mid \mathsf{C} = \mathsf{True}) = 0.2$	$\mathtt{M}_{\mathsf{R}}^{\langle \mathsf{R=False,C=True} \rangle} = 0.2 :: [\mathtt{ff}_\mathsf{R}, \mathtt{ff}_\mathsf{R}, \mathtt{ff}_\mathsf{R}] :- [\mathtt{tt}_\mathsf{C}]$		
$\mathsf{Pr}(\mathsf{S} = \mathsf{True} \mid \mathsf{C} = \mathsf{False}) = 0.5$	$\mathtt{M}_{\mathsf{S}}^{\langle \mathsf{S=True,C=False} \rangle} = 0.5 :: [\mathtt{tt}_\mathsf{S}, \mathtt{tt}_\mathsf{S}] :- [\mathtt{ff}_\mathsf{C}]$	$\mathsf{C}_\mathsf{S}^{\mathtt{ff}_\mathsf{C}}$	$\mathtt{T}_\mathsf{S}$
$\mathsf{Pr}(\mathsf{S} = \mathsf{False} \mid \mathsf{C} = \mathsf{False}) = 0.5$	$\mathtt{M}_{\mathsf{S}}^{\langle \mathsf{S=False,C=False} \rangle} = 0.5 :: [\mathtt{ff}_\mathsf{S}, \mathtt{ff}_\mathsf{S}] :- [\mathtt{ff}_\mathsf{C}]$		
$\mathsf{Pr}(\mathsf{S} = \mathsf{True} \mid \mathsf{C} = \mathsf{True}) = 0.1$	$\mathtt{M}_{\mathsf{S}}^{\langle \mathsf{S=True,C=True} \rangle} = 0.1 :: [\mathtt{tt}_\mathsf{S}, \mathtt{tt}_\mathsf{S}] :- [\mathtt{tt}_\mathsf{C}]$	$\mathsf{C}_\mathsf{S}^{\mathtt{tt}_\mathsf{C}}$	
$\mathsf{Pr}(\mathsf{S} = \mathsf{False} \mid \mathsf{C} = \mathsf{True}) = 0.9$	$\mathtt{M}_{\mathsf{S}}^{\langle \mathsf{S=False,C=True} \rangle} = 0.9 :: [\mathtt{ff}_\mathsf{S}, \mathtt{ff}_\mathsf{S}] :- [\mathtt{tt}_\mathsf{C}]$		
$\mathsf{Pr}(\mathsf{W} = \mathsf{True} \mid \mathsf{R} = \mathsf{False}, \mathsf{S} = \mathsf{False}) = 0$	$\mathtt{M}_{\mathsf{W}}^{\langle \mathsf{W=True,R=False,S=False} \rangle} = 0 :: [\mathtt{tt}_\mathsf{W}] :- [\mathtt{ff}_\mathsf{S}, \mathtt{ff}_\mathsf{R}]$	$\mathsf{C}_\mathsf{W}^{\mathtt{ff}_\mathsf{R},\mathtt{ff}_\mathsf{S}}$	$\mathtt{T}_\mathsf{W}$
$\mathsf{Pr}(\mathsf{W} = \mathsf{False} \mid \mathsf{R} = \mathsf{False}, \mathsf{S} = \mathsf{False}) = 1$	$\mathtt{M}_{\mathsf{W}}^{\langle \mathsf{W=False,R=False,S=False} \rangle} = 1 :: [\mathtt{ff}_\mathsf{W}] :- [\mathtt{ff}_\mathsf{S}, \mathtt{ff}_\mathsf{R}]$		
$\mathsf{Pr}(\mathsf{W} = \mathsf{True} \mid \mathsf{R} = \mathsf{False}, \mathsf{S} = \mathsf{True}) = 0.9$	$\mathtt{M}_{\mathsf{W}}^{\langle \mathsf{W=True,R=False,S=True} \rangle} = 0.9 :: [\mathtt{tt}_\mathsf{W}] :- [\mathtt{tt}_\mathsf{S}, \mathtt{ff}_\mathsf{R}]$	$\mathsf{C}_\mathsf{W}^{\mathtt{ff}_\mathsf{R},\mathtt{tt}_\mathsf{S}}$	
$\mathsf{Pr}(\mathsf{W} = \mathsf{False} \mid \mathsf{R} = \mathsf{False}, \mathsf{S} = \mathsf{True}) = 0.1$	$\mathtt{M}_{\mathsf{W}}^{\langle \mathsf{W=False,R=False,S=True} \rangle} = 0.1 :: [\mathtt{ff}_\mathsf{W}] :- [\mathtt{tt}_\mathsf{S}, \mathtt{ff}_\mathsf{R}]$		
$\mathsf{Pr}(\mathsf{W} = \mathsf{True} \mid \mathsf{R} = \mathsf{True}, \mathsf{S} = \mathsf{False}) = 0.9$	$\mathtt{M}_{\mathsf{W}}^{\langle \mathsf{W=True,R=True,S=False} \rangle} = 0.9 :: [\mathtt{tt}_\mathsf{W}] :- [\mathtt{ff}_\mathsf{S}, \mathtt{tt}_\mathsf{R}]$	$\mathsf{C}_\mathsf{W}^{\mathtt{tt}_\mathsf{R},\mathtt{ff}_\mathsf{S}}$	
$\mathsf{Pr}(\mathsf{W} = \mathsf{False} \mid \mathsf{R} = \mathsf{True}, \mathsf{S} = \mathsf{False}) = 0.1$	$\mathtt{M}_{\mathsf{W}}^{\langle \mathsf{W=False,R=True,S=False} \rangle} = 0.1 :: [\mathtt{ff}_\mathsf{W}] :- [\mathtt{ff}_\mathsf{S}, \mathtt{tt}_\mathsf{R}]$		
$\mathsf{Pr}(\mathsf{W} = \mathsf{True} \mid \mathsf{R} = \mathsf{True}, \mathsf{S} = \mathsf{True}) = 0.99$	$\mathtt{M}_{\mathsf{W}}^{\langle \mathsf{W=True,R=True,S=True} \rangle} = 0.99 :: [\mathtt{tt}_\mathsf{W}] :- [\mathtt{tt}_\mathsf{S}, \mathtt{tt}_\mathsf{R}]$	$\mathsf{C}_\mathsf{W}^{\mathtt{tt}_\mathsf{R},\mathtt{ff}_\mathsf{S}}$	
$\mathsf{Pr}(\mathsf{W} = \mathsf{False} \mid \mathsf{R} = \mathsf{True}, \mathsf{S} = \mathsf{True}) = 0.01$	$\mathtt{M}_{\mathsf{W}}^{\langle \mathsf{W=False,R=True,S=True} \rangle} = 0.01 :: [\mathtt{ff}_\mathsf{W}] :- [\mathtt{tt}_\mathsf{S}, \mathtt{tt}_\mathsf{R}]$		
$\mathsf{Pr}(\mathsf{T} = \mathsf{True} \mid \mathsf{R} = \mathsf{False}) = 0.9$	$\mathtt{M}_{\mathsf{T}}^{\langle \mathsf{T=True,R=False} \rangle} = 0.9 :: [\mathtt{tt}_\mathsf{T}] :- [\mathtt{ff}_\mathsf{R}]$	$\mathsf{C}_\mathsf{T}^{\mathtt{ff}_\mathsf{R}}$	$\mathtt{T}_\mathsf{T}$
$\mathsf{Pr}(\mathsf{T} = \mathsf{False} \mid \mathsf{R} = \mathsf{False}) = 0.1$	$\mathtt{M}_{\mathsf{T}}^{\langle \mathsf{T=False,R=False} \rangle} = 0.1 :: [\mathtt{ff}_\mathsf{T}] :- [\mathtt{ff}_\mathsf{R}]$		
$\mathsf{Pr}(\mathsf{T} = \mathsf{True} \mid \mathsf{R} = \mathsf{True}) = 0.7$	$\mathtt{M}_{\mathsf{T}}^{\langle \mathsf{T=True,R=True} \rangle} = 0.7 :: [\mathtt{tt}_\mathsf{T}] :- [\mathtt{tt}_\mathsf{R}]$	$\mathsf{C}_\mathsf{T}^{\mathtt{tt}_\mathsf{R}}$	
$\mathsf{Pr}(\mathsf{T} = \mathsf{False} \mid \mathsf{R} = \mathsf{True}) = 0.3$	$\mathtt{M}_{\mathsf{T}}^{\langle \mathsf{T=False,R=True} \rangle} = 0.3 :: [\mathtt{ff}_\mathsf{T}] :- [\mathtt{tt}_\mathsf{R}]$		

Fig. 8. Conditional probabilities for variables of the Bayesian network of Fig. 1 and the corresponding probLO methods. Rows are grouped into conditionals and tables according to the third and fourth columns.

Lemma 1. *Let $\mathcal{B}$ be a Bayesian network and Γ a goal containing exactly one formula in $\{\mathtt{tt}_\mathsf{X}, \mathtt{ff}_\mathsf{X}, \mathtt{tt}_\mathsf{X} \& \mathtt{ff}_\mathsf{X}\}$ for each variable X in $\mathcal{B}$. Then, each branch of a successful derivation in the operational semantics of probLO starting from a state with goal Γ, never contains both atoms $\mathtt{tt}_\mathsf{X}$ and $\mathtt{ff}_\mathsf{X}$.*

We can finally prove that, given the encoding of a Bayesian network $\mathcal{B}$ into a probLO program $\mathsf{P}_\mathcal{B}$, the operational semantics of probLO in Fig. 7 correctly computes both joint and marginal probabilities over the variables of $\mathcal{B}$.

Theorem 3 (Computing *probLO*queries). *Let $\mathcal{B} = \langle V, \rightharpoonup, \mathcal{P} \rangle$ be a (Boolean) Bayesian network with variables $V = \{\mathsf{X}_1, \ldots, \mathsf{X}_n\}$. Then:*

1. *the state $p :: \mathsf{P}_\mathcal{B}\ ;\ \mathtt{w}_{\mathsf{X}_1}, \ldots, \mathtt{w}_{\mathsf{X}_n}$ is derivable in the operational semantics of probLO iff $p = \mathsf{Pr}(x_1 \ldots, x_n)$ is the joint probability of all variables in $\mathcal{B}$;*
2. *the state $p :: \mathsf{P}_\mathcal{B}\ ;\ \mathtt{w}_{\mathsf{X}_1}, \ldots, \mathtt{w}_{\mathsf{X}_m}, (\mathtt{tt}_{\mathsf{X}_{m+1}} \& \mathtt{ff}_{\mathsf{Y}_{m+1}}), \ldots, (\mathtt{tt}_{\mathsf{X}_n} \& \mathtt{ff}_{\mathsf{X}_n})$ is derivable in the operational semantics of probLO iff $p = \mathsf{Pr}(X_1 \ldots, X_m)$ is the marginal probability of the variables $\mathsf{X}_1, \ldots, \mathsf{X}_m$ in $\mathcal{B}$ with respect to the (marginal) variables $\mathsf{X}_{m+1}, \ldots, \mathsf{X}_n$.*

Proof (Sketch of Proof). (1) is proved similarly to Theorem 2, taking into account the probability of each method application, while (2) is proven by induction on the number of marginal variables, where the base case is given by the first point, and the inductive step follows from the invertibility of the rule & ([26]).

Corollary 2. *Computing joint and marginal probabilities in probLO costs at most as much as computing them in the standard way directly on the Bayesian network $\mathcal{B}$ i.e., $\mathcal{O}(n)$ for joint probabilities and $\mathcal{O}(n2^k)$ for marginal probabilities, with n the number of variables in $\mathcal{B}$ and k the number of marginal variables*

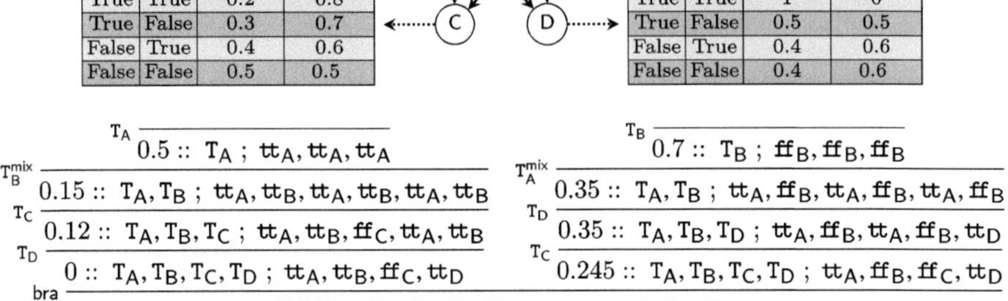

A=True	A=False
0.5	0.5

B=True	B=False
0.3	0.7

A	B	C=True	C=False
True	True	0.2	0.8
True	False	0.3	0.7
False	True	0.4	0.6
False	False	0.5	0.5

A	B	D=True	D=False
True	True	1	0
True	False	0.5	0.5
False	True	0.4	0.6
False	False	0.4	0.6

$$
\dfrac{\dfrac{\dfrac{\dfrac{\dfrac{}{0.5 :: \mathtt{T_A} \; ; \; \mathtt{tt_A}, \mathtt{tt_A}, \mathtt{tt_A}}\,\mathtt{T_A}}{0.15 :: \mathtt{T_A}, \mathtt{T_B} \; ; \; \mathtt{tt_A}, \mathtt{tt_B}, \mathtt{tt_A}, \mathtt{tt_B}, \mathtt{tt_A}, \mathtt{tt_B}}\,\mathtt{T_B^{mix}}}{0.12 :: \mathtt{T_A}, \mathtt{T_B}, \mathtt{T_C} \; ; \; \mathtt{tt_A}, \mathtt{tt_B}, \mathtt{ff_C}, \mathtt{tt_A}, \mathtt{tt_B}}\,\mathtt{T_C}}{0 :: \mathtt{T_A}, \mathtt{T_B}, \mathtt{T_C}, \mathtt{T_D} \; ; \; \mathtt{tt_A}, \mathtt{tt_B}, \mathtt{ff_C}, \mathtt{tt_D}}\,\mathtt{T_D} \qquad \dfrac{\dfrac{\dfrac{\dfrac{}{0.7 :: \mathtt{T_B} \; ; \; \mathtt{ff_B}, \mathtt{ff_B}, \mathtt{ff_B}}\,\mathtt{T_B}}{0.35 :: \mathtt{T_A}, \mathtt{T_B} \; ; \; \mathtt{tt_A}, \mathtt{ff_B}, \mathtt{tt_A}, \mathtt{ff_B}, \mathtt{tt_A}, \mathtt{ff_B}}\,\mathtt{T_A^{mix}}}{0.35 :: \mathtt{T_A}, \mathtt{T_B}, \mathtt{T_D} \; ; \; \mathtt{tt_A}, \mathtt{ff_B}, \mathtt{tt_A}, \mathtt{ff_B}, \mathtt{tt_D}}\,\mathtt{T_D}}{0.245 :: \mathtt{T_A}, \mathtt{T_B}, \mathtt{T_C}, \mathtt{T_D} \; ; \; \mathtt{tt_A}, \mathtt{ff_B}, \mathtt{ff_C}, \mathtt{tt_D}}\,\mathtt{T_C}}{0.245 :: \mathtt{T_A}, \mathtt{T_B}, \mathtt{T_C}, \mathtt{T_D} \; ; \; \mathtt{tt_A}, \mathtt{tt_B} \,\&\, \mathtt{ff_B}, \mathtt{ff_C}, \mathtt{tt_D}}\,\mathsf{bra}
$$

Fig. 9. A Bayesian network together with the computation of the marginal probability $\mathsf{Pr}(\mathsf{A} = \mathsf{True}, \mathsf{C} = \mathsf{False}, \mathsf{D} = \mathsf{True})$ in probLO.

In Fig. 9 we provide an alternative example of application of Theorem 3 with respect to the one in Fig. 2 to further highlight Remark 1.

5 Conclusion, Related and Future Works

We presented probLO, a linear logic programming languages whose multi-head methods are endowed with discrete probability values. This language adopts an operational and modular interpretation of probabilistic reasoning within the framework of Linear Objects (LO). We proved that probLO is expressive enough to encode Bayesian networks, and that its operational semantics correctly captures both joint and marginal probabilities through proof search.

Related Works on Bayesian Networks and Linear Logic. Related works on *Bayesian Proof Nets* provide a proof-theoretic foundation for Bayesian inference based on a graphical interpretation of proof nets of linear logic. In these works, the structure of a Bayesian network is reflected directly in the topology of the net, and probabilistic inferences correspond to normalization [13] or construction [27] steps in the proof net. Our approach differs in both methodology and operational interpretation: probLO implements Bayesian reasoning through computations using probabilistic LO-methods, which are interpreted as proof search in a system of derivable rules in $\mathsf{MALL}^{\mathsf{mix}}$. Said differently, while Bayesian Proof Nets emphasize a global and graph-based representation of probabilistic dependencies relying on the *correctness criterion* of proof nets, probLO adopts a modular rule-based perspective in which each node of the network is encoded as a $\mathsf{MALL}^{\mathsf{mix}}$ bipole (called *Bayesian bipoles* in [27]). Besides proof nets, there are also representations of Bayesian networks based on *Petri nets*, see e.g. [31].

Related Works on Probabilistic Logic Programming. The landscape of probabilistic logic programming is dominated by languages such as ProbLog [11], PRISM [32,33], LPADs [34] and others founded on the distribution semantics. These frameworks extend classical logic programming by attaching probabilities to facts or to rule heads, enabling probabilistic inference through weighted model counting or explanation-based inference. In ProbLog and PRISM, probabilistic choices are represented as sets of annotated alternatives, while LPADs extends Prolog with probabilistic disjunctive rule heads. In probLO, the probabilistic aspect is limited to the measure of the reachability of the goal, and the non-deterministic choices made during proof search are controlled by the goal itself.

Future Work. A direction for future work is to investigate how classical optimization techniques for Bayesian inference can be expressed within our framework. In particular, we aim to study whether algorithms such as *clique tree* (or *junction tree*) [19,23] can be captured by the operational semantics of probLO, by simple extensions of the language (and the underlying logic $\mathsf{MALL}^{\mathsf{mix}}$), or encoded as a collection of probLO methods. The idea is to exploit resource sensitivity of probLO and the modular structure of bipoles to model optimized inference procedures directly at the proof-theoretic level. More generally, we plan to explore the encoding of additional inference strategies, such as *variable elimination* [35] and *belief propagation* [30], to further assess the expressiveness and computational adequacy of probLO for Bayesian reasoning.

References

1. Abramsky, S., Jagadeesan, R.: Games and full completeness for multiplicative linear logic. J. Symb. Log. **59**(2), 543–574 (1994). https://doi.org/10.2307/2275407
2. Acclavio, M., Maieli, R.: Logic programming with multiplicative structures. Electron. Proc. Theor. Comput. Sci. **408**, 42–61 (2024). https://doi.org/10.4204/eptcs.408.3
3. Acclavio, M., Maieli, R.: Probabilistic linear logic programming with an application to bayesian network computations (extended version) (2026). https://arxiv.org/abs/2601.13270
4. Acclavio, M., Manara, G., Montesi, F.: Formulas as processes, deadlock-freedom as choreographies. In: Vafeiadis, V. (ed.) Programming Languages and Systems, pp. 23–55. Springer, Cham (2025). https://doi.org/10.1007/978-3-031-91118-7_2
5. Andreoli, J.M.: Logic programming with focusing proofs in linear logic. J. Log. Comput. **2**(3), 297–347 (1992)
6. Andreoli, J., Pareschi, R.: Lo and behold! concurrent structured processes. ACM SIGPLAN Not. **25**(10), 44–56 (1990). https://doi.org/10.1145/97946.97953
7. Andreoli, J.-M., Pareschi, R.: Logic programming with sequent systems. In: Schroeder-Heister, P. (ed.) ELP 1989. LNCS, vol. 475, pp. 1–30. Springer, Heidelberg (1991). https://doi.org/10.1007/BFb0038690
8. Clocksin, W.F., Mellish, C.S.: Programming in Prolog, 1st edn. Springer, Heidelberg (1981)
9. De Raedt, L., Kimmig, A.: Probabilistic (logic) programming concepts. Mach. Learn. **100**, 5–47 (2015). https://doi.org/10.1007/s10994-015-5494-z

10. De Raedt, L., Kimmig, A., Toivonen, H.: Problog: a probabilistic prolog and its application in link discovery. In: Proceedings of the 20th International Joint Conference on Artificial Intelligence (IJCAI), pp. 2462–2467 (2007)
11. De Raedt, L., Kimmig, A., Toivonen, H.: Problog: a probabilistic prolog for knowledge representation and reasoning. In: Proceedings of the 20th International Joint Conference on Artificial Intelligence (IJCAI), pp. 2462–2467 (2007)
12. Docef, A., Negulescu, R., Prunescu, M.: Using z3 to verify inferences in fragments of linear logic (2023). arXiv preprint arXiv:2309.13796
13. Ehrhard, T., Faggian, C., Pagani, M.: Bayesian networks and proof-nets: a proof-theoretical account of bayesian inference (2024). arXiv preprint arxiv:2412.20540
14. Eng, B., Seiller, T.: Multiplicative linear logic from a resolution-based tile system (2022). CoRR arxiv:2207.08465. https://doi.org/10.48550/arXiv.2207.08465
15. Fierens, D., et al.: Inference and learning in probabilistic logic programs using weighted Boolean formulas. In: Theory and Practice of Logic Programming (2015)
16. Girard, J.: Linear logic. Theor. Comput. Sci. **50**(1), 1–101 (1987). https://doi.org/10.1016/0304-3975(87)90045-4
17. Hodas, J.S., Miller, D.: Logic programming in a fragment of intuitionistic linear logic. Inf. Comput. **110**(2), 327–365 (1994)
18. Horne, R.: The sub-additives: a proof theory for probabilistic choice extending linear logic. In: 4th International Conference on Formal Structures for Computation and Deduction (FSCD 2019), p. 23-1. Schloss Dagstuhl–Leibniz-Zentrum für Informatik (2019)
19. Jensen, F.V.: An Introduction to Bayesian Networks. UCL Press (1996)
20. Kersting, K., De Raedt, L.: Bayesian logic programs. Technical report, arXiv (2000). https://doi.org/10.48550/arXiv.cs/0111058
21. Kobayashi, N.: Concurrent Linear Logic Programming. Ph.D. thesis, University of Tokyo (1996)
22. Kobayashi, N., Yonezawa, A.: Asynchronous communication model based on linear logic. In: Halstead, R.H., Ito, T. (eds.) Parallel Symbolic Computing: Languages, Systems, and Applications, pp. 331–336. Springer, Heidelberg (1993). https://doi.org/10.1007/BF01211602
23. Lauritzen, S.L., Spiegelhalter, D.J.: Local computations with probabilities on graphical structures and their application to expert systems. J. R. Stat. Soc. Series B (1988)
24. Liang, C.C., Miller, D.: Focusing and polarization in linear, intuitionistic, and classical logics. Theor. Comput. Sci. **410**(46), 4747–4768 (2009). https://doi.org/10.1016/j.tcs.2009.07.041
25. Maieli, R.: Retractile proof nets of the purely multiplicative and additive fragment of linear logic. In: Dershowitz, N., Voronkov, A. (eds.) LPAR 2007. LNCS (LNAI), vol. 4790, pp. 363–377. Springer, Heidelberg (2007). https://doi.org/10.1007/978-3-540-75560-9_27
26. Maieli, R.: A proof of the focusing theorem via mall proof nets. In: Proceedings of WoLLIC 2022. Lecture Notes in Computer Science, vol. 13468. Springer, Heidelberh (2022). https://doi.org/10.1007/978-3-031-15298-6_1
27. Maieli, R.: Bayesian proof nets: an encoding of bayesian networks in proof nets of linear logic. In: Lecture Notes in Networks and Systems, vol. 1198, pp. 142–152. Springer, Heidelberg (2025). https://doi.org/10.1007/978-3-031-76459-2_13
28. Miller, D.: A survey of the proof-theoretic foundations of logic programming. Theory Pract. Logic Program. **22**(6), 859–904 (2022). https://doi.org/10.1017/S1471068421000533

29. Miller, D., Nadathur, G., Pfenning, F., Scedrov, A.: Uniform proofs as a foundation for logic programming. Ann. Pure Appl. Logic **51**(1–2), 125–157 (1991). https://doi.org/10.1016/0168-0072(91)90068-W
30. Pearl, J.: Probabilistic Reasoning in Intelligent Systems. Morgan Kaufmann, Burlington (1988)
31. Pinl, A.: Probability Propagation Nets – Unveiling Structure and Propagations of Bayesian Networks by Means of Petri Nets. Phd thesis, Universität Koblenz-Landau, Campus Koblenz, Koblenz, Germany (2007)
32. Sato, T., Kameya, Y.: PRISM: A Logic-Based Probabilistic Modeling Language. Morgan Kaufmann, Burlington (1997)
33. Sato, T., Kameya, Y.: Parameter learning of logic programs for symbolic-statistical modeling. J. Artif. Intell. Res. **15**, 391–454 (2001)
34. Vennekens, J., Denecker, M., Bruynooghe, M.: Logic programs with annotated disjunctions. ACM Trans. Comput. Log. **7**(4), 1–37 (2006)
35. Zhang, N.L., Poole, D.L.: A simple approach to bayesian inference in belief networks. IEEE Trans. Syst. Man Cybern. (1994)

Matrix Coeffect Algebra for Interdependent Context Requirements

Osamu Miyazawa[1(✉)] and Shin-ya Nishizaki[2]

[1] School of Computing, Institute of Science Tokyo, Tokyo, Japan
miyazawa@lambda.cs.titech.ac.jp
[2] Center for Information Infrastructure, Institute of Science Tokyo, Tokyo, Japan
nisizaki@cs.titech.ac.jp

Abstract. Coeffects capture requirements that the environment imposes on programs. Petricek's structural coeffect calculus extends the simply typed lambda calculus with a type-and-coeffect system. In this framework, requirements such as variable reuse counts and the number of past values needed in dataflow languages are represented by scalars drawn from algebraic structures that relax some semiring axioms (coeffect algebras). However, existing scalar- and vector-based coeffect domains combine annotations componentwise and therefore do not naturally capture constraints between interacting contextual quantities, such as travel times between airports and departure times at airports. To address this limitation, we introduce *Matrix Coeffect Algebra*, a matrix-valued coeffect domain whose composition propagates requirements across contextual components, enabling constraints between interdependent quantities. We embed Matrix Coeffect Algebra into Petricek's structural coeffect calculus and prove its type safety via his translational semantics. A flight-timetable case study demonstrates that matrix-based coeffects enable dependency-aware static checking in a coeffect type system. Our technical contribution is a new matrix-valued coeffect algebra, used as an instantiation of Petricek's structural (schematic) coeffect calculus.

Keywords: coeffect calculus · matrix · type system · interdependent information

1 Introduction

1.1 Coeffect Calculus

Verifying how a program interacts with its execution context is a long-standing challenge in programming language research. *Effect systems* track the impact a program has on the outside world [5,7]; by contrast, *coeffect systems* represent requests from the environment to a program [9,11]. The *structural coeffect calculus* by Petricek et al. extends the simply typed lambda calculus by attaching context annotations to each free variable in the typing context [11].

M. Sperber and E. Komendantskaya (Eds.): FLOPS 2026, LNCS 16533, pp. 220–256, 2026.
https://doi.org/10.1007/978-981-92-0184-6_11

Existing coeffect calculi can combine multiple independent requirements by representing annotations as vectors [9], but they cannot easily express interdependent contextual information. We introduce *Matrix Coeffect Algebra* (MCA), a matrix-valued coeffect algebra for such interdependent information. In addition, we instantiate Petricek's structural coeffect calculus by interpreting its schematic rules over MCA (the resulting system is the *Matrix Coeffect Calculus*, MCC). In MCC, annotations are matrices that encode and compose dependencies between contextual quantities, enabling propagation across components.

1.2 Contributions

The main contributions of this paper are summarized below.

1. We define *Matrix Coeffect Algebra* (MCA), a matrix-valued coeffect domain for composing interdependent contextual requirements, and show that it satisfies the axioms of Petricek's structural coeffect framework (including the required algebraic laws and preorder).
2. We obtain the *Matrix Coeffect Calculus* (MCC) by instantiating Petricek's structural coeffect calculus with MCA (i.e., interpreting its schematic typing rules over the matrix domain), enabling dependency-aware static analysis within a type-and-coeffect system.
3. We use *Target Language for Matrix Coeffect* (TLMC), the extension of Petricek's target language with matrix-annotated contextual values and primitives that realize dependency propagation. We then give a type-preserving translation from MCC to TLMC, and establish type safety for MCC via type safety of TLMC.
4. We demonstrate MCC on a flight-timetable case study, showing that it can express and statically check interdependent contextual requirements in a representative scheduling scenario.

Prior scalar- and vector-based coeffect domains combine annotations componentwise, which makes interactions between contextual quantities difficult to express directly. In contrast, matrix-valued coeffects allow composition to mix components and propagate requirements across them, making mutual dependencies representable in the type system.

2 Motivation for Matrix Coeffects

We describe research on representing the interaction between a program and its execution environment, then explain that there are some problems that are difficult to express using these approaches, and finally demonstrate how such problems can be expressed using Matrix Coeffect Calculus.

2.1 Effects and Coeffects

Gifford and Lucassen [5,7] proposed the Effect System as an extension of simply typed lambda calculus to track the impact a program has on the outside world. For example, a typing judgment in the effect system can be expressed as follows:

$$\langle x : \tau \rangle \vdash \mathsf{print}\ x : \mathsf{unit}\ \&\ \{\mathsf{console}\}$$

This means that evaluating the term print x may produce an effect (screen output) on the console.

Meanwhile, Petricek [9,11] introduced the notion of *Coeffect* to represent the external environments that affect a program when it is executed, such as GPS availability or the execution environment, and proposed the Coeffect System, which extends the simply typed lambda calculus by attaching context annotations to free variables. The value used as a context annotation is called *Coeffect Scalar*. A coeffect scalar forms an algebra with two operations: multiplication $\circledast$ and addition $\oplus$. By selecting an appropriate algebra, different static analyses can be expressed uniformly. For example, the coeffect calculus can be used to express dataflow languages like Lucid [14] or Lustre [6]. In this case, the coeffect scalar is a natural number that represents the number of past values each free variable requires [9]. A typing judgment in the coeffect calculus for dataflow language can be expressed as follows:

$$\langle x : \tau, y : \tau \rangle @ \langle 2, 1 \rangle \vdash (\mathsf{prev}(\mathsf{prev}\ x)) + (\mathsf{prev}\ y) : \tau$$

prev, a built-in function in a dataflow language, returns the previous value of the operand. This judgment means that x requires two past values and y requires one past value.

2.2 Multiple Context Information

Existing coeffect calculi can combine multiple independent requirements by representing annotations as vectors [9]. For example, if you want to simultaneously express the number of past values needed in a dataflow language and the number of times a variable appears in bounded linear logic, you can express it as follows:

$$\langle x : \tau, y : \tau \rangle @ \langle \langle 2, 1 \rangle, \langle 0, 2 \rangle \rangle \vdash (\mathsf{prev}(\mathsf{prev}\ x)) + y + y : \tau$$

In this typing judgment, each free variable is annotated with a vector of size 2 as a coeffect scalar. The first component of the vector represents the number of past values needed, and the second component represents the number of times the variable appears. In this example, $\langle x : \tau, \dots \rangle @ \langle \langle 2, 1 \rangle, \dots \rangle$ means that the free variable x requires two past values and appears once in the term.

As previously explained, mutually independent pieces of information can be handled simultaneously by expressing the coeffect scalar as a vector. However, when one type of information depends on another type of information, it is difficult to express this using vectors. Next, as an example, consider a timetable of an international flight route.

2.3 Running Example: Flight-Timetable Constraint Propagation

Figure 1 shows a simple itinerary with three flights: JL43 (HND → LHR), BA318 (LHR → CDG), and AF1240 (CDG → AMS), where HND is Tokyo Haneda Airport, LHR is London Heathrow Airport, CDG is Paris Charles de Gaulle Airport, and AMS is Amsterdam Airport Schiphol. We use this as a running example of *interdependent* contextual information.

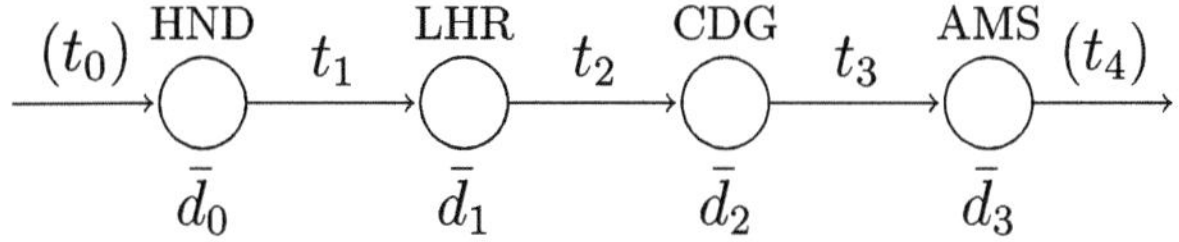

Fig. 1. Route map and timetable information. Each leg i has a duration t_i (given), and a timetable-imposed departure lower bound $\bar{d}_i$ (given). The analysis computes the propagated earliest feasible departure bounds d_i (outputs).

Inputs (Known Quantities). We assume the following are given:

- For each flight (leg) i, a nonnegative integer t_i denoting the *duration* of the leg. Concretely, t_i can include the flight time plus any mandatory transfer (connection) time required to be ready for the next leg.
- For each leg i, a *timetable-imposed lower bound* $\bar{d}_i$ on its departure time. Intuitively, $\bar{d}_i$ is the earliest possible departure time allowed by the published timetable (or other fixed operational constraints that the timetable encodes).
- Optionally, an initial lower bound d_{init} representing the earliest time the traveler can depart from the starting airport (in this example, HND).

Outputs (Unknown Quantities). The goal of the analysis is to compute *propagated lower bounds* $d_0, d_1, \ldots$ where each d_i is the earliest feasible departure time for leg i *after taking preceding legs into account*. Equivalently, we compute the least solution of the constraint system below.

Constraint System (What is Being Solved). For a linear itinerary (a path), the propagated bounds are characterized by:

$$d_0 \geq \max(\bar{d}_0, d_{\text{init}}), \qquad d_i \geq \max(\bar{d}_i,\ d_{i-1} + t_i) \ \ (i \geq 1).$$

Intuitively, leg i cannot depart earlier than (1) what the timetable allows ($\bar{d}_i$), and (2) the earliest time we can reach and be ready for the departure of leg i (from the previous leg), namely $d_{i-1} + t_i$.

Optional Validation (Feasible/Infeasible). If the actual scheduled departure times a_i are also given as inputs, we can additionally *validate* feasibility of the itinerary by checking $a_i \geq d_i$ for all i (and optionally report slack $a_i - d_i$). In this paper, we primarily focus on computing the lower bounds d_i.

The key point is that we must propagate and combine two *interdependent* quantities: durations t_i and departure lower bounds (constraints) $\bar{d}_i$. As explained later, Timetable Matrices (and thus our matrix-valued coeffect instantiation) provide a compact way to express and compose such max-plus propagation.

3 Matrix Coeffect Algebra and Calculus

Petricek's structural coeffect framework [9] validates typing, translational semantics, and type safety by requiring coeffect annotations to form a structural coeffect algebra (a semiring-like structure with relaxed axioms). To capture interdependent contextual requirements, we define *Matrix Coeffect Algebra* (MCA), where matrix composition provides a principled way to mix contextual components while still satisfying the framework's axioms. The resulting Matrix Coeffect Calculus (MCC) supports per-variable dependency propagation and can express interactions that componentwise scalar/vector domains cannot express without bespoke cross-component operators.

As a general rule, we use different letter families for different types of coeffect annotations: coeffect scalars $\mathsf{s}, \mathsf{t}, \ldots$, coeffect vectors $\mathbf{p}, \mathbf{q}, \mathbf{r}, \ldots$, and (timetable) matrices $\mathsf{R}, \mathsf{S}, \mathsf{T}, \ldots$.

3.1 Matrix Coeffect Algebra

Extending the structural coeffect algebra [9], we define the Matrix Coeffect Algebra.

Definition 1. *A matrix coeffect algebra* $(\mathcal{C}, \circledast, \oplus, \mathsf{use}, \mathsf{ign}, \leqslant)$ *is a structure where* $\mathcal{C}$ *is the set of* $n \times n$ *square matrices over a fixed domain (for some fixed* $n \geq 1$*), together with distinguished elements* $\mathsf{use}, \mathsf{ign} \in \mathcal{C}$*, binary operations* $\circledast, \oplus : \mathcal{C} \times \mathcal{C} \to \mathcal{C}$*, such that* $(\mathcal{C}, \circledast, \mathsf{use})$ *and* $(\mathcal{C}, \oplus, \mathsf{ign})$ *are monoids,* $\leqslant$ *is a preorder on* $\mathcal{C}$*, and the following distributivity axioms hold:*

$$(\mathsf{R} \oplus \mathsf{S}) \circledast \mathsf{T} = (\mathsf{R} \circledast \mathsf{T}) \oplus (\mathsf{S} \circledast \mathsf{T})$$
$$\mathsf{T} \circledast (\mathsf{R} \oplus \mathsf{S}) = (\mathsf{T} \circledast \mathsf{R}) \oplus (\mathsf{T} \circledast \mathsf{S})$$

These algebraic elements and operators directly correspond to the typing and structural rules defined later.

The use coeffect annotates each free variable, and the multiplication $\circledast$ is used when composing contexts during function application. The additive identity element ign, the additive operator $\oplus$, and the preorder $\leqslant$ underlie the structural rules of weakening, contraction, and subcoeffecting. In this section, we present two examples of matrix coeffect algebras.

We now give intuitive explanations of ign, use, and $\leqslant$. Informally, ign is the additive identity: adding ign does not increase any requirement, since $\oplus$ is defined componentwise by max. Dually, use corresponds to "no added requirement" at the scalar level (the value 0), and its lifted form yields the identity transformation for sequential propagation under $\circledast$. Finally, $A \leqslant B$ means that B imposes "larger" contextual requirement than A.

MCA's operations, elements, and preorder correspond to type rules of MCC (in Fig. 2). Once the coeffect domain (MCA) is fixed, MCC is obtained by instantiating Petricek's schematic rules. Table 1 summarizes how each algebraic ingredient is reflected in the typing and structural rules. In our timetable instance, $\oplus$ corresponds to taking the pointwise maximum of lower bounds.

Table 1. Correspondence between MCA and MCC.

	meaning in MCA	meaning in MCC	corresponding rule
$\oplus$	addition	requirement join	(CONTR)
$\circledast$	multiplication	requirement propagation	(APP)
ign	additive identity	ignored requirement	(WEAK)
use	multiplicative identity	use of a variable	(VAR)
$\leqslant$	preorder	subcoeffecting	(SUB)

Matrices of Real Numbers and Operations. As a simple example, any set of $n \times n$ real matrices equipped with matrix multiplication with identity matrix, matrix addition with zero matrix, and the pointwise order on entries forms a matrix coeffect algebra in the sense of Definition 1. We omit the routine verification of the axioms.

Timetable Matrix. In order to represent the flight timetables that we mentioned in Sect. 2.2, we define *Timetable Matrix*. First, we define the extended natural numbers (with $-\infty$) and the max operation. These are used in the Matrix Coeffect.

Definition 2. *Let $\mathbb{N}_0$ be the set of nonnegative integers. $-\infty$ denotes negative infinity adjoined to the extended natural numbers, and the following holds:*

- *For all $x \in \mathbb{N}_0$, $x \geq -\infty$*
- *For all $x \in \mathbb{N}_0$, $x + (-\infty) = -\infty + x = -\infty$*

Definition 3. *Let $\hat{\mathbb{N}} := \mathbb{N}_0 \cup \{-\infty\}$ be the set of extended natural numbers, including negative infinity. The binary operation* $\max : \hat{\mathbb{N}} \times \hat{\mathbb{N}} \to \hat{\mathbb{N}}$ *is defined by*

$$\max(x, y) = \begin{cases} x & \textit{if } x \geq y, \\ y & \textit{otherwise.} \end{cases}$$

It is commutative, associative, and idempotent, with identity $-\infty$ *(in other words,* $\max(x, -\infty) = x$*). For a finite nonempty set* $A = \{a_1, \ldots, a_n\} \subseteq \hat{\mathbb{N}}$*, we write* $\max A := \max(a_1, \ldots, a_n)$ *for the iterated binary maximum.*

Next, we define the Timetable Matrix.

Definition 4. *A Timetable Matrix is a* 2×2 *square matrix with natural numbers* $\mathbb{N}_0$ *and negative infinity* $-\infty$ *as its components and has the following structure:*

$$\begin{bmatrix} t & d \\ -\infty & 0 \end{bmatrix}$$

The (1,1) component of the matrix is $t \in \hat{\mathbb{N}}$*, and the (1,2) component is* $d \in \hat{\mathbb{N}}$*. The (2,1) component is always* $-\infty$*, and the (2,2) component is always* 0*. Let the set of Timetable Matrices be the matrix coeffect scalar* $\mathcal{C}$*.*

Definition 5. *The addition* $\oplus$ *of a Timetable Matrix is an operation that takes the maximum value for each component. That is, the following holds:*

$$\begin{bmatrix} t_2 & d_2 \\ -\infty & 0 \end{bmatrix} \oplus \begin{bmatrix} t_1 & d_1 \\ -\infty & 0 \end{bmatrix} = \begin{bmatrix} \max(t_2, t_1) & \max(d_2, d_1) \\ -\infty & 0 \end{bmatrix}$$

The identity element of addition is $\mathsf{ign} = \begin{bmatrix} -\infty & -\infty \\ -\infty & 0 \end{bmatrix}$.

Definition 6. *The multiplication* $\circledast$ *of a Timetable Matrix is an operation in which the sum of elements is replaced by* max *and the product of elements is replaced by* $+$*. That is, the following holds:*

$$\begin{aligned} \begin{bmatrix} t_2 & d_2 \\ -\infty & 0 \end{bmatrix} \circledast \begin{bmatrix} t_1 & d_1 \\ -\infty & 0 \end{bmatrix} &= \begin{bmatrix} \max(t_2 + t_1, d_2 + (-\infty)) & \max(t_2 + d_1, d_2 + 0) \\ \max((-\infty) + t_1, 0 + (-\infty)) & \max((-\infty) + d_1, 0 + 0) \end{bmatrix} \\ &= \begin{bmatrix} t_2 + t_1 & \max(t_2 + d_1, d_2) \\ -\infty & 0 \end{bmatrix} \end{aligned}$$

The identity element of multiplication is $\mathsf{use} = \begin{bmatrix} 0 & -\infty \\ -\infty & 0 \end{bmatrix}$.

Both $(\mathcal{C}, \oplus, \mathsf{ign})$ and $(\mathcal{C}, \circledast, \mathsf{use})$ form monoids; in particular, the set $\mathcal{C}$ is closed under the operations $\oplus$ and $\circledast$.

Observe that the multiplication of timetable matrices mixes different contextual quantities across components: for example, the resulting departure bound $\max(t_2 + d_1, d_2)$ depends on both a travel time and a departure constraint. While the same behavior could be encoded using pairs equipped with an ad hoc binary operation, the matrix representation makes this interaction explicit. Moreover, as discussed in Sect. 7, viewing timetable matrices as the $n = 1$ case of homogeneous transformation matrices suggests a uniform route to higher-dimensional generalizations.

Definition 7. *The preorder $\leqslant$ of a Timetable Matrix is the magnitude relationship between the (1,1) and (1,2) components of the matrix. That is, the following holds:*

$$\begin{bmatrix} t_1 & d_1 \\ -\infty & 0 \end{bmatrix} \leqslant \begin{bmatrix} t_2 & d_2 \\ -\infty & 0 \end{bmatrix} \quad \Leftrightarrow t_1 \leq t_2 \wedge d_1 \leq d_2$$

Since $\leq$ on t and d are preorders, $(\mathcal{C}, \leqslant)$ is also a preorder.

$\circledast$ and $\oplus$ in Timetable Matrices satisfy the distributivity axiom. Therefore,

$$(\mathcal{C}, \circledast, \oplus, \mathsf{use}, \mathsf{ign}, \leqslant)$$

is a matrix coeffect algebra. The proofs of the axioms are shown in Appendix A.

In the Timetable Matrix domain, $\max(\,\cdot\,)$ yields an *earliest permissible departure lower bound.* The realized departure time may be later due to independent operational constraints (e.g., airport occupancy, crew availability). Our typing discipline only requires programs to respect this lower bound; it does not force the realized time to be equal the bound.

Encoding a Leg as an Affine Max-Plus Update. Using Timetable Matrix domain, we can represent Sect. 2.3's problem. For each leg i, define a function on lower bounds:

$$F_i(x) \; = \; \max(x + t_i,\; \bar{d}_i).$$

This maps an incoming lower bound x (earliest possible departure of the previous stage) to the outgoing lower bound for leg i.

We represent F_i by the timetable matrix

$$R_i \; = \; \begin{bmatrix} t_i & \bar{d}_i \\ -\infty & 0 \end{bmatrix}.$$

Path Composition Corresponds to Matrix Multiplication. For the three-leg itinerary (JL43, BA318, AF1240), we form

$$R \; = \; R_2 \circledast R_1 \circledast R_0.$$

By Definition 6, the top-left component accumulates total duration, and the top-right component computes the propagated lower bound after composing the max-plus constraints:

$$R = \begin{bmatrix} t_2 + t_1 + t_0 & \max(t_2 + t_1 + \bar{d}_0,\; t_2 + \bar{d}_1,\; \bar{d}_2) \\ -\infty & 0 \end{bmatrix}.$$

Reading off the Output. If we include an explicit initial bound as a matrix $R_{\text{init}} = \begin{bmatrix} 0 & d_{\text{init}} \\ -\infty & 0 \end{bmatrix}$, then the fully propagated constraint after the itinerary is

$$R \circledast R_{\text{init}} = \begin{bmatrix} t_2 + t_1 + t_0 & \max(t_2 + t_1 + t_0 + d_{\text{init}},\; t_2 + t_1 + \bar{d}_0,\; t_2 + \bar{d}_1,\; \bar{d}_2) \\ -\infty & 0 \end{bmatrix}.$$

The top-right component is exactly the computed output lower bound for the final leg's departure. For intermediate bounds d_0, d_1, one can either (i) inspect partial products $R_0 \circledast R_{\text{init}}$, $R_1 \circledast R_0 \circledast R_{\text{init}}$, or (ii) compute them via the recurrence in Sect. 2.3.

Why the Matrix form Matters. The crucial feature is that multiplication $\circledast$ *mixes* the duration component and the lower-bound component in a principled way (via max-plus composition), which is precisely what we need for interdependent contextual constraints.

Lack of the Absorption Law. Note that Timetable Matrices do not satisfy the absorption law $\mathsf{R} \circledast \mathsf{ign} = \mathsf{ign}$ for all R, which would be required in a strict semiring setting. This is compatible with Petricek's structural coeffect algebra, which relaxes this axiom [9]. The lack of the absorption law means that there is no global "reset" element for sequential propagation ($\circledast$). This is not a drawback for our timetable setting; rather, it is consistent with the fact that previously accumulated constraints cannot be "undone" by later legs.

3.2 Structural Coeffect Calculus

This section reviews Petricek's structural coeffect calculus [9] in its schematic form. We obtain the Matrix Coeffect Calculus (MCC) by instantiating Petricek's framework with our Matrix Coeffect Algebra (MCA). The typing rules are Petricek's schematic typing rules, interpreted over MCA. In the remainder of this paper, we use the term MCC for the system obtained by interpreting the schematic typing rules over our MCA (Definition 1).

Definition 8 (Syntax). *The syntax for the structural coeffect calculus is as follows:*

$$e ::= x \mid n \mid \lambda x{:}\tau.\, e \mid e_1\ e_2 \mid \mathsf{let}\ x = e_1\ \mathsf{in}\ e_2$$
$$\tau ::= \mathsf{num} \mid \tau_1 \xrightarrow{\mathsf{s}} \tau_2$$

The structural coeffect calculus is based on simply typed lambda calculus. Terms are variables, numbers, lambda abstraction, application, and let-binding. Types of terms are number types and function types. s on the arrow of a function type is the coeffect scalar that is annotated to the formal parameter.

Definition 9 (Free Variable Context). *A free variable context is a vector whose elements are free variables and their types. The free variable context is defined as follows:*

$$\Gamma = \langle x_1 : \tau_1, \ldots, x_n : \tau_n \rangle \quad (\forall i, j.\ i \neq j \Rightarrow x_i \neq x_j)$$
$$\mathsf{len}(\langle x_1 : \tau_1, \ldots, x_n : \tau_n \rangle) = n$$

There are no overlaps within a free variable context. The length of the free variable context Γ*, i.e., the number of elements, is denoted as* $\mathsf{len}(\Gamma)$*. The concatenation of free variable contexts* Γ_1 *and* Γ_2 *is represented as* Γ_1, Γ_2*.*

In the structural coeffect calculus, each free variable is annotated with a coeffect scalar. The typing rules express the correspondence between free variable context and coeffect in the following format:

$$\langle x_1 : \tau_1, x_2 : \tau_2, \ldots, x_n : \tau_n \rangle @ \langle \mathsf{s}_1, \mathsf{s}_2, \ldots, \mathsf{s}_\mathsf{n} \rangle$$

Definition 10 (Coeffect Vector). *A vector of coeffect scalars such as* $\langle \mathsf{s}_1, \mathsf{s}_2, \ldots, \mathsf{s}_n \rangle$ *is called a* Coeffect Vector *and is denoted as* $\mathbf{p}, \mathbf{q}, \mathbf{r}$. *The order of the elements in a coeffect vector corresponds to the order of the variables in the free variable context. Similarly to free variable contexts, the length of a coeffect vector* $\mathbf{r}$ *is denoted as* $\mathsf{len}(\mathbf{r})$. *The concatenation of coeffect vectors* $\mathbf{p}$ *and* $\mathbf{q}$ *is denoted as* $\mathbf{p} +\!\!+ \mathbf{q}$.

Definition 11 (Coeffect Vector Multiplication). *We define* $\otimes$, *which extends the coeffect scalar multiplication* $\circledast$ *to the coeffect vector.* $\otimes$ *applies the coeffect scalar multiplication to each element of the coeffect vector. If* t *is a coeffect scalar and* $\mathbf{r} = \langle \mathsf{r}_1, \mathsf{r}_2, \ldots, \mathsf{r}_n \rangle$, *then* $\mathsf{t} \otimes \mathbf{r} = \langle \mathsf{t} \circledast \mathsf{r}_1, \mathsf{t} \circledast \mathsf{r}_2, \ldots, \mathsf{t} \circledast \mathsf{r}_n \rangle$.

Typing Rules

$$\frac{}{x : \tau \,@\, \langle \mathsf{use} \rangle \vdash x : \tau}\ (\textsc{Var}) \qquad \frac{}{\langle\rangle \,@\, \langle\rangle \vdash n : \mathsf{num}}\ (\textsc{Const})$$

$$\frac{\Gamma_1 \,@\, \mathbf{p} \vdash e_1 : \tau_1 \xrightarrow{\mathsf{s}} \tau_2 \quad \Gamma_2 \,@\, \mathbf{q} \vdash e_2 : \tau_1}{\Gamma_1, \Gamma_2 \,@\, \mathbf{p} +\!\!+ (\mathsf{s} \otimes \mathbf{q}) \vdash e_1\, e_2 : \tau_2}\ (\textsc{App}) \qquad \frac{\Gamma, x : \tau_1 \,@\, \mathbf{r} +\!\!+ \langle \mathsf{s} \rangle \vdash e : \tau_2}{\Gamma \,@\, \mathbf{r} \vdash \lambda x{:}\tau_1.\, e : \tau_1 \xrightarrow{\mathsf{s}} \tau_2}\ (\textsc{Abs})$$

$$\frac{\Gamma_1 \,@\, \mathbf{p} \vdash e_1 : \tau_1 \qquad \Gamma_2, x : \tau_1 \,@\, \mathbf{q} +\!\!+ \langle \mathsf{s} \rangle \vdash e_2 : \tau_2}{\Gamma_1, \Gamma_2 \,@\, (\mathsf{s} \otimes \mathbf{p}) +\!\!+ \mathbf{q} \vdash \mathsf{let}\ x = e_1\ \mathsf{in}\ e_2 : \tau_2}\ (\textsc{Let})$$

Structural Rules

$$\frac{\Gamma \,@\, \mathbf{r} \vdash e : \tau}{\Gamma, x : \tau_1 \,@\, \mathbf{r} +\!\!+ \langle \mathsf{ign} \rangle \vdash e : \tau}\ (\textsc{Weak}) \qquad (x \notin \Gamma)$$

$$\frac{\Gamma_1, x : \tau_1, y : \tau_2, \Gamma_2 \,@\, \mathbf{p} +\!\!+ \langle \mathsf{s}, \mathsf{t} \rangle +\!\!+ \mathbf{q} \vdash e : \tau}{\Gamma_1, y : \tau_2, x : \tau_1, \Gamma_2 \,@\, \mathbf{p} +\!\!+ \langle \mathsf{t}, \mathsf{s} \rangle +\!\!+ \mathbf{q} \vdash e : \tau}\ (\textsc{Exch})$$

$$\frac{\Gamma_1, y : \tau_1, z : \tau_1, \Gamma_2 \,@\, \mathbf{p} +\!\!+ \langle \mathsf{s}, \mathsf{t} \rangle +\!\!+ \mathbf{q} \vdash e : \tau}{\Gamma_1, x : \tau_1, \Gamma_2 \,@\, \mathbf{p} +\!\!+ \langle \mathsf{s} \oplus \mathsf{t} \rangle +\!\!+ \mathbf{q} \vdash e[z, y \leftarrow x] : \tau}\ (\textsc{Contr})$$

$$\frac{\Gamma \,@\, \mathbf{p} +\!\!+ \langle \mathsf{s}' \rangle +\!\!+ \mathbf{q} \vdash e : \tau}{\Gamma \,@\, \mathbf{p} +\!\!+ \langle \mathsf{s} \rangle +\!\!+ \mathbf{q} \vdash e : \tau}\ (\textsc{Sub}) \qquad (\mathsf{s}' \leqslant \mathsf{s})$$

Fig. 2. Typing rules and structural rules

The combination of a free variable context and its corresponding coeffect vector $\Gamma @\mathbf{r}$ is collectively called a *context.*

Definition 12 (Typing Rules and Structural Rules). *The typing of a term takes the following form:*

$$\Gamma @\mathbf{r} \vdash e : \tau$$

The typing rules and structural rules are shown in Fig. 2. The typing rules follow the usual reading. (Var) annotates a variable with the unit coeffect use, whereas (Const) assigns no requirements to constants. (App) propagates contextual demands from formal to actual parameters via scalar multiplication, and (ABS) internalizes the coeffect of the bound variable into the function type; (LET) can be derived from these. The structural rules (WEAK), (EXCH), (CONTR), and (SUB) correspond to weakening, exchange, contraction, and subcoeffecting, and are justified by the identity element ign, the commutative structure of coeffect vectors, the additive operator $\oplus$, and the preorder $\leqslant$, respectively.

We use the structural coeffect calculus of Fig. 2 as a schema and interpret its annotations in the Matrix Coeffect Algebra. We call the resulting matrix-annotated system the Matrix Coeffect Calculus.

Definition 13 (Matrix Coeffect Calculus). *Let* $(\mathcal{C}, \circledast, \oplus, \mathsf{use}, \mathsf{ign}, \leqslant)$ *be the Matrix Coeffect Algebra of Definition 1. The Matrix Coeffect Calculus is defined by interpreting the schema of Fig. 2 over* $\mathcal{C}$*. Concretely, coeffect scalars range over* $\mathcal{C}$*, and multiplication, addition, the units* use *and* ign*, and the preorder are interpreted as* $\circledast, \oplus, \mathsf{use}, \mathsf{ign}, \leqslant$*, respectively.*

4 Translational Semantics and Type Safety

We give MCC an operational interpretation by translating closed programs to a comonadic target language where contextual values and their composition are explicit. This translation makes dependency propagation by matrix annotations operationally concrete and supports a modular type-safety argument.

In this section, we adapt Petricek's translational semantics for the structural coeffect calculus [9] to MCC. Concretely, we translate MCC programs into a *target language*—an extension of the simply typed lambda calculus with comonadic constructs. We then define reduction rules for the target language and establish type safety.

4.1 Translational Semantics

Target Language for Matrix Coeffect. Following Petricek [9], we use a comonadic target language as our compilation target. We call this language *Target Language for Matrix Coeffect* (TLMC), which is an extension of the Petricek target language for matrix coeffect annotations. Overall, TLMC is based on Petricek's target language: we keep the same induced-semantics architecture via contextual values and comonadic structure. Our extensions are (i) replacing scalar/vector annotations with matrix annotations and (ii) adding a small number of domain-specific primitives (e.g. leg for timetables, explained later) that update matrix annotations to realize dependency propagation at runtime. All other constructs and reduction rules are inherited unchanged.

Contextual Value Mc. Following Petricek's translational semantics of coeffects, TLMC makes run-time contexts explicit as *contextual values* as follows:

$$\mathsf{Mc}\langle (S_0, v_0), \ldots, (S_k, v_k) \rangle$$

A contextual value packages the values of free variables (corresponding to v_i) together with their annotations in an indexed comonad type; in our setting, these annotations are *matrices* (corresponding to S_i) that record how contextual requirements propagate and interact.

Type Constructor C. The type constructor C classifies such contextual values Mc; for example, C takes the following form:

$$C^{\langle \mathsf{S}_1,\ldots \mathsf{S}_k\rangle}(\llbracket\tau_1\rrbracket\times\cdots\times\llbracket\tau_k\rrbracket)$$

Intuitively, it is the type of contexts storing values of types $\llbracket\tau_i\rrbracket$ (corresponding to Mc's v_i) together with matrix annotations S_i (corresponding to v_i's annotation S_k).

Standard Operations. The translation uses the standard comonadic operations as follows:

$$\mathsf{counit}_{\mathsf{use}} : C^{\langle \mathsf{use}\rangle}\tau \to \tau$$

$$\mathsf{cobind}_{\mathsf{s},\mathbf{r}} : (C^{\mathbf{r}}\tau_1 \to \tau_2) \to (C^{\mathsf{s}\otimes\mathbf{r}}\tau_1 \to C^{\langle \mathsf{s}\rangle}\tau_2)$$

counit extracts the underlying value from a contextual value (discarding the context information), and cobind lifts a computation that inspects a contextual value into one that produces a contextual value. In our translation, counit is only used on single-component contextual values. Operationally, cobind is the mechanism by which translated terms evaluate with access to their surrounding context, and it ensures that subsequent computations can continue to observe and propagate matrix annotations through contextual values.

Structural Operations. In addition to standard operations, TLMC provides structural operations as follows:

$$\begin{aligned}
\mathsf{merge}_{\mathbf{p},\mathbf{q}} &: C^{\mathbf{p}}\tau_1 \times C^{\mathbf{q}}\tau_2 \;\to\; C^{\mathbf{p}+\!\!+\mathbf{q}}(\tau_1\times\tau_2)\\
\mathsf{split}_{\mathbf{p},\mathbf{q}} &: C^{\mathbf{p}+\!\!+\mathbf{q}}(\tau_1\times\tau_2) \;\to\; C^{\mathbf{p}}\tau_1 \times C^{\mathbf{q}}\tau_2\\
\mathsf{dup}_{\mathsf{s},\mathsf{t}} &: C^{\langle \mathsf{s}\oplus\mathsf{t}\rangle}\tau \;\to\; C^{\langle \mathsf{s},\mathsf{t}\rangle}(\tau\times\tau)
\end{aligned}$$

These operations realize the structural manipulations of contexts required by the structural coeffect calculus (weakening, contraction, and exchange). These primitives operate directly on matrix-annotated contextual values, reflecting the algebraic combination of requirements computed by the source typing rules.

Syntax, Typing Rules, and Reduction Rules for TLMC. The extension to the syntax of the target language is shown below:

$$\begin{aligned}
v &::= \cdots \mid \mathsf{Mc}\langle (S_0, v_0), \ldots, (S_k, v_k)\rangle\\
e &::= \cdots \mid \mathsf{Mc}\langle (S_0, e_0), \ldots, (S_k, e_k)\rangle
\end{aligned}$$

The full syntax is shown in Appendix B.1. According to the addition of Mc into the target language, we extend typing rules and reduction rules, as shown in Fig. 3. The typing and reduction rules for the target language are given in Appendices B.2 and B.3.

Translational Form. Each typing judgment $\Gamma \mathbin{@} \mathbf{r} \vdash e : \tau$ in MCC is interpreted as a function $f : [\![\Gamma \mathbin{@} \mathbf{r}]\!] \to [\![\tau]\!]$ in TLMC by translation rules. This interpretation preserves types and reflects coeffect annotations in the context, forming an indexed comonad structure. The translation of contexts and types is defined as follows:

$$\begin{aligned}
[\![\langle x_1 : \tau_1, \ldots, x_n : \tau_n\rangle @ \langle \mathsf{s}_1, \ldots, \mathsf{s}_n\rangle]\!] &= C^{\langle \mathsf{s}_1, \ldots \mathsf{s}_n\rangle}([\![\tau_1]\!] \times \cdots \times [\![\tau_n]\!]) \\
[\![\mathsf{num}]\!] &= \mathsf{num} \\
[\![\tau_1 \xrightarrow{\mathsf{t}} \tau_2]\!] &= C^{\langle \mathsf{t}\rangle}[\![\tau_1]\!] \to [\![\tau_2]\!]
\end{aligned}$$

Based on these mappings, each typing rule is translated into a function in the target language. If $\Gamma = \langle x_1 : \tau_1, \ldots, x_k : \tau_k\rangle$ then we may write $[\![\tau_1]\!] \times \cdots \times [\![\tau_k]\!]$ as $[\![\Gamma]\!]$.

Typing Rule

$$\frac{\forall i \in \{0, \ldots, k\}.\, \Gamma \vdash e_i : \tau_i}{\Gamma \vdash \mathsf{Mc}\langle (S_0, e_0), \ldots, (S_k, e_k)\rangle : C^{\langle \mathsf{S}_0, \ldots, \mathsf{S}_k\rangle}(\tau_0 \times \cdots \times \tau_k)}\ (\text{Mc})$$

Reduction Rules

$$\begin{aligned}
&(\mathit{counit})\ \mathsf{counit}_{\mathsf{use}}\ \mathsf{Mc}\langle(\mathsf{use}, v_0)\rangle \rightsquigarrow v_0 \\
&(\mathit{cobind})\ \mathsf{cobind}_{\mathsf{S}, \langle \mathsf{T}_0, \ldots, \mathsf{T}_k\rangle}\ f\ \mathsf{Mc}\langle (S \circledast T_0, v_0), \ldots, (S \circledast T_k, v_k)\rangle \\
&\qquad \rightsquigarrow \mathsf{Mc}\langle (S, f(\mathsf{Mc}\langle (T_0, v_0), \ldots, (T_k, v_k)\rangle))\rangle \\
&(\mathit{merge})\ \mathsf{merge}_{\langle \mathsf{S}_0, \ldots, \mathsf{S}_k\rangle, \langle \mathsf{T}_0, \ldots, \mathsf{T}_l\rangle}\ (\mathsf{Mc}\langle (S_0, v_0), \ldots, (S_k, v_k)\rangle, \mathsf{Mc}\langle (T_0, v_0'), \ldots, (T_l, v_l')\rangle) \\
&\qquad \rightsquigarrow \mathsf{Mc}\langle (S_0, v_0), \ldots, (S_k, v_k), (T_0, v_0'), \ldots, (T_l, v_l')\rangle \\
&(\mathit{split})\ \mathsf{split}_{\langle \mathsf{S}_0, \ldots, \mathsf{S}_k\rangle, \langle \mathsf{T}_0, \ldots, \mathsf{T}_l\rangle}\ \mathsf{Mc}\langle (S_0, v_0), \ldots, (S_k, v_k), (T_0, v_0'), \ldots, (T_l, v_l')\rangle \\
&\qquad \rightsquigarrow (\mathsf{Mc}\langle (S_0, v_0), \ldots, (S_k, v_k)\rangle, \mathsf{Mc}\langle (T_0, v_0'), \ldots, (T_l, v_l')\rangle) \\
&(\mathit{dup})\ \mathsf{dup}_{\mathsf{S}, \mathsf{T}}\ \mathsf{Mc}\langle (S \oplus T, v)\rangle \rightsquigarrow (\mathsf{Mc}\langle (S, v)\rangle, \mathsf{Mc}\langle (T, v)\rangle)
\end{aligned}$$

Fig. 3. Extension of typing and reduction rules for target language

Translation Rules. We present two representative translation rules: abstraction and application. Complete translation rules are given in Appendix B.4.

Abstraction

$$\frac{[\![\Gamma, x : \tau_1 @ \mathbf{r} +\!\!+ \langle \mathsf{s}\rangle \vdash e : \tau_2]\!] = f}{[\![\Gamma @ \mathbf{r} \vdash \lambda x{:}\tau_1.\, e : \tau_1 \xrightarrow{\mathsf{s}} \tau_2]\!] = \lambda\rho.\lambda\nu.f(\mathsf{merge}_{\mathbf{r}, \langle \mathsf{s}\rangle}(\rho, \nu))}$$

where,

$$\begin{aligned}
f &: C^{\mathbf{r} +\!\!+ \langle \mathsf{s}\rangle}([\![\Gamma]\!] \times [\![\tau_1]\!]) \to [\![\tau_2]\!] \\
\rho &: C^{\mathbf{r}}[\![\Gamma]\!] \\
\nu &: C^{\langle \mathsf{s}\rangle}[\![\tau_1]\!] \\
\mathsf{merge}_{\mathbf{r}, \langle \mathsf{s}\rangle} &: C^{\mathbf{r}}[\![\Gamma]\!] \times C^{\langle \mathsf{s}\rangle}[\![\tau_1]\!] \to C^{\mathbf{r} +\!\!+ \langle \mathsf{s}\rangle}([\![\Gamma]\!] \times [\![\tau_1]\!])
\end{aligned}$$

Thus,

$$\lambda\rho.\lambda\nu.f(\mathsf{merge}_{\mathbf{r},\langle\mathsf{s}\rangle}(\rho,\nu)) : C^{\mathbf{r}}[\![\Gamma]\!] \to (C^{\langle\mathsf{s}\rangle}[\![\tau_1]\!] \to [\![\tau_2]\!]).$$

This corresponds to the interpretation of $[\![\Gamma@\mathbf{r} \vdash \lambda x{:}\tau_1.e : \tau_1 \xrightarrow{\mathsf{s}} \tau_2]\!]$. The merge operation combines the contexts according to the coeffect annotations. It combines the ambient context ρ with the argument contextual value ν to form the extended context expected by f.

Application

$$\frac{\begin{array}{r}[\![\Gamma_1@\mathbf{p} \vdash e_1 : \tau_1 \xrightarrow{\mathsf{s}} \tau_2]\!] = f \\ [\![\Gamma_2@\mathbf{q} \vdash e_2 : \tau_1]\!] = g\end{array}}{[\![\Gamma_1,\Gamma_2@\mathbf{p}{+\!\!+}(\mathsf{s}\otimes\mathbf{q}) \vdash e_1e_2 : \tau_2]\!] = \lambda\rho.\mathsf{let}\ (ctx_1, ctx_2) = \mathsf{split}_{\mathbf{p},\mathsf{s}\otimes\mathbf{q}}\ \rho\ \mathsf{in}\ f\ ctx_1(\mathsf{cobind}_{\mathsf{s},\mathbf{q}}\ g\ ctx_2)}$$

where f, g are translations of e_1, e_2. The split operation partitions the combined context, and cobind pushes the function's coeffect annotation s to the argument context (componentwise via $\otimes$), ensuring correct coeffect handling.

A concrete example of translation and reduction is given in Appendix E.

4.2 Type Safety of TLMC

This section provides the two technical ingredients used to justify stuck-freedom for closed MCC programs under the induced execution model (translate, then evaluate): (i) the translation from MCC to TLMC preserves typing (Theorem 1), and (ii) TLMC is type safe (Theorem 4). We define execution of a closed MCC judgment by evaluating its TLMC translation, following Petricek's translational-semantics approach [9]. Combining (i) and (ii), well-typed closed source terms never get stuck under this induced operational behavior. Due to space limitations, full proofs of the theorems and auxiliary lemmas are presented in Appendix C.

Theorem 1 (Well-typedness of the translation from MCC to TLMC). *Given a typing derivation of the closed MCC judgment $\langle\rangle@\langle\rangle \vdash e : \tau$, let f be its TLMC translation, written as follows:*

$$\frac{[\![(\dots)]\!] \quad = (\dots)}{[\![\langle\rangle@\langle\rangle \vdash e : \tau]\!] = \quad f}$$

Then f is well-typed: $\vdash f : [\![\langle\rangle@\langle\rangle]\!] \to [\![\tau]\!]$.

Here, the ellipses $(\dots)$ on the left stand for the premises of the MCC typing derivation (i.e., the immediate sub-judgements of the last typing rule). The corresponding $(\dots)$ on the right denote the TLMC translations of those premises, which are functions taking a contextual value as an argument. The translation is defined by recursion on the typing derivation; the complete set of translation clauses is given in Appendix B.4. Intuitively, $[\![\langle\rangle@\langle\rangle]\!]$ is the type of contextual values (a matrix-annotated context) supplied to the translated program.

Lemma 1 characterizes the possible canonical forms of well-typed terms and is used in the proof of the progress theorem.

Lemma 1 (canonical forms of TLMC). *For all terms e and types τ, if $\vdash e : \tau$, and e is a value, then:*

1. *If $\tau = \mathsf{num}$ then $e = n$ for some n*
2. *If $\tau = \tau_1 \to \tau_2$ then $e = \lambda x.e'$ for some x, e'*
3. *If $\tau = \tau_1 \times \cdots \times \tau_n$ then $e = (v_1, \ldots, v_n)$ for some v_i*
4. *If $\tau = C^{\langle \mathsf{S}_0, \ldots, \mathsf{S}_k \rangle}(\tau_0 \times \cdots \times \tau_k)$ then $e = \mathsf{Mc}\langle (S_0, v_0), \ldots, (S_k, v_k) \rangle$ for some matrices S_i and v_i.*

Lemma 2 (preservation under substitution of TLMC). *For all Γ, e, e', τ, τ', if $\Gamma, x : \tau \vdash e : \tau'$ and $\Gamma \vdash e' : \tau$ then $\Gamma \vdash e[x \leftarrow e'] : \tau'$.*

Theorem 2 (type preservation of TLMC). *If $\Gamma \vdash e : \tau$ and $e \rightsquigarrow e'$ then $\Gamma \vdash e' : \tau$.*

Theorem 3 (progress of TLMC). *If $\Gamma \vdash e : \tau$ then either e is a value or there exists e' such that $e \rightsquigarrow e'$.*

Theorem 4 (type safety of TLMC). *If $\Gamma \vdash e : \tau$ and $e \rightsquigarrow^* e'$, then*

1. *$\Gamma \vdash e' : \tau$*
2. *either e' is a value, or there exists e'' such that $e' \rightsquigarrow e''$*

5 Example: Timetable Matrix

5.1 Timetable Language

In this section, we present a small Timetable Language as an instance of the Matrix Coeffect Calculus. It extends the structural coeffect calculus with its own syntax and typing rules to address the multiple-context problem introduced in Sect. 2.2, using the Timetable Matrix from Sect. 3.1 as a coeffect scalar. The syntax and typing rules added by the Timetable Language are shown below:

Syntax

$$e ::= \cdots \mid \mathsf{leg}\ S\ e$$

Typing Rule

$$\frac{\Gamma @ \mathbf{r} \ \vdash \ e : \tau}{\Gamma @ \mathsf{S} \otimes \mathbf{r} \ \vdash \ \mathsf{leg}\ S\ e : \tau}\ (\textsc{Leg})$$

The term $\mathsf{leg}\, S\, e$ represents one leg e of an itinerary, with a Timetable Matrix S as its constraint. Its typing rule (Leg) treats S as a coeffect scalar and updates the coeffect vector of e by multiplying by S. Figure 4 illustrates a derivation for $(\lambda w{:}\tau.\, \mathsf{leg}\, S_2(\mathsf{leg}\, S_1\, w))(\mathsf{leg}\, S_0\, x)$, where the final constraint on x is $(\mathsf{S}_2 \circledast \mathsf{S}_1) \circledast \mathsf{S}_0$.

$$\dfrac{\mathcal{D}_A \qquad \dfrac{\dfrac{}{x : \tau \,@\, \langle \mathsf{use} \rangle \vdash x : \tau}\ (\textsc{Var})}{x : \tau \,@\, \langle \mathsf{S}_0 \rangle \vdash \mathsf{leg}\ S_0\ x : \tau}\ (\textsc{Leg})}{x : \tau \,@\, \langle \mathsf{S}_2 \circledast \mathsf{S}_1 \circledast \mathsf{S}_0 \rangle \vdash (\lambda w{:}\tau.\, \mathsf{leg}\ S_2(\mathsf{leg}\ S_1\ w))(\mathsf{leg}\ S_0\ x) : \tau}\ (\textsc{App})$$

$\mathcal{D}_{\mathbf{A}}$:

$$\dfrac{\dfrac{\dfrac{\dfrac{}{w : \tau \,@\, \langle \mathsf{use} \rangle \vdash w : \tau}\ (\textsc{Var})}{w : \tau \,@\, \langle \mathsf{S}_1 \rangle \vdash \mathsf{leg}\ S_1\ w : \tau}\ (\textsc{Leg})}{w : \tau \,@\, \langle \mathsf{S}_2 \circledast \mathsf{S}_1 \rangle \vdash \mathsf{leg}\ S_2(\mathsf{leg}\ S_1\ w) : \tau}\ (\textsc{Leg})}{\langle\rangle @ \langle\rangle \vdash \lambda w{:}\tau.\, \mathsf{leg}\ S_2(\mathsf{leg}\ S_1\ w) : \tau \xrightarrow{\mathsf{S}_2 \circledast \mathsf{S}_1} \tau}\ (\textsc{Abs})$$

Fig. 4. An example of type derivation for timetable language

A more concrete example of a derivation tree is given in Appendix E.

5.2 TLMC-TT: A Target Language Instance for Timetable Language

To execute well-typed Timetable programs, we define an induced execution model for well-typed Timetable programs via translation to a target language, following the induced-semantics pattern of Sect. 4.2. A well-typed closed Timetable term is executed by translating it to a target term and evaluating the result in the target semantics.

Syntax $\quad e ::= \cdots \mid \mathsf{peel}_{\mathsf{S},\mathbf{p}}\, e \qquad K ::= \cdots \mid \mathsf{peel}_{\mathsf{S},\mathbf{p}}\, \_$

Typing

$$\dfrac{\Gamma \vdash e : C^{\langle \mathsf{S}\circledast\mathsf{P}_0, \ldots, \mathsf{S}\circledast\mathsf{P}_k \rangle}(\tau_0 \times \cdots \times \tau_k)}{\Gamma \vdash \mathsf{peel}_{\mathsf{S},\langle \mathsf{P}_0,\ldots,\mathsf{P}_k\rangle}\, e : C^{\langle \mathsf{P}_0,\ldots,\mathsf{P}_k\rangle}(\tau_0 \times \cdots \times \tau_k)}\ (\textsc{Peel})$$

Translation

$$\dfrac{[\![\Gamma @ \mathbf{p} \vdash e : \tau]\!] = f}{[\![\Gamma @ (\mathsf{S} \otimes \mathbf{p}) \vdash \mathsf{leg}\, S\, e : \tau]\!] = \lambda \rho.\, f(\mathsf{peel}_{\mathsf{S},\mathbf{p}}\, \rho)}\ (\mathrm{leg})$$

Reduction

$$(\mathit{peel}) \quad \mathsf{peel}_{\mathsf{S},\langle \mathsf{P}_0,\ldots,\mathsf{P}_k\rangle}\, \mathsf{Mc}\langle (S \circledast P_0, v_0), \ldots, (S \circledast P_k, v_k) \rangle \rightsquigarrow \mathsf{Mc}\langle (P_0, v_0), \ldots, (P_k, v_k) \rangle$$

Fig. 5. TLMC-TT (we assume $\mathbf{p} = \langle \mathsf{P}_0, \ldots, \mathsf{P}_k \rangle$).

TLMC-TT and the peel *Primitive.* We denote by TLMC-TT the extension of TLMC for the Timetable Language. The only domain-specific extension needed here is a single target-level primitive, which we call peel. Intuitively, peel accounts for one itinerary segment at run time: it removes ("peels off") an outer timetable matrix S that has been propagated to the current contextual value. Concretely, it maps a contextual value whose annotations have the shape $\mathsf{S} \circledast \mathsf{P}_i$ back to one whose annotations are P_i.

We deliberately distinguish names between the source and target levels. In the Timetable Language instance, the source construct leg is translated to the target primitive peel (Fig. 5). More generally, for any MCC instance with domain-specific source primitives, we expect to introduce corresponding target primitives—peel-like operations—that realize the operational behavior of those source primitives on contextual values, while keeping the rest of TLMC unchanged.

Why Well-Typed Programs do not get Stuck. The PEEL typing rule ensures that peel can only be applied to contextual values with annotations of the form $\mathsf{S} \circledast \mathsf{P}_\mathsf{i}$, so the reduction rule for peel is always applicable in the new progress case introduced by timetables. Apart from peel (and its evaluation frame), TLMC-TT inherits the syntax, typing, and reduction rules of TLMC unchanged. Appendix D proves that translating and evaluating a well-typed closed Timetable term does not get stuck (i.e., it either is a value or can take a reduction step) via (i) well-typedness of the translation and (ii) type safety of TLMC-TT.

6 Related Work

Research on coeffects has developed along several complementary lines. Petricek et al. introduced the first coeffect calculus, which initially assigned a single annotation to whole expressions (flat coeffects) [10]. This was later refined into the structural coeffect calculus, where coeffects are tracked per variable [11]. The structural calculus admits structural rules such as weakening, exchange, contraction, and subcoeffecting, each justified by corresponding algebraic properties of the coeffect domain. By selecting suitable algebraic structures, one can recover both the flat and structural styles of analysis. Our key difference from prior structural-coeffect domains is how annotations combine: matrix multiplication provides a principled way to mix components, so requirements on one contextual quantity can constrain another. This yields a per-variable coeffect analysis that captures interactions that componentwise scalar- and vector-based domains do not naturally express without bespoke cross-component operators.

Brunel et al. proposed a quantitative type system grounded in linear and bounded linear logic [1]. Brunel et al.'s system differs from Petricek's in several respects: it relies on semirings rather than relaxed algebraic structures, composes coeffects additively during function application rather than multiplicatively, and includes a dedicated typing rule, written (coeff), for language-specific co-handlers such as resource consumption [1]. While Petricek's calculus does not feature such a rule, extensions via translational semantics and type-safety proofs can incorporate primitives in a similar spirit, as shown in his dataflow case studies. Unlike Brunel et al.'s system, which assumes strict semiring properties, our approach is based on a relaxed semiring structure that better accommodates practical contextual dependencies.

Ghica and Smith proposed a resource-aware typing discipline for program scheduling, parameterized by a resource semiring; one notable instance uses 2×2

homogeneous matrices to represent one-dimensional affine transformations [3,4]. Our use of matrices is different in both role and interpretation. In their setting, matrices encode *numeric resource transformations* that support scheduling analyses, whereas in our setting a matrix is a *coeffect annotation* that encodes dependencies between contextual quantities and supports propagation across components within a type-and-coeffect discipline. In particular, our matrices are not restricted to a fixed 2×2 form: their dimension is determined by the number of contextual quantities being tracked, and entries represent cross-component interaction (interdependence) that is difficult to express with componentwise scalar/vector domains.

The underlying algebraic structure also differs. Ghica and Smith instantiate their framework with conventional numeric semiring structures (e.g., standard arithmetic on numbers, yielding affine-style composition), while our timetable analysis is based on $\hat{\mathbb{N}}$ with max as the additive operator and ordinary addition as the multiplicative operator, reflecting constraint combination and sequential accumulation of durations, respectively. Moreover, our development is explicitly an instantiation of Petricek's structural coeffect calculus with a matrix-valued coeffect algebra, together with an induced (translational) semantics and type-safety result. Thus, although both lines of work employ matrices, they do so for different semantic purposes and with different algebraic and metatheoretic commitments.

Gaboardi et al. proposed a method for combining effects and coeffects by introducing graded distributive laws for graded monads and comonads [2]. In contrast, our work focuses solely on coeffects, although one could imagine taking matrices as grades, which we leave for future work.

Several works have applied coeffects to practical software problems. To address dependency hell, where a single program simultaneously requires multiple incompatible versions of a library, Tanabe et al. developed the λ_{VL} calculus [12,13]. By mapping versions to computational resources, their type system can be understood as an instance of Brunel et al.'s quantitative coeffect system. Matsuyama introduced effects and coeffects into choreographic programming [8]. By representing endpoints using effect and coeffect annotations, their system can statically restrict the endpoints that may participate in a communication. This framework is inspired by Gaboardi et al.'s combined effect-and-coeffect setting. In contrast to these works, which use scalar coeffects to track a single class of requirements (such as versions or endpoints), our contribution is to extend the structural coeffect calculus with matrix-valued coeffects in order to capture interdependent contextual quantities.

7 Conclusion and Future Work

7.1 Conclusion

We presented the Matrix Coeffect Calculus, a matrix-based coeffect system that supports interdependent contextual requirements by allowing annotations to propagate constraints across components. We defined the Matrix Coeffect Algebra, provided an operational interpretation via TLMC, proved type safety, and demonstrated the approach using timetable constraints.

7.2 Future Work

The Timetable Matrices introduced in this work can be seen as the case $n = 1$ of the general $(n+1) \times (n+1)$ homogeneous transformation matrix. In our formulation, rather than manipulating homogeneous coordinate vectors directly, we use matrices corresponding to diagonal homogeneous transformations; these form a restricted yet expressive subclass. For clarity of exposition, we restricted our study to the one-dimensional setting. However, higher-dimensional generalizations of Timetable Matrices are expected to be useful for applications involving multiple interdependent contextual constraints. Future work includes developing generalized Matrix Coeffect Algebras based on such higher-dimensional structures and studying their typing and semantic properties.

Furthermore, we plan to explore additional application domains for the Matrix Coeffect Calculus, implement it in a practical programming language with type inference and tooling, and investigate systematic methods for designing domain-specific matrix coeffect algebras. In the short term, we plan to implement a prototype type checker that computes matrix-valued coeffects for a small DSL (e.g., a realistic checker for flight itineraries based on the Timetable Language). In the long term, we plan to investigate integration as an extension of an existing coeffect-aware language (e.g., Granule). Key challenges include inferring matrix sizes/indices, producing user-friendly error messages for violated constraints, and scaling up matrix operations.

Other Potential Instances. While our running example is flight timetables, the matrix-valued approach is not specific to that domain. In general, one might choose a scalar domain that models a notion of requirement (e.g., lower bounds with $(\hat{\mathbb{N}}, \max, +)$) and then use matrices to express cross-component interaction and propagation. As further instances, we might expect: (i) build systems and data pipelines, where matrix annotations propagate interdependent bounds such as lower bounds on completion time (and, potentially, freshness/version constraints) across a dependency graph; (ii) power/thermal throttling, where component-wise budgets are coupled by a shared global constraint, making cross-component interaction essential; and (iii) multi-stage real-time and streaming constraints, where latency, jitter, and buffering requirements interact and must be propagated together. A key challenge in such instances is designing the underlying scalar operators and corresponding domain-specific target primitives (such as peel in TLMC-TT) so that they satisfy the structural coeffect requirements while faithfully capturing the intended constraint propagation.

A Properties of the Timetable Matrix

We show that the Timetable Matrix satisfies the axioms required of a structural coeffect algebra in the sense of Petricek [9]. In this section, suppose $\mathcal{C}$ is a set of Timetable Matrices.

A.1 Monoid: Associativity and Identity Element

Lemma 3. *Associativity of addition*

$$\forall \mathsf{R}_1, \mathsf{R}_2, \mathsf{R}_3 \in \mathcal{C}.\ (\mathsf{R}_1 \oplus \mathsf{R}_2) \oplus \mathsf{R}_3 = \mathsf{R}_1 \oplus (\mathsf{R}_2 \oplus \mathsf{R}_3).$$

Proof. Let $\mathsf{R}_1 = \begin{bmatrix} t_1 & d_1 \\ -\infty & 0 \end{bmatrix}$, $\mathsf{R}_2 = \begin{bmatrix} t_2 & d_2 \\ -\infty & 0 \end{bmatrix}$, $\mathsf{R}_3 = \begin{bmatrix} t_3 & d_3 \\ -\infty & 0 \end{bmatrix}$.

$$\begin{aligned} (\mathsf{R}_1 \oplus \mathsf{R}_2) \oplus \mathsf{R}_3 &= (\begin{bmatrix} t_1 & d_1 \\ -\infty & 0 \end{bmatrix} \oplus \begin{bmatrix} t_2 & d_2 \\ -\infty & 0 \end{bmatrix}) \oplus \mathsf{R}_3 \\ &= \begin{bmatrix} \max(t_1, t_2) & \max(d_1, d_2) \\ -\infty & 0 \end{bmatrix} \oplus \begin{bmatrix} t_3 & d_3 \\ -\infty & 0 \end{bmatrix} \\ &= \begin{bmatrix} \max(t_1, t_2, t_3) & \max(d_1, d_2, d_3) \\ -\infty & 0 \end{bmatrix} \end{aligned}$$

$$\begin{aligned} \mathsf{R}_1 \oplus (\mathsf{R}_2 \oplus \mathsf{R}_3) &= \mathsf{R}_1 \oplus (\begin{bmatrix} t_2 & d_2 \\ -\infty & 0 \end{bmatrix} \oplus \begin{bmatrix} t_3 & d_3 \\ -\infty & 0 \end{bmatrix}) \\ &= \begin{bmatrix} t_1 & d_1 \\ -\infty & 0 \end{bmatrix} \oplus \begin{bmatrix} \max(t_2, t_3) & \max(d_2, d_3) \\ -\infty & 0 \end{bmatrix} \\ &= \begin{bmatrix} \max(t_1, t_2, t_3) & \max(d_1, d_2, d_3) \\ -\infty & 0 \end{bmatrix} \end{aligned}$$

Therefore, $(\mathsf{R}_1 \oplus \mathsf{R}_2) \oplus \mathsf{R}_3 = \mathsf{R}_1 \oplus (\mathsf{R}_2 \oplus \mathsf{R}_3)$.

Lemma 4 (Identity element of addition). *For any matrix* R,

$$\mathsf{R} \oplus \mathsf{ign} = \mathsf{ign} \oplus \mathsf{R} = \mathsf{R}.$$

Proof. Let $R = \begin{bmatrix} t & d \\ -\infty & 0 \end{bmatrix}$.

$$\begin{aligned} R \oplus \mathsf{ign} &= \begin{bmatrix} t & d \\ -\infty & 0 \end{bmatrix} \oplus \begin{bmatrix} -\infty & -\infty \\ -\infty & 0 \end{bmatrix} \\ &= \begin{bmatrix} \max(t, -\infty) & \max(d, -\infty) \\ \max(-\infty, -\infty) & \max(0, 0) \end{bmatrix} \\ &= \begin{bmatrix} t & d \\ -\infty & 0 \end{bmatrix} \end{aligned}$$

$$\begin{aligned} \mathsf{ign} \oplus R &= \begin{bmatrix} -\infty & -\infty \\ -\infty & 0 \end{bmatrix} \oplus \begin{bmatrix} t & d \\ -\infty & 0 \end{bmatrix} \\ &= \begin{bmatrix} \max(-\infty, t) & \max(-\infty, d) \\ \max(-\infty, -\infty) & \max(0, 0) \end{bmatrix} \\ &= \begin{bmatrix} t & d \\ -\infty & 0 \end{bmatrix} \end{aligned}$$

Therefore, $\mathsf{R} \oplus \mathsf{ign} - \mathsf{ign} \oplus \mathsf{R} = \mathsf{R}$.

Theorem 5. *Monoidality of addition* $(\mathcal{C}, \oplus, \mathsf{ign})$ *is a monoid.*

Proof. By Lemma 3 and Lemma 4.

Lemma 5 (Associativity of multiplication).

$$\forall \mathsf{R}_1, \mathsf{R}_2, \mathsf{R}_3 \in \mathcal{C}.\ (\mathsf{R}_1 \circledast \mathsf{R}_2) \circledast \mathsf{R}_3 = \mathsf{R}_1 \circledast (\mathsf{R}_2 \circledast \mathsf{R}_3).$$

Proof. Let $\mathsf{R}_1 = \begin{bmatrix} t_1 & d_1 \\ -\infty & 0 \end{bmatrix}$, $\mathsf{R}_2 = \begin{bmatrix} t_2 & d_2 \\ -\infty & 0 \end{bmatrix}$, $\mathsf{R}_3 = \begin{bmatrix} t_3 & d_3 \\ -\infty & 0 \end{bmatrix}$.

$$\begin{aligned}
&(\mathsf{R}_1 \circledast \mathsf{R}_2) \circledast \mathsf{R}_3 \\
&= (\begin{bmatrix} t_1 & d_1 \\ -\infty & 0 \end{bmatrix} \circledast \begin{bmatrix} t_2 & d_2 \\ -\infty & 0 \end{bmatrix}) \circledast \mathsf{R}_3 \\
&= \begin{bmatrix} t_1{+}t_2 & \max(t_1{+}d_2, d_1) \\ -\infty & 0 \end{bmatrix} \circledast \begin{bmatrix} t_3 & d_3 \\ -\infty & 0 \end{bmatrix} \\
&= \begin{bmatrix} t_1{+}t_2{+}t_3 & \max(t_1{+}t_2{+}d_3, \max(t_1{+}d_2, d_1)) \\ -\infty & 0 \end{bmatrix} \\
&= \begin{bmatrix} t_1{+}t_2{+}t_3 & \max(t_1{+}t_2{+}d_3, t_1{+}d_2, d_1) \\ -\infty & 0 \end{bmatrix}
\end{aligned}$$

$$\begin{aligned}
&\mathsf{R}_1 \circledast (\mathsf{R}_2 \circledast \mathsf{R}_3) \\
&= \mathsf{R}_1 \circledast (\begin{bmatrix} t_2 & d_2 \\ -\infty & 0 \end{bmatrix} \circledast \begin{bmatrix} t_3 & d_3 \\ -\infty & 0 \end{bmatrix}) \\
&= \begin{bmatrix} t_1 & d_1 \\ -\infty & 0 \end{bmatrix} \circledast \begin{bmatrix} t_2 + t_3 & \max(t_2 + d_3, d_2) \\ -\infty & 0 \end{bmatrix} \\
&= \begin{bmatrix} t_1{+}t_2{+}t_3 & \max(t_1{+} \max(t_2{+}d_3, d_2), d_1) \\ -\infty & 0 \end{bmatrix} \\
&= \begin{bmatrix} t_1{+}t_2{+}t_3 & \max(t_1{+}t_2{+}d_3, t_1{+}d_2, d_1) \\ -\infty & 0 \end{bmatrix}
\end{aligned}$$

Therefore, $(\mathsf{R}_1 \circledast \mathsf{R}_2) \circledast \mathsf{R}_3 = \mathsf{R}_1 \circledast (\mathsf{R}_2 \circledast \mathsf{R}_3)$.

Lemma 6 (Identity element of multiplication). *For any matrix* R,

$$\mathsf{R} \circledast \mathsf{use} = \mathsf{use} \circledast \mathsf{R} = \mathsf{R}.$$

Proof. Let $R = \begin{bmatrix} t & d \\ -\infty & 0 \end{bmatrix}$.

$$\begin{aligned}
R \circledast \mathsf{use} &= \begin{bmatrix} t & d \\ -\infty & 0 \end{bmatrix} \circledast \begin{bmatrix} 0 & -\infty \\ -\infty & 0 \end{bmatrix} \\
&= \begin{bmatrix} t{+}0 & \max(t + -\infty, d) \\ -\infty & 0 \end{bmatrix} \\
&= \begin{bmatrix} t & d \\ -\infty & 0 \end{bmatrix}
\end{aligned}$$

$$\mathsf{use} \circledast R = \begin{bmatrix} 0 & -\infty \\ -\infty & 0 \end{bmatrix} \circledast \begin{bmatrix} t & d \\ -\infty & 0 \end{bmatrix}$$
$$= \begin{bmatrix} 0+t & \max(0+d, -\infty) \\ -\infty & 0 \end{bmatrix}$$
$$= \begin{bmatrix} t & d \\ -\infty & 0 \end{bmatrix}$$

Therefore, $\mathsf{R} \circledast \mathsf{use} = \mathsf{use} \circledast \mathsf{R} = \mathsf{R}$.

Theorem 6. *Monoidality of multiplication* $(\mathcal{C}, \circledast, \mathsf{use})$ *is a monoid.*

Proof. By Lemma 5 and Lemma 6.

A.2 Preorder: Reflexivity and Transitivity

Lemma 7. *Reflexivity of* $\leqslant$ *For any matrix* $R \in \mathcal{C}$, $R \leqslant R$.

Proof. Let $R = \begin{bmatrix} t & d \\ -\infty & 0 \end{bmatrix}$, then $(t \leq t) \wedge (d \leq d)$. Therefore, by the definition of $\leqslant$, $\begin{bmatrix} t & d \\ -\infty & 0 \end{bmatrix} \leqslant \begin{bmatrix} t & d \\ -\infty & 0 \end{bmatrix}$.

Lemma 8. *Transitivity of* $\leqslant$

$$\forall R_1, R_2, R_3 \in \mathcal{C}.\ ((R_1 \leqslant R_2) \wedge (R_2 \leqslant R_3)) \Rightarrow R_1 \leqslant R_3.$$

Proof. Let $\mathsf{R}_1 = \begin{bmatrix} t_1 & d_1 \\ -\infty & 0 \end{bmatrix}$, $\mathsf{R}_2 = \begin{bmatrix} t_2 & d_2 \\ -\infty & 0 \end{bmatrix}$, $\mathsf{R}_3 = \begin{bmatrix} t_3 & d_3 \\ -\infty & 0 \end{bmatrix}$. From the assumption,

$$(t_1 \leqslant t_2) \wedge (d_1 \leqslant d_2)$$
$$(t_2 \leqslant t_3) \wedge (d_2 \leqslant d_3)$$

Therefore, $(t_1 \leqslant t_3) \wedge (d_1 \leqslant d_3)$, and by the definition of $\leqslant$,

$$\begin{bmatrix} t_1 & d_1 \\ -\infty & 0 \end{bmatrix} \leqslant \begin{bmatrix} t_3 & d_3 \\ -\infty & 0 \end{bmatrix}$$

Theorem 7 (preorder). $(\mathcal{C}, \leqslant)$ *is a preorder.*

Proof. By Lemma 7 and Lemma 8.

A.3 Distributivity

Lemma 9 (Distributivity). *For all matrices* $R_1, R_2, R_3 \in \mathcal{C}$,

$$\mathsf{R}_1 \circledast (\mathsf{R}_2 \oplus \mathsf{R}_3) = (\mathsf{R}_1 \circledast \mathsf{R}_2) \oplus (\mathsf{R}_1 \circledast \mathsf{R}_3)$$
$$(\mathsf{R}_1 \oplus \mathsf{R}_2) \circledast \mathsf{R}_3 = (\mathsf{R}_1 \circledast \mathsf{R}_3) \oplus (\mathsf{R}_2 \circledast \mathsf{R}_3).$$

Proof. Let $\mathsf{R}_1 = \begin{bmatrix} t_1 & d_1 \\ -\infty & 0 \end{bmatrix}$, $\mathsf{R}_2 = \begin{bmatrix} t_2 & d_2 \\ -\infty & 0 \end{bmatrix}$, $\mathsf{R}_3 = \begin{bmatrix} t_3 & d_3 \\ -\infty & 0 \end{bmatrix}$.

$$\begin{aligned}
&\mathsf{R}_1 \circledast (\mathsf{R}_2 \oplus \mathsf{R}_3) \\
&= \begin{bmatrix} t_1 & d_1 \\ -\infty & 0 \end{bmatrix} \circledast \begin{bmatrix} \max(t_2, t_3) & \max(d_2, d_3) \\ -\infty & 0 \end{bmatrix} \\
&= \begin{bmatrix} t_1 + \max(t_2, t_3) & \max(t_1 + \max(d_2, d_3), d_1) \\ -\infty & 0 \end{bmatrix} \\
&= \begin{bmatrix} \max(t_1+t_2, t_1+t_3) & \max(t_1+d_2, t_1+d_3, d_1) \\ -\infty & 0 \end{bmatrix}
\end{aligned}$$

$$\begin{aligned}
&(\mathsf{R}_1 \circledast \mathsf{R}_2) \oplus (\mathsf{R}_1 \circledast \mathsf{R}_3) \\
&= \begin{bmatrix} t_1+t_2 & \max(t_1+d_2, d_1) \\ -\infty & 0 \end{bmatrix} \oplus \begin{bmatrix} t_1+t_3 & \max(t_1+d_3, d_1) \\ -\infty & 0 \end{bmatrix} \\
&= \begin{bmatrix} \max(t_1+t_2, t_1+t_3) & \max(\max(t_1+d_2, d_1), \max(t_1+d_3, d_1)) \\ -\infty & 0 \end{bmatrix} \\
&= \begin{bmatrix} \max(t_1+t_2, t_1+t_3) & \max(t_1+d_2, t_1+d_3, d_1) \\ -\infty & 0 \end{bmatrix}
\end{aligned}$$

Therefore, $\mathsf{R}_1 \circledast (\mathsf{R}_2 \oplus \mathsf{R}_3) = (\mathsf{R}_1 \circledast \mathsf{R}_2) \oplus (\mathsf{R}_1 \circledast \mathsf{R}_3)$. The proof of $(\mathsf{R}_1 \oplus \mathsf{R}_2) \circledast \mathsf{R}_3 = (\mathsf{R}_1 \circledast \mathsf{R}_3) \oplus (\mathsf{R}_2 \circledast \mathsf{R}_3)$ is similar.

Theorem 8 (Matrix Coeffect forms a Coeffect Algebra). *The structure* $(\mathcal{C}, \circledast, \oplus, \mathsf{use}, \mathsf{ign}, \leqslant)$ *satisfies all conditions of the structural coeffect algebra defined by Petricek.*

Proof. We verify each axiom in turn.

Additive monoid. By Lemma 3 (associativity of $\oplus$) and Lemma 4 (identity element ign), $(\mathcal{C}, \oplus, \mathsf{ign})$ forms a monoid (Theorem 5).

Multiplicative monoid. By Lemma 5 (associativity of $\circledast$) and Lemma 6 (identity element use), $(\mathcal{C}, \circledast, \mathsf{use})$ is also a monoid (Theorem 6).

Preorder. Reflexivity and transitivity follow from Lemma 7 and Lemma 8, thus $(\mathcal{C}, \leqslant)$ is a preorder (Theorem 7).

Distributivity. Left and right distributivity are shown in Lemma 9.

Hence, $(\mathcal{C}, \circledast, \oplus, \mathsf{use}, \mathsf{ign}, \leqslant)$ satisfies all axioms of a structural coeffect algebra.

B Full Syntax and Rules of Target Language

B.1 Syntax

The full syntax of the target language is shown below:

$$\begin{aligned}
v &::= n \mid \lambda x.e \mid (v_1, \ldots, v_n) \mid \mathsf{Mc}\langle (S_0, v_0), \ldots, (S_k, v_k) \rangle \\
e &::= x \mid n \mid \pi_i e \mid (e_1, \ldots, e_n) \mid e_1 e_2 \mid \lambda x.e \mid \mathsf{Mc}\langle (S_0, e_0), \ldots, (S_k, e_k) \rangle
\end{aligned}$$

$$\mid \mathsf{cobind}_{\mathsf{s},\mathbf{r}}\ e_1\ e_2 \mid \mathsf{counit}_{\mathsf{use}}\ e \mid \mathsf{merge}_{\mathbf{p},\mathbf{q}}\ e \mid \mathsf{split}_{\mathbf{p},\mathbf{q}}\ e \mid \mathsf{dup}_{\mathsf{s},\mathsf{t}}\ e$$

$$\tau ::= \mathsf{num} \mid \tau_1 \times \cdots \times \tau_n \mid \tau_1 \rightarrow \tau_2 \mid\ C^{\mathbf{r}}(\tau_1 \times \cdots \times \tau_k)$$

$$K ::= (v_1, \ldots, v_{i-1}, \_, e_{i+1}, \ldots, e_n) \mid v\ \_ \mid \_\ e \mid \pi_i\ \_$$

$$\mid \mathsf{cobind}_{\mathsf{s},\mathbf{r}}\ \_\ e \mid \mathsf{cobind}_{\mathsf{s},\mathbf{r}}\ v\ \_ \mid \mathsf{counit}_{\mathsf{use}}\ \_ \mid \mathsf{merge}_{\mathbf{p},\mathbf{q}}\ \_ \mid \mathsf{split}_{\mathbf{p},\mathbf{q}}\ \_ \mid \mathsf{dup}_{\mathsf{s},\mathsf{t}}\ \_$$

$$\mid \mathsf{Mc}\langle (S_0, v_0), \ldots, (S_i, \_), \ldots, (S_k, e_k) \rangle$$

We define a set $\mathcal{K}$ of (syntactic) *context frames* K, i.e., one-hole contexts that select the next subterm to be evaluated in our call-by-value reduction. In the literature, these are sometimes called evaluation frames; we use the term "context frame" to avoid confusion with recursive contexts. We write $K[e]$ for plugging e into the hole of K. We employ these context frames in the operational semantics and in the proof of Theorem 11 (the progress theorem).

B.2 Typing Rules

The full typing rules of the target language are shown in Fig. 6.

$$\frac{x : \tau \in \Gamma}{\Gamma \vdash x : \tau}\ (\textsc{Var}) \qquad \frac{}{\Gamma \vdash n : \mathsf{num}}\ (\textsc{Num})$$

$$\frac{\Gamma, x : \tau_1 \vdash e : \tau_2}{\Gamma \vdash \lambda x.e : \tau_1 \rightarrow \tau_2}\ (\textsc{Abs}) \qquad \frac{\Gamma \vdash e_1 : \tau_1 \rightarrow \tau_2 \quad \Gamma \vdash e_2 : \tau_1}{\Gamma \vdash e_1\ e_2 : \tau_2}\ (\textsc{App})$$

$$\frac{\Gamma \vdash e : \tau_1 \times \cdots \times \tau_i \times \cdots \times \tau_n}{\Gamma \vdash \pi_i\ e : \tau_i}\ (\textsc{Proj}) \qquad \frac{\forall i \in \{1, \ldots, n\}.\ \Gamma \vdash e_i : \tau_i}{\Gamma \vdash (e_1, \ldots, e_n) : \tau_1 \times \cdots \times \tau_n}\ (\textsc{Tup})$$

$$\frac{\Gamma \vdash e : C^{\langle \mathsf{use} \rangle} \tau}{\Gamma \vdash \mathsf{counit}_{\mathsf{use}}\ e : \tau}\ (\textsc{Counit})$$

$$\frac{\Gamma \vdash e_1 : C^{\mathbf{r}}(\tau_1 \times \cdots \times \tau_k) \rightarrow \tau \quad \Gamma \vdash e_2 : C^{\mathsf{s} \otimes \mathbf{r}}(\tau_1 \times \cdots \times \tau_k)}{\Gamma \vdash \mathsf{cobind}_{\mathsf{s},\mathbf{r}}\ e_1\ e_2 : C^{\langle \mathsf{s} \rangle} \tau}\ (\textsc{Cobind})$$

$$\frac{\Gamma \vdash e : C^{\mathbf{p}}(\tau_1 \times \cdots \times \tau_l) \times C^{\mathbf{q}}(\tau_{l+1} \times \cdots \times \tau_k)}{\Gamma \vdash \mathsf{merge}_{\mathbf{p},\mathbf{q}}\ e : C^{\mathbf{p} + \!\!\! + \mathbf{q}}(\tau_1 \times \cdots \times \tau_k)}\ (\textsc{Merge})$$

$$\frac{\Gamma \vdash e : C^{\mathbf{p} + \!\!\! + \mathbf{q}}(\tau_1 \times \cdots \times \tau_k)}{\Gamma \vdash \mathsf{split}_{\mathbf{p},\mathbf{q}}\ e : C^{\mathbf{p}}(\tau_1 \times \cdots \times \tau_l) \times C^{\mathbf{q}}(\tau_{l+1} \times \cdots \times \tau_k)}\ (\textsc{Split})$$

$$\frac{\Gamma \vdash e : C^{\langle \mathsf{s} \oplus \mathsf{t} \rangle} \tau}{\Gamma \vdash \mathsf{dup}_{\mathsf{s},\mathsf{t}}\ e : C^{\langle \mathsf{s},\mathsf{t} \rangle}(\tau \times \tau)}\ (\textsc{Dup})$$

$$\frac{\forall i \in \{0, \ldots, k\}.\ \Gamma \vdash e_i : \tau_i}{\Gamma \vdash \mathsf{Mc}\langle (S_0, e_0), \ldots, (S_k, e_k) \rangle : C^{\langle \mathsf{S}_0, \ldots, \mathsf{S}_k \rangle}(\tau_0 \times \cdots \times \tau_k)}\ (\textsc{Mc})$$

Fig. 6. Typing rules for target language

B.3 Reduction Rules

The full reduction rules of the target language are shown in Fig. 7.

$$
\begin{aligned}
(fn)\ & (\lambda x.e)\, v \ \rightsquigarrow\ e[x \leftarrow v] \\
(prj)\ & \pi_i\,(v_1, \ldots, v_n) \ \rightsquigarrow\ v_i \\
(ctx)\ & K[e] \rightsquigarrow K[e'] \quad \text{where } e \rightsquigarrow e' \\
(counit)\ & \mathsf{counit}_{\mathsf{use}}\ \mathsf{Mc}\langle (S_0, v_0)\rangle \ \rightsquigarrow\ v_0 \\
(cobind)\ & \mathsf{cobind}_{\mathsf{S},\langle \mathsf{R}_0,\ldots,\mathsf{R}_k\rangle}\ f\ \mathsf{Mc}\langle (S \circledast R_0, v_0), \ldots, (S \circledast R_k, v_k)\rangle \\
& \rightsquigarrow \mathsf{Mc}\langle (S, f(\mathsf{Mc}\langle (R_0, v_0), \ldots, (R_k, v_k)\rangle))\rangle \\
(merge)\ & \mathsf{merge}_{\langle \mathsf{P}_0,\ldots,\mathsf{P}_k\rangle,\langle \mathsf{Q}_0,\ldots,\mathsf{Q}_l\rangle}\ (\mathsf{Mc}\langle (P_0, v_0), \ldots, (P_k, v_k)\rangle, \mathsf{Mc}\langle (Q_0, v_0'), \ldots, (Q_l, v_l')\rangle) \\
& \rightsquigarrow \mathsf{Mc}\langle (P_0, v_0), \ldots, (P_k, v_k), (Q_0, v_0'), \ldots, (Q_l, v_l')\rangle \\
(split)\ & \mathsf{split}_{\langle \mathsf{P}_0,\ldots,\mathsf{P}_k\rangle,\langle \mathsf{Q}_0,\ldots,\mathsf{Q}_l\rangle}\ \mathsf{Mc}\langle (P_0, v_0), \ldots, (P_k, v_k), (Q_0, v_0'), \ldots, (Q_l, v_l')\rangle \\
& \rightsquigarrow (\mathsf{Mc}\langle (P_0, v_0), \ldots, (P_k, v_k)\rangle, \mathsf{Mc}\langle (Q_0, v_0'), \ldots, (Q_l, v_l')\rangle) \\
(dup)\ & \mathsf{dup}_{\mathsf{S},\mathsf{T}}\ \mathsf{Mc}\langle (S \oplus T, v)\rangle \rightsquigarrow (\mathsf{Mc}\langle (S, v)\rangle, \mathsf{Mc}\langle (T, v)\rangle)
\end{aligned}
$$

Fig. 7. Reduction rules for target language

B.4 Translation Rules

The full translation rules of the target language are shown in Fig. 8.

C Proofs of Translation from MCC to TLMC and Type Safety of TLMC

This appendix provides full type-safety proofs for TLMC, focusing on matrix-annotated contextual values and the operations that implement dependency propagation. We adapt the translation-based proof structure to these primitives and include the complete derivations for self-containment.

Theorem 9 (Well-typedness of the translation from MCC to TLMC (restatement of Theorem 1)). *Given a typing derivation of the closed MCC judgment $\langle\rangle @ \langle\rangle \vdash e : \tau$, let f be its TLMC translation, written as follows:*

$$
\frac{[\![(\ldots)]\!]}{[\![\langle\rangle @ \langle\rangle \vdash e : \tau]\!]} = \frac{(\ldots)}{f}
$$

Then f is well-typed: $\vdash f : [\![\langle\rangle @ \langle\rangle]\!] \to [\![\tau]\!]$.

Proof. By induction on the derivation of the translation. The well-typedness of the translation can be rephrased as the following proposition:

$$\frac{}{[\![x:\tau@\langle\mathsf{use}\rangle \vdash x:\tau]\!]} = \frac{}{\lambda\rho.\mathsf{counit}_{\mathsf{use}}\rho} \quad \text{(var)}$$

$$\frac{}{[\![\langle\rangle@\langle\rangle \vdash n:\tau]\!]} = \frac{}{\lambda\rho.n} \quad \text{(num)}$$

$$\frac{[\![\Gamma, x:\tau_1@\mathbf{r}+\!\!+\langle\mathsf{s}\rangle \vdash e:\tau_2]\!] = f}{[\![\Gamma@\mathbf{r} \vdash \lambda x{:}\tau_1.\, e:\tau_1 \xrightarrow{\mathsf{s}} \tau_2]\!] = \lambda\rho.\lambda v.f(\mathsf{merge}_{\mathbf{r},\langle\mathsf{s}\rangle}(\rho, v))} \quad \text{(abs)}$$

$$\frac{\begin{array}{r}[\![\Gamma_1@\mathbf{p} \vdash e_1:\tau_1 \xrightarrow{\mathsf{s}} \tau_2]\!] = f\\ [\![\Gamma_2@\mathbf{q} \vdash e_2:\tau_1]\!] = g\end{array}}{\begin{array}{rl}[\![\Gamma_1, \Gamma_2@\mathbf{p}+\!\!+(\mathsf{s}\otimes\mathbf{q}) \vdash e_1e_2:\tau_2]\!] = & \lambda\rho.\mathsf{let}\ (ctx_1, ctx_2) = \mathsf{split}_{\mathbf{p},\mathsf{s}\otimes\mathbf{q}}\ \rho\\ & \mathsf{in}\ f\ ctx_1(\mathsf{cobind}_{\mathsf{s},\mathbf{q}}\ g\ ctx_2)\end{array}} \quad \text{(app)}$$

$$\frac{[\![\Gamma@\mathbf{r} \vdash e:\tau]\!] = f}{\begin{array}{rl}[\![\Gamma, x:\tau_1@\mathbf{r}+\!\!+\langle\mathsf{ign}\rangle \vdash e:\tau]\!] = & \lambda\rho.\mathsf{let}\ (ctx_1, \_) = \mathsf{split}_{\mathbf{r},\langle\mathsf{ign}\rangle}\ \rho\\ & \mathsf{in}\ f\ ctx_1\end{array}} \quad \text{(weak)}$$

$$\frac{\begin{array}{r}[\![\Gamma_1, x:\tau_1, y:\tau_2, \Gamma_2@\mathbf{p}+\!\!+\langle\mathsf{s},\mathsf{t}\rangle+\!\!+\mathbf{q}\\ \vdash e:\tau]\!] = f\end{array}}{\begin{array}{rl}[\![\Gamma_1, y:\tau_2, x:\tau_1, \Gamma_2@\mathbf{p}+\!\!+\langle\mathsf{t},\mathsf{s}\rangle+\!\!+\mathbf{q} = & \lambda\rho.f(\mathsf{nest}_{\mathbf{p},\langle\mathsf{t},\mathsf{s}\rangle,\langle\mathsf{s},\mathsf{t}\rangle,\mathbf{q}}(\lambda\phi.\\ \vdash e:\tau]\!] & \quad \mathsf{let}\ (ctx_1, ctx_2) = \mathsf{split}_{\langle\mathsf{t}\rangle,\langle\mathsf{s}\rangle}\ \phi\ \mathsf{in}\\ & \quad \mathsf{merge}_{\langle\mathsf{s}\rangle,\langle\mathsf{t}\rangle}(ctx_2, ctx_1))\ \rho)\end{array}} \quad \text{(exch)}$$

$$\frac{\begin{array}{r}[\![\Gamma_1, y:\tau_1, z:\tau_1, \Gamma_2@\mathbf{p}+\!\!+\langle\mathsf{s},\mathsf{t}\rangle+\!\!+\mathbf{q}\\ \vdash e:\tau]\!] = f\end{array}}{\begin{array}{rl}[\![\Gamma_1, x:\tau_1, \Gamma_2@\mathbf{p}+\!\!+\langle\mathsf{s}\oplus\mathsf{t}\rangle+\!\!+\mathbf{q} = & \lambda\rho.f(\mathsf{nest}_{\mathbf{p},\langle\mathsf{s}\oplus\mathsf{t}\rangle,\langle\mathsf{s},\mathsf{t}\rangle,\mathbf{q}}\mathsf{dup}_{\mathsf{s},\mathsf{t}}\ \rho)\\ \vdash e[z, y \leftarrow x]:\tau]\!] & \end{array}} \quad \text{(contr)}$$

Assuming the following auxiliary definitions:

$$\begin{aligned}\mathsf{nest}_{\mathbf{p},\mathbf{s},\mathbf{s}',\mathbf{q}} \;=\; & \lambda f.\lambda\rho.\\ & \mathsf{let}\ (ctx_1, ctx') = \mathsf{split}_{\mathbf{p},\mathbf{s}+\!\!+\mathbf{q}}\ \rho\ \mathsf{in}\\ & \mathsf{let}\ (ctx_2, ctx_3) = \mathsf{split}_{\mathbf{s},\mathbf{q}}\ ctx'\ \mathsf{in}\\ & \quad \mathsf{merge}_{\mathbf{p},\mathbf{s}'+\!\!+\mathbf{q}}(ctx_1, \mathsf{merge}_{\mathbf{s}',\mathbf{q}}(f\ ctx_2, ctx_3))\end{aligned}$$

Fig. 8. Translation rules to target language.

If the judgment $\Gamma@\mathbf{r} \vdash e:\tau$ (where $\Gamma = \langle x_1:\tau_1, \ldots, x_n:\tau_n\rangle$ and $\mathbf{r} = \langle \mathsf{r}_1, \ldots, \mathsf{r}_n\rangle$) holds in the source language, then the function produced by the translation has the type $C^{\mathbf{r}}([\![\tau_1]\!]\times\cdots\times[\![\tau_n]\!]) \to [\![\tau]\!]$.

We verify whether the above proposition holds for each translation rule. In the following proof, the translation of the context $\Gamma@\mathbf{r}$ is also denoted as $C^{\mathbf{r}}[\![\Gamma]\!]$.

(var) case From the pre-translation context, the type of the argument ρ of the post-translation lambda abstraction is $C^{\langle\mathsf{use}\rangle}[\![\tau]\!]$. Since the type of $\mathsf{counit}_{\mathsf{use}}$ is $C^{\langle\mathsf{use}\rangle}\alpha \to \alpha$, the body of the post-translation lambda abstraction, $\mathsf{counit}_{\mathsf{use}}\ \rho$, has the type $[\![\tau]\!]$. Therefore, the type of the entire post-translation lambda abstraction is $C^{\langle\mathsf{use}\rangle}([\![\tau]\!]) \to [\![\tau]\!]$, and the proposition holds.

(num) case Since the pre-translation context is empty, the type of the argument ρ of the post-translation lambda abstraction is $C^{\langle\rangle}()$. Also, since the type of the number n is num, the type of the body of the post-translation lambda abstraction is $[\![\mathsf{num}]\!] = \mathsf{num}$. Therefore, the type of the entire post-translation lambda abstraction is $C^{\langle\rangle}() \to \mathsf{num}$, and the proposition holds.

(abs) case From the pre-translation context, the type of ρ is $C^{\mathbf{r}}[\![\Gamma]\!]$ and the type of v is $C^{\langle \mathsf{s}\rangle}[\![\tau_1]\!]$. Here,

$$\mathsf{merge}_{\mathbf{r},\langle \mathsf{s}\rangle} : C^{\mathbf{r}}\alpha \times C^{\langle \mathsf{s}\rangle}\beta \to C^{\mathbf{r}+\!\!\!+\langle \mathsf{s}\rangle}(\alpha \times \beta) \quad (\because \text{Definition of merge})$$

$$\text{Thus, } \mathsf{merge}_{\mathbf{r},\langle \mathsf{s}\rangle}(\rho, v) : C^{\mathbf{r}+\!\!\!+\langle \mathsf{s}\rangle}([\![\Gamma]\!]\times[\![\tau_1]\!])$$

Also, by the induction hypothesis, $f : C^{r+\langle s\rangle}([\![\Gamma]\!] \times [\![\tau_1]\!]) \to [\![\tau_2]\!]$. Therefore,

$$f(\mathsf{merge}_{\mathbf{r},\langle \mathsf{s}\rangle}(\rho, v)) : [\![\tau_2]\!].$$

Consequently, the type of the entire post-translation lambda abstraction is $C^{\mathbf{r}}[\![\Gamma]\!] \to C^{\langle \mathsf{s}\rangle}[\![\tau_1]\!] \to [\![\tau_2]\!]$, and the proposition holds.

(app) case From the pre-translation context, the type of ρ is $C^{\mathbf{p}+\!\!\!+(\mathsf{s}\otimes\mathbf{q})}([\![\Gamma_1]\!] \times [\![\Gamma_2]\!])$. By $\mathsf{split}_{\mathbf{p},\mathsf{s}\otimes\mathbf{q}}$, the types of ctx_1 and ctx_2 are $C^{\mathbf{p}}[\![\Gamma_1]\!]$ and $C^{\mathsf{s}\otimes\mathbf{q}}[\![\Gamma_2]\!]$, respectively. Here,

$$g : C^{\mathbf{q}}[\![\Gamma_2]\!] \to [\![\tau_1]\!] \quad (\because \text{Induction hypothesis})$$

$$\mathsf{cobind}_{\mathsf{s},\mathbf{q}} : (C^{\mathbf{q}}\alpha \to \beta) \to (C^{\mathsf{s}\otimes\mathbf{q}}\alpha \to C^{\langle \mathsf{s}\rangle}\beta) \quad (\because \text{Definition of } \mathsf{cobind})$$

$$\text{Thus, } \mathsf{cobind}_{\mathsf{s},\mathbf{q}}\ g\ ctx_2 : C^{\langle \mathsf{s}\rangle}[\![\tau_1]\!]$$

Also, by the induction hypothesis, $f : C^{\mathbf{p}}[\![\Gamma_1]\!] \to (C^{\langle \mathsf{s}\rangle}[\![\tau_1]\!] \to [\![\tau_2]\!])$. Therefore,

$$f\ ctx_1 : C^{\langle \mathsf{s}\rangle}[\![\tau_1]\!] \to [\![\tau_2]\!]$$

$$\text{Consequently, } f\ ctx_1\ (\mathsf{cobind}_{\mathsf{s},\mathbf{q}}\ g\ ctx_2) : [\![\tau_2]\!].$$

From the above, the type of the entire post-translation lambda abstraction is $C^{\mathbf{p}+\!\!\!+(\mathsf{s}\otimes\mathbf{q})}([\![\Gamma_1]\!]\times[\![\Gamma_2]\!]) \to [\![\tau_2]\!]$, and the proposition holds.

(weak) case From the pre-translation context, the type of ctx is

$$C^{\mathbf{r}+\!\!\!+\langle \mathsf{ign}\rangle}([\![\Gamma]\!]\times[\![\tau_1]\!]).$$

Therefore, by applying $\mathsf{split}_{\mathbf{r},\langle \mathsf{ign}\rangle}\ \rho$, the type of ctx_1 becomes $C^{\mathbf{r}}[\![\Gamma]\!]$. By the induction hypothesis, $f : C^{\mathbf{r}}[\![\Gamma]\!] \to [\![\tau]\!]$, so $f\ ctx_1 : [\![\tau]\!]$. Consequently, the type of the entire post-translation lambda abstraction is

$$C^{\mathbf{r}+\!\!\!+\langle \mathsf{ign}\rangle}([\![\Gamma]\!]\times[\![\tau_1]\!]) \to [\![\tau]\!],$$

and the proposition holds.

(exch) case Let us call the lambda function $\lambda\phi.\mathsf{let}(ctx_1, ctx_2) = \ldots$ provided in the translation rule the $\mathsf{exchange}$ function. The type of the $\mathsf{exchange}$ function is $C^{\langle \mathsf{t},\mathsf{s}\rangle}(\sigma_2\times\sigma_1) \to C^{\langle \mathsf{s},\mathsf{t}\rangle}(\sigma_1\times\sigma_2)$. Also, from the pre-translation context,

$$\rho : C^{\mathbf{p}+\!\!\!+\langle \mathsf{t},\mathsf{s}\rangle+\!\!\!+\mathbf{q}}([\![\Gamma_1]\!]\times[\![\tau_2]\!]\times[\![\tau_1]\!]\times[\![\Gamma_2]\!]).$$

Therefore,

$$\mathsf{nest}_{\mathbf{p},\langle \mathsf{t},\mathsf{s}\rangle,\langle \mathsf{s},\mathsf{t}\rangle,\mathbf{q}}\ \mathsf{exchange}\ \rho : C^{\mathbf{p}+\!\!\!+\langle \mathsf{s},\mathsf{t}\rangle+\!\!\!+\mathbf{q}}([\![\Gamma_1]\!]\times[\![\tau_1]\!]\times[\![\tau_2]\!]\times[\![\Gamma_2]\!])$$

By the induction hypothesis,

$$f : C^{\mathbf{p}+\langle \mathsf{s},\mathsf{t}\rangle+\mathbf{q}}([\![\Gamma_1]\!]\times[\![\tau_1]\!]\times[\![\tau_2]\!]\times[\![\Gamma_2]\!]) \to [\![\tau]\!].$$

Thus,

$$f(\mathsf{nest}_{\mathbf{p},\langle \mathsf{t},\mathsf{s}\rangle,\langle \mathsf{s},\mathsf{t}\rangle,\mathbf{q}}\ \mathtt{exchange}\ \rho) : [\![\tau]\!]$$

From the above, the type of the entire post-translation lambda abstraction is

$$C^{\mathbf{p}+\langle \mathsf{t},\mathsf{s}\rangle+\mathbf{q}}([\![\Gamma_1]\!]\times[\![\tau_2]\!]\times[\![\tau_1]\!]\times[\![\Gamma_2]\!]) \to [\![\tau]\!]$$

and the proposition holds.

(contr) case The argument is similar to the (exch) case, replacing the $\mathtt{exchange}$ function with $\mathsf{dup}_{\mathsf{s},\mathsf{t}} : C^{\langle \mathsf{s}\oplus\mathsf{t}\rangle}\alpha \to C^{\langle \mathsf{s},\mathsf{t}\rangle}(\alpha\times\alpha)$.

Lemma 10 (canonical forms of TLMC (restatement of Lemma 1)). *For all terms e and types τ, if $\vdash e : \tau$, and e is a value, then:*

1. *If $\tau = \mathsf{num}$ then $e = n$ for some n*
2. *If $\tau = \tau_1 \to \tau_2$ then $e = \lambda x.e'$ for some x, e'*
3. *If $\tau = \tau_1\times\cdots\times\tau_n$ then $e = (v_1, \ldots, v_n)$ for some v_i*
4. *If $C^{\langle \mathsf{S}_0,\ldots,\mathsf{S}_k\rangle}(\tau_0\times\cdots\times\tau_k)$ then $e = \mathsf{Mc}\langle(S_0, v_0), \ldots, (S_k, v_k)\rangle$ for some matrices S_i and v_i.*

Proof. For each of the cases, by focusing on the last typing rule used to derive the type judgment. The final typing rule used in each case uniquely determines the shape of e: (Num) for case (1), (Abs) for (2), (Tup) for (3), and (Mc) for (4).

Lemma 11 (preservation under substitution of TLMC (restatement of Lemma 2)). *For all Γ, e, e', τ, τ', if $\Gamma, x : \tau \vdash e : \tau'$ and $\Gamma \vdash e' : \tau$ then $\Gamma \vdash e[x \leftarrow e'] : \tau'$.*

Proof. By induction on the typing derivation of e.

(Var) case If $e = y$, there are two subcases. If $x = y$, then $e[x \leftarrow e'] = e'$, hence $\Gamma \vdash e[x \leftarrow e'] : \tau'$ by assumption. If $x \neq y$, then $e[x \leftarrow e'] = y$, and since $\Gamma, x : \tau \vdash y : \tau'$ implies $y : \tau' \in \Gamma$, we also have $\Gamma \vdash e[x \leftarrow e'] : \tau'$.

(Num) case It is obvious because $n[x \leftarrow e'] = n$.

(Proj) case If $e = \pi_i\, e_0$, the typing rule (Proj) gives $\Gamma, x : \tau \vdash e_0 : \tau_1 \times \cdots \times \tau_n$ with $\tau' = \tau_i$. By the induction hypothesis, $\Gamma \vdash e_0[x \leftarrow e'] : \tau_1 \times \cdots \times \tau_n$, hence $\Gamma \vdash \pi_i(e_0[x \leftarrow e']) : \tau_i$.

(Tup) case If $e = (e_1, \ldots, e_n)$, each component satisfies $\Gamma, x : \tau \vdash e_i : \tau_i'$. By induction, $\Gamma \vdash e_i[x \leftarrow e'] : \tau_i'$ for all i, thus $\Gamma \vdash (e_1[x \leftarrow e'], \ldots, e_n[x \leftarrow e']) : \tau_1' \times \cdots \times \tau_n'$.

(App) case If $e = e_1 e_2$, we have $\Gamma, x : \tau \vdash e_1 : \tau_1 \to \tau_2$ and $\Gamma, x : \tau \vdash e_2 : \tau_1$. By induction, $\Gamma \vdash e_1[x \leftarrow e'] : \tau_1 \to \tau_2$ and $\Gamma \vdash e_2[x \leftarrow e'] : \tau_1$. Hence $\Gamma \vdash (e_1[x \leftarrow e'])(e_2[x \leftarrow e']) : \tau_2$.

(Abs) case If $e = \lambda y.e_0$ (with $y \neq x$), then $\tau' = \tau_1 \to \tau_2$ and the rule (ABS) gives $\Gamma, x:\tau, y:\tau_1 \vdash e_0 : \tau_2$. By induction, $\Gamma, y:\tau_1 \vdash e_0[x \leftarrow e'] : \tau_2$, thus $\Gamma \vdash \lambda y.e_0[x \leftarrow e'] : \tau_1 \to \tau_2$.

(Counit) case If $e = \mathsf{counit}_{\mathsf{use}}\ e_0$, then $\Gamma, x:\tau \vdash e_0 : C^{\langle \mathsf{use} \rangle}\tau'$. By induction, $\Gamma \vdash e_0[x \leftarrow e'] : C^{\langle \mathsf{use} \rangle}\tau'$, hence $\Gamma \vdash \mathsf{counit}_{\mathsf{use}}\ e_0[x \leftarrow e'] : \tau'$.

(Cobind) case If $e = \mathsf{cobind}_{\mathsf{s,r}}\, e_1\, e_2$, then by (COBIND),

$$\Gamma, x:\tau \vdash e_1 : C^{\mathsf{r}}(\tau_1 \times \cdots \times \tau_k) \to \tau_0, \quad \Gamma, x:\tau \vdash e_2 : C^{\mathsf{s} \otimes \mathsf{r}}(\tau_1 \times \cdots \times \tau_k).$$

By induction, both judgments hold with x substituted, so $\Gamma \vdash e[x \leftarrow e'] : C^{\mathsf{s}}\tau_0$.

(Merge), (Split), (Dup), (Mc) cases Each follows analogously from the induction hypothesis and the corresponding typing rule.

Theorem 10 (type preservation of TLMC (restatement of Theorem 2)). *If $\Gamma \vdash e : \tau$ and $e \rightsquigarrow e'$ then $\Gamma \vdash e' : \tau$.*

Proof. By induction over the reduction rule $\rightsquigarrow$. Using Lemma 2, we show that typing is preserved across each reduction rule:

(*fn*) case If $e = (\lambda x.e_0)\, v$, then by Lemma 2 we have $\Gamma \vdash e_0[x \leftarrow v] : \tau$.

(*prj*) case If $e = \pi_i(v_1, \ldots, v_n)$, then $\Gamma \vdash e : \tau_i$ by (PROJ), and $e' = v_i$ by (*prj*). Hence, $\Gamma \vdash e' : \tau_i$.

(*ctx*) case If $e = K[e_0]$ and $e' = K[e'_0]$, the same typing rule applies to both by the induction hypothesis; hence $\Gamma \vdash e' : \tau$.

(*counit*) case If $e = \mathsf{counit}_{\mathsf{use}}\ \mathsf{Mc}\langle(R_0, v_0)\rangle$, then $\Gamma \vdash \mathsf{Mc}\langle(R_0, v_0)\rangle : C^{\langle \mathsf{use} \rangle}\tau$ by (COUNIT) and $\Gamma \vdash v_0 : \tau$ by (MC). Hence, typing is preserved across the reduction rule (*counit*).

(*cobind*) case If $e = \mathsf{cobind}_{\mathsf{S}, \langle \mathsf{R_0}, \ldots, \mathsf{R_k} \rangle}\ e_1\ \mathsf{Mc}\langle(S \circledast R_0, v_0), \ldots, (S \circledast R_k, v_k)\rangle$, then by (COBIND), $\Gamma \vdash e : C^{\langle \mathsf{S} \rangle}\tau'$ where

$$\Gamma \vdash e_1 : C^{\langle \mathsf{R_0}, \ldots, \mathsf{R_k} \rangle}(\tau_0 \times \cdots \times \tau_k) \to \tau'$$
$$\Gamma \vdash \mathsf{Mc}\langle(S \circledast R_0, v_0), \ldots, (S \circledast R_k, v_k)\rangle : C^{\langle \mathsf{S \circledast R_0}, \ldots, \mathsf{S \circledast R_k} \rangle}(\tau_0 \times \cdots \times \tau_k).$$

Focusing on post-evaluation, $e' = \mathsf{Mc}\langle(S, e_1(\mathsf{Mc}\langle(R_0, v_0), \ldots, (R_k, v_k)\rangle))\rangle : C^{\langle \mathsf{S} \rangle}\tau'$. Hence, typing is preserved across the reduction rule (*cobind*).

(*merge*), (*split*), (*dup*) cases Each case follows by the corresponding typing rule and Lemma 2.

Theorem 11 (progress of TLMC (restatement of Theorem 3)). *If $\Gamma \vdash e : \tau$ then either e is a value or there exists e' such that $e \rightsquigarrow e'$.*

Proof. By induction on the typing derivation of e. Each case mirrors the structure of Lemma 1: values are normal forms, and non-values have an applicable reduction rule.

(Num) case There exists some n such that $e = n$, therefore e is a value.

(Abs) case There exists some x, e' such that $e = \lambda x.e'$, therefore e is a value.
(Var) case Since the expression is closed, this case is not possible.
(App) case $e = e_1\, e_2$, and e is not a value. By the induction hypothesis, e_1 is either a value or reducible. If it is reducible, apply the (ctx) rule for the syntactic context frame $(\_\ e_2)$. If both e_1 and e_2 are values, then by Lemma 1, $e_1 = \lambda x.e'$, so the (fn) rule can be applied.
(Proj) case $e = \pi_i\, e_0$, and let $\tau = \tau_1 \times \cdots \times \tau_n$. If e_0 is reducible, apply the (ctx) rule for the context frame $\pi_i\_$. Otherwise, by Lemma 2, $e_0 = (v_1, \ldots, v_n)$, so the (prj) rule is applied.
(Tup) case $e = (e_1, \ldots, e_n)$, and if any e_i for some $i \in \{1, \ldots, n\}$ is not a value, apply the (ctx) rule for the syntactic context frame K, defined as

$$K = (v_1, \ldots, v_{i-1}, \_, e_{i+1}, \ldots, e_n).$$

Otherwise, all subexpressions are values, so e is also a value.
(Counit) case Let $e = \mathsf{counit}_{\mathsf{use}}\, e_1$. If e_1 is not a value, apply the (ctx) rule for the syntactic context frame $\mathsf{counit}_{\mathsf{use}}\ \_$. Otherwise, e_1 is a value, and by Lemma 1, $e_1 = \mathsf{Mc}\langle(S_0, v_0)\rangle$, so the $(counit)$ rule is applied.
(Cobind) case Let $e = \mathsf{cobind}_{\mathsf{S},\langle \mathsf{R}_1,\ldots,\mathsf{R}_k\rangle}\, e_1\, e_2$. If e_1 is not a value, apply the (ctx) rule for the syntactic context frame K_1; if e_2 is not a value, apply the (ctx) rule for the syntactic context frame K_2. The contexts are defined as follows:

$$\begin{aligned} K_1 &= \mathsf{cobind}_{\mathsf{S},\langle \mathsf{R}_1,\ldots,\mathsf{R}_k\rangle}\ \_\ e_2 \\ K_2 &= \mathsf{cobind}_{\mathsf{S},\langle \mathsf{R}_1,\ldots,\mathsf{R}_k\rangle}\ v\ \_ \end{aligned}$$

If both e_1 and e_2 are values, then by Lemma 1,

$$\begin{aligned} e_1 &= \lambda x.e' \\ e_2 &= \mathsf{Mc}\langle(\mathsf{S} \circledast R_0, v_0), \ldots, (S \circledast R_k, v_k)\rangle, \end{aligned}$$

so the $(cobind)$ rule can be applied.
(Merge), (Split), (Dup), (Mc) cases Each case follows by the corresponding reduction rule and Lemma 1.

Theorem 12 (type safety of TLMC (restatement of Theorem 4)). *If $\Gamma \vdash e : \tau$ and $e \rightsquigarrow^* e'$, then*

1. *$\Gamma \vdash e' : \tau$*
2. *either e' is a value, or there exists e'' such that $e' \rightsquigarrow e''$*

Proof. By rule induction using Theorem 2 and Theorem 3.

D Type Safety of the Timetable Language

Here, we prove the type safety of the Timetable Language.

Theorem 13 (Well-typedness of the translation from Timetable Language to TLMC-TT). *Given a typing derivation of the closed Timetable Language judgment* $\langle\rangle@\langle\rangle \vdash e : \tau$*, let* f *be its TLMC-TT translation, written as follows:*

$$\frac{[\![(\dots)]\!] \quad = (\dots)}{[\![\langle\rangle@\langle\rangle \vdash e : \tau]\!] = \quad f}$$

Then f *is well-typed:* $\vdash f : [\![\langle\rangle@\langle\rangle]\!] \to [\![\tau]\!]$.

Proof. By induction on the derivation of the translation. As in the proof of Theorem 9, we verify whether the proposition holds for each translation rule.

(var), (num), (abs), (app), (weak), (exch), (contr) cases Same as Theorem 9.

(leg) case From the pre-translation context, the type of ρ is $C^{\mathbf{S}\otimes\mathbf{p}}[\![\Gamma]\!]$. Here,

$$\mathsf{leg}_{\mathbf{S},\mathbf{p}} : C^{\mathbf{S}\otimes\mathbf{p}}[\![\Gamma]\!] \to C^{\mathbf{p}}[\![\Gamma]\!] \quad (\because \text{Definition of } \mathsf{leg})$$

Also, by the induction hypothesis, $f : C^{\mathbf{p}}[\![\Gamma]\!] \to [\![\tau]\!]$. Therefore,

$$f(\mathsf{leg}_{\mathbf{S},\mathbf{p}}\ \rho) : [\![\tau]\!]$$

Consequently, the type of the entire post-translation lambda abstraction is

$$C^{\mathbf{S}\otimes\mathbf{p}}[\![\Gamma]\!] \to [\![\tau]\!],$$

and the proposition holds.

Lemma 12 (preservation under substitution of TLMC-TT). *For all* Γ, e, e', τ, τ', *if* $\Gamma, x{:}\tau \vdash e : \tau'$ *and* $\Gamma \vdash e' : \tau$ *then* $\Gamma \vdash e[x \leftarrow e'] : \tau'$.

Proof. By induction on the typing derivation of e. For (Var), (Num), (Proj), (Tup), (App), (Abs), (Counit), (Cobind), (Merge), (Split), (Dup), (Mc) cases, the same as Lemma 11.

(Leg) If $e = \mathsf{leg}_{\mathbf{S},\mathbf{p}}\ e_0$, then:

$$\tau' = C^{\mathbf{p}}(\tau_0 \times \cdots \times \tau_k)$$
$$\Gamma, x{:}\tau \vdash e : C^{\mathbf{S}\otimes\mathbf{p}}(\tau_0 \times \cdots \times \tau_k)$$

By induction, $\Gamma \vdash e[x \leftarrow e'] : C^{\mathbf{S}\otimes\mathbf{p}}(\tau_0 \times \cdots \times \tau_k)$, hence

$$\Gamma \vdash \mathsf{leg}_{\mathbf{S},\mathbf{p}}\ e_0[x \leftarrow e'] : C^{\mathbf{p}}(\tau_0 \times \cdots \times \tau_k).$$

Theorem 14 (type preservation of TLMC-TT). *If* $\Gamma \vdash e : \tau$ *and* $e \rightsquigarrow e'$ *then* $\Gamma \vdash e' : \tau$.

Proof. By induction over the reduction rule $\rightsquigarrow$. Using Lemma 12, we show that typing is preserved across each reduction rule. For (*fn*), (*prj*), (*ctx*), (*counit*), (*cobind*), (*merge*), (*split*), and (*dup*) cases, the same as Theorem 10.

(*leg*) case If $e = \mathsf{leg}_{\mathsf{S},\langle\mathsf{P}_0,\ldots,\mathsf{P}_k\rangle}\,\mathsf{Mc}\langle(S\circledast P_0, v_0),\ldots,(S\circledast P_k, v_k)\rangle$, then by the typing rule (Leg),

$$\Gamma \vdash e : C^{\langle\mathsf{P}_0,\ldots,\mathsf{P}_k\rangle}(\tau_0\times\cdots\times\tau_k).$$

Focusing on post-evaluation

$$e' = \mathsf{Mc}\langle(P_0, v_0),\ldots,(P_k, v_k)\rangle : C^{\langle\mathsf{P}_0,\ldots,\mathsf{P}_k\rangle}(\tau_0\times\cdots\times\tau_k)$$

Hence, typing is preserved across the reduction rule (*leg*).

Theorem 15 (progress of TLMC-TT). *If $\Gamma \vdash e : \tau$ then either e is a value or there exists e′ such that $e \rightsquigarrow e'$.*

Proof. By induction on the typing derivation of e. Each case mirrors the structure of Lemma 1: values are normal forms, and non-values have an applicable reduction rule. For (Num), (Abs), (Var), (App), (Proj), (Tup), (Counit), (Cobind), (Merge), (Split), (Dup), and (Mc) cases, the same as Theorem 11.

(Leg) case Let $e = \mathsf{leg}_{\mathsf{S},\mathbf{p}}\, e_1$ and $\mathbf{p} = \langle\mathsf{P}_0,\ldots,\mathsf{P}_k\rangle$. If e_1 is not a value, apply the (*ctx*) rule for the syntactic context frame $\mathsf{leg}_{\mathsf{S},\mathbf{p}}\,\_$. Otherwise, e_1 is a value, and by Lemma 1, $e_1 = \mathsf{Mc}\langle(\mathsf{S}\circledast\mathsf{P}_0, v_0),\ldots,(\mathsf{S}\circledast\mathsf{P}_k, v_k)\rangle$, so the (*leg*) rule can be applied.

Theorem 16 (type safety of TLMC-TT). *If $\Gamma \vdash e : \tau$ and $e \rightsquigarrow^* e'$, then*

1. *$\Gamma \vdash e' : \tau$*
2. *either e′ is a value, or there exists e″ such that $e' \rightsquigarrow e''$*

Proof. By rule induction using Theorem 14 and Theorem 15.

E A Worked Timetable Example: Derivation and Translation

E.1 Concrete Instance (JL43, BA318, AF1240)

Consider the itinerary shown in Fig. 9. All times are in GMT. The scheduled departure times are fixed by the timetable.

For computation, we encode times as minutes since 00:00 (GMT):

$$\begin{aligned}\bar{d}_0 &= 00{:}50 &&= 50\\ \bar{d}_1 &= 17{:}20 &&= 1040\\ \bar{d}_2 &= 20{:}15 &&= 1215\\ \text{arr}(\text{JL43}) &= 15{:}15 &&= 915\\ \text{arr}(\text{BA318}) &= 18{:}40 &&= 1120\\ \text{arr}(\text{AF1240}) &= 21{:}25 &&= 1285\end{aligned}$$

The flight durations and transfer durations are:

$$\begin{aligned}t_0 &= 0\\ t_1 &= arr(\text{JL43}) - \bar{d}_0 &&= 915 - 50 = 865 &&(\text{JL43})\\ t_2 &= arr(\text{BA318}) - \bar{d}_1 &&= 1120 - 1040 = 80 &&(\text{BA318})\\ t_3 &= arr(\text{AF1240}) - \bar{d}_2 &&= 1285 - 1215 = 70 &&(\text{AF1240})\end{aligned}$$

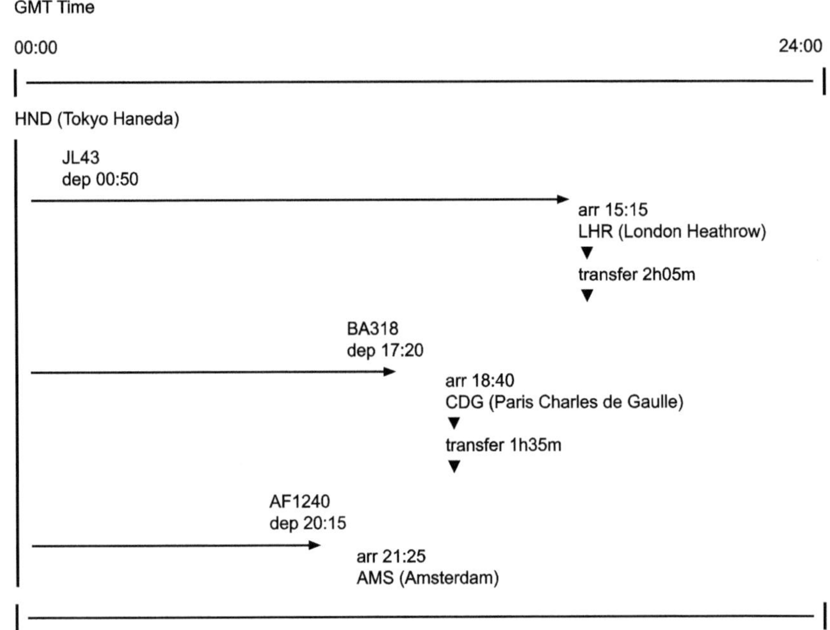

Fig. 9. The flight itinerary used in the running example.

E.2 Known Timetable Bounds Vs Propagated Bounds

We separate two roles that were conflated in the main text:

Known inputs (timetable-imposed bounds):

$\bar{d}_i$ scheduled earliest departure times
t_i flight times

Unknown outputs (propagated bounds):

d_i earliest feasible departure times computed from the itinerary

Let d_{init} be an initial lower bound on the first departure (here we take $d_{\text{init}} = 0$). Let $\bar{d}_3$ be $-\infty$ because there are no flights scheduled to depart from AMS for this itinerary. Then the propagated bounds are computed by:

$$d_0 = \max(\bar{d}_0,\ d_{\text{init}})$$
$$d_1 = \max(\bar{d}_1,\ d_0 + t_1)$$
$$d_2 = \max(\bar{d}_2,\ d_1 + t_2)$$
$$d_3 = \max(\bar{d}_3,\ d_2 + t_3)$$

For this instance:

$$\begin{aligned}
d_0 &= \max(50, 0) & &= 50\\
d_1 &= \max(1040, 50 + 865) &= \max(1040, 1040) &= 1040\\
d_2 &= \max(1215, 1040 + 80) &= \max(1215, 1215) &= 1215\\
d_3 &= \max(-\infty, 1215 + 70) &= \max(-\infty, 1285) &= 1285
\end{aligned}$$

Thus the itinerary is feasible and achieves the scheduled departures exactly.

E.3 Timetable Matrices (numeric) and Composition

We package the above propagation in the timetable matrix form. We work over the max-plus style operators (as in the main paper), with bottom element $-\infty$ ("no constraint") and multiplicative identity 0 ("do nothing"), and with matrix composition $\circledast$.

For this concrete instance, define four matrices:

$$S_0 = \begin{bmatrix} t_0 & \bar{d}_0 \\ -\infty & 0 \end{bmatrix} = \begin{bmatrix} 0 & 50 \\ -\infty & 0 \end{bmatrix}$$

$$S_1 = \begin{bmatrix} t_1 & \bar{d}_1 \\ -\infty & 0 \end{bmatrix} = \begin{bmatrix} 865 & 1040 \\ -\infty & 0 \end{bmatrix}$$

$$S_2 = \begin{bmatrix} t_2 & \bar{d}_2 \\ -\infty & 0 \end{bmatrix} = \begin{bmatrix} 80 & 1215 \\ -\infty & 0 \end{bmatrix}$$

$$S_3 = \begin{bmatrix} t_3 & \bar{d}_3 \\ -\infty & 0 \end{bmatrix} = \begin{bmatrix} 70 & -\infty \\ -\infty & 0 \end{bmatrix}$$

Composition yields:

$$S_3 \circledast S_2 \circledast S_1 \circledast S_0 = \begin{bmatrix} t & d \\ -\infty & 0 \end{bmatrix}$$

where

$$\begin{aligned}
t &= t_3 + t_2 + t_1 + t_0\\
&= 70 + 80 + 865 + 0\\
&= 1015\\
d &= \max(t_3 + t_2 + t_1 + \bar{d}_0,\ t_3 + t_2 + \bar{d}_1,\ t_3 + \bar{d}_2,\ \bar{d}_3)\\
&= \max(1065, 1190, 1285, -\infty)\\
&= 1285.
\end{aligned}$$

If we apply the composed matrix to the initial bound $d_{\text{init}} = 0$ (encoded as a contextual quantity), the top-right entry recovers the propagated lower bound $d_3 = 1285$ for the final departure.

E.4 An MCC Term and Its Full Typing Derivation

We now connect the numeric matrices above to a concrete MCC typing derivation. Consider the term:

$$e \triangleq (\lambda w : \tau.\, \mathsf{leg}\, S_3\, (\mathsf{leg}\, S_2\, (\mathsf{leg}\, S_1\, w)))(\mathsf{leg}\, S_0\, x).$$

Assume the (schematic) typing behavior of leg is:

$$\frac{\Gamma @ \mathbf{r} \vdash e : \tau}{\Gamma @ (\mathsf{S} \otimes \mathbf{r}) \vdash \mathsf{leg}\, S\, e : \tau}\ (\textsc{Leg})$$

Then a full derivation tree for e is as follows:

$$\dfrac{\mathcal{D}_B \qquad \dfrac{\dfrac{}{x : \tau\, @\, \langle \mathsf{use} \rangle \vdash x : \tau}\ (\textsc{Var})}{x : \tau\, @\, \langle \mathsf{S}_0 \rangle \vdash \mathsf{leg}\ S_0\ x : \tau}\ (\textsc{Leg})}{x : \tau\, @\, \langle (\mathsf{S}_3 \circledast \mathsf{S}_2 \circledast \mathsf{S}_1) \circledast \mathsf{S}_0 \rangle \vdash (\lambda w{:}\tau.\, \mathsf{leg}\ S_3(\mathsf{leg}\ S_2(\mathsf{leg}\ S_1\ w)))(\mathsf{leg}\ S_0\ x) : \tau}\ (\textsc{App})$$

$\mathcal{D}_{\mathbf{B}}$:

$$\dfrac{\dfrac{\dfrac{\dfrac{\dfrac{}{w : \tau\, @\, \langle \mathsf{use} \rangle \vdash w : \tau}\ (\textsc{Var})}{w : \tau\, @\, \langle \mathsf{S}_1 \rangle \vdash \mathsf{leg}\ S_1\ w : \tau}\ (\textsc{Leg})}{w : \tau\, @\, \langle \mathsf{S}_2 \circledast \mathsf{S}_1 \rangle \vdash \mathsf{leg}\ S_2(\mathsf{leg}\ S_1\ w) : \tau}\ (\textsc{Leg})}{w : \tau\, @\, \langle \mathsf{S}_3 \circledast \mathsf{S}_2 \circledast \mathsf{S}_1 \rangle \vdash \mathsf{leg}\ S_3(\mathsf{leg}\ S_2(\mathsf{leg}\ S_1\ w)) : \tau}\ (\textsc{Leg})}{\langle\rangle @ \langle\rangle \vdash \lambda w{:}\tau.\, \mathsf{leg}\ S_3(\mathsf{leg}\ S_2(\mathsf{leg}\ S_1\ w)) : \tau \xrightarrow{\mathsf{S}_3 \circledast \mathsf{S}_2 \circledast \mathsf{S}_1} \tau}\ (\textsc{Abs})$$

Thus the coeffect annotation on the only free variable x is the composed matrix $(\mathsf{S}_3 \circledast \mathsf{S}_2 \circledast \mathsf{S}_1) \circledast \mathsf{S}_0$, which is exactly the numeric matrix computed in Appendix E.3.

E.5 A Concrete TLMC Translation and One Reduction Step

We sketch the corresponding TLMC translation. Let $\mathsf{s} \triangleq \mathsf{S}_3 \circledast \mathsf{S}_2 \circledast \mathsf{S}_1$ as above, and let f and g be the translations of the function and argument:

$$f \triangleq [\![\langle\rangle @ \langle\rangle \vdash \lambda w : \tau.\, \mathsf{leg}\, S_3(\mathsf{leg}\, S_2(\mathsf{leg}\, S_1\, w)) : \tau \xrightarrow{\mathsf{s}} \tau]\!]$$
$$g \triangleq [\![x : \tau @ \langle \mathsf{S}_0 \rangle \vdash \mathsf{leg}\, S_0\, x : \tau]\!].$$

Then, the translation of the application has the characteristic App shape:

$$[\![x : \tau @ \langle \mathsf{s} \circledast \mathsf{S}_0 \rangle \vdash e : \tau]\!] = \lambda \rho.\, \mathsf{let}\ (ctx_1, ctx_2) = \mathsf{split}_{\langle\rangle, \langle \mathsf{s} \circledast \mathsf{S}_0 \rangle}\ \rho \quad \mathsf{in}\ f\ ctx_1 \big(\mathsf{cobind}_{\mathsf{s}, \langle \mathsf{S}_0 \rangle}\ g\ ctx_2\big).$$

Intuitively, split separates the context for the function from that for the argument, and cobind pushes the annotation s to the argument context so that it matches the translated arrow type.

A Single Reduction Step (Illustrating Annotation Propagation). Take a single-component run-time context value

$$\rho \;=\; \mathsf{Mc}\langle\!\langle s \circledast S_0,\ v_x \rangle\!\rangle.$$

By the TLMC reduction rule (*cobind*) (Fig. 3 in the main text),

$$\mathsf{cobind}_{\mathsf{s},\langle S_0\rangle}\ g\ \rho \;\rightsquigarrow\; \mathsf{Mc}\langle\!\langle s,\ g(\mathsf{Mc}\langle\!\langle S_0, v_x\rangle\!\rangle)\rangle\!\rangle.$$

That is, cobind factors out the outer annotation s (which corresponds to the function's coeffect), applies g to the stripped context $\mathsf{Mc}\langle\!\langle S_0, v_x\rangle\!\rangle$, and rewraps the result with annotation s. This step makes the operational behavior reflect the same coeffect composition $(\mathsf{S}_3 \circledast \mathsf{S}_2 \circledast \mathsf{S}_1) \circledast \mathsf{S}_0$ computed by the MCC typing derivation.

References

1. Brunel, A., Gaboardi, M., Mazza, D., Zdancewic, S.: A core quantitative coeffect calculus. In: Shao, Z. (ed.) ESOP 2014. LNCS, vol. 8410, pp. 351–370. Springer, Heidelberg (2014). https://doi.org/10.1007/978-3-642-54833-8_19
2. Gaboardi, M., Katsumata, S.Y., Orchard, D., Breuvart, F., Uustalu, T.: Combining effects and coeffects via grading. In: Proceedings of the 21st ACM SIGPLAN International Conference on Functional Programming, ICFP 2016, pp. 476–489. Association for Computing Machinery, New York, NY, USA (2016). https://doi.org/10.1145/2951913.2951939
3. Ghica, D.R., Smith, A.I.: From bounded affine types to automatic timing analysis (2013). https://arxiv.org/abs/1307.2473
4. Ghica, D.R., Smith, A.I.: Bounded linear types in a resource semiring. In: Shao, Z. (ed.) ESOP 2014. LNCS, vol. 8410, pp. 331–350. Springer, Heidelberg (2014). https://doi.org/10.1007/978-3-642-54833-8_18
5. Gifford, D.K., Lucassen, J.M.: Integrating functional and imperative programming. In: Proceedings of the 1986 ACM Conference on LISP and Functional Programming, LFP 1986, pp. 28–38. Association for Computing Machinery, Cambridge, Massachusetts, USA (1986). https://doi.org/10.1145/319838.319848. https://dl.acm.org/doi/10.1145/319838.319848
6. Halbwachs, N., Caspi, P., Raymond, P., Pilaud, D.: The synchronous data flow programming language LUSTRE. Proc. IEEE **79**(9), 1305–1320 (1991). https://doi.org/10.1109/5.97300. https://ieeexplore.ieee.org/document/97300
7. Lucassen, J.M., Gifford, D.K.: Polymorphic effect systems. In: Proceedings of the 15th ACM SIGPLAN-SIGACT Symposium on Principles of Programming Languages, POPL 1988, pp. 47–57. Association for Computing Machinery, San Diego, California, USA (1988). https://doi.org/10.1145/73560.73564. https://dl.acm.org/doi/10.1145/73560.73564
8. Matsuyama, K.: Formalizing a Choreographic Programming Language as an Effect-and-Coeffect System (2025). https://prg.is.titech.ac.jp/papers/pdf/thesis-b/2025-matsuyama.pdf
9. Petricek, T.: Context-aware programming languages. Technical report, UCAM-CL-TR-906, University of Cambridge, Computer Laboratory (2017). https://doi.org/10.48456/tr-906. https://www.cl.cam.ac.uk/techreports/UCAM-CL-TR-906.pdf

10. Petricek, T., Orchard, D., Mycroft, A.: Coeffects: unified static analysis of context-dependence. In: Fomin, F.V., Freivalds, R., Kwiatkowska, M., Peleg, D. (eds.) ICALP 2013. LNCS, vol. 7966, pp. 385–397. Springer, Heidelberg (2013). https://doi.org/10.1007/978-3-642-39212-2_35
11. Petricek, T., Orchard, D., Mycroft, A.: Coeffects: a calculus of context-dependent computation. SIGPLAN Not. **49**(9), 123–135 (2014). https://doi.org/10.1145/2692915.2628160. https://dl.acm.org/doi/10.1145/2692915.2628160
12. Tanabe, Y., Aotani, T., Masuhara, H.: A context-oriented programming approach to dependency hell. In: Proceedings of the 10th ACM International Workshop on Context-Oriented Programming: Advanced Modularity for Run-Time Composition, pp. 8–14. Association for Computing Machinery, New York, NY, USA (2018). https://doi.org/10.1145/3242921.3242923
13. Tanabe, Y., Lubis, L.A., Aotani, T., Masuhara, H.: A functional programming language with versions. Art Sci. Eng. Program. **6**(1) (2021). https://doi.org/10.22152/programming-journal.org/2022/6/5
14. Wadge, W.W., Ashcroft, E.A.: Lucid, the Dataflow Programming Language. Academic Press (1985)

Test Your Polymorphic Functions with Boolean Values

Akimasa Morihata(✉)

The University of Tokyo, Tokyo, Japan
morihata@graco.c.u-tokyo.ac.jp

Abstract. Testing of parametrically polymorphic functions is nontrivial because an inappropriate type instantiation may lead to overlooking bugs. Several studies have discussed sufficient conditions for *complete testing*, i.e., a set of tests that can find every incorrect input-output behavior. This paper studies *finite complete testing*, namely complete testing by instantiating type parameters with finite-domain types (Boolean type, in particular). The finiteness brings not only exhaustive testing but also simpler test cases and debugging than the existing state-of-the-art method, which may derive complicated types whose elements are costly or even computationally infeasible to identify. Based on the theory of parametric polymorphism, known as relational parametricity or Wadler's free theorem, we formulate a sufficient condition for finite complete testing; moreover, we provide a transformation that yields functions more suitable for applying the theorem. Our theory only examines types and hence applies even to black-box testing. A preliminary experiment with the Haskell 98 Prelude library demonstrated the promise of the current proposal, enabling finite complete testing of 57 functions among 79 polymorphic functions.

Keywords: Polymorphic Function · Testing · Relational Parametricity

1 Introduction

Parametric polymorphism is essential in typed functional programming. Many functions in the standard libraries are polymorphic, serving their application-independent usage.

Despite their ubiquity, the testing of polymorphic functions poses a subtle issue. An inappropriate type instantiation may lead to overlooking bugs. For example, consider the *filter* function that extracts the elements satisfying the given predicate.

$$\mathit{filter} :: \forall \alpha.\ (\alpha \to \mathit{Bool}) \to [\alpha] \to [\alpha]$$

Since the parametric polymorphism signifies the independence of the function from the type parameter α, any type seems appropriate for its testing. However, the instantiation with the unit type (consisting of only a single element) fails

M. Sperber and E. Komendantskaya (Eds.): FLOPS 2026, LNCS 16533, pp. 257–273, 2026.
https://doi.org/10.1007/978-981-92-0184-6_12

to check the usage of the predicate. Then, how about instantiation with the Boolean type?

Several studies [3,4,9,22] have identified this issue and developed methods for *complete testing*, i.e., a set of tests that can find every incorrect input-output behavior. These methods calculate type instantiations such that the resulting monomorphic types are isomorphic to the original polymorphic types. For instance, a complete testing of *filter* on a list of n elements consists of lists of integers from 1 to n and predicates over positive integers. The intuition behind this testing is that the function can be aware of only the position of the element (of type α).

This paper tries to take a step forward: when does an instantiation to finite-domain types (Boolean, in particular) suffice for complete testing? The idea underlying the development is to focus on the value identifications. For example, consider the standard *reverse* function.

$$\mathit{reverse} :: \forall \alpha.[\alpha] \to [\alpha]$$

For this function, we can locate every bug by identifying each element, i.e., checking whether the first element of the output is the last one of the input, and so on. Now, suppose a bug places a value incorrectly in the output as follows.

$$\mathit{reverse}\ [1,2,3,4] = [4,4,2,1] \qquad (\neq [4,3,2,1])$$

Note that due to the polymorphic type, *reverse* cannot observe the list elements or alter its behavior according to them. Therefore, the bug must be present even if we use, instead of the incorrect value (4 in this case), the results of applying to each value ($\equiv 4$), i.e., the identifications of the incorrect value.

$$\mathit{reverse}\ [\mathit{False}, \mathit{False}, \mathit{False}, \mathit{True}] = [\mathit{True}, \mathit{True}, \mathit{False}, \mathit{False}]$$

Testing the *filter* function is more involved. Consider the following test case, in which "3" is wrongly output.

$$\mathit{filter}\ \mathit{isOdd}\ [1,2,3] = [1,3,3]$$

One might be tempted to use *True* for the wrongly output value and *False* for the others. However, this approach disregards the presence of the parameter predicate, *isOdd*. The wrong behavior might be because *isOdd* results in *False* from 2. This issue can be resolved by considering the following test instead.

$$\mathit{map}\ \mathit{fst}\ (\mathit{filter}\ \mathit{snd}\ [(1, \mathit{True}), (2, \mathit{False}), (3, \mathit{True})]) = [1,3,3]$$

Here, each integer element in the input list is tagged by the result of *isOdd*, and hence, the LHS expression is equivalent to *filter isOdd* $[1,2,3]$. Now that no predicate observes the integer list element, the instantiation with the Boolean type works well.

The use of the finite-domain type has several potential benefits. First, it makes failing test cases smaller and debugging easier. As seen in the case of *reverse*, it commonly isolates the source of failure by tagging it as *True*, leaving others as *False*. Second, it naturally leads to exhaustive testing, e.g. testing

$$
\begin{array}{ll}
id :: \forall \alpha . \alpha \to \alpha & map :: \forall \alpha, \beta . (\alpha \to \beta) \to [\alpha] \to [\beta] \\
id\ x = x & map\ f\ [\,] \quad\ \ = [\,] \\
 & map\ f\ (a : x) = f\ a : map\ f\ x \\
fst :: \forall \alpha, \beta . (\alpha, \beta) \to \alpha & snd :: \forall \alpha, \beta . (\alpha, \beta) \to \beta \\
fst\ (x, y) = x & snd\ (x, y) = x \\
reverse :: \forall \alpha . [\alpha] \to [\alpha] & filter :: \forall \alpha . (\alpha \to \mathbf{2}) \to [\alpha] \to [\alpha] \\
reverse\ [\,] \quad\ \ = [\,] & filter\ p\ [\,] \quad\ \ = [\,] \\
reverse\ (a : x) = reverse\ x +\!\!+ [a] & filter\ f\ (a : x) = \mathbf{if}\ p\ a\ \mathbf{then}\ f\ a : filter\ p\ x \\
 & \qquad\qquad\qquad\quad \mathbf{else}\ filter\ p\ x
\end{array}
$$

Fig. 1. Standard functions used in this paper

reverse by inputting arbitrary Boolean lists.The exhaustivity not only guarantees completeness but also provides a foundation for analyzing the efficiency of the testing. Third, the simplicity of the type guarantees efficiency of processing each test case, in contrast with the existing state-of-the-art method [9] that, in the worst case, derives higher-order types and hence verifying the test results becomes computationally infeasible (see Sect. 5.2 for details).

We formulate the ideas as a theorem and a transformation (Sect. 3). The theorem presents a sufficient condition for when instantiating type parameters with finite-domain types leads to complete testing (hereinafter referred to as *finite complete testing*). The transformation leads to functions more suitable for applying the theorem. They are based on the theory of parametric polymorphism known as relational parametricity [17] or Wadler's free theorems [21]. Our theory only examines types and hence applies even to black-box testing.

Finite complete testing is not always possible. Nevertheless, a preliminary experiment with the Haskell 98 Prelude library [16] demonstrated the promise of the current proposal. Among 79 polymorphic functions, our theory brought finite complete testing of 57 functions.

2 Preliminaries

We use $f, g, h, x, y, z, \ldots$ to denote variables. Capital letters such as $A, B, T, \ldots$ denote types or type constructors. Greek alphabet $\alpha, \beta, \gamma, \ldots$ are type variables.

We describe programs using Haskell. For readability, we denote the lambda abstraction $\lambda x.\ e$ instead of $\backslash x \to e$ and use $\equiv$, $\not\equiv$, $\circ$, and $+\!\!+$ to denote the equality, nonequality, function composition, and list concatenation operators, respectively. $\mathbf{1}$ denotes the unit type that consists of only (). The Boolean type, which consists of $\mathbf{T}$ and $\mathbf{F}$, is denoted by $\mathbf{2}$. $\mathbb{Z}$ denotes the types for the integers.

Figure 1 lists the Haskell functions used in this paper.

Given a polymorphic expression $e :: \forall \alpha.\ T(\alpha)$, we let $e^{[\alpha := A]} :: T(A)$ denote its instantiation of the type variable α by the type A. If the type variable is apparent from the context, we may write e^A instead. For brevity, "a value of type α" refers to "a value of type A under the instantiation e^A with a certain type A" without specifying A. We assume the standard type isomorphisms, including currying, uncurrying, and the one between T and $\mathbf{1} \to T$.

We borrow the notion of functors from category theory. A covariant functor F consists of two mappings: one from each type A to type $\mathsf{F}A$, and the other from each function $f :: A \to B$ to $\mathsf{F}f :: \mathsf{F}A \to \mathsf{F}B$. The function mapping must satisfy $\mathsf{F}id^A = id^{\mathsf{F}A}$ and $\mathsf{F}f \circ \mathsf{F}g = \mathsf{F}(f \circ g)$. For brevity, functors refer to covariant functors in this paper. A typical functor is the list type constructor $\mathsf{L}X = [X]$, for which the *map* function maps functions. In general, a type constructor T consisting of products, coproducts, constants, functions, and functors is a functor if α appears only covariantly in $T(\alpha)$. We use $\mathsf{F}, \mathsf{G}, \mathsf{H}, \ldots$ to denote functors.

The theory developed here is based on the *parametricity* of the polymorphic types [17,21]. We restrict our scope to types and semantics that can be expressed in System F, which makes the parametricity principle hold. Note that our results remain applicable even to programs involving partial functions so long as their execution terminate without errors regardless of the evaluation strategy [5].

We will use the following lemma, whose proof is immediate from parametricity.

Lemma 1. *Consider a polymorphic function*

$$g :: \forall \alpha.(\mathsf{F}_0\alpha \to \mathsf{G}_0\alpha) \to (\mathsf{F}_1\alpha \to \mathsf{G}_1\alpha) \to \cdots \to (\mathsf{F}_{n-1}\alpha \to \mathsf{G}_{n-1}\alpha) \to \mathsf{H}\alpha$$

where each of $\mathsf{F}_i, \mathsf{G}_i$, *and* H *is a functor. Then, given functions* $f_i :: \mathsf{F}_i A \to \mathsf{G}_i A$, $f'_i :: \mathsf{F}_i B \to \mathsf{G}_i B$, *and* $h :: A \to B$ $(0 \le i < n)$, *the following equation holds:*

$$\mathsf{H}h\ (g^A\ f_0 \cdots f_{n-1}) = g^B\ f'_0 \cdots f'_{n-1},$$

provided that $\mathsf{G}_i h \circ f_i = f'_i \circ \mathsf{F}_i h$ *for every* $0 \le i < n$. □

3 Finite Complete Testing of Polymorphic Functions

3.1 Classifying Situations

Consider testing a polymorphic function, $g :: \forall \alpha.\ T_1(\alpha) \to T_2(\alpha)$. We instantiate the type parameter α with a certain type A, pass an input $v :: T_1(A)$ to $g^A :: T_1(A) \to T_2(A)$, and verify whether $g^A\ v :: T_2(A)$ equals the intended value. For complete testing, A must satisfy some requirements, depending on T_1 and T_2.

1. If $T_2(\alpha)$ is independent of α, such as $g :: \forall \alpha.\ [\alpha] \to \mathbb{Z}$, then α does not affect the output, and thus, no restriction is posed on A.
2. If T_1 and T_2 are functors, such as $g :: \forall \alpha.\ [[\alpha]] \to [\alpha]$, values of type α are typically stored in containers[1]. Erroneous behaviors can be usually detected by comparing the shape and elements of the output container with the expected

[1] In particular, $T(\alpha)$ is a container type if T is constructed from the products, coproducts, constant, and containers [1,2].

results. In this process, the element verification can be reduced to the check of the suspicious element (tagged by **F**, in particular). This pattern typically enables finite complete testing. Note that this case includes those using generator functions, such as $g :: \forall\alpha.\ (\mathbb{Z} \to \alpha) \to [\alpha]$.
3. If $T_1(\alpha)$ involves types corresponding to observations on α, such as $g :: \forall\alpha.\ (\alpha \to \mathbf{2}) \to [\alpha] \to [\alpha]$, the naive tagging approach mentioned above is insufficient. The behavior may depend on the result of the observations.
4. If $T_1(\alpha)$ involves types enabling computation on α, such as $g :: \forall\alpha.\ (\alpha \to \alpha) \to \alpha \to \alpha$, finite complete testing is commonly impossible. The parameter function (of type $\alpha \to \alpha$) may be repeatedly applied, and the behavior may depend on the number of applications. For instance, the type of g above is the Church encoding of natural numbers, suggesting the impossibility of perfectly investigating the behavior on the finite domain.
5. If $T_2(\alpha)$ involves function types, such as $g :: \forall\alpha.\ [\alpha] \to [\alpha \to \mathbb{Z}]$, we cannot test the equality on the output. Unless type isomorphisms (such as uncurrying) aid this situation, the testing-based approach is impossible.

We study the first two cases (Sect. 3.2), and then propose a transformation that reduces the third situation to the first two (Sect. 3.3). The last two cases are conceptual limitations of the current approach. We will empirically evaluate the severity of the limitations later (Sect. 4).

3.2 Sufficient Condition for Finite Complete Testing

For testing a polymorphic function $g :: \forall\alpha.\ \mathsf{T}_1\alpha \to \mathsf{T}_2\alpha$, where T_1 and T_2 are functors, we need to care about how to observe the output. It is natural to assume T_2 to be a container type [1,2], in which the shape and contents identify each value. Following this idea, we define two kinds of verifications over outputs.

Definition 1. *Given a functor* H, *a* structural property *is a polymorphic function* $sp :: \forall\alpha.\ \mathsf{H}\alpha \to \mathbf{2}$. *A verification of* $v :: \mathsf{H}(A)$ *against it is* $sp^A\ v$.

Definition 2. *Given a functor* H *and type* A, *an* element property *is a pair of functions* $ep :: (\forall\alpha.\ \mathsf{H}\alpha \to \alpha, A \to \mathbf{2})$. *A verification of* $v :: \mathsf{H}(A)$ *against it is* **let** $(acc^A, p) = ep$ **in** $p\ (acc^A\ v)$.

The first component of an element property is an *accessor* to an element. The polymorphic types of the structural property and an accessor signify their irrelevance to the elements of type α.

We assume that each test consists of a set of verifications against structural and element properties. For example, the complete identification of a list of length n consists of one about the length (a structural property) and the others for each element accessed via the index (an element property). Similarly, a dictionary (key-value store) is identified by checking the domain (a structural property) and each value accessed via the key (an element property).

The following lemmas are for reasoning about structural and element properties. Their proofs are straightforward from the parametricity principle.

Lemma 2. *Every structural property* $sp :: \forall\alpha.\ \mathsf{H}\alpha \to \mathbf{2}$ *for a functor* H *satisfies the following equality:*

$$sp^A = sp^{\mathbf{1}} \circ \mathsf{H}erase,$$

where $erase :: \forall\alpha.\ \alpha \to \mathbf{1}$ *is a function defined by* $erase\ a = ()$. □

Lemma 3. *Every element property* $(acc, p) :: (\forall\alpha.\ \mathsf{H}\alpha \to \alpha, A \to \mathbf{2})$ *for a functor* H *satisfies the following equality:*

$$p \circ acc^A = acc^{\mathbf{2}} \circ \mathsf{H}p.$$ □

These lemmas, together with Lemma 1, lead to the following finite complete testing.

Theorem 1. *Consider a polymorphic function*

$$g :: \forall\alpha.\ \mathsf{F}_0\alpha \to \mathsf{F}_1\alpha \to \cdots \to \mathsf{F}_{n-1}\alpha \to \mathsf{H}\alpha,$$

where F_i $(0 \le i < n)$ *and* H *are functors.*

1. *For any structural property* sp *for* H*, we can substitute the verifications of the outputs of* $g^{\mathbf{1}}$ *against* $sp^{\mathbf{1}}$ *for those of* g^A *against* sp^A.
2. *For any element property* (acc, p) *for* H*, we can substitute the verifications of the outputs of* $g^{\mathbf{2}}$ *against* $(acc^{\mathbf{2}}, id^{\mathbf{2}})$ *for those of* g^A *against* (acc^A, p).

Proof. The following reasoning proves the case of structural properties.

$$\begin{aligned}
& sp^A\ (g^A\ f_0 \cdots f_{n-1}) \\
= & \ \{\ \text{Lemma 2}\ \} \\
& sp^{\mathbf{1}}\ (\mathsf{H}erase\ (g^A\ f_0 \cdots f_{n-1})) \\
= & \ \{\ \text{Lemma 1, where } f_i' = \mathsf{F}_i erase\ f_i\ \} \\
& sp^{\mathbf{1}}\ (g^{\mathbf{1}}\ f_0' \cdots f_{n-1}')
\end{aligned}$$

The case of element properties is similar.

$$\begin{aligned}
& p\ (acc^A\ (g^A\ f_0 \cdots f_{n-1})) \\
= & \ \{\ \text{Lemma 3}\ \} \\
& acc^{\mathbf{2}}\ (\mathsf{H}p\ (g^A\ f_0 \cdots f_{n-1})) \\
= & \ \{\ \text{Lemma 1, where} f_i' = \mathsf{F}_i p\ f_i\ \} \\
& acc^{\mathbf{2}}\ (g^{\mathbf{2}}\ f_0' \cdots f_{n-1}')
\end{aligned}$$ □

Example (*reverse*). As an example, consider $reverse :: \forall\alpha.[\alpha] \to [\alpha]$ and its reference implementation REVERSE. Suppose that the result for a list $v :: [A]$ violates an element property (acc, p), namely, $p\ (acc^A\ (reverse^A\ v)) \neq p\,(acc^A\ (\text{REVERSE}^A\ v))$. Then, from the type of *reverse* (and REVERSE), Theorem 1 guarantees that inputting $v' = map\ p\ v$ causes the same wrong behavior:

$$\begin{aligned}
p\ (acc^A\ (reverse^A\ v)) &= acc^{\mathbf{2}}\ (reverse^{\mathbf{2}}\ v') \\
&\neq acc^{\mathbf{2}}\ (\text{REVERSE}^{\mathbf{2}}\ v') = p\ (acc^A\ (\text{REVERSE}^A\ v)).
\end{aligned}$$

In other words, Theorem 1 enables shrinking the failed test-case $v :: [A]$ to a Boolean list $v' :: [\mathbf{2}]$. Similarly, the instantiations with $\mathbf{2}$ are sufficient for verifying $zip :: \forall\alpha, \beta. [\alpha] \to [\beta] \to [(\alpha, \beta)]$ against element properties.

Example (*length*) The instantiation with $\mathbf{1}$ suffices for verifying $length :: \forall\alpha.[\alpha] \to \mathbb{Z}$. The return value is free from α, and hence, structural properties suffice for the verification. The same holds even for the generic *length* function in Haskell 2010, $length :: \forall\alpha, \tau.\ Foldable\ \tau \Rightarrow \tau\alpha \to \mathbb{Z}$, as long as the type constructor parameter τ is a functor.

3.3 Eliminating Observations

Recall the *filter* function.

$$filter :: \forall\alpha.\ (\alpha \to \mathbf{2}) \to [\alpha] \to [\alpha]$$

It takes a predicate of type $\alpha \to \mathbf{2}$. Since $T(X) = X \to \mathbf{2}$ is not a (covariant) functor, Theorem 1 cannot apply. Now, consider testing the following $filter'$ instead.

$$\begin{aligned} &filter' :: \forall\alpha.\ [(\alpha, \mathbf{2})] \to [\alpha] \\ &filter'\ x = map\ fst\ (filter\ snd\ x) \end{aligned}$$

It regards the second value of each element as the filtering condition. As the following equation shows, $filter'$ can simulate the arbitrary behavior of *filter*.

$$filter\ p\ x = filter'\ (map\ (\lambda a.(a, p\ a))\ x)$$

Thus, testing $filter'$ suffices. The absence of the predicate enables Theorem 1 to apply to it.

The intuition behind this is that the polymorphic type restricts the use of the predicate. Only the elements of the input list can provide the input of the predicate, namely, a value of type α. In other words, the predicate is unnecessary if the elements are associated with its result. The following theorem formalizes this idea.

Theorem 2. *Consider a polymorphic function*

$$g :: \forall\alpha.\ (\alpha \to \mathsf{F}_0\alpha \to \mathsf{G}_0) \to (\mathsf{F}_1\alpha \to \mathsf{G}_1\alpha) \to \cdots \to (\mathsf{F}_{n-1}\alpha \to \mathsf{G}_{n-1}\alpha) \to \mathsf{H}\alpha,$$

where F_i, G_i $(0 \le i < n)$, *and* H *are functors. Note that* G_0 *must not contain* α. *For verifications of outputs of* g^A *(against either a structural or element property), we can substitute those of outputs of the following* g'*:*

$$\begin{aligned} &g' :: (\mathsf{F}_1 B \to \mathsf{G}_1 B) \to \cdots \to (\mathsf{F}_{n-1} B \to \mathsf{G}_{n-1} B) \to \mathsf{H} B \\ &g'\ f_1' \cdots f_{n-1}' = \mathsf{H} fst\ (g^B\ f_0'\ f_1' \cdots f_{n-1}'), \end{aligned}$$

where $B = (A, \mathsf{F}_0 A \to \mathsf{G}_0)$ *and* $f_0'\ x\ y = snd\ x\ (\mathsf{F}_0 fst\ y)$.

Proof. We prove $g^A\ f_0 \cdots f_{n-1} = g'\ f'_1 \cdots f'_{n-1}$, where each f'_i $(1 \leq i < n)$ is defined as follows:

$$f'_i = \mathsf{G}_i mkpair_{f_0} \circ f_i \circ \mathsf{F}_i fst \quad \textbf{where } mkpair_{f_0}\ a = (a, f_0\ a).$$

The proof consists of the following equational reasoning.

$$\begin{array}{ll} & g'\ f'_1 \cdots f'_{n-1} \\ = & \{ \text{ definition of } g' \ \} \\ & \mathsf{H} fst\ (g^B\ f'_0\ f'_1 \cdots f'_{n-1}) \\ = & \{ \text{ Lemma 1 (the premise will be confirmed later) } \} \\ & \mathsf{H} fst\ (\mathsf{H} mkpair_{f_0}\ (g^A\ f_0\ f_1 \cdots f_{n-1})) \\ = & \{ \ fst \circ mkpair_{f_0} = id \text{ and } \mathsf{H} \text{ is a functor } \} \\ & g^A\ f_0\ f_1 \cdots f_{n-1} \end{array}$$

The application of Lemma 1 requires the following two conditions.

- $f_0\ x\ y = f'_0\ (mkpair_{f_0}\ x)\ (\mathsf{F}_0 mkpair_{f_0}\ y)$
- $\mathsf{G}_i mkpair_{f_0} \circ f_i = f'_i \circ \mathsf{F}_i mkpair_{f_0}\ (1 \leq i < n)$

The latter is easy from $fst \circ mkpair_{f_0} = id$ and the property of functors. The former can be verified as follows.

$$\begin{array}{ll} & f'_0\ (mkpair_{f_0}\ x)\ (\mathsf{F}_0 mkpair_{f_0}\ y) \\ = & \{ \text{ definition of } f'_0 \ \} \\ & snd\ (mkpair_{f_0}\ x)\ (\mathsf{F}_0 fst\ (\mathsf{F}_0 mkpair_{f_0}\ y)) \\ = & \{ \ \mathsf{F}_0 \text{ is a functor } \} \\ & snd\ (mkpair_{f_0}\ x)\ (\mathsf{F}_0 (fst \circ mkpair_{f_0})\ y) \\ = & \{ \ fst \circ mkpair_{f_0} = id \text{ and } \mathsf{F}_0 id^A = id^{\mathsf{F}_0 A} \ \} \\ & snd\ (mkpair_{f_0}\ x)\ y \\ = & \{ \text{ definitions of } mkpair_{f_0} \text{ and } snd \ \} \\ & f_0\ x\ y \end{array}$$

□

Remark. One might consider that the testing of *filter′* may lead to false positives, owing to the possibility of an argument, such as $[(\mathbf{T}, \mathbf{T}), (\mathbf{T}, \mathbf{F})]$, that cannot arise from associating the results of the predicate. In reality, this cannot happen, because *filter′* is essentially an instance of *filter*. Every erroneous behavior of *filter′* is due to *filter*.

Example (*filter*) Consider applying Theorem 2 to the *filter* function. Since $\alpha \to \mathbf{2} \simeq \alpha \to \mathbf{1} \to \mathbf{2}$, $\mathsf{F}_0\alpha = \mathbf{1}$ and $\mathsf{G}_0 = \mathbf{2}$. Thus, $B = (A, \mathbf{1} \to \mathbf{2}) \simeq (A, \mathbf{2})$, $f'_0 :: B \to \mathbf{2}$ is $f'_0\ x = snd\ x$, and in consequence, we obtain *filter′* mentioned earlier.

Example (map) Next, consider $map :: \forall \alpha, \beta.(\alpha \to \beta) \to [\alpha] \to [\beta]$. We apply Theorem 2 by regarding only α as the type parameter (i.e., β as a constant) and obtain the following function.

$$map\ snd :: \forall \alpha, \beta.[(\alpha, \beta)] \to [\beta]$$

Observe that the return value does not contain α; hence, from Theorem 1, the instantiation of α with $\mathbf{1}$ suffices.

$$map^{[\alpha:=\mathbf{1}]}\ snd :: \forall\beta.[(\mathbf{1},\beta)] \to [\beta]$$

Because $(\mathbf{1},\beta)$ is isomorphic to β, this result is equivalent to the folklore about *map*: testing *map id* is sufficient for *map* [3,9]. We can further instantiate β with $\mathbf{1}$ or $\mathbf{2}$, according to which structural or element properties we would like to verify.

3.4 Limitation

Theorem 2 relies on the finiteness of the functions that observe values of type α. Hence, it cannot deal with functions whose input may contain an arbitrarily many observation functions, such as $f :: \forall\alpha.[\alpha \to \mathbf{2}] \to [\alpha] \to \mathbf{2}$. Although appearing to be artificial, Theorem 2 sometimes yields such a type.

For instance, consider $nubBy :: \forall\alpha.(\alpha \to \alpha \to \mathbf{2}) \to [\alpha] \to [\alpha]$, which takes an equivalence relation (the first argument) and retains only the representatives of the equivalence class. Applying Theorem 2 results in $nubBy' :: \forall\alpha.[(\alpha, \alpha \to \mathbf{2})] \to [\alpha]$. In return for the elimination of the first argument, the second argument now contains a list of observations, and neither of Theorems 1 nor 2 applies anymore[2]. A function taking a binary relation as an argument often causes a similar problem. This problem is somewhat natural because $\alpha \to \alpha \to \mathbf{2}$ can encode $\alpha \to \alpha$, which hinders finite complete testing.

Careful modifications of the interfaces sometimes solve the problem. For example, consider $elemBy :: \forall\alpha.\ (\alpha \to \alpha \to \mathbf{2}) \to \alpha \to [\alpha] \to \mathbf{2}$, which checks whether the given list contains an element equivalent to the given element according to the given equivalence relation. As in the case of *nubBy*, finite complete testing appears to be impossible. However, this interface is loose. We do not need to compare list elements with each other! A better type is $elemBy' :: \forall\alpha,\beta.\ (\alpha \to \beta \to \mathbf{2}) \to \alpha \to [\beta] \to \mathbf{2}$. Applying Theorem 2 to $elemBy'$ results in $elemBy'' :: \forall\alpha,\beta.\ (\alpha, \beta \to \mathbf{2}) \to [\beta] \to \mathbf{2}$, which justifies instantiating α with $\mathbf{1}$. A further application of Theorem 2 (after currying) yields $elemBy''' :: \forall\beta.\ \mathbf{1} \to [(\beta, \mathbf{2})] \to \mathbf{2}$. Instantiating β with $\mathbf{1}$ safely eliminates all the type variables. In summary, the verification of $elemBy'$ is possible by instantiating α and β with $\mathbf{1}$ and $\mathbf{2}$, respectively.

4 Experiment

We evaluate the applicability of our theory by conducting an experiment on the polymorphic functions in the Prelude library of Haskell 98.

[2] This failure is essential. Instantiation with T consisting of n values cannot detect bugs that occur only in a long output, because $nubBy^T$ cannot output any list containing more than n elements.

4.1 Benchmark Functions

Among the 196 functions (including constants) in the Prelude library, 79 polymorphic functions were selected by excluding those matching the following conditions.

- Monomorphic functions, such as $\mathit{and} :: [\mathbf{2}] \rightarrow \mathbf{2}$. (25 functions)
- Those whose every type parameter is quantified by a numeric type class, such as *Num*: Since they essentially concern numeric computations, their finite complete testing is hopeless. A typical example is $(+) :: \forall\alpha.\ \mathit{Num}\ \alpha \Rightarrow \alpha \rightarrow \alpha \rightarrow \alpha$. (66 functions)
- Those whose types each have at most one inhabitant, such as $\mathit{fst} :: \forall\alpha, \beta.(\alpha, \beta) \rightarrow \alpha$: Their verifications require no testing. (15 functions)
- Those that are necessary for defining type classes, such as $(\equiv) :: \forall\alpha.\ \mathit{Eq}\ \alpha \Rightarrow \alpha \rightarrow \alpha \rightarrow \mathbf{2}$: They are in reality a collection of monomorphic implementations defined for every instance. (11 functions)

35 functions out of 79 involved type classes. We eliminated these type class constraints by the "dictionary-passing" transformation [8,15], which introduces extra parameters to receive the methods necessary for defining the type class. For example,

$$\mathit{lookup} :: \forall\alpha, \beta.\ \mathit{Eq}\ \alpha \Rightarrow \alpha \rightarrow [(\alpha, \beta)] \rightarrow \mathit{Maybe}\ \beta$$

is transformed to the following, because $(\equiv) :: \forall\alpha.\ \mathit{Eq}\ \alpha \Rightarrow \alpha \rightarrow \alpha \rightarrow \mathbf{2}$ is the requirement for the *Eq* class.

$$\mathit{lookup} :: \forall\alpha, \beta.\ (\alpha \rightarrow \alpha \rightarrow \mathbf{2}) \rightarrow \alpha \rightarrow [(\alpha, \beta)] \rightarrow \mathit{Maybe}\ \beta$$

A few type classes have more than one minimal way to define. For instance, one can define the *Eq* class via either $(\equiv)$ or $(\neq)$. For these classes, the author selected one that seemed the most natural. The selection did not affect the result.

4.2 Method

Theorems 1 and 2 were applied to all 79 benchmark functions. In this process, we assumed that type constructors, namely lists, tuples, *Maybe*, *Either*, and *IO*, are functors accompanied by appropriate accessor functions. The assumption is invalid for *IO* in a precise sense, but reasonable for our experiment. The *IO* in the Prelude library only involves files (or standard streams) and errors, and hence, is merely a variant of the state monad or error monad if we regard the files and the standard streams as the extra parameters. For example, the $\mathit{print} :: \forall\alpha.\ \mathit{Show}\ \alpha \Rightarrow \alpha \rightarrow \mathit{IO}\ \alpha$ function can be regarded as $\mathit{print} :: \forall\alpha.\ \mathit{Show}\ \alpha \Rightarrow \alpha \rightarrow (\mathit{stdout} \rightarrow (\mathbf{1}, \mathit{stdout}))$, and the detail of *stdout* does not affect the finite complete testing.

The experiment was conducted manually. The automation is future work.

4.3 Results

Among 79 benchmark functions, Theorem 1 could directly apply to 24 functions. Theorem 2 was effective for 33 out of the remaining 55 functions. Our method could not apply to 22 functions. The detail is presented in the Appendix.

We can categorize the sources of the inapplicabilities into the following two.

The primary source was the computation on α (cf. Sect. 3.1). This category includes all the inapplicabilities of functions without type classes (9 functions) and those concerning monads (8 functions). As we have discussed, it is natural to expect that finite complete testing is impossible for these functions.

The other source was the comparison operator on α (5 functions). They all come from type classes *Eq* and *Ord*. As discussed in Sect. 3.4, this is a conceptual limitation. Nevertheless, a close investigation reveals potential improvements.

- For the three functions from *Eq* (*elem*, *notElem*, and *lookup*), the interface was inappropriate. The types derived by the dictionary-passing transformation are less polymorphic than the actual semantics and hinder the applications of our theorems (cf. Sect. 3.4).
- For the two functions from *Ord* (*maximum* and *minimum*), ideally, complete testing with Boolean is possible. This fact follows from Donald Knuth's 0–1 principle for sorting networks [10], which states that sorting networks can be verified by a Boolean sequence. Unfortunately, the polymorphic type alone is insufficient because of the neglect of the properties of ordering.

In summary, for polymorphic functions in the Prelude libraries, Theorems 1 and 2 enable finite complete testing was possible for about 72% of functions. The identification of the possibilities was rather precise. These results show the promise of finite complete testing. Nevertheless, for dealing with type classes, there seems to be room for further investigation, particularly for exploiting the algebraic properties.

5 Related and Future Work

5.1 Methods for Testing Polymorphic Functions

Several studies have investigated the testing of functions with parametric polymorphism. To the author's knowledge, the first persons who discussed this issue are Bernardy et al. [3]. At roughly the same time, Christiansen and Seidel [4] developed a similar method in the context of strictness analysis. Xia [22] considered the categorical dual of the one by Bernardy et al. Hou and Wang [9] developed a precise and general formalism from the perspective of type theory. Unfortunately, none of them focused on finiteness. The current study is the first in-depth investigation into the finite complete testing of polymorphic functions.

Existing methods can be classified into two. The first type [3,4,9] counts the number of *occurrences* of values of type α (thus, "logarithm" [9] matters—logarithm counts the number of multiplications). The other type, particularly the one by Xia, tries to distinguish the *observations*. Our method is another observation-based method. Hou and Wang (Sect. 8.3 of [9]) conjectured that the observation-based approach would reduce the size of the test case. Our method answers the conjecture.

Our method is orthogonal to the occurrence-based methods. For example, existing occurrence-based methods certify that a list consisting of different integers, $[1, 2, \ldots, n]$, is sufficient to test *reverse*. Combining this result with ours, i.e., mapping the existence of the erroneous element, indicates that testing every Boolean list containing exactly one **T** suffices for the complete testing of *reverse*.

The blog post by Xia [22] is the first consideration on observation-based methods. In addition to the focus on complete finite testing, our method contains the following two essential refinements.

First, our method regards the *testing as an implicit observation*. Recall the *reverse* function. If we disregard the testing, it seems impossible to instantiate the type variable with the Boolean type, because $\forall\alpha.\ [\alpha] \to [\alpha]$ is not isomorphic to $\forall\alpha.\ [\mathbf{2}] \to [\mathbf{2}]$. Regarding the testing as an *explicit* observation also hinders complete finite testing. For instance, consider a variant of *reverse*, say *reverse_test*, which checks whether it outputs the same value as the reference implementation.

$$\mathit{reverse\_test} :: \forall\alpha.\ (\alpha \to \alpha \to \mathbf{2}) \to [\alpha] \to \mathbf{2}$$

As in the case of *nubBy* (Sect. 3.4), finite complete testing does not apply to a function having this type.

Second, Theorem 2 enables us to combine occurrence-based and observation-based methods by *incrementally* eliminating the observation function parameters. Xia's method is unsuitable for cooperation with occurrence-based methods because of its monolithic instantiation of type variables.

5.2 Efficiency of Complete Testing

Our method focuses on *finite* complete testing. One might expect that the finiteness improves the efficiency of the verification. In reality, our method leads to more testing using simpler test cases. Therefore, it is slower if the number of test cases matters, while the simplicity of the test cases is sometimes valuable.

Here, we compare ours with the existing state-of-the-art occurrence-based method by Hou and Wang [9]. For verifying the *reverse* function on a list of length n, our method requires 2^n-times testing with Booleans, whereas the existing method needs only a single testing with $\log n$ bits integers. However, complex types make the comparison more subtle. Consider $g_1 :: \forall\alpha.([\mathbf{2}] \to \alpha) \to \mathbb{Z} \to \alpha$. Unlike ours, the existing method instantiates α with $[\mathbf{2}]$, which increases the cost of the output verification. For $g_2 :: \forall\alpha.((\mathbb{Z} \to \mathbb{Z}) \to \alpha) \to [\alpha]$, it instantiates α with a function type, $\mathbb{Z} \to \mathbb{Z}$, thereby making the output verification infeasible.

5.3 Relationship to Knuth's 0–1 Principle

Our method appears to be related to Knuth's 0–1 principle for sorting networks [10]. Day et al. [6] indicated a connection between this principle and relational parametricity. Using relational parametricity, Voigtländer [19] developed the 0-1-2 principle for prefix-sum networks, which enables complete testing with a type of three values. Morihata [14] investigated sufficient conditions for complete testing of prefix-sum networks with Boolean values. Our theory cannot derive these results, perhaps because it cannot handle type classes precisely.

5.4 Future Work

We have developed a theory for finite complete testing of polymorphic functions. Yet, several developments are left.

A natural direction is automation. Taking type isomorphisms into account is particularly nontrivial. The automation might require reformulation of the proposed method along the course of Hou and Wang [9].

The discussion in Sect. 5.2 indicates that both the occurrence-based and observation-based methods have their own strengths and weaknesses. Their combination seems worth investigating.

The appropriate treatment of algebraic properties is also an issue. It seems necessary to deal precisely with type classes and deriving the 0–1 principle. Systematically developing nontrivial variations of the 0–1 principles [7, 11–14, 19] may be a milestone. Studies on relational parametricity under the presence of type classes [18, 20] may be informative for this direction.

We have considered structural and element properties. However, some natural properties, such as "arranged in ascending order" or "containing no duplication", fall into neither category. Breaking them into a series of structural and elemental properties may reduce the efficiency of testing, even if possible. Their efficient verification requires further investigation.

Our theory leads to a type instantiation with a type with a reasonably small domain. However, the type is not necessarily the minimal. For example, while our approach uses $(\mathbf{2}, \mathbf{2})$ for the *filter* function, the author currently doubts the necessity of four different values. Chasing the minimality might open a new interesting theory.

Acknowledgments. The author is grateful to anonymous reviewers for their careful and valuable comments, which helped improve the presentation of this paper, and to Atsushi Ohori for his insight on the connection between the current subject and Church encoding. The author is supported by JSPS Kakenhi 23K11044.

Disclosure of Interests. The authors have no competing interests to declare except the grant mentioned above.

A Detailed Experimental Results

Tables 1 and 2 list the results of the experiment. The "Th1" column shows whether Theorem 1 is applicable. The "w/Th2" column indicates whether Theorem 2 makes Theorem 1 applicable ("–" denotes that Theorem 2 is unnecessary).

Table 1. Experiments with Prelude functions (without type classes)

name	type	Theorem 1	w/Theorem 2
catch	$IO\ \alpha \to (IO\ Error \to IO\ \alpha) \to IO\ \alpha$	Yes	–
concat	$[[\alpha]] \to [\alpha]$	Yes	–
maybe	$\beta \to (\alpha \to \beta) \to Maybe\ \alpha \to \beta$		Yes
zipWith	$(\alpha \to \beta \to \gamma) \to [\alpha] \to [\beta] \to [\gamma]$		Yes
(!!)	$[\alpha] \to \mathbb{Z} \to \alpha$	Yes	–
(++)	$[\alpha] \to [\alpha] \to [\alpha]$	Yes	–
all	$(\alpha \to \mathbf{2}) \to [\alpha] \to \mathbf{2}$		Yes
any	$(\alpha \to \mathbf{2}) \to [\alpha] \to \mathbf{2}$		Yes
asTypeOf	$\alpha \to \alpha \to \alpha$	Yes	–
break	$(\alpha \to \mathbf{2}) \to [\alpha] \to ([\alpha], [\alpha])$		Yes
concatMap	$(\alpha \to [\beta]) \to [\alpha] \to [\beta]$		Yes
cycle	$[\alpha] \to [\alpha]$	Yes	–
drop	$\mathbb{Z} \to [\alpha] \to [\alpha]$	Yes	–
dropWhile	$(\alpha \to \mathbf{2}) \to [\alpha] \to [\alpha]$		Yes
filter	$(\alpha \to \mathbf{2}) \to [\alpha] \to [\alpha]$		Yes
foldl	$(\alpha \to \beta \to \alpha) \to \alpha \to [\beta] \to \alpha$		
foldl1	$(\alpha \to \alpha \to \alpha) \to [\alpha] \to \alpha$		
foldr	$(\alpha \to \beta \to \beta) \to \beta \to [\alpha] \to \beta$		
foldr1	$(\alpha \to \alpha \to \alpha) \to [\alpha] \to \alpha$		
head	$[\alpha] \to \alpha$	Yes	–
init	$[\alpha] \to [\alpha]$	Yes	–
iterate	$(\alpha \to \alpha) \to \alpha \to [\alpha]$		
last	$[\alpha] \to \alpha$	Yes	–
length	$[\alpha] \to \mathbb{Z}$	Yes	–
map	$(\alpha \to \beta) \to [\alpha] \to [\beta]$		Yes
null	$[\alpha] \to \mathbf{2}$	Yes	–
readParen	$\mathbf{2} \to ReadS\ \alpha \to ReadS\ \alpha$	Yes	–
repeat	$\alpha \to [\alpha]$	Yes	–
replicate	$\mathbb{Z} \to \alpha \to [\alpha]$	Yes	–
reverse	$[\alpha] \to [\alpha]$	Yes	–
scanl	$(\alpha \to \beta \to \alpha) \to \alpha \to [\beta] \to [\alpha]$		
scanl1	$(\alpha \to \alpha \to \alpha) \to [\alpha] \to [\alpha]$		
scanr	$(\alpha \to \beta \to \beta) \to \beta \to [\alpha] \to [\beta]$		
scanr1	$(\alpha \to \alpha \to \alpha) \to [\alpha] \to [\alpha]$		
span	$(\alpha \to \mathbf{2}) \to [\alpha] \to ([\alpha], [\alpha])$		Yes
splitAt	$\mathbb{Z} \to [\alpha] \to ([\alpha], [\alpha])$	Yes	–
tail	$[\alpha] \to [\alpha]$	Yes	–
take	$\mathbb{Z} \to [\alpha] \to [\alpha]$	Yes	–
takeWhile	$(\alpha \to \mathbf{2}) \to [\alpha] \to [\alpha]$		Yes
until	$(\alpha \to \mathbf{2}) \to (\alpha \to \alpha) \to \alpha \to \alpha$		
unzip	$[(\alpha, \beta)] \to ([\alpha], [\beta])$		Yes
unzip3	$[(\alpha, \beta, \gamma)] \to ([\alpha], [\beta], [\gamma])$		Yes
zip	$[\alpha] \to [\beta] \to [(a, \beta)]$		Yes
zip3	$[\alpha] \to [\beta] \to [\gamma] \to [(\alpha, \beta, \gamma)]$		Yes
zipWith3	$(\alpha \to \beta \to \gamma \to \delta) \to [\alpha] \to [\beta] \to [\gamma] \to [\delta]$		Yes

Table 2. Experiments with Prelude functions (involving type classes)

name	type	Theorem 1	w/Theorem 2
enumFrom	$Enum\ \alpha \Rightarrow \alpha \to [\alpha]$		Yes
enumFromThen	$Enum\ \alpha \Rightarrow \alpha \to \alpha \to [\alpha]$		Yes
enumFromThenTo	$Enum\ \alpha \Rightarrow \alpha \to \alpha \to \alpha \to [\alpha]$		Yes
enumFromTo	$Enum\ \alpha \Rightarrow \alpha \to \alpha \to [\alpha]$		Yes
pred	$Enum\ \alpha \Rightarrow \alpha \to \alpha$		Yes
succ	$Enum\ \alpha \Rightarrow \alpha \to \alpha$		Yes
$(\neq)$	$Eq\ \alpha \Rightarrow \alpha \to \alpha \to \mathbf{2}$		Yes
elem	$Eq\ \alpha \Rightarrow \alpha \to [\alpha] \to \mathbf{2}$		
lookup	$Eq\ \alpha \Rightarrow \alpha \to [(a, \beta)] \to Maybe\ \beta$		
notElem	$Eq\ \alpha \Rightarrow \alpha \to [\alpha] \to \mathbf{2}$		
$(=<<)$	$Monad\ m \Rightarrow (\alpha \to m\ \beta) \to m\ \alpha \to m\ \beta$		
$(>>)$	$Monad\ m \Rightarrow m\ \alpha \to m\ \beta \to m\ \beta$		
applyM	$Monad\ m \Rightarrow (\alpha \to m\ \beta) \to m\ \alpha \to m\ \beta$		
sequence	$Monad\ m \Rightarrow [m\ \alpha] \to m\ [\alpha]$		
*sequence_*	$Monad\ m \Rightarrow [m\ \alpha] \to m\ \mathbf{1}$		
mapM	$Monad\ m \Rightarrow (\alpha \to m\ \beta) \to [\alpha] \to m\ [\beta]$		
*mapM_*	$Monad\ m \Rightarrow (\alpha \to m\ \beta) \to [\alpha] \to m\ \mathbf{1}$		
$(<)$	$Ord\ \alpha \Rightarrow \alpha \to \alpha \to \mathbf{2}$		Yes
$(>)$	$Ord\ \alpha \Rightarrow \alpha \to \alpha \to \mathbf{2}$		Yes
$(\geq)$	$Ord\ \alpha \Rightarrow \alpha \to \alpha \to \mathbf{2}$		Yes
compare	$Ord\ \alpha \Rightarrow \alpha \to \alpha \to Ordering$		Yes
max	$Ord\ \alpha \Rightarrow \alpha \to \alpha \to \alpha$		Yes
maximum	$Ord\ \alpha \Rightarrow [\alpha] \to \alpha$		
min	$Ord\ \alpha \Rightarrow \alpha \to \alpha \to \alpha$		Yes
minimum	$Ord\ \alpha \Rightarrow [\alpha] \to \alpha$		
read	$Read\ \alpha \Rightarrow String \to \alpha$	Yes	–
readIO	$Read\ \alpha \Rightarrow String \to IO\ \alpha$	Yes	–
readList	$Read\ \alpha \Rightarrow ReadS\ [\alpha]$	Yes	–
readLn	$Read\ \alpha \Rightarrow IO\ \alpha$	Yes	–
reads	$Read\ \alpha \Rightarrow ReadS\ \alpha$	Yes	–
print	$Show\ \alpha \Rightarrow \alpha \to IO\ \mathbf{1}$		Yes
showList	$Show\ \alpha \Rightarrow [\alpha] \to ShowS$		Yes
shows	$Show\ \alpha \Rightarrow \alpha \to ShowS$		Yes
showsPrec	$Show\ \alpha \Rightarrow \mathbb{Z} \to \alpha \to ShowS$		Yes

References

1. Abbott, M.G., Altenkirch, T., Ghani, N.: Categories of containers. In: Gordon, A.D. (ed.) Foundations of Software Science and Computational Structures, 6th International Conference, FOSSACS 2003 Held as Part of the Joint European Conference on Theory and Practice of Software, ETAPS 2003, Warsaw, Poland, April 7-11, 2003, Proceedings. LNCS, vol. 2620, pp. 23–38. Springer, Cham (2003). https://doi.org/10.1007/3-540-36576-1_2
2. Abbott, M.G., Altenkirch, T., Ghani, N.: Containers: constructing strictly positive types. Theor. Comput. Sci. **342**(1), 3–27 (2005)
3. Bernardy, J., Jansson, P., Claessen, K.: Testing polymorphic properties. In: Gordon, A.D. (ed.) Programming Languages and Systems, 19th European Symposium on Programming, ESOP 2010, Held as Part of the Joint European Conferences on Theory and Practice of Software, ETAPS 2010, Paphos, Cyprus, March 20-28, 2010. Proceedings. LNCS, vol. 6012, pp. 125–144. Springer, Berlin, Germany (2010). https://doi.org/10.1007/978-3-642-11957-6_8
4. Christiansen, J., Seidel, D.: Minimally strict polymorphic functions. In: Schneider-Kamp, P., Hanus, M. (ed.) Proceedings of the 13th International ACM SIGPLAN Conference on Principles and Practice of Declarative Programming, 20–22 July 2011, Odense, Denmark, pp. 53–64. ACM (2011). https://doi.org/10.1145/2003476.2003487
5. Danielsson, N.A., Hughes, J., Jansson, P., Gibbons, J.: Fast and loose reasoning is morally correct. In: Morrisett, J.G., Peyton Jones, S.L. (eds.) Proceedings of the 33rd ACM SIGPLAN-SIGACT Symposium on Principles of Programming Languages, POPL 2006, Charleston, South Carolina, USA, 11–13 January 2006, pp. 206–217. ACM (2006). https://doi.org/10.1145/1111037.1111056
6. Day, N.A., Launchbury, J., Lewis, J.: Logical abstractions in Haskell. In: Proceedings of the 1999 Haskell Workshop. Utrecht University Department of Computer Science, Technical Report UU-CS-1999-28, Utrecht, Netherlands (1999)
7. Even, G., Levi, T., Litman, A.: Optimal conclusive sets for comparator networks. Theor. Comput. Sci. **410**(14), 1369–1376 (2009)
8. Hall, C.V., Hammond, K., Peyton Jones, S.L., Wadler, P.: Type classes in Haskell. ACM Trans. Program. Lang. Syst. **18**(2), 109–138 (1996)
9. Hou, K., Wang, Z.: Logarithm and program testing. Proc. ACM Program. Lang. **6**(POPL), 1–26 (2022). https://doi.org/10.1145/3498726
10. Knuth, D.: The Art of Computer Programming, vol. 3, second edn. Addison Wesley, USA Longman, Boston, MA (1998)
11. Li, S.R.: Unified algebraic theory of sorting, routing, multicasting, and concentration networks. IEEE Trans. Commun. **58**(1), 247–256 (2010)
12. Marić, O., Sprenger, C., Basin, D.: Cutoff bounds for consensus algorithms. In: Majumdar, R., Kunčak, V. (eds.) CAV 2017. LNCS, vol. 10427, pp. 217–237. Springer, Cham (2017). https://doi.org/10.1007/978-3-319-63390-9_12
13. Miltersen, P.B., Paterson, M., Tarui, J.: The asymptotic complexity of merging networks. J. ACM **43**(1), 147–165 (1996)
14. Morihata, A.: When does 0–1 principle hold for prefix sums? New Gener. Comput. **41**(3), 523–531 (2023)
15. Ohori, A.: A polymorphic record calculus and its compilation. ACM Trans. Program. Lang. Syst. **17**(6), 844–895 (1995)
16. Peyton Jones, S. (ed.): Haskell 98 Language and Libraries: The Revised Report. Cambridge University Press, Cambridge, UK (2003)

17. Reynolds, J.C.: Types, abstraction and parametric polymorphism. Inf. Process. **83**, 513–523 (1983)
18. Seidel, D., Voigtländer, J.: Proving properties about functions on lists involving element tests. In: Mossakowski, T., Kreowski, H. (eds.) Recent Trends in Algebraic Development Techniques - 20th International Workshop, WADT 2010, Etelsen, Germany, 1–4 July 2010, Revised Selected Papers. LNCS, vol. 7137, pp. 270–286. Springer, Cham (2010).https://doi.org/10.1007/978-3-642-28412-0_17
19. Voigtländer, J.: Much ado about two (pearl): a pearl on parallel prefix computation. In: Necula, G.C., Wadler, P. (eds.) Proceedings of the 35th ACM SIGPLAN-SIGACT Symposium on Principles of Programming Languages, POPL 2008, San Francisco, California, USA, 7–12 January 2008, pp. 29–35. ACM, New York, NY, USA (2008). https://doi.org/10.1145/1328438.1328445
20. Voigtländer, J.: Free theorems involving type constructor classes: functional pearl. In: Hutton, G., Tolmach, A.P. (eds.) Proceeding of the 14th ACM SIGPLAN international conference on Functional programming, ICFP 2009, Edinburgh, Scotland, UK, August 31 - September 2, 2009, pp. 173–184. ACM (2009). https://doi.org/10.1145/1596550.1596577
21. Wadler, P.: Theorems for free! In: FPCA'89 Conference on Functional Programming Languages and Computer Architecture. Imperial College, London, England, 11–13 September 1989, pp. 347–359. ACM, New York (1989). https://doi.org/10.1145/99370.99404
22. Xia, L.: A terminal view of testing polymorphic functions. Blog post (2017). https://blog.poisson.chat/posts/2017-06-29-terminal-monomorphization.html

Automatic Knowledge Gap Detection and Plan Validation Using Counterfactual Justifications

Alexis R. Tudor[1(✉)], Joaquín Arias[2], and Gopal Gupta[1]

[1] University of Texas at Dallas, Richardson, TX, USA
alexisrenee1@gmail.com
[2] CETINIA, Universidad Rey Juan Carlos, Madrid, Spain

Abstract. Given the increased importance of physical AI, reliable planning in dynamic environments remains a critical function of embodied systems. In particular, care must be taken in how they interact with situations outside the boundaries of their training. While planning languages such as PDDL or STRIPS tend to be highly problem-dependent, LLMs can be applied to broader and more general tasks in dynamic environments, but remain prone to hallucinations. Logic-based systems, in contrast, provide frameworks for a wide variety of problems and offer justifications for complete and correct plans, but offer no explanation when they cannot generate a plan. For example, VECSR, a planning system based on the s(CASP) answer set programming system, can create plans for unseen tasks by generalizing from a small number of training tasks. However, this generalization is limited to tasks achievable with actions learned during training. To address this limitation, we propose and build the *Counterfactual Generation Module*, which exploits the justification framework of s(CASP) to identify counterfactuals for unachievable tasks. These counterfactuals allow us to detect missing actions that should be incorporated into VECSR's knowledge base to enable task completion. We validate our proposal by asking VECSR to generate action plans for 55 tasks outside the 10 it was trained on. For 16 tasks, VECSR could not produce plans, and the counterfactuals "identified" the actions that need to be learned to complete 13 of them. Next, we evaluated 56 plans generated by GPT-4o, observing that the module's assessment of plan correctness corresponded to human evaluation, supporting that the module itself is correct.

Keywords: Commonsense Reasoning · Counterfactual Reasoning · Logic Programming

1 Introduction

Physical AI, which is the use of AI for embodied systems, is widely considered to be the next frontier of AI. For systems to carry out tasks in an embodied environment reliably, solving the planning problem for real-world environments

M. Sperber and E. Komendantskaya (Eds.): FLOPS 2026, LNCS 16533, pp. 274–292, 2026.
https://doi.org/10.1007/978-981-92-0184-6_13

becomes critical. There is an additional challenge when porting traditional planning approaches to an embodied environment in that it is impossible to train an AI for everything it may encounter in real environments. Thus, special care must be taken in how they interact with concepts outside of those they have learned in training. We posit that a truly trustworthy planning system requires two traits. Firstly, any planning system must have the ability to validate whether the plan it produces is theoretically correct and executable. We define a theoretically correct and executable plan as lacking any obvious flaws that would prevent the plan from being carried out even in ideal conditions. Secondly, a system must be able to identify and explain gaps in its own knowledge that result in being unable to produce a correct plan for a given unseen task.

Several approaches to the traditional planning problem exist, each with positive and negative aspects. Planning languages, like PDDL [20] or STRIPS [11], are designed with planning in mind, but lack the ability to generalize from a specific domain to others. Even within a single domain, systems built for learning with planning languages (like LOCM [8], LSONIO [23], or ARMS [31]) require large quantities of data and may often learn inaccurate plans which need to be reviewed by a domain expert when the data is noisy. Deep learning approaches, including large language models (LLMs), are trained on more general data, allowing them to plan for a wider range of domains. While these systems are often trained on even larger, noisier datasets than the previously mentioned planning language-based systems, the effect of the noisy data is typically smaller [26]. However, requiring large datasets has a downside, as data can be difficult and expensive to require and often contains unknown errors which can be internalized by the model. Additionally, while these systems are able to create plans to execute tasks, they often cannot explain why they have produced that solution, undermining trust in the results [22]. Worse, deep learning systems can produce an incorrect answer rather than correctly identifying that it cannot identify the answer based on its training. In LLMs, this behavior is referred to as "hallucination" and poses a major concern if used in real systems [3,15].

Logic-based systems, in contrast, provide more flexibility and ability to generalize than planning-specific languages and provide justifications for complete plans, increasing trust. However, they do not provide any justification when a complete and correct plan cannot be provided. In particular, we focus on the Virtually Embodied Common Sense Reasoning (VECSR) system, a logic-based planning system built for an embodied household environment and built on a foundation of goal-directed answer set programming [28]. VECSR is therefore highly explainable while making plans that have been verified to be correct against the constraints of the simulation. Additionally, VECSR is capable of generalizing from a small set of training data (in this case, tasks with action plans) to compute plans for unseen tasks in a simulated environment. This provides an advantage over the systems above, as it becomes trivial in most cases to find high-quality data when the amount of data required is small. However, it is only able to complete tasks which use actions and concepts learned in training, and not those tasks which require entirely novel concepts. In cases where VECSR does not have enough information to generate a task plan, it fails to produce a plan at all. This behavior is an improvement to over-confidently providing an incorrect answer, but does not provide any insight into why it has failed.

In this work, we have developed a Counterfactual Generation (CG) module (i) that can check if a plan is correct, and (ii) if incorrect, it can identify where the plan fails and why. The design of the CG module is a continuation of VECSR's design paradigm of using a small amount of training data to learn how to interact in an embodied environment. The module is implemented using s(CASP), an answer set programming solver that executes in a top-down goal-directed manner and constructs a proof tree for any solved query. By using this capability both for successful queries and the negation of failed queries, this proof tree provides transparency for correct and incorrect answers. Using s(CASP) we have created a knowledge base of environmental constraints in the embodied environment (such as being unable to grab an object without being close to it) extracted from the VirtualHome simulator. Many of constraints are enforced in the original VECSR knowledge base (hence the ability to create demonstrable correct plans based on learned actions from the training tasks), however because of the encoding of the original VECSR knowledge base it is not possible to identify the reason why a plan could not be created or why a plan would fail. VECSR creates plans by traversing lists, much like traditional planning solutions, however these lists prevent negated queries from providing meaningful explanations. The proposed CG module encodes these constraints directly, which means that using it to computer plans is intractable but the negation of failed plans is informative. Thus, it is easier to make a validation system (the CG module) than a reasoner (VECSR). A knowledge base expressed in rules (and constraints) can be expanded, refined, validated, and modified easily by adding new rules. Additionally, using this secondary knowledge base, and the fact that the planner can explain its decisions in natural language, allows us to detect errors in the knowledge base—so we can discard a plan, fix the knowledge base, and request a new plan. We include a Python interface to integrate the CG module with different plan systems, in particular with VECSR and GPT-4o, an LLM by OpenAI [17].

We use the CG module to improve the plan generation of VECSR. When VECSR is not able to provide a plan, we relax the constraints included in the VECSR knowledge base to guarantee generation of a plan, though the plan will be incorrect. We can then detect why the plan is not correct using the counterfactual module and take corrective actions. The module can also be used to check action plans for correctness, and evaluate it on action plans generated by GPT-4o and using the methods by Huang et al. [16].

We validate these two use cases on task and plan pairs generated by VECSR, by GPT-4o, and by an LLM system by Huang et al. [16]. VECSR was originally trained on 10 tasks, and then tested on 55 additional unseen tasks, of which it could achieve 39. We evaluate the remaining 16 tasks using the integrated VECSR with CG module, finding that we could reasonably generate counterfactuals, indicative of the missing knowledge in VECSR, for 13 of those tasks. To verify that the CG module correctly indicates a valid or invalid action plan, we also evaluate 56 LLM-generated plans with the CG module (10 generated by GPT-4o in the original VECSR validation [28] and 46 generated by Huang et al. [16]). We found that the correctness evaluation of the CG module provided results in line with that of human evaluation. The primary contributions of this paper are as follows:

- The Counterfactual Generation module, a standalone component designed with integration into VECSR in mind
- An analysis of the use of counterfactuals and justifications for detection of knowledge gaps with an explanation of what is missing
- A comprehensive validation that the accuracy of the Counterfactual Generation module aligns with human evaluation

2 Background

2.1 ASP and S(CASP)

Logic-based systems have high levels of inherent explainability, giving them an advantage over deep learning systems. Answer set programming (ASP), in particular, is a powerful declarative paradigm that uses stable model semantics to generate answer sets based on a given program. Implementations of ASP systems that require grounding, such as Clingo [12], are limited to programs that are considered safe (that is, that every variable appears in at least one positive goal). On the other hand, s(CASP), a goal-directed implementation of ASP, is executed in a top-down fashion that eliminates the need for grounding [2].

Using ASP, and particularly s(CASP), in this work allows for complex representations of real-world commonsense rules. In this section, we will cover a few of the features of s(CASP) that are of particular use for this work. Our knowledge base uses *even loops over negation* and *odd loops over negation*, which are essentially *abducibles* and *contradictions* or *denials*[1]:

- Abducibles can be used to generate multiple possible worlds in an answer, allowing for assumptions to be made in the absence of denial information. For example:

  ```
  p :- not q.                                   q :- not p.
  ```

  Generates two worlds, one where only `p` is true, and another world where only `q` is true.
- Contradictions, conversely, to bar worlds from existing where certain conditions are true. Adding `r :- target(X),not r.`, where target(X) is some constraint, prevents any model from being created where target(X) is true.

[1] Note that s(CASP) uses the same syntax as Prolog, where `p :- not q.` can be read as not q implies p.

The most important feature of s(CASP) for counterfactual reasoning is the capability of s(CASP) to generate justification trees for each answer set [1]. Because the semantics of s(CASP) use backwards chaining, the justification trees it generates are intuitive to read and indicative of why an answer for a particular goal is correct. The s(CASP) justification tree can be generated for a successful query and for the negation of a failed query. For example, given the query `?- p.` to the following program:

```
s.                    p :- not q.                    q :- s.
```

There would be `no models` containing `p`, meaning that a solution cannot be found for this query. On the other hand, the query `?- not p` would generate the justification tree:

```
not p :-
    q :-
        s.
```

Indicating that `not p` succeeds because `q` holds which, in turn, holds because `s` holds, allowing for justification of both successful and unsuccessful queries. We can leverage this justification feature of s(CASP) to successfully reason with counterfactuals.

2.2 VECSR and VirtualHome

The Virtually Embodied Common Sense Reasoning (VECSR) [28] system combines the s(CASP) reasoner with various simulation environments for commonsense reasoning. VECSR can solve several planning problems in a variety of domains by converting facts about a simulated world state into a s(CASP) representation for reasoning. Additionally, due to the large size of most simulation fact bases, VECSR comes with several static analysis tools to reduce the computation time of the resultant s(CASP) program. VECSR is highly generalizable and designed to function in simulated embodied environments, and can be modified with new rules without the need for additional data. VECSR is open source and available at https://github.com/Alexandara/vecsr. VECSR works with multiple simulation environments [29], however, the focus of this work is the use of VECSR with VirtualHome.

VirtualHome [24] is a simulated apartment that provides an API for embodied actions run by an autonomous agent and has robust documentation available online at http://virtual-home.org/. Additionally, VirtualHome provides a large dataset of domestic tasks alongside human-generated breakdowns. This dataset contains 549 tasks, each of which contain at least one human-created plan breakdown, making it an excellent resource for training. The VirtualHome documentation provides the preconditions and postconditions of any actions in the simulation. For example, the "grab" action has a precondition of being close to the object being grabbed and a postcondition of the object being held.

VECSR was trained on ten tasks in the VirtualHome database, and is able to generate plans in the environment that are guaranteed to be correct and executable by the constraints of the simulation environment. VECSR takes into account the existing items in the simulation when formulating its plan, and when it lacks the knowledge to produce a plan, it produces no plan.

3 Design of the Counterfactual Generation Module

The Counterfactual Generation module is a standalone contribution that can be used with any simulation-based generated action plans. We posit that it could be a valuable addition at the end of any planning solution's pipeline. We discuss integration with one such planning solution in Sect. 3.1. In this section, we describe the counterfactual generation process as described in Algorithm 1. The algorithm is primarily implemented in Python, but interacts with the CG s(CASP) reasoner when calling SET_INITIAL_WORLD_STATE, ACTION_POSSIBLE, and UPDATE_WORLD_STATE.

Algorithm 1 Counterfactual generation algorithm

Input A where A = Ordered List of Actions in Plan

$time \leftarrow 1$
SET_INITIAL_WORLD_STATE
for $a_n \in A$ **do**
    ACTION_POSSIBLE(a_n, $time$) ▷ Where Success is true if the action is possible
    if Success **then**
        UPDATE_WORLD_STATE(a_n)
        $time \leftarrow time + 1$
    else if !Success **then**
        ACTION_POSSIBLE(a_n, $time$)
        return Justification ▷ s(CASP) tree for why Action_Possible failed
    end if
end for

a) **First**, the input to the CG module is an ordered list of actions A which represent the steps in the plan. The CG module takes the form of a s(CASP) program created by formalizing the simulation constraints from the VirtualHome environment (but could be adapted from any simulation environment) in order to evaluate domestic task plans. It is notable that the constraints used to build the CG module are different from the knowledge base used to train VECSR originally. The former consist of physical constraints in the simulation defined by preconditions as described below, and the latter is a knowledge base of human-created plans. Of those plans, 10 were used to train the original VECSR. This difference in knowledge base is primarily due to the encodings required to generate plans being different from the encodings required to perform a negated query and receive a meaningful justification tree.

The Counterfactual Generation module is based on iterating over a known quantity of time steps (`time(Time).` starting with $Time \leftarrow 1$) and checking against the constraints for each action defined in the VirtualHome documentation. For example, the preconditions for using the "walk" action on the "obj1" object are defined as follows:

- character is not sitting
- obj1 is reachable (not inside some closed container) or obj1 is a room.
- obj1 is not grabbed

This can be formalized in s(CASP) as[2]:

```
action_valid(walk,Object,Time) :- rooms(Object),
                                  not -action_valid(walk, Object, Time).
action_valid(walk,Object,Time) :- -rooms(Object),
                                  not sitting(character1, Time),
                                  reachable(Object, Time),
                                  inside(character1, Room, Time),
                                  inside(Object, Room, Time),
                                  not -action_valid(walk, Object, Time).
```

Where `reachable/2` is defined as:

```
reachable(Object, Time) :- not -reachable(Object, Time).
-reachable(Object, Time) :- inside(Object, Container, Time),
                            closed(Container, Time).
```

The above rules make use of strong negation, so that we assume if something is not explicitly unreachable, it is reachable. In addition to the constraints imposed by the simulator itself, we allow for exceptions [30] using `not -action_valid/3`. However, for most actions, the only area where `-action_valid/3` succeeds is where the object does not exist, as in `-action_valid(_,Object, _) :- not exists(Object).`.

We also include (i) global constraints for commonsense rules provided by the simulator that are inviolable, such as that the agent only has two hands and can therefore only hold two things:

```
:- held(Object1, Time), held(Object2, Time), held(Object3, Time),
   Object1 \= Object2, Object1 \= Object3, Object2 \= Object3.
```

And, (ii) abducibles using simple even loops, such as whether something is open or closed:

```
open(Object, Time) :- not closed(Object, Time).
closed(Object, Time) :- not open(Object, Time).
```

Note that while `closed/2` could be represented as `-open/2`, we match the convention of the VirtualHome simulation by having `closed/2` and `open/2`.

b) Second, if an action is successful, we execute lines 5 to 7 in Algorithm 1. For each successful action executed, we update the world state of the simulation with the postconditions of that action. Following the previous example, the postconditions for the "walk" action on "obj1" at time *Time* are defined by VirtualHome as follows:

[2] Note that the dash (-) before a predicate is an example of classical negation.

- character will move at a distance close to the object, making sure it is visible.
- if obj1 is a room, character will move to the center of the room

When the CG module updates the state with these postconditions, it takes the form of adding the rule `close(character,obj1, Time)` as well as `inside(character,obj1, Time)` if obj1 is a room. This allows commonsense constraints to enforce proper sequencing of actions. For example, if another action in the list is to grab obj1 at time $Time2$, and a precondition to grab is that obj1 is close to the character, it follows that $Time2$ cannot be smaller than $Time$. After updating the world state for successfully taken actions, time is incremented and the process starts over for the next action.

c) Eventually, for unachievable action plans, an action will fail to be carried out (invalid action) given the constraints of the simulation and current world state (line 8 of Algorithm 1). When an invalid action is found, the corresponding subgoal is negated and executed as a query to obtain the justification for why that action is invalid. The Appendix includes an example of an invalid plan for the task "Put shoes and coats [on]", which produces the following justification tree:

```
not action_done(walk,coat3205,8) :- time(8),
    action(walk),
    not action_valid(walk,coat3205,8) :-
        not rooms(coat3205),
        -rooms(coat3205) :-
            proved(not rooms(coat3205)).
        not sitting(character1,8),
        not held(coat3205,8),
        not reachable(coat3205,8) :-
            -reachable(coat3205,8) :-
                inside(coat3205,closet114,8),
                closed(closet114,8).
```

Analysis of the counterfactual provided by this justification tree identifies that the action is not achievable because `coat3205` is not `reachable/2` at time `8` because it is inside `closet114` which is `closed/2`. Therefore, the facts at the bottom of the justification tree would be what needs to be different at $time = 8$ for this action to have been achievable. The CG module is highly scalable, as execution for even the longest tested plans takes only a few seconds.

3.1 Integration of CG with VECSR

We integrated the CG module as an enhancement to VECSR as demonstrated in Fig. 1. Creating the CG module as a standalone component was required due to the unsuitability of the VECSR system's knowledge representation for counterfactual generation. The original VECSR knowledge base is designed around state and action plans being manipulated as lists, which means that one cannot negate a query and receive a justification tree, which is critical to counterfactual analysis using s(CASP) [10]. VECSR performs a loop consisting of five main steps, depicted in the top half of Fig. 1:

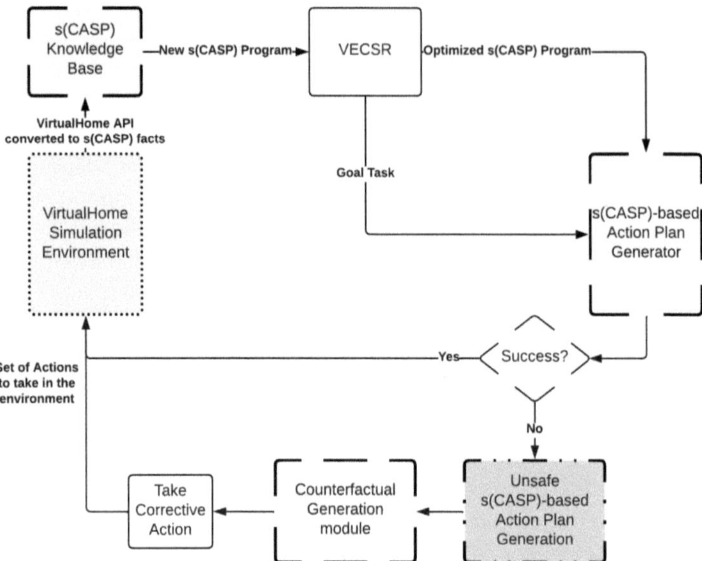

Fig. 1. The VECSR system with the Counterfactual Generation module added.

1. Convert a simulation (VirtualHome) to s(CASP) facts
2. Merge those facts with a knowledge base
3. Perform optimizations on the newly created s(CASP) program
4. Use s(CASP) to generate action plan to complete a task
5. Perform actions in the simulation environment

The integration of the CG module starts after step four (represented with the addition of a "Success?" block in Fig. 1). If generating a plan succeeds, the loop continues as above. However, if it fails, the desired task and initial world state are used again in an "unsafe" version of VECSR that is guaranteed to produce a plan, but is not guaranteed to produce a *correct* plan. That plan then becomes the input to the CG module, which finds the step at which the plan becomes incorrect and the justification for why it is not correct based on the parameters given by the simulation. This information can then be reviewed, and various corrective actions taken depending on the nature of the system.

The input to this process is the same as the input to the original VECSR: a task $t \in T$ to complete, where T is the set of all tasks in the VirtualHome database. If the task is successfully achieved, then the CG module is not called and the process is the same as described by Tudor et al. (2025). If the task is not achievable, the CG module process begins on line 3 of Algorithm 2.

First, t is input to an "unsafe" version of VECSR. Our definition of unsafe is that the plans it produces are not guaranteed to be correct as per the original work. This change guarantees it to produce a plan for any input task, however these plans are often flawed and are not feasible given the constraints of the

Algorithm 2 Integration of CG module and VECSR.

```
Input t ∈ T where T = Set of All VirtualHome Tasks
A = VECSR(t)        ▷ Guaranteed to produce a correct answer, or no answer
if Success then return A
else if Failure then
    A = VECSR_UNSAFE(t)        ▷ Guaranteed to produce an answer
    CG_MODULE(A)
end if
```

simulation environment. The original VECSR produced only actions that were constrained to be legal, it fails otherwise. This paradigm is formalized below:

```
choose_action(Action, State1, State2) :- suggest(Action, State1, State2),
                                         legal_action(Action, State1).
choose_action(Action, State1, _) :- legal_action(Action, State1).
```

where `Action` is the next action to take, `State1` is the current world state, and `State2` is the desired outcome given the input task. When an unachievable task is input, its failure is reported by s(CASP), namely, that a model cannot be found. This was the case in 16 of the tasks evaluated with VECSR in 2025 [28]. To guarantee generation of plans, whether they are correct or not, we add

```
choose_action(Action, State1, State2) :- suggest(Action, State1, State2).
```

in between the two previously existent `choose_action/3` rules. This additional rule allows for actions that may lead to task completion, regardless of if those actions are legal, given the current state of the world. This invalid action plan becomes the input to Algorithm 1, which returns the justification for why the action plan is invalid. The version of VECSR extended with CG is also available at https://github.com/Alexandara/vecsr/releases/tag/v1.1.0.

The example "Put shoes and coats [on]" above is one of the failed tasks from the original VECSR, which had an action plan generated for it by the "unsafe" VECSR. Analyzing that counterfactual indicates a need for the "open" action to change `closed/2` so that the coat can be accessed. This was noted in the original VECSR research as an action that wasn't learned from the ten examples VECSR was built around. Using the CG module, we have thus identified a gap in VECSR's knowledge base. Though not covered in the scope of this paper, identifying these gaps allows for corrective action to be taken (such as learning the "open" action to open the doors of a cupboard; the "open" action learned will help complete other tasks that could not be achieved earlier) or to provide awareness of the limitations of a system.

3.2 Integration of CG with LLMs

In the same way that the CG module was integrated with VECSR, we posit that it could be integrated with LLMs. We perform a surface level integration with GPT-4o to evaluate the correctness of the CG module. Similar to the integration in Algorithm 2, we used GPT-4o to generate action plans, which became the input to the CG module. Some translation was required between the natural language of GPT-4o (a notable weakness of LLM planning) and the executable language of VirtualHome for the integration, which we performed by hand[3].

This kind of integration could further be used to validate that the final output of an LLM is not hallucinatory (which we do below) but also during training or fine-tuning to provide automated evaluation of the correctness of a given output. However, the primary integration of this work is the CG module with VECSR. We use GPT-4o generated plans to validate the correctness of the CG module compared to other research.

4 Evaluation and Validation of CG

4.1 CG for Increasing Task Coverage in VECSR

VECSR was originally trained on 10 tasks and then evaluated on 55 additional tasks randomly selected from the VirtualHome task database. VECSR could only achieve 39 of those tasks, providing no models for the remaining 16. We evaluated the CG module on those remaining tasks, *producing action plans for all 16 originally unachievable plans.* The CG module provided a justification-based counterfactual for each task, and for 13 of those tasks the counterfactual provided a clear knowledge gap that resulted in the task being unachievable. The "open" action knowledge gap at the end of Sect. 3 prevented 8 (out of the 13) of those tasks from being accomplished. Another example of a knowledge gap that prevented task completion is knowledge of the outside of the house. One such task is "Prepare letter for mailing", which produces a non-viable action plan (See the Appendix for an example).

The agent needs to be inside the same area as an object to walk to it. However, the knowledge base only contained the information for the rooms of the apartment and did not include information about leaving the apartment. Thus, the action plan was unable to be executed as the agent could not locate the mailbox to walk to it. Figure 2 contains a breakdown of the knowledge gaps identified, and how many tasks of the 16 were affected by that knowledge gap. The other two knowledge gaps include activities done with other agents ("Get

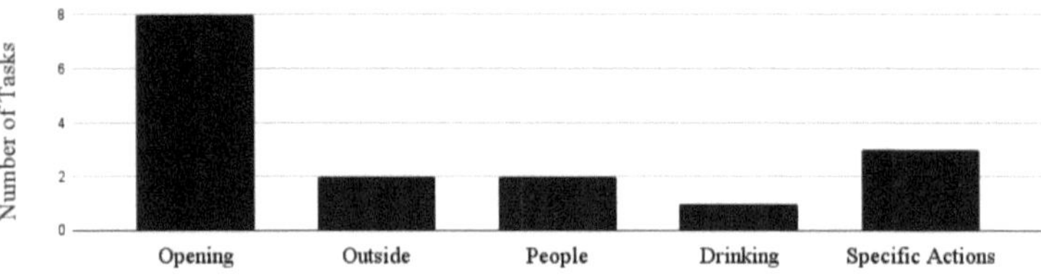

Fig. 2. Number of failed tasks by required concept for task completion.

[3] This primarily took the form of syntactic corrections, e.g. translating "Walk to your home office" to "Walk to homeoffice".

in way of guests trying to leave") and drinking something rather than eating it ("Have ice coffee").

However, three of the tasks from VECSR's original evaluation did not have clear counterfactual solutions. To explain this, we define the set of known concepts in VECSR's knowledge base (C_k) as our in-distribution data, learned by the original VECSR by reviewing 10 randomly selected tasks. The tasks which required concepts α where $\alpha \in C_k$ are achievable, and the 16 unachievable tasks T_u requiring concepts outside C_k require concepts in a separate set C_u, containing all concepts not included in C_k. C_u contains two kinds of concepts of interest for this work. The first concepts could be said to fall in C'_k, which are complements of actions of C_k that can be defined by actions in C_k. For example, the action *open* in C_u is approximately equal to $close'$ (complement of *close*), where $close \in C_k$. This also applies to concepts that aren't actions, such as $outside \approx inside'$ and $inside \in C_k$.

Conversely, the second type of concepts in C_u are made up of our three remaining tasks. These require actions or concepts that cannot easily be quantified as complements or combinations of concepts in C_k. For example, one such task is "Do free-style dance routine", requiring the concept of dancing. However, dancing cannot be easily described by the concepts existent in C_k. While the Counterfactual Generation module can easily discover flaws in action plans requiring the first type of concept in C_u, it cannot fill the knowledge gaps required for the second, which is true out-of-distribution data. Nonetheless, this identifies the missing knowledge required for incomplete tasks in 81% of cases, and if corrective action is taken based on the generated counterfactuals, the generalized task completion of VECSR could be increased from 70.91% to 94.55%.

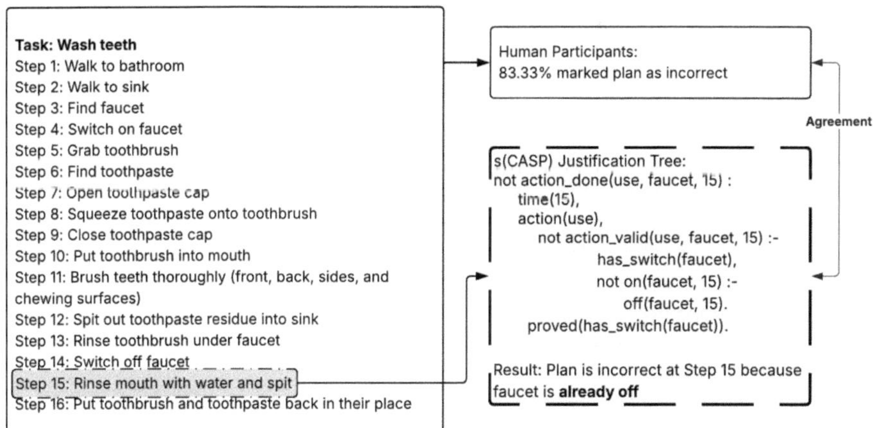

Fig. 3. Example task generated by GPT-4o previously marked incorrect by human participants, also validated as incorrect by the VECSR counterfactual analysis.

Table 1. Human correctness evaluation of GPT-4o generated plans vs. CG validation (Yes/No), along with the first wrong step of the incorrect plans.

Task	Correctness Evaluation		
	Humans	CG	Wrong Step
Go To Sleep	83.33% (±0.39)	Yes	—
Browse Internet	**50.00%** (±0.52)	**No**	Step 3
Wash Teeth	**16.67%** (±0.39)	**No**	Step 15
Brush Teeth	91.67% (±0.29)	Yes	—
Vacuum	83.33% (±0.39)	Yes	—
Change Sheets [...]	91.67% (±0.29)	Yes	—
Wash Dirty Dishes	83.33% (±0.39)	Yes	—
Feed Me**	**33.33%** (±0.49)	Yes	—
Breakfast	**25.00%** (±0.45)	**No**	Step 3
Read	66.67% (±0.49)	Yes	—
Valid tasks*	6/10	7/10	

(*)A task rated as correct by over 50% is counted as Valid.
(**)Feed Me is marked as incorrect by the humans, but is correct.

4.2 CG vs. Human Validation of LLM Plans

We seek to validate the correctness of the plan evaluation by the CG module using the analysis of action plans generated by LLMs. The two primary metrics by which a generated action plan can be measured are correctness and executability [16]. In a simulated environment such as VirtualHome, executability can be easily measured without a human in the loop by trying the action plan in the simulation. If it fails to parse the plan, then it is not executable. However, correctness poses a different issue. There are often times where a plan can be executable, but not correct. An example for the task "Browse internet" is provided in the Appendix which contains looking at a computer that is off. The generated plan is executable, but common sense dictates that the task is only completed correctly if the computer is also on. Previous research has used human evaluation to determine whether these commonsense constraints are followed in addition to executability, but human evaluation is expensive and slow. Having an automated correctness analysis would allow for better training of LLMs and constraining the output of the LLM so that it does not confidently hallucinate a wrong answer.

In our previous work, human evaluators marked GPT-4o-generated plans for 10 tasks, whether they are correct or incorrect. For our comparison, we used those same tasks with the CG module. One such example is in Fig. 3, where an incorrect task is correctly identified by the CG module as being invalid. In addition to matching the human evaluation of the task, the CG module also provides an explanation of why the plan is invalid.

As noted in the original work [28], almost all the tasks generated by an off-the-shelf GPT-4o instance are not executable in VirtualHome, so we translated them into an executable form in a way that most favors the GPT-generated plan. For example, the instruction "Walk to the storage area where the vacuum cleaner is kept." would be translated into the VirtualHome action "Walk to bedroom 74", where the vacuum is located. This evaluation does not measure how the plan matches the actual simulation (as GPT has no context awareness), rather if the actions are correct when executed with most favorable starting conditions.

We validated the LLM-generated plans in all but one case. The results of the CG module agree with human correctness ratings, where "correct" is assumed to be the case where human evaluators rated it as correct over 50% of the time. We include the results of the user study by Tudor et al. [28], augmented with our results from the CG module (including the step at which a plan is marked incorrect) in Table 1.

4.3 CG vs. Human Evaluation of Executability and Correctness

In this section, we compare CG module validation with the evaluation performed by Huang et al. [16] to evaluate with state-of-the-art. In the original paper, Huang et al. created a system of LLM models designed to constrain the output of an LLM to correct and executable VirtualHome plans (with correctness and executability as defined in Sect. 4.2). Using this system, they generated action plans for tasks from the VirtualHome dataset, which were each evaluated for correctness by 10 human participants. Although not every task and plan was made available from the original research, 46 plans were provided. We ran all 46 available plans through the CG module and found that 17 (36.96%) were marked correct by the CG module. The results of our evaluation are available in Table 2. We evaluated the 46 plans by hand and found that the 17 plans marked correct by the CG corresponded with our assessment of which plans were correct.

Of the plans created by the best system of Huang et al., 73.05% were executable and 66.13% were correct, but only 35.23% were executable *and* correct. While the executability percentage is calculated as the direct portion of plans that can be achieved, the correct percentage represents an aggregate of participant ratings for each task averaged together. Hence, we cannot directly compare our measurement of achievability to theirs. However, taking these measures alongside our review of the plans matching the CG module's, provides a reasonable amount of confidence in its ability to evaluate plans correctly.

Table 2. Human Evaluation vs. CG Validation of 46 LLM plans of Huang et al. [16]

Humans			CG	
Correct	Executable	Achievable	# Valid	Achievable
73.05%	66.13%	**35.23%**	17/46	**36.96%**

5 Related Works

The idea behind counterfactual generation to identify and correct knowledge gaps is not new, as much work has been done in this field and the closely related fields of explainable AI (XAI) [21], plan/model repair [4], and unsolvability in planning [25]. While much of the focus in XAI is concentrated on explanations for existent solutions, less attention is paid to an explanation for a lack of solution or why a solution fails. The planning community has focused on "making unsolvable problems solvable or fixing models based on plan traces" [4]. Bercher et al. [4] provide a survey of such approaches, however, they consider plan repair research to still be in its early stages. Significant examples of work in this direction are by Sreedharan et al. [27], which explains why a successful plan was chosen by explaining why failed plans were not, and by Das et al. [9], which focuses on repairing plans that have failed because of interaction with the environment. Our system is designed to evaluate cases where a plan is chosen, but ends up being incorrect due to commonsense constraints that were not taken into account by the planner, such as in the case where the action "rinse mouth" is taken after the action "switch off faucet". Our work is also an effort towards automating plan repair but it is distinct in that it relies on *direct* counterfactual reasoning. Additionally, we have designed our solution to be planner agnostic. As the CG module is distinct from the planners themselves, it can be used to evaluate plans from any planner in the VirtualHome domain (we demonstrated on LLMs and VECSR). Other systems are interconnected with specific planners and therefore not as extensible as the CG module [6,13,14]. Additionally, a common constraint of other planners is the disallowance of negative preconditions [4,18]. For example, a positive precondition could include that in order to drink something, it must be drinkable, while a negative precondition could say that a drink must *not* have already been drunk. Using s(CASP) default rules with exceptions and strong negation, the representation of these becomes straightforward (see Drink example in Appendix A) .

Finally, other works focus solely on assessment of generated plans and not on explanation and assessment [5,7,19]. The explainability of the CG module is a useful trait when paired with its human and machine-readable assessment of plans from a variety of planners, making our combined solution a novel contribution.

6 Conclusion

The ability to autonomously detect knowledge gaps and validate the commonsense correctness of generated plans is critical for creating trustworthy systems. The Counterfactual Generation module is a versatile contribution that can address this problem for a variety of task-breakdown tools. The counterfactual explanations, made possible by the goal-directed justifications of s(CASP), provide critical explainability on why a plan is invalid. Our evaluation found that the CG module is accurate and helpful for the detection of knowledge gaps in

VECSR's knowledge base. In the future, for truly embodied real-world planning, the constraints used to create the CG module could be discovered experimentally through use of an actual autonomous agent.

Appendix

Example: Put Shoes and Coats. Note, we follow the example of Huang et al. [16] to translate the actions from machine-readable format ([walk] <object> 1) into natural language for ease of reading (Walk to object 1):

1. Walk to bedroom 74
2. Walk to shoe 3203
3. Grab shoe 3203
4. Walk to shoe 3204
5. Grab shoe 3204
6. Put shoe 3203 on character 1
7. Put shoe 3204 on character 1
8. Walk to coat 3205
9. Grab coat 3205
10. Walk to character 1
11. Put coat 3205 on character 1

Example: Prepare Letter for Mailing

1. Grab paper 303
2. Walk to bedroom 74
3. Walk to envelope 3218
4. Grab envelope 3218
5. Put paper 303 in envelope 3218
6. Walk to kitchen 207
7. Walk to bedroom 74
8. Walk to mailbox 3219
9. Put envelope 3218 in mailbox 3219

Which fails at step 8 with the following abridged justification tree[4]:

```
not action_done(walk,mailbox3219,8) :-
  time(8),
  action(walk),
  not action_valid(walk,mailbox3219,8) :-
    [...]
    not close(character1,mailbox3219,8) :-
      not close(mailbox3219,character1,8) :-
        chs(not close(character1,mailbox3219,8)).
```

[4] Note that not close(character1,mailbox3219,8) holds because s(CASP) detects that close(character1,mailbox3219,8) was called through an even number of intervening negations, indicated by chs/1.

```
  proved(not held(mailbox3219,8)).
not inside(character1,Var1 | {Var1 \= bedroom74,Var1 \= kitchen207},8),
[...]
inside(character1,kitchen207,8),
not inside(mailbox3219,kitchen207,8).
```

Example: Browse Internet

1. Walk to computer 176
2. Sit on chair 109
3. Look at computer 176

Example: Feed Me

1. Walk to dining room.
2. Walk to table where you are seated.
3. Find a chair for me to use (if needed).
4. Pull chair closer to table.
5. Sit on the chair (if I were human).
6. Locate plate for you.
7. Locate food for you.
8. Grab food for you.
9. Place food on your plate.
10. Hand you the food or assist you with eating.

```
action_valid(drink, X, T) :-
drinkable(Y), not action_invalid(drink, X, T).
action_invalid(find, X, T) :- Before .<. T, action_done(drink, X, Before).
```

References

1. Arias, J., Carro, M., Chen, Z., Gupta, G.: Justifications for goal-directed constraint answer set programming. In: TC of the 36th International of Conference on Logic Programming, TC-ICLP'20. EPTCS, vol. 325, pp. 59–72 (2020). https://doi.org/10.4204/EPTCS.325.12
2. Arias, J., Carro, M., Salazar, E., Marple, K., Gupta, G.: Constraint answer set programming without grounding. Theory Pract. Log. Program. **18**(3–4), 337–354 (2018). https://doi.org/10.1017/S1471068418000285
3. Bai, Z., et al.: Hallucination of multimodal large language models: a survey. arXiv preprint arXiv:2404.18930 (2024)
4. Bercher, P., Sreedharan, S., Vallati, M.: A survey on model repair in AI planning. In: 34th International Joint Conference on Artificial Intelligence, p. 26. IJCAI Organization (2025)
5. Caglar, T., Belhaj, S., Chakraborty, T., Katz, M., Sreedharan, S.: Can LLMs fix issues with reasoning models? Towards more likely models for AI planning. In: Proceedings of the AAAI Conference on Artificial Intelligence, vol. 38, pp. 20061–20069 (2024)

6. Chen, G., et al.: Language-augmented symbolic planner for open-world task planning. arXiv preprint arXiv:2407.09792 (2024)
7. Chrpa, L., Dodaro, C., Maratea, M., Mochi, M., Vallati, M.: Comparing planning domain models using answer set programming. In: Gaggl, S., Martinez, M.V., Ortiz, M. (eds.) Logics in Artificial Intelligence. JELIA 2023. LNCS, vol. 14281, pp. 227–242. Springer, Cham (2023). https://doi.org/10.1007/978-3-031-43619-2_16
8. Cresswell, S.N., McCluskey, T.L., West, M.M.: Acquiring planning domain models using LOCM. Knowl. Eng. Rev. **28**(2), 195–213 (2013)
9. Das, D., Banerjee, S., Chernova, S.: Explainable AI for robot failures: generating explanations that improve user assistance in fault recovery. In: Proceedings of the 2021 ACM/IEEE International Conference on Human-Robot Interaction, pp. 351–360 (2021)
10. Dasgupta, S., Arias, J., Salazar, E., Gupta, G.: CoGS: causality constrained counterfactual explanations using goal-directed asp. arXiv preprint arXiv:2407.08179 (2024)
11. Fikes, R.E., Nilsson, N.J.: STRIPS: a new approach to the application of theorem proving to problem solving. In: Proceedings of the 2nd International Joint Conference on Artificial Intelligence, pp. 608–620. IJCAI'71, Morgan Kaufmann Publishers Inc., San Francisco, CA, USA (1971)
12. Gebser, M., Kaminski, R., Kaufmann, B., Schaub, T.: Multi-shot ASP solving with clingo. Theory Pract. Log. Program. **19**(1), 27–82 (2019). https://doi.org/10.1017/S1471068418000054
13. Göbelbecker, M., Keller, T., Eyerich, P., Brenner, M., Nebel, B.: Coming up with good excuses: what to do when no plan can be found. In: Proceedings of the International Conference on Automated Planning and Scheduling, vol. 20, pp. 81–88 (2010)
14. Gragera, A., Fuentetaja, R., García-Olaya, Á., Fernández, F.: A planning approach to repair domains with incomplete action effects. In: Proceedings of the International Conference on Automated Planning and Scheduling, vol. 33, pp. 153–161 (2023)
15. Huang, L., et al.: A survey on hallucination in large language models: principles, taxonomy, challenges, and open questions. ACM Trans. Inf. Syst. **43**(2), 1–55 (2025)
16. Huang, W., Abbeel, P., Pathak, D., Mordatch, I.: Language models as zero-shot planners: extracting actionable knowledge for embodied agents. In: Chaudhuri, K., Jegelka, S., Song, L., Szepesvari, C., Niu, G., Sabato, S. (eds.) Proceedings of the 39th International Conference on Machine Learning. Proceedings of Machine Learning Research, vol. 162, pp. 9118–9147. PMLR (2022). https://doi.org/10.48550/arXiv.2201.07207, https://proceedings.mlr.press/v162/huang22a.html
17. Hurst, A., et al.: GPT-4o system card. arXiv preprint arXiv:2410.21276 (2024)
18. Lin, S., Bercher, P., et al.: Change the world-how hard can that be? On the computational complexity of fixing planning models. In: IJCAI, pp. 4152–4159 (2021)
19. McCluskey, T.L., Vaquero, T.S., Vallati, M.: Engineering knowledge for automated planning: towards a notion of quality. In: Proceedings of the 9th Knowledge Capture Conference, pp. 1–8 (2017)
20. McDermott, D., et al.: PDDL-the planning domain definition language (1998). https://api.semanticscholar.org/CorpusID:59656859
21. Mersha, M., Lam, K.N., Wood, J., AlShami, A.K., Kalita, J.: Explainable artificial intelligence: a survey of needs, techniques, applications, and future direction. Neurocomputing **599**, 128111 (2024)

22. Morales, E.F., Murrieta-Cid, R., Becerra, I., Esquivel-Basaldua, M.A.: A survey on deep learning and deep reinforcement learning in robotics with a tutorial on deep reinforcement learning. Intel. Serv. Robot. **14**(5), 773–805 (2021). https://doi.org/10.1007/s11370-021-00398-z
23. Mourao, K., Zettlemoyer, L.S., Petrick, R., Steedman, M.: Learning STRIPS operators from noisy and incomplete observations. arXiv preprint arXiv:1210.4889 (2012)
24. Puig, X., et al.: VirtualHome: simulating household activities via programs. In: Proceedings of the IEEE Conference on Computer Vision and Pattern Recognition, pp. 8494–8502 (2018)
25. Sarwar, M.M.S., Ray, R.: Exploring inevitable waypoints for unsolvability explanation in hybrid planning problems **24**(6) (2025)
26. Song, H., Kim, M., Park, D., Shin, Y., Lee, J.G.: Learning from noisy labels with deep neural networks: a survey. IEEE Trans. Neural Netw. Learn. Syst. **34**(11), 8135–8153 (2022)
27. Sreedharan, S., Srivastava, S., Smith, D., Kambhampati, S.: Why can't you do that hal? Explaining unsolvability of planning tasks. In: International Joint Conference on Artificial Intelligence (2019)
28. Tudor, A.R., Arias, J., Gupta, G.: VECSR: virtually embodied common sense reasoning system. In: Proceedings 41st International Conference on Logic Programming, The University of Calabria, Arcavacata CS, Italy, 12–19 September 2025. Electronic Proceedings in Theoretical Computer Science, Open Publishing Association (2025)
29. Tudor, A.R., Kimbrell, K., Gupta, G.: Using goal-directed answer set programming for orchestration of neuro-symbolic UAV autonomy. In: Hawaii International Conference on System Sciences 2026 (2026)
30. Wang, H., Gupta, G.: FOLD-SE: an efficient rule-based machine learning algorithm with scalable explainability. In: Gebser, M., Sergey, I. (eds.) Practical Aspects of Declarative Languages. PADL 2024. LNCS, vol. 14512, pp. 37–53. Springer, Cham (2023). https://doi.org/10.1007/978-3-031-52038-9_3
31. Yang, Q., Wu, K., Jiang, Y.: Learning action models from plan examples using weighted MAX-SAT. Artif. Intell. **171**(2–3), 107–143 (2007)

Dynamic Programming and Tabled Logic Programming for Encoding Single-Constant Multiplication Into SAT (Declarative Pearls)

Neng-Fa Zhou[1(✉)], Chufeng Jiang[1], Hendrik Bierlee[3], and Peter Stuckey[2]

[1] City University of New York, New York, USA
nzhou@brooklyn.cuny.edu, cjiang@gradcenter.cuny.edu
[2] Monash University & OPTIMA ARC Industry Training and Transformation Centre, Melbourne, Australia
peter.stuckey@monash.edu
[3] Department of Computer Science, KU Leuven, Leuven, Belgium
henk.bierlee@kuleuven.be

Abstract. Encoding single-constant multiplication (SCM) constraints into SAT is essential for solving a wide range of combinatorial problems involving integer arithmetic. Although optimal SAT encodings for SCM are known, they are often prohibitively expensive to generate for large constants. This paper introduces a dynamic programming (DP) approach that offers a practical balance between encoding quality and encoding time. The proposed method recursively decomposes the binary representation of the target constant into chunks and eliminates common subexpressions across the chunks and their one's complements. The objective is either to minimize the number of additions (the *min-k* objective) or to minimize the number of half/full adders (the *min-a* objective). The DP algorithm is naturally expressed and efficiently implemented using mode-directed tabling in Picat. Although the approach does not guarantee optimality, experimental results show that it produces high-quality encodings while substantially reducing encoding time. This makes SAT-based techniques considerably more practical for applications involving SCM constraints. The full implementation is publicly available at: https://github.com/nfzhou/Picat/blob/master/scm.pi.

Keywords: SCM · SAT · Dynamic programming · Declarative programming · Tabled Logic Programming

1 Introduction

The performance of Boolean Satisfiability (SAT) solvers has improved dramatically over the past two decades, making it feasible to tackle many combinatorial optimization problems by encoding them into SAT instances and solving them

M. Sperber and E. Komendantskaya (Eds.): FLOPS 2026, LNCS 16533, pp. 293–305, 2026.
https://doi.org/10.1007/978-981-92-0184-6_14

using SAT solvers. Nevertheless, for many integer programming problems, SAT-based solvers still struggle due to the lack of optimizations in the encodings for integer-domain constraints.

One fundamental integer-domain constraint is single-constant multiplication (SCM), of the form $c \cdot x = y$, where c is a fixed constant, and x and y are integer-domain variables. In SAT, SCM constraints are typically encoded using multiple additions, subtractions, and bit-shifts (i.e. multiplications by powers of two). Since subtractions can always be represented as additions, and bit-shifts and additions with zero bits are free in SAT, the encoding quality is primarily determined by minimizing the number of additions (the *min-k* objective) and the number of half/full adders (the *min-a* objective). The former objective only depends on c, while the latter also depends on the bit-width of x.

The SCM problem is well studied in the context of hardware design [4]. It is NP-hard to minimize the number of additions/subtractions for SCM [3]. Previous approaches to SCM are either based on graph methods [8], Common Subexpression Elimination (CSE) [14], Integer Linear Programming (ILP) [10], SAT-based solvers [11,13], as well as various heuristic methods [9,12]. The *min-a* objective was first covered by [5]. For the Multiple Constant Multiplication (MCM) problem, the generalization of SCM, where a set of constants should be covered by the circuit, both optimal and heuristic methods have been developed [1].

Unlike in hardware design, where the time required to find an SCM solution does not affect the performance of the resulting circuit, in SAT solving, the encoding time directly contributes to the total solving time. Although precomputed databases of optimal SCM encodings for relevant coefficients and bit-widths can reduce this cost [2], such databases cannot feasibly cover the full range of coefficients and bit-widths required in practice. As a result, for any coefficient and bit-width combination outside of the database, a naive fallback is used to encode the multiplication.

In this paper, we propose a dynamic programming (DP) approach to SCM encoding that offers a practical balance between encoding quality and generation time. The proposed method recursively decomposes the binary representation of the target constant into chunks and eliminates common subexpressions across the chunks and their one's complements. The method fits within the general framework of decomposing a given integer c using one of three operator types, namely, $(c_l \ll s) + c_r$ (SPLUS), $(c_l \ll s) - c_r$ (SMINUS), or $c_l - (sc_r \ll s)$ (MINUSS) [2], where $\ll s$ denotes left shift of s bits or equivalently multiplying by 2^s. Because the decomposition is guided by the binary representation of c, the search space for c_l, c_r, and s is considerably reduced.

We implemented the proposed DP algorithm using tabling in Picat [18,20]. The implementation models SCM as a planning problem, where a solution is represented as a set of operations. For each decomposition step, it takes the union of the sub-plans generated for the chunks, thereby eliminating duplicate operations. The use of mode-directed tabling enables concise modeling of both the *min-k* and *min-a* objectives. The entire program is under 100 lines and serves as an excellent example of declarative programming and illustrating its expressiveness for arithmetic encoding problems.

Although the program does not guarantee optimality, it is designed to strike a favorable trade-off between encoding quality and encoding time, and the experimental results demonstrate strong practical performance. For the *min-k* objective, the *DPmin-k* encoder solves all 1023 instances in the SCM database [2] in under one second and produces optimal encodings for over 93% of them. For the *min-a* objective, the *DPmin-a* encoder similarly solves all 16,368 database instances within one second, achieving optimal encodings for more than 57% of the cases. The approach also scales to very large constants efficiently. For example, it returns in 8.75 s a 7-operation plan for 171398451, only 1 operation away from the known optimal solution [11], while the *min-k* and *min-a* models given in [2] fail to solve it within 24 h.

The remainder of this paper is organized as follows. Section 2 describes the proposed DP approach in detail. Section 3 presents the Picat implementation using tabling. Section 4 reports experimental results and analysis. Finally, Sect. 5 concludes the paper and outlines future research directions.

2 A Dynamic Programming Approach to SCM Encoding

Dynamic programming is not a natural approach to SCM encoding because a fundamental assumption of dynamic programming, optimal substructure, does not hold. Given all optimal solutions to SCM for coefficients c_l and c_r it may not be possible to create an optimal solution to SCM for $c = (c_l \ll s) + c_r$. This is because a non-optimal recipe for c_l that shares many intermediate results with a non-optimal recipe for c_r may overall generate a better solution than combining any two optimal solutions. In practice, however, this behavior is rare allowing us to take advantage of the efficiency of DP without too much loss of optimality.

Example 1. Consider computing the constant integer 55415. We can decompose it as $55415 = (6143 \ll 3) + 6271$. The optimal solution for $c_l = 6143$ requires two additions and $c_r = 6271$ requires three additions, respectively. Combining these optimal solutions yields six additions in total:

$$
\begin{aligned}
&55415 \cdot x = (6143 \cdot x) \ll 3 + 6271 \cdot x\\
&6143 \cdot x = x \ll 13 - 2049 \cdot x\\
&2049 \cdot x = x \ll 11 + x\\
&6271 \cdot x = (49 \cdot x) \ll 7 - x\\
&49 \cdot x = x \ll 6 + 15 \cdot x\\
&15 \cdot x = x \ll 4 - x
\end{aligned}
$$

However, by using non-optimal recipes that share intermediate results (i.e. 6143), we can achieve a better overall solution only using 4 additions in total:

$$\begin{aligned}
&55415 \cdot x = (6143 \cdot x) \ll 12 + 6271 \cdot x \\
&6143 \cdot x = x \ll 12 + 2047 \cdot x \\
&6271 \cdot x = x \ll 7 + 6143 \cdot x \\
&2047 \cdot x = x \ll 11 + x
\end{aligned}$$

As the SCM problem violates the optimal substructure, DP does not guarantee optimality. To mitigate the issue, the proposed DP approach uses a union operation when constructing the solution recursively. Instead of independently merging sub-plans, the approach takes the union of the sub-plans computed for different chunks and dynamically eliminates redundant intermediate operations. Although this strategy does not restore the optimal substructure, it enables the identification and sharing of common intermediate values across chunks, leading to high-quality encodings in practice.

2.1 Problem Definition and Notation

The single-constant multiplication (SCM) constraint has the form $c \cdot x = y$, where c is a fixed constant, and x and y are integer-domain variables. When $c = 0$ or $c = 1$, the constraint can be trivially encoded as an equality constraint. When c is even, the constraint $c \cdot x = y$ can always be rewritten as $c' \cdot x \ll s = y$, where c' is an odd integer and $\ll$ denotes the left-shift operator. In the remainder of this paper, we assume that c is odd, meaning that its binary representation always ends with a 1.

The target constant c can be decomposed using one of the following operator types when $c > 1$:

$$\begin{aligned}
&c = (c_l \ll s) + c_r \text{ (SPLUS)} \\
&c = (c_l \ll s) - c_r \text{ (SMINUS)} \\
&c = c_l - (c_r \ll s) \text{ (MINUSS)}
\end{aligned}$$

The *min-k* objective aims to minimize the number of operations. Since additions with zero bits are free in SAT, the SPLUS operation could be free depending on the bit-width of x. For example, the addition

$$(5 \times x) \ll 4 + x$$

is free if the bit width of x is less than 5. The *min-a* objective aims to minimize the number of one-bit adders required in the final encoding by counting out free additions.

The DP approach decomposes the binary representation of c into chunks using one of the operator types when c is not a base case, and it recursively applies the method to each chunk or its complement. When multiple decompositions are possible, the DP approach explores all of them.

In the following, the constant c is always given in binary format, and the following notations are used to express pattens and operations on binary strings:

- $.^n$: indicates a binary string of length n. In particular, 0^n indicates a string of 0 s, and 1^n indicates a string of 1 s.

- $|\alpha|$: indicates the length of binary string α.
- $\bar{\alpha}$: indicates the 1's complement of α.

2.2 Details of the Dynamic Programming Formulation

The Base Case: When $c = 1$, the empty set is returned as the recipe.

The SPLUS Rule: The SPLUS rule decomposes c's binary representation into α and β, where both α and β are an odd integers. Let $c_l = \alpha$, $c_r = \beta$, and s be $|\beta|$. The rule recursively applies the DP approach on c_l and c_r, respectively. This rule returns a recipe that takes the union of the recipes from c_l and c_r with the following SPLUS operation added:

$$c = (c_l \ll s) + c_r$$

Example 2. The binary string `110101` (53) has the following three SPLUS decompositions:

$$\begin{array}{lllll} \alpha = 1101 & \beta = 01 & c_l = 1101 & c_r = 1 & s = 2 \\ \alpha = 11 & \beta = 0101 & c_l = 11 & c_r = 101 & s = 4 \\ \alpha = 1 & \beta = 10101 & c_l = 1 & c_r = 10101 & s = 5 \end{array}$$

The SMINUS Rule: The SMINUS rule decomposes c's binary representation into α and β, where α's lowest bit is 0. Let $c_l = \alpha + 1$, $c_r = \bar{\beta} + 1$, and $s = |\beta|$. The rule recursively applies the DP approach on c_l and c_r, respectively. This rule returns a recipe that takes the union of the recipes from c_l and c_r with the following SMINUS operation added:

$$c = (c_l \ll s) - c_r$$

It is obvious that the SMINUS equation holds since $(1 \ll |\beta|) - \bar{\beta} - 1 = \beta$.

Example 3. The binary string `110101` has the following three SMINUS decompositions:

$$\begin{array}{lllll} \alpha = 11010 & \beta = 1 & c_l = 11011 & c_r = 1 & s = 1 \\ \alpha = 110 & \beta = 101 & c_l = 111 & c_r = 11 & s = 3 \\ \alpha = 0 & \beta = 110101 & c_l = 1 & c_r = 1011 & s = 6 \end{array}$$

The MINUSS Rule: The MINUSS rule decomposes c's binary representation into α and β, where α's lowest bit is 0 and $\alpha \neq 0$. Let $c_l = (1 \ll |\alpha\beta|) - (1 \ll |\beta|) + \beta$, $c_r = \bar{\alpha}$, and $s = |\beta|$. The rule recursively applies the DP approach on c_l and c_r, respecitvely. This rule returns a recipe that takes the union of the recipes from c_l and c_r with the following MINUSS operation added:

$$c = c_l - (c_r \ll s)$$

It is not difficult to see that the MINUSS equation holds since

$$(1 \ll |\alpha\beta|) - (1 \ll |\beta|) - (\bar{\alpha} \ll |\beta| = (\alpha \ll |\beta|)$$

Example 4. The binary string `110101` has the following two MINUSS decompositions:

$$\begin{array}{lllll} \alpha = 11010 & \beta = 1 & c_l = 11111 & c_r = 101 & s = 1 \\ \alpha = 110 & \beta = 101 & c_l = 11101 & c_r = 1 & s = 3 \end{array}$$

Discussion. The DP approach is incomplete: some encodings, possibly optimal in terms of the number of additions, cannot be generated. For example, for the SCM $1965 \cdot x$, an optimal encoding (shown below) only requires three additions [2]:

$$\begin{array}{l} 1965 \cdot x = (131 \cdot x) \ll 4 - 131 \cdot x \\ 131 \cdot x = x \ll 7 + 3 \cdot x \\ 3 \cdot x = x \ll 1 + x \end{array}$$

However, the best encoding obtained via DP requires four additions. The limitation stems from the fact that DP's decompositions are driven by the target integer's binary representation, and some integers, such as 131 in the example, never appear as a chunk or as the complement of a chunk in that representation.

The major advantage of this restriction is that there at most $O(\log c)$ ways of splitting the coefficient c along its binary encoding, rather than $O(c)$ if we considered each possible split for SPLUS.[1]

3 Implementation Using Tabling

Tabling, also known as memorization in logic programming, is a program-evaluation strategy in which the system tables the results of subgoal calls and reuses them to avoid redundant computation and infinite loops [16,17,21]. Mode-directed tabling, which was introduced in [6,7] and later incorporated in other systems (e.g., [15,19]), lets the programmer declare modes on tabled predicate arguments to control which arguments are used for variant checking and how answers are tabled based on the modes. Mode-directed tabling is particularly useful to express dynamic programming algorithms. This section gives an implementation of the DP algorithm presented in the previous section using tabling in Picat [20].

In Picat, in order to have all of the calls and answers of a predicate or function tabled, users just need to add the keyword `table` before the first rule. Picat also supports mode-directed tabling. For example, the predicate `sp(X,Y,Path,W)`, defined below, searches for a path with the minimum cost from `X` to `Y` in a graph specified by the `edge` predicate.

[1] Even more for MINUSS since $c_l > c$.

```
table(+, +, -, min)
sp(X, Y, Path, Cost) ?=>
    Path = [(X, Y)],
    edge(X, Y, Cost).
sp(X, Y, Path, Cost) =>
    Path = [(X, Z)|Path1],
    edge(X, Z, W),
    sp(Z, Y, Path1, Cost1),
    Cost = W + Cost1.
```

The mode + indicates an input argument, the mode - indicates an output argument, and the mode `min` instructs Picat to only table one optimal answer for the same input arguments.

Recently, Picat has been extended to support the table modes `mmin` and `mmax`, which instruct the system to table all optimal answers. If `min` were replaced with `mmin` in the example above, the predicate could be used to enumerate all lowest-cost paths between a given pair of nodes.

The following Picat program implements the DP approach:

```
import ordset.

table (+, +, mmin, -)
scm(1, XBits, Cost, Plan) =>
    Cost = 0, Plan = [].
scm(C, XBits, Cost, Plan) =>
    (split_pp(C, C1, C2, S),          % SPLUS: C = (C1 << S) + C2
     OP = $splus(C, C1, C2, S)
    ;
     split_pn(C, C1, C2, S),          % SMINUS: C = (C1 << S) - C2
     OP = $sminus(C, C1, C2, S)
    ;
     split_np(C, C1, C2, S),          % MINUSS: C = C1 - (C2 << S)
     OP = $minuss(C, C1, C2, S)
    )
    comp_op_cost(XBits, OP, ThisCost),
    scm(C1, XBits, _Cost1, Plan1),
    scm(C2, XBits, _Cost2, Plan2),
    Plan12 = union(Plan1, Plan2),
    Plan = Plan12.insert((OP, ThisCost)),
    Cost = sum([T : (_, T) in Plan]).
```

As a plan is represented as an ordered set, the program imports the `ordset` module in the beginning.

The predicate `scm(C, XBits, Cost, Plan)` returns a plan (`Plan`) with cost (`Cost`) for the multiplication `C*X`, where `XBits` is the bit-width of `X`.

The first rule handles the base case when `C = 1`.

The second rule encodes the DP recurrences using a disjunction of three branches. After decomposing the binary representation of `C` into `C1` and `C2`, the rule recursively obtains a plan `Plan1` for `C1` and a plan `Plan2` for `C2`. It then forms a plan for `C` by taking the union of `Plan1` and `Plan2`, adding the newly derived operation together with its associated cost. The total cost is the sum of the costs of all operations in the resulting plan. Note that the disjunction introduces nondeterministic search: if one branch fails, the next branch is automatically tried.

The `comp_op_cost(XBits, OP, Cost)` predicate binds `Cost` to the cost of operation `OP`. For the *min-k* objective, the cost is always 1. For the *min-a* objective, the cost is the number of adders needed for the operation, which is dependent on `XBits`.

Note that the table mode `mmin` is used, which instructs Picat to table all minimum-cost solutions. If the `min` table mode were used instead, the final solution might not be as optimal.

4 Experimental Results

To evaluate the performance of the DP-based encoders (*DPmin-k* and *DPmin-a*), we conducted experiments across a range of problem scales—from small instances with known optimal solutions to medium and very large integers that challenge existing optimal solvers. The DP encoders were compared against a baseline shift-and-add model implemented in Picat (*Baseline*) and two models implemented in MiniZinc [2], *min-k*, which minimizes the number of addition operations, and *min-a*, which minimizes the number of one-bit half/full adders, both of which can guarantee optimality. All experiments were conducted on a system running Ubuntu 22.04 under WSL2, equipped with an Intel Core i7-12700H processor (2.30 GHz), and 32 GB of RAM.

4.1 Evaluation on Small-Sized Integers

DP-based encoders were first evaluated on small-sized integers with bit widths ranging from 1 to 16 bits, for which the optimal solutions obtained from MiniZinc *min-k* and *min-a* models are available [2]. The *min-k* recipe includes optimal encodings for 1023 odd integers up to 2047. *DPmin-k* found encodings for all the 1023 integers in 0.137 s. Among the encodings, 952 (93%) of them are optimal, and 71 are near optimal with each requiring only one more addition than the optimal one.

A similar evaluation was conducted for *DPmin-a*. The *min-a* recipe includes 16368 encodings for 1023 odd integers up to 2047 and bit widths from 1 to 16 bits. *DPmin-a* found encodings for the 16368 cases in 0.903 s. Among the encodings, 9424 (57.58%) are optimal in terms of the number of half/full adders, and an additional 5298(32.37%) are near-optimal, requiring no more than five extra half/full adders. A further 1471 (8.99%) exhibit a moderate overhead of six to ten extra half/full adders, and the remaining 175 encodings (1.07%) incur a high overhead, requiring between eleven and sixteen more.

4.2 Evaluation on Medium-Sized Integers

Table 1 compares *DPmin-k* and *Baseline* on time and encoding quality using ten randomly generated medium-sized integers with bit widths ranging from 17 to 25. Although *DPmin-k* incurs higher encoding time, it generates much higher-quality encodings in a compact way. For example, for the integer 30261031, the *Baseline* encoding requires 17 additions, while the *DPmin-k* encoding only requires 5 additions. The MiniZinc *min-k* model failed to produce an encoding within 24 h.

Table 1. Comparison of encoding time (in seconds) and encoding quality (number of additions) between *Baseline* and *DPmin-k* on medium-sized integers.

c	*Baseline*		*DPmin-k*	
	time	#adds	time	#adds
464571	0.001	12	0.153	6
7137249	0.001	14	0.201	5
8176693	0.001	12	0.467	6
9330001	0.001	12	1.265	6
11895821	0.001	10	0.494	6
14049001	0.001	15	0.915	6
15055315	0.001	15	0.798	6
16532753	0.001	11	0.599	5
27587603	0.001	12	0.868	6
30261031	0.001	17	0.757	5

Table 2 presents the corresponding comparison between *DPmin-a* and *Baseline* under an 8-bit variable-width assumption on the same set of integers. Although *DPmin-a* is slower than *Baseline*, it achieves notable improvements in encoding quality. Specifically, for the integer 30261031, the number of required half/full adders is reduced from 128 in the *Baseline* encoding to 60 in the *DPmin-a* encoding. As with *min-k*, the MiniZinc-based *min-a* encoder is not able to handle any of these tested instances within 24 h.

4.3 Evaluation on Large Integers

The DP-based encoders are capable of handling large integers of 26 bits or more. For example, for $c = 171398451$, *DPmin-k* returns the following encoding in 8.755 s:

Table 2. A comparison on encoding time (seconds) and quality (the number of half/full adders) between *Baseline* and *DPmin-a* under an 8-bit variable-width assumption on medium-sized integers.

c	*Baseline*		*DPmin-a*	
	time	#adders	time	#adders
464571	0.001	88	0.01	43
7137249	0.001	104	0.02	44
8176693	0.001	88	0.02	57
9330001	0.001	88	0.026	60
11895821	0.001	72	0.028	58
14049001	0.001	112	0.025	51
15055315	0.001	112	0.024	51
16532753	0.001	80	0.018	56
27587603	0.001	88	0.034	62
30261031	0.001	128	0.021	60

```
5 = 1 * (1 << 2) + 1
13 = 1 * (1 << 3) + 5
653 = 5 * (1 << 7) + 13
10461 = 653 * (1 << 4) + 13
167381 = 10461 * (1 << 4) + 5
307 = 5 * (1 << 6) - 13
171398451 = 167381 * (1 << 10) + 307
```

which only uses one more addition than the known optimal encoding [11].

DPmin-a returns the following encoding for $c = 171398451$ and $|x| = 8$ in 0.061 s

```
5 = 1 * (1 << 2) + 1
13 = 1 * (1 << 3) + 5
77 = 1 * (1 << 6) + 13
205 = 1 * (1 << 7) + 77
268435251 = 1 * (1 << 28) - 205
268434739 = 268435251 - 1 * (1 << 9)
268432691 = 268434739 - 1 * (1 << 11)
268391731 = 268432691 - 5 * (1 << 13)
267867443 = 268391731 - 1 * (1 << 19)
263673139 = 267867443 - 1 * (1 << 22)
255284531 = 263673139 - 1 * (1 << 23)
171398451 = 255284531 - 5 * (1 << 24)
```

which uses 68 half/full adders. For this instance, no optimal encoding is known.

The difference in encoding times between *DPmin-k* and *DPmin-a* for large integers results from the fact that *DPmin-a* tables fewer answers than DPmin-k. For example, for $c = 3626291$, *DPmin-k* returns 14 encodings, while *DPmin-a* only returns 6 encodings for $|x| = 8$.

Overall, the experimental results provide strong quantitative evidence that the proposed DP-based encoders achieve a favorable trade-off between encoding quality and computational efficiency across a wide spectrum of problem scales. On small-sized instances with known optimal solutions, *DPmin-k* and *DPmin-a* closely match optimal encodings, validating their effectiveness. On medium-sized integers, the DP-based encoders consistently outperform the baseline approach in terms of encoding quality, albeit at the cost of increased encoding time. Finally, the proposed DP-based encoders scale naturally to very large integers, producing high-quality encodings even for instances far beyond the limits of existing optimal solvers.

5 Conclusion

In this paper, we have introduced a DP based method to solve SCM problems by utilizing the binary representation of the target constant at acceptable encoding times. Our DP-based encoders yield optimal solutions over a variety of small instances at the cost of theoretical optimality, and scales efficiently to large constants where optimal encoders break down. Our approach is succinctly and declaratively implemented in Picat, due to its mode-directed tabling. The current implementation is ready for deployment in SAT encoders, and can also be used to compute tight bounds to speed up optimal encoders.

Our work could be extended in different ways. An important direction would be to adapt the approach to MCM problems, as multiple constants often share common subexpressions, and there are opportunities to reuse intermediate results. The proposed DP framework is well-fitted to this setting by using `union` operation to represent such common intermediate values across different constants.

Second, machine learning can make the search decisions and pruning more knowledgeable at least for *DPmin-k*. In contrast, *DPmin-a* adopts a cost model to steer its way through pruning, while *DPmin-k* simply counts the number of operations per each decomposition path even when there are many unnecessary paths explored. Learned strategies can help direct the search toward more promising decompositions.

Third, it may be possible to improve optimality and speed by looking at other number representations or hybrid strategies. These advancements offer opportunities to close the gap between generating efficient encodings and solving arithmetic constraints efficiently with high-quality SAT-based solvers.

References

1. Aksoy, L., Flores, P.F., Monteiro, J.: Exact and approximate algorithms for the filter design optimization problem. IEEE Trans. Signal Process. **63**(1), 142–154 (2015). https://doi.org/10.1109/TSP.2014.2366713
2. Bierlee, H., Dekker, J.J., Lagoon, V., Stuckey, P.J., Tack, G.: Single constant multiplication for SAT. In: Dilkina, B. (ed.) CPAIOR 2024, Part I. LNCS, vol. 14742, pp. 84–98. Springer, Cham (2024). https://doi.org/10.1007/978-3-031-60597-0_6
3. Cappello, P., Steiglitz, K.: Some complexity issues in digital signal processing. IEEE Trans. Acoust. Speech Signal Process. **32**(5), 1037–1041 (1984)
4. de Dinechin, F., Kumm, M.: Multiplication by Constants. In: de Dinechin, F., Kumm, M. (eds.) Application-Specific Arithmetic, pp. 365–426. Springer, Cham (2024). https://doi.org/10.1007/978-3-031-42808-1_12
5. Garcia, R., Volkova, A.: Toward the multiple constant multiplication at minimal hardware cost. IEEE Trans. Circuits Syst. I Regul. Pap. **70**(5), 1976–1988 (2023).https://doi.org/10.1109/TCSI.2023.3241859
6. Guo, H.-F., Gupta, G.: Simplifying dynamic programming via tabling. In: Jayaraman, B. (ed.) PADL 2004. LNCS, vol. 3057, pp. 163–177. Springer, Heidelberg (2004). https://doi.org/10.1007/978-3-540-24836-1_12
7. Guo, H.F., Gupta, G.: Simplifying dynamic programming via mode-directed tabling. Softw. Pract. Exper. **38**(1), 75–94 (2008)
8. d Gustafsson, O.: Towards optimal multiple constant multiplication: a hypergraph approach. In: 42nd Asilomar Conference on Signals, Systems and Computers, ACSSC 2008, Pacific Grove, CA, USA, 26–29 October 2008, pp. 1805–1809. IEEE (2008). https://doi.org/10.1109/ACSSC.2008.5074738
9. Gustafsson, O., Dempster, A., Johansson, K., Macleod, M., Wanhammar, L.: Simplified design of constant coefficient multipliers. Circuits Syst. Signal Process. **25**, 225–251 (2006). https://doi.org/10.1007/s00034-005-2505-5
10. Kumm, M.: Optimal constant multiplication using integer linear programming. IEEE Trans. Circuits Syst. II Express Briefs **65-II**(5), 567–571 (2018). https://doi.org/10.1109/TCSII.2018.2823780
11. Lagoon, V., Metodi, A.: Deriving optimal multiplication-by-constant circuits with a sat-based constraint engine. In: Proceedings of the MODREF 2020 Workshop (2020)
12. Lefèvre, V.: Multiplication by an integer constant. Technical report N4192, INRIA (2001)
13. Ma, S., Ampadu, P.: Optimal SAT-based minimum adder synthesis of linear transformations. In: Lee, H., Geiger, R.L. (eds.) 62nd IEEE International Midwest Symposium on Circuits and Systems, MWSCAS 2019, Dallas, TX, USA, 4–7 August 2019, pp. 335–338. IEEE (2019). https://doi.org/10.1109/MWSCAS.2019.8885033
14. Macleod, M.D., Dempster, A.G.: Common subexpression elimination algorithm for low-cost multiplierless implementation of matrix multipliers. Electron. Lett. **40**(11), 651–652 (2004)
15. Santos, J., Rocha, R.: Mode-directed tabling and applications in the YapTab system. In: Simões, A., Queirós, R., da Cruz, D.C. (eds.) 1st Symposium on Languages, Applications and Technologies, SLATE 2012, Braga, Portugal, June 21-22, 2012. OASIcs, vol. 21, pp. 25–40. Schloss Dagstuhl - Leibniz-Zentrum für Informatik (2012). https://doi.org/10.4230/OASICS.SLATE.2012.25
16. Tamaki, H., Sato, T.: OLD resolution with tabulation. In: ICLP, pp. 84–98 (1986)

17. Warren, D.S.: Memoing for logic programs. Comm. ACM, Spec. Sect. Log. Program. **35**, 93–111 (1992)
18. Zhou, N.F., Fruhman, J.: A user's guide to Picat. https://picat-lang.org (2013–2026). Accessed 22 Apr 2026
19. Zhou, N.F., Kameya, Y., Sato, T.: Mode-directed tabling for dynamic programming, machine learning, and constraint solving. In: ICTAI, pp. 213–218 (2010)
20. Zhou, N., Kjellerstrand, H., Fruhman, J.: Constraint Solving and Planning with Picat. Springer Briefs in Intelligent Systems. Springer, Cham (2015). https://doi.org/10.1007/978-3-319-25883-6
21. Zhou, N.F., Sato, T., Shen, Y.D.: Linear tabling strategies and optimizations. Theory Pract. Logic Program. **8**(1), 81–109 (2008)

Author Index

M. Sperber and E. Komendantskaya (Eds.): FLOPS 2026, LNCS 16533, p. 307, 2026.
https://doi.org/10.1007/978-981-92-0184-6

MIX
Papier aus verantwortungsvollen Quellen
Paper from responsible sources
FSC® C105338

If you have any concerns about our products,
you can contact us on
ProductSafety@springernature.com

In case Publisher is established outside the EU,
the EU authorized representative is:
Springer Nature Customer Service Center GmbH
Europaplatz 3, 69115 Heidelberg, Germany

Printed by Libri Plureos GmbH
in Hamburg, Germany